Botanica's

ORGANIC GARDENING

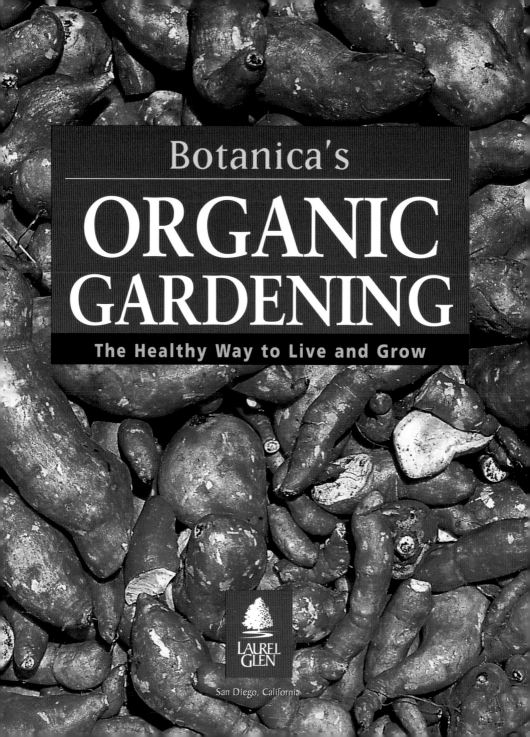

Botanica's

ORGANIC GARDENING

The Healthy Way to Live and Grow

LAUREL GLEN

San Diego, California

Laurel Glen Publishing
An imprint of the Advantage Publishers Group
5880 Oberlin Drive, San Diego, CA 92121-4794
www.laurelglenbooks.com

ISBN 1-57145-818-2

Library of Congress Cataloging-in-Publication Data available
upon request

1 2 3 4 5 06 05 04 03 02

Author:	Dr. Judyth McLeod
Publisher:	James Mills-Hicks
Editors:	Jan Hutchinson
	Rob Paratore
	Sue Grose-Hodge
	Scott Forbes
	Amber Cameron
Photography:	Keith McLeod
	Random House Picture Library
Designer:	Jenny Mansfield
Picture Researcher:	Monika Paratore
Production Manager:	Linda Watchorn
Publishing Assistant:	Monika Paratore
Printed by:	Sing Cheong Printing Co. Ltd,
	Hong Kong
Film Separation:	Pica Digital Pte Ltd,
	Singapore

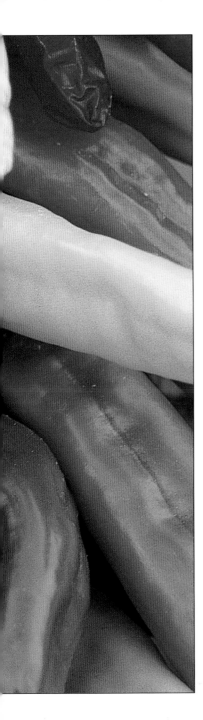

Contents

Contents

Preface

Organic gardening is a mind shift. It isn't about rules and
regulations. Rather, it's about living in trust with Nature,
and respecting all life on the planet. This book will take
you on the gentle path to recognising that we are part of
the living world, not separate from it. It's about appreciating
life's simple pleasures and reaping the benefits to be found
in the beautiful, diverse, and sometimes unexpected
environment of our own gardens.

It was never an option for me not to garden organically.
As a plant ecologist, it was unthinkable that I would choose
to damage the beauty I saw around me. As a lover of Nature,
I couldn't help but be entranced by observing the intricacies
of the tiny inter-related lives that pass unnoticed by most of
us. I discovered the two great loves of my life—my partner,
and the organic movement—in the same place and married
both of them. Neither of them have ever failed me.

Maybe this is what living in an organic way is really about—
love. I think, perhaps, it is about loving the life force in all
things, in respecting them and helping them grow.

Dr Judyth McLeod

Sydney, Australia

2002

Introduction

Organic gardening is not rocket science. Yet some organic gardening manuals simply swap the prescriptive recommendations for chemical gardening for equally prescriptive organic theories and methodologies. They totally miss the point that Nature is only too willing to forgive mistakes, provided that a reasonable attempt is made to cooperate with natural systems instead of trying to dominate them.

Even if 'green side up' is recent news to you, there is no need to panic. First, you are never going to be handling poisonous chemicals or concentrates, just rich soil that will be ever-increasingly charged with life force the longer you garden organically. No matter whether your garden is in pots on a balcony, in a tiny patch of soil, on a recently abandoned piece of land, in a large garden or on a farm, the principles remain the same and are easy to understand. Second, gardening is meant to be fun! Sometimes hard work, often good exercise, but always fun.

Organic gardening should be a rest from our busy lifestyles. The garden should be our retreat, our meditation space, a place to recharge ourselves daily with the energies of the planet. It can also become our gift back to the Earth—one small piece of the world where we have restored the natural balance. If enough people in enough places try to create a garden by working with Nature, our planet will be at least partially healed.

Part 1

ORGANIC GARDENING

Chapter 1

THE ORGANIC APPROACH

The history of organic gardening

Consider the nature of gardening before the 20th century. There were no such things as pesticides, and fertilizers were known as 'manures' since animal droppings were the only really practical way of applying nutrients to the garden. The methods of agriculture that were used had been tried and tested over hundreds of years. Then came the advent of chemical gardening, which offered 'quick fix' solutions to pest and disease control and nutrient deficiencies. Once the long-term effects of these methods were observed, however, some people realized that the costs often outweighed the benefits.

Sir Albert Howard (1873–1947)

This British agricultural officer working in India between 1905 and 1931 observed the sustainability of local agricultural practices. Based on his experiences, he wrote the seminal organic farming book, *An Agricultural Testament* (1947). Howard's particular legacy was his focus on the role of humus and composting in maintaining healthy soil. He developed the principles behind rapid composting, using a technique now known as the Indore Method.

Louis Bromfield (1896–1956)

Louis Bromfield's account of rescuing and restoring a worn-out, eroded piece of land in Ohio that he named 'Malabar Farm' was recounted in his book, *Pleasant Valley*. He documented his use of the deep-rooted alfalfa to bring up nutrients from the glacial sediments that lay beneath his soil. Successive cuts off the alfalfa were turned into the exhausted soil to remineralize it as well as to add desperately needed organic matter.

Bromfield, a Pulitzer Prize winner and author of 30 major books, studied agriculture at Cornell University before going to Columbia University to study journalism. A contemporary of Steinbeck, Hemingway, Sinclair Lewis, Pearl S

Mount Vernon, in Virginia, was home to the first president of the United States, George Washington, for over 45 years. A strong environmentalist, it was here, on his family estate, that he practiced many pioneering farming methods.

Buck, and F Scott Fitzgerald, he was a foundation staff member of *Time* magazine. He moved to France as his writing career escalated, spending almost 12 years there. It was in France that he was able to contrast the sustainable methods of traditional European farming with the then current practices in his native Ohio that had simply mined the land of its nutrients, causing farms to be abandoned within three generations.

His reputation as a conservationist and farmer grew worldwide until they equaled his reputation as a writer, and he has been honored both in the United States and abroad for his visionary and innovative techniques and ideas, which were adopted around the world. *Malabar Farm* and *From My Experience*, the continuing story of the restoration of his farm, are also inspirational classics of organic farming.

Much of the movement that is today called sustainable or organic agriculture had its roots in those books, and in Bromfield's restoration of the worn-out 1,000 acres (405 ha) of 'Poverty Knob', as the farm had previously been called. In a few short years he turned it into one of the most productive farms in Richmond County, tripling the yields by using only natural methods. Agriculturalists and farmers came not only from all over the country but from all around the world to learn about his farming system.

J I Rodale (1898–1971)

An influential figure in the early organic movement in the United States, Rodale coined the term 'organic' in 1940, arguing that the use of chemical fertilizers and pesticides was destructive of the environment. His legacies are the Rodale Press, which he founded and which to this day publishes the magazine *Organic Gardening*, and the Rodale Institute, based in Pennsylvania, which

researches and disseminates a wealth of literature on organic methods. Much of this information is available on the Internet.

Percival (P A) Yeomans (1905–1984)

Yeomans, an Australian farmer, was one of a number of people invited by Louis Bromfield to Ohio. In the 1940s he had, quite independently, developed keyline farming, an integrated method for effectively spreading and retaining rainwater on farms, combined with the creation of biologically fertile soil to increase productivity, a system which has now been adopted in many parts of the world. Yeomans' methods emphasized improving the soil organic matter levels by using deep, non-inversion tillage, and the renewal of pasture by cyclical grazing or cutting, effectively treating pasture as a green manure crop. He envisaged and created a permanent agricultural system, one that would constantly improve soil fertility the longer the land was farmed.

Yeomans purchased his original farm of twin blocks totaling 1,000 acres in 1943, on what at the time was considered at best marginal land for farming in an area that can suffer intense drought, at North Richmond, 35 miles (56 km) northwest of Sydney in New South Wales. The property was originally managed by his brother-in-law, who tragically died

US President Thomas Jefferson was a dedicated organic gardener and, at his Monticello farm, cultivated over 250 varieties of vegetable alone.

when a wildfire swept throught the property in 1944.

The killer fire was the trigger for Yeomans to design a farming system that would put moisture into the soil and provide great reservoirs of water to be held across the entire farm. Previous work as a geological engineer, and quite separately in the earthmoving industry, had given him a unique perspective to design and carry out the work. His concepts for tilling, sheet-composting, and green manure crops came out of his own experiences and also the influence of farmers abroad such as Friend Sykes, T J Barrett, Edward Faulkner (author of *Ploughman's Folly*), and many others. He not only read extensively in his field but also corresponded actively with many leading 'alternative' agriculturalists of his period around the world.

Yeomans is the single most influential agriculturalist produced by Australia, and his name is known far beyond his original sphere of

An ornamental garden consisting entirely of vegetables.

influence. His last book, *The City Forest*, published in 1971, was in some ways a precursor to the work of another Australian whose influence has spread worldwide—Bill Mollison, co-founder of the Permaculture Movement. Yeomans' book remains a highly influential text for contemporary urban designers and architects. Today, although his farm is now surrounded by creeping urbanization, its green, rolling hills, lush pasture, and extensive keyline system of dams and off-contour water channels remain a monument to his vision. The farm is currently being used as a cattle-fattening property, maintained under the guidelines that Yeomans laid down.

Rachel Carson (1907–64)

During the 1960s, doubts about chemical agriculture were intensifying as the long-term effects of the heavy usage of pesticides such as DDT were becoming apparent. A book about the subject by Rachel Carson, *Silent*

Spring, became recognized by the organic movement and society in general as a wake-up call about the downside of what had been a rush to jump aboard the chemical train.

Masanobu Fukuoka (1913–)

In Japan in the middle of last century, a microbiologist was also becoming increasingly disenchanted with the narrow solutions that modern science was providing. Masanobu Fukuoka became a farmer dedicated to seeking a more sustainable system that adopted many of the principles of ancient Japanese agriculture. He wrote *The One-Straw Revolution: An Introduction to Natural Farming*, a book that has become a classic for organic gardeners. In it, he recounts how he rescued a worn-out farm and restored it to health, high productivity, and a state of balance with nature. One of his methods was to use the huge Japanese daikon radish, which can grow up to 40 in (1 m) long or more, to loosen and aerate the ground, as well as to bring up subterranean minerals to enrich the topsoil. A world away from Bromfield, he solved the same problem of demineralized, highly compacted, humus-free soils by the same method, differing only in the plant he chose to grow in his fields. Fukuoka's sequel work, *The Natural Way of Farming*, is also well worth reading for its ecological and philosophical insights.

Friend Sykes

In England in 1936, Friend Sykes was plagued by an outbreak of tuberculosis that affected two-thirds of his prize-winning Friesian dairy herd, as well as contagious abortion in his most valuable thoroughbred breeding mare. The animals had all been raised on lush, chemically fertilized, lowland soils at 'Richings Park' in Buckinghamshire. He eventually left this farm and bought an almost derelict, windswept, and bleak 750-acre (300-ha) Wiltshire upland property on the eastern escarpment of Salisbury Plain. This land had been in production for perhaps as long as 4,000 years and over the previous 60 years several farmers had given up on its thin, unproductive soils before Sykes purchased it.

There he created mixed leys of pasture species, using them as green manure crops to gradually return structure, microbial life, and fertility to the soil. His leys were on a four-year rotation and included chicory, fescues, sweet clover, kidney vetch, burnet, Italian ryegrass, and timothy. He rotated dairy cattle, followed by beef cattle, and then sheep over his pastures, acquiring three kinds of urine and manure along the way. Each field, with its rich green manure ley crops and complement of dung and urine, was then harrowed and allowed to sheet-compost while lying fallow. That was when what Sykes called 'the farmer's best friend and unpaid labor force'—thousands of earthworms encouraged by the soil's aeration, warmth, and organic matter—worked together to release abundant plant foods back into the topsoil for the next planting. Vast quantities of compost were also prepared on the farm with the help of mechanization, and used to grow all the winter feeding crops needed on the farm as well as making the household self-sufficient. Sykes staked his organically fertilized wheat against all comers grown from 'artificials' for the flavor of the bread it made.

Using only natural techniques, and despite the doubts of his farmer friends, he gradually created a second prize-winning herd and converted his farm from barrenness to lushness, balance, and health based on green manuring. His book, *Humus and the Farmer*, is another classic in the world of sustainable farming.

The way we are now

Modern civilization relies on factory-style agriculture and horticulture that is motivated by profitability and economic rationalism. Unfortunately, this drives farmers to try and squeeze the maximum productivity out of their land in a way that is often unsustainable. Governments and society can no longer afford, however, to ignore the massive problems of soil erosion, salinity, weed invasion, and chemical pollution that have become the inevitable consequences of unsustainable farming practices. This zero tolerance of pests, diseases, and imperfections makes it almost impossible for farmers to work in sustainable ways.

We are bombarded daily in the media with new reports of the problems being created by technologies that have been imposed on society in the name of progress. Food additives, packaging and processing, and now genetically modified organisms, are all issues that are raising questions about whether we have gone too far with technology.

All plants benefit from the organic approach. Whether you're starting a new garden from scratch, or are beginning to use organic methods in your existing space, you'll soon see an amazing difference.

The great paradox of modern agriculture and horticulture is that while plant breeding has played a very significant role in the enormous gains in food production, it has also resulted in a disastrous phenomenon known as 'genetic erosion'. New varieties have been developed that are high yielding and fit easily into mechanized agribusiness, resulting in the vast majority of the old varieties that were used to breed these plants being discarded.

Advances in many crops have been made through what are known as F1 hybrids, produced by commercial plant breeders for their uniformity and high productivity. The big problem for organic gardeners is that seed produced by F1 hybrids does not come true to type, and while it is possible to collect and grow them, they will not have the same characteristics as their parents.

Genetically modified plants present a different set of problems. Genetic engineers are combining genetic material from organisms in ways that have never been possible in Nature. Going on previous scientific experience we know that changing one part of an ecosystem will always result in some kind of knock-on effect, resulting in unforeseen changes in other directions that lead to environmental problems.

A possible example of such problems lies in the breeding of genetically modified plants that have resistance to the widely used herbicide glyphosate (sold under tradenames such as Roundup and Zero). This work is being done with crops such as tomatoes that have wild relatives that are weeds. It is conceivable that the gene for herbicide resistance could be transferred to the wild relatives by bees and other insects transferring pollen at random from crop to weeds. This could result in strains of 'super weeds' that are resistant to glyphosate.

What makes organic gardening different?

Organic gardening is all about sustainable gardening that creates a balance between the plants we wish to grow and the various other organisms that inevitably come to co-exist with them. It is simply unnatural for plants to grow blemish-free, and if we can accept that we do not need to exterminate pests, diseases, and weeds, but rather learn to manage them, then we can create gardens that are safe, sustainable, satisfying, and productive.

The key to the success of the organic approach lies in sustainability through diversity of plants and the organisms that associate with them, creating a healthy balance of organisms in the soil. This allows us to establish an ecological balance and maintain it through more natural methods of pest and disease control.

Organic gardening gives us the opportunity to regain control over one of the basic needs in life—food.

The vast majority of gardeners would prefer not to use toxic chemicals if they can be avoided. Growing and consuming a diverse range of chemical-free food plants provides us with a diet that is much more in tune with how we have evolved as a species. Freshly ripened organic produce can provide an extraordinary diversity of nutritionally important components for our diet, making us healthier and happier on a daily basis. Successful organic gardeners would also point to the tremendous satisfaction of growing healthy plants and then enjoying the wonderful flavor and texture of chemical-free fruit and vegetables.

Organic produce is not just better to the taste, it also has higher vitamin levels and lasts longer. Research is still unlocking the nutritional effects of eating organic foods, but the story also involves hidden benefits such as natural antibiotics formed by microorganisms in composted soils. We co-evolved with our food plants grown by natural means, and it seems that the lesson, repeated in so many areas, is that our bodies are best served by working with the pattern long evolved by Nature.

Inspirational People

Kent Whealy

Kent is director and co-founder of the Seed Savers Exchange (SSE), a nonprofit organization of 8,000 gardeners, orchardists, and plant collectors who maintain and distribute heirloom varieties of vegetables, fruits, grains, flowers, and herbs. In 1986, he began developing Heritage Farm, a unique educational facility near Decorah, Iowa, in the United States, that maintains and displays collections of 19,000 heirloom vegetables and fruits and herds of Ancient White Park cattle.

Kent Whealy began his campaign to save heirloom varieties in the early 1970s by writing to gardening magazines about the loss of precious heirloom vegetables. He received an enthusiastic response from readers and began a small seed saving and swapping group of six members. A year later, one member had died but her precious 'Bird Egg' bean' that her grandmother had brought to Missouri in the 1880s was preserved, saved by that early network. It is now owned by hundreds of gardeners and is safely stored in the repositories of SSE, along with 4,000 other rare and heirloom varieties of beans. There are

also 4,000 varieties of heirloom tomatoes, 950 peas, 1,200 peppers, and 850 lettuces among a total of 18,000 varieties.

The Seed Savers Network, officially begun in 1975 with a total of 29 members, now consists of 8,000. Today, the annually published *Seed Savers Yearbook* listing seed for exchange has 21,000 members listed. The SSE has received much support not only from gardeners and farmers, but also from scientists and plant breeders caught up in the same battle to preserve genetic diversity in edible crops.

At Heritage Farm Kent then took on another monumental task—to record every vegetable variety available in the United States, together with every known source. The aim was to hold documented evidence of seed becoming threatened with commercial extinction, or lost from the lists. Every threatened variety is taken under the care of the SSE and five editions of the vegetable seed inventory have now been completed. An underground storage facility now protects this irreplaceable germplasm collection.

There are ten isolation gardens around the farm to prevent crosspollination and allow for crop rotation. Netted isolation boxes are used for some crops such as peppers. The orchard is filled with precious collections of apples, crabapples, and cold-hardy varieties of grapes.

In recent times, the SSE has collaborated with the Vavilov Institute in St Petersburg, Russia, once the world's greatest seedbank, and has donated money to sustain vital plant-collecting expeditions. Part of the Vavilov collection is now safely replicated in Iowa, as are some of the collections once preserved in East Germany. Kent and the SSE have also joined the fight to prevent the patenting and locking up of plant genes by modern bioengineering companies.

Kent Whealy of Seed Savers Exchange.

Bill Mollison

In the latter half of the 1970s Bill Mollison decided to set about designing planting systems for human settlement that would more closely reflect the stable structure of natural plant ecosystems. His aim was to design systems that were economically profitable and ecologically sound. His concept, permaculture—from permanent and culture—is now a worldwide movement.

Encouraged by the response to a radio broadcast in Australia about his ideas to revolutionize agriculture, Bill went to print in 1978 with *Permaculture One*. From the huge interest that this book generated all around Australia arose a need to do something concrete with these new ideas and to meet up with those who felt similarly inspired. Out of this emerged an association with a quarterly journal, which evolved to become the *International Permaculture Journal*. More publications followed over the years. In 1999, Bill wrote *The Permaculture Book of Ferment and Human Nutrition*, aimed at modern city dwellers.

Permaculture design essentially created highly productive, inter-dependent planting systems that mimicked those in Nature. Structural and species diversity, exploitation of site diversity, and a true understanding of the local ecology were the structural underpinnings of this new philosophy.

As Bill says, 'Permaculture designs are human constructs. Nowhere in Nature will you find them. We needed a system that would produce enough energy to give a sustainable yield. Nature … produces greater sustainability … by producing a more complex system. That's what we did. But Nature doesn't have gardens like this, so incredibly rich in functional plants.'

David Cavagnaro

A master gardener in Iowa philosophically dedicated to organic gardening, David Cavagnaro maintains that human beings need to understand and respect the principles of Nature that govern natural ecosystems, and that we should model our co-creative gardening process after those principles.

David, who is largely self-taught, believes that we should have the courage to experiment and evaluate the results, and then through the process of trial and error to arrive at solutions that work. He also believes we should read and learn from the experience of others, but primarily he is keen on encouraging people to try things on their own and come to their own conclusions and solutions.

David Cavagnaro

One of the skills that David considers essential is to learn how to observe intelligently and accurately in the garden, to understand the life cycles of insect pests and disease organisms, and to develop interventions accordingly. David seldom eliminates diseases and pests in his garden, saying, 'Clearly an organic approach involves all of these organisms existing together in some form of balance, so in a sense everybody gets something to eat. And we should never use any poisons or any interventions that are designed to annihilate anything, but rather to keep things in some kind of balance.'

David's approach to garden design is somewhat unusual. At the start of winter he goes through his seed collection, collecting or ordering in more seeds that he wants to grow. The seeds are then sorted into different bags correlated according to planting time—so he will have an early spring greenhouse and cold frame bag of seeds, an early spring vegetable bag and an early spring flower bag for direct sowing outside, and a warm weather planting bag of each as well. When each of those planting cycles comes around, he gets all of those seeds out on the table, spreads them out, and starts planting.

In the back of his mind, David likes to keep a clear idea of what his garden spaces are, and he tries to visualize different combinations and different ways that he might want to arrange these plants, and in what volumes. He tends to overplant as a result, and is never sure until he actually goes out into the garden just how many plants of each crop he is going to put in.

The result is often like an abstract painting gradually revealed, which is unique each year. 'It is all very instinctive but nevertheless the skill involved is based on years of experience in terms of knowing when to plant things, how to care for them, and what kind of conditions they need.'

David's season begins in spring with the removal of prodigious amounts of leaf mulch and litter protection, liberating the plants that have been protected over the winter. During March and April, he germinates in the greenhouse and the cold frame those plants that will go out as soon as the frost has passed. Cool weather seeds that can go straight into the garden, such as peas and sweet peas, are planted out. His season gradually escalates through April and May, and then at the end of May and early June there is a two-week period for planting, during which all else is set aside.

'Theoretically, June is a quieter month, because everything is in and we are just waiting for things to grow. But in actual fact, it isn't quite so. There is plenty to do! The weeds come on and mulching has to be done. Particularly the mulching! All the winter mulch that came off the winter-protected plants goes back out on beds and paths for weed control and moisture retention. And then the work escalates through the summer as the crops need harvesting, and the produce bottling, and drying, and processing for winter.'

There is no let-up for David in fall, because he will need to haul many pickup loads of packed, chipped leaves from the leaf dump in town in order to mulch those plants that need to be protected over the winter. He aims to have everything done and ready before the first snow falls, usually some time between the end of October and the end of November.

Once winter arrives, the year slows down, and he takes the opportunity to catch up on desk work and other neglected tasks until the cycle starts again in April.

As a master gardener, David has a refreshing attitude toward weeds. 'Well, of course, we eat them!' he says. 'You know the old saying that one man's junk is another man's treasure. Well, that is a philosophy that applies to weeds as well. The term "weed" is very subjective. It simply means something that one doesn't like, something that seems out of place, or competitive ... In Iowa, where the vegetation grows rampantly as though we lived in the tropics, you have to cut some of the introductions down with a chainsaw because of the size they get to. [But] there has to be some kind of balance created in the garden between the domestic plants we enjoy for beauty or for sustenance and those that are

aggressively competing. So we do have interventions of various kinds in our garden, particularly mulching, and prodigious amounts of weeding which everyone grumbles about, but like all gardeners we face those issues. But once again we try to live in balance with these things, and strike some kind of balance in terms of how much time we spend at it versus the end result.'

As someone who has planted out more than 15,000 cultivars during his career, David is in a good position to recommend the exceptional performers of the vegetable world. Among the tomatoes, he likes 'Amish Paste' and 'Green Zebra'. When it comes to lettuces, David prefers to grow varieties across a broad range of colors, and often chooses decorative varieties such as 'Lollo Rosso' and 'Lollo Bionda', the frilly red and yellow varieties, as well as 'Australian Yellowleaf' for its magnificent pale chartreuse color, which he plants side by side with 'Ibis', a dark, almost black lettuce.

David has one—and only one— favorite green bean cultivar, the famous Italian pole bean 'Romano'. For either fresh eating or freezing, this delicate bean hardly requires any cooking and far outstrips anything else he has encountered.

Old fashioned country flowers growing at the Seed Saver Exchange, Iowa, U.S.

Chapter 2

UNDERSTANDING
HOW PLANTS GROW

Beneath the ground

Roots

'Out of sight, out of mind' is an expression that is most applicable to plant roots, as they are a greatly neglected facet of successful gardening. More often than not poor performance above the ground is due to problems with the root system. A plant's root system is the means by which it takes up nutrients and water. Finely structured hairs at the extremities of the root system do the majority of the work.

The traditional belief that a taproot penetrates deeply into the soil to anchor the plant and then branches laterally to find nutrients and water is often not accurate. In fact, roots will go wherever it is easiest and most rewarding, and so if the soil is compacted underneath, they will stick to the topsoil where they can easily penetrate. If there is a source of water nearby such as a broken drain, the roots will concentrate in that area.

Perhaps the most basic of all factors in successful plant growth is the creation of a balance between air and water (since nutrients in the soil are dissolved in water) in the soil. In between the particles of sand, silt, clay, and organic matter are voids or pore spaces that can contain either air or water. The smaller spaces hold water against the force of gravity and the larger spaces hold air most of the time, providing drainage and allowing the roots and soil organisms to breath. Digging in lots of organic matter glues the soil particles together and builds soil structure which is the key to getting the right balance between large and small pore spaces.

Microorganisms

A healthy organic soil is brimming with all sorts of organisms, from the highly visible types such as earthworms down to microscopic single-celled creatures such as bacteria, as well as a multitude in between such as fungi and algae. The presence of healthy and abundant soil microflora is the key factor that sets organic gardening apart from other methods. The way to encourage these small organisms is by using composts and manures in generous quantities.

The place where microorganisms live is the rhizosphere, a narrow zone of soil directly adjacent to plant roots, containing root exudates, leaked and secreted chemicals, sloughed root cells, and mucilages. This complex mixture of organic compounds provides nutrients for the microorganisms, many of which are capable of forming relationships with the plant. The most important of these is symbiosis, the mutually beneficial relationship between two organisms. Beneficial soil organisms include fungi, bacteria, and nematodes.

Well-prepared soil is the key to a good harvest.

Mycorrhizal fungi—literally translated, this term means 'fungus roots'—are one of the most common forms of symbiosis in the plant world. Basically, a friendly species of fungus grows in intimate contact with the root cells, and the fine threads of the fungus (known as mycelia) act as extensions of the root system, making the plant much more efficient at taking up water and nutrients, especially if these are in limited supply. This type of symbiosis is particularly common in woody plants, and the secret to making it happen lies in enriching your soil with compost. Not only do mycorrhizal fungi help the plant to take up water and nutrients, but they also protect the roots from infection by harmful pathogenic fungi.

There are also beneficial types of bacteria that can have profoundly positive relationships with certain types of plants. The best example of this is **Rhizobium**, which lives in the roots of a family of plants known as legumes, which includes peas, beans, soybeans, clovers, acacias, and a host of others. The bacteria enter the roots and, as the colonies increase, they form swellings known as nodules. Inside these nodules, the bacteria absorb nitrogen gas from the air in the soil and convert it into a mineral form that can be absorbed by the plant. As nitrogen is required by plants in relatively large quantities and is often in limited supply in the soil, the action of Rhizobium makes it possible for legumes to thrive in soils where other plants struggle for adequate nutrition.

The relationship between legumes and Rhizobium has been known for many decades. While the bacteria are found in most soils, they are also commonly introduced by coating seed with a slurry containing Rhizobium.

Nematodes are microscopic, worm-like creatures that inhabit the soil in huge numbers. Perhaps the best

known of these soil-dwelling creatures are those that cause harm to plants, such as the root knot nematode. However, soil biologists are discovering many beneficial species that combat pests and diseases that are injurious to plants. They are all part of the natural balance that is characteristic of a healthy soil ecosystem.

The great thing about these beneficial organisms is that they are already present in most soils, and simply by enriching your soil with composts and manures on a regular basis, you will introduce even more as well as encouraging those that are already there. Castings from worms are also a potent source of beneficial microorganisms.

Commercial preparations of these naturally occurring biological agents are starting to be made available to farmers. Some are already available to home gardeners in countries such

The bacterium Rhizobium lives in the roots of leguminous plants such as acacias and helps the plant to absorb beneficial nutrients.

as the United States. As awareness of the benefits increases undoubtedly they will become available to gardeners worldwide.

Nutrient deficiencies

Nutrient deficiencies can result from a variety of circumstances and are generally of two distinct types. First, a large range of nutrients can be depleted from the soil when we grow a crop and harvest it at the end of the season. Symptoms of such generalized nutrient deficiency will include a general stunting and yellowing of the plant. To correct such problems, apply a fertilizer that has a balance of the essential nutrients that plants require. Because most organic fertilizers (such as compost and various animal manures) are based on the breakdown of plant materials, they tend to supply a complete range of nutrients with a

Trees drop their leaves when a combination of climatic features to which they are sensitive indicate that winter has arrived.

balance that replenishes the nutrients that a crop takes out of a soil.

Generally speaking, digging in a 4 in (10 cm) thick layer of compost or manure when preparing the soil will supply the complete range of nutrients required to establish the crop. For perennial plants, apply the materials as mulch on top of the soil. They will gradually work their way into the soil as a form of slow-release fertilizer.

Second, a specific nutrient such as nitrogen or calcium may be lacking, so a concentrated source of that nutrient will correct the deficiency. Deficiencies in specific nutrients often reflect imbalances in the soil such as an extremely acidic or alkaline condition. Often, a dose of a balanced organic fertilizer will also correct these specific deficiencies. If not, it is best to seek advice from a horticulturist or a soil-testing laboratory to find out what the deficiency is and how to correct it organically.

Above the ground

Temperature and day length

Plants have all sorts of subtle ways in which they sense the seasons and use the signals to trigger off events such as flowering and fruiting. This is often the reason why a species will grow well in one particular location but not in another. Species that have evolved in cool climates, such as apple trees, need a sequence of cool night temperatures to tell them that winter has come and gone, and that it is time to flower. Grow them in warmer temperatures, and they will not flower properly.

The farther away from the equator one is, the greater the variation in day length between seasons, and many plant species use this as the signal to tell them when to flower. So a species that requires a short or long day length to flower will not grow well near the equator, where it will remain vegetative and never flower.

An organic approach would be to consider these factors and favor those species which thrive best in your particular area.

Light

A vital part of organic gardening lies in understanding the way in which plants have evolved to thrive in their environmental niche. Too much light can be as harmful to a shade-loving plant grown away from its natural habitat as too little light could be to an arid area species. For instance, plants from rainforest environments often have to survive in low light conditions and have evolved large, dark green leaves to trap whatever sunlight falls their way. Desert plants, on the other hand, often have leaves reduced to spines or even less as light is so abundant. Therefore, consider the natural adaptation of the species you wish to grow in terms of their innate requirements for light.

Natural defences

If you follow organic principles, it shouldn't be necessary to take drastic action when your garden is attacked by pests and diseases. If a plant is healthy it will have a greater capacity to resist them, and it will also heal more quickly if damage does occur. Plants have a rudimentary immune system that is triggered off by infection with pests and diseases. Substances called phytoalexins are produced that are toxic to alien organisms. The sap of woody plants is another method used to counteract pests. Attack by borers stimulates a prolific sap flow that literally drowns out the pest and allows the healing process to begin via special callus cells that grow like a scab over the wound.

The brilliant colors of deciduous leaves in fall. Shorter days are the signal for many trees to commence their preparations for winter.

Chapter 3

CREATING LIVING
SOILS

Many gardening books are full of contingency plans for a thousand disasters. To read them is to fear hordes of mysterious diseases and voracious insects heading for your bit of earth. To take them seriously is to never attempt to create a garden. Well, things do go a little astray in earthly paradises—nothing is perfect. But if you can get your soil into balance, everything else will come into balance too. While insects and diseases are attracted to the weak and feeble in the garden, healthy soils grow healthy plants, and while minor attacks may still occur, they will not be devastating ones, provided that the constitution of your plants is strong and built on sound nutrition.

This chapter will tell you how to create living soil, the kind of soil that smells nutty and sweet, that you can literally dig with your hands—soil full of fat, wriggling earthworms. Seen through a microscope, such a soil is a world of its own, full of tiny micro-arthropods such as mites, spiders, and other insects, one-celled protozoa, slender white laceworks of fungal mycelia, and swarms of minuscule bacteria, all with their part to play in recycling the precious minerals in the topsoil, the upper 4 in (10 cm) where most plant root growth is concentrated.

Compare such a soil with the dead soils left behind in many gardens and farms totally depleted of organic matter. Here, sandy soils run lifeless through your fingers and heavy soils are so compacted that a pickax is needed to break them up. There are no earthworms, no signs of the busy, swarming microscopic world of a good, organic soil. These soils are biologically dead, or nearly so, and they produce plants with multiple deficiencies, prone to diseases and predators. With soils like these, you really do need that set of contingency plans for a thousand garden disasters.

The basis for all organic gardens is organic matter. The precious minerals in the topsoil are continuously returned in the cycle of life to death to life in the plant world. The nutrients locked up in organic matter are released by the activities of a number of different groups of soil organisms. This is carried out in the process

Manure, blood and bone, and compost add nutrients to the soil.

called composting. Long before we knew about the life cycles of all those anonymous soil organisms or had solved the biochemistry of their activities, gardeners were producing abundant and beautiful crops by observing natural processes and following them closely.

In addition to compost, there are many other additives that can be fed to the soil to enrich it, such as well-rotted manures, natural mineral dusts, wood ashes, hay and fallen leaves, worm castings, various vegetable meals, blood and bone, the hulls and shells of peanuts, rice, oats and other grains, broken-up cuttle shells found on beach forages and seaweed washed free of salt. Even coffee grounds and used tea leaves are valuable. In addition, green mulches can be grown as part of a crop rotation and chopped into the soil to be sheet-composted.

Of course, you will not be adding all of these materials to the soil at once, nor probably will you find all these things. Some, at least, are regional specialties. They are just a list of desirable delicacies for your precious topsoil that can be added when, and if, you come by them. The major point is that the organic garden runs on natural substances, and the chief of all these is compost. Now that you know this, nothing organic should ever find its way into your trash can again.

Soil types and soil pH

Whatever type of soil you start out with—no matter how sandy or clay-filled or compacted and hard it may be—the organic approach will turn it into a rich and productive area, the envy of all who see it! The first step is learning about your soil type.

Make a vertical cut into the ground. A series of layers will be revealed, known as 'horizons'. Starting from the top, the uppermost

The basis of any organic garden is the recycling of all green material.

layer of natural mulch, also called the litter layer, is O horizon. Many garden soils lack this layer which is generally only found in forests and other wild, undisturbed situations, and also in well-managed organic gardens. Below that is a darkish layer of topsoil, the A horizon, which may be very thin but in better soils averages 4–6 in (10–15 cm) in depth. Below that is the subsoil or B horizon, which is lighter in color and often higher in clay content. Below that again is the C horizon, the parent rock material. It is perfectly possible, from personal experience, to begin with a 2 in (5 cm) A horizon and no O horizon, particularly in urban situations.

The roots of many plants, particularly annual flowers and vegetables, explore no deeper than the A horizon, the topsoil layer, at most 12 in (30 cm) below the ground. The B horizon can be an obstacle course for any roots attempting to penetrate deeper. It is often stony or may contain a very compacted layer called a 'hardpan'.

Next, you need to find out the pH of the soil to determine what plants will flourish in your particular area, in combination with prevailing climatic factors. A scale of 14 points measures from powerful acids at pH 1 to powerful alkaline substances at pH 14. Neutral soils are pH 7. Soils are increasingly acidic as the pH drops below 7, and increasingly more alkaline as the pH rises above 7. The majority of garden plants prefer a pH of 6–7.5. Mountainous acid soils that grow camellias, heaths, azaleas, and rhododendrons are acidic, and usually in the pH range 5–6. Peat soils associated with swamps are the most acidic of all soils, with a pH as low as 3. Some arid zone soils, so-called alkaline hotspots, are in the pH range 8.5–10.

The importance of soil pH lies in its effect on the availability of soil nutrients, and also the effect that this has not only on plants but also on soil fungi and bacteria. In very acidic soils with a pH of less than 5.5, phosphorus can become restricted in availability. On the other hand, soils that are alkaline progressively lock up nutrients such as iron, manganese, copper, zinc, and boron as the pH increases.

The pH of the soil can be manipulated with soil additives, but it is far easier to adjust the pH upward than downward. Lime or dolomite may be applied to raise the pH of the soil. Compost is slightly acidifying, and its regular addition to alkaline soils gradually reduces the soil pH. The addition of sulfur to the soil will also reduce alkalinity.

Natural dolomitic and acidic soils occur around the world, and whole regional floras are adapted to those extremes. It is a good idea to use plants that have been pre-adapted by natural selection if you garden on a fairly extreme pH. Working with the grain is far easier on the garden and the gardener, and also on the environment. Many highly desirable ornamental plants and trees can be found to suit either markedly acidic or markedly alkaline soils. In the productive part of the garden, in the vegetable garden and home orchard, the addition of copious compost and of lime or dolomite in acid soils will help to bring the soil closer to a desirable pH level.

To determine the pH of your soil, a number of commercial kits are available for a very reasonable price. Few gardens, even smaller ones, have the same soil conditions across the entire garden so several samples should be tested across the area as the pH may vary.

Soil pH is a crucial factor to consider when planning which crops to grow in your garden.

Rock dusts

The crushed gravels left by retreating glaciers after the last Ice Age were a legacy that enriched the farmlands of Europe, North America, and New Zealand. Australia's thin, ancient soils missed out.

In previous centuries, gardeners and farmers knew that rock dusts remineralized depleted soils so they left small rocks in the earth, knowing that over time they would gradually contribute minerals to the soil. As well, gravels and crushed rock were added.

The value of this natural soil remineralization was recognized by both soil scientists and food nutritionists in the 19th century. However, the theory was to suffer a setback after the German scientist Baron Justus von Leibig published his research involving analysis of the constituents of ashed plants in his 1840 book, *Organic Chemistry in its Application to Agriculture and Physiology*. He had found that the elements common to all ashed plants were nitrogen (N), phosphorus (P), and potassium (K). This led to the production of chemical fertilizers formulated to various NPK ratios to suit various crops. Von Leibig had no way of measuring elements present in small amounts, so the all-important trace elements were entirely absent from his theory.

The work, though groundbreaking in a sense, was incredibly crude both analytically and in terms of understanding the complexity of soil science. It could scarcely have been otherwise, given the period in which it was carried out. But his ideas were extraordinarily influential, with an irresistible combination of simplifying and codifying Nature, and the powerful promise of being able to control soil fertility and, by definition, Nature herself.

From that time the interests of agriculturalists were increasingly focused on the provision of specific chemical compounds to supply what was perceived as the required plant elements.

This simplistic approach seemed at first to live up to everyone's hopes. Plants responded with visible results to the addition of the new simple chemicals. Yet even von Leibig came to realize and later to write of his error in oversimplifying the case. He had come to see how intricate and self-sustaining was the process of the recycling of nutrients in the precious topsoil. Sadly, many of his followers were not so self-questioning.

Farmers ceased their old practices of feeding their soils with organic matter such as manures and compost, seaweeds, hoof and horn, and blood and bone. The soil was no longer supplemented with crushed rock and rock dusts. It was so much easier to rip open clean bags of pure chemicals and distribute them over the soil. Chemical companies used highly persuasive marketing to sell their products as the modern way to farm. And it was certainly less time consuming. Humus levels in the soils dropped, and many of the ingredients in NPK-based fertilizers either suppressed or killed many valuable soil microorganisms responsible for providing nutrients in the usable state to plants.

Robbed of the microorganisms capable of feeding the soil with nutrients, the soils in effect became hooked on the artificial fertilizers and farmers and gardeners needed more and more of them to achieve the same effect. Soils also became increasingly acidic, causing additional fertility problems as the supply of some nutrients became locked up by low pH levels. Humus formation was increasingly suppressed, and with it the capacity of the topsoil to hold nutrients. Instead, these were leached into the watertable, in some areas dangerously contaminating house wells with nitrates and other inorganic compounds. As humus levels dropped, soil compaction increased. Farmers began walking off their farms as crop yields dropped below economically sustainable levels, leaving behind them dead soils but not the huge debts they had accumulated.

In some parts of the world where traditional practices were never abandoned, despite continuous land usage for cropping, the soil remains fertile and alive, fed a steady diet of slow-release, organically based fertilizers that are completely in accord with the natural system. These are soils that have been continuously used for thousands of years. They have never worn out, because the natural cycle has been followed and recycling of precious mineral nutrients has always been ensured. Yet

Adding rock dusts to your soil can remineralize depleted areas.

researchers at the University of Wisconsin recently estimated that the overuse of synthetic nitrogen-based fertilizers during the past 40 years has caused the equivalent damage of 5,000 years of natural aging.

We now know how the hard particles of rock dusts release their nutrients to the soil. Weathering can account for some release of minerals, but only over a long time. The whole process is greatly speeded up by the organic (humic) acids released from decomposing organic matter and also by soil microorganisms (including malic and acetic acids). Weak though these acids are, they have been demonstrated to release the constituent elements from rock dust in a usable, soluble form. Once released, these can be held attached to soil colloids such

as those of humus and clay, and accessed by the plants through the principle of positive ion exchange.

To be effective, rock dusts need to be incorporated into the soil with the addition of compost that will help provide the necessary organic acids to speed up mineral release. If a green manure crop is to be grown, rock dusts can be applied to the crop, and the whole slashed down at maturity and incorporated into the soil. When you construct your compost heap, add a good dusting of ground rock on each successive layer so that the organic acids that are formed in the composting process will begin to break down the dusts. Granite dust is the exception to the rule, and is usually applied with compost directly to the soil.

A number of mineral dust fertilizers are commonly used. Dusts are the preferred form as they offer a large surface area for organic acids to attack. These include:

Rock phosphate

In trials, rock phosphate dust incorporated with compost into the soil has equaled the addition of single phosphate. However, depending on where it was mined, rock phosphate can be contaminated by other minerals that are not desirable. If you purchase it through an organic supply company, this should not be a problem, and the company will be able to tell you the source. In other cases, you'll need to find out yourself. One way of doing this is to send samples to a mineral laboratory for tests. One great benefit of rock phosphate is that, being slow working, an over-generous application does not matter.

Dolomite

Dolomite is used interchangeably with lime by many gardeners, but is more valuable as it consists of both calcium carbonate and magnesium carbonate. It is particularly useful in sandy soils

and also in low magnesium soils. As well, it adjusts the pH upward in the same manner as lime. **Crushed limestone** has the same effect but is pure calcium carbonate.

Natural gypsum

Powdered natural gypsum is particularly valued for its ability to break up sticky clay soils so that they can be cultivated. The calcium content is also valuable for crops.

Greensand

Greensand is the crushed product from a sandy rock or sediment that contains a high amount of glauconite, a greenish-black mineral formed in shallow marine deposits. Glauconite in turn contains, among others, the elements potassium, phosphorus, iron, and magnesium, and has been commercially marketed for over a century as a natural mineral fertilizer and soil improver for both crops and potted plants in the United States. It has long been a favorite of organic growers, as it slowly releases potassium and phosphorus without causing the tip burn associated with fast-release chemical fertilizers. Greensand also has the ability to absorb large amounts of water.

Crushed basalt

Basalt rock, originating from volcanic activity, is used in quantity in road building, and the dust from the preparation of basalt gravel, known as 'belt dust', is quite readily available in many areas. It is an excellent source of minerals, including silica (used in cell structure and in phosphorus and calcium uptake), and makes an optimum additive where it is available.

Granite dust

This is an excellent source of slow-release potash or potassium. Granite dusts vary in composition but usually contain 3–5 percent potassium.

The vexed question of trace elements

Trace elements—boron, zinc, copper, iron, manganese, and molybdenum—are vital for plant growth though they are only needed in very tiny amounts. Younger geological soils such as those of North America and New Zealand are very unlikely to display major trace element deficiencies. However, some areas of inland Australia are seriously lacking in one or more trace elements. Human beings and grazing animals living off such soils take on the same trace element deficiencies. In a well established organic garden you should not have a problem with trace element deficiencies as the continuous process of recycling organic matter in the soil will prevent them from occurring. If, however, you are at an early stage of creating your organic garden and are planning to live on the produce you raise, it might be worth getting a full analysis done on your soil. Make sure you also receive an interpretation of the results from a competent person as they will mean very little in raw figures to a lay person. Deficiences can be remedied by the addition of seaweed, which accumulates trace elements, to compost heaps, as well as the use of seaweed 'soup', seaweed sprays, and seaweed mulches to the soil. Basalt and other mineral dusts are also useful for this purpose.

To dig or not to dig?

One of the controversies in organic gardening is the question of whether it is better to thoroughly dig the garden before planting each crop or to minimally disturb the soil once it has been prepared. Given the effort and time involved in thorough digging, it is deeply satisfying to be able to confirm that laziness, for once, has its own rewards. There is no doubt that redigging the land for each successive crop is damaging both to soil structure and to the life in the soil.

Every time soil is thoroughly dug (or rototilled or plowed conventionally), the exposure to air causes a rapid increase in decomposition of organic matter. As well, the entire complex, interwoven community of soil biota is severely disturbed.

Sometimes, however, digging is unavoidable. Many urban gardens in particular have been very severely

Digging too deeply can harm the delicate infrastructure of microorganisms beneath the soil's surface.

compacted and are acidic due to past industrial activities. Often, they are virtual deserts, with few signs of worms or microscopic life. In these circumstances, digging is necessary, but it is important to preserve the soil's natural horizons. The general rule in preparing a new garden bed is to loosen the deeper soil with a garden fork by pushing it in and then moving it backward and forward, and then to turn the topsoil shallowly, if at all.

Once the garden bed has been prepared, it can be sheet-mulched with progressive layers of alfalfa (lucerne) hay or pea straw, salt hay, or other organic mulches, and dusted with additives such as rock dusts, powdered seaweed, bone meal, dolomite, and so on. The mattress of mulch should initially be about 18 in (45 cm) deep or more. Make pockets in the mulch and fill them with rich compost, into which large seeds such as squash may be directly planted, or well-grown seedlings of Asian greens, brassicas, or tomatoes. Chitted potatoes can be placed in the middle layer of the mulch sandwich. The bed should then be thoroughly watered. Make sure it receives regular watering until the mulch begins to settle, or the plant roots may dry out.

As the mulch settles and composts, it will form a cool, moist, rich root run for the plants. Beneath the mulch, the soil will now contain active earthworms. Soon the soil will smell sweet and nutty, and it will be swarming with life. An annual relayering of the garden can be continued indefinitely if necessary. Gardens on sandy beach soils, for instance, are exceedingly hungry for organic matter and could be sheet-mulched in this manner annually, or on rotation. Alternatively, the 'no-dig' garden can be conventionally planted after the first year (without disturbing the soil) and mulched.

There is a more absolute form of 'no-dig' gardening, in which the

Healthy soil contains all the essential nutrients plants need to grow.

garden is pegged out on turf and then sheet-mulched very heavily, with no prior ground preparation. It works perfectly well. In fact, with this technique, gardeners have been known to grow a good harvest of vegetables on concrete.

It is a personal choice, but I prefer to loosen the lower soil of flower gardens that will be in the public eye, then lightly turn the top 4–6 in (10–15 cm) and incorporate into the soil generous quantities of well-rotted compost. The bed can then be planted and mulched. In this way the soil is only disturbed once, in the initial preparation of the garden. Thereafter, compost and regular mulches only need to be applied to the surface. Aesthetically, these beds never look displeasing and are rapidly activated to become very healthy and productive. The vegetable garden can be managed on a rotational 'no-dig' garden basis, which enriches the soil. Vegetables requiring a fine tilth can be grown in 'no-dig' beds 12–18 months after construction. All new beds can also be created by this method, but the soil should always be loosened first.

If you apply these methods to a very heavy soil, you'll improve initial drainage, soil wettability, the rate of soil improvement, and the increase in worm population. It's worth remembering that these principles can always be adapted if necessary. What works well in one area, soil, or climate may need modifying for another.

Is sludge safe?

Sludge is the solid sediment left behind after municipal wastewater has been treated. Sludge is very rich in recovered nutrients but can also contain amounts of heavy metals and other pollutants. Depending on where you live, these will either be of concern or within permissible limits. Is the risk of using this product acceptable? The standards applied in most countries are variable, and few are as conservative as those of some European governments. Perhaps in the matter of

sludge it is sensible to be cautious. As far as we know, soil contaminants are long-lived, and mistakes are likely to be equally long-lived.

Compost

Earth is the greatest composter, processing millions of tons of dead material daily, recycling the nutrients that are locked up within decaying matter, and returning them back to the soil so that they are once again available for plants. Even without lifting a finger in your garden, composting will happen. Making compost has more to do with speeding up a natural process that might otherwise take years in cooler climates, and with retaining the abundant nutrients once they are produced.

Good compost smells like rich, moist, woodland earth—sweet and nutty. If you run it through your

Rich, moist organic material will enrich the soil and improve the productivity of any plant.

fingers it feels irresistibly sensuous, cushiony, crumbly, and cool. In theory, you should be able to dig the earth with your hands if it is well composted. In fact, you shouldn't be able to resist doing so!

Nutrients are slowly and steadily released to plants by the compost so that natural growth rates and seasonal hardening off occurs. Compost is the finest of all soil improvers, whether in heavy clay soils or the sandy soils of coastal areas. Its spongy nature is vital to successful gardening in sandy soils as it holds water and prevents the rapid leaching of nutrients from the topsoil, while heavy soils on the other hand are improved in texture, aeration, and drainage.

The end point of composting is a substance called 'humus', a complex mixture of sticky brown colloidal substances. It is the colloids in humus that ultimately release nutrients to the plant roots and keep the soil aerated and fluffy. In heavy clay soils, colloids act as binding agents for the clay particles, sticking them together into granular aggregates. Instead of a dense impenetrable clay, tiny holes appear between the clay aggregates, which then allow air and water to penetrate with much greater ease. Colloids are quite stable chemically, but they do eventually break down. Adding compost to the soil annually replaces colloids lost to the soil, as well as continuing to improve soil texture and fertility.

There are two quite opposite approaches to composting. One involves dumping endless piles of wet, compacted, mown summer grass in a forlorn corner of the garden, occasionally enlivened with the odd unwanted lettuce leaves and brussels sprouts. This turns in relatively little time into a squelchy, slimy, green and brown mound that exudes strangely odorous vapors when kicked with a garden boot. The second involves advanced mathematical calculations,

intricate formulae and at least a nodding acquaintance with university-level chemistry. Undoubtedly, this is a source of satisfying challenge, and an absorbing interest for some. Both approaches have been responsible for many gardeners abandoning a project to compost garden and kitchen wastes.

In reality, a skill for sandwich making and the possession of a few guiding principles are all that is required to succeed in making plentiful, sweet, nutty-scented, rich brown compost. And, this way, there will be no complaints from the neighbors. Understanding what drives the process of composting will put you in charge of the compost heap, and able to easily adjust your technique to suit different circumstances.

How to make a compost heap

The materials for a compost heap depend on what is readily at hand. The father of the modern compost heap—an odd but honorable distinction—was Sir Albert Howard, who developed the principles behind rapid composting. He discovered that layering different organic materials in a heap caused decomposition to become both more rapid and more complete. He created what were effectively giant sandwiches, with successive layers composed of a good carbon source (such as hay, shredded

In warmer climates, a compost heap can generate an enormous amount of heat as the organic material in it decomposes.

cardboard and paper, weeds, grass clippings, sawdust, prunings from shrubs and trees), a rich source of nitrogen (manures, washed seaweed, comfrey leaves, hops, tomato wastes, pea and bean wastes, bone meal, fish meal, blood and bone), a sprinkling of lime or dolomite, and a light layer of garden loam. He also discovered that aerating the pile improved the process, and that a minimum critical mass of material was necessary to produce rapid breakdown. His discoveries remain the basis for composting techniques today.

In Sir Albert Howard's day, manures were the easiest of things to come by. In cities these days, the most likely sources are riding stables, poultry farms, and spent mushroom compost from your local garden center. All of these materials are rich not only in nitrogen but also in the appropriate microorganisms. The other suggested nitrogen sources are often easier to come by. Nitrogen-rich comfrey leaves are an ideal accelerator for the compost heap. Comfrey is an exceptionally generous plant that soon forms a large clump that can be

readily harvested for its large leaves. A warning about comfrey: place the clump where you will not resent its pioneering ways as it is not easy to completely remove once established. Substances such as fish meal and blood and bone are already very concentrated and need only be used as a sprinkled layer. A sprinkling of rock dust can be applied at the same time.

Broken down into its simplest formula, these are the four basics of composting: air, an equal ratio of carbon and nitrogen sources, control of excessive acidity, and moisture. Those nasty smells that emanate from compacted little piles are the result of air being excluded from the pile. In the absence of air, a form of composting occurs using microorganisms that do not require oxygen, a process called 'anaerobic fermentation', and it is the cause of many closed windows.

To avoid this, begin your compost heap by marking out a space about 5–6 ft (1.5–2 m) square in a convenient and fairly sunny area of your vegetable garden. Drive four sturdy posts (metal star posts are quick and easy) into the ground and wrap wire netting around

Compost bins are available in a wide range of designs and will fit in the smallest garden.

three sides, using wire ties to keep the netting in place. There is absolutely no need to remove the turf. Criss-cross a latticework of prunings and branches from trees on the ground to form an open mattress about 4 in (10 cm) deep. This layer will allow air to circulate freely under the growing pile and will draw the air up through the pile, speeding up the rate of decomposition in the same way that a fire burns more fiercely when a draft of air passes upward. The wire netting sides also increase air access to the pile.

Now you can form your heap on the twig mattress, spreading each layer evenly out to the sides. Compost heaps make wonderful family or even neighborhood projects. Ask everyone to save all their old papers and have a paper-shredding morning out in the sunshine. It is the sort of group exercise that gets rid of tension and is very satisfying as the piles grow. Let everyone know that grass clippings are welcome, and bags of vegetable scraps (but not meat, which will attract vermin). With the enticement of an *al fresco* meal and cold drinks, you may find yourself well provided with mountains of compostable material, and very popular as neighbors and family gather to help and learn. That first huge compost heap may be only one weekend away.

If, however, you have to make the compost heap alone, no matter. Create one full layering of carbon and nitrogen-based materials sprinkled with dolomite, lime, or sources of calcium such as crushed eggshells and wood ashes, and top it with a thin layer of soil. Repeat each time the kitchen pail is full of vegetable scraps.

To further improve aeration, drive three or four stakes into the ground when you begin the pile. After the pile is completed at about 5 ft (1.5 m), wriggle each of the stakes around to make a hole, then withdraw the stakes.

Now you need to provide your heap with the right amount of moisture. Without sufficient moisture, the microorganisms needed to decompose the pile are not activated. Excessive water, on the other hand, fills the air spaces between material and causes undesirable anaerobic bacteria to activate. Make sure the last layer of the pile is a capping of soil, then water the heap to thoroughly wet the contents without making them soggy. The mattress of twigs and branches at the base of the pile provides the additional advantage of allowing the pile to drain correctly.

A well-made compost heap can reach temperatures of 158°F (70°C). It can scald if a hand is placed inside, and will steam gently in the air. If you are concerned about weed seeds in compost, don't be. If it is well made, the pile will reach sufficiently high temperatures for long enough to kill the seed. After a few days at peak heat, the pile will begin to lose temperature.

If you haven't been able to add compost to the garden, feeding plants directly is a priority. Always water well after fertilising.

You could leave it to continue composting more slowly. Alternatively, the pile can be turned over by forking it out and throwing it all back again, loosely mixed. It is extra effort but is rewarded by a second rapid increase in heat. In midsummer, a compost pile may have broken down sufficiently for it to be used within two to three weeks if a second turning is made.

While the first pile is composting, peg out an adjacent second area so that a new heap can be started. There is something magical about the way a huge sandwiched pile heats up so quickly and within weeks sinks to a fluffy, rich, sweet-smelling, brown pile about half the volume of the original. Anything that has not sufficiently composted in your first pile can always be put onto the new pile for recomposting.

One other point is helpful. The smaller the pieces of material placed into the compost heap, the greater the surface area for the microorganisms to attack. Bashing, shredding, and cutting material greatly increases the exposed surface area. Use a hammer or the back of a spade on tough fibrous materials such as corn cobs, corn and cabbage stalks, and twigs. You might want to buy a shredder if you are creating compost heaps in larger gardens. The adage of all compost makers is: Anything that has lived once can live again.

As the compost heap cools down, earthworms will move in and help further aerate and enrich the pile with worm castings. Never cover the floor below the heap with concrete or plastic in the mistaken belief that it is cleaner and neater. The pile will not drain as freely, water will gather, creating anaerobic conditions, and earthworms will not find their way in. Never put earthworms into the compost pile when you make it. You will end up with steamed earthworms! They will find their own way in when the conditions in the pile are ready for them.

Don't worry if your compost heap is not perfect. Nature will still create compost from it. The process will just be slower. In cool climates composting takes longer. If a compost pile still contains fairly rough material at the end of the season, you could leave it to compost over winter or spread it thickly over soil to be planted in

Fallen leaves are ideal additions to any compost heap as they provide a large surface area for the microorganisms to work on.

spring. It will still protect and enrich the soil, and earthworms will pull material down piece by piece and process it further. Roughly made compost is infinitely more desirable than no compost.

The easiest way to apply compost is to use it as a mulch applied directly to the surface of the soil. It can also be turned through the top 4 in (10 cm), disturbing the soil as little as possible.

Sheet-composting

Composting in heaps involves very little effort for smaller gardens, but supplying sufficient compost every year for a very large garden or small farm is not quite so simple, although mechanization can make the movement of raw materials and the turning of compost piles considerably easier. An alternative technique sometimes used is sheet-composting or deep-litter mulching. It consists of composting directly onto the garden soil surface, laying down a thick mulch of any or all of the materials listed for compost production. Once composted, the materials can be turned into the soil or left on the surface as a fertile mulch. Any existing old mulch can be incorporated into the layers of the sheet compost.

Once a heavy layer of hay mulch or something similar is put around crops in summer, you can tuck the household vegetable and fruit peels under the mulch regularly. Your kitchen scraps will be all but fully composted in a couple of weeks as the earthworms rapidly multiply and the microbial population quickly recycles the nutrients back into the soil.

A green manure crop (discussed below) can also be planted and turned into the soil for composting. If necessary, let weeds form a green cover crop and turn them into the soil before they flower. Clean and neat though finely tilled soil may look, it is vital to keep humus levels up and the soil covered to prevent topsoil loss.

Manures

The days when manures were easily come by are gone. However, many enterprising farmers bag and sell horse and cow manures, and a number of large zoos equally enterprisingly sell 'zoopoo', an exotic mixture that may contain anything from elephant droppings to giraffe and peacock contributions. Horse stables are also a likely source of manure, although they are increasingly contracted to supply firms producing commercial compost. Dried, pulverized manures are bagged and commercially available in many places.

Treat chicken manure pellets with some care. If the manure has not come from a certified source, it may be contaminated with veterinary chemicals. It is also highly con-centrated and quite capable of burning plant roots in the same manner as the excessive use of nitrogen-based chemical fertilizers. Provided that you are satisfied with the quality of the product, it can be scattered through the compost heap and used as a nitrogen-rich compost accelerator.

Within reason, the origin of manures is not so important as the fact that they have been obtained. To purists, this is heretical stuff, but I believe that the occasional sourcing from a non-organic farm or stable is allowable (unless, of course, you are producing certified produce). Just try to make sure that it has not come from intensive production units, as it will then be laced with veterinary chemicals. Old-fashioned, free range farms tend to produce equally old-fashioned manure with little contamination. Manures stored for six months are normally fairly free of veterinary pollutants. Organic farmers rightly work within a closed system, recycling their farm-produced manures to feed their own crops. So for newcomers to organic gardening, the probability of obtaining manures from a certified (or even non-certified) organic farm is in fact remote.

Some manures decompose very rapidly, releasing sufficient heat to physically scald plants, and may release nitrogen so rapidly that they will cause similar damage to that caused by the excessive use of chemical fertilizers. In general, dryish concentrated manures, such as rabbit droppings, poultry manure, and horse and sheep dung are likely to have this effect, and they are referred to as 'hot manures'. Cow manure is an example of a 'cool manure'.

All of these manures are desirable and can be used in the organic garden. But, as a rule of thumb, it is best to layer them through the compost heap rather than dig them directly into the garden. As a bonus,

Check crops for potassium deficiency if you use animal manure.

the composting process is particularly hot and rapid when manures are added. Once layered within the pile, the valuable nutrients in manures are absorbed into the material. Never leave a steaming pile uncovered to the elements and the air. A substantial amount of its nutritional value will be lost to leaching by rain and to the atmosphere. If nothing else is available, cover it with waterproof sheeting.

Once composted, manures can be turned through the top 4 in (10 cm) of soil, and are particularly valuable for crops such as squash of all kinds, potatoes, tomatoes, chard, lettuce and endive, Asian greens, and brassicas. If manures just don't fit on your shopping list, don't worry. Although manure is an admirable substance, compost, green manures, and the other additives described here will more than provide you with the richest and most productive of soils.

Speaking of manure, it has been said that the best manure is the footsteps of the gardener. Patrolling the garden and keeping an eye out for problems, as well as learning from observation, is indeed as great a contributor to the garden's productivity as the most magical of manures ... even unicorn zoopoo.

Manure 'soups'

Once you know about manure soup, you might find that it becomes a secret vice! It makes a very effective side-dressing for struggling plants, and is also an effective foliar spray. The one drawback is that it is a trifle smelly, so the bin should be placed away from commonly used areas.

First, choose a plastic bin that can be dedicated to the process. The next step is to tie a sack of manure or compost and suspend it in the bin, which you then fill with water. The lid can be laid slightly askew on top. The process that follows is not merely leaching of the nutrients in the

manure, but fermentation. Occasional bubbles plop to the surface, so a tightly sealed bin would be disastrous. Gradually, over two weeks, a rich brown soup is formed. This can be scooped out, diluted 1:10 with water, and applied to the base of plants or sprayed or splashed onto leaves as a foliar feed. The solution, when it is applied, should be no darker than a cup of weak tea.

Once the soup is brewed, additions can be made at any time, topping up the water level to the top of the bin for each brew. A trip to the beach after rough weather will often reveal a wealth of seaweed in the flotsam and jetsam of the tidal line. After washing an armful of seaweed free from salt, suspend a bagful in the bin of water. The resulting solution, formed two weeks later, is nearly miraculous stuff, benefiting everything to which it is applied. Seaweed soup is rich in a range of trace elements. It is also a reasonable deterrent to fungal attack due to its agar content, and it confers resistance to aphid attack. Like manure soup, it should be applied in a dilution of 1:10 with water.

Valuable, mineral-rich plants such as comfrey leaves, stinging nettles, and chamomile can be fermented in this way too. Each soup is rich in its own spectrum of nutrients and activities, and it is a good idea to use either a mixture of soups or a variety of soups over time. Birds seem to love to gargle with this stuff, so expect to share it with your feathered friends. They probably regard it as a pick-me-up tonic.

Earthworms

The 'solid' earth beneath our feet is positively heaving with activity. In every acre (.5 ha) of organically managed soil, it has been calculated that there are 1–2 million earthworms producing up to 40 tons of castings per year, moving a ton or more of soil per day. They can burrow up to 6$\frac{1}{2}$ ft (2 m) into the ground, providing micro-irrigation systems underground, and allowing easy access routes for

Earthworms are the hidden engine-room of the organic garden, converting mulch into high-quality, soil-improving nutrients.

water to find its way through the soil to plant root systems.

Sadly, not everyone appreciates these creatures which have contributed so much to the formation and maintenance of the world's topsoil that feeds us all. Some gardeners even poison them with ammonium sulfate because their castings are considered to spoil the perfection of manicured lawns.

Earthworms are in fact remarkable processors of organic materials in the soil. Dragging mulch or leaves down into the soil, they chew the material and excrete castings that contain partially and wholly undigested fibers. These castings are an excellent, high-fertility soil improver. Charles Darwin devoted an entire book to them, such was his belief in the significance of their contribution to soil health. In Africa, many tribal people graze cattle where worm castings on the surface are densest, knowing that the pasture will be most nutritious in that place.

Worm farms

Should you start a worm farm? It's something only you can decide. Worm farming is a small art of its own, and it may be more than you want to take on when you manage your organic garden. In any case, if the garden is rich in organic matter, it should also be rich in large natural earthworm populations. If you decide you need a helping hand to begin with, a worm farmer can supply you with worms, although once your soil is being regularly fed the organic way, native earthworms will move in from every direction, mysteriously obtaining the message that your garden has become an eco-friendly place to live.

It is also possible to use an earthworm farm as a recycling device for kitchen scraps, although this has its traps. A dead worm farm is at once an evil-smelling and a deeply reproachful object capable of engendering strong feelings of guilt. If you have little spare time, or go away for longish periods, or live a busy, erratic lifestyle, then worm farms are not for you. Fortunately, you can buy the resultant worm compost from worm farmers or organic garden suppliers, and this can provide many benefits to your garden, most

Potted plants, such as this Aloe vera, *benefit from an annual dressing of worm castings.*

particularly for potted plants as it has good water-holding capacity.

You can find many uses for worm compost in the garden. It makes an excellent additive to potting mixes and is particularly useful in producing strong, healthy seedlings under glass for spring planting. Potted houseplants revel in worm castings, and a layer of about $4/5$ in (2 cm) placed on top of the soil is a spring treat for them. It also makes a very good top dressing for plants that are heavy feeders in both the vegetable and flower garden, especially in the early stages of growth. Squash and melon plants, tomatoes, peppers, and eggplants are among those that benefit most.

If you would like to use a worm farm to recycle kitchen scraps, rather than using a compost heap, then there are a number of very cleverly designed models available, or you might want to design your own. It is important to remember that even earthworms have their limits. There is just so much that they can eat per day, and piling in masses of peelings and vegetable leaves will result in the excess kitchen wastes putrefying. In that condition they have no attraction at all for the worms, and they will soon die under the weight of blackened, slimy vegetable matter. A healthy worm farm smells sweet and earthy and slightly nutty. Unpleasant smells are a warning that something rather nasty has happened. Even a well-managed farm should receive a sprinkling of dolomite from time to time to 'sweeten' conditions for the worms.

Earthworms function best at temperatures of around 54.5–77°F (12.5–25°C). Natural earthworms in garden soil can move vertically to escape excessive cold or heat and continue to function as much as possible in their optimum temperature range. They are able to survive quite low temperatures, but their effectiveness in processing organic matter is greatly reduced. In a worm farm, however, there is no escape for them. It is important to position the farm in a place where temperatures will not greatly vary. Many a neat housekeeper has stationed the farm outside the kitchen door only to find a bin full of steamed earthworms in the evening. It should be placed in a covered and cool area in summer, and a warm area or covered with insulation by mid-autumn.

Another potential problem to be addressed is the liquid produced by the worm farm. Commercially designed farms for household use are usually provided with a drainage tap at the bottom of the bin. At intervals, the excess liquid can be drained away. Many home-made models deal with this problem by removing the bottom of the container and placing it directly in contact with the earth. This is a simple design solution that prevents any liquid build-up from occurring. But it also means that the farm is only transportable with great difficulty when seasonal temperatures make it necessary to move its location.

There are some wastes that should never be added to a worm farm. These include meat and fish scraps and bones, animal feces, remnant dairy products from yoghurt to cheese, and large quantities of citrus peels. Of course, nothing that is not of living origin should ever be added either to a worm farm or to a conventional compost heap.

Mulches

Mulches are an essential part of organic gardening, particularly in warm to tropical areas. In these places heat 'burns' organic matter out of the soil at a remarkable rate, and soils are often pounded by heavy rains. Mulch does much to preserve the soil's organic content and structure from compaction when the soil dries out and prevents erosion caused by rain. As well, mulches dampen the daily oscillation in soil temperature so that soil organisms, earthworms, and the roots of plants are not subjected to the maximum soil temperature extremes. Soil moisture is better maintained with the use of mulches, reducing the level of water usage in the garden. Mulches also protect the soil from the effects of people walking over garden beds.

Best of all, the use of mulches controls weeds in crops, greatly reducing a gardener's workload. Constant disturbance of the soil with hoeing, forking, or even the hand-removal of large weeds, simply brings more seeds from the soil's long-lived seedbank to the surface, where they germinate when exposed to light.

Mulches should be applied once young plants are fully established and growing strongly. Until that time, hand-weeding is the best method of control, removing weeds while still very small so as to cause minimal soil disturbance.

Organic mulches such as hay and straw are clean and effective. Alfalfa (lucerne) and hay and pea straw are particularly valued, and more expensive if purchased, because they are made from nitrogen-fixing plants and are richer in nutrients. Oat, wheat, and barley straw can also be used but are lower in nutrients. 'Spoiled hay' is often offered for sale, particularly after prolonged rains. While it is useless for animals, it is cheap and in the first stage of composting.

Straws and hays allow some light through to the soil surface, and this can be prevented by putting down an initial layer of 8–10 sheets of newsprint (not colored magazines). Sugar-cane bagasse is an excellent mulch in areas where it is readily available.

Dried leaves can also be used, as can rough compost, dried and roughly chopped seaweeds (superb for potatoes, chard, asparagus, beetroot, and tomatoes), shredded prunings, wood shavings, sawdust

Ornamental plants can be used to cover steep or awkward-to-get-at sites. They are, in effect, living mulches because they form a protective carpet over the ground, helping to prevent soil erosion.

and woodchips. The latter three, while having useful physical qualities, temporarily cause nitrogen loss from the soil, as the bacteria responsible for composting them require nitrogen to do their work. Plants mulched with wood shavings, woodchips, and sawdust often show some yellowing (chlorosis) of the leaves as the bacteria make temporary withdrawals from the soil's nitrogen bank. A sprinkling of blood and bone can correct this situation, or a foliar feeding with seaweed solution or manure 'tea'. Alternatively, mix any wood-based mulches with well-rotted cow manure or one of the seed meals. Wood products must not be derived from treated wood.

Lawn cuttings are frequently piled onto the garden after mowing. There they compact and slime. Their high nitrogen levels can also cause damage by burning young seedlings. Mix the grass cuttings with fallen leaves to produce a much better mulch. Pine needles and shredded bracken fern can be used as mulches, but when they are fresh they both contain plant growth inhibitors. They can be used once they are aged and brown, although they are more effective if mixed with other materials.

Mulches should not be applied directly to dry soil or to soil that has not properly warmed from winter. Thoroughly water the soil before applying mulch, as not only does mulch cap moisture loss upward from the soil but it also reduces water penetration downward. In cold areas, raised beds will warm faster in spring. Once the soil is warm, mulch can be applied. Organic mulches are doubly rewarding. They are progressively composted and at the end of the growing season their remains can be dug into the soil as an additional source of organic matter, or simply left on the surface and topped up with fresh mulch to nurture the next planting in the crop rotation.

Mulch should never be applied too close to the plant as this encourages fungal attacks due to the increased humidity it creates. Mulch can also encourage large populations of slugs and snails. Place beer traps—shallow cans half-filled with beer and buried at ground level—under a sheet of black plastic near the offending mulch. Check early in the morning and dispose of your victims. There will probably be an amazing number of them. Make sure that you can recognize the good guys from the bad. Some slugs and snails are predators

Left: A straw mulch will help protect plants from extremes of hot or cold.

Right: Apply a mulch between plants to suppress weeds and conserve moisture.

A pile of stable straw ready for summer mulching.

on other slugs and snails, or do not eat living plants. These should be spared.

In hot dry areas, a triple mulch consisting of a layer of chopped alfalfa (lucerne) hay, followed by woodchips or another wood-based product, topped with a couple of layers of flat rocks placed around fruit trees can make a remarkable difference to growth and productivity. Pebbles and gravel can be used in many gardens as an aesthetic, permanent, insulating ground cover.

There is also a range of artificial mulches such as black polythene sheeting and weedmat that are effective. That said, they are decidedly unattractive and lack the ambience of a natural mulch. As well, no matter how hard the soil's microorganisms try, they will never release any beneficial plant food from nylons and high-density industrial plastics. Quite the reverse, in fact. Black polythene can find use in warming soil in spring; however, summer temperatures beneath it can reach 140°F (60°C) in hot climates, a highly destructive temperature that

will sterilize much of the microflora and damage the roots that are concentrated in the upper soil layer. Weedmat is permeable and far less damaging to the soil. On ornamental areas, composted bark gives an excellent appearance and is a good insulator. It does not temporarily rob the soil of nitrogen as do other wood products, and it also acts as a soil conditioner.

Green mulches

Green mulches are cover crops that are turned into the soil when they are fully grown. Choose a nitrogen-fixing crop such as vetches or tares, lupins, alfalfa (lucerne), red clover, sweet clover, trefoil, fenugreek, small-seeded field-grown forms of broad, or fava bean such as 'Egyptian Brown', and cowpeas. Buckwheat, phacelia (*Phacelia tanacetifolia*, which is also an excellent attractor of beneficial insects if allowed to flower), mustard (which should not be allowed to flower unless you are happy for a large volunteer crop in your next vegetable crop), sorghum, timothy, and grazing rye can also grown to add large quantities of organic matter.

All of these crops can be slashed down and then turned into the soil to compost, which will improve not only soil fertility but also soil structure. At a pinch, even a crop of weeds can be used as a green mulch (which makes an admirable excuse for the lazy gardener). Simply cut them down and turn them into the soil before they flower and set seed.

Green mulches provide several important benefits to the soil. Without plant cover, valuable topsoil is lost permanently every time the wind blows. Just as the soil needs covering from heat and wind, so it also needs protection from the impact of heavy rain, which can cause severe erosion of topsoil, the compaction of heavier soils, and the leaching of nutrients into lower horizons, making them unreachable by most crop plants. As well as these benefits, green mulches are excellent weed suppressors once they are established. Long and extensively rooted cover crops also help to open and aerate the soil, improving its structure.

Green mulches can be built into a crop rotation pattern, always followed by a crop that copes with a rough tilth, such as beans, squash, melons, potatoes and sweet potatoes, or well-grown seedlings of brassicas and Asian greens.

Some green mulches provide additional benefits by sending long or extensively developed roots deep down into the earth, over 3 ft (1 m) deep or more, retrieving nutrients from far below. These crops have the additional value of breaking up the substrate and opening and aerating the soil to improve its structure. They include alfalfa (lucerne), chicory, and Japanese daikon radish.

The same techniques can be applied in the home garden. The scale may be different, but the results will be the

same. If you choose to use the 'no-dig' cultivation method, cut the crop down to the ground, allow it a few days to dry out, and plant your new crop into the garden, treating the slashed cover crop as a garden mulch.

Shallow folding in of trashed sorghum to build up organic matter.

Alfalfa *Medicago sativa*
Alfalfa (lucerne) is exceptionally deep rooted and may reach depths of 6$^1/_2$ ft (2 m) or morenutrients from deep below the surface and helping to break up the subsoil. It is a fairly long-lived perennial, and will

Alfalfa hay is nitrogen-rich which makes it particularly sought after as a mulch.

provide many cuts of nitrogen-rich hay. Once grown, it is an excellent weed suppressor. Alfalfa is a nitrogen-fixing plant that is planted from spring to midsummer. It is unsuitable on soils with a pH below 6.5, or on poorly drained soils. The fresh or dried flower heads and tips can be mixed with red clover heads and spearmint to make an excellent herbal tea. Perennial cover crops such as alfalfa, sorghum, and rye will regrow after each cut is taken from the crop. Either mulch heavily to exclude light or use the opportunity to plant a potato crop directly on the soil surface and then mulch heavily.

Black Medic *Medicago lupulina*

This hardy, biennial, nitrogen-fixing crop, also called yellow trefoil or hop clover, is planted in spring to mid-summer and matures within 3 months. It can be left in the soil until the following early summer, and will grow on quite dry, light soils, preferring alkaline conditions. The tips can be eaten as a potherb.

Blue Lupin *Lupinus angustifolius*

This annual crop, also known as narrow-leaved lupin, is planted in spring to midsummer and matures within two to three months. It is ideally suited for lighter soils with a pH below 7. **Sweet White Lupin** (*L. albus saccharatus*) is another good choice but needs a slightly longer growing time. It has the added benefit of being edible. The immature pods are sliced and prepared like snap beans, while the dried seeds when ground make an excellent flour used for lupin pasta. The roasted seeds can be eaten like roasted peanuts. This non-bitter form was not isolated until 1928 in Germany, after thousands of lines had been tested.

Buckwheat *Fagopyrum esculentum*

This semi-hardy annual is planted from late spring to late summer and is a bee attractant if allowed to flower, although the honey made from it is dark and strong. The hulled seeds make an excellent breakfast cereal, and the flour can be used to make buckwheat pancakes. As a cover crop, it is available for use within 2–3 months.

Buckwheat, Fagopyrum esculentum, *was once grown in the Netherlands. An ideal crop for poor sandy soils, it virtually disappeared after the advent of artificial fertilizers. As a ground cover, it can be used as a green mulch.*

Crimson Clover *Trifolium incarnatum*
Seed of this annual clover should be
planted in early spring to late summer
for a harvest in 2–3 months. It prefers
a light soil. The dried flowers are used
to make a herbal tea.

Fenugreek *Trigonella foenum graecum*
Fenugreek is a semi-hardy annual that
is planted from early spring to late
summer, matures within two to three
months and is an excellent nitrogen
fixer. It prefers a well-drained soil.
The aromatic leaves are used as a
popular potherb in India, and the
seeds are one of the principal
ingredients of curry powder.

Field Bean *Vicia fava*
This is a small-seeded form of the
broad or fava bean. The seeds are
sown in fall to early winter, and the
plants, which are nitrogen-fixing,
flower in the following spring when
they are returned to the soil.

Red Clover *Trifolium pratense*
Red clover is a hardy, short-lived,
nitrogen-fixing perennial that prefers
to grow on loam soils, and is very

The field bean, Vicia
Fava, *is a nitrogen-fixing
plant also valued as a
cover crop.*

fetching with its beautiful coloring.
The fresh young leaves and honey-
scented flower heads can be used fresh
in salads. It is planted from early
spring to late summer, takes 3 months
to mature and will survive quite cold
winters if left in the ground.

Red clover, Trifolium
pratense, *is Vermont's
state flower. Though it is
not a native, it is
important to the dairying
industry. Like other
legumes, it enriches the
soil with nitrogen.*

Chapter 4

MANAGING YOUR GARDEN

Pests and diseases: a gentle approach

We have made great strides in recent times in our understanding of pests and diseases. With more information about the reproductive systems of many garden and farm pests and diseases, it is now possible to use strategies to break the life cycle at a vulnerable stage, to avoid the damage being done to our crops. This is a far more environmentally friendly attitude than existed 20 or even 10 years ago. As a result many new and helpful approaches are available to the organic gardener.

In this book, you will find no detailed prescriptions for dealing with every predator and disease, although useful suggestions have been made with the appropriate crops. Instead, a policy of reasonable tolerance is advocated, and an acceptance that one of three things is probably wrong with a crop under attack: it is either out of place, out of time, or out of sorts.

Out of place: you may have been tempted to grow a crop that is ill suited to your particular climate, or soil, or both. Such a crop will be stressed from the beginning, and stressed plants are the target of both diseases and pests. Recent research has confirmed what organic gardeners long suspected from observation, that predators can detect weakened or sick plants even though to our eyes they look little different, and it is these plants that are first attacked. It seems to be Nature's way of dealing with any weaklings in the plant world.

Out of time: a spring crop planted near summer, a summer crop planted after the longest day or a winter crop not planted until late fall will all struggle to catch up. The plants will have had insufficient time to grow to full size and accumulate adequate reserves before seasonal changes initiate flowering and fruiting. As a result, the plants will be stressed and become a target for predators and diseases.

Out of sorts: the third likely cause of disease attack could be poor nutrition—plants grown in poor soils suffer one or many deficiencies—or genetic weakness. Your plant may have inherited a poor genetic constitution or you may be using an old batch of seed that has been genetically damaged.

To give your plants the strongest chance in life, choose varieties that are suited to your soil and climate, plant them at the correct time, and introduce them into a garden well supplied with nutrients and with a soil that is in the correct pH range. The seed used should be fresh and should have been kept sealed and cool since harvest. By following those simple rules, you'll give individual plants the maximum opportunity to realize their full growth potential and vigor, to be less vulnerable to attack, and to be in the best position to outgrow any attacks that do occur.

Diversity
This is one of the gardener's best friends. Where there are many species in a garden, pests and diseases are not given the chance to concentrate their

Not all slugs are pests. Large ones, like this leopard slug, Limax maximus, *feed on dead organic matter and fungi and will not harm your garden plants.*

Sap-sucking aphids attack plants in summer, causing distortion of new shoots and young leaves. They can be controlled by introducing natural predators, such as hoverflies and ladybugs, or using insecticidal soaps and sprays.

attack and have no chance to multiply. This is why tropical forest ecosystems are so resistant to some of the planet's most aggressive insects. Species are interspersed throughout the forest, forming a mosaic within a diverse group of species. This is a good model for planting the garden.

Companion planting

Some believe companion planting is hocus pocus, but in fact it is a real phenomenon that is backed by solid research. Broadly, it means that

there is a cultural advantage to planting two species together. At its very simplest, one plant may positively modify the physical environment of another plant—for instance, by providing shade for a shade-loving plant. The well-known combination of borage with strawberries is an example. There are certainly other factors at play, but shading is significant.

All plants produce a range of waste products that are exuded though their roots and shoots, and that chemically

Mildew is a fungus that creates a powdery residue. Mulching can help prevent the build-up of the damp conditions in which it thrives.

Leaf discoloration or distorted foliage can be a sign of disease or pest attack. If you monitor your plants closely, you may be able to treat the problem in its early stages.

modify the environment of adjacent plants. Some plants, notably the herbs, but also tomatoes, nasturtiums, African and French marigolds and various others, contain strong-smelling volatile substances that are emitted by their leaves. These substances can swamp the odor signals emitted by other plants and confuse insects seeking out a target. The long-established idea of planting strongly scented herbs randomly throughout the vegetable garden is well founded, and it will certainly help your crops to avoid insect problems.

Root exudates can also have a powerful effect. The marigolds, *Tagetes* spp., exude a chemical that discourages nematodes (sometimes known as eel worms), the microscopic worms that burrow into the vascular tissue of the roots of plants such as tomatoes. The first time you know that nematodes are in the soil may be when a plant wilts for no apparent reason. When you dig it up, gall-like knots will be found on the roots. To clean soils of nematodes, plant a crop of French marigolds, *T. patula*, or the weedy *T. minuta*. Professional garlic growers use this same technique. Chop the marigold

crop back into the ground before the seed ripens in the flowers.

Substances formed in the foliage of some plants act as growth stimulants, others as plant growth retardants or seed germination inhibitors. Substances leached from the leaves of some species by rain are designed to inhibit competition. Attempts are being made to harness this phenomenon for use in vegetable cropping.

Crop rotation

A useful practice in the garden, and one that has long been known for its ability to reduce the build-up of diseases in crops, is crop rotation. It is a simple procedure that involves never replanting the same crop or closely related crops in the same soil for a period of at least three to four years. A seasonal plan should be recorded in your garden notebook each year to ensure that two similar crops never follow each other. A four-crop rotation is the usual aim for garden crops. Count any member of the same family as one crop rotation—for example, only one *Brassica* crop, such as kale, cauliflower, cabbage, broccoli or brussels sprouts, should be planted in the four-crop cycle. It is a good idea to use different vegetables harvested for different purposes in the plan for any one garden bed. An example might be potatoes (no more *Solanaceae* are then allowed, thus no tomatoes, eggplants, peppers, or tobacco), followed by celery, followed by beets, followed by lettuce. These vegetables are not at all closely related, are harvested for different products, and are unlikely to share in any common diseases. The infection cycle and build-up of pathogens is therefore prevented.

Sanitation

Cleaning up any plant debris left at the end of the growing season helps prevent overwintering colonies of insects from gaining a rapid foothold on crops in the following season.

Monitoring

Become familiar with the useful insects in your garden—insects that prey on garden pests or that are responsible for other activities such as pollination. Finding out about the 'good guys' and the 'bad guys' of the garden is all part of good organic management.

Although it sounds old-fashioned, walking around the garden regularly and hand-picking the pest insects can do much to control damage, particularly insects such as katydids and beetles. Keep a regular watch for caterpillars. A night stroll with a torch can be an eye-opener. Lay a few simple traps. Halved oranges with the flesh removed and laid cut side down in the garden will almost certainly be housing a few slugs the next morning. Even a moist sack or a small sheet of timber laid flat on the ground will be found to harbor slugs and snails. The deluxe version is a shallow can half-filled with beer and buried level with the soil surface. Slugs are drawn irresistibly to the beer, fall in, and drown in a beery oblivion.

Floating row covers have rapidly become a frontline defence against flying insect pests. These should be employed wherever possible as they are the least troublesome of all preventatives to use. Just be sure you don't exclude the 'good' insects as well. If your crop needs to be fertilized by bees, then the row cover should be rolled back or the flowers hand-fertilized.

Regularly monitor your crops as you walk through the garden. A few insect pests are normal and nothing to worry about. But if the numbers seem to be increasing fairly rapidly, a decision needs to be made. The first question involves the general health of the plants in which pest build-up is occurring. If the plants don't look well, first aid can be applied with seaweed emulsion diluted to the recommended strength. If there appears to be no improvement after a week and the plants are continuing to come under attack, consider removing them. If the plants seem to be growing well, administer the seaweed solution to improve the general status of the plant. Then consider one of the options below.

Roses are susceptible to black spot, a fungal disease. Collecting and burning the diseased leaves will help prevent infecting other plants.

Using natural predators

On commercial crops, biological control is carried out by releasing insects that are natural predators on insect pests. These are now available for a range of crop pests. Lacewings are commonly found in organic gardens, and both the larvae and adults feed on a variety of insects and mites. Predator mites are available from a number of companies, and they attack spider mites while doing no damage to plants. There are several tiny wasps that are used commercially to attack the immature stages of the whitefly in greenhouses. Tiny trichogamma wasps are used to parasitize and control caterpillar invasions. A voracious relative of the ladybug, the cryptolaemus beetle in both its adult and larval stages feeds on mealy bugs. Some ladybugs are among the best and most aggressive of all predators on garden pests. Both in the adult and larval stages, ladybugs will feed on spider mites, aphids, and mealy bugs. There is also a tiny wasp, *Aphytis melinus*, marketed to control red scale. Lacewings, ladybugs and spined soldier beetles all prey on Colorado beetle, which attacks any crops in the *Solanaceae* family.

In the organically managed garden, many of these predators are naturally present and act to maintain the status quo, ensuring that pest populations do not reach serious proportions.

Sprays, dusts, and insecticides

Resist the temptation to resort to standard garden sprays, as they will wipe out the steadily building populations of many natural predators and will set back the progress of ecological balance.

There are a number of zero or low ecological impact dusts and sprays used by organic gardeners. For many caterpillars, a biological control containing the bacterium *Bacillus thuringiensis B.t.*, marketed as Dipel among other tradenames, is quite effective. The caterpillars normally die within two to three days after consuming treated leaves. It is safe for humans, even if used near the harvest stage. A strain of this bacillus, *B.t. tenebrionis*, can be used against the Colorado beetle.

B.t. is much less effective against cutworms, which live under the soil during the day but come out to feed at night, attacking the stems of young seedlings. Cardboard drinking cups

Caterpillars feed on leaves and new growth, but you may feel the price of a few plants is worth paying to enjoy the resulting butterflies.

from which the bases have been removed can be partially sunk into the ground around a seedling to provide good physical protection. Parasitic nematodes are used as a commercially available biological control.

Cutworms are also likely to be responsible for those unsightly bare patches that grow rapidly in green lawns. The offenders can be flushed to the surface by diluting a tablespoon of soft soap in a bucket of water and flooding the area. (Note: A fungus can also be responsible for brown rings in the lawn.)

A number of useful botanically derived insecticides are also available. Sprays based on garlic and chile peppers are commonly used. Ryania is a botanical insecticide that can be used to control codling moth, asparagus beetle, and corn earworm. Pyrethrin, derived from the *Pyrethrum* daisy, is useful against a range of insect pests, including flying insects, and it breaks down within a few hours of exposure to sunlight.

Longer-lived and more toxic synthetic pyrethroids are sometimes used commercially, but preferably not in an organic garden. Derris dust, or rotenone, is used to control chewing insects on vegetables, but it should never be used where it might come into contact with fish. In any event, it should be viewed with caution as its effect on human health is still being investigated. Sabadilla, another botanical insecticide used against caterpillars and leafhoppers, should be totally avoided as it is highly toxic to birdlife.

Other organically acceptable treatments for insect pests come in the form of dusts, oil sprays, and soaps. Contact dusts act by scarifying the exterior of the pest insect so that it dies by desiccation. Diatomaceous earth is effective when used for this purpose, but what the powder can do to an insect's exoskeleton it can most certainly do to your lungs, and all due care should be taken in handling

this substance. Diatomaceous earth is particularly used to discourage ants, snails, and slugs. Silica aerogel, used for drying living flowers for craftwork, can be applied to kill small insects by drying them out. Boric acid can also be used, either in the form of a powder or a paste, inside traps.

Gardeners in the past swore by soapy water, and it was never wasted. Instead, it was tossed over rosebushes and other shrubs to keep them free of infection. Now insecticidal soaps are also an acceptable control measure. These are mixtures of particular fatty acids which have low toxicity for humans but will effectively control most small problem insects, including mites. They are fast in action, leave no residual effect, and are approved for use on crops. Certain plants are damaged by some of the soaps available, and so these mixtures should not be used indiscriminately on delicate leaves. If you have any doubts, test-spray a few leaves first. Manufacturers of these products recommend that the soap solutions be made up with soft water.

Oil sprays are another useful control measure that is acceptable both environmentally and with regard

When disease has spread too far it will be necessary to remove the damaged leaves. Always burn the infected leaves rather than adding them to your compost.

Divide your vegetable garden into areas and rotate crops to control pests and diseases.

to your own safety. These newer oils are highly refined and are designed to smother insects and their eggs. The winter oils or dormant oils are used in winter, and in cooler areas in early spring, to control insects that over-winter on deciduous shrubs and trees. This severely reduces the initial population in the garden in spring, and at no stage should you need to deal with epidemic proportions of the target insects during the summer months. Summer oils are applied after trees and shrubs have leafed out and turned their regular summer color. Even so, some species are sensitive to summer oils, and a test spray should be done to ensure that no major damage will be done. Summer oils are also used to spray on citrus trees. They have a wide range of effectiveness because they rely for effect simply on their capacity to smother. They are effective against scale insects and aphids, and will smother the eggs of a variety of summer insects, as well as pear psylla.

A number of powders and sprays can be used against fungal diseases in the garden. One of the most effective is also one of the most simple, a soft soap spray made from drugstore soft soap (not detergent), which is diluted at the rate of 1:100 with water. Research carried out in Great Britain to test this old-fashioned anti-fungal drench against various chemical fungicides proved that it was as effective, or almost as effective, as the major chemicals in controlling classic garden fungal problems such as rust and blackspot on roses.

Old-fashioned sulfur dust is still quite an effective treatment for rust, scab, and powdery mildew. It can be applied as a wettable powder or as a dry dust. Equally old-fashioned lime sulfur is the plant world's general defense and is available as a preventative spray for peach leaf curl and powdery mildew. It also finds use as a dormant spray in controlling scale insects and some kinds of mites.

If your roses have been severely affected by fungal diseases, use seaweed fertilizer as remedial therapy. The agar in the seaweed appears to have an inhibiting effect on the further spread of the fungus, while the nutrient boost provides a rapid recovery. Any remaining infected leaves are shed and a fresh foliage quickly leafs out.

Xeriscaping: solutions for dry areas

The days are gone when water resources could be used without thought. Water is rapidly becoming a valuable commodity on this planet. Changing weather patterns worldwide are exposing many areas to more frequent and more acute drought cycles, as was accurately predicted by the world's leading climatologists. These changing circumstances have combined with a movement to create more naturalistic landscapes—landscapes that emerge out of consideration for the climate, the soils, and the natural vegetation of the area in which the garden is constructed. The rationale is that by enhancing what is already natural to the landscape, rather than imposing exotic plants from different climates and soils which may require considerably different growing conditions, a low energy, highly sustainable garden should result.

Xeriscaping was developed to cope with the effects of prolonged aridity while using minimal water, and creating as little impact as possible on a more fragile environment.

Not every gardener deals with drought as a regular occurrence, but increasingly people are settling in lower rainfall environments with wide open skies—areas of sparse beauty with the clean air of the inland. Some beautiful chapparal gardens have been created in California, for instance, with comparable gardens in Texas and Australia, as well as some stunning dry prairie gardens in places such as Iowa.

Windbreaks

How do you raise crops with relatively little water? If you conserve the available resources, it can be possible. The planting of natural windbreaks is one method of reducing windspeed, and hence soil evaporation rates, in the garden. This can make a remarkable difference to the volume of

Miniature gardens can be created in window boxes and planters. Water-retaining agents can be added to soil in containers.

Ivy, Hedra helix 'Goldheart', is a good choice for ground cover in shade where grass has difficulty growing. It is also less waterdependent.

water required to sustain a garden without altering any other factor. The species used should be suited to the conditions of your area and should require little or no supplementary watering after becoming fully established. Choose a native plant, or one that comes originally from a comparable ecological niche and is already proven to grow well in your area. It needs to be deeply rooted, with minimal lateral roots so that it doesn't rob soil moisture from adjacent plantings, and should be fire retardant (so don't choose eucalypts or conifers, for example).

On larger properties where space is not at a premium, double and even triple stepdown hedges can be constructed to further reduce severe windspeeds. The outermost hedge is the tallest, the second or middle hedge shorter, and the innermost hedge the shortest. The shrubs or small trees chosen can be purely functional, or you can select them for their attractiveness, or even because they also produce fruit, nuts, leaf teas, or mulching materials. Mixed hedges look charming and relaxed in appropriate gardens.

An alternative to lawns

Lawns are major consumers of garden resources, especially water. Many xeriscapers advocate the use of tussock grasses to replace the conventional grass lawn as they are low consumers of water and require no mowing. For arid zone gardens, the tussock grasses are handsome and blend well with their surroundings, but they can pose a fire hazard. In urban areas, they are a less useful solution as they do not fit comfortably with the aesthetics of urban living. As well, children cannot play on tussock grasses, and dogs tend to consider them a thoughtful adjunct to whatever tree trunks are in the garden and bestow their usual favors upon them. Somewhere between the high-consuming, fine green lawn and the tussock grass replacement of the arid zone garden lies a compromise. Rather than eliminating turf, the area put down to grass can probably be halved to advantage in the average suburban garden. First, consider flagging or other paving, particularly where grass is struggling to grow. Paved areas near the house provide excellent places for entertaining or simply for permanent garden furniture to be arranged for family relaxation. A patio or decking can often add great value to a home and improve the quality of living for everyone.

Other ground covers much less greedy of resources may be appropriate where grass grows poorly. Under densely shading trees, for instance, ivy and the blue-flowered periwinkle both look neat and will grow well, requiring clipping back once or at most twice a year. Beside the sea, dense, clump-forming, cheerfully flowered gazanias will rapidly carpet sandy slopes which have full sun and salt exposure. Simple but good quality mulches can also be used to reduce the total area of lawn, and additional garden beds added where appropriate. Ultrafine grass cultivars can be replaced by drought-resistant species that will at the same time take much more wear and tear. By using a mixture of strategies like these, it is possible to at least halve the volume of water used on your lawn

and greatly reduce unproductive gardening time.

Foundation plantings

Much of the art of xeriscaping lies in making appropriate choices for the foundation plantings of the garden. Most plantings should be able to cope with no more than natural rainwater once they are established. This sounds restrictive, but really is not. It is a rule that applies well to any garden, whether in a dryland situation or in an urban setting. You will soon find that some things just can't help growing well for you. Although you neglect them cruelly, they reward you loyally with a magnificent show annually. These foundation plants are all but impervious to pests and diseases. The trick is to plan our garden around these loyal plants, including the annuals that self-seed and fill corners so admirably with little encouragement. That way, the garden will always have substance, will always

The candelabra aloe, Aloe arborescens, is a tough, shrubby succulent that thrives in dry conditions.

perform well, and will be virtually without need of additional water.

For those who live in semiarid areas, the choice of plants is larger and far more delightful than might be imagined. The southwest United States has a long list of plants from which to choose, and California is particularly rich in spectacular dryland plants that have since been adapted worldwide. To these can be added many of the plants of inland Spain, lower Provence in France, Greece, the Middle East, North Africa, and the semiarid zones of Australia (particularly the flora of Western Australia), and Chile. Salvias in particular offer a huge variety in form and color, and many are attractors of hummingbirds in the Americas and honeyeaters in Australia.

Free of many pests and diseases that are easily spread in densely settled areas, the arid zone garden can be a great pleasure, particularly in spring when the many desert ephemerals reach their full glory in the dry inland heat. Dryland trees such as peppercorns provide pleasurable shade and are well adapted to the heat.

Mulches

Productive plants such as vegetables, fruit trees and, to some degree, nut trees do require water, especially after harvesting. However, even with these plants, the water budget can be dramatically reduced even in hot, arid zone areas. The use of heavy mulches is effective. These should be applied after the ground has warmed up in spring and after the soil has been watered to field capacity. In its early stages, mulch is almost as effective in excluding water applied overhead as it is in retaining moisture below. In dry areas, a two-tiered mulch of compost covered by a second layer of rock mulch is effective in maintaining cool, moist soil under fruit and nut trees. Always keep the mulch away from tree trunks or it will encourage collar rot.

Terracing

For gardens on a slope, terracing is helpful in maximizing the retention of natural rainfall. Terraces allow rainwater to slowly percolate into the soil. Slopes, on the other hand, encourage rainfall to run off rather than penetrate the soil. For much the same reason as terraces are used, plantings should always be made on the contours of slopes, meaning that trees or shrubs should be planted in rows at right angles to the slope. As rainfall runs down the slope, it will be progressively interrupted by the rows of plantings. As the water slows down, it percolates into the soil around the plants. Some arid zone plants native to Australia actually self-plant on the contour to maximize their harvest of rare desert rainfall. Conversely, never plant in

Dry area gardens can be as colorful and productive as those in higher rainfall areas if you choose suitable plants and take steps to avoid water loss.

Drip systems are far more ecomomical with water than sprinklers.

rows vertically down a hill. Not only is much of the natural rainfall totally wasted in run-off, but the rows between plantings channel the water unimpeded down the slope, causing erosion.

Drip irrigation

A xeriscaped garden should be largely independent of supplementary watering, except under occasional extreme conditions. Watering of productive crops is achieved mainly by variations on the idea of drip irrigation. This technique delivers very small amounts of water accurately targeted to the roots of plants. It was developed in Israel to make the best possible use of scarce water resources to grow extensive orchards of export-quality fruit. The equipment to drip irrigate is now affordable, easily found, and easy to set up anywhere in the garden.

Weeds: a different viewpoint

Weeds have long been viewed with disdain. The general feeling is that we don't control them, they will control us. The puritanical zeal with which such plants are attacked is saddening.

The weeds are symptoms, not causes, of disturbance.

Another kinder and more useful definition of weeds is that they are plants for which we have not yet found a use. This is at least a sympathetic interpretation, but the inference remains that the plant kingdom is answerable to us. It is true that there are a few 'super competitors' among the world's plants, highly aggressive species that easily outcompete native flora and that need campaigns of eradication. But many others are simply filling niches we have created. Despite this definition, many of the common field weeds distributed around the world by European migration do have known uses.

For many gardeners, weeds are the bane of their lives. This is a great shame because weeds are so useful, busy repairing the damage we constantly do with our farming and gardening, sustaining the lives of countless insects, providing free fresh food for those in the know, attracting bees and butterflies, and providing free mulch.

If you walk into an undamaged piece of natural land, there are no weeds. They are found only in disturbed ecosystems such as our

The leaves of young dandelions, long regarded as a weed, can make a delicious salad.

farms and gardens. It is probably the sheer exuberance of weeds in our gardens that tends to daunt us. You clear the garden so that everything is clean and brown, turn your back for a second, or so it seems, and there is a fine green fuzz of weeds over everything. In fact, clean, brown earth is the opposite of good gardening and farming practice. Topsoil should never be left exposed. The nutrient degradation begins immediately, as well as the sheer loss of volume of the precious topsoil.

A green manure

Weeds are the best, the toughest, and the fastest plant species that Nature has developed to begin the healing process for the earth and to conserve the topsoil against erosion by wind and rain. They are the frontline troops designed to hold the land against further damage until a succession of longer-lived plants can restore full cover to the damaged earth. Whether the damage is caused by natural events such as landslides or floods, or by agriculture and gardening, the same succession of plant communities occurs until a stable community finally covers the damaged area. Just as farmers once burned off the trash from crops in order to clean the land,

a practice now seen as hugely wasteful of precious organic matter for the soil, gradually the idea of clean brown earth is becoming less acceptable, particularly in warmer areas. Those weeds that annoy us so intensely and take so much abuse continue to silently and rapidly repair the damage we do by being too neat in the garden and on our farms.

Although weeds compete most effectively with our domesticated crops, we could do much worse than allow weeds to cover a spare patch until we are ready to plant it, treating the weed cover as a green manure crop and turning it in when the first flower buds emerge. If we are still not ready to plant, the weed will rapidly oblige with a second green manure crop, quickly increasing the organic content of the soil.

Preventing weeds: the deep-dig method

Understanding how weeds flourish is the first step to learning how to control them organically. The soil holds a seedbank of weed seed. Even if no weed seed floated in from elsewhere, the soil would continue to produce multiple crops each year for about nine years. Some species would persist beyond that. Light is the trigger for germination of tiny weed seeds. There is no point in their germinating unless they are very near or at the surface. Every time you diligently dig the soil, a fresh batch of seeds reaches the light and is triggered into germinating. Armed with this knowledge, there are two obvious things you can do: never dig the soil and exclude light from the soil surface.

The first of these principles, to turn the garden over as little as possible, is the basis of the deep-dig method used in different variations in many Asian countries as well as in some parts of Europe. Prepare a garden bed thoroughly when you first make it. The topsoil (and only the topsoil) should be well dug and broken up, then compost and any soil additions such as rock dusts are added. If you can resist the temptation to ever dig the garden again, your struggle with weeds will soon be over. Mulch the bed heavily, water well, and allow it to stand for a few days. The mulch will settle, excluding all light. Seeds that were triggered into germination by their brief exposure to light will be pale and withering beneath the mulch. After a week, pull the mulch aside just sufficiently to plant seedlings into the soil, or large seeds such as sunflowers, melons, beans, and peas. In the following years, top up the bed with a layer of compost and an occasional dusting of dolomite to ensure that the soil does not become increasingly acidic. Underneath the surface, the continuous activity of earthworms will be aerating the soil as well as any digging could achieve, pulling organic matter down to the root zone and improving the soil structure.

Weeds as food

If everyone knew how delicious 'eating on the wild side' can be, there would be far fewer weeds in the average garden. Before you rush out to start foraging for edible weeds, however, you will need a good identification manual. There are also short courses and evening courses on wild foods offered in many educational institutions. Among the wide variety of weeds used for salads are young dandelion leaves (the rosette of leaves can be gathered up and tied at the top with a rubber band for a few days to blanch any excessive bitterness), the leaves of chickweed, the tender tip leaves of fat hen, the tender new leaves of mallow, corn salad, wild arugula (rocket), portulaca, chicory, and some of the small cresses.

A simple vinaigrette, with lemon juice substituted for the vinegar, is the perfect salad dressing. Serve the salad as they do in Greece with some

Wild radish and wild turnip—weeds to some but delicious salad ingredients to the organic gardener.

Even the humble nettle has its uses. It can be eaten as a spinach substitute, turned into a soup, and can even be used as a dye for woollens.

creamy cheese and a couple of slices of good strong bread with which to mop up the juices. Similar wild salads were traditionally gathered all over Europe as the spring weeds appeared. The flowers of English daisy, *Bellis perennis*, and wild radish are also used. The flowers of true dandelions make a refreshing, golden summer wine of greater potency than might be anticipated, and the roasted and ground roots can be made into dandelion coffee.

Brick walls can alter the microclimate of a garden and provide some protection against frost.

Extending the growing season in cold areas

Few places outside the true tropics and near tropics are free from the threat of frosts. The best rule for planting is to always plant to the known extremes of your climate. Most plants will do well while conditions remain mild, but if your district experiences occasional severe frosts or very low temperatures, or soaring temperatures or severe drought, then the more permanent members of the garden—the perennials, shrubs and trees—should be capable of withstanding those extremes. This way, no matter what Nature throws at your garden, the damage will be temporary and its structure and character will not be destroyed. Gardens not planted to the norm of a district sooner or later are wiped out by extreme weather. If climatic extremes have happened before, then they certainly will again. A few risky choices can be added for pleasure, knowing that you will probably lose the plant one day but enjoying it while you have it.

If a severe frost does come, as is the rule with wildfires, don't immediately prune back. Some of the plant may still be alive. Wait until spring is underway and new growth has begun. If you cut back after initial damage has been done, the plant may be accidentally stimulated into producing new tender growth that will be vulnerable to a subsequent frost.

Small gardens can offer microclimatic advantages for plants. Frost can be mitigated by the warmth radiated at night from brick walls exposed to sunshine during the day. In the northern hemisphere, the warmest situation is a planting against a south-facing brick wall. In the southern hemisphere, a north-facing brick wall is the warmest. Overhead cover reduces the effect of frost too. Plants beneath the eaves of houses and underneath evergreen trees will receive some frost protection.

Cold air tends to move down slopes to the lowest point, pooling around any structures that impede its movement, such as a house or barn built into a slope. Plantings in hollows will be the most affected. The areas behind buildings built into slopes, where cold air can collect, are also severely affected.

Plants are far more able to cope with frosts if they are hardened off during late summer and fall. For gardens in areas that are frost susceptible, organic feeding is ideal. Don't use fast-release fertilizers toward the end of summer as they will promote a new flush of growth that will have no opportunity to properly harden off before winter arrives. The slow, steady release of nutrients from compost incorporated into the soil in the spring is ideal for producing slower growth that is easily winter hardened. Watering should also be reduced as fall approaches, to improve the hardening of the season's growth. But do not allow the soil to dry out. Moist soil releases more warmth than dry soils.

Unseasonal frosts are the most damaging. Frosts early in fall, before plants have fully hardened, or the black frosts of spring that hit after plants have leafed out and commenced flowering can never be ruled out. Covering plants with sheets of plastic or burlap can prevent damage to vulnerable plants if the frost is predicted.

Some simple devices are also available to reduce frost damage to young plants. Floating row covers placed over vegetable crops to protect them from attack by flying insects also protects the plants from frost. Cold frames help protect young plants grown from seedlings or from cuttings. They are the equivalent of a mini-glasshouse, consisting of shallow boxes, usually constructed of wood,

with a slanted lid that can be left open during the day to harden young plants, and closed at night. The lid is made from a transparent material such as plastic or glass. Various devices have been invented to protect plants, from individual bell-shaped glass covers to cloches, the equivalent of miniature polytunnels. Greenhouses provide the best protection of all and are invaluable for extending the season for gardeners in cold areas. Seedlings can be raised under cover, and then

A simple cloche and small greenhouse can extend the growing season.

A greenhouse is by far the best method of extending the growing season.

A sheet of polythene can be used to create a mini-greenhouse.

the survival rate of your plants. The mulches are pulled back when spring is fairly advanced, to allow the soil to warm and growth to commence again.

Harvesting and storing

Many people who are converts to organic gardening make excellent resolutions about producing all the family's food, or at least most of it. We plan extensive bottling and freezing sessions to regularly use up the ever-mounting harvests that we intend to take from the garden. But the reality is that we are usually so busy with other things that the wheels come off the grand plan every year with monotonous regularity.

Although the arts of bottling, making chutney, or even drying foods are mysteries to many of us, once mastered, it is surprisingly satisfying and easy to fill a sizable pantry with the finest quality foods for use in the winter months. Preparing food for deep-freezing takes a little time but is another achievable skill. Vegetable bottling does requires some expertise, and you will need instructions from a competent home bottler or follow a good book on the subject to the letter.

Start by setting aside an area to store food reserves. Everything should be off the floor and on shelves. Check carefully that no rats or mice can enter, and clean the area out thoroughly, finishing with a wipe-over with cider vinegar.

moved to be gradually hardened off in cold frames.

Never be tempted by a few days of mild delightful spring weather to rush out and begin planting before recommended dates. Early plantings are often blighted by a late cold snap. Even if no late frosts occur, plants do not grow well until the soil is fully warmed, and early plantings usually have no advantage over later plantings.

Mulches are very important for gardeners in severe winter areas. Heavy mulches piled onto the winter-prepared garden can make a great difference to

Collecting seeds for planting the following season is an economical way of maintaining your garden.

Beans

No matter how you try, the bean harvest will get ahead of you. There are only so many beans you can eat, so leave the remainder of the crop to run to seed. 'Romano' is a variety that is equally delicious as a green bean, fresh shelled, or used dry. Bean seed is prone to attack by a small weevil that bores neat holes in the seed, leaving telltale traces of sawdust behind. Place all bags of bean seeds in the freezer compartment of the refrigerator to eliminate this pest.

Herbs

Progressively harvest all culinary herbs. Most can be hung to dry, and then rubbed down and stored in sealed, labeled bottles. Other herbs lose their delicate flavor easily. Parsley can be chopped and frozen in ice cubes or in ziplock bags in the freezer. Tarragon dries relatively poorly (it is freeze-dried commercially, as is parsley), but readily confers its flavor to vinegar, and can be stored as tarragon vinegar, or it can be deep-frozen in the same manner as parsley. Chives are also best stored deep-frozen.

Fruits

Many fruits are readily stored by deep-freezing or by bottling, or they can be used to make conserves, chutneys, sauces, or jellies.

This is nowhere near what might be achieved, but with a little effort you will have frozen vegetables and fruits for winter use, bottled fruits, a huge

array of dried herbs for teas and flavorings, dried beans for winter dishes, and more chutneys, sauces, conserves, and jellies than you are ever likely to need.

Finally, as the bounty from your garden grows, you can always swap your excess harvest for the different organic produce of organic growers and friends living in other areas and climates.

Parsley should be chopped and frozen in ice to preserve its flavor throughout the winter months.

With careful planning you can ensure a constant supply of seasonal produce.

Multiplying your plants

Plants grown from seed, cuttings, or division are a good way of cheaply increasing the number of plants in your garden.

Growing from seeds

This is much less expensive and can be more fun than buying cuttings or mature plants. Annuals like poppies and nasturtiums can be raised easily from seed and will often self-seed once established. The simplest method is to sow seeds straight into the spot in the garden where you want the plants to grow. This is especially effective if you want to achieve a mass planting of one particular variety, if the seeds are tiny (like carrot seed), or if the seedlings are from plants that don't like to be moved once established.

To prepare the ground, rake the area, removing any weeds. Scatter the seeds over the soil surface, then rake again gently to distribute them. Ensure the seeds are kept moist and thin out the seedlings as they develop.

If you are sowing seed in pots or trays, use a commercial seed soil rather than garden soil. Fill the container with moist mix and lightly firm it down. Then scatter or space the seeds evenly. Sprinkle on a light cover of soil mix. Keep moist and

Many plants can be grown cheaply and easily from seed. Healthy seedlings can be produced by placing several cuttings in a pot and using a plastic bottle to create a mini-greenhouse.

provide even light and temperature until shoots appear. Once the seedlings have developed a set of leaves you can gently separate them out and transfer them to individual containers. They can be transplanted to the garden when they are 4 in (10 cm) tall.

Growing from cuttings

Small segments of stem or leaf sections can be removed from one plant to generate a completely new one, genetically identical to its parent.

Fleshy-stemmed plants like begonias, busy lizzies, nasturtiums, and pelargoniums can be grown easily from cuttings. Remove a new shoot, cutting just below the third set of leaves from the tip. Trim off the lowest set of leaves and make a fresh cut at the base of the stem. Insert the cutting into a pot of cuttings compost. Cover the plant with a plastic bag or the top half of a plastic bottle to conserve moisture and keep it in a light, airy place until a root system develops. The plants can then be transplanted to a large pot and gradually moved outside.

In mild climates, cuttings can be taken at almost any time of year, although rose cuttings are usually taken in very early spring. Cuttings taken from shrubs can be placed straight into fine soil and kept outside

Tuberous-rooted plants can be propogated by division. Remove the plant from its pot, gently cut or pull the plant into sections and repot each section as a new plant.

in a sheltered spot. Several cuttings can be packed tightly into one pot and the survivors potted on when there are signs of good root and leaf growth.

Cuttings, seedlings, and small immature plants grow best in even temperatures and in light, but not sun-bright positions. Keep moisture levels fairly constant and provide shelter. Some air circulation is essential.

Division
This is a quick and easy method of propagating clump-forming perennials such as anemones and campanulas. Use a fork to loosen and lift the entire plant, then gently cut or pull apart the roots so that the plant is divided neatly into sections. To survive, each section must have both roots and above-ground shoots. Replant the divided sections as you would any new plant. The best time to divide plants is when they are dormant.

Tuberous-rooted plants, like begonias, can also be propagated by division. Lift the tubers, choosing one with at lease three shoots, and use a

sharp knife to cut the tuber into sections. Each section must have a shoot. The sections can then be replanted. Once bulbous plants, like daffodils and lilies, have been established for a few years you can divide them by removing the young bulblets that form on the main bulb. Dig up the bulbs when dormant, gently remove the small bulblets from the parent bulb, and replant. They may take a few years to flower again.

African violets and succulents can be propagated from a single leaf or leaf segment. Remove a leaf with its stalk, or a segment from a succulent, and place the cutting in a pot of fine propagating soil. Provide even temperatures and moisture levels until the cutting takes root.

Most clump-forming perennials can be divided easily.

Repotting and transplanting

There is nothing complicated about moving or repotting plants unless they are enormous. A large tree, for example, will require professional help, but the principles are much the same.

Pot plants

The health of a pot plant will start to deteriorate if it has out-grown its container. Roots trailing from the bottom of the pot, leaf drop, and depleted soil are signs that the plant needs repotting. One or two pot sizes larger is usually sufficient. Don't be too eager to repot everything. Some plants (especially ferns) actually prefer slightly cramped conditions and many flowering plants bloom more prolifically if they are a little pot-bound.

Before repotting, water the plant well. When the water has drained away, invert the pot, lightly tapping the sides to release the mass of roots and any that are soggy and brown. Add some potting mix to the new pot, then insert the plant so that it sits at the same surface level as before. If you like, you can add some slow-release fertiliser to the potting mix to save on feeding later on. Surround the plant with some more soil mix and firm in. Water the plant well.

Garden plants

Plants established in the garden may also need moving if they have outgrown their site or are unhappy in a particular position. If possible, try to move them when they are dormant (usually in winter), avoiding extreme weather. If you have to move plants in summer, they will often benefit from some temporary shade while they re-establish themselves. Cover the plant with some lightweight fabric or an inverted basket and apply a mulch to protect the roots.

When moving a medium-sized tree or shrub, it is best to work gradually to reduce damage and trauma. Water the ground thoroughly, then loosen the soil in a wide circle around the plant. Leave for a few days then repeat the process, gradually digging deeper until it is possible to lift out the root mass. Always use a sharp spade, and if roots look ragged or bruised, re-trim them cleanly with secateurs.

If you have to move a plant some distance to a new site, wrap its root ball in a piece of plastic or hessian. Plants that are difficult to handle can be pruned before transplanting. Prune

To repot a plant, tap the pot, invert it, and carefully remove the plant. Trim off any damaged roots and firm into new pot with extra soil.

them back by up to one-third to reduce the shock to their system.

Immediately transfer the plant to its new hole, adding fresh compost. Firm the soil around the plant and water in well. Some people like to apply a hormonal root stimulant when transplanting large shrubs. If you do this, follow the directions carefully and do not overdose.

If the plant is to have a period in a pot before it is planted out, then choose a container only slightly larger than the root ball. Fill any gaps between the roots and the sides of the container with potting mix and water well both before and after potting. Only feed if the pot-bound period is to be an extended one.

A certain amount of transplant shock is almost inevitable with a mature specimen. Reactions can vary. The plant may look a bit weedy, or it may drop its leaves. If the latter happens, treat it with consideration— don't let it dry out or drown—and it should recover with time.

Seedlings

Seedlings are easy to transplant as they haven't had time to develop an extensive root system. If they have been grown in groups, separate them by gently pulling them apart or, if they have delicate roots, cut them apart with a sharp knife. Make a small hole in the ground, then position the plants, firming the soil gently around them. Water the seedlings in well and ensure they are kept moist.

Indoor seedlings may need hardening off before transplanting. Place them in a sheltered place outside for a few hours each day, gradually increasing exposure to full sun and night temperatures over a few weeks.

Seedlings in the garden can be re-established in a new site that better fits your garden scheme. Dig them out carefully, retaining as much accompanying soil as possible, then plant them as above.

Transplant seedlings when they have a few leaves. Make a hole large enough to fit the seedling's root mass. Now loosen the soil and gently separate the roots. Place each seedling in a hole, firm in, and water well.

Chapter 5

STARTING UP

Diversity is the key to creating abundance

Mother Nature has given us the perfect model for sustainable ecosystems—diversity. Diversity is a major factor in preventing pest and disease build-up because of the way in which organisms interact in the natural world. When any one species begins to predominate in an area, its predators will move in to take advantage of the bounty. Eventually they will reduce the numbers of the dominant species, restoring the balance of Nature.

In the past, farmers relied on natural methods of farming because chemicals were not available to them. Now, it is possible to grow crops as monocultures because the use of pesticides has given us a way of controlling competition. This unnatural form of agriculture has created a range of unintended problems. We can learn from these mistakes by planting a diverse range of species in our gardens, thus naturally reducing pests and diseases.

The advantages of heirloom varieties

Heirloom plants are varieties that have been handed down through decades or even centuries from farmer to farmer and gardener to gardener. For roughly 12,000 years, human civilization has been based on agriculture and horticulture, and during this time thousands of genetically unique strains of fruit and vegetables have been selected and bred by farmers and gardeners. They represent a genetic heritage that is disappearing from commercial horticulture, where large-scale factory-type production demands that plants conform to strict guidelines to fit into mechanized systems.

By contrast, heirloom varieties are a celebration of genetic diversity whose greatest strength is the fact that there are individuals within each crop that mature a bit earlier or are more resistant to pests and diseases. Such characteristics are a tremendous advantage in the organic garden where the produce does not have to fit into a narrow commercial window.

Fortunately, there are many gardeners who recognize the value of maintaining genetic diversity for future generations. Consequently, around the world various non-profit organizations have been formed to store seed or to help gardeners and farmers form networks that enable them to swap seed and vegetative material of heirloom plant varieties.

Some examples of organizations that provide access to heritage varieties include:

Seed Savers Network
PO Box 975
Byron Bay
NSW 2481
AUSTRALIA

Contrasting foliage textures and colors mix with blooms in a cottage-style border.

National Council for the
Conservation of Plants and Gardens
C/o Wisley Garden
Woking
Surrey GU23 6QB
UK

Abundant Life Seed Foundation
PO Box 772
Port Townsend
WA 948368
USA

Seed Savers Exchange
PO Box 70
Decorah
IA 52101
USA

The many vital roles of herbs and flowers

Introducing a range of herbs and flowers into your organic garden will have all sorts of beneficial consequences. They will help attract an increased range of birds, insects, lizards, and other animals. Insects and birds will act as pollinators for your fruit and vegetables resulting in increased yields. Many of these creatures will also help to control pests. Inevitably, there will also be some negative consequences, such as birds feeding on fruit, but the diversity you create will be your insurance policy in that if one food crop is decimated there will be a host of others that can replace it.

Herbs often have aromatic oils that give their foliage and flowers a characteristic perfume. Herbs such as pyrethrum and garlic can be used to create organic remedies for pest and disease problems. In addition, such plants release oils into the air and soil that surrounds them, thereby helping to repel pests from your garden.

Garden fresh produce is free of all the fungicides and pesticides used to extend the shelf-life of commercially produced crops.

Planning

Much of the history of landscaping has involved the imposition of a beautiful patterned design or concept upon the submissive earth. The site was unimportant or, worse, an impediment to the design, to be configured into a more acceptable form. Compliance was what was required of the site. Design was imposed from the outside, not generated from within.

Yet the design pendulum occasionally swung back through the centuries, and sometimes there was an acknowledgment of the role of the site, of the possibility of working with the natural contours of the land and using them as a starting point for the creative design process. Out of such a fashion swing came the idea of 'spirit

Terracing is an effective way to manage a steep incline or unstable soil.

of place', which remains the best way to design, for both amateur or professional, and offers some guarantee that no major design errors will occur. In essence, this means having the patience to get to know your site properly. Walk around the area you plan for your garden, sit in it for an hour or so, move around it to see different viewpoints. Every site talks if you will listen.

When you believe you have a feel for the place, then you can begin to plan the design. Now the site will shape the design—the reverse of the classical design process.

There are many things we need to know about a site before we can begin to transform it into a garden. In urban areas the list will be longer and more complex. The first thing to do is to measure the area out as accurately as possible and draw it to scale. Locate any major permanent items such as large trees, buildings, and other structures. Locate north on your site analysis. Topography, or the shape and fall of the land, is important too. You will want to know how and where the land slopes and how steeply. Try to determine the way rainwater would run off the site, or visit on a day of fairly heavy rain. It is a good idea to make several photocopies of your scale drawing so that all the information you obtain can be easily recorded without too much clutter. It can be summarized later. The site may also be limited by water availability, the depth of soil, the type of soil, and the pH level.

Look next at the effect of the environment on the site. There are two major concerns here. First, the natural environment, which includes the directions of severe prevailing winds during the year and any special considerations such as salt-laden winds for beachside properties, or the historical line of wildfire approach for country properties. Second, the built environment needs particular

Attracting wildlife should be an important consideration when planning a garden.

consideration for city properties. Are there unreasonable levels of noise coming from the road? Are there unsightly views to be eliminated? What utilities are buried underground and where are they? What is overhead? Locate sewerage pipes, water pipes, telephone lines, and any other utilities on the scaled diagram of the site. Locate existing paths.

Every site offers opportunities. There may be a pleasant view from some angle or perhaps a well-grown mature tree. Existing feature trees can give an instant look of maturity to the garden.

Finally, use one-word descriptions to record your impressions of the spaces in the garden. Enter information also about the surrounds to the property. Take soil samples from the major areas of the garden and check the soil pH. This can be a severe constraint on what you will be able to plant, though luckily most soils are within one scale point of neutral (pH 7).

By now you should feel that you really know your site. Perhaps as you worked through this process, you began to see how some things might be changed or improved. This is the time to visualize all the features you would like in your garden and to make a list. The key checklist words at this point are style, coherence, and scale. In terms of style, do you like things to be homely and comfortable and perhaps a bit untidy, or do you prefer neatness and order? Do you go for elegant simplicity, or the romantic semi-wilderness of the true cottager's garden? Remember that the house itself may dictate the garden design to quite an extent. Perhaps a theme might trigger your imagination.

Now think about coherence. Does everything relate well together? Grand or modern houses, for instance, look silly if juxtaposed with a cottage garden of meandering home-made paths.

Matching the scale of the garden to the house is important too. Tiny gardens can be the best fun of all. They are like little jewels. The idea here is to mix textures and colors together, to add fruits and flowers and herbs in incredible profusion. Buy containers and pots and make them as beautiful as you can. The days when organic meant brown and functional have gone.

Break all the rules in your planting schemes. Trust your instincts. Observing the way things work together in Nature is part of the pleasure of organic gardening. Create a balance of restfulness and brightness, of sun and shade, a living tapestry intricately woven from every plant that you love.

The topography of your site should form the basis of your garden plan. Try to work with its natural features, not against them.

The commuter's evening garden

It is ironic that the demands of modern living often result in our working so hard to earn our dream place that we rarely have the time or opportunity to see it. Commuters will be all too familiar with the frustrations of leaving for work in the dark and returning in the dark to their tiny piece of paradise.

Although it isn't the same without sunshine, it is possible to enjoy a night garden, a place that can work as a great de-stresser. Why not make a night garden a special project, a reward to look forward to?

A porch, patio, or deck provides the ideal focus for the project. You will need a place where potting and propagation and messing around is possible. A small conservatory would be ideal, but a screened outdoor room makes a good compromise. This allows the cool of the night air in, excludes insects, and puts a screen between you and the outside world. You will need good lighting, a work table, and an old cupboard in which to store secateurs, gloves, trowels, pots, trays, and the like. A couple of bins can be used to hold potting mix and seedling mix made up during weekends. In winter, a small greenhouse can be a magical world of warmth filled with the smells of growing plants and rich earth. It can be located close to the house and a strong spotlight used to illuminate the area. Use an internal lock on the door if you are nervous about security.

Summertime gardens can be enjoyed at night if you concentrate on areas close to the house. As the sun goes down, the color drains from the landscape. Flowers become pale moons swimming in the dark. Night-scented flowers begin to breathe out their fragrance on the air to attract pollinators. Some of the evening-scented flowers are exquisite.

Borrowing ideas

Cottage gardening has been successfully practiced for many centuries. The basic concept is to grow a diverse range of plant species in somewhat random fashion throughout the garden. This creates a more natural meadow-like appearance and, apart from being aesthetically pleasing, it also reduces the risk of attack by pests and diseases by scattering the plants and making them harder to find than large plantings of the same species.

Observe gardens in your neighborhood and join any local gardening clubs to learn what will thrive in your area. Local garden centres can also be a wonderful source of information on this subject as they have a big interest in steering you in the right direction.

The evening primroses glow in the dim light and pour forth intense lemon and tuberose fragrance. The slightly earthy day scent of English honeysuckle becomes pure sweetness in the cool night air. Night-scented stocks, so insignificant by day, pour spices from their tiny throats. White ginger lilies and annual phlox will drift the purest of fragrances toward open doors and windows.

Gather a bunch of scented flowers during the day and test each during the night. You might be surprised at the changes they display.

A garden in pots can easily be accessed at night if it is near the house. Why not keep a duplicate culinary herb garden on the patio or around the porch? Nothing replaces the pleasure of freshly harvested herbs in cooking. Use lightweight imitations of good pots so that you can easily move them when the nights draw in.

Sound is an extra dimension to the garden unaffected by darkness. Add some large wind chimes with rich clear notes to your garden. The sound of running water, even from a small bubble fountain, has a cooling effect on hot summer nights.

Imagine at the end of your working day coming back to the cool sweetness

of the evening-scented flowers, a herb garden in pots ready for easy harvest, and perhaps a living salad bar of lettuce, baby tomatoes, tiny radishes, and spring onions.

Think about planning the garden to suit the way you live. If you don't get home until late, placing pots near the house will at least enable you to enjoy the fragrance of night-blooming plants.

Pretty and sweet-scented, the Mexican Orange Blossom Choisya ternata *is the perfect choice for a night-time garden.*

A child's secret garden

For small children, a garden is a big world filled with possibilities. Even the simplest garden can be a place of mystery and excitement. But gardens can offer so much more. The best ones are filled with special places, sunny glades, trellises dripping with sweet raspberries and crisp sugary peas, pumpkin vines rampaging on fences, clumps of milky cob corn to be gathered and nibbled, each small kernel popping creamy sweetness, rampant pools of nasturtiums with nectar to be sucked from peppery horns, snapdragons to be snapped, ants to watch for hours, clouds to see strange worlds in, jungles of summer leaves to hide in, teepees of sweetpeas to read beneath.

Fortunately, in the organic world, provided that no poisonous plants are grown, children can play freely. Ponds, however, even shallow ones, should be kept out of bounds until children are old enough for ornamental pools to cease to be a hazard.

Children love to imitate what we adults do. Allocate a small area of the garden to children. Give them a really good piece of land, one that has been well cultivated and composted. First results with gardening have a way of staying with us and compacted, poor soil in a shady corner is a recipe for early disillusionment with gardening.

Large-seeded plants are easiest for young fingers to manage. Corn is a good choice. Make sure that many seeds are planted. Draw a circle on the soil and encourage your child to plant it evenly with seed. Sunflowers are an easy crop. So too are zucchini (courgettes), tomatoes, nasturtiums, marigolds, beans, peas, and strawberries.

Include children in planning garden plantings for the season. Vegetables become special when you own them or have helped care for them. Make

A thyme lawn is easy to grow and an ideal way of introducing children to the magic of organic gardening.

midsummer will be a memory to treasure. Use a simple motif such as a white duck against blue water with a yellow sun, or a pattern of squares.

Creating a thyme lawn, a planter pot filled with strawberries or a hanging basket full of flowers, or constructing a teepee for climbing beans are all simple projects that will bring the magic of gardening into young lives ... and older ones. Don't forget the simplest of pleasures—threading daisy chains and coronets, making floral carpets on trays, creating miniature gardens. A few fairytales, myths and magic can complete a perfect summer memory.

Gardening within limitations

There is something healing about gardening, and such a positive energy flow takes place. Tired, stressed bodies relax, optimism replaces pessimism, anger is blunted. But it isn't just the psychological effect of gardening, it is the physical effect too. Gardening can be the perfect exercise, driven not by a preoccupation with

Corn, with its large seeds, is one of the most rewarding plants for young children to grow.

harvesting a privilege and supply a personalized basket to make the job special. Create projects that you can do together, such as planting a flower carpet. Design it together, choosing the pattern and the colors, selecting the right dwarf plants, buying or raising seedlings together, drawing the pattern on the soil and filling it in. The living picture in glowing color in

Succulents are ideal pot dwellers.

body image, but by the need to nurture tiny plants.

All sorts of problems can inhibit our garden activities, however, from a temporary setback such as a broken bone to long-lasting arthritic pain. Faced with such limitations, many of us are reluctant to give up the pleasures that gardening gives, or the positive way it contributes to our wellbeing. Fortunately, some simple adjustments can be made so that gardening remains our favorite hobby.

There are many specially created gardening aids that are now available. They range from knee pads and kneelers that protect sensitive joints to ergonomically designed secateurs, garden spades, forks and other garden instruments that use much enhanced leverage ratios to compensate for lost strength or pain when exerting pressure.

If your movement is restricted, beautiful, satisfying gardens can still be created in large pots that can be tended while sitting on a chair. Raising garden beds with stonework, bricks, or timber can also make gardening much easier. It is an expense to raise garden levels, but the reward of being able to work at waist height is worth it.

Large concrete trough gardens created with stones and pebbles and filled with precious miniature alpines can also fill many happy hours. Moss gardens planted in stone troughs can be fascinating projects. There are hundreds of mosses to choose from, all the way up to the world's largest, the Australian *Dawsonia*, which looks like a miniaturized fir tree, standing 10–12 in (25–30 cm) high.

Perhaps the biggest boon to gardeners as they age and the earth seems to retreat a little further from reach every year is the no-dig garden system so passionately advocated by Esther Dean in the 1970s in Australia. To see such a garden is to be instantly converted. (*See Creating Living Soils.*)

No space is too small for an organic garden.

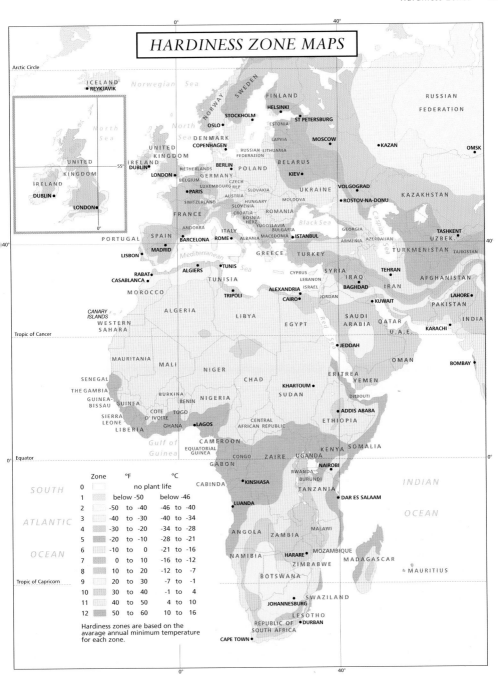

HARDINESS ZONE MAPS

Zone	°F	°C
0	no plant life	
1	below -50	below -46
2	-50 to -40	-46 to -40
3	-40 to -30	-40 to -34
4	-30 to -20	-34 to -28
5	-20 to -10	-28 to -21
6	-10 to 0	-21 to -16
7	0 to 10	-16 to -12
8	10 to 20	-12 to -7
9	20 to 30	-7 to -1
10	30 to 40	-1 to 4
11	40 to 50	4 to 10
12	50 to 60	10 to 16

Hardiness zones are based on the avarage annual minimum temperature for each zone.

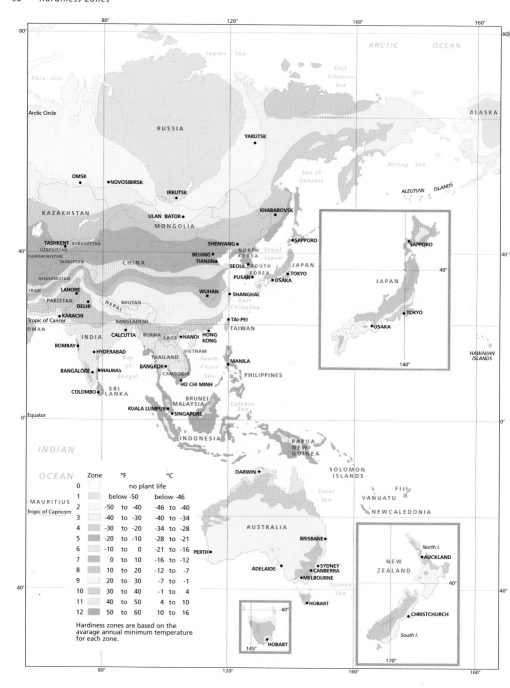

Hardiness zones are based on the
avarage annual minimum temperature
for each zone.

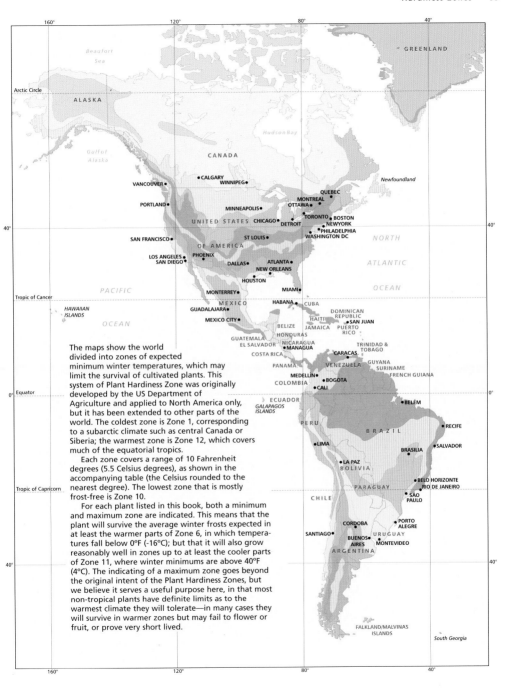

The maps show the world divided into zones of expected minimum winter temperatures, which may limit the survival of cultivated plants. This system of Plant Hardiness Zone was originally developed by the US Department of Agriculture and applied to North America only, but it has been extended to other parts of the world. The coldest zone is Zone 1, corresponding to a subarctic climate such as central Canada or Siberia; the warmest zone is Zone 12, which covers much of the equatorial tropics.

Each zone covers a range of 10 Fahrenheit degrees (5.5 Celsius degrees), as shown in the accompanying table (the Celsius rounded to the nearest degree). The lowest zone that is mostly frost-free is Zone 10.

For each plant listed in this book, both a minimum and maximum zone are indicated. This means that the plant will survive the average winter frosts expected in at least the warmer parts of Zone 6, in which temperatures fall below 0°F (-16°C); but that it will also grow reasonably well in zones up to at least the cooler parts of Zone 11, where winter minimums are above 40°F (4°C). The indicating of a maximum zone goes beyond the original intent of the Plant Hardiness Zones, but we believe it serves a useful purpose here, in that most non-tropical plants have definite limits as to the warmest climate they will tolerate—in many cases they will survive in warmer zones but may fail to flower or fruit, or prove very short lived.

Part 2

ORGANIC PLANT ENCYCLOPEDIA

Section 1

VEGETABLES

Asian Greens

Chinese Cabbage or **Pe-tsai** *Brassica rapa* var. *pekinensis*; **Chinese Flat Cabbage** or **Tatsoi** *B. rapa* var. *rosularis*; **Chinese Mustard** or **Gai Choy** *Brassica juncea* var. *rugosa*; **Chinese White Cabbage** or **Pak Choi** *Brassica rapa* var. *chinensis*; **Mizuna** and **Mibuna** *Brassica rapa* var. *nipposinica*, *Brassica rapa* var. *japonica*

A healthy diet includes ultra-fresh vegetables in quantity and Asian greens are a good choice for home gardens. They are fast-growers that can be cultivated with ease provided that adequate attention is paid to soil preparation.

Growing and Harvesting

Chinese gardeners use deep bed methods combined with organic additions and regular watering to tender greens. A single short bed about 6¹/₂ ft (2 m) wide and 13 ft (4 m) long would keep a family richly supplied with Asian greens. Incorporate as much well rotted organic matter as possible into the soil to form beds up to 12 in (30 cm) high with sloping sides. The top should be raked flat. Traditional methods favor regulated flooding between rows to ensure thorough deep watering, but overhead watering can also be used. Liquid compost and manure 'soups' should be regularly applied to ensure there is no nutritional setback. As soon as the crops are harvested they should be replaced with a new crop. Root vegetables grown in these beds penetrate deeply and easily, and in turn help to loosen the soil and keep it aerated. Add compost to the surface of the soil before planting new crops of Asian greens.

Above: With many Asian vegetables the whole plant can be eaten— leaves, stems, and shoots.

Below: Asian greens wilt soon after picking, so are best eaten as fresh as possible.

Chinese Cabbage *or* Pe-tsai
Brassica rapa var. *pekinensis*   Zones 7–11

This is perhaps the most commonly encountered Chinese vegetable. It is also known as celery cabbage, *wong bok*, *siew choy*, and Peking cabbage. It forms densely packed, creamy, large, upright heads which may be slender to barrel-shaped to almost round, depending on the cultivar. The leaves are more tender than the European cabbage, and their flavor is sweeter and milder with a faint mustard tang. They are designed for the shortest of cooking periods so are perfect for stir-fried and steamed dishes, or as a last-minute addition to soups.

Growing and Harvesting
Chinese cabbages require deep, well drained, nutrient-rich soils in a sunny position. They prefer a pH of 6.5–7.0. Their optimal temperature range is achieved in most areas in spring and fall. In tropical areas, this is a winter crop. Seed can be directly sown into the garden in rows, spacing the plants about 14 in (35 cm) apart. There is little to be gained by planting seed in flats and transplanting seedlings as they can run to flower as a result of the additional stress. Seeds germinate in 2–3 days at 68°F (20°C). They can be harvested at any time up to full development, and individual outer leaves can also be picked, leaving the central leaf core to grow on, as a cut-and-come-again vegetable. Dense-hearted cultivars store well in winter.

Recommended Cultivars
China's immense regional differences have resulted in the development of over 200 cultivars. Among these are 'Tokyo Giant', 'Winter Giant', 'China King', 'Wong Bok', 'Spring Giant', 'Kasumi', and 'Michichili'. In recent times a plethora of hybrids have also been released.

Chinese Flat Cabbage *or* Tatsoi
Brassica rapa var. *rosularis*   Zones 7–11

This is one of the handsomest and easiest to grow Chinese greens, forming a dense, flat layered rosette of glossy, thick, dark green leaves with pale green petioles. It is ideal for winter soups or braised dishes, and can be used as a spinach substitute. It is remarkably cold-hardy, surviving severe frosts and living under snow without protection. The seeds are sown in fall. Warm weather will cause the plants to bolt rapidly. It is also known as Chinese flat black cabbage.

Chinese cabbages, Brassica rapa var. pekinensis, large and barrel-shaped, look different to the European variety. The plants mature more quickly and the leaves have a finer texture.

The Chinese flat cabbage resembles cos lettuce, but has strongly veined leaves. The leaves are commonly tied together around the developing heart.

Chinese Mustard
or Gai Choy

Brassica juncea var. *rugosa*   Zones 6–11

Chinese mustards were developed as a result of hybridization between Chinese cabbages *B. rapa* and black mustard *B. nigra*. The result is a very diverse group which somewhat resembles open cabbages or kales and have inherited a marked but by no means unpleasant mustard flavor.

Growing and Harvesting
Chinese mustard is grown in the same manner as Chinese cabbage. It is more tolerant of acidic soils than other Chinese greens, and will grow on less well prepared soils. The plants can be harvested at any stage, and if some run to flower the seed can be popped in oil and added to various dishes to add flavor.

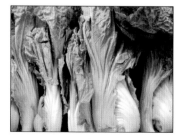

Chinese mustard, Brassica juncea var. rugosa, is used mainly as a vegetable, but can also be used for pickling.

Recommended Cultivars
Four groups are recognized: the **'Swatow Mustard'** types that can be used like lettuce (in moderation) in mixed salads and include highly ornamental types like **'Osaka Purple'**, the delicately flavored **'Wrapped Heart Mustard'**, and **'Bamboo Mustard'**, a group with curled and finely cut leaves resembling curly kales that can overwinter well, a peppery flavored winter salad group with fine-cut edges of which **'Green-in-the-Snow'** is a member, and a group with thickened leaf stalks eaten together with the young shoot tips as a winter crop.

Chinese White Cabbage
or Pak Choi

Brassica rapa var. *chinensis*   Zones 7–11

Other names for these open-headed cabbages are *bok choi*, *tsoi sum*, and flowering white cabbage. It is characterized by succulent crisp thick leaf stalks and smooth broad leaves. Chinese white cabbage is used in salads and stir fries, and can be braised, steamed, or pickled. These tender-leafed vegetables have a delicious, faintly hot and bitter tang if they are not over-cooked.

Growing and Harvesting
These are grown in the same manner as Chinese cabbage. They germinate in about 7 days at 68°F (20°C). The plants are thinned to 10 in (25 cm) apart and the thinnings make excellent additions to stir fries. They are sown in spring and fall, and in tropical areas in winter.

Recommended Cultivars
Many cultivars have been developed which may look quite unlike each other. Among those easily available and of excellent quality are **'Shanghai Pak Choi'**, also known as green stalk, **'Lei Choy'** (developed in Holland and popular in California), and **'Chinese Bok Choi'**. **'Canton

'Dwarf' is very heat-tolerant and is ideal for semi-tropical climates. 'Tsoi Sum' and 'Hong Kong Yow Choy' are good forms of flowering cabbage varieties.

Mizuna and Mibuna

Brassica rapa var. *nipposinica, B. rapa* var. *japonica*   Zones 7–11

Mizuna is a traditional Japanese salad green forming a dense, non-hearting clump of long, narrow, very finely dissected, tender green leaves that look beautiful in salad mixes and have a slight cabbage and mustard flavor. Mibuna is thought to be closely related to mizuna except that its leaves tend to be longer and narrower, with rounded tips. The plants are exceptionally easy to grow in spring or fall, directly planted into a well-drained, well-composted soil, and are moderately hardy, making them an ideal salad vegetable for early winter months.

Crisp stalks form the main bulk of the Chinese white cabbage, Brassica rapa var. chinensis. The plants run to seed quickly, so should be sown in small groups every 10 days.

Mizuna, Brassica rapa var. nipposinica, can grow on a wide range of soil types but prefers rich, loamy soils with high water retention.

Beans

Broad Beans *Vicia faba;* **Cowpeas** *Vigna unguiculata* ssp. *unguiculata;* **Dry Beans** *Phaseolus vulgaris;* **Hyacinth Beans** *Dolichos lablab;* **Lima Beans** *Phaseolus lunatus;* **Nunas** *P. vulgaris;* **Runner Beans** *P. coccineus;* **Shelling Beans** *P. vulgaris;* **Snake Beans** *Vigna unguiculata* ssp. *sesquipedalis;* **Snap Beans** *Phaseolus vulgaris;* **Soybeans** *Glycine max;* **Tepary Beans** *Phaseolus acutifolius, P. a.* var. *tenuifolius*

Most of the thousands of bean varieties grown around the world belong to just one species, *Phaseolus vulgaris.* Some have been developed for their fleshy, tender pods, some for their seeds, the peas, and some for drying for winter storage. These groups are further sub-divided into dwarf, semi-vining, and pole or climbing beans. There are also highly developed subgroups such as the flageolet beans (a group of gourmet shelling bean cultivars developed in France), and the cranberry (or horticultural) beans which are characterized by pods and seeds that are brightly splashed and striped with red.

Above: The broad bean, Vicia faba, *is believed to be one of the earliest domesticated crop plants.*

Right: Beans display great variation in pod, seed, and growth characteristics. They are thought to be a cultivated derivative of a wild species from the northern Andes.

Broad Beans
Vicia faba   Zones 7–10

Broad beans, also called fava beans, are among the oldest crops in the Old World and were extensively grown by the ancient Egyptians, the Greeks, and the Romans. They are the hardiest of the beans and were a staple food in the Middle Ages. There are four different groups of beans available within this species today: the broad bean or fava, the horse bean, the tic bean, and a group closely allied to the tic bean.

Broad beans should never, ever be grown to the size of those leathery monsters sold in stores. Instead, they should be harvested young, sweet, and while they still have thin seed coats. After steaming or boiling, slip the seeds out of their coats as the French do and encounter a sweet, tender vegetable of rare delight.

Growing and Harvesting
Broad beans need to be planted in cool temperatures, during fall in warmer areas, or in either fall or early spring in cool areas. They require a protected, sunny position and well-prepared soil to which compost and some ground rock phosphate has been added. Some gardeners dust the seed

with *Rhizobia* innoculent before planting. Sow the seed 4–6 in (10–15 cm) apart at a depth of 1 in (2.5 cm) to allow the tall plants mutual support. Most cultivars grow to about 4 ft (1.2 m).

Hot weather is detrimental to flowering and pod set. Some gardeners pinch plants back to hasten maturity, but with our increasingly erratic weather patterns this is becoming less advisable. If you do pinch out the flowering tops, try steaming them and tossing in a little butter for a deliciously different new vegetable. Harvest regularly to encourage setting of flowers. Little bean pods can be cooked whole.

Rust, which appears as reddish pustules on the leaves, should be treated immediately with sulfur dust. Black aphids may also be a problem and should be sprayed with insecticidal soap or pyrethrins, taking care to target the spray or dust accurately.

Broad beans can self-pollinate or cross-pollinate with other broad beans. If you can place a net cage around a group of plants, it will ensure the purity of the seed to be saved for planting the following year, as well as excluding insects.

Recommended Cultivars
'Aquadulce Claudia' — This is the finest of the early cultivars and can be planted in fall or early spring.

'Green Windsor' — A broad bean of superb flavor, and exceptionally popular among gardeners. The seed remains deep green even when cooked. Introduced in 1831, other than seed color it is similar in all respects to **'Broad Windsor'**.

Red Epicure — This is considered the finest flavored broad bean in the world with beautiful red flowers and deep red-brown seeds that taste like chestnuts when cooked. It requires a cool to mild climate where it is hardy and a heavy cropper.

Cowpeas
Vigna unguiculata ssp. *unguiculata*   Zones 10–11

Cowpeas belong to the subspecies *unguiculata*, and are thought to have originated in Ethiopia where they were developed for their seeds. Today they are widely grown across the Mediterranean, Africa, the Middle East, India, South America, and southern areas of the United States. They are also known as blackeye peas or crowders and are indispensible to the cuisine of the south.

Growing *and* Harvesting
Most modern cultivars are dwarf so the plants do not require support. Seeds should be planted in rows in spring, in a sunny position, when the ground has warmed sufficiently.

The broad bean, Vicia faba, has small flowers, usually borne in clusters from the leaf axils. Flowers can be white, pink, purple, or pale yellow. The pods that follow are often hairy or downy.

The attractive seeds of the cowpea, Vigna unguiculata ssp. unguiculata can be eaten fresh, as immature pods, or dried.

Many bean varieties grow so tall that they need support in the form of trellises.

The 'Black Delgado' dry bean, Phaseolus vulgaris, *was a staple ingredient in the diet of the Zapotecs in Mexico.*

Dry Beans

Phaseolus vulgaris   Zones 7–11

Dry beans or field beans are invaluable harvests to store in the winter pantry. As well as being beautifully colored with intricate patterning, they are nutritious, keep very well if stored correctly, and are an ideal addition to winter dishes. In the past dry beans have been used as survival food through long, cold winters though they are also popular in the cuisines of warmer countries such as South America, Mexico, and parts of the Mediterranean.

Growing and Harvesting

While some dried beans are readily available, many of the best sorts for cooking are not grown commercially so the only way to enjoy them is to grow your own. Dry beans are grown in the same way as snap beans. To harvest them, pull out the whole plant when the pods are dry and most of the leaves have dried and fallen. The plants can then be hung upside-down to fully dry. Small quantities of pods can be shelled by hand, a calming activity. Larger quantities need to be handled differently, placing them in a container of some kind such as a sack and threshing them with a wooden flail. Allow the seed to dry thoroughly before storage.

A universal curse is the presence of bean weevils, small, beetle-like insects that bury into the seed creating small round holes and leaving behind a powder. Stored seed is eventually destroyed if infested. Freezing will kill weevils. Place the seed into large, ziplocked plastic bags or plastic-topped glass jars in a deep freeze for one week before storing in the normal way in an airtight container.

Recommended Cultivars

Among the many old cultivars still available are the dryland farmed 'Hopi Black'; ancient 'Black Delgado' used by the Zapotecs in Mexico; 'Mitla Black' from Oaxaca in Mexico; 'Swedish Brown'; green seeded pre-1750s' 'Hutterite Soup'; 'Anasazi', the bean of the cliff dwellers of the southwest United States; New England's 'Soldier Bean'; the ancient American-Indian cultivar 'Arikara'; and the old Maine bean 'Yellow Eye' or 'Molasses Face'.

*Rows of hyacinth beans,
Dolichos lablab, growing
at Monticello, Virginia,
USA. The foliage of this
plant is a beautiful,
vibrant green and purple
and the flowers are
bright purple and white.*

Hyacinth Beans
Dolichos lablab   Zones 10–12

Also known as the bonavista bean and Egyptian bean, the hyacinth bean has long been suspected of being poisonous and gardeners once anxiously warned visitors of the perils of the purple beans and the exquisite, two-toned purple flowers. The beans are perfectly edible, however, as is the thick root, so perhaps this idea came from a wish to protect the vines from flower arrangers. These are the hardiest of climbing beans with no notable pests or diseases. They should be planted into prepared soil in spring when the ground temperature has warmed. Hyacinth beans will grow well in warm rather than hot summers. In tropical areas the plants flower best in fall and again in the following spring.

Lima Beans
Phaseolus lunatus   Zones 10–12

Lima beans are also known as butter beans and Madagascar beans. They occur as small seeded cultivars known as *sieva* (sometimes called 'Carolina') beans whch originated from Mexico.

This is a tropical, lowland species although some cultivars are adapted to cooler and higher altitude conditions. The seeds are the part of the plant that is eaten and they have a melting, buttery texture and unique delicious flavor. They require a long growing season and are an ideal crop in the southern United States, much of Australia, Mediterranean areas, North Africa, Madagascar, and the North Island of New Zealand, apart from their native Mexico. Green limas contain good amounts of beta carotenes and useful levels of vitamins B1, B2, and C together with calcium, phosphorous, and iron.

*The lima bean cultivar
'Christmas', Phaseolus
lunatus, heirloom bean
dates back to the 1840s.
Its vines are vigorous
and produce heavy
yields. It grows well,
even in extreme heat.*

Large seeded Lima beans, Phaseolus lunatus, were developed around the capital of Peru at least 7,300 years ago.

Growing and Harvesting

Limas are cold-sensitive and planting into soil that has not fully warmed after winter will result in the seed rotting in the ground. In general they should be planted at least two weeks after snap beans. They require a well-drained soil in a sunny position. Heavy, wet, clay soils are unsuitable unless they have been enriched with compost for a few seasons to improve soil aeration and tilth.

Climbing forms require support similar to that for climbing or pole snap beans. The seed of bush limas should be planted 6 in (15 cm) apart in rows 30 in (75 cm) apart and at a depth of 1 in (2.5 cm). Pole or climbing limas should be planted at intervals of 10 in (25 cm). If the weather is uncertain, seed can be raised in small pots for transplanting until warmer temperatures have settled in. Plants should be mulched once they are 6 in (15 cm) high.

Pick the pods as they swell. They should not be left on the plants too long if you intend to use them fresh. For dry limas, allow the pods to dry on the vine and pull up the whole vines, treating them in the same way as for **Dry Beans** above.

Recommended Cultivars

'Christmas' syn. large speckled calico — This is a very beautiful pole cultivar with large, flat, white seeds speckled with crimson. It is popular in the United States and Australia.

'Florida Butter' syn. Florida speckled butter. — This is an ideal pole lima for areas with a subtropical climate. It grows to 8 ft (2.5 m) and bears small, delicious, buff seed spotted with reddish brown. The pods are borne in prolific quantities.

'Fordhook' — This productive 1907 cultivar is still popular. It has 3–4 large, plump, creamy white to pale green seeds per pod.

'Henderson' — Gardeners appreciate this older bush cultivar (dating from 1883) for its excellent quality, creamy white seed on short plants to 12 in (30 cm) high.

'King of the Garden' — A popular pole cultivar with 4–6 large, pale green, flat seeds per pod of excellent quality. The vines grow to 10 ft (3 m).

Seed Saving Note

Lima beans need to be separated by a minimum distance of 10 ft (3 m) to prevent cross pollination. As this is impractical in most gardens, if you are saving seed and growing two or more cultivars, temporarily cover some flower heads with net bags, tapping the flowers to ensure pollen falls on the stigma. Once the pods are set the bag can be removed and the inflorescence marked with a tied colored thread. Alternatively, grow only one cultivar each year, well separated from other plants.

Nunas

Phaseolus vulgaris   Zones 7–11

Nunas are the bean world's equivalent of popcorn. While frijoles or boiled beans were the mainstay of the Incan diet at lower altitudes, at very high altitudes in the Andes, water boiled at too low a temperature to cook beans. Instead, people relied on a strain of *Phaseolus vulgaris* which could be cooked in oil. When the oil heats the plump, oval, hard-shelled beans the contents pop, expelling the soft contents, which taste a little like peanuts and, being high in protein, are very nutritious. The beans are exceptionally pretty, looking like birds' eggs speckled and splashed with almost every imaginable color.

They are popularly grown from Equador to southern Peru and were virtually unknown outside this area until recent times. Now they are grown in cooler areas for their usefulness as a nutritious snack food. Nuna plants can be grown in the same way as common beans, and as they have a vining habit they are often grown up cornstalks. They are adapted to cool growing conditions and appear to be unable to tolerate temperatures over 77°F (25°C). At the other end of the spectrum they will not cope with temperatures much below 42°F (5.5°C). Research on nunas is concentrating on removing their requirement for a short day length and they have great promise in the near future. At least 100 strains exist but few are known beyond their local area. Among the finest are the grey and white speckled *pava*, the pure white pigeon egg *huevo de paloma*, and the beautifully red and white splashed *parcollana*.

Runner Beans

Phaseolus coccineus   Zones 9–11

Native to Mexico, the runner bean was domesticated about 2,200 years ago. John Gerard's *Herball or General Historie of Plantes* of 1597 records it as being introduced into England as an ornamental in the 16th century by John Tradescant. And an ornamental it remained, people believing that its brilliant scarlet flowers were a clear warning of danger. The first Englishman to brave the perils of the runner bean was Phillip Miller who, in the early 18th century, instructed his cook to prepare pods gathered in the Chelsea Physic Garden for his lunch. Then, in the best tradition of scientific inquiry, he sat down to meticulously record his own symptoms and death agonies should he be wrong in his assumptions. Since then, the runner bean has proved an admirable alternative for snap beans in the cooler conditions of the British Isles.

Today, white-flowered, red-flowered, pink-flowered, and half-red/half-white flowered varieties exist and there are dwarf as well as tall cultivars. The pods should be harvested and sliced while still young or they will become too fibrous. Some cultivars such as **'Giant Greek White'** are grown not for their pods but their

This white flowered runner bean, Phaseolus coccineus, is one of many different varieties of runner bean.

Runner beans are perennial, and last for several years, though they bear most heavily in their first year.

seeds, which, when cooked, can be used in salads and, in their dry form, stored dry for winter use.

Growing and Harvesting

Runner beans are perennial and in mild climates will die back, coming up again each spring. They will not tolerate temperatures below 37°F (3°C). Although they will grow perfectly well in very warm to hot areas, it is only in the cooler fall months that the flowers will set and yield pods. The climbing cultivars are quite substantial plants requiring support.

Seed should be planted after the last frost, when the soil has warmed up, placing it 1 in (2.5 cm) deep and 6 in (15 cm) apart. In cold districts, seed

'Scarlet Runner', a Phaseolus coccineus cultivar, is planted mostly as an ornamental because of its abundance of large, brightly colored flowers.

can be started indoors in individual pots ready to be planted when conditions are favorable. Compost should have plenty of rotted manure or compost incorporated. The plants need a protected position to flourish. Mulching and deep watering are both helpful with flower setting.

Runner beans have few enemies but poorly drained soils can cause root rot. Harvest vines regularly when the pods are still tender, if they are to be eaten fresh or, in those cultivars used as dry beans, leave the pods to dry on the vine. See *Seed Saving Note* for Lima Beans above.

Recommended Cultivars

'Black-seeded Runner' — First described in 1654, the large seeds of this climbing cultivar are a glossy jet black. The young pods have excellent flavor.

'Giant Greek White' — This tall climber is grown for its large white seed which is harvested when dried. It is popular in Greek cuisine.

'Hammond Dwarf' syn. Hammonds' scarlet runner bush — This widely grown dwarf cultivar is useful at all stages, as a green bean when young, and later as a shelling bean.

'Painted Lady' — Known since the early 19th century, this climbing cultivar has racemes of flowers with red upper petals and white lower petals.

'Scarlet Runner' — syn. scarlet emperor — This is the most popular cultivar in Australasia and remains very popular in Great Britain. It dates back to at least the 19th century but it may be very much older. The flowers are a brilliant scarlet, large, and handsome. Seeds are purple, stippled with black.

Shelling Beans
Phaseolus vulgaris   Zones 7–11

The shelling beans include the gourmet French flageolet beans and the horticultural beans some of which are traditional American or Italian cultivars. Shelling beans have leathery pods which pop open easily like podded peas. The beans are meaty and full of flavor and can be used in soups, as a vegetable like peas, or boiled and cooled for summer salads. Once rare in Australasia, the United States, and Europe (except for Italy) they are now common. In the United Kingdom and Australasia they tend to be marketed as **borlotti** beans, regardless of the cultivar, and in the United States as **cranberry** beans, again regardless of the cultivar.

Growing and Harvesting
Shelling beans are grown in the same way as snap beans, but should be harvested when the pods have fully swollen in the manner of podded peas.

Recommended Cultivars
'Bert Goodwin's' — This New Hampshire heirloom is grown in the United States and Australasia and is a bush form with large seeds of exceptional flavor.

'Chevrier' syn. *chevrier vert*, flageolet green — This classic 1870s' bush bean is one of the classics of the French summer garden and shells out jade-green seed of exquisite flavor.

'Cranberry Pole' — A pole bean bearing very large, purple-tinged pods with exceptionally large seeds which are pale buff slashed with deep red.

'Low's Champion' syn. dwarf red cranberry — This bush cultivar forms large, plump, wonderfully flavored, broadly oval seeds when used as a shelling bean. It can be eaten fresh when young, and as a dried bean when fully matured.

'Tongue of Fire' syn. Tierra del Fuego, *horto* — A widely grown bush cultivar from Argentina. It has long pods of plump, large buff seed splashed cranberry-purple. Of excellent flavor.

'Vermont Cranberry' — This is a very popular bush form, a New England heirloom grown also in Australasia. It has plump, cranberry colored seed, striped maroon.

'Wren's Egg' syn. London horticultural, speckled cranberry, bird's egg — A shorter growing climber with large, plump, oval, very meaty and flavorful seeds.

This *South American native* 'Tongue of Fire' Phaseolis vulgaris *can be picked early and used as snap beans or left to form pods of 6 in (15 cm) in length.*

Snake beans Vigna unguiculata ssp. sesquipedalis *can form pods up to 3 ft (1 m) in length. They are best eaten when young.*

Snake Beans

Vigna unguiculata ssp. sesquipedalis   Zones 10–11

Snake beans, named for their length, are also known as yard-long beans and asparagus beans. They are the mainstay of subtropical to tropical bean crops, and many people regard them as the finest of beans. Sliced, steamed, and served with a little butter, they possess a unique nutty flavor. They are also a favorite of southern Chinese and South East Asian cooks, and are grown extensively in warmer parts of Australia.

Growing and Harvesting
These beans can only be grown in areas with long, hot summers. Some dwarf cultivars of snake bean exist but these are somewhat self-defeating given the length of the pods. Snake bean seeds should be planted in spring in well-prepared earth to which compost has been added. Supports will help to produce well-shaped beans, and to hold the beans out of mud splash and prevent rotting in monsoonal summers. They have few enemies in their preferred climate and can be harvested from week 14.

Recommended Cultivars
'Dixielee' and 'Extra Early Blackeye'. About 12 cultivars are readily available including 'Purple-podded', 'Extra Long Black-seeded', the highly productive, delicious and tender 'Green Pod Kaohsiung', and the Japanese 'Orient Wonder' which has tender, fleshy, well-flavored beans and is best suited to cooler, drier areas.

Snap Beans

Phaseolus vulgaris   Zones 7–11

These beans are also known as green beans, French beans, kidney beans, and string beans. They are grown for their low fiber, tender pods. Recent selection has produced stringless beans. Dwarf snap beans were first grown in Europe in the early 18th century. Early cultivars were all climbers requiring support. Green podded forms are the commonest, but there are also purple podded cultivars which turn rich green when cooked, and yellow podded forms called wax or butter beans. Ultra slender, ultra tender green beans are a French gourmet specialty and those cultivars are well worth seeking out and planting. Flower color in snap beans also varies from white and cream to pink, lilac, and purple, and the seeds come in an amazing range of colors, sizes, shapes, and patterns.

Growing and Harvesting
Snap beans require a sunny position and a well-drained, well-aerated soil. They grow best in districts with warm to hot summers, and the seed should not be planted until after the last frost date for your district and when the soil temperature reaches a minimum of 65°F (18°C). The addition of compost to the soil in moderate quantities will help in retaining moisture.

Dwarf snap beans, Phaseolus vulgaris, *can grow without support.*

Dwarf snap beans should be planted directly into the soil in rows, the seed spaced approximately 4 in (10 cm) apart and 1 in (2.5 cm) deep. Mulching is as important to maintaining even soil moisture as regular watering, although many of the original South American cultivars are very drought-hardy.

In a protected position beans require no support though semi-twiner cultivars are scramblers and need a low support of about 4 ft (1.2 m).

Many forms of support are suitable for pole or climbing beans. Panels of welded steel mesh, used for fencing, is easy to use, dismantle, and store when not in use. Simply put sturdy posts into the ground and tie the panels to them with wire. The trellis can be dismantled in a couple of minutes at the end of the season and set up in a new site the following spring to allow for rotation of crops. Temporary trellises can be constucted from cheap bamboo canes which can be recycled for a few years in the garden.

Prettiest of all are teepees, which are freestanding conical structures made by sticking an uneven number of 2 ft (1.8 m) slender bamboo canes at intervals of about 8 in (20 cm) around a circle drawn on the ground of about 40 in (1 m) in diameter. Secure the canes at the top with a couple of stout rubber bands reinforced by strong raffia or thick garden twine ties. Weave a couple of rows of twine at intervals around the teepee structure to provide extra growing support. Larger teepees are needed for more vigorous cultivars and can be constructed in the same way using slightly thicker, taller canes of 8–10 ft (2.5–3 m) well embedded into the soil. The flowering, bean-covered structure also makes a wonderful secret summer retreat for children if a gap is left in the side. Use slender canes tied in one or two rows around larger teepees to reinforce their structure, rather than using twine.

Beans form nodules near the top of the roots which contain a nitrogen-fixing bacterium. Follow a bean crop with a high nitrogen requiring crop to make maximum use of this free fertilizer.

Beans yield abundantly when regularly picked, and are at their best

Snap beans, Phaseolus vulgaris, require a sunny position and well-drained, aerated soil.

Bean teepees are the prettiest forms of support for pole or climbing beans. A crop of radishes, open leaf lettuce, or Chinese greens can be planted inside the structure to make use of the space until the crop has matured.

when half sized and very tender. Avoid many of the modern cultivars and hybrids which flower and crop over a very short interval and have been bred to maximize a once-over mechanical harvest of field-grown beans. Remember that the seed of hybrids cannot be saved for your next crop.

While beans can be affected by any number of fungal diseases, they are rarely a problem if the crop is grown in a sunny position with no overshading of plants and with good air circulation. Crop rotation will also prevent the build-up of diseases. Mexican beetle is a pest in the United States, creating holes in the leaves. It can be controlled by dusting with pyrethrum or derris dust used with due precaution.

The 'Rattlesnake' bean, Phaseolus vulgaris tolerates heat and drought and is a prolific bearer.

Recommended Cultivars

'Beurre de Rocquencourt' — This is a bush wax or butter bean cultivar, highly productive, with slender, straight, deep golden, stringless beans. Resistant to cold and wet.

'Black Valentine' — Grown since 1897, this is still a classic bush snap bean, highly productive with slender, straight green pods and distinctive flavor.

'Blue Lake Stringless' — This has long been one of the most popular pole or climbing beans with meaty, very well flavored beans.

'Frenchie' — A gourmet European cultivar with very slender deep green pods, sweet and crisp, borne prolifically. Mosaic virus-resistant.

'Purple King' — Another purple podded climbing bean that grows exceptionally well.

'Purple Teepee' — A dwarf cultivar with smooth, rounded, slender, tender, pods full of flavor.

'Rattlesnake' — It would be difficult to imagine a more prolific climbing bean with round, green, firm pods distinctively striped and streaked with purple. Tolerant to heat and drought.

'Romano' — This is a pole cultivar recognized for its outstanding flavor and meaty, stringless, green pods. It is also used as a shelling bean.

'Roq d'Or' — Another gourmet French cultivar.

'Slenderette' — Prolific slender, straight, deep green pods borne over an exceptionally long period for a bush bean.

'Triomphe de Farcy' — This is one of the most popular traditional French fillet beans, with prolific, utterly delicious, tender, rich deep green slender pods.

'Viola Cornetti' — A traditional Italian pole or climbing bean bearing abundant crops of delicious, tender, stringless pods of superb quality.

Seed Saving Note

All beans from the species *Phaseolus vulgaris* are self-pollinating and need be separated by no more than 6$\frac{1}{2}$ ft (2 m) to ensure that the seed saved will breed true to type.

Soybeans

Glycine max   Zones 9–11

These beans, also known as soya beans, originate in tropical Asia and have been grown in China for at least 5,000 years. The seeds are exceptionally high in protein and are eaten cooked, or subjected to processing and fermentation to produce a wide range of products such as soy milk, soy cheese, soy flour, tofu, tempeh, miso, and soy sauce. Some cultivars have been bred for green seed use and are harvested as soon as the pods have filled out. They are steamed before shelling out like peanuts as a healthy snack food.

Growing and Harvesting

Seeds should be planted out directly into the soil after the last frost date, spaced 4–6 in (10–15 cm) apart and 1 in (2.5 cm) deep. They form compact bushes and require no support. Many soybeans are bred as long season plants but those recommended will cope with shorter seasons. Soya beans for dried use are harvested and treated in the same manner as **Dry Beans** above.

Recommended Cultivars

'**Butterbeans**' — Popular in the United States, this widely adapted cultivar has buttery textured, sweet, bright green seeds which can be cooked fresh for shelling or freezing.

'**Envy**' — This is a fresh shelling, bright green seeded cultivar adapted to shorter seasons.

'**Lammer's Black**' — A high-yielding, well-known heirloom cultivar which is used for tofu and tempeh.

Tepary Beans

Phaseolus acutifolius, P. a. var. tenuifolius
Zones 7–11

These beans from the Sonoran Desert are also called tepari, pavi, and Texas beans. They are perfectly adapted to dryland farming and produce dried beans that can be eaten cooked or boiled. Once cooked, they have a light but meaty texture and a rich flavor. The plants grow and pod very rapidly as they are adapted to take advantage of the brief storm rains that come through the desert. Tepary beans are planted extensively in the American southwest and Mexico. About 30 selected cultivars are available including '**Blue Speckles**', '**San Filipe Pueblo**', '**Golden**', '**Sonoran**', '**Mitla Black**', and '**Warihio White**'. For dryland cultivation, plant teparies to coincide with summer rains, but use irrigation to extend the season and increase the yield. Wild teparies are also harvested from the desert and used as food.

Above left: The soya bean, Glycine max *is an ancient Chinese crop and has been used for at least 5,000 years as a food and medicine.*

Below: Tepary beans, Phaseolus acutifolius, *mature quickly and are tolerant of the low desert heat, drought and alkaline soils.*

Beets and Chards

Beets *Beta vulgaris*; **Mangelwurzel** *B. vulgaris* Crassa Group; **Sea spinach** *B. vulgaris* ssp. *maritima*; **Sugar beet** *B. vulgaris* Crassa Group; **Swiss chard** *B. vulgaris cicla*

Although superficially they look quite different, beets and chards have been developed from the same species, *Beta vulgaris*. In beets and sugar beets, the sweet-tasting root has been developed. In the chards, the foliage has been selected for abundance, flavor, and tenderness. The steamed leaves and stems of beets are a much neglected vegetable in their own right with a tender texture and sweet, mild flavor. Both beets and chards can be boiled or baked and served with melted butter.

Although they're different in appearance, beets and chards share much in terms of cultural requirements, and in the management of pests and diseases.

Beets

Beta vulgaris   Zones 5–10

In the past, beets were largely treated as a winter root crop. The bulbs were slowly baked to enhance their sweet flavor or made into borsch, a Russian soup, often served with sour cream.

Beets, Beta vulgaris, once grown only for their leaves, are now enjoyed for their roots as well. These range in color from crimson, through red to golden. This old Italian favorite, the 'Chioggia' beet, has alternating red and white layers inside, making it an attractive salad vegetable.

Crops for winter use were lifted in fall, the tops twisted off, and the roots stored to prevent frost damage. Winter storage beets were substantial in size, with rough 'shoulders' and long, tapered shapes. Culinary fashions have changed since then and it was discovered that beets also made good summer eating. New varieties were developed in the United States and became popular in Australasia and Europe. These tender, young, sweet beets were ideal for salads, grated raw, and particularly delicious served with a dressing of fresh orange juice. They could also be steamed or boiled and served hot or cold. Beets have come a long way from the ubiquitous vegetable pickled in malt vinegar many of us remember disliking in our childhoods.

Beets are positively brimming with nutritional goodness including folic acid (necessary for normal foetal development), vitamin C, and potassium. The fashion now is for small beets and so they are harvested much younger than in the past, the preferred size being about 2–3 in (5–7.5 cm) in diameter.

Growing and Harvesting

To grow beets you need a warm and sunny site, with well-drained soil. Ideally, it should be enriched with organic matter and slightly acidic, with a pH of around 6.5. If your soil is too acidic (under 6.5), add dolomite or lime. If you live near the sea, growing beets is not a problem. Many vegetables dislike salt-laden winds, but beets are not sensitive to sodium chloride, thanks to their coastal origins. Beets are susceptible to boron deficiency, which shows in the young leaves at the top of the plant, deforming them so that the leaves roll downward toward the base. This is less likely to be a problem in the relatively geologically young soils of North America and Europe, but in the ancient, eroded soils of Australia this

Beets are relatively easy vegetables to grow for the home gardener. They thrive in well-drained soil enriched with compost.

is one of several micro-nutrients that may be undersupplied. A once-off application of a commercial formulation of trace elements should remedy the deficiency, provided garden wastes are always composted so that trace elements are tightly recycled.

Start crops for summer use in spring, either sowing directly in rows into the ground when it has warmed up, or starting indoors in early spring. Beets do not in general grow as well if transplanted, so the former method is best. The seeds occur in tiny balls of 2–6 seeds within the dried husks of the fruit and will germinate better and more evenly if pre-soaked in warm water for an hour or two before planting. Seeds should be sown thinly, about $^3/_5$ in (1.5 cm) deep, in rows 16 in (40 cm) apart and well watered in. When the crop is 4–6 in (10–15 cm) high, the rows need to be thinned so that the remaining seedlings are about 4 in (10 cm) apart. You can use the thinnings as a colorful salad green, used either on their own or added to mesclun. *(See Salad Greens.)* For a continuous supply of young beets, an

extra row can be planted every 4 weeks up to the last 12 weeks before the first frost date in cold areas and the last 6 weeks in milder areas. In subtropical climates, beets can be planted year-round avoiding only the hot months of midsummer. Summer plantings need to be deeper, approximately 2 in (5 cm) apart to allow for sufficient soil moisture.

Regular watering is essential to produce tender vegetables. Weed competition interferes with water uptake, so make sure you clear the area around your seedlings. Hand weeding should be followed by heavy mulching. Pull the mulch up well around the growing roots. Unlike most root crops, beets benefit from extra nitrogen, so after thinning the crop, add a side dressing of cottonseed meal or blood and bone or other nitrogen-rich organic fertilizer. Apply it in a band parallel to the crop rows and about 2 in (5 cm) from the seedlings.

Beets are blessedly free of any significant pests and diseases, provided you follow a few rules: enrich the soil with compost, water regularly and

Modern day beets are derived from the sea beet which grows wild on the coasts of Europe, North Africa and Asia.

maintain a strict crop rotation to prevent a build-up of problems in the soil.

You can harvest your crop whenever you choose, from baby beet stage up to full size. Set aside some to provide the next season's seed. If you live in a warm climate, they can be left to overwinter in the ground. In places with frost, the plants should be stored in a cool, dry, dark area. They can be replanted to form seed in spring.

Recommended Cultivars
'Boltardy' — As its name suggests, this beet is resistant to bolting. Though the roots are not as uniform as some other varieties, it crops well and tastes good.

'Cylindra' — This is a slim, elongated beet with roots that can grow to 10 in (25 cm). Developed to give uniform slices, the dark-red flesh is rich and tender.

'Derwent Globe' — A popular variety with a sweet taste and good texture. Sow after frost is over.

'Detroit Dark Red' — A good beet to grow at home with a sweet taste and good texture. Sow after frost is over.

'Golden Beet' — One of the sweetest varieties, this beet doesn't 'bleed' like its red relative and its unusual yellow flesh provides a good color contrast in salads. It has globe-shaped roots with light green leaves which can also be eaten if picked young.

Mangelwurzel
Beta vulgaris Crassa Group   Zones 5–10

This vegetable is thought to have arisen from a cross between the garden beet and wild beet, and has given rise to massive beets that may weigh as much as 30 pounds (14 kilograms) and are coarse textured, mainly reserved for cattle fodder. A few cultivars, however, are very good for the table if harvested while young and tender, including the cultivar **'Mammoth Long Red'**.

Sea Spinach
Beta vulgaris ssp. *maritima*   Zones 5–10

Some believe that this original species (also known as Wild Sea Beet) still has the finest flavor of all, surpassing the efforts of farmers, gardeners and plant breeders through the century. The younger leaves are used for salads, and the mature leaves are used as a spinach substitute, steamed or boiled. The seed can be gathered from wild plants along the Mediterranean and Atlantic coasts, and is available from specialist seed suppliers. It should be grown in the same way as swiss chard.

Sugar Beet
Beta vulgaris Crassa Group   Zones 5–10

Sugar beet are principally grown for the commercial extraction of sugar in areas where sugar cane will not survive. They are grown in the same manner as beetroot, but may reach a huge size. However a few are also suited to table use when young, particularly when baked, including the cultivar **'White Forage'**.

Swiss Chard

Beta vulgaris var. *cicla*   Zones 5–10

Swiss chard is known by many names: silverbeet, sea kale, Indian spinach, and leaf beets. Chard has been developed for its tender leaves which can be used as a spinach substitute. Perpetual spinach beet, another relative, is smaller with succulent leaves. It is bred for its great resistance to bolting.

Growing and Harvesting

Chards and leaf beets are among the easiest and most rewarding of plants to grow, provided they are initially given a well enriched soil with plenty of com-post and regular adequate watering, as the plants require high nutrition to develop to their productive best. Potash, in the form of greensand or wood ash, should be added to the soil before planting. In cool climates, seed can be raised indoors in early spring for transplanting in mid-spring, or directly planted in the soil in mid-spring. A second planting can be made in late summer. In areas with hot, wet, monsoonal summers, chard and perpetual beet are planted in fall for winter harvests. The final planting distance is 10 in (25 cm). This crop has few pests and diseases, apart from slugs and snails.

Recommended Cultivars

'Erbette' syn. verde di taglio — This is a leaf beet grown as a cut-and-come-again vegetable which has exceptionally fine-tasting, smooth-textured leaves. It produces over a very long season.

'Lucullus' — This very productive cultivar has extremely large, thick, very crumpled, light green leaves. The stalks are pure white. It has excellent flavor.

'Perpetual' syn. perpetual spinach, spinach beet, cutting chard — This is an old European leaf beet which is hardy,

drought-tolerant, and resistant to bolting in hot weather. The leaves are smooth and succulent, dark green, and of excellent quality.

'Rhubarb Chard' — This beautiful variety has been available in England since the 16th century. It is sown in spring or fall.

'Southern European' — The leaves are large, pale green, only lightly puckered, and broad. They are sweeter and less stringy than standard cultivars.

Swiss chard is grown for its leaf rather than its root.

'Rhubarb Chard', Beta vulgaris var. *cicla, can be cooked like spinach while the stems are excellent creamed or used as a substitute for asparagus.*

The Cabbage Family

Broccoli *Brassica oleracea* Cymosa Group syn. var. *italica*; **Brussels Sprouts** *B. oleracea* Gemmifera Group syn. var. *gemmifera*; **Cabbages** *B. oleracea* Capitata Group syn. var. *capitata*; **Cauliflower** *B. oleracea* Botrytis Group syn. var. *botrytis*; **Chinese Broccoli** *B. oleracea* Alboglabra Group syn. var. *alboglabra*; **Kale** B. oleracea Acephala Group syn. var. *acephala*; **Kohlrabi** *B. oleracea* Gongylodes Group syn. var. *gongylodes*

Countless generations have tried to emphasize and improve the usefulness and flavor of different parts of the original polymorphic species of cabbage. The many members of this family now look very different from each other, yet under the skin are so closely related that only minor adjustments to growing practices are required to produce each one. The whole group is, in turn, very closely related to the Chinese cabbages, and to turnips, rutabagas (swedes), oil seed rape, and other mustards.

The original wild cabbage, *B. oleracea* subsp. *oleracea*, can still be found growing along the southern coast of England, the western coast of France and the north-western coast of Spain. The cultivation of wild cabbages and closely related species spread from there to the rest of Europe, the Middle East, and into Asia thousands of years ago.

The true wild cabbage looks rather like a sprouting broccoli with red-tinged leaves and multiple branched stalks of buds. When in flower, it produces masses of attractive golden-yellow, four-petalled flowers arranged in a crucifix shape; this gave rise to the old name for the family to which these vegetables belong, *Cruciferae*.

The ancient Celts cultivated cabbages all over Europe and are reponsible for many of the names. Their word *kal* or *kol* became the

Above right: The diverse foliage of cabbage cultivars can add color and variety to your vegetable patch.

Right: Versatile vegetables with a range of culinary uses, cabbages are also highly nutritious. They have been shown to increase resistance to cancer.

English 'kale' and German *kohl*, the Celtic word *kap* became *kappes* in German and 'cabbage' in English.

Detailed studies of the members of this vegetable group indicate that they contain compounds that inhibit the growth of some tumors, including cancer of the colon. Cabbages and Brussels sprouts have been shown to effectively lower levels of low-density lipoproteins (LDL), the so-called 'bad' cholesterol, in the blood. The juice of cabbage has also been used in the treatment of *Candida* yeast infections. All of this makes those beds of organic cabbages, broccoli and their ilk in your vegetable patch look like a great health-insurance policy as well as a source of delicious, fresh greens!

The sulfur smell given off by vegetables in the cabbage family deters some people from eating these valuable foods. However, the odour is usually eliminated by steaming the vegetable until just tender. This retains flavor and vital nutrients, as does the cooking of Brassicas in soups. Many people who dislike cooked broccoli or cauliflower enjoy them if the heads are broken up into small florets and used to scoop up dips. Very few will turn down cabbages if presented in a crisp, sweet coleslaw with a flavor-packed dressing.

Broccoli

Brassica oleracea Cymosa Group syn. var. *italica*
Zones 6–11

Broccoli is reputed to have come from Italy, but may have originated in Crete or Cyprus. By the 18th century, it was referred to as 'Italian Asparagus'. The

flowering heads were selected for their flavor, density, and productivity.

The original broccoli cultivars produced numerous tightly budded branches, but with the introduction of mechanical harvesting plant breeders developed cultivars in which all the heads flower at the same time, allowing for a single harvest. Home gardeners, who generally prefer their crop to flower slowly over a longer period, will therefore find that many of the older and Italian varieties are better suited to their purposes.

As a small aside, it was the family of Albert Broccoli, producer of 15 James Bond films, that brought broccoli to America—a fact that adds a certain glamor to this vegetable!

Growing and Harvesting

Like cauliflower, broccoli forms dense flower heads that hold for a sustained period in the bud stage. Broccoli is, however, easier to grow; it also has excellent flavor, at least in the traditional varieties, and great health benefits. In addition, the traditional varieties are all cut-and-come-again cultivars, which provide food for six to eight weeks. So, by planting a few early-, mid-season- and late-flowering cultivars, you can have fresh broccoli on your table almost year-round. About 10 to 12 plants are enough to supply an average family, particularly if small successive sowings are made.

Older and Italian broccoli cultivars with several branches have a flavor that is seldom matched by the modern, large, single-headed hybrids.

Traditional varieties of broccoli typically have numerous sideshoots. These sprouting broccolis are sometimes referred to as calabrese.

Many broccoli cultivars do well in subtropical climates if grown through the cool winter months.

Soil preparation for broccoli is the same as for cabbages (*see Cabbages*). Especially with cut-and-come-again cultivars, the soil should be as enriched as possible with compost and well rotted manure. A couple of light applications of fertilizer during the growing period will help to ensure continuous rapid growth and tender stalks and heads. Pelleted organic fertilizer, blood and bone, and liquid fertilizer are all suitable.

Broccoli seed emerges in seven to ten days. In cool climates, cultivars for summer eating should be raised in flats or pots in the greenhouse to lengthen their growing season. In milder climates, seeds can be directly sown into beds, about $1/2$ in (1.5 cm) below the surface and spaced about 24 in (60 cm) apart in rows 30 in (75 cm) apart. Seedlings should be similarly spaced. **'Romanesco'**, however, requires 36 in (90 cm) between each seed.

The deep purple shoots of the 'Early Purple Sprouting' cultivar turn emerald green when cooked.

After the main head is harvested, you may wish to thin a few plants out; they will then continue to expand as they develop side shoots. Regular watering is essential.

Broccoli has few significant enemies, the most notable being the caterpillar stage of the cabbage white butterfly. In some areas, root maggots, flea beetles and aphids infest plants. (For information on the treatment of these problems, *see Cabbages*.) Most of the other diseases of broccoli can be avoided using crop rotation. Cutworms may attack seedlings; they can be thwarted by placing a heavy paper collar around the stem of each seedling. Cardboard cups with the bottoms cut out are ideal.

The broccoli crop can be harvested as soon as the first heads form. Indeed, young, tender heads provide the best eating. Little dots of yellow are an indication that a shoot is about to run to flower; such heads should be harvested at once. Side shoots are particularly valued, but if the main head is allowed to break into flowers, the side shoots will never develop because the plant will put all its energy into seed production. Heads should be cut with stems of around 3 in (7.5 cm).

Recommended Cultivars

Calabrese syn. 'Green Sprouting Calabrese', 'Early Green Calabrese' — This superb traditional broccoli produces a medium-sized, solid central head

followed by large numbers of tender sideshoots over a long period. It is both a main crop cultivar and, once the central head is cut and side shoots develop, a good cut-and-come-again broccoli.

'De Cicco' — A favorite with market and home gardeners for its richly flavored, tender central head and even more delicious side heads. The young leaves are eaten like kale.

'Early Purple Sprouting' — This traditional cultivar is ideal for cooler areas. Planted in spring or early summer, it will grow on through the winter to form a tall plant with abundant, succulent, tender, sweet-tasting, deep purple shoots that can be harvested during the following spring.

'Romanesco' — The 'Romanesco' style broccoli was developed in northern Italy where it is grown widely. It is characterized by large, lime-green, conical heads constructed of dense, spiraling buds. Its flavor is superb.

'White Sprouting' — This multiple-headed broccoli produces almost endless supplies of small white heads with excellent flavor and texture late in the season. It will survive cold winters; in areas with such a climate, it should be planted in late spring to early summer and harvested in the following spring.

Brussels Sprouts

Brassica oleracea Gemmifera Group syn. var. *gemmifera*   Zones 6–11

Brussels sprouts were first recorded in Belgium around 1750 and appear to have reached France and England at the start of the 19th century. However, a similar plant had already been described in the 14th century.

Over the centuries, Brussels sprouts have gradually changed. They still have leaves evenly spaced along their tall stems, but the lateral buds no longer grow into normal side shoots as they once did. Instead, the compressed stems overlap to form something like a baby cabbage. If not harvested, these sprouts open, grow into flowering branches and form seed.

Growing and Harvesting

Brussels sprouts require a long growing season. In warm climates, they are planted in late summer for harvest in late autumn and winter—this is one brassica that cannot be tricked into producing a bumper crop by starting it in winter in warm to hot areas. In cool and cold climates, broccoli are started as seedlings in flats or cells in early spring, then rowed out in early summer.

Plants should be spaced 18 in (45 cm) apart, in rows 24–30 in (60–75 cm) or more apart. When the soil

The bright green, spiral buds of 'Romanesco' are reminiscent of coral. The plant's flavor is more akin to cauliflower than other types of broccoli.

With Brussels sprouts, bigger is seldom better. Small, tightly formed sprouts tend to be more tender and have more flavor than larger ones.

Brussels sprouts are frost-resistant. Indeed, sprouts often develop better in cold or slightly frosty weather.

has warmed, and approximately four months before the first frost date, a second sowing can be made, using seeds planted directly into rows. The seeds should be sown about 6 in (15 cm) apart and covered with $1/2$ in (1 cm) of soil. Regular water is required to ensure even germination.

The rows should be regularly thinned to the recommended spacing for seedlings, retaining the strongest plants. Mature plants are frost hardy.

Sprouts require the same soil preparation as cabbages, but many growers include an extra step, adding a little bonemeal to the soil below each plant. A foliar spay of seaweed or fish emulsion applied once or twice during growth acts as a booster and is also useful against some pests and diseases. Brussels sprouts suffer from the same pests and diseases as cabbages, and these should be dealt with in the same way (*see Cabbages*).

Nothing is worse than overcooked sprouts, apart from similarly treated cabbage. Sprouts should be steamed until tender to retain their color and sweet, nutty flavor. A touch of melted butter is all the embellishment they need, or, at most, a hollandaise sauce.

Don't abandon Brussels sprout plants at the end of winter. They move into a new phase in spring, producing delicious, tender, gourmet-quality shoots similar to sprouting broccoli.

Recommended Cultivars

'Bedford Fillbasket' — This traditional cultivar is high yielding and produces excellent-quality sprouts from mid-autumn to mid-winter on strong plants.

'Early Half Tall' syn. 'Continuity' — This Danish cultivar grows to 18–20 in (45–50 cm). It is heavy cropping, producing small, tight, deep blue-green sprouts from mid-autumn to mid-winter, and copes well with exposed, windy conditions.

'Long Island Improved' — Dating from the 1890s, this cultivar is

semi-dwarf, growing to 20–24 in (50–60 cm) high and providing good yields of medium-sized sprouts.

'Noisette' — This is a favorite traditional French gourmet cultivar with a long cropping season that continues through winter into spring. The small to medium-sized, tightly formed sprouts have a delicious flavor reminiscent of hazelnuts.

'Rubine' — This is a large, handsome, cultivar that is deep red-purple in color. It is late maturing and flavoursome. It is also an ideal variety for landscaping, and is said to be less attractive to cabbage white butterfly. A few drops of vinegar added to cooking water will help preserve its color.

Cabbages

Brassica oleracea Capitata Group syn. var. *capitata*
Zones 6–11

As far as is known, modern cabbages, including both the red and white types, originated in Germany. The Savoy cabbage is believed to have come from northern Italy. All these types have been selected for their ability to create a large tight head of overlapping leaves by compressing the distance between the leaves on the stem (the internodes).

Savoy cabbages are a good choice in cool regions, being able to withstand cold winters, including hard frosts.

Growing and Harvesting

Cabbages require cool weather to develop good heads and are generally cold-resistant. In warm climate areas, they are grown from autumn to spring, whereas in cooler areas they are started as a spring crop, with the large, keeping varieties being held for winter consumption. Farmers tend to classify cabbages according to the season in which they are harvested or their shape, which may be conical with pointed heads (almost absurdly so in some varieties), globe-shaped, or broad and flat like a drum.

The Savoy cabbage is the most cold-resistant group. It is distinguished by its highly puckered leaves which are characteristically sweet and tender, with a slightly different flavor from other kinds of cabbage.

Make sure to check the packet to determine that the species you are planting is a cultivar of *B. oleracea*. The Chinese cabbage group *B. rapa* is grown differently.

In cooler areas, if planting in spring for the first sweet cabbages of summer, seedlings should be started early in a greenhouse, in tubes or cells or soil blocks, or otherwise in a seedbed. The plants will be ready to be rowed out in their permanent position six to eight weeks later. The seeds of winter cabbages can be planted directly into the soil about two or three months prior to the first frost date.

Cabbages prefer a well-drained soil enriched with compost or manure, and a sunny, open position. Cottonmeal or composted seaweed will help the plant along. If you have no time to compost seaweed, it can be washed free of salt and used with hay as a valuable, slow rotting, soil-conditioning mulch that will release a rich supply of essential nutrients and trace elements.

The optimum soil pH for cabbages is 6.0–6.5. No additional nutrients should be supplied during the growing

By choosing a range of culltivars that mature at different times, you can have a steady supply of cabbages year-round.

Spraying salty water over cabbages in the evening will hellp eliminate caterpillars. It will also clear out lurking slugs.

season as slower, sturdier growth results in better-quality heads. Moreover, a number of pests and diseases such as cabbage whitefly are favored by excessive additions of nitrogen-rich fertilizers. Ample water is required for good growth.

Cabbage white butterfly can be a problem with virtually all brassicas, and particularly with cabbages. The sight of dancing white butterflies above the crop is not a sight to lighten the gardener's heart. For in a short time, eggs will be laid, and green caterpillars (sometimes called cabbage worms) will emerge to chew their way through the leaves. Cabbages in rich, well-watered soils are less likely to be skeletonized, but the heads will certainly be less appetizing.

Planting sweet alyssum, Lobularia maritimum, around your cabbage s will attract Trichogamma wasps, natural predators of the green caterpillar.

In areas that are prone to this problem, a floating row cover can be erected over the crop to keep the butterflies out. Trichogamma wasps are natural predators of this caterpillar and can be encouraged by planting sweet alyssum, *Lobularia maritimum*, at the edge of the crop. *Bacillus thuringiensis* (Bt), marketed as Dipel, can also be used as a control. It is dangerous only to the caterpillars and will not affect other life in the garden. Salty water sprayed over the plants in the early evening is another non-toxic method of killing the young caterpillars. Garlic spray is of no value in this instance. You will only end up with garlic flavored caterpillars.

Catherine Osgood Foster's solution for dealing with the cabbage white butterfly, set out in her 1972 book *Organic Gardening*, creates a memorable mental image: 'But best of all, get out there with the tennis racket when they appear, and whack them'. The suggestion is likely to improve the fitness of the gardener, but unlikely to cope with persistent winged hordes.

Traditionally, derris dust, more correctly known as Rotenone, was used to control caterpillars on brassica crops. However, in 2000, derris dust was shown to produce the symptoms of Parkinson's disease in laboratory rats that ingested high regular doses. There is no clear evidence yet that it has the same effect on humans, but precautions should be taken. Rotenone is also toxic to fish and should not be used where they might be affected by run-off or drifting dust.

Other problems affecting cabbages include flea beetles, root maggots and mealy aphids. The first two can also be foiled by the use of floating row covers; aphids can be controlled with insecticidal soap spray. Limonene, a substance found in lemon peel, is also effective as an aphid repellent. To make a spray, grate the rind of two lemons and steep overnight in four cups of boiling water. Filter the liquid through coffee filter paper, then add three drops of detergent to improve the mixture's spreading ability before using as a spray. Garlic spray is also effective against aphids. Apply all these sprays early in the morning or evening to prevent possible leaf burn.

Most other diseases can be controlled by crop rotation, which prevents buildup of infestations in the soil. The rotation must, however, incorporate closely related brassicas from another group, such as mustards, turnips, or broccoli rabe.

Clubroot is a threat in some soils, and is caused by nematodes. One solution is to plant the cabbages between rows of marigolds *Tagetes*. The marigolds' root exudates are an effective deterrent to nematodes. You can prepare the ground for next year's brassica crop by planting a patch of marigolds, then chopping them into the soil at the end of the season.

Cutworms may also be a problem. These are the larvae of various species of cutworm moths. They remain underground during the day, coming to the soil surface to chew young seedlings. A stiff paper collar (such as a paper cup with a hole in the bottom) placed around individual seedlings will block the larvae.

Cabbage whitefly, which resembles the whitefly in glasshouses, can create difficulties in some regions. It can be passed from old overwintering plants to newly planted spring seedlings. Cleaning up and burning old, infested plants—or at least their lower leaves—before spring planting will help. White-fly eggs are laid on the underside of lower leaves, and the immobile pupae look like tiny brown scales. The adult population is easily detected as clouds of small, white, winged insects fly up into the air if the bush is disturbed. Although the flies do little harm to a healthy crop, the honeydew which they exude is the perfect growing medium for sooty moulds. The application of an insecticidal soap spray to the underside of the leaves at weekly

Marigolds, Tagetes, planted between rows of cabbages will keep nematodes at bay and help avoid clubroot.

intervals in spring and summer will contain any infestation.

Companion planting with flowering fennel, lovage, and carrot, including 'Queen Anne's Lace' and the pretty annual *Phacelia tanacetifolia*, is recommended by the Henry Doubleday Research Organisation. These plants attract the parasitic wasps *Aphelinus* which feed on the whitefly. Lacewings are another enemy of cabbage whitefly and can be attracted to your cabbage patch by plantings from the family Asteraceae, such as English daisy, *Bellis perennis*, in spring, yarrow, *Achillea*, and chamomile, *Anthemis*, in summer, and Michaelmas daisies, *Aster*, in autumn. Dandelions in flower are also attractors of *Aphelinus*.

A powerful jet of water, trained under the leaves, can dislodge whitefly, honeydew, and sooty mould. Even walking regularly through your crop and can be enough to disrupt the white cabbage fly's feeding patterns.

Despite this daunting list of potential problems, you are unlikely to suffer from many, if any, provided your soil is in good health, plenty of organic matter has been added, and the crop is regularly watered. In any case, mild infestations will make little difference to your harvest.

Cabbages (and their relatives) should always be kept weed free. Because the root system lies close to the surface, avoid hoeing around the plant. Instead, regularly remove small weeds by hand until the plants have begun to grow, then apply a mulch.

Cabbages should be harvested only after a solid head has formed. The heads of some varieties are prone to splitting if left in the ground too long. One way of countering this is to twist fully developed cabbages so that some of their root systems break, thereby preventing further enlargement of the heads. Harvested cabbages should be kept in a cool, dark place.

Cabbages have marked apical dominance, but once the head has been harvested side shoots can develop. To assist this process, cut a cross about 1 in (1.25 cm) deep in the top of the cut stem. A cluster of baby cabbages will form around the top of the stem, providing at least two more meals per plant for you and your family.

Recommended Cultivars

'April Green' — This excellent cool-temperate European cultivar is very long-lasting. Ideal for home gardeners, it has deep green foliage, a solid head, and good flavor.

'Early Jersey Wakefield' syn. 'Jersey Wakefield', 'Sugarloaf' — Originating in Yorkshire, England, in 1788, this is believed to be the oldest cultivar still in existence. It is planted in

Cabbages are ready for harvesting once a soild head has formed. Cut them with a sharp knife, just above the soil.

spring for summer eating and forms a small conical head. The flavor is sweet and excellent. A German truck farmer in New Jersey reselected this old strain to create a more even and earlier maturing crop. '**Early Jersey Wakefield**' was released in 1865 and went on to become a successful commercial variety and the darling of home gardeners. In warmer areas, it is planted in autumn as a winter variety. In the American South, '**Southern Jersey Wakefield**' is favored. This same cabbage is grown as '**Sugarloaf**' in north-eastern Australia, where it performs well under subtropical conditions when planted in autumn for a reliable winter crop.

'**January King**' syn. 'Pontoise', 'Winter', 'Chou Milan de l'Hermitage', 'Blaugruner' — This cold-resistant, 19th-century French cultivar is planted in late summer for late autumn and winter use. It has a strong flavor.

'**Mammoth Red Rock**' syn. 'Red Rock' — Forming a large, solid, flattened, purple-red head up to 5 in (12.5 cm) in diameter, this cultivar has a full flavor and is used for pickling, sauerkraut, and boiling. It keeps well through winter.

'**Minicole**' — Perfect for the small garden or container planting, this cultivar forms round or oval, dense, compressed heads on compact plants that lend themselves to dense planting. The heads stand for up to four months without splitting.

'**Offenham Flower of Spring**' syn. 'Flowers of Spring' — Introduced around 1905, this is still one of the most popular cultivars for home gardeners in England. Its medium-sized, solid, conical heads are full of sweet flavor. It should be planted in early spring and autumn.

'**Ormskirk Late**' syn. 'Irish Giant Drumhead' — Favored for its cold resistance and reliability, this tasty

cultivar forms large, dark green, solid heads with deeply crinkled leaves. It is planted in late spring or early summer for harvesting in mid-winter through to early spring, and will stand for a long time.

'**Primo**' — Adaptable to most soils, this cultivar is sown in spring for an early crop of medium, dense, round-headed cabbages of excellent quality. It is tender and delicately flavored. Some gardeners grow no other crop, simply planting a succession of these cultivars from late winter to the end of summer.

'**Red Acre**' — This is a globe-shaped cultivar with deep purple-red heads up to 6 in (15 cm) in diameter. Firm and solid, it holds well without splitting and stores very well. It is planted in spring for spring to summer harvests.

'**Red Drumhead**' — Dating from around 1867, this variety is still

Its ability to resist cold has made 'Ormskirk Late' a popular choice in cooler parts of the world such as the UK and Tasmania in Australia.

outstanding. It forms a large, tightly packed, deep purple-red drumhead with a sweet flavor. It is used raw (in coleslaws), cooked, or pickled, and retains its color well.

'Savoy Chieftain' — Forming large, heavy, slightly flattened, densely packed, deep green heads, this cultivar is of excellent quality. Its frost resistance allows it to stand through winter in cool areas.

'Yellow Acre' — This is a very early-maturing, round-headed variety that is planted in spring for summer harvests. It is excellent raw in coleslaws or cooked. Resistant to the 'yellows' virus, it keeps for about two months; it will bolt if left in the ground after mid-summer.

Cauliflower

Brassica oleracea Botrytis Group syn. var. *botrytis*
Zones 6–11

Cauliflowers, like broccoli, were originally selected for their ability to form dense inflorescences. Cauliflowers form a single head; though the majority of heads are white or cream,

purple and pink varieties are also available. A broccoli–cauliflower hybrid called 'floccoli' now exists, sporting lime green curds.

Growing and Harvesting

Timing of planting is particularly important in growing cauliflower and, depending on your needs, three types are available: the first is planted in spring for a late winter/early spring harvest; the second in mid-autumn for an early to mid-summer harvest; the third is planted mid- to late spring for a late summer and autumn harvest. In warm areas with few frosts, late summer plantings will be ready to harvest by late winter or early spring.

Cauliflower should be grown in soil that is moisture-retentive and prepared with generous quantities of compost. No additional sources of nitrogen should be supplied. Cauliflowers prefer a higher pH to most other brassicas and the soil should be well limed before planting if naturally acidic—for most garden soils, a good handful lime per sq yd

The white cauliflower has been a popular eating vegetable since the Renaissance.

(sq m) should be adequate. Seedlings should be planted approximately 36 in (90 cm) apart in rows a similar distance apart. Regular watering is vital for good growth, as is weeding until the crop is tall enough to mulch. Cauliflower is affected by the same pests and diseases as cabbage, which should be treated in the same way, too (*see Cabbages*).

Many new cultivars have been bred so that the leaves curl over and conceal the curds, naturally blanching them. For blanching to take place in other cultivars, the leaves have to be gathered up and tied with soft raffia or twine. The currently fashionable colored cauliflowers, which have excellent flavor, do not require blanching. They are especially suited to being eaten raw in salads. The large-headed cultivars of the past are often too large for today's smaller families; as a result, mini cauliflowers are popular with many gardeners.

Recommended Cultivars

'All the Year Round' — This is the most popular cultivar in Europe. It forms large, compact, self-blanching heads that hold well and do not bolt for a long time, even in hot weather. It can be sown at most times but is favored for spring seedling production under glass, and autumn planting.

'Limelight' — This cultivar forms small to medium heads of lime green curds which have excellent flavor and require no blanching. It is sown in late spring in cool areas for harvest in mid-autumn. **'Alverda'** is another excellent example of a lime-green-curded cauliflower; it is sown and harvested at the same times.

'Purple Cape' — This is a tolerant, hardy cultivar sometimes classified as a broccoli. It has excellent flavor and purple curds that of course need no blanching. In cool climates, it is planted in late spring for harvesting during the following spring.

Chinese Broccoli

Brassica oleracea Alboglabra Group syn. var. *alboglabra*   Zones 6–11

Also known as Chinese Kale, Gai Lohn, Kaai Laan and Gai Choi, Chinese broccoli has thick, tender, green stems and small, broccoli-like heads of buds. Its flavor is delicate and sweet. It is a true cabbage, and it has been postulated that its ancestor was introduced into China by the Portuguese, who first had contact with Canton in 1517. It appears to be most closely related to couve tronchuda and has been selected to produce a number of cultivars.

Growing and Harvesting

Some Chinese broccoli cultivars are grown in winter in hot areas; others have adapted to growing in hot summer conditions. When cultivated in cool climates, Chinese broccoli is best planted in mid-summer.

Many cultivars have heads that blanch naturally as a result of being covered by their large, curled leaves.

Once fully developed, some Chinese broccoli cultivars can produce flowering heads for up to six months.

Recommended Cultivars

'Full White' — This cultivar grows well in both hot and cold weather, producing tender, thick leaves. The stems are harvested after the buds develop and are used in stir-fries.

'Green Lance' — This hybrid cultivar is exceptionally heat-resistant. It has thicker stems than most cultivars, and grows rapidly. Like older forms of true broccoli, once the main stem is cut numerous side stalks develop, each bearing a small broccoli-like head.

'Large Leaf' — Resistant to both hot and cold weather, this cultivar has crisp stems and unusually large, rounded leaves that are ideal for braising, steaming, and stir-frying.

Chinese broccoli has broader leaves, longer stems and smaller heads than normal broccoli.

Kale

Brassica oleracea Acephala Group syn. var.
acephala   Zones 6–11

Kale is a non-heading brassica which was originally grown for its ornamental curled and laciniated foliage. It is also called borecole.

Growing and Harvesting

Kale is cold-resistant but also grows well in warmer climates during the cooler months. In cool to cold areas, seeds should be sown directly into the ground in late spring for autumn and winter harvesting. To maintain a supply of tender young leaves, an additional final planting can be made six to eight weeks before the first frost. In warm areas, seeds should be sown directly into the ground in late summer and early autumn for winter and spring harvests.

Kale requires the same growing conditions as cabbages, but is more tolerant of less than optimal soils. Seeds should be planted in rows $1/_2$ in (1.5 cm) below the surface, with about 24 in (60 cm) between seeds and 30 in (75 cm) between rows. Regular watering will ensure that the leaves remain tender. The lower leaves should be harvested regularly throughout the season, a leaf or two at a time.

Kales are generally less prone to pests and diseases than other brassicas, but can suffer similar problems. For methods of treatment, see Cabbages. Strict crop rotation will avoid soil-borne diseases.

Recommended Cultivars

'**Cavolo Nero**', 'Tuscan Black Palm', black cabbage — Now popular in the USA, the UK, Australia and New Zealand, this is a highly ornamental form of kale. A northern Italian gourmet cultivar, it is hardy, rises to 24–36 in (60–90 cm), and has very dark green, strap-like, recurved, rugose leaves that form an upward-growing rosette. Freezing weather deepens its flavor, which lies some-where between that of cabbage and kale. The young upper leaves are harvested, and often used in soups and stews.

'**Dwarf German Kale**' syn. borecole — Introduced into America by the Dutch in the early 18th century, this cultivar forms short plants up to 24 in (60 cm) tall, with frilly, blue-green leaves. It is highly reliable and easy to grow. The seeds should be rowed out in the field six weeks before the first frost date. Another Pennsylvanian Dutch cultivar, '**Mosbacher Grunkohl**' tastes like broccoli, looks like a cross between couve tronchuda and 'Tall Green Curled' kale, and is also valued as an ornamental plant.

'**Marrow Stem**' — This heirloom variety is valued for its mild flavor and very thick stem, which is up to 5 ft (1.5 m) high and 3–4 in (7.5–10 cm) wide, and swollen in its upper two-thirds. It is normally harvested when the stem is about 2 in (5 cm) wide. This cultivar represents an intermediate form between kale and kohlrabi.

'**Pentland Brig**' — This old English cultivar has finely curled leaves of excellent quality. It arose from a cross between 'Thousand Headed' kale and the curled-head kales. A cut-and-come-again variety that is also strongly cold-resistant, its over-wintered plants produce numerous delicious, broccoli-like sprouts.

As well as bringing intriguing flavors to the kitchen, ornamental forms of kale add attractive shapes and colors to the garden.

'Walking Stick Cabbage', a type of kale, takes its name from the practice of fashioning sturdy walking sticks out of the plant's straight stems.

'Red Russian' syn. 'Ragged Jack', 'Buda Kale', 'Canadian Broccoli' — This Russian cultivar has wavy-edged, smooth, grey green leaves reminiscent of oak leaves, with deep rose to purple veins. It grows up to 36 in (90 cm) and has excellent flavor and a tender texture. If allowed to stand until spring, it produces small broccoli-like clusters of buds.

'Tall Green Curled' syn. 'Tall Green Scotch', 'Tall Scotch Curled' — This is a highly ornamental 19th century cultivar with a large, terminal, dense rosette of long, narrow, clear green leaves that are tightly curled and have frilled margins. It grows to 24–36 in (60–90 cm) and is exceedingly cold hardy, providing gourmet-quality, tender, richly flavored greens in the heart of winter. **'Dwarf Green Curled'** is a similar but low-growing form dating from prior to 1865.

'Thousand Headed' syn. branching borecole — This highly productive heirloom cultivar originated in France. It is tall and striking, with many stems rising from the base of the plant, but only the tender young leaves are worthy of the table.

'Walking Stick Cabbage' syn. 'Jersey Island Kale', 'Chou Cavalier', 'Giant Jersey Kale' — Admittedly more exciting to grow than eat, this ancient cultivar is still widely available. It will reach 6 ft (1.8 m) with ease, and produce a terminal cluster of large, non-curled, blue-green leaves. The young leaves are good when used as kale, and the older tougher leaves provide fodder.

The highly attractive cultivar known as 'Red Russian' kale is said to have been introduced to North America by early Russian traders.

The straight, tall stems can be stripped of their bark, then dried and polished to make handsome walking sticks—hence the name.

Kohlrabi

Brassica oleracea Gongylodes Group syn. var. *gongylodes*   Zones 6–11

When harvested and put on display in shops, kohlrabi looks deceptively like a root vegetable, but, as is apparent in the garden, it is the short stem that swells to produce a vegetable.

Growing and Harvesting

Kohlrabi should be sown directly into the ground rather than transplanted as seedlings, and small plantings should be made throughout the growing season. Rows should be kept weed free, and mulched on either side. Kohlrabi are fairly drought tolerant. They are prone to many of the potential afflictions suffered by cabbages, but most can be avoided by crop rotation.

Kohlrabi are best harvested when young and tender, and about the size of a tennis ball. They should be peeled before grating, slicing or cooking. To prevent discoloration of the raw vegetable, dip it into a solution of water and a few drops of lemon juice.

Recommended Cultivars

'**Giganté**' — This remarkable Czech heirloom cultivar, now quite widely available, forms huge globes measuring up to 12 in (30 cm) in diameter. Remarkably, it remains crisp, tender, and delicately flavored. It is resistant to root maggots and stores well for winter.

'**Green Delicacy**' — An old, globe-shaped cultivar that originated in the 1880s, it has pale green skin and finely textured flesh of good flavor. It can be sown progressively from early spring to mid-summer, and is more prone to frost damage than the purple form.

'**Purple Delicacy**' — This is a purple-skinned cultivar otherwise similar to '**Green Delicacy**'. It is sown in late summer for harvest in early autumn and winter, and is slow to bolt.

'**White Vienna**' — Dating from prior to 1865, this is still the standard white cultivar. It is early-maturing and low growing, and has glossy, white, medium-sized bulbs with a mild turnip flavor and crisp, white flesh. '**Purple Vienna**' is similar, except for the skin color.

Seed Saving Note

All members of the cabbage family are self-incompatible, meaning that they cannot fertilize themselves and require another plant to achieve fertilization. They are pollinated by bees and will readily interbreed, both with other cultivars in the group and with others in different groups. They may also cross with closely related weeds belonging to the brassica family.

To prevent unwanted cross-breeding while achieving successful pollination and seed production, place netted cages over the plants. Otherwise, a separation distance of several hundred yards is required.

Seeds are shelled out of the dried pods or siliquas, and can be stored for three or four years in zip-locked bags or tightly sealed glass bottles kept in a cool, dry, dark place—ideally the bottom of a refrigerator.

Kohlrabi should be harvested when the bulbous stem is about the size of a tennis ball.

Celery and Celeriac

Celeriac *Apium graveolens* var. *rapaceum*;
Celery *A. graveolens* var. *dulce*; **Leaf Celery**
A. graveolens var. *secalinum*

Celeriac, celery, and leaf celery come
from the same species of wild celery,
once called smallage, a widely
distributed species in Europe and
Asia. It is associated with stream
banks and tidal marshes near river
estuaries, often growing under slightly
saline conditions. The wild form is
intensely flavored verging on pungent.

The British diarist John Evelyn
described celery as a new vegetable in
the 1690s. It appeared in its modern
form in Italy in the 16th century. The
leaf petioles (stalks) of celery were
selected to be crisp, juicy, enlarged,
and sweet, and by the end of the
19th century there were pink, red,
and yellow stemmed forms (all still
available) as well as green (which
could be blanched to white). Today
the useful self blanching cultivars
predominate on the market.

Celeriac is grown for its bulbous
corms, celery for its stalks, and leaf
celery for its foliage.

Celeriac has been selected over time
for its large swollen basal stem which
has a mild celery-like flavor and
smooth textured, solid, crisp flesh. It
became known in Europe later than
celery and was introduced from
Alexandria in Egypt to England by
nurseryman Stephen Switzer in the

*Above: Celery and
celeriac need rich, moist
soil to grow well.*

Below: Celeriac, Apium
graveolens *var.*
rapaceum, *is grown
for its corm, unlike
celery, which is grown
for its leaves.*

1720s. Early celeriacs were rather knobbly creatures, and breeders are still refining their outer appearance, but the flesh in newer cultivars is often of superb quality. Celeriac has long been a favorite with Europeans— in France, it is a prized vegetable—but is not so well known in Australasia and the United States. It is good in winter soups and stews, excellent mashed with potatoes, served *au gratin*, or braised with butter or with ham as it is in France. It can also be served as a salad in fall, sliced and cooked in salted water until just tender, then tossed in a vinaigrette to which a few drops of walnut oil and a little raw sugar has been added.

Leaf celery has been selected for its flavorful curly foliage which is used as a herb in soups, stews, and casseroles in the same way as parsley. It is a cut-and-come-again vegetable, producing new foliage after cutting. Of the three groups, it remains closest to wild celery. Allied forms are found in China and are sold as Chinese celery or *kintsai*.

Celery has great value too as a natural medicine. The seeds, stalks, and the fresh juice contain a compound believed to be effective in reducing high blood pressure. It has been used traditionally in Chinese medicine for this purpose. The same juice may help you if you are under stress—in combination with some time in the garden! Freshly juiced celery and apple juice over ice is truly delicious.

Celeriac
Apium graveolens var. rapaceum   Zones 5–10

Celeriac is also known as knob celery and celery root. It is produced in the same way as self-blanching celery and shares its need for a rich, well-worked soil. Space seedlings 8 in (20 cm) apart, leaving 18 in (45 cm) between rows. The bulbous stem base enlarges partly above and partly below the soil, and should be hilled up keep the flesh white, tender, and crisp throughout. The roots can be harvested at any stage after swelling begins, but should not be left in the ground after fall as the plants can become over large, tough-skinned, and woody in the center.

Recommended Cultivars
'Alabaster' — This variety should be harvested when still small, about 2–4 in (5–10 cm) in diameter. It is smooth and round with white skin and fine-textured flesh which remains pure white when cooked.

'Giant Prague' syn. large smooth Prague — Maturing in 120 days, this very large bulbed cultivar introduced in 1885 remains a standard market cultivar with an even, round shape, smooth white skin, and fine, mild-flavored flesh. A good keeper.

Celery
Apium graveolens var. dulce   Zones 5–10

Celery has never left behind its wild longings for the rich, moist, peaty soils of its ancestors, despite centuries of domestication. It still grows best in enriched, moist soils, whether naturally occurring or created with garden compost. Unless watered very regularly, the stems will end up tough,

Celery, Apium graveolens var. dulce, *has been domesticated for over 2000 years. Selection and breeding has produced numerous cultivars.*

Celeriac corms are rough-textured and need peeling to cook. Once exposed to air, the roots discolor, though the taste is not affected.

stringy, and lacking in crispness. It is also one of those vegetables that prefer the cold, developing a real zing in taste after the first frosts of fall, the flavor and sweetness both intensifying, along with the crispness factor. (If you live in a warmer climate, Chinese celery is a better choice, growing well and providing abundant harvests in well-watered, well-composted soils.)

Common celery, Apium graveolens var. dulce, *is characterized by its long stalks and leafy green tops. It can be eaten cooked or raw.*

The old way is still the best way with celery, even if it takes a little effort. Dig a shallow trench about 12 in (30 cm) deep and 18 in (45 cm) wide, keeping the sides as vertical as possible. Pile the excavated soil progressively along one side of the trench. You can use it to blanch the crop toward the end of the growing season. Fill the trench one-third with good rich compost or well-rotted manure and fork it through the soil. Celery is tolerant of fairly acid conditions, so do not add lime or dolomite.

Seeds are sown in late winter in flats or shallow pots filled with a free-draining mixture of sifted loam, fine textured compost, and sharp sand in a ratio of approximately 3:1:1. Press the mix down firmly and evenly, and place in a tray of shallow water, about 1 in (2.5 cm) deep so that capillary action will draw water up to the top of the pot or flat, to thoroughly wet the mix. Once the surface is wet, remove the flat from the water bath and thinly sow the seeds over the surface, covering them with a thin layer of the mix. The seeds require a temperature of around 60°F (16°C) to germinate so in cold climates place seed trays in a greenhouse, covered with a sheet of glass until the seedlings emerge. The glass sheet should then be removed. Make sure the seedlings are kept close to light, or they will become elongated and weak. Once the plants have produced a pair of true leaves, the seedlings are pricked out into small pots—a little tedious, although any activity in the warmth of a greenhouse in winter tends to be pleasurable! Pot-grown celery will develop into large plants. Alternatively, the seedlings can be rowed out into a second, bigger box filled with the same mixture as before. A watering from beneath with a weak seaweed solution at the recommended dilution will prevent any transplant shock.

Keep the young plants in the warmth of the greenhouse, gradually hardening them off until they are ready to be planted out in late spring or the beginning of summer, depending on the district. Unlike the mature plants, the seedlings are frost-susceptible. Never let the seedlings dry out. Months later your sins will find you out when some of the crop runs to seed during the growing season. Plantings should be held back until early summer because if the seedlings are put out in spring, the plants often run to flower.

Plant the seedlings out at 12 in (30 cm) intervals and water them regularly throughout the growing season. The application of seaweed solution at the recommended dilution helps the plants to grow actively, and seems to forestall many problems. Once the plants have attained a good height (about two months after planting outside), gather up each plant into a bunch and tie the top with raffia or string. The body of the celery should then be wrapped around with thick paper or, better, a sheet of waxed paper which will prevent soil getting between the stems of the plant.

Celery is tolerant of fairly acid conditions.

Now you need to fill the trench with the reserve soil in order to commence the blanching process which takes from 5–7 weeks. Blanching the stalks is necessary to produce sweeter, more succulent, crisper, and paler stalks. Celery that is only intended to flavor winter soups and stews need not be blanched and is higher in vitamins, but the extra effort is repaid the first time your blanched celery is served with a few favorite cheeses in fall.

Blanched celery can be harvested as needed until well into winter. The remainder of the crop should then be protected by covering it with a cloche, or by throwing a thick layer of hay over the patch at night. The hay can be left to one side during the day. In cold areas, plants should be lifted, the roots and tops trimmed off, and then stored, packed in sand.

If you find blanching too much trouble, there are self-blanching varieties available. Although these are less succulent than home-produced results, they are certainly easier to grow. 'Golden Self-Blanching' is the exception to the rule. Plants are raised in the same manner as for ordinary celery, but are planted on the top of raised beds in late spring or early summer. The beds should be mulched, and water regularly applied. The plants

Celery needs careful thinning-out as it is difficult to plant the tiny seeds in an organized manner.

are due for harvesting by late summer. They will not tolerate frosts and should be enjoyed while in season.

Slugs can be a nuisance with this crop in its early stages and steps should be taken to discourage them. Other problems are leaf miner and fungal leaf spots. Many gardeners swear by the use of a very diluted manure 'tea' sprayed over the growing celery once a week as a deterrent to leaf miner, a routine which has the advantage of also boosting the crop's growth. The smell of the solution also appears to discourage the celery fly from laying its eggs. If not dealt with, the maggots of this fly will tunnel through the leaves. Burn any leaves that are found to be affected. Fungal leaf spots mainly affect young plants. Remove any affected leaves and burn immediately.

Recommended Cultivars

'Clayworth Prize Pink' — This is a trench variety form developed in the Victorian era when it was a great favorite. Its full flavor emerges after a frost. It is a standard market cultivar in Great Britain.

'Giant Pascal' — A self-blanching variety harvested in fall with thick solid stems that blanch to creamy white and have a nutty, sweet flavor. It forms tender crisp hearts. It is resistant to blight.

'Giant Red' — Grown as a trench variety, the stalks are pink when blanched. The plants are compact with excellent quality stems. It was known before 1877 and is exceptionally hardy, standing well into winter.

'Giant White' — A trench variety with delicious cream-colored stalks that when blanched are crisp, sweet, and of good flavor. It is frost resistant.

'Golden Self Blanching' — This is an old French variety with succulent, tender, delicately flavored, stringless stems that blanch to yellow and form a dense heart. It is also disease resistant and a true gourmet delight.

'Solid White' — Known since before 1877, this vigorous old trenching variety is still very popular with tender, crisp, solid stalks that blanch to ivory with good flavor and quality. All you need are a few walnuts, a couple of favorite cheeses and a glass of red wine— which is just how this celery was consumed in the 19th century.

'South Australian White' — This is the foundation of the Australian celery industry and is a self-blanching, tall, vigorous, thick-stemmed, crisp cultivar of excellent flavor.

'Utah' syn. Utah tall green — Popular in both the USA and Australia for commercial crops, this cultivar produces excellent quality green celery with stocky, compact plants to 24 in (60 cm) in height. The stalks are thick, solid, succulent, crisp and stringless with excellent flavor. It is effectively self-blanching as the stems wrap tightly around each other.

Leaf Celery

Apium graveolens var. secalinum   Zones 5–10

Leaf celery, also known as French celery, Chinese celery, soup celery, and cutting celery, is grown in the same manner as self-blanching celery. Given regular watering and a well-enriched soil, it is vigorous and healthy and not liable to suffer any major pests or diseases. Most cultivars form small suckers to enlarge the clump.

Recommended Cultivars

'French Dinant' — Full of rich celery flavor and used fresh or dried, this cultivar forms a fountain of fine foliage resistant to light frosts.

'Kintsai' — An excellent, easy-to-grow Chinese cultivar to be harvested young.

'Par-Cel' — This European heirloom, now widely available, grows to 18 in (45 cm) with parsley-like foliage and a warm aromatic flavor.

'Zwolsche Krul' — A very hardy Dutch heritage cultivar popular in Europe for its dark green, curly, intensely flavored leaves which can be used fresh or dried.

Seed Saving Notes

Celery cultivars will cross with each other and with celeriac and leaf celery. They are all biennial, flowering in their second year. For gardeners in cold areas, to produce seed requires selecting a few good representatives of each cultivar grown, cutting them back and overwintering them to grow for a second season. In milder districts most cultivars will come through a few frosts with ease. Flowers need to be bagged with nylon net or similar to prevent cross-pollination, or isolated in a temporary netted cage.

The seeds are harvested when the seedheads have dried. As the seed ripens from the outside of the head toward the inside, progressive harvesting by hand is recommended. Store in zip lock bags labelled with the name of the cultivar and date, place in an airtight container, and store in the bottom of the refrigerator or in a cool, dry, dark place. Celery seed will be viable up to 8 years.

As its name suggests, leaf celery, Apium graveolens *var.* secalinum, *is grown for its foliage rather than its stalks, which are more stringy than common celery. Its ancestor, smallage, was used by the Chinese as a medicine, and by the Greeks and Romans as a seasoning.*

Corn

Corn *Zea rugosa;* **Indian Corn**
Z. indurata; **Popcorn** *Z. praecox*   Zones 7–11

There is no such thing as wild corn. The modern crop appears to be derived from a wild grass which grows in Mexico, Guatemala, and Honduras. Its name, *teosinte*, means 'God's maize'. Another wild genus, *Tripsacum*, also seems to have been involved. Just what crossed with what remains a botanical mystery. What is certain is that those early forms of corn were subsequently selected by thousands of generations of farmers to produce large, dense cobs enclosed in tightly sheathed bracts. The different kinds of corn we know today are all varieties of a single species, *Zea mays*.

Long before Columbus made his voyage to the New World, corn was grown from Chile to southern Canada. It was one of the 'three sisters', the staples grown by Native Americans, the others being squash and beans.

Above: Corn comes in an amazing variety of colors. Bicolor hybrids, like these, are grown for sweetness.

Below: You'll need plenty of space to grow corn. This variety, Zea rugosa, also known as sweetcorn, can grow to about 6¹/₂ ft (2 m).

The earliest cobs that have been found were excavated at Tehuacan in Mexico. They were very small in size and approximately 5,500 years old. From Mexico, corn spread south into the Andes where cobs 3,000 years old were discovered. It was also carried north but the earliest record of its cultivation in North America as a staple crop was far more recent, about 1,200 years ago.

Corn is now grown around the world and essential to the cuisine of many countries, not least that of Mexico where it originated. There are a number of types, including ornamental corn (of which Indian corn is a variety), popcorn, and corn, often known outside the United States as sweetcorn. Generally, only sweetcorn can be cooked and eaten fresh; most other corns must be dried before they can be ground into cornmeal or flour.

Indian corn can be grown just for its decorative multi-colored kernels though it is also used in cooking.

Popcorns are bred for their ability to split open when heated and invert their soft, cooked contents.

Some corn cultivars have undergone a mutation that prevents them from converting sugars to starches so that the kernels taste sweet. 'Sugar enhanced' and 'Supersweets' are modern sweetcorn hybrids that have very high sugar levels, like candy, though to some they lack the true corn flavor.

Growing and Harvesting

Corn is a warm weather crop. Seeds are directly planted into the ground when the temperature has risen to at least 72°F (22°C). To grow corn in cool areas, seed can be planted into individual small pots in spring and grown outside in a frame. You can help to warm the soil in cool areas by covering it in black plastic weighted down around the edges, or covering it with a cloche.

Corn needs a well enriched soil, so add generous quantities of rotted manure or compost. Ground rock phosphate is recommended, together with kelp, and if the soil is fairly acid (pH 5.5 or less) when tested, add dolomite at the rate of 2 handfuls per sq yd (sq m). Slightly acidic soils need no adjustment.

Choose a sunny, warm position where the crop has not been grown for several years. Allow for the height of the crop when planning your garden layout for the season as it can overshadow other crops.

As corn is wind-pollinated, it should be planted in blocks composed of rows placed closely together. This ensures that the pollen will drift onto the corn silks, the elongated styles from the female plant's ovaries. Any silks not pollinated will result in a gap in the developed cob. At least 4, and preferably at least 8, rows should be planted in each block to achieve maximum exposure. Seed can be grown 2 per hole and 1 in (2.5 cm) deep, the holes spaced at 10 in (25 cm) intervals. As an alternative, plant seeds in clusters of 5–6, separating the seeds by about 4 in (10 cm). Each cluster should be separated from the next by a distance of about 40 in (1 m). Fill the holes with soil, firm it down, and water well.

Seed should emerge in 6–10 days depending on the cultivar and temperature. When the seedlings are about 2–3 in (5–7.5 cm) high, thin out the weaker of each of the seedling pairs.

Most corn cultivars need ample water to do well, and crops should be kept weeded while young, and then heavily mulched to conserve soil

Corn is ready for harvesting when the silks have turned brown. Inside, the kernels will be plump and full.

Corn needs to have full
exposure to the sun.
Indian corn should be
planted 2–3 weeks after
sweetcorn, or the two
varieties may cross.

moisture. In warmer areas most corn cultivars are ready to harvest within 90 days. Corn which is grown in healthy soils with regular watering rarely suffers major problems. Once germinated, corn will grow despite cool weather.

Cobs are harvested as soon as the silks have browned and the kernels are plump and full. There's no need to run to the pot with the cobs as was once advised, but it is true that the sooner they are eaten after picking, the more delicious they are. Indian corn and popcorn need to be dried before cooking.

Recommended Cultivars

Corn (Zea rugosa)

'Country Gentleman' syn. shoe peg — This 1890 Connecticut cultivar is still popular in Australia and the UK as well as in its native land. Its cobs of white kernels are tender, milky and sweet, perfect steamed or creamed.

'Golden Bantam' — If you can find this 1902 variety, treasure and save it. Still stocked by a number of the better seed houses, it remains the standard by which sweetcorns are judged, but it has been disappearing off world lists rapidly in the face of a flood of 'supersweet' hybrids pouring onto the markets. It is arguably still the best flavored of all sweetcorns, tasting deliciously of corn as well as sugar, with perfect, succulent, plump kerneled, golden cobs.

'Golden Midget' — This is a mini corn ideal for small gardens, growing to 30–36 in (75–90 cm) high, and bearing 3–5 very sweet, juicy little golden cobs that are deliciously flavored and only 4 in (10 cm) long.

'Rainbow Inca' — This modern corn cultivar was created by Dr Alan

'Rainbow Inca', Zea rugosa, is a cross between ornamental corn and sweetcorn, resulting in a vegetable that looks and tastes good.

The 'Strawberry', a Zea praecox *cultivar,* produces strawberry-shaped maroon-colored cobs, excellent for popping or as a decoration.

Kapuler. He started with colored corn cobs and mixed them with the large white chokelo variety of Peru and the heirloom sweetcorns. The seeds were planted in a special pattern, according to his belief in a mystical connection to the earth. After selection and stabilization of his new cultivar, he had created a new variety with multi-colored cobs that were sweet and delicious raw or steamed.

'Stowell's Evergreen' — Despite the fact that this cultivar originated in New Jersey prior to 1848, it continues to be very popular indeed as a market and home gardeners' cultivar, prized for its sweet, tender, white kernels at the milk stage and its ability to remain fresh over a long period. It has been called 'the most widely known and appreciated variety ever produced'.

Indian Corn (Zea indurata)

'Anasazi' — The Anasazi were 'the ancient ones', Indian tribes who once lived in the southwest of North America. Indian corn, with its beautiful multi-colored cobs, is thought to be an ancestor of many of the colored corns now grown in that region.

'Hopi Turquoise — This exquisitely colored corn has large ears of kernels in every shade of blue from navy to turquoise. It is prized for grinding for tortillas and also for decorative use.

'Oaxacan Green' — An exceptionally beautiful cultivar with a mixture of smooth and dented emerald-green kernels, used for centuries by the Zapotec Indians in Mexico for green tamales.

Popcorn (Zea praecox)

'Lady Finger' — This Amish cultivar from Ohio, Indiana, and Iowa bears many slender, small cobs on short, stout plants. The tiny, deep yellow kernels pop well with a delicate, delicious flavor and tender texture.

'Ontos White' — Almost the shape and size of a golfball, the cobs are densely packed with small, oval-shaped white kernels. The plants grow to $6^{1}/_{2}$ ft (2 m)

'Strawberry' — Resembling a strawberry in shape and color, this cultivar is used for popping and ornamental purposes.

'Tom Thumb' — This is a very early cultivar that will perform well in short summer areas. Reselected from a New Hampshire heirloom, it is dwarf growing with small ears of rich golden-yellow kernels that pop very well.

Cucumbers

Cucumber *Cucumis sativus*　　　Zones 9–12

There are many different varieties of the cucumber. Eaten raw or cooked, they can also be picked young and pickled.

Cucumbers were originally cultivated at least 3,000 years ago and were known to both the ancient Greeks and Romans. Various types of cucumbers have been developed from the species *Cucumis sativus* to suit different cuisines and climates.

Cucumbers come in many varieties and shapes from the tiny French *cornichon* cultivars used for pickling, to fruits grown in greenhouses for salads (not included here, as they require specialized knowledge) and those grown in the open. The Middle Eastern *beit alpha* cucumber is smooth-skinned, tender, crisp and sweet, and requires no peeling. The African horned cucumber *C. metuliferus* is as much fruit as vegetable and is delicious in salads. The Armenian cucumber *C. melo* is a mild, sweet fruit. The West Indian gherkin *C. anguria* has oval, spined fruits that are used for pickles.

Growing and Harvesting

Cucumbers are climbing or sprawling plants. Fences, walls, or trellises can be used to support the plants above the ground. To achieve a long straight form, the vines must be trained upwards. If space is a problem, cucumbers are very amenable to being grown in large containers such as a half wine barrel. Cucumbers require mild to warm conditions to be grown in the open. In more marginal areas, crops need to be started in small pots in a seedling bed under a glass frame, and planted out when all danger of frost has passed.

Cucumbers are tolerant of a wide range of soils, provided they are well drained, but they do require high levels of humus. To ensure this, incorporate generous quantities of compost into the soil before planting time. If the soil is not free-draining, create a raised bed for the cucumber crop. This will also allow the soil to warm more rapidly after winter. If the soil is markedly acidic (pH 5.5 or less), lime or preferably dolomite should be added at the rate of 2 cupfuls to the sq yd (sq m). In areas with hot summers, seed can be directly planted $3/5$ in (1.5 cm). below the surface. Plants should have a final spacing of 36 in (90 cm), and if you are direct-sowing seed it is best to plant 4–5 seeds at each site so that the strongest 2 plants can be selected to continue growing. Use scissors to cut off the excess plants so that the root systems of the remaining plants are not disturbed.

Cucumbers love warmth and do well in rich soil with plenty of sunshine. Here, they have been left to mature for seed.

Regular watering is absolutely essential to the production of cucumbers, and mulch should be applied to retain soil moisture. If the leaves begin to wilt, apply additional water.

The plants are very susceptible to frost and should be covered both at the beginning and end of the growth period to protect against an out of season frost.

By pinching the tips out of the young plant trailers the female flowers, which form the fruits, will develop on the laterals.

Cucumber vines grown in healthy, clean soils and, if regularly watered, are vigorous and rarely show problems until near the end of their life, some cultivars becoming more susceptible to fungal diseases of the leaves with age. If the young plants

A very old white-skinned apple-type variety of Cucumis Sativus, which is a prolific bearer.

The slender ribbed fruits of the Armenian cucumber, Cucumis melo, can grow up to 3 ft (90 cm) on bushy vines.

The fast growing 'African Horned Cucumber', Cucumis metuliferus, is also known as the hedgehog gourd for its spiky skin. It has a good yield, and loves organic, rich soil.

have been eaten through at ground level, cutworms may be the problem. Mosaic disease strikes some cultivars, causing yellowish marbling and distortion of the leaves. Any affected plants should be removed and burned. (*See Pests and Diseases.*)

Cucumbers should be regularly harvested as productivity drops once the plants are allowed to mature their fruits.

Recommended Cultivars

'African Horned Cucumber' syn. kiwano, jelly melon — This species has become quite widely spread around the world in warmer areas. The very long-keeping fruits are small, plump, and orange, with short rounded spikes, or 'horns'. The flesh tastes like a cross between a cucumber and a melon, with a flavor compounded of lime and banana.

'**Armenian**' syn. yard long, burpless, snake cucumber — A slender, pale green, ribbed cucumber that can grow up to 36 in (90 cm).

'**Boston Pickling**' — Exceedingly popular with home gardeners, this is an early, highly productive cultivar producing long, oval, deep green fruit up to 7 in (18 cm) long, with crisp, tender flesh ideal for dilled and sweet pickles.

'**China Long**' syn. Chinese long green — This oriental cultivar produces abundant, slender, ridged, deep green fruits up to 20 in (50 cm) long. The flesh is firm and mild with a small seed cavity. The vigorous plants have mosaic virus resistance and are widely adapted. The species was introduced into the West in the 1860s.

'**Crystal Apple**' syn. white lemon — An excellent, very prolific 1930 Australian cultivar which is widely grown around the world, forming plump, oval, creamy-white skinned fruits. The flesh is exceptionally crisp, white and sweet.

'**Giant Russian**' — This remarkable cultivar forms prolific, very large fruits with yellow skin that turns to orange-brown, averaging 8 in (20 cm) in length and 5 in (12.5 cm) in diameter. No matter how mature, the flesh remains crisp, sweet, and acid-free, and the fruits will store for several months. It is resistant to mildew.

'**Green Gem**' syn. poinsett — A highly productive cultivar strongly resistant to downy and powdery mildew and resistant to anthracnose, producing dark green cylindrical fruits with crisp, juicy flesh.

'**Lebanese**' — A small, smooth and very thin-skinned green cucumber with crisp mild flesh and a small, solid seed cavity.

'**Telegraph**' syn. Rollinson's telegraph, English telegraph — This traditional English cultivar, introduced before 1885, produces deep green, smooth-skinned, slender fruits up to 18 in (45 cm) long with solid, crisp, white flesh.

'**Vert Petit de Paris**' — A classic, very popular French cultivar grown for the production of tiny pickling cucumbers. It is vigorous and enormously productive.

Eggplants

Eggplant or **Aubergine** or **Brinjal**
Solanum melongena   Zones 9–12

From the family *Solanaceae*, the family of the sun, the eggplant (or aubergine or brinjal) originated in tropical Asia. India alone has approximately 20 indigenous species. Several species are known to have been cultivated in China by the 5th century BC, and eggplants made their way to northern Africa with Arab travelers before reaching Spain in the 15th century.

Right: Eggplants or aubergines, Solanum melongena, *can come in an array of colors and shapes, though the large purple oval form is the most commonly known.*

Below: Beautiful purple and white striped eggplants or aubergines are to be found in sunny Mediterranean markets.

While eggplants were sub-tropical to tropical in origin, many varieties have been developed that will thrive in areas with warm summers which consistently reach temperatures of at least 70°F (21°C).

Eggplants can come in the most beautiful array of colors and shapes, though the large purple oval form is the most commonly known. Eggplants range from tiny emerald-green pea-sized Thai varieties used in the famous Thai green curries to slender purple finger-shaped Japanese varieties, globose deep-orange varieties, ivory eggs, the beautiful purple and white striped fruits found in sunny Mediterranean markets, and huge rose-pink striped varieties of the most delicate flavor and texture.

Growing and Harvesting

The culture of eggplants is similar to that for peppers. Seeds are planted 8–10 weeks before moving seedlings to the garden. As eggplants are particularly cold-sensitive, planting out should take place at least 2 and preferably 3 weeks after the last frost date for your area. In the tropics, they can be grown year round. There is no advantage to rushing planting out as plants tend not to move ahead until the days are reliably warm, and fruit will not set when temperatures fall below 70°F (21°C). Seedlings should be well hardened off and spaced 18–24 in (45–60 cm) apart in rows approximately 3 ft (1 m) apart. Mulch should not be applied until the soil has warmed up. In cool districts some growers use black plastic over the soil to absorb the sun's warmth and increase the soil temperature, replacing the plastic with straw mulch once the temperature of the soil has risen adequately.

To encourage production, pick fruit as they ripen. With most varieties, large fruits are not the highest quality. When sliced, the seed should be milky in color. Brown seeds are fully matured and can be dried and saved for next year's planting, but the fruit from which they came is overripe.

The fruits are ready for harvest when the skin is fully colored for type with a glossy skin, and yield to gentle pressure.

Trouble Shooting

If the leaves of young plants appear to be shot-holed, various leaf-chewing insects are responsible. Derris dust or pyrethrum should be used.

In the United States the Colorado potato beetle has become a problem and is controlled organically by inspecting below the leaves and squashing any orange egg masses. The beetle chews beneath the leaves and can be controlled by removing the beetle and crushing any adults or egg masses.

Eggplants come in a range of colors and sizes and have a wide variety of culinary uses.

The most serious fungal problem is soil-borne verticillium wilt, which should be suspected if leaves on a plant curl and wilt, and the edges yellow. Remove the infected plant from the garden. This disease is best controlled by practicing crop rotation for the family *Solanaceae* in your garden. *(See Tomatoes.)*

Recommended Varieties

'Burgundy' syn. Osaka Honnoga — One of the most cold-resistant varieties, capable of withstanding light frosts, the tall, to 4 ft (1.2 m), plant bears burgundy fruits up to $7^1/_2$ in (18 cm) long.

'De Barbentane' syn. Debarbentane — The traditional eggplant used to make ratatouille, and named for a

The Italian eggplant 'Rosa Bianca' bears large, squat, pear-shaped fruit of soft lavender-pink over white and has wonderfully flavored flesh.

town in France, this is a 19th century French variety bearing long, cylindrical, shiny, black-purple fruits.

'Early Long Purple' — The slender, dark purple fruits, harvested when 8 in (20 cm) long and 1 in (2.5 cm) wide, are ideal for many Asian dishes, for frying and pickling, and are tender and well flavored. A Taiwanese variety, **'Pintong Long'**, is of similar shape with rosy purple fruits up to 14 in (35 cm) long. It is hardy and disease resistant, maturing in 90 days from seed.

'Imperial Black Beauty' — This variety, developed in 1910, remains the market standard and bears about 8 large, deepest purple, smooth oval fruits of excellent flavor. It is a good choice for areas that do not greatly exceed 70°F (21°C) in summer as it requires less warmth than most.

'Listada De Gandia' — This is an excellent variety for warm to hot summer areas and is drought tolerant. The fruit is egg-shaped and up to 6 in (15 cm) long with beautiful white skin irregularly striped with purple. The thin non-bitter skin does not need to be peeled before cooking.

'Louisiana Long Green' syn. Green Banana — This variety is excellent in hot, humid areas yet surprisingly is resistant to light frosts. It bears long, slender, pale green fruits, up to $7^1/_2$ in (18 cm), striped cream at the end.

'Rosa Bianca' — This old Italian variety bears large, squat, pear-shaped fruit of soft lavender-pink over white and has meaty, creamy, superbly flavored flesh.

'Thai Green' syn. Thai Long Green and Elephant Tusk — This traditional variety from Thailand has very long, up to 14 in (35 cm), slender, cylindrical, light green fruits borne abundantly on sturdy 2 ft (60 cm) plants. The flesh is mild flavored and tender.

'Thai Green Pea' — This very distinctive variety is only suitable for hot, humid summer areas. It bears clusters of tiny, round, green fruits about $1/_2$ in (1–1.2 cm) in diameter on 4 ft (1.2 m) bushes. It is the classic ingredient in Thai green curries.

'Tiger Stripe' syn. Lao Green Stripe — A traditional Laotian variety now quite widely available, bearing prolific quantities of small 1 in (2.5 cm) globose cream and green tiger-striped fruits that are well flavored, non-bitter and seedy. A related type from the region is of similar size and shape but striped lavender and white, while another is pure lavender. Bushes grow up to 4 ft (1.2 m).

'Turkish Orange' syn. Turkish Italian *S. integrifolium* — This variety is sometimes called the **'African Scarlet Eggplant'** or the **'Tomatoes of the Jews of Constantinople'**. The Ladinos, a Jewish tribe, are believed to have originally collected this variety in Northern Africa before they were expelled from Timbuktu c. 1400 A.D. From there, they travelled to Spain where they were evicted c. 1500 A.D., moving on to their final home in Constantinople (now modern Istanbul). The variety grows to 3 ft 3 in (1 m) and is sturdy, producing up to 25 spherical fruit up to 4 in (10 cm) across, with quite seedy white flesh that is fragrant with excellent flavor. They are usually picked green and are excellent in curries.

The 'White Beauty' eggplant has creamy-white flesh that is truly delicious.

A number of red or orange skinned varieties are popular in Asia, including **'Sweet Red'** and **'Small Ruffled Red'** (**'Red Ruffies'** and **'Hmong Red'**).

'Violetta di Firenze' — A beautiful variety with very large, squat, rounded fruit, deep lavender striped with white. Excellent fried or stuffed.

'White Beauty' — A productive variety for hot, humid areas bearing egg-shaped fruit up to 6 in (15 cm) in diameter with white skin and well flavored creamy-white flesh.

Eggplants 'Violetta di Firenze' and 'Listada De Gandia', which has beautiful white skin irregularly striped with purple.

Garden Grains
and Edible Seed

Amaranth, *Amaranthus* spp., *Amaranthaceae*;
Buckwheat and **Tartarian Buckwheat**
Fagopyrum esculentum, F. tartaricum; **Chia**
Salvia spp.; **Quinoa** *Chenopodium quinoa*;
Sesame *Sesamum orientale* syn. *S. indicum*;
Sunflower *Helianthus annuus*;

The cultivar 'Amaranth Burgundy' with deep, rich red flowers and white seeds.

It would not be feasible to grow many of the field grains in a small domestic garden. However, the plants gathered here all serve multiple purposes in the organic garden, and yield large harvests for the space they occupy. They all provide interesting grains and seeds that can be used in all sorts of ways to create wonderful new flavors and foods. Allow quite small spaces for a couple of experimental crops each year. A space 13 x 6$^{1}/_{2}$ ft (4 x 2 m) will yield a surprising amount. A number of these plants are more than pretty enough to justify a place in the most distinguished flower garden if space is a problem.

Amaranth

Amaranthus spp., *Amaranthaceae*   Zones 8–11

Many of the amaranths are grown as ornamentals, but few gardeners know that these same plants, beautiful though they are, were really grown for their seeds, which were used as a grain crop in their native South America and Mexico. Inca wheat or kiwicha (pronounced kee-wee-cha) or pendant amaranth, *Amaranthus caudatus*, is one of the prettiest crops in the world, with very long, dense heads of red, purple or gold flowers and beautifully colored foliage growing in blazingly colored fields. Kiwicha is not found in the wild, and has been a domesticated crop in the Andes for over 4,000 years.

The seeds are very small—only a little larger than poppy seeds—but are borne in extraordinary abundance. It has been calculated that there are more than 100,000 seeds per plant. When the seeds are heated, they can be popped like popcorn to produce a delicious, crisp, nutty product that can be eaten as a snack, or as a cereal, or made into a sweet with honey or raw sugar called 'boroco'. The grain can also be ground into a flour or flaked. The seeds are extraordinarily nutritious, indeed one of the most nutritious foods in the world, being richer in protein than any major cereal and having a near perfect amino acid balance.

This species was one of the key

crops in maintaining the health of the Incas, but it was almost forgotten outside South America. Now it is becoming well known, even fashionable, and the flour is used to improve the nutritional status of many bakery products. The popped grain is also included in a number of cereals in health food shops and supermarkets. It is becoming an increasingly popular crop in the United States.

Mexican grain amaranth, *A. cruentus*, has been in use as a grain for at least 6,000 years in Central America and is also cultivated for its seed, which is ground or popped or sprouted. The flowers are used to color tortillas, and the leaves are steamed and used as a spinach substitute.

Mercado grain amaranth, *A. hypochondriacus*, has been in use for at least 1,500 years and was the species used by the Aztecs. It also produces quantities of small seeds, which are toasted, ground to a flour to create tortillas, or used in sustaining drinks somewhat like barley water. The seed are also made into sweet cakes with honey or used popped as a cereal.

Growing and Harvesting

Amaranth is a highly adaptable crop that will grow on virtually any soil type, although richer soils will yield larger heads on larger plants. Seeds should be planted after the last frost date, sowing them thinly about $^1/_4$ in (0.5 cm) deep in rows 12 in (30 cm) apart. Plants are thinned to about 3 in (7.5 cm) apart and then watered to settle the crop back. With a small crop, thin with scissors or pinch off between finger and thumb so as not to disturb the roots of the young remaining plants. Weekly deep watering is more effective than daily surface watering. The huge flower heads are harvested on a sunny dry day before the first harvest when the seed begins to fall from the heads. They are laid out on tarpaulins in the sun to fully dry and mature, shedding

Grown as beautiful ornamentals, Inca wheat is cultivated for its seeds in South America.

their seed in the process. Cover with a sheet of plastic each night to protect from dew and possible rain.

Among the finest and most easily found cultivars are **'Burgundy'**, which reaches 6 ft (1.8 m), with deep, richest red, dense long plumes of flowers with white seeds, the equally ornamental and statuesque **'Golden Giant'**, which is a very heavy yielder, and **'Mercado'**, with beautiful emerald-green cockscombs and tan seed. The best popping cultivar readily available is **'Mercado Dreadicus'** from Mexico and Guatemala.

Buckwheat *and* Tartarian Buckwheat

Fagopyrum esculentum, F. tartaricum   Zones 3–9

Buckwheat, also known as soba, is a pretty, pink-blossomed or white-flowered member of the same family as bistort and sorrel, and is widely cultivated around the world. The hulled kernels of the triangular seeds have a delicious nutty flavor and are used in various breakfast cereal dishes, while the flour is used to make the famous buckwheat pancakes, as well as noodles and breads. Beer is also brewed from the seeds, and a high quality spirit distilled from it. The young plants are

The famous buckwheat pancakes have a delicious nutty flavor.

sold in health food stores as buckwheat lettuce for adding to salads. Several cultivars are available including **'Giant American'** and **'Mancan'**. The seeds are rowed out in spring, and prefer a well-drained loam in a sunny position. It has no major pests or diseases.

Tartarian buckwheat, also known as duck wheat, is cultivated for its seed, which is ground into a flour. Only one cultivar is readily available, the tradi-tionally used **'Madawaska'**. Tartarian buckwheat is idea for those in areas with short cool growing seasons and poor soils.

Chia

Salvia spp. *Labiatae*   Zones 7–11

Scientific evidence indicates that chia seeds were first used as food as early as 3500 B.C. The have many uses and come in three main varieties.

Mexican chia, *Salvia columbariae,* is cultivated in Central Mexico and yields nutritious seeds that swell in water to form a gelatinous mass. They are added to fruit juices and are also used to make puddings. The seeds can also be ground into a flour for baked products.

The seed of golden chia, *S. hispanica,* was originally used by Native Americans ground into a nutritious pinole or made into a refreshing drink of lime or lemon with sugar and water. The seeds swell in water in the same way as Mexican chia. They can be sprouted for salads, and the leaves are used in place of garden sage in stuffings.

Tarahumara chia or lindenleaf sage, *Salvia tiliafolia,* is the prettiest of all three sages, with electric blue-flowered bushes growing to 6 ft (1.8 m). It was used by the Chumash Indians of southern California and the Tarahumara Indians of northern Mexico. The very nutritious seeds, which are popularly

Tarahumara Chia, Salvia tiliifolia, *is planted in spring and harvested in autumn.*

sold in Mexican markets, are roasted and ground. When added to water, they form a gel that is used to sustain long distance runners. Tarahumarans are famed for distance running; they say that 1 tablespoon will sustain a runner for 24 hours. The seed of the well-known, rich blue-flowered ornamental **Blue Sage** or **Prairie Sage**, *Salvia azurea*, is used popped, roasted or combined with other grains.

All three sages are easily raised from seed planted in spring, and the abundant seed is harvested in autumn. Germination usually takes place within 2 weeks. and the seedlings should be put into individual pots when they are large enough to handle. Plant out in late spring or early summer. A well-composted soil and regular watering improves both the size of the plants and the seed yield. Chia seed is readily available from specialist seed firms in most areas.

Quinoa

Chenopodium quinoa   Zones 8–11

Also known as mother grain of the Incas, this annual profuse seed-bearing plant was a staple food of the Andean mountain people. It has become very popular in recent times in the United States. The highly nutritious seeds are ground and incorporated into a wide range of baked goods. The cooked grains remain fluffy and separate, and have a nutty flavor. They are incorporated into a range of healthy breakfast foods. The sprouted seeds are used in salads, and the tender young leaves are used as a pot herb. Nutritionally, they compare favorably with spinach, with the added advantage of being very low in oxalates. Quinoa can contain twice the protein of con-ventional cereal crops, and has been grown successfully as a productive crop as far north in North America as Manitoba in the grain belt.

The seeds of most cultivars contain bitter-tasting constituents in the outer layers of the seed coats. These are mostly water-soluble saponins, and the seed is either soaked and washed or milled before use.

A very close relative is **'Kaniwa'**, *C. pallidicaule*, which produces small seed that are toasted before grinding into a nutritious, nutty-flavored flour that is used in baked foods, in break-fast cereals, and in a warm drink similar to hot chocolate.

Growing and Harvesting

Quinoa and kaniwa are grown in the same manner as grain amaranth, paying particular attention to good drainage. Hundreds of cultivars of quinoa exist, some of the best being the highly adaptable sea-level cultivar **'Faro'**, the traditional higher altitude cultivar **'Kaslala'**, the spectacular pink or golden-headed traditional cultivar **'Isluga'**, and the drought-tolerant, highly adaptable **'Lipez'**. All are available from specialist seed firms.

Sesame

Sesamum orientale syn. *S. indicam*   Zones 9–12

Sesame is a significant Middle Eastern crop, and the seed are a good source of calcium. The crop is easy to grow in warmer areas and is exceptionally pretty, making it a welcome plant in the ornamental garden or even in pots.

The seed is planted directly into the ground after the last frost date.

Pods containing the edible sesame seeds burst with a pop when the small seeds are mature. Since this process scatters the seeds, the pods are often harvested before they are fully ripe.

Sesame seeds come in a variety of colors depending on the plant variety, including shades of brown, red, black and yellow.

The seeds are sown thinly, about $^2/_5$ in (1 cm) deep in rows 12 in (30 cm) apart. A sunny position and good drainage are important, but a rich soil is unnecessary. Weeding, mulching and regular, deep, weekly waterings are required for good seed yields. The plants are ready for harvesting when $^1/_4$ to $^1/_3$ of the seedpods have opened. Apart from using the seed on baked goods and pan roasted as a salad topping, try making your own 'gomasio', a delicious sprinkle made from the lightly roasted seed coarsely ground with sea salt.

Sunflower
Helianthus annuus   Zones 4–11

Sunflowers are a delight in the garden. There is something so benevolent and friendly about their huge golden heads nodding like huge golden suns. And at the end of their spectacular flowering comes densely packed, swirled seed-heads that may in some cultivars be the size of dinner plates. The seed are hulled and used as nibble food, used like nuts in cooking, sprouted, boiled, roasted, or used to make sunflower butter. The germinated seed are also

The seed is developing in this sunflower, which is one of the easiest and most colorful plants to grow.

Sunflowers are popular in many gardens for their huge golden heads, and at the end of flowering their seeds are edible.

fermented with water to make seed yoghurt and seed cheese. The young seedlings are sold as sunflower lettuce through health food outlets, and the young flower receptacles are steamed and eaten in the manner of globe artichokes, to which they are related. Sunflower seeds are rich in vitamin B1 and are sources of vitamins B2 and B3 as well as calcium and iron.

Growing and Harvesting

Sunflowers are the easiest and most rewarding plants to grow, and always give great pleasure to children for their ease of growing and sunny dispositions. They are tolerant of a wide variety of soils but require a sunny position where they will not overshadow other crops. They are as well placed with ornamental flowers as with vegetables. While they are very willing plants, a fertile, well-composted soil will produce truly beautiful, productive flowers. Regular watering is required. Sow the seed after the last frost date directly where the plants are required at a depth of about $2/5$ in (1 cm) and 12 in (30 cm) apart. Germination is rapid under warm conditions, often taking only 3–5 days. The plants should be weeded when young and mulched to stop further weed growth when the plants are about 12 in (30 cm) high.

The heads are ready to harvest when they nod over. They can be hung upside down in a dry protected area for a few extra days to thoroughly dry out before rubbing off the seed and storing it for use. Save a few long-stalked heads to hang up for the birds as natural feeders when the days shorten.

Recommended Cultivars

'Italian White' — A beautiful, creamy-white flowered cultivar that yields high quality seed.

'Mammoth' — This golden-flowered sunflower is tall growing, with huge heads that may reach 16 in (40 cm) wide, with thin-shelled seed.

'Russian Giant' — This classic cultivar has huge heads on stalks to 10 ft (3 m) with thin-shelled, striped seed in quantity.

'Tarahumara' — This traditional, drought-resistant, golden-flowered cultivar produces one very large seedhead per plant. The seed are white-shelled.

Gourds

Bottle Gourd *Lagenaria siceraria*; **Cucuzzi**
L. siceraria 'Longissima'; **Snake Gourd**
Trichosanthes cucumerina

Bottle Gourd

Lagenaria siceraria   Zones 10–12

The bottle gourd or calabash is native
to Africa—and not only can it hold
water but also the unexplained. In a
highly intriguing horticultural mystery,
there is archeological evidence of
bottle gourds being grown in southern
Africa 9,000 years ago, and remains
have been found in Mexico dated to
between 1,500 and 2,000 years ago.
The scientific rationale to explain this
is that gourds survived an accidental
sea journey. Certainly gourds can float
in seawater for at least seven months
without the seed losing viability.

Above right: Gourds are popular vegetables and are very easy to grow.

Below: The bottle gourd Lagenaria siceraria, has fruit that can be used raw, steamed, boiled or cooked.

However, such epic voyages were
certainly also made by sailors long
before Columbus, and the distance is
less than 2,000 miles (3,200
kilometers) at the nearest point. It is
tempting to think of expeditions
thousands of years ago, perhaps made
by raft or some more sophisticated
craft, accompanied by the seed of what
must have been one of the most vital
species in the African continent for
survival purposes. (Thor Heyerdahl
proved it was possible to cross the very
much wider Pacific from South
America to landfall in Queensland by
nothing more than a raft.)

The plants are annual, and only
young fruit the size of a small zucchini
are usually eaten. However, there are
a number of selected cultivars in India
and China that are excellent to eat

when much larger, and recommended cultivars include '**Pusa Summer Prolific Long**' and '**Summer King**'. The mature fruit are cleaned inside and dried thoroughly to make an excellent fresh water container. They were used in Egypt for this purpose at least 6,000 years ago.

Cucuzzi
Lagenaria siceraria 'Longissima'   Zones 10–12

The cucuzzi or New Guinea bean is an annual that forms long, straight to slightly curved pale green fruit up to 4 ft (1.2 m) long and about 3 in (7.5 cm) in diameter. It is preferable to grow it over a support to produce straight, long fruit. The fruit are usually harvested when still quite small to be used raw in salads, or steamed, boiled, cooked as fritters, used in curries, fried, or stuffed and baked. The texture is fine grained and tender, and the taste is like beans. If well grown, they remain edible even when full-sized.

Snake Gourd
Trichosanthes cucumerina   Zones 10–12

The snake gourd looks uneasily like a long, slender, green snake writhing on the prolific, up to 10 ft (3 m) vines. To prevent this natural 'writhing', a small stone is often tied to the bottom of developing fruit to encourage them to grow straight. The fruit can reach about 6 ft (2 m) or more, but are usually harvested when young. They are peeled, and boiled and eaten like beans, or used in curries or in stews.

A bright red pulp found around the ripe seeds is also used as a tomato substitute. It is an annual and native to tropical Asia, but will grow anywhere there is a fairly hot summer, as will the other two gourds listed here.

Growing and Harvesting
All three species require a strong trellis support, but a pergola or arch may be used, or the sunny side of a garden building to which is firmly fixed metal netting. The plants require full sun, a well-enriched soil with plenty of compost and wood ash if available worked through, and regular watering directed to the roots. They have few enemies apart from occasional chewing insects which can be removed by hand. In cool climates, they are started in individual pots, and grown on in a glasshouse.

Left: Flowers of the cucuzzi, Lagenaria siceraria *'Longissima'.*

Below: Snake Gourds, Trichosanthes cucumerina, *are peeled and boiled and eaten like beans, or can be used in curries or stews.*

Onions

Garlic *Allium Sativum*; **Globe Onion** and **Spring Onion** *A. cepa*; **Leek** *A. porrum* syn *A. ampeloprasum* var. *porrum*, *A. a. babingtonii*; **Potato Onion** *A. cepa*; **Shallot** *A. cepa*; **Tree Onion** *A. cepa* var. *proliferum*; **Welsh Onion** *A. fistulosum*; **The Other Alliums**

Of all the vegetables grown in home gardens, the onion tribe are the most popular. They are close relatives of the lily family and number around 300 species in the genus Allium, of which around 70 are cultivated while many of the others are wild harvested. They all share in varying degrees that hot, mouth-watering, savoury pungency that has made them indispensible to cooking worldwide. Also included

Garlic, Allium sativum, is valued around the world for cooking and medicinal purposes.

here is the very closely related leek. The importance of onions in medicine is another reason for their popularity over many thousands of years; they are the perfect example of Hippocrate's recommendation 2,400 years ago: '*Let food be your medicine, and medicine be your food*'.

Onion soup was considered a prime restorative for ladies in the 19th century and the widespread aphrodisiac reputation of the onion family has done nothing to detract from its popularity.

Garlic

Allium sativum   Zones 7–10

Otherwise alluded to by the unflattering epithet of 'the stinking rose', garlic is now one of the most fashionable of foods. Festivals and restaurants are quite rightly dedicated to it, and life without garlic is unthinkable for many people on the planet. It is without doubt the most fashionable and sought after allium in North America today. The town of Gilroy in California claims, probably correctly, to be the world's largest producer. Garlic wine, garlic ice-cream, garlic candy—anything is possible in Gilroy.

Apart from its immense culinary importance, garlic is a significant natural medicine around the world and the subject of much research. It has significant antibiotic and antibacterial properties. In World War I, in the absence of the as yet undiscovered penicillin, surgeons used garlic juice to prevent field wounds turning septic. It has been used in outbreaks of cholera and plague. It is also used to expel intestinal worms and ticks, and as a prophylactic in lead poisoning.

Ongoing research is confirming that the juice lowers blood sugar levels in diabetic patients, dilates blood vessels and as a result reduces high blood pressure, and reduces cholesterol levels in the blood. It is also a diuretic, and is considered effective as a remedy for constipation. In the form of a syrup, it is used as an expectorant. As if all this were not enough, garlic is one of the few dietary sources of selenium, a powerful antioxidant that acts to prevent the free radical damage to cells which contributes to the aging process.

Garlics are divided botanically into two groups, those with 'soft necks' which belong to the var. *sativum*, and those called 'hardnecks', referred to as Rocambole, serpent garlic, Ophio garlic, or Spanish garlic which belong to the var. *ophioscorodon*.

Garlic does not exist in the wild, although it is closely related to *A. longicuspis*. It no longer produces fertile seed and is entirely dependent on humans for its propagation, a true symbiotic relationship of immense mutual benefit.

Growing and Harvesting
Softnecks

This group is propagated by planting single plump cloves taken from around the edge of the bulb. (The small inner cloves often simply enlarge during the growing season rather than dividing to produce a number of new cloves.) The soil is prepared as for onions and needs to be very freely draining and formed into raised beds.

In cool climates, cloves are planted in spring. They require a long growing season, and sometimes in cool, short season climates they will simply form a solid bulb in their first year, splitting into multiple cloves in their second year. The plants can also be subject to damage by severe frosts. The best way to overcome these problems is to initially plant the cloves individually into small pots and place them into a cold frame until the end of winter by which time they will have filled the pot with roots. Ideally, garlic should be planted into cool soil, so there is

no need to wait for the soil to warm up past 50°F (10°C). They are then tapped out of the pots and planted in rows in the open, having gained a couple of months growing time. In warm, longer season areas, garlic is planted in late fall to be harvested the following mid to late summer. Plant the cloves vertically with the pointed tip covered by about 1 in (2.5 cm) of soil. A distance of 6 in (15 cm) between plants and twice that between rows is ideal. It is important to maintain weed-free beds.

The green tops of the growing plants are gourmet food, with a mild, garlicky scent delicious in a stir fry and braised dishes, or finely chopped in omelettes, scrambled eggs, and

Universally popular, onion soup is made in a variety of ways around the world.

Garlic is unknown in the wild, but closely related plants are found in central Asia.

The English rocambole garlic is a hardneck variety and is usually left in the ground for two years before lifting and harvesting.

soups. It is well worth sacrificing a few plants for these delights. When the leaves turn yellow the garlic is ready for harvesting and the bulbs should be lifted, and left to dry out on top of the soil for a couple of days. They can then be brought in to a warm, dry, well-aired place to complete the curing process. If the bulbs are to be braided, they should be left until the tops are thoroughly dry when they will resemble raffia.

Hardnecks or Rocambole

These are propagated by planting the topset bulbils in the same manner as onion sets. They are perennial and are usually left in the ground for two years before lifting and harvesting. They prefer cooler, moister, richer conditions and are extremely cold hardy.

Recommended Cultivars
Softnecks

'California Early' — This is an important market cultivar, with 10–12 plump, even sized, mild flavored cloves in a flattened bulb, easily peeled, and of excellent appearance. The skin is papery white, streaked with purple, off-white skin. It stores for only 4–6 months.

'Chets' — This excellent keeping garlic is a reselected strain of **'Italian Purple'** and is a large artichoke type (cloves arranged in dense tiers, superficially resembling the buds of globe artichokes) with 15–20 fairly mildly flavored cloves per bulb. The skin is papery white with streaks of purple.

'Clermont Ferrand' — From the Massif Central of France, a large cloved garlic adapted to cold weather and poorer soils.

'Inchelium Red' — This extraordinary heirloom variety was found on the Coleville Indian Reservation at Inchelium, Washington, U.S. It has superb flavor and is a very productive, extremely vigorous artichoke variety. The bulbs are marbled with reddish-purple and the cloves white.

'Italian Red' — The garlic of connoisseurs, with an outstandingly strong flavor and fragrance. The bulbs are very large and long keeping, the cloves large, even, plump, red skinned, and easily peeled. **'Early Italian Red'** is an artichoke type with somewhat smaller bulbs, reddish-purple color, milder flavor, excellent for braiding, and is harvested two weeks earlier.

'Purple' — This is an exported Chilean variety, also grown in California, with beautiful, rich purple, medium-sized bulbs that are superbly flavored.

'Silverskin' — This is a classic culinary garlic and one of the finest of the white skinned types, forming large, firm, long-keeping, white bulbs with reddish-purple, strongly flavored cloves.

Hardnecks or Rocamboles

Around 15 named varieties are readily available commercially, of which two varieties are listed here.

German Red Garlic — This is a medieval garlic still available in Europe, and brought to North America by 18th century German settlers. It is now disseminated by specialist suppliers, and grows up to 6 ft (1.8 m), forming a large bright purple basal bulb of 8–15 strongly flavored, lemon fleshed cloves. It also produces large topsets. This variety thrives on cold. It is not a long keeper.

Spanish Roja — Very widely available and popular, this is a gourmet garlic forming a very large, reddish skinned bulb with approximately 10 cloves per bulb. The cloves are easy to peel and have an intense fragrance and flavor. This is a very winter hardy variety, an heirloom from Portland, Oregon, and will not grow well outside cold areas.

Globe Onion *and* Spring Onion

Allium cepa   Zones 4–11

'*Onions are the truffles of the poor.*' The soft tissued onion left little behind for archeologists to find, and the origins of onion domestication remain guesswork. Some believe that onions were first domesticated in the area between modern Iran and Pakistan, but other authorities believe that domestication began in central Asia. Certainly, onions were in cultivation in Egypt 3,500 years ago, and were among the provisions left for the dead in tombs. In a text from 2,400 B.C. which told of the ploughing of a city governor's field, there is evidence that the Sumerians were growing onions a

millennium before that. The Romans reputedly introduced the onion from Egypt, and excavations in Pompeii unearthed evidence of a field of onions, the empty globe-shaped depressions marking the exact site where Pliny the Elder had described them to be flourishing.

We would still recognize the onions of ancient Sumeria, Egypt, India and Rome. They have changed relatively little and have been known in white, yellow, and red flesh colors and globe, spindle, and oblate shapes for centuries. However quite extensive breeding in the 19th and 20th centuries has developed many varieties with immunity to various diseases and pests, extended their climatic range, and by removing most of the pungency developed the very popular 'sweet onions'.

The onion, Allium cepa, grows best in well tilled, well drained soils to which plenty of organic matter has been added.

Growing and Harvesting

Onions are sensitive to daylength (photoperiod) and tend to make bulbs poorly if grown in the wrong daylength area. Choosing the right variety of onion is important, particularly for storage onions. Onion varieties have now been bred to grow everywhere from the tropics to cold climate areas, and are frost tolerant. The best production technique for onions begins with planting the seeds to take advantage of the cool spring days which will allow the longest possible time for the growth of green tops before the bulbs begins to swell. The minimum temperature for germination is 41°F (5°C). In cool climate areas, gardeners can also take advantage of greenhouses to sow seed in late winter, usually in jiffy pots or peat blocks, with around 6 seeds per pot and covered with a thin layer of coarse sand, so that young 6–8 week old plants can be gradually hardened off and rowed out in spring when they will receive an excellent head start on growth. Warm to hot summers with low humidity are ideal for bulb formation.

In many areas, an early autumn planting is also possible, but very well drained soils are required, and it should be noted that the crop will occupy garden space for around 42 weeks as opposed to 24 weeks for spring sown varieties. This is an important consideration in a small garden. Another potential problem lies in timing the planting of seed if planting in autumn. If planted too early for a particular area, the plants are prone to run to flower ('bolt') in spring. In general, the milder the area the later should be the planting.

While onions are usually grown from seed, in cold climates a crop can be grown by the small trick of growing the seed in two stages. In the first growing season, the seed is sown to produce miniature onions which die back to tiny bulbs and are then known as 'sets'. In the second growing season, the sets are planted ('set') out to grow into full sized bulbs. In cooler areas, sets are usually widely available from suppliers and provide a very simple way for the gardener to stock the kitchen with good sized onions, but far fewer cultivars are available compared to the number of cultivars offered as seed.

Onions grow best in well tilled, well drained soils to which plenty of organic matter in the form of finely broken down compost has been added. A lot is made of the rule that onions only grow well on sandy soils, but that is only true of heavier soils that have little or no added organic matter. Heavy soils such as clay loams are certainly unsuitable to begin with,

A young onion crop.

but after the addition of generous quantities of compost the soil will have improved drainage, be better aerated, and will then grow good crops for the home garden. After 3 years of generous mulching and compost additions, the most recalcitrant heavy soil will begin to grow excellent onions, and improve with every passing year. It is also an ideal crop to follow a heavily composted crop in a garden rotation. The short root systems of onions need a rich soil to adequately feed the growing bulbs.

Onions are very sensitive to excessively acid soils and a pH of 6.2–6.8, just on the acid side of neutral, is desirable. In markedly acid soils, dolamite (by preference) or lime should be added to the soil to raise the soil pH. Regular watering is also necessary for good quality bulbs. Plant the onion seed as early in spring as possible, sowing thinly and around $^1/_2$ in (1 cm) deep, in rows 12 inches (30 cm) apart. Onion sets are planted 3 in (7.5 cm) apart in rows 12 inches (30 cm) apart in early spring, the pointed end upward and just visible at the soil surface.

Keeping a crop of globe onions weed free is absolutely essential in order to obtain good results, and careful, regular hand weeding that does not disturb the short roots is vital. A mulch can be applied to the soil, but only after the crop is partially grown. The mulch will help to retain even soil moisture, prevent soil compaction, and suppress weeds. For those living in high summer rainfall areas, the mulch needs to be kept well clear of the developing bulbs in order not to encourage fungal or bacterial rots.

Globe onions have a built in indicator for harvesting. They are ready when the green tops have fallen over and yellowed. Sometimes the crop ripens unevenly. Bend over by hand the tops of any that are still growing as this will stop further growth. Wait until the tops have died. Choose a dry, breezy period to pull the onions and leave them on their sides to dry off for a couple of days in the field before taking them in to cure. If the weather is unpredictable, it is wiser to gather the bulbs in and lay them out on the floor of a porch, garage or shed for initial drying. Onions are susceptible to various rots during long term storage unless properly cured. This process consists of moving them into storage in a dry, well ventilated, warm area, spacing the bulbs out, and leaving them until the necks of the bulbs have thoroughly dried out, which usually takes about two weeks.

Onions for use as spring or green onions are harvested at early stages from the crop. Thinnings from the early sowing of seed can be used progressively as spring onions, eventually leaving an ideal space of 3 in (7.5 cm) between plants to mature into large bulbs for winter storage. Commercial growers of spring onions plant the seeds or sets much closer together than normal and harvest when the plants reach full

Onion varieties have now been bred to grow everywhere from the tropics to cold climate areas, and are generally frost tolerant.

Onions should be left to die down naturally before harvesting for storage.

Keeping a crop of onions weed free is important in order to obtain good results.

height but have not begun to swell at the base. Baby onions can also be grown in this manner and harvested when the bulbs are around $1^{1}/_{2}$–2 in (4–5 cm) in diameter. At this stage they are delicious steamed, then braised in a little butter with a sprinkle of brown sugar and freshly ground nutmeg, or marinated in olive oil and lemon juice, and lightly sprinkled with finely chopped parsley. Every variety of onion can be used to grow spring onions (or scallions), but some varieties favored by growers include **'White Lisbon'** ('**White Portuguese'**), **'Yellow Globe'**, **'Southport White Globe'**, and

'Ebenezer'. Cultivars of the Welsh or Bunching Onion *A. fistulosum* are also used as spring onions or scallions. (*See below: Welsh Onions*) 'Pickling onions', on the other hand, are onion sets which have completed their first season of growth and formed several protective papery outer coats of protective scales, or alternatively are naturally small bulbed cultivars like **'Paris Silverskin'** and **'Purplette'** which are further restricted in their growth by fairly dense planting.

Recommended Cultivars of Globe Onion

'Ailsa Craig' — This favorite of growers in Australia and the United Kingdom was bred in Scotland c. 1889 and quickly forms golden skinned, very large, globe-shaped bulbs with extremely firm, sweet, mild flesh, and long keeping qualities. It is a traditional winner on the show bench. It can be planted in spring or early autumn.

'Australian Brown' — This is a superb keeping onion forming medium sized, somewhat flattened bulbs with exceptionally thick, dark reddish-brown skin and firm, light yellow flesh that is very pungent. It is popular and widely grown as sets. It is also grown from seed throughout Eastern Australia, and the coastal areas of central California.

'Bedfordshire Champion' — Released in 1885, this superbly flavored onion is still exceptionally popular. It has large, globe-shaped bulbs about 5 in (12.5 cm) in diameter with light brown skin and mildly pungent, firm flesh. An excellent keeping and heavy yielding variety, it is susceptible to downy mildew.

'Giant Zittau' — This cultivar from 1880 is one of the longest keeping of all onions, and has large, flattish bulbs about 5 in (12.5 cm) in diameter with golden salmon skin and pungent flesh.

A trial crop of exceptionally rare onion varieties.

'James Long Keeping' — Still a favorite among both commercial growers and home gardeners in England, this cultivar introduced c. 1834 produces small to medium, pear-shaped bulbs with coppery red skin. It is an excellent keeper.

'Kelsae Sweet Giant' — This is the onion cultivar which holds the world record for size. It is extremely large and solid, with a very sweet, delicious, mild flavor. A good keeper, it is a long day type and matures by early autumn. It is a favorite cultivar in Maine in North-Western United States and Canada, and is favored in England as a show bench cultivar where it takes many awards.

'Long Red Florence' syn. 'Rouge de Florence' — Popular with gardeners and market growers, this remarkable onion produces exceptionally long, spindle shaped bulbs about 6 in (15 cm) long which are pinkish red with sweet, very mild, crisp flesh ideal for salads. It can be sown in spring or autumn.

'Paris Silverskin' — This is the favorite pickling onion. It is planted from mid–to late spring, sown thickly in rows. When harvested, the bulbs are very small, white skinned and white fleshed.

'Pukehoe' — This is an exceptionally long-keeping, highly productive, intermediate day type originating from New Zealand, and producing large, round, golden-brown bulbs with firm, white, pungent flesh.

'Red Brunswick' syn. 'Rouge de Brunswick' — This 19th century cultivar produces small, very flat bulbs with intensely dark violet-red skins and firm, juicy, mildly pungent white flesh. It stores well and remains popular in the United States and United Kingdom.

'Red Torpedo' syn. 'Italian Red Bottle' — This Italian gourmet cultivar produces an elongated spindle-shaped bulb with red skin, and red and white, sweet, mild flesh. It does not keep well and is principally used in salads.

'Red Wethersfield' syn. 'Large Red' — This 19th century cultivar can grow to an impressive 6–8 in (15–20 cm) in diameter and is a good storage variety with purple-red skin and hot, purple-white flesh. It was introduced prior to 1865 and is still popular in the United States.

'Southport White Globe' syn. 'White Globe' — This is a long day type forming medium sized, globe shaped, smooth white skinned, white fleshed, pungent bulbs. It is also widely used for green bunching spring onions.

'Vidalia' — In general, hybrids have been excluded in this book but an exception is made for this remarkable short day cultivar which is now synonymous with the state of Georgia. Very large, golden skinned, and with a white flesh so sweet that Georgia claims it as the 'sweetest onion in the world', it is also resistant to bolting. It is widely grown around Vidalia, Georgia, and an entire cuisine and tourist industry has sprung up around its use.

'Walla Walla Sweet' — A large, early onion with white flesh that is crisp and sweet. It is exceptionally cold hardy and performs well in the Pacific North West of the United States, the South Island of New Zealand, Victoria and Tasmania.

'White Lisbon' syn. 'White Portuguese', 'White Portugal', 'Philadelphia White', 'Philadelphia Silver Skin' — Grown around the world, this variety was introduced into the United States from Portugal c. 1780, and a little later into Australia. The bulb is white and flattened in shape, and is an ideal choice for pickling and green bunching onions onions when sown thickly.

'White Sweet Spanish' syn. 'White Spanish' — This is a popular variety in Australia, southern Europe, and warmer areas of the United States. It is grown as a spring onion, and also as a good keeping, mild fleshed onion planted in autumn and in spring. It is a standard white keeping onion for long day areas.

'Yellow Danvers' syn. 'Round Yellow Danvers', 'Yellow Globe Danvers' — This very productive, round, moderately pungent, white fleshed, coppery-yellow skinned cultivar was introduced c. 1865. It forms bulbs which are 3 in (7.5 cm) across, and the seed is planted in spring. Productive, long keeping, and very popular for the home and market gardener, this cultivar is also grown for sets.

'Yellow Ebenezer' — A long day cultivar forming medium sized, slightly flattened, mild flavored bulbs with creamy white flesh, this cultivar introduced from Japan c. 1900 is highly productive, keeps well, and is widely used to produce sets.

The stunning blue leaves of the St. Victor leek can make any garden both productive and attractive.

Leek

Allium porrum syn. *A. ampeloprasum* var.
porrum, A. a. var. *babingtonii*   Zones 5–10

The first gardeners to grow leeks appear to have been the ancient Egyptians, with the earliest records of their cultivation dating back to 3200 BC.

The modern leek was derived from *A. ampeloprasum*, a very variable species endemic to all of southern Europe, North Africa, Turkey, and Iran. Today it is grown for its thickened, white, somewhat fleshy, leaf bases which are tightly wrapped around each other. Selection has resulted in varieties which vary from those with very long, slender, white shanks through to the impressive pot leeks which are remarkably fat but shorter shanked. Selection has also provided a number of markedly cold resistant varieties, often characterized by distinctive blue or violet colored leaves.

The British Leek, *A. ampeloprasum* var. *babingtonii*, is a perennial leek which is widespread through Western Ireland, the Scilly Isles and South Western England. It is believed to have originated as a garden escape, and is tall growing to over 39 in (1 m). The flowering umbels consist of a few flowers mixed with many bulbils up to $3/4$ in (1.5 cm) long. This leek is often associated with ancient Christian monastery sites and it is thought that it was popularly grown by monks. A close variant *A. ampeloprasum* var. *bulbiferum* is found around the coast of Western France and the Scilly Isles and has smaller bulbils in the inflorescence.

Leeks have a far milder and more delicate flavor than that of onions and find wide use in the classic potato and leek soup (vichyssoise when served cold), or braised and served hot with melted butter and cold with a vinaigrette, or the traditional English style white or cream sauce.

Growing and Harvesting

Leeks respond readily to organically enriched soil. A combination of soil amply supplied with compost (and manure also, if available) not only supplies the needs of leeks for high levels of organic matter and nitrogen, but will also improve soil drainage. In colder areas, a march is stolen on the season by sowing seed indoors in mid-to late winter. These seedlings are grown on and planted out into their permanent position in mid-to late spring when the soil is fully warmed. A second planting is made in early spring in a seedbed to be planted in their final position in the summer months.

To obtain those desirably ice-white, thick, juicy leeks needed for most recipes, the plants need to be blanched at the base. This is easily achieved by opening up a V-shaped trench about 6 in (15 cm) deep. The young leeks are then spaced roughly 6 in (15 cm) apart along the base of the trench and sufficient soil pulled back over the roots to settle the plants in place. Leeks intended for the local show bench need twice the spacing between plants. Leeks need regular watering through-out the growing stages, and a feed with compost or mature tea mid-season is helpful.

Always let some leek run to flower so that seed may be collected for future plantings.

Alternatively, apply seaweed solution as a foliar feedant. As the plants grow, progressively fill the trench in. This results in the desired blanching and, as a result, delicacy of flavor and texture. Mulching should be used both for weed control and to retain even soil moisture.

As an alternative, 6 in (15 cm) holes can be dibbled into the ground and a seedling dropped roots first into each hole. The plants are then watered into place. The second alternative is an easy way to proceed, but as a rule the first produces the finest quality. In warmer climates, or as a second crop, leek seed can be directly sown into beds and covered with about $1/2$ inch (0.5 cm) of soil. The resulting crop is crowded, slender, and has pale green, stringier shanks than blanched plantings. Nevertheless, for very little effort, these can be a wonderful standby for soups, casseroles, and stews.

Soil which has been maintained with generous mulch and compost grows such healthy crops of leeks that problems virtually never occur. However, until soils reach full health, leeks can be susceptible to rust fungus which appears as orange patches on the leaves. Infected plants should be removed and burned immediately. The onion fly maggot is an occasional problem in some areas. Leeks can also be prone to nematode (eel worm) damage. The plants become distorted

and finally collapse. Interplanting the crop with colorful French marigolds that produce root exudates to deter nematodes is an easy solution. The marigolds should be dug under the soil when the crop is finished, which will keep the soil nematode free for some time.

Harvesting can begin at any stage as leeks are useful from scallion size onwards, although they are sweetest after the first frost.

Recommended Cultivars

'American Flag' — This is a favorite home and market garden variety, consistently producing high quality, long, thick stalks to 2 in (5 cm) in diameter which blanch to pure white and have a fine, delicate flavor. It grows to 18 in (45 cm) and has excellent cold resistance.

'Bleu de Solaise' — This is a highly ornamental and flavorful 19th century heirloom French cultivar with blue-green leaves that turn almost violet in cold weather. It can withstand cold winters in the ground, standing until spring. Similar in coloring, productivity and hardiness is the old traditional French cultivar **St Victor** which produces excellent stems of superb flavor.

'Cutting Leek' syn. 'Schnittporree' — Unlike the other leeks listed, this

Traditional leek and potato soup.

cultivar is selected for its wonderfully flavored, dark green, slender leaves and stems which are used like scallions, or finely chopped for similar uses to chives.

'Levant Garlic' or **Perennial Sweet Leek** or **Garlic Leeks** or **Yorktown Onion** *A. ampeloprasum* — This cultivated species from the Mediterranean region and the Middle East develops large basal bulbs consisting of a few very large cloves which have a mild garlic flavor and can be either eaten raw or used in sauces, stir fries, pickles and chutneys.

'King Richard' — This is a popular variety in the United Kingdom. Excellent for summer and autumn harvesting, it has exceptionally long white flanks with a mild flavor. It will take heavy frosts but will not overwinter in cold areas.

'Monstrueux de Carentan' or **'Giant Carentan'** — A beautifully fat leek which can be harvested up to mid-winter. Planted early enough in spring, the fairly short shanks can attain a diameter of 4 in (10 cm) and have excellent flavor.

'Musselburgh' syn. 'Scotch Flag', 'Giant Musselburgh' — Introduced in 1834, and still one of the greatest standards for its class, grown around the world, this cultivar was derived from **'London Flag'** (still grown in the United Kingdom, United States, Australia, and New Zealand), being selected to survive under the much colder conditions of Scotland, with shorter shanks and a lighter green color. It has proved wonderfully adaptable.

'The Lyon' syn. 'Mr Lyon's Leek' — This is a fast growing cultivar first released in 1880 and forms slender, tall plants with well blanched bases.

'Verina' — Ready for harvest in early autumn, it forms long shanks and is highly rust resistant. It is popular in the United Kingdom.

Potato Onion

Allium cepa Aggregatum Group   Zones 4–11

Like many vegetables favored in the 19th century, the potato onion (or nest onion, hill onion, or pregnant onion) was unfairly eclipsed by the plethora of new vegetable cultivars released in the 20th century. Now they are being rediscovered and are delighting a new century of gardeners. Fortunately in places like Tasmania, England, Illinois, Indiana, and other cooler areas of the United States, many farmers and gardeners treasured their potato onions through the decades in which they lost popularity, vowing that they needed no other onion in their garden. The Potato Onion is a form of shallot that earns its name from the basal 'nest' of small, tender, mild flavored onions it produces below the ground, reminiscent of a nest full of eggs, or for others the riches revealed in the cluster of potatoes formed at the base of the potato plant. The bulbs keep well for 12 months and are propagated by

'Mammoth Blanche' Allium porrum *is typical of the very fat leeks, grown for their thick and fleshy stems.*

The Potato Onion, Allium cepa, var. aggregatum, is also known as the Underground Onion because its bulbs multiply beneath the soil.

bulbs in spring or autumn. Many of the finest gourmet onions are to be found in this group and the closely associated shallots. Specialist suppliers now offer several varieties of this easy to grow, infinitely rewarding, gourmet vegetable and the Seed Savers Exchange in Iowa is also a source. Grow in soil prepared in the same way as for onions.

Recommended Cultivars

'White Potato Onion' or **'White Multiplier Onion'** — This white skinned, white fleshed, gourmet variety originated and thrives in Tasmania. It is also found in the United States where it is grown in the South as a winter onion and in the North it is planted in spring. It is cold hardy, long keeping, and produces a nest of around 15 underground small bulbs which can be used as pearl onions for pickling as well as in any dish calling for their superb flavor. The delicate green tops are often treated as bunching onions.

'Yellow Potato Onion' or **'Yellow Multiplier Onion'** This cultivar divides underground to produce a nest of up to 15 onions of excellent mild flavor that keep for up to 12 months. It will grow over a wide range of soils and climate.

Multiplier Onion 'Yellow Potato Onion' divides underground to produce a nest of up to 15 onions of excellent mild flavor.

Shallot

Allium cepa Aggregatum Group   Zones 4–11

Shallots, or eschalot, or scallions, divide evenly from one bulb to form a cluster of small even-sized bulbs, each with a separate stem, above ground. In the 19th century in North America, it was the tops that were favored rather than the delicately flavored bulbs. The refined, sweeter flavor of the bulbs lends itself to many dishes where the strong flavor of onions would swamp the balance of flavors, and they are a cornerstone of French cuisine.

Thanks to the greatly increased interest in shallots associated with food trends, shallots are quite easy to obtain from specialist suppliers, and a number of varieties are now available.

Growing and Harvesting

The natural growth pattern for shallots is to bulk up as much as possible, spit into several even cloves, then fill them out to small onion size before mid-summer when the plant will initiate flowering while the leaves begin to die back. To avoid flowering, the bulbs are rowed out as early as possible and harvested by mid-summer. The old rule was always to plant shallots on the shortest day and harvest on the longest, instructions easier to follow in milder districts. Elsewhere the sets are planted in early spring.

Recommended Cultivars

'Dutch Yellow' — This is an excellent, long keeping cultivar producing clusters of 8–12 shallots up to 2 in (5 cm) in diameter when grown well. It is widely adapted, being grown in Europe, the United States, and Australia. The flesh is cream to yellow and the skin golden brown.

'French Shallot' or **'Shallot'** — Widely used for the delicate garlic flavor it lends to soups, salads, omelettes, this hardy cultivar produces a

cluster of about 6–8 bulbs with a deep orange-brown skin and purple-white flesh. It stores well.

'Frog's Leg' or **'Brittany'** or **'Chicken's Legs'** — This is an exceptionally mild, sweet variety with elongated bulbs said to resemble the legs of bull frogs, with purple tinged white flesh and deep orange-brown skin. It is highly productive.

'Golden Gourmet' A reliable variety with a sweet mild flavor, forming a number of small–to medium–sized, light golden-skinned bulbs.

'Grey Shallot' or **'Eschalot Grise'** This is generally regarded as the finest of the French gourmet cultivars. The bulbs are large and elongated, about 4 in (10 cm) long with greyish-brown skin and purplish-white flesh which is distinctively and deliciously different. It has a high multiplication rate of around 20 bulbs per original set. It does not store well.

'Hative de Niort' — This good traditional French cultivar is a show bench winner for its beautiful appearance, forming clusters of 3–4 flask-shaped, large shallots with polished chestnut brown skin and reddish flesh.

Tree Onion

Allium cepa var. *proliferum*   Zones 4–11

Other names for this remarkable onion are Egyptian onion, walking onion or topset onion and each seeks to describe the peculiar characteristics of this onion which appears to have arrived in the English vegetable garden c. 1790 with remarkably little comment. The onion initially forms a stem of about finger thickness. At the base the original bulb often divides into several shallot-like bulbs. The flowering stem bears not flowers but a terminal inflorescence of plump, small, excellently flavored, crisp bulbils, ideal for pickling in the manner of pearl onions. The weight of the head can bow the bulbils to the ground where they will grow, repeating the process and looping the onion progressively into new territory each year. References to this as the Canada tree onion are also incorrect. The tree onion appears to have no exact counterpart in the wild and is believed to have originated as an accidental garden hybrid.

Top left: Shallots divide evenly from one bulb to form a cluster of small even-sized bulbs, each with a separate stem, above ground.

Left: The fine layers of purple shallots make them ideal for slicing and scattering over salads, or for deep frying to make a crisp and tasty garnish

The flowering stem of the tree onion bears a terminal inflorescence of plump, small, excellently flavored, crisp bulbils, ideal for pickling in the manner of pearl onions.

Deliberate breeding for new varieties of the tree onion was carried out by a nurseryman in Catawissa, Pennsylvania, F.F. Merceron, in the mid-19th century. He planned to produce strains for the onion pickling industry and produced three extraordinary cultivars of tree onions— a red, a white, and a yellow—all of which grew secondary plants arising out ot the bulbils in the inflorescence, creating two-storeyed plants that were so tall that they reached 5 ft (1.5 m) and required support to prevent storm damage. These became widely disseminated in the United States, supporting a tree onion industry in the South and Bermuda, as well as around Indiana. Surprisingly, hundreds of different tree onions have been conserved by families around the world and the Seed Savers Exchange in Iowa has a remarkable collection. The very early emergence of leaves from the bulbs make the tree onion as valued in some places for its fresh spring foliage as for its later bulbils, and it is grown in place of bunching onions.

The tree onion belongs to the Proliferum Group *which bears small bulbs at the top of the flower stalks.*

Growing and Harvesting

Tree onions are planted in early spring using bulbils from the inflorescence of the previous crop. They are planted in the same manner as onion sets, using the same spacing and soil preparation. The topsets form in summer and make excellent baby pickled onions, which are delicious boiled and then caramelized in butter, brown sugar, and nutmeg. (This cooking method is ideal for any small, pickling onion.) The parent onion is perennial, and can be left in situ for a few years. Like all onions, a weed-free environment is vital for good quality and mulching between rows should be used.

Recommended Cultivars

'**Fleener's Top Setter**' — Reputedly a cross between a potato onion and a tree onion, this is an excellent variety. The base of the plant produces a cluster of shallots while the bulbils at the top are perfect miniature pearl onions making this the perfect lazy gardener's onion.

'**Red Catawissa**' — This mid-19th century vigorous cultivar is tall growing to 5 ft (1.5 m), often forming a secondary plant growing out of a bulbil in the original inflorescence. The second set of bulbils at the top of the plant usually produce green leaves.

'**Moritz Egyptian**' — This Missouri heirloom is of exceptional quality and is popular with seed saving exchanges. It is a dark, red-purple colored cultivar with larger than average bulbils and may form a second set of bulbils around the middle of the stalk.

Welsh Onion

Allium fistulosum   Zones 6–9

Variously known as Poor Man's leek, bunching onion, ciboule, scallions and *Chang Fa*, the Welsh onion should not be confused with the true leek. The Welsh onion certainly grows in the manner of a leek, but has hollow leaves which are round in cross-section like those of an onion. It is a long lived perennial in many places, and is extremely hardy, forming new plants by dividing and multiplying at the base to form a clump. The dense, rounded cone-shaped flowering heads supported by hollow stems form prolific seed. Although perennial, most modern varieties are usually cultivated as an annual. It has been domesticated in China since prehistoric times where it is favored for stir fried and braised dishes, and to add a finishing layer of freshness to long cooked dishes, finely chopped and raw.

While the Welsh onion, introduced into England in the early 17th century (from Siberia via Switzerland, not Wales!) is a tall, coarse plant intended originally for poultry feed, many far more delicate bunching onions were developed in places like France and Asia.

Most closely resemble coarse leaved chives. Japan has been res-ponsible for breeding a number of excellent varieties in recent times, together with hybrids *A. fistulosum* and *A. cepa*. The varieties favored today form clumps of delicate green onions esteemed for their flavor and value in a wide variety of dishes. Markets rarely distinguish between pulled and bunched immature onions and the true bunching onion, often selling both as 'spring onions' or 'scallions'. It should be noted that 'scallion' is also a name quite com-monly applied to shallots in the United States, and to confound the issue further, true spring onions are fre-quently known in Australia as 'shallots'. The term Welsh onion is thought to be derived from the German word *welsche* meaning foreign.

Growing and Harvesting

Welsh onions can be propagated either by the offshoot bulbs around the sides of the clumps, or by the seed which is produced prolifically, and often self sows if undisturbed. The seed can just be scattered over the soil, raked in, and with regular watering a good yield can be expected. However to grow quality

The Welsh Onion grows in the manner of a leek, but has hollow leaves that are round in cross-section like those of an onion.

The red Welsh bunching onion is a strongly flavored cultivar which produces 3 to 4 coppery red stalks.

has good resistance to thrips, smut, and pink root.

'Ever-ready Onion' or 'Everlasting Onion' *A. cepa* 'Perutile' — This has been claimed to be the most productive onion in existence, and it is certainly possible. This is a hardy, perennial true onion which forms clumps of pink-skinned and fleshed shanks with foliage that is finer in texture and milder in flavor than true Welsh onion, but as it is grown and used in the same manner it is included here. Many modern hybrid bunching onions share *A. cepa* as a parent.

'Evergreen White Hardy Bunching' — This is a very hardy cultivar forming slender shanks with excellent flavor. It is resistant to bolting. Widely available, it matures in around 65 days, and has resistance to thrips, pink root, and smut.

'Hikari' — A cultivar forming only slight bulbs and with good resistance to the cold and to bulb rot fungus Botrytis. The clumps consist of about 6 erect stems, and both the stems and leaves are tender are delicately flavored. It is planted 3 times a year, in spring, summer, and autumn, and is popular in both the United Kindom and the United States.

'Kujo Green' — This excellent bunching onion, popular in the United Kingdom, produces around 4 slender white stalks which are exceptionally tender and full of flavor, ideal for stir fried dishes.

'Red Beard' — An unusual Japanese cultivar being grown in the United States as a gourmet item, having attractive deep red stems which are white inside, and dark green foliage. It is planted in late summer and harvested in around 60 days when the bulbs are just starting to swell. It is a vigorous grower and develops coloring with cooler weather. It is delicious char-grilled. The strongly flavored old

crops, the seed is sown fairly densely in rows 6–12 in (15–30 cm) apart in raised, well prepared, well drained beds of soil enriched by compost. The rows are mulched to control weeds and retain moisture, and the crop is regularly watered to ensure optimum flavor and quality. The Welsh onion can occasionally suffer from mildew in prolonged wet weather but the application of a dusting of lime sulphur or soot will contain the problem. Other growing problems are very rare if they are cared for as above.

Recommended Cultivars

'Beltsville Bunching' — This is a very widely adapted variety, capable of producing good quality crops even in hot, dry weather. The long white stems are smooth with virtually no bulb formation, tender and mild but flavorful. It was developed by the USDA, matures in 65 days, and

Garlic chives have a mild garlic flavor and can be an attractive addidion to any flower border..

cultivar **'Red Welsh'** syn. 'Early Red', 'Ciboule Commune Rouge' resembles the original Welsh onion and is perennial, very cold hardy, and produces 3–4 coppery red stalks. It is ideal for flavoring soups and stews, and can be sown by seed or propagated by division.

'Tokyo Long White' — This is a single stalk type with virtually no bulb, ideal for summer and autumn harvesting, maturing in 65–70 days. The stalks are exceptionally long, white and succulent, reaching a diameter of up $1^1/_2$in (3–4 cm), and are tender fleshed with full flavor. It is widely available.

The Other Alliums

Many alliums are grown as excellent, often spectacular ornamentals (although the slightest touch to their foliage gives their origins away), but mentioned here are just a few of the lesser alliums that are widely cultivated for their delicious onion flavor. They are ideal for the organic gourmet grower, as close to pest free and 'grow themselves' vegetables as anyone could hope for.

Canada Onion or **Meadowleek** or **Wild Garlic** *A. canadense* — Native to North America, this scallion-like species is cultivated for its crisp white bulbs and deliciously onion scented foliage. It forms topset bulbils and, in cultivation, may form clusters of onions. It is grown as for scallions. Zones 4–9.

Chinese Onion or **Rakkyo** *A. chinensis* — An Asian species cultivated in North America with wispy hollow green leaves and crisp textured small bulbs with a strong onion flavor that are popular raw, cooked, and in Japan pickled in sake, or vinegar, soy sauce, and honey. The umbels containing 15–20 flowers appear in autumn along with the emergent young leaves. It is perennial, grown as for onion chives. Zones 6–9.

Chinese onion has wispy hollow green leaves and crisp textured small bulbs with a strong onion flavor.

The stems and flowers of the Garlic chive can be eaten. The flowers stay crisp if cooked quickly in a wok.

Chives or Onion Chives

A. schoenoprasum — This is the wellknown onion chives grown around the world for its finely textured, dense tufts of tubular leaves which have a delicate onion flavor. A number of varieties are extensively grown, including **Extra Fine Leaved** which is favored for bunching, and the very productive **'Grolau'**. Zones 5–10.

Fragrant Garlic Chives *A. odorum* —

This Central Asian species is grown for its leaves which are used in a similar manner to chives. It has pretty umbels of white flowers, each with a red stripe down the centres of the petals. It is propagated from seed and grown in a similar manner to Onion Chives. Zones 7–11.

Garlic chives have been cultivated for centuries in India and China. It is now widely grown for its leaves, which are used as a green vegetable.

Garlic Chives or Chinese Leek or Chinese Chives *A.tuberosum* —

Indispensable in the home garden, and able to be used in any way as onion chives are, the plants grow larger and have flat, straplike leaves that have a mouth watering, mild garlic flavor. The ornamental flowering heads composed of garlic-scented, starry-white flowers are excellent scattered over dips and salad dishes. The plants tiller to form clumps. A number of cultivars exist including **'Broad Leaved'** which blanches well and is used in stir fry dishes, **'Flowering'** or **'Gow Choy Fah'** or **'Chinese Flower Leek'** which has been selected for its plump flower buds and leek flavor and is used in stir fry dishes, soups and pickles, **'New Belt'** with prolific thick green leaves which is eaten both for its stalks and buds, and **'Vietnamese'** which is the giant garlic chive of Vietnam, prized for its plump flower buds which are stir fried, steamed, and used in soups. All may be propagated from seed or by division of the parent clump. Zones 7–11.

Nodding Onion or Lady's Leek

A. cernuum — A North American species grown for its intense onion flavor. It is perennial and propagated from seed or bulbs in a similar way to onion chives. Zones 3–9.

Ramps or Wood Leek *A. tricoccum* —

An early spring emergent in rich woodlands and native to North America. They form scallion-like bulbs and broad, flat leaves. They occur from North Carolina to Canada, and West Virginia holds a number of celebrations and festivals to coincide with the emergence of ramps. Their name comes from the woodland ramsons of England. Ramps have a unique flavor that combines that of onions with that of strong garlic. Although more potent, they are used in any way that leeks might be, such as boiled and served with cream sauce, fried, finely chopped into salads and used in creamed soups. They are easily cultivated in a moist site enriched with compost. Zones 4–9.

Ramsons or **Bear's Garlic** *A. ursinum* — This super garlicky species is grown for its leaves. The bulbils are pickled and used as caper substitutes. It is grown as for onion chives, and a number of selections exist. Zones 5–9.

Sand Leek or **Russian Garlic** or **Giant Garlic** *A. scorodoprasum* — Cultivated in Russia, Eurasia, and Australia, this species develops large basal bulbs with a mild garlic flavor. Zones 5–10.

Seed Saving Note

All the seed forming species and varieties above belong to the Genus *Allium*. The individual flowers, which are born in a terminal inflorescence, each have both male and female parts present but the flowers cannot self pollinate. The inflorescence continues to open over a period of about 30 days. New anthers continuously ripen and shed fresh pollen while new stigma surfaces are revealed by the opening flowers. The flowers are pollinated by a number of different insects and will readily cross within species. The recommended separation distance to maintain pure seed is as much as 3 miles (5 km) over flat countryside.

To preserve your own pure breeding seed, use fine net bags (squares of white nylon net will do) tied over the inflorescence. Each day, remove the bag and gently brush over the inflorescense to transfer the pollen, then re-bag. A cheap children's paintbrush is ideal but never use the same brush for a different cultivar. The seeds are harvested when the heads are dry and the seed capsules beginning to split. Enclose the head(s) in a paper bag and tie upside down for a week in a dry, warm place. The seed will fall into the bag. Give the bag a few sharp taps to release the seed and store in zip lock bags labeled with the name of the variety and date. Store all your seed in an airtight plastic container, and preferably at the bottom of the refrigerator, or in some other cool, dark place. Warmth and moisture rapidly reduce the germination rate of your precious *allium* seeds.

Chinese onion,
Allium Chinensis.

Peas

Field Pea *P. sativum* var. *arvense*; **Shelling Pea** *P. sativum*; **Snap Pea** *P. sativum* var. *macrocarpon* ; **Snow Pea** *P. sativum* var. *macrocarpon*

Peas are among our most ancient vegetables and have been grown in the Near East and southern Europe for at least 8,000 years. They were probably first cultivated in Turkey, where archeological digs have unearthed seeds that are over 7,500 years old. Pea seeds have also been found during excavations of ancient Jericho, in the ruins of 4,000-year-old Troy, and at Neolithic sites in Hungary.

Chinese snow peas are used extensively in stir-fries. The plant begins to produce peas quickly and the pods must be picked young.

Heinrich Schliemann, the famous archeologist who rediscovered ancient Troy in 1870 using Homer's *Iliad* as his guide, found caches of peas in the ruins. In an act that dramatically bridged the centuries, forming an almost supernatural connection with ancient humanity, he and his team then ate a meal made with some of the peas. Schliemann later described the meal as having 'supped from peas from Priam's larder'.

Rich in soluble fibre, peas help reduce detrimental LDL cholesterol. In addition, they are an excellent source of vitamin C, and a significant source of vitamin B1, folic acid, vitamin K, and potassium.

For gardening purposes, peas are generally categorised as field peas, shelling peas, snap peas or snow peas.

Growing and Harvesting

The essential requirement of all pea cultivars, which are otherwise highly adaptable, is a well-drained, moisture-retentive soil. Peas are particularly prone to rotting if grown in poorly drained soils, and also resent dry soils.

Dig a modest amount of compost through the soil to ensure moisture retention, and create raised beds about 6 in (15 cm) high. If the soil is strongly acidic—pH 5.5 and below—it should be limed at the rate of about two cupfuls per sq yd (sq m).

Excessive compost addition should be avoided. Peas are able to fix nitrogen directly from the atmosphere through the agency of specialized symbiotic bacteria associated with nodular formations on the roots (these are not to be confused, however, with the nematode-caused outgrowths found on the roots of some crops). This also means that they do not require a nitrogen-rich soil. Indeed, once planted, the peas will raise the nitrogen level of the soil, which in turn helps prevent disease. This makes them useful for crop rotation.

Peas are essentially a cool-weather crop. In warm areas, they should be planted in mid-autumn for winter and early-spring cropping. In cool areas, they should be rowed out in early spring, although some cultivars will grow satisfactorily through the winter, especially if given the added protection of a cloche during cold snaps.

Generally, a sunny position is required and seeds should be sown directly, in a double row. Plant them $3/4$ in (2 cm) deep with about 3 in (7.5 cm) between seeds and 12 in (30 cm) between rows. The double rows allow the plants to support each other in windy conditions.

After planting, water the seeds, but when the seedlings emerge water only sparingly to prevent rot. More regular watering can take place once the plants are well established. When the crop is half grown, an application of blood and bone can be beneficial.

Many pea cultivars require trellises. Such structures can easily be made using a few panels of steel mesh wired to pairs of 6-ft (1.8-m) metal star posts. These materials can be put into storage once the season is over; they can also be used for sweetpeas and climbing beans. Alternatively, you can create attractive teepees from 6-ft (1.8-m) slender bamboo canes stuck deep into the ground in a circle roughly 40 in (1 m) in diameter and tied at the top. Place thin, dry sticks at the base to assist plants in the initial stage of climbing.

The major threats to established plants are slugs and snails, which will graze high into tall-growing cultivars during wet periods. They can be dealt with by hand-picking at night and by using beer traps. Birds may eat both flowers and pods, as may mice, and the pea moth may be a problem in some areas. Powdery mildew can threaten susceptible cultivars; to inhibit mildew, do not water the tops of plants in the evenings.

Trends in modern breeding include modification of cultivars to produce more tendrils and fewer leaves. This reduces the available leaf area and hence the incidence of leaf disease. Most other recent developments in breeding relate to the needs of the frozen vegetable market. For example, even maturation has been encouraged so that a maximum number of pods reach their optimum size at the same time, allowing for a single mechanical harvest. This, however, is at odds with the needs of the home gardener, who normally seeks to avoid a glut. Older cultivars spread the harvest better, so that the pleasure of fresh peas can be enjoyed for at least six to eight weeks.

A line of slender sticks will provide adequate support for many of the low-growing climbers.

Climbing vegetables allow for effective use of garden space.

Pea seeds germinate more quickly if they are soaked in water for an hour prior to planting.

Field Peas

Pisum sativum var. *arvense*   Zones 3–10

Also called dry peas, field peas are usually grown for their dried seeds, which can be stored. The seeds are used to make soups and other dishes, and also fed to animals. Some dried peas are also fermented, or roasted to make a coffee substitute.

Growing and Harvesting
Peas for drying are left on the vine and harvested only when the pods have turned a light brown and are quite dry.

Recommended Cultivars
'Blue Pod Capucijners' — Developed by Capuchin monks in the 17th

Many excellent cultivars that yield late and for long periods can be lost if not carefully trellised.

century, this is a highly productive, semi-vining type that grows to 4 ft (1.2 m) and has purple pods and grey-brown seeds.

'Raisin Capucijners' — Though normally dried, this cultivar can also beused as a green shelling pea. A productive dwarf vine, it grows to 2 ft (60 cm).

Shelling Peas

Pisum sativum   Zones 3–10

Shelling peas can be eaten when soft, immature and high in sugar; left until fully mature and dried as a winter storage food for soups and stews; or puréed for 'mushy peas'. The famed Rounceval pea, which the Owl and the Pussycat of children's nursery rhyme fame dined on, was considered a great delicacy; this shelling pea was even described by author and farmer Thomas Tusser in the Tudor period.

Growing and Harvesting
Shelling peas are harvested when the pods feel full when gently pressed between thumb and forefinger. (Young pods swell deceptively ahead of the seed.) They should always be picked while sweet and young; later they will be large but starchy.

Recommended Cultivars
'Early Onward' — Introduced in 1908 and still one of the most popular English cultivars, it is used for spring sowing and forms vigorous, very productive vines growing to around 24 in (60 cm).

'Feltham First' — This hardy cultivar is suitable for autumn and early-spring sowing, short growing to 18 in (45 cm), and heavy cropping.

'Hurst Green Shaft' syn. 'Greenshaft' — This productive cultivar has self-supporting vines that grow to 30 in (75 cm) and bear long, packed pods of flavorsome peas which freeze well.

'Kelvedon Wonder' — A dwarf plant that is popular in England and

grow to 16 in (40 cm). It is resistant to wilt, and produces exceptionally sweet, deep green peas.

'Lincoln' syn. 'Homesteader' — Favored in warmer areas for its resistance to heat, this cultivar has compact 24 in (60 cm) vines that produce long, pods packed with sweet, tender peas. It also does well in cooler areas.

'Little Marvel' — Introduced in 1908, this cultivar is a favorite of home growers and forms a dwarf, prolific vine reaching 18 in (45 cm). It is resistant to wilt, and produces peas of exceptional quality. **'Early Frosty'** is a **'Little Marvel'** type with a higher yield.

'Petit Pois' — This is the original French cultivar prized by gourmets for its sweet, tender, small peas. The vines are highly prolific, hardy, and grow to 20 in (50 cm). **'Petit Provencal'** is a very hardy **'Petit Pois'** type cultivar of similar height which can be sown in autumn and winter in milder climates.

'Tall Telephone' syn. 'Alderman' — Introduced around 1878 and still very popular, this cultivar grows to 6 ft (1.8 m) and is a heavy bearer of large pods, each containing up to 10 sweet, tender peas per pod.

Tasmania, Australia, it bears prolific medium pods of sweet peas.

'Knight' — A favorite of home and market gardeners, it forms vigorous plants that grow to 24 in (60 cm) and are resistant to powdery mildew, wilt, and viruses.

'Lacy Lady' — This mildew-reistant, semi-leafless dwarf form produces numerous extra tendrils.

'Laxton's Progress' — This is a favorite early garden and market cultivar with dwarf, compact, vigorous, productive vines that

Peas thrive in the cool, moist, root-run of the no-dig garden.

Many snow pea cultivars, most notably 'Carouby de Maussane', produce attractive purple flowers.

Snap Peas

Pisum sativum var. macrocarpon   Zones 3–10

Snap peas—also known as sugar snap peas—are classified as the same variety as snow peas. But whereas the maturation of snow-pea seeds is delayed, snap pea seeds develop at the natural rate so that a crispy, whole, filled-out pod is produced.

Growing and Harvesting
Snap peas are normally harvested when they have just filled out, and should always be destringed.

Recommended Cultivars
'**Sugar Ann**' — Ideal for small gardens, or even pot culture, and widely adapted, this self-supporting, dwarf cultivar grows to 22 in (55 cm). It was an All America Selections winner in 1984 and remains very popular for its delicious, sweet, crisp, bright-green pods.

'**Sugar Mel**' — A fine, reliable cultivar that bears large quantities of crisp, sweet, thick, round pods on vigorous, mildew-resistant vines. It grows to 48 in (1.2 m).

'**Sugar Rae**' — This is an unusual cultivar in that it sends up multiple vines from the base. It is a dwarf, growing to just 30 in (75 cm), mildew resistant, and a prolific producer of crisp, sweet pods borne over a long period.

'**Sugar Snap**' — This is an early-bearing cultivar that produces plump, succulent, crisp, sweet pods borne on vigorous, wilt-resistant vines rising to 6 ft (1.8 m).

Snow Peas

Pisum sativum var. macrocarpon   Zones 3–10

Selection over centuries created a line of peas in which the fibre content of the pods was reduced so that they were tender and succulent when full sized, and swelling and maturation of the seed was delayed. These crisp, sugar-sweet, flat-podded peas became known variously as snow peas, sugar peas and *mangetout* ('eat all'). They were known to John Gerard in London, who wrote about them in his famous *Herball* of 1597, together with three other different kinds of edible peas. Fearing Burr described no less than nine cultivars of snow peas in the USA in his seminal 1863 book *Field and Garden Vegetables of America*, together with 65 other pea cultivars, a number that is astonishing in our era of limited offerings. Peas reached China via India during the T'ang Dynasty and it was the snow pea and the sweet-tasting pea shoots gathered from the growing plants that were favored and further refined in China.

The effort of creating a trellis is fullly repaid by the excellent yield and succulent seeds of the 'Tall Telephone' cultivar.

Snow peas are at their best when the pods are flat and thin and the bulge of the tiny seed is only just visible.

Growing and Harvesting

Snow-pea cultivars can be harvested regularly before the seeds begin to swell. The strings need to be removed on some cultivars, but harvesting at about three-quarters of full size usually produces a higher-quality harvest with no need to destring.

Pea shoots, also known as *dau miu* or *hoh laan tau*, can be gathered from any tender-shooted, taller cultivar. When growing for this purpose, do not allow the plants to flower; this will divert the sugars into the shoots.

Recommended Cultivars

'Carouby de Maussane' syn. 'Roi de Carouby' — Originating near Avignon, this vigorous cultivar grows to 5 ft (150 cm) and has very attractive purple flowers which are followed by tender, sweet pods. They should be eaten before any swelling of the pods occurs.

'Dwarf White Sugar' — Particularly popular in the USA, this prolific cultivar grows to 30 in (75 cm) and bears stringless, tender pods.

'Golden Sweet' — Collected originally in India, this cultivar is now available in the USA. It has beautiful two-toned purple flowers and clear lemon-yellow pods which are harvested and eaten young.

'Mammoth Melting Sweet' — A favorite with home gardeners for its large, sweet, succulent pods. The vines grow to 5 ft (150 cm), and are productive, hardy and wilt-resistant.

'Oregon Sugar Pod' — This is a highly productive, vigorous, short-vined plant that grows to 30 in (75 cm). The pods are sweet and crisp, and good for freezing. The plants are resistant to viruses and fusarium wilt, and bear over a long period.

The seeds of the 'Raisin Capucijners' cultivar are the principal ingredient in Dutch pea soup.

Peppers

Aji *Capsicum baccatum;* **Bell Pepper** and
Chile Pepper *C. annuum* var. *annuum;*
Habanero Pepper and **Scotch Bonnet**
Pepper *C. chinense;* **Rocoto** *C. pubescens;*
Tabasco Pepper *C. frutescens*

Right: Capsicum
annuum, Longum Group
cultivar, has elongated,
moderately hot to very
hot fruits.

Below: Peppers come
in all sizes, shapes and
colors, and vary in
flavor from sweet and
mild to very hot.

The hot chile peppers and their sweet
pepper cousins have been used for so
many centuries in the cooking of
India, China, Japan, Asia, the Middle
East and Mediterranean Europe that
many people imagine that peppers
originate from these areas. But all
species came originally from South
America and Meso America.

Christopher Columbus was not the
first European visitor to the Americas,
but he was the first to introduce chile
peppers to the Iberian Peninsula, from
where it was dispersed around the

Mediterranean and Aegean regions.
It is often noted that Columbus discovered the wrong spice in the wrong
country. (He was hoping to find black
pepper, *Piper nigrum,* and other spices
in East India, instead discovering the
islands that would become known
as the West Indies, and confusingly
labeling their inhabitants 'Indians' and
their entirely unrelated hot spice 'pepper'.) But no-one can deny that he was
entirely successful in contributing to
the evolution of Mediterranean, Middle
Eastern and North African cuisines.
The divine heat of peppers was destined to enliven the taste buds of all
who lived in those regions. Columbus
recorded his own encounter in his
ship's diary in 1493, noting that the
Indians ate *'aji, which is their pepper
and nobody partakes without it,
because they consider it so healthful'.*

The confusion begun by Columbus
about peppers has been further
extended by European spellings of the
Spanish word 'chile'. In the United
States and Mexico, 'chile pepper' is
used for both the plant and its fruit.
The word 'chile' is reserved for a stew
made with chiles or chile powder. But,
as peppers spread around Europe,
every possible variation on the
spelling was invoked, from 'chilli' and
'chillie' to 'chile', 'chilee' and even

Potted chile peppers in village markets add heat to local dishes.

'chilly'. Leading dictionaries prefer 'chile' and 'chilli' to other spellings. Here we defer to America.

Our earliest record of C. *annuum* chiles being eaten in Central Mexico is 7000 B.C., and the domestication of chile preceded corn and squash, and probably occurred simultaneously with that of beans. Certainly crops of chile recognizably modern in form were being grown in the Tehuacán Valley in Mexico c. 4000 B.C. The chile had spread north into what is now southern Texas and south to Argentina by c. 1400 A.D.

Peppers are far more than a hot aromatic spice. They are also a health food and a herbal medicine. Peppers, hot or sweet, contain very significant levels of vitamins. Vitamin C was first extracted from capsicums by Nobel prize winner Albert Szent-Györgyi, and they contain much higher levels than the commonly recommended oranges. The level of vitamin C in peppers varies with growing conditions, variety and maturity of the fruit, but it is always exceptionally high in terms of natural plant sources. Perhaps even more surprising, peppers are approximately three times as rich in vitamin A as

carrots. They also contain very useful levels of the B vitamins thiamine, riboflavin and niacin, as well as iron and magnesium. Add to all this the fact that they are low in calories and have notable antioxidant levels, particularly when eaten raw, and it becomes clear that peppers are a superfood for the 21st century.

Chile peppers also have various medicinal and therapeutic uses, and have found their way into a number of pharmaceutical and home herbal preparations. The heat-causing components of chile peppers are substances called 'capsaicinoids'. Each chile pepper contains its own combination of capsaicinoids, each with its own specific qualities of fragrance and flavor, and its own special way of delivering heat to the mouth. These capsaicinoids became the target of intensive clinical research in the 1980s and 1990s, and were found to be effective in the treatment of many conditions, confirming many old-fashioned remedies. Topical creams containing capsaicinoids were found to be very effective when rubbed into hands and joints to reduce the pain of osteoarthritis and rheumatoid arthritis.

Capsaicinoid creams are also effective in reducing the extreme pain of shingles for many patients, and are useful in treating neuralgia as well as a num-ber of annoying or painful skin conditions. Used as a nasal spray, it is effective for many sufferers of cluster headaches.

Nor do the health benefits of peppers stop there. Reliable medical evidence indicates that chile peppers help the body to metabolize fat, are natural anticoagulants helping to prevent blood clots that can lead to strokes and heart attacks, and lower cholesterol and triglycerides while maintaining the so-called good cholesterol HDL. Predictably, they can prevent scurvy because of their high levels of vitamin C. Their high levels of antioxidants also appear to be involved in inhibiting some cancers. It should be added that there can, of course, be too much of a good thing, and excessive long-term use can be detrimental. But for men suffering from hair loss, a Caribbean cure involving rubbing chile-impregnated

This mix of peppers shows the variety available for cooking.

oil into the scalp may be worth trialing. It most likely works by increasing circulation. For the same reason, an old trick for warming cold feet was to sprinkle powdered dried chiles into socks.

For the gardener, there is one more important use for chile peppers in the garden. They can be used to make very effective home-made pest repellents.

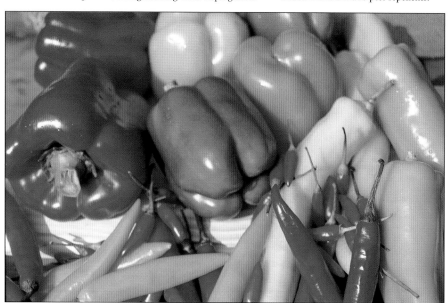

Growing and Harvesting

Selecting the right varieties is the key to successfully growing peppers organically, and a wide variety have been described here so that optimum choices can be made. Most species of peppers originated in hot, long summer areas. The exception is the species *C. pubescens*, which came from the Andean highland areas. As peppers were transported around the world, they were reselected constantly by local farmers and gardeners so that now there are many varieties adapted to areas where the original pepper varieties could never have grown. By selecting optimal varieties for your garden, and planting at the right time, you will have little trouble producing a good crop. Many *C. annuum* varieties selected for cooler climates are actually short-lived perennials but will die with the first frost, having expended their energy in flowering and fruiting. But for gardeners in frost-free to tropical areas, many varieties of *C. annuum* can persist from two to several years, and varieties of *C. pubescens*, *C. chinense*, *C. frutescens* and *C. baccatum* may last for a number of years. While full sun and heat are necessary for peppers to flourish in cooler areas, in sub-tropical to tropical areas they appreciate light dappled shade or protection from the hot afternoon sun, and are often grown between fruit trees such as pawpaws in the home garden, or professionally under a light shadecloth.

Peppers are very cold-sensitive and should not be planted out until at least two weeks after the last frost date has passed and when the soil temperature has reached at least 65°F (18°C). In cool areas, black plastic laid around the plants can warm the soil considerably by absorbing the heat of the sun. It can be removed once the days are reliably warm and replaced with a thick mulch. Cloches may also be used or row covers in

areas with cool summers. *(See Recommended Varieties.)*

Seed should be sown in flats of well-drained seedling mix, and planted 8–10 weeks before the last frost date. A mixture of 2 parts coarse washed river sand to 1 part well-sieved compost is ideal. Seedlings are prone to the fungal disease 'damping off', which appears as pinching and browning of the base of the stem, followed by wilting and dying. The microorganisms that cause wilting are soil borne. To sterilize the soil mix, place the equivalent volume of a flat in a large heavy duty clear plastic bag, seal the end temporarily (clothes pegs will do) and place the bag flat in a very cool oven (around 112°F (50°C)

Early summer peppers grow out at Heritage Farm, Iowa.

By selecting optimal varieties of pepper plants for your garden, and planting at the right time, you will have little trouble producing a good crop.

Capsicum annuum, Grossum Group cultivar, bearing fruit.

for 30 minutes. In warm to hot areas, the sun will act as an oven. Simply lay the sealed bag flat in full sunshine for an hour. Pour the now pasteurized soil into a flat, smooth over, press the mix down evenly, and plant the seed about $^1/_5$ in (0.7 cm) below the surface. Seed may also be planted into individual cells. Water gently. It is essential that the seed be kept at 75–85°F (24–29°C) for good germination, which takes 2–3 weeks for most varieties, and up to 4 weeks. Continue watering as needed to keep the mix moist but well drained, and use tepid rather than cold water. When the seedlings become too large for the flat or pot, they should be individually planted into 5 in (12.5 cm) pots. Peppers need plenty of root space and usually will not develop into heavy yielding plants if they have had limited root space as seedlings. As planting out time approaches, harden the plants off by exposing them to increasing amounts of sunlight and air movement on warmer days. It is easy to be excited by the first few warm days of spring and to want to plant these seedlings into the ground, but the soil will be too cold and night temperatures too low. Be patient and wait until the soil temperature has reached 65°F (18°C). Then there will be no check in growth, and plants will quickly come into bearing.

Peppers thrive in a rich, well-composted, freely draining soil and prefer a pH of 6.5 to 7.0. The planting distance for annual plantings of *C. annuum* is 12–18 in (30–45 cm), depending on plant size. Other species grown in frost-free environments can attain a considerable size of 4–6 ft (1.2–2 m) or more in 2–3 years, and a 3 ft 3 in (1.2–2 m) gap should be left between plants of larger varieties.

Plants should be heavily mulched from early to mid-summer onward once the ground is thoroughly warmed. Blossom drop can occur in low humidity conditions, causing poor

fruit set. This is mainly a problem in areas with hot, dry summers and is partly overcome by planting peppers the minimum distance apart. Regular applications of seaweed or fish emulsion liquid fertilizers in the early stages of growth is beneficial but should be stopped once the plants are near to flowering. The high nitrogen levels in these fertilizers encourage growth but reduce flowering and therefore yields. High phosphorus, on the other hand, maintains fruit production. The plants of sweet peppers can become top heavy when fruiting, and staking is recommended.

Fruits can be harvested at any stage after reaching full size, from green to fully ripe, but the flavor is more intense and the vitamin C levels much higher when the fruit have reached full color.

Trouble Shooting
Like tomatoes, peppers are susceptible to tobacco mosaic virus. Smokers should never smoke around the plants or handle plants without first washing their hands. Peppers are quite disease resistant but are susceptible to the fungal disease anthracnose.

Crops should never be planted in the same soil for a period of at least 3–4 years, and a strict crop rotation should be followed using vegetables that are not in the family *Solanaceae*. Occasionally, blossom end rot (rotting of the bottom of the fruit) occurs in *C. annuum* varieties due to low calcium levels (incorporate dolomite or crushed eggshells into the soil), or an uneven water supply. The latter is overcome by the use of a thick mulch applied when the soil is thoroughly warmed.

Important Tip

The capsaicin in hot peppers can cause a severe burning sensation in the fingers that may last a couple of days. Total numbness of the fingertips may even ensue for a day or more. When de-seeding fruits of very hot varieties, for seed saving or for cooking, use a protective pair of gloves. Never touch your face until you have thoroughly washed your hands with soap. They will still be mildly lethal weapons if you have de-seeded a number of hot fruits. A final wash in water with a little ammonia added is a professional tip for seed savers as it stops the burning. Of course, ammonia cannot be used to reduce the hellfire effects caused internally by a very hot pepper. Cold water helps momentarily, but capsaicin is not water soluble. Casein, found in milk, yoghurt, cheese and milk-based ice-cream, is very effective in reducing the heat quickly as it breaks the bond between capsaicin and the pain receptors in the mouth. Mixing alcohol and chiles can cause severe stomach reactions in the sensitive, and a preliminary slice of cheese offers some useful protection.

Sweet, slightly spicy, multicolored and irregular, these are the true provincial peppers.

*'Bishop's Crown'
chile pepper.*

Recommended Varieties

Several species of peppers are widely grown. It can be a delightful treasure hunt to discover, grow and taste test peppers. They are so variable in flavor, aroma and heat, in size and shape, and come in a range of jewel colors. Botanically, they can be distinguished by their flowers, leaf and bush form, and fruit attachment. The fruits are of little assistance botanically, with many 'look-alikes' from various species.

Aji

Capsicum baccatum   Zones 9–12

Varieties of this species are known throughout South America as aji and originated in Peru or Bolivia. The flowers usually have golden or tan spots on the corollas and yellow anthers. Areas with reliably warm, long summers can easily grow the suggested varieties and many more. These are tall-growing plants reaching 5 ft (1.5 m) in some instances, and need up to 120 days to reach maturity. They are heavily productive, can be very hot at 8 on the heat scale, and are extremely variable in size, color and form of fruit.

Recommended Cultivars

'Aji Amarillo' — From the Andes region, this is a variety used to color and spice foods, with beautiful, pendulous, rich yellow, elongated fruits up to $2^1/_2$ in (6.25 cm) long and $^1/_2$ in (1.25 cm) wide borne in profusion.

'Peri-Peri' — A Portuguese variety of very pretty form with green fruits turning red like Chinese lanterns dangling along the open branches, fruits $2^1/_2$ in (6.25 cm) wide and 2 in (5 cm) long, and mild to medium heat. **'Bishop's Crown'** is close in form.

'Peru Yellow' syn. Aji Limon — Indispensable to a chile aficionado, this variety has upward or sideways pointing, clear yellow fruits to $1^1/_2$ in (3.75 cm) long and $^1/_2$ in (1.25 cm) wide, with a strong lemon note to its fragrance and flavor, and moderate heat (7+ on the heat scale).

Bell Pepper *and* Chile Pepper

Capsicum annuum var. annuum   Zones 8–12

This species occurs in many hundreds of varieties and includes heat-free bell peppers as well as many very hot varieties. In warmer climates with long summers, gardeners will easily succeed with almost all varieties. By starting plants early under protection, a number of specially bred varieties will also do well in cooler climates.

Varieties for Cool Climates

Bell Pepper or Sweet Capsicum

'Canape' — An early maturing Japanese variety now very widely available, bell-shaped, green-skinned, with medium-thick, sweet mild flesh. Can be grown in frames or outdoors.

'Corona' — This Dutch variety with medium-sized, 3- or 4-lobed orange fruits when ripe is notable for its sweetness and rich flavor.

'Golden Summit' — One of many excellent Yugoslavian varieties now becoming available, this forms

short plants bearing heavy crops of bell peppers that turn bright orange-yellow before turning deep red, with thick, juicy, sweet flesh.

'Merrimack Wonder' — Released in 1942, this variety reliably sets fruit even in cool areas. It produces blocky, 4-lobed fruit, 3^1/$_2$ in (9 cm) wide and long, with medium sweet flesh.

'Permagreen' — This is a recent variety developed for Canada and the northern states of the United States. It forms 3-lobed, elongated fruits that are glossy green when mature with thin, crisp flesh of excellent flavor.

'Sweet Banana' syn. Yellow Banana, Hungarian Wax Sweet — This widely grown and popular variety is exceptionally heavy yielding, bearing tapered 6 in (15 cm) long fruits ripening from pale green turning yellow to orange. The thin crisp flesh is sweet.

'Yolo Wonder' syn. Californian Wonder— Resistant to mosaic disease, a blocky, medium to large bell type with sweet flavor, dark green turning clear red.

Chile Pepper

'Czechoslovakian Black' — A beautiful very early variety that would ornament any garden, or for pot culture, with green foliage tinged and striped purple, white flowers striped lavender, and small, bluntly conical fruits that turn deep red overlaid with purple-black, like smoldering coals.

'Hungarian Wax' syn. Hot Banana — Long, tapered fruits to 7 in (17.5 cm) long and 1^1/$_2$ in (4 cm) wide, turning from pale green to yellow and then crimson, with medium hot spicy flavor.

Capsicum annuum, Grossum Group cultivar.

'Hot Banana' peppers have long, tapered fruit that turn from pale green to yellow and then crimson, with a medium hot spicy flavor.

'Corno di Toro' is a traditional Italian frying pepper with long and curved, spicy fruit.

Varieties for Warm to Hot Climates

Of many hundreds of suitable varieties, as an excellent beginning you could try:

Bell Pepper or Sweet Capsicum

'Aconcagua' Syn. Giant Aconcagua — An Argentinian variety bearing long, large peppers to 11 in (27.5 cm) long, sweetly flavored, turning pale green to orange to red, used fresh, fried or roasted. The 30 in (75 cm) plants bear so heavily they must be staked.

'Almapaprika' — A beautiful 'flattened tomato'-shaped fruit turning from ivory through gold to red, this Hungarian paprika variety is sweet-fleshed and non-spicy.

'Bull Nose' syn. Large Sweet Spanish — This is an heirloom variety from India with large, thick-walled, 4-lobed, sweet-fleshed fruits.

'Corno di Toro' — A traditional Italian frying pepper that can be obtained as a yellow or red type, the fruits of this variety are long and curved, up to 8 in (20 cm) long with a spicy flavor. Excellent in hot, dry summers.

'Cubanelle' — Richly flavorful, the fruits are 6 in (15 cm) long, turning pale green to orange to red, and are used fresh, fried or stuffed.

'Nardello' syn. Jimmy Nardello's Sweet Frying — An heirloom Italian frying pepper, heavy cropping, with masses of slender fruit to 7 in (18 cm) long, this is a very sweet variety when red. Superb in Italian sauces.

'Pimento' — One of many 'pimentos', this bears heart-shaped fruits. ripening deep orange-red, with thick sweet flesh.

'Quadrato d'Asti Giallo Rosa' — An excellent variety for hot dry summers, with large, broad, golden fruits ripening red, and a very sweet and spicy flavor.

Chile peppers thrive in a rich, well-composted, freely draining soil.

Cayenne peppers are available in a number of varieties and are all elongated, slender, tapered, thin walled and hot to very hot.

'**Sweet Cherry**' — A 19th century variety as popular as ever, with cherry-sized, very sweet fruits to 1–1¹/₄ in (2.5–3 cm), ideal for fresh snacks or pickling. Exceedingly productive.

'**Sweet Chocolate**' — Rich chocolate-brown, blocky bell peppers with deep red, slightly spicy, delicious flesh.

'**World Beater**' syn. Ruby Giant — Developed before 1912 and still very popular, this variety is well named, with tall plants bearing very large, blocky, red fruits with thick, very sweet flesh, averaging 5 in (12.5 cm) in length.

Chile Pepper

'**Anaheim**' syn. Long Green Chile — Cultivated in New Mexico for over 300 years and usually stuffed and roasted or used in salsas when green, or dried when red to be ground into powder. Anaheim is only mildly pungent to medium hot, and fruits are long and tapering, up to 10 in (25 cm) long and 1³/₄ in (4.5 cm) wide.

'**Black Cuban**' — A very hot, small, broadly oval, upward-facing chile, ¹/₂ in (1.25 cm) long and wide, black-purple maturing brilliant red with black-purple foliage.

'**Cabai Burong**' — A very hot Malaysian variety with small, upward-pointing, slender red fruits on an open bush, 2 in (5 cm) long and ¹/₂ in (1.25 cm) wide.

'**Cascabel**' — This variety has cherry-shaped fruits that mature reddish-brown, are thick walled, with mild to medium heat, and are usually dried and ground for flavoring.

'**Cayenne**' — Available in a number of varieties including '**Charlston Hot**', '**Golden Cayenne**', '**Hot Portugal**', '**Long Red Cayenne**', '**Long Slim**', and '**Ring of Fire**', these are all elongated, slender, tapered peppers approximately 6 in (15 cm) long and ³/₅–⁷/₈ in (1.5–2 cm) wide, somewhat to markedly transversely wrinkled and curved, thin walled and hot to very hot. The fruits are easily dried and usually prepared as powdered cayenne.

'**Chile de Comida**' — This is a very popular Mexican variety with medium heat, and fruits that are dark red when mature, 4 in (10 cm) long and 1 in (2.5 cm) wide.

'**Chiltepin**' — A wild variety now becoming well known among aficionados, found originally in southwest USA and Mexico, with tiny, blindingly hot, (10 plus on the heat scale), oval to small conical red fruits $1/4$ in (0.5 cm) wide and $1/2$–$3/4$ in (1.5–2 cm) long.

'De Arbol' — Also known as the **tree chile**, this variety bears elongated, slender, red, thin-walled, hot fruit to 3 in (7.5 cm).

'Desi Teekhi' — A very hot cayenne-like pepper originating from Asia, this very productive variety bears slender and tapering, curved and transversely wrinkled fruits $3^1/2$ in (8.75 cm) long and $1/2$ in (1.25 cm) wide.

'Guajillo' — Brownish-burgundy when ripe and up to 5 in (12.5 cm) long, this thin-walled chile pepper is used in sauces and for cooking.

'Holiday Cheer' — A delightful ornamental variety (but of course edible), very low growing and smothered in marble-sized, round fruit, yellow turning red.

Right: 'Peruvian Purple' is one of the most beautiful chile peppers, with deep purple-green foliage and small conical purple fruit ripening to deep red.

Below: 'Peru Yellow' and 'Peter Pepper', which has medium to high heat and is excellent in sauces, pickled or dried for chile powder.

'Jalapeno' — A Mexican variety producing abundant quantities of 3 in (7.5 cm) long green fruits, smooth, of low to medium heat. Used fresh in sauces and salsas and to flavor stews and casseroles, also pickled or smoked.

'Malahat' — Intensely pungent, this Turkish variety has tapering, downward-pointing fruit, green turning red, 4 in (10 cm) long and $3/4$ in (1.8 cm) wide.

'Numex Sunset' — Derived from 'Anaheim', this is one of a series of excellent large-fruited varieties that have come from the breeding program of New Mexico State University, mildly pungent, with long tapered pods averaging $7^1/2$ in (19 cm), green turning a brilliant clear orange. Dries superbly.

'Pasilla' — Raisin-scented, with a rich mellow flavor, and dark brown, to 12 in (30 cm) long tapered fruit, with gentle to medium heat, borne prolifically. Indispensable in Mexican cooking where it is smoked to make mole sauces. Superb.

'Peruvian Purple' — One of the most beautiful chiles and perennial in frost-free areas, with deep purple-green foliage and small conical purple fruit ripening to deep red. Medium to hot.

'Peter Pepper' — The 'X-rated' pepper shaped like a penis. Available in yellow and red forms, up to 4 in (10 cm) long, of intermediate to high heat, excellent pickled, in sauces and for chile powder.

'Poblano' — This variety bears large tapered fruit 4 in (10 cm) long and $2^1/2$ in (6.5 cm) wide, of mild to medium heat. Two varieties – **'Ancho'** maturing red and **'Mulatto'** maturing brown – are stuffed, used in sauces, roasted or dried. This is the most popular pepper in Mexico.

'Serrano' — Despite belonging to C. *annuum*, this is a reliable perennial variety in frost-free areas, with lipstick-shaped $2^1/4$ in (5.5 cm) long and $^1/_2$ in (1.5 cm) wide fruits that are pendant, thin walled, deep green turning red, and hot. It is used for salsas, pickling, sauces and seasoning.

'**Szentesi**' — Resembling a bell pepper, somewhat tapering, ivory-lemon maturing red, $4^1/_4$ in (10.5 cm) long and 2 in (5 cm) wide, this is a Hungarian variety that is hot and used as a spice when dried and powdered.

'**Takanotsume**' — Meaning 'claw of the eagle', this Japanese variety has clusters of very hot tapering fruit $1^1/_2$ in (3.75 cm) long and $^1/_2$ in (1.25 cm) wide, green turning lacquer red.

'**Thai Hot**' syn. Hang Pri — This is the most common hot red pepper encountered in Thai dishes, a productive variety bearing slim, tapering fruits $3^1/_2$ in (9 cm) long and $^1/_2$–$^3/_4$ in (1.25–2 cm) wide that are slightly wrinkled and mind-blowingly hot. They can reach a perfect 10 on the heat scale.

'**Tiny Samoa**' — An immensely productive variety surviving 3 or

more years in frost-free areas, with upward-pointing, small conical fruit $^2/_5$–$^4/_5$ in (1–2 cm) long, immensely hot, on neat dense small bushes.

'**Yatsafusa**' — A Japanese variety on a sturdy bush to 2 ft 8 in (80 cm), with clusters of upward-pointing, tapering fruits $2^1/_2$ in (6.5 cm) long and $^1/_4$ in (0.6 cm) wide, coloring green to bright red, and very hot. (The Chinese variety '**Chichien**' is close in form.)

'Rooster Spur' is a flavorful Japanese pepper that has tapering, hot fruit.

There are numerous South American varieties of chile peppers.

Habanero Pepper *and* Scotch Bonnet Pepper

Capsicum chinense   Zones 10–12

This group flourishes in areas with hot summers, and the fruits are often blindingly hot. The species originated in the Amazon Basin (despite its disastrously incorrect naming by the Dutch physician and collector of plants in the Caribbean, Nikolaus von Jacquin, in 1776) and is variable in form and size. The flowers are white or green with purple anthers, and they set 2 to 6 fruit per node. The fruit often resemble Chinese lanterns, or bonnets, or elongated variations of this shape, but all varieties fit this pattern. The leaves are large and wrinkled. On the heat scale, 10 represents 100,000 Scovile units or more. *C. chinense* varieties range from 0 to an off-the-scale 577,000 (for the notorious **'Red Savina'** variety). The shape of fruit is no indication of heat level. Most varieties are short-lived perennials in hot climates.

Recommended Varieties

'Habanero' — From the Yucatán Peninsula of eastern Mexico and neighboring Belize, this variety bears campanulate, undulating fruit pointed at the end and brilliant clear orange in color. It is exceptionally hot with fruits that

are $2^{1}/_{2}$ in (6.25 cm) long and 1 in (2.5 cm) wide.

'Jamaican Red Bonnet' (close to **'West Indian Red'**) — A prolific bearing variety usually grown under broken shade in Jamaica, with campanulate, pointed, undulate, brilliant lacquer fruits that are only for the brave, but are flavorful and used to prepare escabeche of fish in Jamaica. The fruits are approximately $2^{1}/_{2}$ in (6.25 cm) long and 1 in (2.5 cm) wide.

'Rocatillo' — Shaped like a flared bell with crimped edges, or like a very squashed Tam O'Shanter, with medium to thick walls, deep red when ripe, 2 in (5 cm) wide and long, with wonderful flavor, spicy rather than hot.

'Scotch Bonnet' — Shaped like a Scottish Tam O'Shanter, or like a rather squashed Chinese lantern, these are clear yellow or orange fruits, exceedingly hot at 10+, thin walled, fruity, up to $2^{1}/_{2}$ in (6.5 cm) wide and $1^{1}/_{2}$ in (4 cm) long, and broadly ridged around the equator.

Rocoto

Capsicum pubescens   Zones 9–12

Distinguished by its purple flowers and jet black seeds, rocotos were the favored pepper of the Incas, grown in Meso America and northern South America. Most resemble small, blocky, smooth-skinned apples. Compressed, pear-shaped, finger-like and lobed varieties exist. The color ranges from

Rocotos are pear-shaped peppers prized for their unique flavor and they are also very hot.

yellow to orange or red in mature fruits and they are prized for their unique flavor (if you can distinguish it from the heat, which rates a 9 on the heat scale.) Various names for the rocoto include **chile manzano (apple pepper)**, **chile perón (pear pepper)**, and **chile caballo (horse pepper)**. In frost-free mountain gardens it can reach, in time, 13–16 ft (4–5 m), forming an open, sprawling, finely hairy bush which is perennial. Its natural habitat is cooler tropical highlands but it can also thrive in cooler coastal gardens. It prefers a light canopy of trees above.

Tabasco Pepper

Capsicum frutescens   Zones 9–12

The tabascos, the malaguetas of Brazil's Amazon Basin and bird peppers belong in this group. They are all easy to grow in areas with long hot summers. Plants of C. *frutescens* are compact and grow up to 4 ft (1.2 m) high. They are perennial in frost-free areas, lasting at least 3 to 4 years, and enormously productive. The flowers are a distinguishing feature, greenish-white with no spots, and purple anthers. The fruits are held upward and are small, with a high heat rating of 8 or 9 on the heat scale.

'**Tabasco**' — Tabasco was selected from a pepper brought to Louisiana during the war between the United States and Mexico (1846–47). The McIlhenny family made a sauce on Avery Island, Louisiana, by salting and fermenting the peppers and ageing the resulting blindingly hot liquid. Their famous Tabasco Pepper Sauce is now marketed around the world. This ornamental chile with attitude is exceptionally productive, growing to 4 ft (1.2 m), with hundreds of upward-pointing fruits, to $1^1/_2$ in (3.75 cm) long and $^1/_2$ in (1 cm) wide, pale yellow maturing to orange then bright red, all colors borne at the same time on the bush. In southern United States, a fungal wilt affected this variety in the 1960s and it has been replaced with the resistant '**Greenleaf Tabasco**', but the orig-inal variety will thrive elsewhere. Other tabascos worth growing include '**Wild Grove**', '**Zimbabwe Bird**' and the Cambodian '**Angkor Sunrise**'.

Potatoes and other tuberous crops

Achira *Canna edulis*; **Cassava** *Manihot esculenta*; **Day Lily** *Hemerocallis* spp.; **Jerusalem Artichoke** *Helianthus tuberosus*; **Jicama** *Pachyrhizus erosus* syn. *P. tuberosus*; **Lotus Root** *Nelumbo nucifera*; **Mashua** *Tropaeolum tuberosum*; **Oca** *Oxalis tuberosa*; **Potato** *Solanum tuberosum*; **Sweet Potato** *Ipomoea batatas*; **Taro** *Colocasia esculenta*; **Ulluco** *Ullucus tuberosus*; **Water Chestnut** *Eleocharis tuberosa*; **Yacon** *Polymia sonchifolia*; **Yams** *Dioscorea* spp.

While the potato is the best known of all tuber crops, there are many other crops grown for their edible tubers, particularly in the sub-tropics and tropics. All are prized as rich sources of carbohydrate. Also listed here are vegetables that are technically corms or rhizomes but develop large, tuber-like carbohydrate storage organs, and which are almost invariably refered to as tubers. The group shares many common techniques for use, cooking, production and storage.

As propagation by vegetative means is regularly used within this group, each cultivar will remain true to name even after many years of saving seed tubers and replanting. Another advantage of tuber and corm crops is

Above Right: Achira, Canna edulis, is easy to grow, forming huge, succuoent, tuber-like rhizomes just below the ground, which are either baked or boiled as a vegetable.

Below: There are many edible tubers including yams, taro, jicama and lotus.

that many different cultivars can be planted in a small garden, allowing the gourmet gardener to enjoy a wide range of tastes, textures, colors and shapes. Many tuber and corm crops have the additional advantage of lending themselves to pot culture. Many good meals can be harvested from a few pots grown on a patio, and most are also handsome ornamentals.

Achira
Canna edulis   Zones 9–12

Achira, also known as edible canna, originates from South America and is closely related to the ornamental cannas with lush, lily-like leaves. It is considered to have been one of the first plants to be domesticated in the Andes. It is exceptionally easy to grow, forming huge, succulent, tuber-like rhizomes just below the ground. The rhizomes are either baked or boiled as a vegetable or shredded and extracted for their starch, which is cooked to a transparent mixture.

Achira is easily propagated by rhizome tips with a couple of whole tips attached, or with whole tubers. The sections are planted into furrows to conserve moisture, covered with soil, regularly watered, and will quickly make new clumps. Weeding is necessary while the crop is young, but the lush, abundant foliage will suppress weeds later in the cycle of the crop.

Achira is harvested at about 6 months. It is widely grown around the world including China, South East Asia, and Queensland, Australia. Grasshoppers and beetles may be a problem.

Cassava

Manihot esculenta   Zones 10–12

Cassava, which is also known as manioc, yuca, tapioca, Brazilian arrowroot or mandioca, forms a bush to around 6–7 ft (2 m) high with dull green, palmate leaves. The tubers are formed in a cluster just beneath the soil. When fully developed, the tubers are swollen and long-oval in shape, deep red-brown, brown or grey with a white, fibrous flesh, and may be 39 in (1 m) long in primitive forms. This was the staple diet of the Caribbean Indians and remains so today. It is estimated that approximately 300 million people around the world consume cassava daily as their principal carbohydrate source. One of its great advantages is its astonishingly high yields, as much as 19.6 tons (20 tonnes) to 0.4 hectares (1 acre), and the total lack of production skills required to achieve this figure. Cassava never existed in the wild, a not uncommon situation with a number of South American and Meso American crops, including corn. It is considered to be a hybrid of two or more wild species and is believed to have originated in Peru 1,000 years ago.

The tubers of the more primitive bitter cassava contain a deadly poison which must be removed by prolonged boiling, or by grating, washing, pounding and then squeezing and drying the tubers. The lethal component is a glycoside of hydrocyanic acid HCN which is an inhibitor of a respiratory enzyme and precipitates death by asphyxiation. (The Arawak Indians reputedly chose death by eating uncooked cassava in preference to being tortured by the invading Spaniards.) Bitter cassava, also known as *kii*, has high levels of hydrocyanic glucocide. So-called sweet cassava or makasera consists of a complex of selected forms which also contains hydrocyanic glucosides but in lower levels (less than 50 ppm).

The tubers of sweet cassava are usable after simple cooking and are usually roasted, boiled or fried as chips. The detoxified tubers are also pounded to make a paste known in West Africa as *fufu*. The prawn crackers of Indonesia, *krupuk*, are also prepared from cassava. A flour is made from the detoxified tubers, called *farinha* or *gari* which is used to prepare flatbreads and biscuits. The refined starch is known as *tapioca* and is prepared by the gentle heating of the starchy pulp over heat until the starch forms small translucent balls which can then be dried for storage. It forms the basis of tapioca pudding and as a thickening agent for sauces. The juice of the tubers is boiled to make a condiment known as *cassareep*, and it is also fermented into alcoholic beverages such as *chicha* and *kaschiri*.

Cassava is the highest producer of carbohydrates among all the staple crops.

Cassava, Manihot esculenta, have tubers formed in a cluster just beneath the soil, which are swollen and long-oval in shape, deep red-brown or grey with white flesh.

Growing and Harvesting

Cassava may well be the world's most easily grown crop. Stem cuttings are planted and require no tending until they are subsequently harvested some 6–8 months later. Cassava has no significant enemies, whether pest or disease. The crop flourishes anywhere the growing season is warm and wet followed by a dry period such as in the dry tropics. If left in the ground too long, the tubers eventually become woody.

Day Lily

Hemerocallis spp.   Zones 4–11

It may seem to be hugely wasteful and unappreciative to even contem-plate eating the beautiful day lily, and given the prices of the beautiful modern hybrid cultivars you would undoubtedly be correct. But several species of day lilies and their ancient cultivars have long been a part of Chinese and Japanese cuisine, and have become widely appreciated elsewhere. Virtually all parts of the two commonest species are eaten, the Asian **Tawny day lily** *H. fulva*, now naturalized in the United States, together with its ancient double form '**Kwanso**', and the delightfully fragrant **Yellow day lily** or **Lemon lily** *H. flava*.

Hemerocallis fulva 'Flore Pleno' has double orange flowers with sepals curved back and a red eye. In China and Japan the flower buds are sold as food.

The beautiful trumpet-shaped blooms are cooked in the manner of squash blossom, the green buds hidden in a fragile encasement of tempura batter and deep fried or steamed and served with butter and a squeeze of lemon, while the opened flowers can be stuffed with savory rice, added to omelettes, or used in soups. The spring shoots are steamed and tossed in butter like new season asparagus or cooked in stir fry dishes. The small tubers that form in a cluster at the base of the stem have the most delicious flavor when steamed or boiled, and are prepared in a similar manner to potatoes including mashed, in salads, and in fritters. The dried flowers of tawny day lily, known as golden needles, are traditionally used in soups and stews. These can easily be prepared by loosely threading the flowers together and hanging them in an airy place out of direct sunlight to dry thoroughly before storing in an airtight container. The tubers of '**Kwanso**' also yield a useful starch.

Other species of day lily that have traditionally been used as a vegetable include: the **Edible day lily** *H. middendorfii* var. *esculenta* with leaves that are stir fried and flowers that are pickled; the **Grassleaf day lily** *H. minor* from China and Japan, the tubers of which are variously steamed, baked, roasted and sliced in stir fry dishes, the flowers used in soups, and the young shoots steamed; and *H. dumortieri*, the **Narrow day lily**, the flowers of which are used in tempura or dried to make a tea, or to add to soups.

Growing *and* Harvesting

Day lilies are remarkably easy and resilient creatures. It has been said that 'if you can't grow a day lily you should give up gardening'. That is extreme, but certainly they are rugged perennials, tolerant of drought, high summer temperatures, cold (including the sub-zero temperatures of places

Day Lily , Hemerocallis Lilioasphodelus, has a range of uses in herbal medicine and although some parts may be eaten, others can be hallucinogenic.

like Canada), and of a wide range of soil types including alkaline, sandy, and heavy clays. They are usually planted in spring or fall but will survive summer planting in the hottest of areas, provided watering is attended to while they settle in.

The only enemy of the day lily is an occasional attack by snails or slugs after a prolonged period or rain, and this is normally overcome by using beer traps or taking a torch out at night to pick them off. You may prefer to use only the species described above as vegetables, as these have a delicacy of texture that is unsurpassed. But the thousands of modern hybrid day lilies all yield fully edible flowers and other parts. Of the modern varieties, **'Stella d'Oro'** is popular among those growing edible flowers for markets, its heavy repeat flowering habit resulting in high yields of smallish golden flowers over a long season. While not absolutely necessary, lifting and dividing day lily clumps every 3–4 years assures an excellent supply of flowers annually, and the opportunity to harvest the tubers, although the latter can be done at any time of the year provided the ground is not frozen. An application of compost around the clumps once or twice during the growing season is

beneficial to the quality and quantity of flower production in daylilies, particularly with highly bred, modern hybrids.

Jerusalem Artichoke

Helianthus tuberosus   Zones 4–10

Neither an artichoke nor from Jerusalem, this mysterious vegetable conundrum for gardeners, is a species native to North America. In the same genus as the sunflower *Helianthus annuus*, it was cultivated by the people of the First Nation for centuries, and was introduced into Europe via Holland, reaching England in 1617.

Hemerocallis Hybrid 'Stella d'Oro' has clear golden-yellow flowers of almost circular outline.

Specimens were also dispatched from Cape Cod to France where they became known as *batatas de Canada* or pommes de Canada, and from there cultivation subsequently spread to Italy where they thrived.

The tubers have particular value for diabetics as they store their carbohydrate in the form of insulin rather than the sucrose and starches that are found in most tubers. The tall plants grow to 8 ft (2.5 m) and bear small, decorative yellow flowers. The tubers are quite knobbly when gathered from the wild, but cultivated forms are smoother skinned which makes them easier to peel. Even the varieties which first entered Europe were far superior to wild dug tubers, and were evidence of early selection in this vegetable. More recently, breeding and selection has resulted in much shorter varieties, around 4 ft (1.2 m). Tuber colors vary from white and cream to red, reddish-orange and purple.

While the Jerusalem artichoke has never wavered greatly in the public's esteem in Europe, until around 30 years ago it was almost a forgotten vegetable in its native North America. Now its high levels of free amino acids in combination with its desirable sugar, high levels of pantothenic acid, and useful levels of most of the other B group vitamins and vitamins A and C, and nutty flavor have resulted in a re-evaluation of this historic vegetable.

In Europe the tubers were at first used principally to make rich pies, partnered with dried fruits like raisins and dates, and fortified wine, or they were boiled, peeled, sliced and tossed in a pan with butter and wine. A popular modern variation of that recipe is to parboil the peeled tubers, slice, and sauté in butter, tossing in finely chopped chives or rosemary. They are also boiled, steamed, and baked. The latter are quite delicious as the sweet nutty flavor is intensified. In southern and eastern France where they were widely cultivated in the 19th century, they were served as a

Jerusalem atichoke, Helianthus tuberosus, is native to North America and is a vegetable with a delicious nutty flavor.

The frost hardy Jerusalem artichoke can be left in the ground until it is ready to be eaten.

fritter. But most popular of all is its use in making a classic creamy soup. The raw tubers are crisp and sweet, and can be sliced and used in the manner of Chinese water chestnuts, eaten like radishes, or sliced into winter salads.

The Jerusalem artichoke is completely frost hardy. Tubers that are not harvested will reshoot from the ground in spring. This benefit is also its undoing in the eyes of some gardeners who find it a difficult crop to contain.

The names Sunroot and Sunchoke are both used currently in promoting the Jerusalem artichoke. Strictly speaking, 'Sunchoke' should be applied to the cross between the sunflower and the Jerusalem artichoke which was developed as a potential future sugar crop. A natural hybrid of the Jerusalem artichoke, *Helianthus x laetiflorus* known as **Showy Sunflower**, has edible tubers with a flavor identical to that of the parent Jerusalem artichoke. The closely related **Maximilian's Sunflower** *H. maximilianii*, native to North America, is a perennial sunflower which produces subterranean tubers that can be eaten raw, or boiled, or roasted. While recent cultivars such as **'Prairie Gold'** have been selected, none appear to be markedly better than the already excellent older strains. The **Wood Sunflower** *Helianthus strumosus* also forms excellent edible underground tubers. The showy sunflower, Maximilian's sunflower, and the wood sunflower can all be propagated in a similar manner to Jerusalem artichokes.

Growing and Harvesting

As it is virtually impossible to find every tuber from a previous crop, it is advisable to allocate a piece of ground semi-permanently to the Jerusalem artichoke.

Ignore claims that this vegetable makes an excellent windbreak. It does, but not until late summer, and by then it is easily knocked over by the heavier winds of fall.

Rich sandy loams are ideally suited to the Jerusalem artichoke. It needs a minimum growing season of 125

Jerusalem artichoke, Helianthus tuberosus, spreads rapidly, making a forest of slender stems terminating in small yellow flowerheads.

days, moist soil conditions, and is tolerant of a wide climatic range although it will not succeed in the tropics. Heavy and clay soils will still grow an excellent crop of large tubers provided they are first well dug, then generous quantities of compost forked through. Likewise, poorer sandy soils will yield a good crop with the addition of plenty of rotted manure or compost. The tubers are planted as early as the soil can be worked in spring 4 in (10 cm) deep and 18–24 in (45–60 cm) apart in both directions. This produces a self supporting crop that will effectively smother most weeds. A light mulch applied once the plants are at least 12 in (30 cm) above the ground will retain soil moisture and suppress any weed problem. Alternatively, tubers are rowed out 18–24 in (45–60 cm) apart with a

Jerusalem artichoke, Helianthus tuberosus, flower.

spacing between rows of 36 in (90 cm). While whole tubers are usually planted, segments of tuber can be planted, but the smaller the piece the lower the yield per plant. Pests and diseases are rarely a problem.

As the tubers of the Jerusalem artichoke are not frost sensitive, once the top growth is finally stopped by a severe fall frost, the tops can be cut off and added to the compost bin, or cut up into lengths and used as a rough winter mulch over the bed. Jerusalem artichokes have a thin tender skin and do not store well for more than a couple of weeks. Instead supplies are dug as needed from the first frost of fall to spring. In areas with severe frost where the ground freezes hard, once the early fall harvests have been taken the bed is covered with a thick mulch of garden leaves, garden trash, and hay so that the soil temperature is mitigated. Tubers can then be dug through the winter. Dig under the clump with a garden fork and gently lever upward rather than using a hoe which often chops tubers. The crop can also be lifted in late fall and stored in damp sand. Connoiseurs of the Jerusalem artichoke often consider that the crop should never be eaten until it has been through a good frost.

Recommended Cultivars

In the United States in particular, a number of heirloom varieties exist which are often found in limited areas. The Seed Savers' Exchange in Iowa holds a collection of these heirloom varieties, many of the rarest having been originally collected and preserved by Will Bonsall of Farmington, Maine whose Scatterseed Project is famous for its seed and stock distribution. As tubers remain true to variety, a number of different varieties can be planted, although because of their rambling nature each variety shoud be well separated to prevent varieties trespassing.

'Dwarf Sunray' — Despite the name, this cultivar is only somewhat reduced in height at 5–7 ft (1.5–2.1 m), but it forms sturdy, bushy plants with an abundance of flowers that are excellent for picking. The tubers are crisp, tender, very thin skinned, and do not require peeling.

'French Mammoth White' — This standard older cultivar is quite commonly grown in England, the United States and Australia. It is very reliable, tall growing to 8–10 ft (2.5–3.0 m), late maturing, vigorous and a heavy yielder. The tubers are large and white skinned but have the disadvantage of being knobbly and therefore difficult to peel.

'Fuseau' — This is an old French cultivar which matures early in around 95 days. The plants are tall growing to 7–9 ft (2.1–2.7 m), yielding a good crop of very smooth, pale brown, elogated, tapered tubers approximately 4–5 in (10–12.5 cm) long and approximately $1^{1}/_{2}$ in (3–4 cm) in diameter.

'Golden Nugget' — This variety is notable for its carrot-like, long, thin tubers which are reddish-orange, smooth-skinned, and around 3 in (7. 5 cm) long and $^{1}/_{2}$–1 in (1.25–2.5 cm) wide.

Jicama

Pachyrhizus erosus syn. *P. tuberosus*   Zones 10–12

Native to Meso America where it has been grown since 8,000 BC, jicama or yam bean has swollen tubers which are crisp and sweet, somewhere between an apple and a potato. Jicama is now widely cultivated throughout the tropics and long, hot summer areas of the world, including California, Texas, Australia (Queensland and northern New South Wales), and New Zealand. The plump single tuber can weigh between 1–6 lbs (450 g–2.7 kg) and can reach diameters of 3–6 in (7.5–15 cm). The flesh is similar in crispness to the Chinese chestnut for which it can be substituted in any recipe. The tubers add crunch and sweetness to any salad, or salsa, or stir fry dish, and are also used cut into crunchy slices to serve with guacamole and other dips. It can also be cooked in the same manner as sweet potatoes, steamed, baked, mashed, or fried, or added to casseroles and stews. Also known as yam bean, *P. erosus* forms a vine with trifoliate leaves. The flowers are very attractive, in white or purple, and very fragrant, but both these and the seeds are highly toxic, and all parts of the plant are discarded except the tuber.

In Mexico, a common street food snack consists of slices of crisp jicama with a squeeze of lime juice and a sprinkle of chili powder, and jicama is one of the four elements used in the Festival of the Dead which is a celebration of the continuity of life held on 1 November each year. This is a time when it is believed that those who have passed on return to visit their families and should be entertained with flowers such as bright golden marigolds, and foods and decorations traditional to the festival.

The fibrous brown skin of the tuber must be completely stripped off before the tuber is used. A closely related species *P. tuberosus* is native to the

Jicama, Pachyrhizus erosus, *has swollen tubers that are crisp and sweet, with the taste of an apple and a potato.*

Amazon area and cultivated in the Equadorian Andes. It is also widely cultivated in the Carribean and China.

Growing and Harvesting

Jicama is propagated from seed or by small tubers retained from the previous crop. The seeds should be pre-soaked in warm water for 24 hours, placing the container somewhere safely away from children and animals, and also safely disposing of the soak water. In areas with long growing seasons, the seed are rowed out directly into well dug raised beds into which compost and wood ash or another source of potash has been incorporated. Seed should be sown 2 in (5 cm) deep and about 10–12 in (25–30 cm) apart. In areas with long growing seasons, but where frosts occur, seed can be started in pots indoors and can be planted out as soon as danger of frost has passed.

Once the plants are well established, a thick mulch of clean straw or sawdust is applied. As the mulch will temporarily deprive the crop of some nitrogen and the crop will continue to demand high levels of potash, many growers add a side dressing of wood ash or compost, or use a foliar feedant. The vines will grow unmanageably long if unattended, and are regularly pruned back to around 3–5 ft (1.0–1.5) m.

Very large tubers can only be obtained in areas where there are no frosts and the perennial vine can grow for 12–16 months. However, the tuber is delicious at all stages, and small tubers can be harvested at the end of a 4–5 month growing season, before frosts begin. Some growers pick off and dispose of the beans as they appear so as to direct the plant's energies into enlarging the tuber. The plant has few problems in terms of pests and diseases. The tubers will not survive underground during the winter months in places where frosts occur. They should be dusted but not washed before storage.

Lotus Root

Nelumbo nucifera   Zones 8–12

Lotus, or sacred lotus or pink lotus, is indigenous to tropical Australia, Asia including the Indian subcontinent, and the Middlle East, and is now cultivated world wide. The flowers are huge and exquisite, most commonly single and pink, but there are many very beautiful cultivars in white, shades of pink and deep crimson, with a number of double forms. A number of cultivars have also been selected for desirable eating qualities. The flowers have an exotic, sweet fragrance and, like the leaves which are flat and circular with undulate margins and tall stalks, are borne well above the water. The seedpods are shallow bowl shaped and the seed are shaken out through holes in the top. The fleshy underwater rhizomes are narrowly pinched at the nodes, and when cut through reveal large air spaces which assist the plant to respire in its underwater environment. The tuberous rhizomes are eaten boiled, pickled, preserved in syrup, stir fried, and in tempura. A starch is also extracted from them. The stamens are used as a fragrant flavoring for tea, the tender young leaves are used in salads and to wrap food parcels for steaming, and the seeds are eaten raw, popped like popcorn, roasted, boiled, candied, or used as a coffee substitute.

Lotus is the symbol of Buddha who is often depicted sitting within the centre of the pure, unsullied flower. Bunches of lotus are an offering made within Buddhist temples and the lotus was mentioned in many legends from India and Egypt. The sun god Atum was even said to have emerged from a lotus blossom.

Growing and Harvesting

If you have an ornamental pool or perhaps a pond or dam, lotus can be quite easily grown. Lotus are planted into large pots sunk in shallow water. The pots – traditionally very large glazed jars – are filled with a mixture of well rotted cow manure and good loam in the ratio of 3:1. The mixture needs to be cured underwater before planting can take place and the pots of soil should be left just under the water for two weeks.

Lotus are propagated from the tuberous underwater rhizomes in

Lotus Root, Nelumbo nucifera, *is cultivated worldwide and has tuberous rhizomes that are eaten boiled, pickled, preserved in syrup and stir fried.*

The flower of the Lotus has an exotic, sweet fragrance and, like the leaves which are flat and circular with undulate margins and tall stalks, are borne well above the water.

spring. Pieces of rhizome 2 or 3 segments long are planted in the pre-cured pots of mix with the upper end just emergent above water. As the plant begins to grow, the pots are moved into progressively deeper water. In the tropics, they may eventually be sunk 6$\frac{1}{2}$ ft (2 m) or more as lotus prefers a temperature range of 68–86° F (20–30°C). In milder climates the pots may be kept quite shallow to allow the underwater temperature to warm adequately.

The rhizomes are harvested year round in tropical climates once the plants are established. In cooler areas, plants will begin to initiate rhizomes in fall and can be harvested then, never taking more than 80% of the total rhizomes. If there is danger of the rhizomes freezing in winter, they should be lifted and stored in moist sand where frost will not affect them. All named cultivars must be propagated from rhizomes or they will not come true to type. Lotus seed has extraordinary longevity, in the order of hundreds of years, under the right conditions. Before planting, the seed should be filed at one end to create a hole in the seed coat while not damaging the flesh of the seed. The

seed are then placed in water in a warm, well lit position and the water changed daily. They can be transplanted to pots that are sunk level with the water of the pond once the seedlings are thriving.

Mashua

Tropaeolum tuberosum   Zones 8–10

Mashua, or anu, or tuberous nasturtium, is a species of nasturtium native to the High Andes where it may be grown in mixed fields with potatoes, oca, or ulluco and its tubers, leaves, and flowers are all edible. This is the dream crop for those with cool, wet summers, and the plants which are slightly frost tolerant will perform well even in poor soils, and are exceptionally high yielding. In addition to all these virtues the plant repels many insects, as well as nematodes, and many pathogens. Quite charming when grown as an ornamental plant, this species is a climber with abundant, long spurred, hooded, small flowers in red or yellow, and peltate, fan-shaped leaves.

The tubers are crisp and fairly hot, like radish roots when eaten raw. Once boiled, usually for about 10 minutes,

they lose their heat and are quite sweet to taste. They are elongated, sometimes club-shaped, and somewhat constricted at the nodes.

Growing and Harvesting

This crop responds to the incorporation into the soil of plenty of rotted leaves or compost which should be well dug through with a garden fork. Planting is carried out after the last frost date, the tubers being planted about 2 in (5 cm) below the soil. The vines can create a very attractive screen during the summer months.

The plants grow rapidly but are easily set back by drought, and regular watering is essential. Once the vines die back with frost, the tubers should be gently lifted and stored protected where they will not reach freezing point. Alternatively, a dense, thick mulch can be spread over the ground to protect the tubers. They can then be dug as required during the winter months. Like many High Andean crops, the formation of tubers is triggered by daylength, and most cultivars will not form tubers until the daylength drops below 12 hours.

Recommended Cultivars

'Ken Aslet' — This cultivar was developed in England, and was distributed and popularized in the United Kingdom by Ken Aslet, a former superintendent of the rock garden at the Royal Horticultural Society's grounds at Wisley. It has the advantage of being daylength neutral, meaning that the daylength does not need to drop below 12 hours before tuber formation is initiated. It forms large tubers that are longitudinally striped with red over a yellow background, and belongs to the *var. lineamaculatum*.

Oca

Oxalis tuberosa   Zones 7–10

This is a very common crop in the Andes region of South America, second only to the potato, and with its high altitude origins has always had the potential for being grown in cooler areas of the world where the potato has been proven to thrive. It will tolerate far harsher conditions than the potato, and will often give twice the yield of potatoes grown in the same field. Yet for a long time it was overlooked. New Zealand

In some South American communities the mashua is believed to act as a anti-aphrodisiac!

exports and markets oca under the name 'New Zealand yams'. There are indications that oca was originally introduced into New Zealand in 1869 from Chile.

The plants are semi-vining, with clover-like leaves and orange flowers, growing to 2–2½ ft (60–75 cm). The underground tubers are formed in a similar manner to potatoes and are usually elongated and about 4 in (10 cm) long, although some Andean varieties are round. Buds (or eyes) are distributed fairly evenly along the length of the tuber. The skin is shiny and tubers may be pink, white, yellow, orange or apricot. They are prepared by boiling for about 10 minutes, or are parboiled and then roasted, and have a flavor like a potato. Depending on the variety, there may be a slight sourness due to oxalic acid which has led to them being called 'potatoes that don't need sour cream'. In the Andes sour varieties are placed out in the sun for a few days to become sweet and floury textured. The tubers yield a quality starch for use in desserts and porridges which can be used successfully in place of wheat flour.

Growing and Harvesting
The limiting factor for oca cultivation is its requirement for a long growing season. The tubers only begin to form when the daylength falls below 9 hours, but top growth must be maintained at the same time. Areas with a prolonged fall are best for oca culture, but in less suitable areas plants can be induced to grow a good crop of tubers by extending the growing period with the use of a frame or polytunnel. Alternatively, oca can easily be grown by planting into large pots of compost enriched soil in spring. They can be taken outside once the danger of frosts have passed, and will grow lush tops. At the end of the season and before the first frosts of fall begin, the plants should be brought under cover to complete their growing cycle. Oca is grown in a similar manner to potatoes, hilling the plants up with soil during the growing season to encourage extra layers of tubers to form.

Plant breeders are now working to mitigate the limitations imposed by daylength requirement. With the help of breeding and selection, oca is poised to become one of the future major crops of cool temperate countries, in the way that the potato was poised to conquer the world in the 16th century. Over 1,000 accessions have been made in the last decade by universities in the region as a result of field collections in Peru, Ecuador, and Bolivia, and the

Oca, Oxalis tuberosa, has a shiny skin and the tubers may be pink, white yellow or orange .

improved yields for farmers. Tubers are stored for long keeping at 35–37° F (1–2° C), approximately that of the domestic refrigerator, at 90–100% humidity.

Potato

Solanum tuberosum   Zones 6–11

It used to be said that there was little point in growing your own potatoes as the potato is generally the easiest and cheapest of vegetables to buy.

But all argument about the value of potato growing disappeared when the heirloom varieties, with their remarkable range of flavors, were rediscovered. We became potato connoiseurs. Different varieties were suited to different uses and as consumers and gardeners we wanted that choice. And it is easy and satisfying to grow several little patches of favorite varieties, to be able to dig tender new season potatoes from your garden, rush them to a pot on the stove, add garden fresh herbs and sweet butter. Indeed, it is one of the world's great culinary pleasures.

huge genetic diversity represented by this collection should ensure some wonderful varieties to come from breeding programs. Production rates are already 39–49 tons (40–50 tonnes) per $2^1/_2$ acres (1 hectare), easily comparable with and often better than the best potato yields.

Oca has no notable diseases. The major pest is the weevil, and integrated control through cultivation practises, the use of resistant varieties, biological control, and good post harvest management has led to greatly

Potato, Solanum tuberosum, *comes in a variety of shapes, colors, sizes and flavors. Most of its nutrients are located in the thin layer immediately below the skin.*

Potato varieties are divided for culinary purposes according to their starch content. Those with a high starch content are floury in texture, and are used for baking, frying, and mashing. The other group of potatoes tend to have a waxy texture, and hold together well when boiled. These are ideal for potato salads, for gratin dishes, and for any recipe in which you want the potato to hold together after cooking. With their high water content they are a poor choice for frying as they will never crisp satisfactorily.

Potatoes are a good source of vitamins B and C, as well as minerals such as potassium and these nutrients are almost entirely located in the thin layer immediately below the skin. For this reason, cleaned potatoes should be steamed or boiled in their jackets, or baked, roasted or chipped with skin on. The flavor is also greatly enhanced.

South America, the home of the potato, literally holds thousands of varieties. Every market throughout the continent holds its own treasure chest of unique cultivars in an unbelievable variety of shapes, colors, sizes, and flavors. The heirloom varieties that emerged into production in the 1990s were perfectly suited to new food fashions and gained instant acceptance with chefs and gourmets. The possibilities are endless. Flesh colors available include rich rose, blossom pink, blue, purple, golden yellow, lemon, rich cream and white, as well as marbled colors such as lemon and blue, with a contrasting or matching skin color. The shapes range from long, slender fingerlings to blocky oblong, rounded, oval and pear shapes. Some are tiny at harvest, others weigh two pounds or more. The differences in flavor are as much a revelation as the difference in colors.

Potatoes are native to the cool tropical high Andean regions of Bolivia, Peru and Ecuador, and they were very easily adapted to many areas. They were introduced into Europe by the Spanish, and Sir Walter Raleigh has been credited with introducing the potato into Ireland.

Elsewhere in Europe, the potato had an ill-founded reputation as an aphrodisiac, or was feared as a poison. The latter was not entirely without foundation; the leaves of potatoes contain a poisonous alkaloid as does the outer greened skin of tubers exposed to the light.

Allowing potatoes to sprout is commonly called 'greensprouting' or 'chitting'.

Growing and Harvesting

Ideally, certified virus free seed potatoes are used to plant a crop. Organic certified potato seed of some cultivars are also available. Shop bought potatoes, or potatoes you have saved from strong, healthy plants in your own garden, are usually quite low risk for use as a starter for a home crop. As this crop is intended for your own pleasure, choose a few tubers of several varieties rather than a lot of one cultivar.

Place undamaged tubers of your chosen varieties in a well lit, well ventilated place, spread out in a single layer. The eyes will be concentrated toward one end of the potato. Arrange the potatoes eye-side upward. The potatoes will turn a bright green and after four to five weeks will begin to sprout, forming stubby shoots from the eyes. Any tubers that sprout thin, spindly, atypical shoots are likely to be carrying virus and should be discarded. Large tubers can be cut into a few pieces 1–2 hours before planting, each with one strong eye shoot. The cut surface should be dry before planting. Whole tubers rather than pieces are recommended for planting in poorer soils.

Prepare the ground before planting by digging the soil over to a spade depth and incorporating generous quantities of compost. The site should be well drained or the tubers will rot. Do not add lime to the soil. Rake the ground over, then open up shallow trenches about 6 in (15 cm) wide and 8 in (20 cm) deep. The rows need to be approximately 3 ft (90 cm) apart. Plant the sprouted tubers with the sprout side upward and about 12 in (30 cm) apart, then cover with soil. While it is not essential, some growers create slightly deeper trenches and line them with about 2 in (5 cm) depth of hay or other clean dry mulch which can help keep tubers clean and less prone to rotting. A side dressing of a nitrogen rich organic fertilizer such as

blood and bone or a seaweed extract applied once or twice during the growing period at the advised rate helps growth to carry on unchecked. Make sure solid fertilizers are not in direct contact with the tubers.

Tubers should be planted about two weeks before the last frost date for your area so that they emerge into a frost free environment. To gain a head start in cold districts, a small early crop can be grown under cloches or in a polytunnel which will provide harvests in time for summer salads.

Once the plants emerge above the ground, hill the soil up around them leaving the uppermost 3–5 in (7.5–12.5 cm) of shoot above ground. This has the effect of promoting tuber growth; it also improves growing conditions, prevents potatoes greening from sun exposure, and as a bonus suppresses weed growth. Hilling up is carried out 2 or 3 times in the growing period. A mulch of clean straw applied around the fully grown plants at flowering time helps to hold moisture in the ground during hot weather, and to exclude light.

Early in the season, potato tubers are much sweeter than later when most of the sugars have been converted to starches. Once the flowers have bloomed, the tiny early formed potatoes can be a bonus crop with a flavor that is irresistible. Carefully dig into the side of the

To gain a head start in planting in cold districts, a small crop of potatoes can be grown in a polytunnel.

Once the flowers have bloomed, the tiny early formed potatoes, Solanum tuberosum, *can be a bonus crop.*

potato hill, harvest enough for an early meal, and replace the soil. These early sugary potatoes are one of the delights of growing your own food, and taste quite different to store bought potatoes.

Mature crops are ready to dig once the stems of the potato vines have yellowed and died back for a couple of weeks. The skins on the tubers will by then have firmed and it is easier to harvest without damage. Choose a sunny, dry day for harvesting, and lift the crop gently with a garden fork to minimize damage to the tubers. Allow the harvest to sit on the ground for a few hours to dry the tubers. Sort out any damaged, scabbed or blemished specimens. These are for immediate use. Transfer the remainder of the crop to a dark, cool, dry, vermin proof area for storage. Bins, hessian bags, or

If space is at a premium, a good crop of potatoes can be grown inside a pile of old tyres.

wooden crates are ideal for storage. Potatoes tubers are susceptible to frost and it is important that the storage area does not drop to freezing point. Always choose a new site to grow potatoes each year so that diseases do not build up in the soil.

Potatoes have parachute-shaped flowers in pink, lavender, purple or white, borne in clusters. Even if you have only a tiny sunny plot filled mainly with flowers, you can grow potatoes and they will not look out of place.

If space is at a premium, a good crop of potatoes can be grown in inside a pile of old tyres, or in an area about 1 yard (1 meter) square walled by straw bales. Fill the initial space with a mixture of compost and soil, and plant 1–2 tubers which have already formed shoots. As the plants grow, add extra layers of tyres or extra rows of hay bales, and continue to fill in with soil compost mix, leaving the uppermost 3 in (7. 5 cm) of plant above the soil. With this technique, an amazing harvest can be achieved as tier after tier of potato tubers are formed. To harvest, simply dismantle the pile of tyres or hay bales.

Potatoes are also a good crop for container growing. Choose large

Scabs will usually affect the skin and not the flesh of the potato. Several varieties of potato are scab resistant.

containers with adequate drainage holes. Even an inverted plastic bin with the base cut out will work well. Potatoes need a sunny, warm, protected place to grow, but not a hot position. Soil in pots will heat more rapidly than in the ground. Half fill the containers, plant one or two chitted potatoes, and progressively add more soil and compost mix as the plant grows.

Another useful organic technique which results in easy-to-find, clean, well-shaped potatoes is to grow potatoes on hay. Place the green sprouted seed potatoes on the surface of the soil and shake a loose layer of hay over them to a depth of 8–10 in (20–25 cm). As the potato plants emerge, continue to hill up with additional layers of mulch. It is vital to maintain a good depth of mulch in order to exclude light from the developing tubers or they will green and be useless for eating. To harvest, simply pull back the mulch whenever potatoes are on the menu. Sadly it is almost as easy for rodents and other pests to harvest so that the technique is not suitable for every garden. To provide nitrogen for spring potato crops, some gardeners place deep rows of compostable material on the

ground in fall. The nitrogen rich material is largely rotted down by spring, and the seed potatoes are rowed out on top, then covered in a deep bed of fresh hay.

Potatoes are an excellent crop for improving soil tilth for a following crop. Early potato crops will be finished by mid-summer and a leafy crop makes an ideal follow-up to ensure no wasted space in the garden. In some areas, farmers use potatoes as a crop for clearing weedy land. Weeds are slashed and the green shooted potato seed rowed out. Instead of hilling up to exclude light however, the whole row is covered with black polythene. When the plants push through and begin to lift the plastic, a cross is slashed in the plastic above each plant to allow it to emerge. The weeds are suppressed by the black polythene, and the crop is harvested by rolling back the polythene. This is an easily adopted technique to clean a weedy patch in the vegetable garden.

Water the soil regularly, particularly at flowering time when the tubers are just beginning to swell. Scab, a skin blemish affecting sections of the potato skin causing it to crack and discolor, is prevented by maintaining an even soil moisture. Varieties bred to be scab resistant include 'Sebago', early maturing 'Kennebec', 'Bison', 'Chieftain', 'Norgold Russet', 'Arran Pilot', 'Cherokee', and 'Superior'. A crop of marigolds *Tagetes* grown and then dug under in the season before a crop of potatoes is grown will deter possible nematode damage to the crop. Dusting seed potatoes with sulphur before planting reduces the possiblity of bacterial rot.

In areas where the purple-black and cream striped Colorado beetle is a problem, weekly spraying with insecticidal soap will help to keep them at bay. Slugs can be a problem, and beer traps should be used if slug damage is noticed. Greenfly can be dealt with by the use of derris dust, but care should be taken. It is a fish poison and has recently been implicated in neurological disorders in laboratory rats.

The potato blight, infamous for causing the Irish potato famine in the mid-1840s and for the emigration of 3 million Irish to the United States, Australia and other countries, is caused by a fungus *Phytophthora infestans*. Late blight causes rotting of the tubers and apart from ensuring good air movement and sunlight exposure for the crop, in areas where

the disease is a problem, selection of blight resistant varieties is the best insurance. Areas with warm, wet summers are more prone to the disease which appears as chocolate to black, rapidly growing blotches on the leaves, progressing to the stems and reducing the plant to a rotted mess.

The varieties 'Kennebec', 'Essex', 'Bison', 'Cherokee', 'Estima', 'Pink Pearl', 'Spunta' and 'Maris Peer' all have good blight resistance. Early crops are rarely affected.

Smokers should always wash their hands before entering the potato patch. Tobacco and potato are in the same family and smokers often have tobacco viruses on their hands that will transmit to potatoes. Any potatoes that appear spindly or abnormally wilted or generally sick should be removed and burned well away from the crop.

Seed Saving Notes

Potatoes set what are called seedballs after flowering. These are formed commonly in warmer areas but less so in cool. The ripe seed will not grow true to type. If you are growing more than one variety together, cross pollination between varieties may also have happened. A wonderful new variety might lie hidden in those seedballs. The famous American plant breeder Luther Burbank founded his commercial success on a single seedball of 'Early Rose'. It yielded one of the most important potato varieties of all time, the 'Russet Burbank' (1873), also known as the 'Idaho Potato'. Plant seed in spring, and row out the seedlings when they are sturdy plants about 6 in (15 cm) tall. There may be an exceptional performer among your seedlings. It is a long shot, but a fascinating exercize.

If you are saving your own seed potatoes, store them in brown paper bags labelled with variety and date. Store them in a cool, dark place that will not reach freezing point.

A fridge full of heirloom potatoes at the Seed Savers Exchange, Iowa, USA.

Recommended Cultivars

There are many hundreds of cultivars of potatoes available around the world and those listed here are but a tiny sample of the incredible range of gourmet potatoes awaiting your discovery. Cultivars are divided into early season types (first earlies), mid-season types (second earlies), and late season types (main crop). The length of the growing season for each type varies considerably according to climate. Choose a few cultivars for each of the three harvest periods.

Like many vegetatively propagated plants, over long periods of time potatoes accumulate viruses. Tissue culture techniques have offered the opportunity to 'clean up' some of the greatest old varieties, and virus free material is being released so that we can grow some of the greatest potatoes of the past in all their glory. A very important non-governmental contributor to this program is the Seed Savers Exchange in Iowa, where hundreds of heirloom varieties are now being maintained in a tissue culture bank and progressively freed of viruses.

Our current potatoes are derived almost exclusively from one species. There are 8 other cultivated species of potatoes grown in the Andes that await the discovery of the rest of the world.

'All-Blue' — A very pretty variety of American origin with deep blue skin and lavender-blue flesh. It is high yielding, with an outstanding flavor when baked or boiled, and has good keeping abilities. *Mid-season variety.*

'Arran Pilot' — This 1931 United Kingdom variety is noted for its ease of growing, drought and disease resistance, and its very well flavored, white skinned, white waxy fleshed tubers. Early season variety. The Scottish variety **'Arran Victory'** syn. Irish Blues (1918), is also coming back into fashion for its superb flavor and floury texture. *Late season variety.*

'Bintje' syn. Yellow Finnish Bintje — This highly reliable 1911 Dutch variety is very high yielding, producing small to medium oval tubers with a yellow skin and finely textured waxy yellow flesh. It is superb baked or boiled, with a distinctive

Heritage potatoes, including 'Blue Congo', 'Pink Fir Apple', 'Blue Bismark' and 'Kipfler'.

The blue skin of the 'Edzell Blue' potato fades to white when cooked. Good for mashing but too small for baking.

excellent flavor. It is grown extensively around the world. *Late season variety.*

'Bison' — Bred for resistance to late blight and scab, this variety from North Dakota is excellent for baking, full of flavor, and has red skinned, medium sized, uniform, round tubers with pale yellow flesh. *Early season variety.*

'Blossom' — Not only excellent for baking, this is an irresistibly pretty variety producing masses of large, beautiful, pink blossoms that would not be at all out of place in the flower garden. The tubers are almost as attractive, oblong and tapered, with a rich pink skin and exquisite blossom pink flesh. *Late season variety.*

'Blue Victor' — This hardy, very pro-ductive, vigorous American heir-loom is still a favorite with its blocky, large tubers which are lavender colored sometimes marbled white, with white flesh of very good flavor. It has few disease or pest problems and reliably tolerates cool nights during the growing period. *A late season cultivar.*

'Candy Stripe' — A gourmet potato which has delightful flavor whether fried, baked, or boiled. This Californian variety produces medium sized, oval tubers which are white striped with red, with fine textured white flesh. *Mid-season cultivar.*

'Chieftain' — This is the most popular red skinned cultivar for Canadian commercial growers, bred in 1968 in Iowa, with oblong tubers that have smooth red skin and white flesh. It is productive and scab resistant. *Late season cultivar.*

'Congo' — This cultivar, available in Australia and the United States, has beautiful purplish foliage, purple flowers, and long, thin, somewhat knobbly, intensely purple–skinned tubers with purple flesh used for salads and mashing, retaining its color. *Late season cultivar.*

'Cow Horn' — This very popular New Hampshire heirloom has curved fingerling tubers which are purple skinned and purple fleshed. It is an excellent keeper and prized as a superb salad potato, retaining its vivid color when cooked. *Late season cultivar.*

'Desirée' — This is the most popular mainline crop in Europe and is the most popular potato cultivar in the world. It is a heavy yielding, disease resistant, all purpose, well flavored Dutch cultivar producing large, smooth tubers with rose pink skins and cream flesh. *Mid-to late season cultivar.*

'Duke of York' — This popular lemon skinned, lemon fleshed cultivar for home growers originated in Aberdeenshire in 1891. It is prized for its fine, firm texture and outstanding sweet, intense potato flavor, finding use for boiling, baking, and roasting. *Early season cultivar.* **'Duke of York Red'** has a red skin and lemon flesh, and is used for boiling and salad variety. *Late season cultivar.*

'Early Rose' — An 1857 Vermont favorite, known for its excellent flavor and its long, pretty, salmon pink tubers with white flesh streaked with pink. It is a short keeper, but is high yielding. *Medium to late season cultivar.*

'Early Ohio' — Very easy to grow and resistant to disease and pests, this pre-1885 heirloom is still treasured by older gardeners. It forms rounded-oblong tubers with pinkish-tan skin and white flesh, and is an excellent tasting all-rounder for chips, baking, or boiling, with very good flavor. *Mid- to late season cultivar.*

'Edgecote Purple' — Renowned for its exceptional flavor, this English cultivar has purple skinned tubers with yellow flesh. *Mid-season cultivar.*

'Edzell Blue' — This pre-World War I Scottish variety with its deep blue skin and clean white, floury textured, flavorful flesh makes delicious soups and creamed potatoes.

'Epicure' — A traditional Ayrshire variety introduced in 1897 and popular today in Scotland and Canada, Epicure is exceptionally hardy and highly productive, with round, white fleshed tubers of outstanding flavor when boiled or baked. *Early season cultivar.*

'Garnet Chile' — This famous, vigorous, high-yielding old cultivar bred in New York in 1853 has delicious flavor and a floury texture when cooked. The tubers are large, rounded to oblong, long keeping, with garnet colored skin and white flesh. *Late season cultivar.*

'German Butterball' — This high yielding cultivar comes naturally buttery flavored, with large, uniform, oblong tubers that are smooth, gold skinned, gold fleshed, and of exceptional flavor and quality for steaming and boiling. *Late season cultivar.*

'Gladstone' — This old English cultivar is an excellent high starch variety suitable for baking and making fluffy mashed potatoes. It has marbled red and yellow skin. *Mid-season cultivar.*

'Golden Wonder' — This is sometimes rated the finest flavored of all British cultivars and produces russet skinned fingerling tubers with golden flesh. It is medium yielding but very reliable. *A late season cultivar.*

'Green Mountain' — Introduced c. 1885, this is a favorite old Vermont cultivar. Yielding high starch, the blocky tubers with light brown skins and pure white flesh, are perfect for chips, potato pancakes, and gratin dishes. It grows best on sandy soils in cool climates. *Late season cultivar.*

'Irish Cobbler' — This widely available old cultivar has a sweet nutty flavor. It performs well on heavy soils and is still widely grown for its very reliable heavy yields. It produces medium to large oblong, white fleshed, brown skinned tubers excellent for boiling, mashing, and baking. *Early season cultivar.*

'Katahdin' — This very fine 1932 variety is widely available in the United States, Australasia, and Canada. The tubers are flattened-elliptical and shallow-eyed, with smooth white skin and flesh, ideal for boiling. *Mid-to late season cultivar.*

'Kerr's Pink' — Raised in 1907 in Scotland, this cultivar has rounded,

'Pink Fir Apple' has a sweet nutty flavor. It has knobbly elongated tuber that have a waxy lemon flesh.

The 'Purple Peruvian' potato has a medium starch content so is a good all purpose potato.

pink skinned tubers and cream, floury flesh when cooked. It is used for baking, roasting, mashed potatoes, and boiling. *Mid-to late season cultivar.*

'Maris Peer' — Released in the United Kingdom in 1962, this is a popular variety for chips, boiling, salads, and after maturing is considered ideal for wedges. The tubers are oval, cream skinned and cream fleshed. *Mid-season variety.*

'Maris Piper' — This 1964 British cultivar is one of the most popular potatoes in the United Kingdom particularly for that much loved dish, fish and chips. The tubers are oval, with cream skin and cream flesh. *Mid-season cultivar.*

'Pink Fir Apple' syn. 'Tannenzapfen' — This is one of the finest of all salad cultivars. It originated in France c. 1850, and has a sweet nutty flavor. It is highly productive with knobbly elongated tubers that have a waxy lemon flesh. It is a good keeper, and is available in Australia, France, the United Kingdom, and the United States. *Late season cultivar.*

'Pink Pearl' — As pretty as it sounds and becoming increasingly popular with home growers, the tubers of this blight resistant cultivar are oval, pink skinned with shallow eyes; they keep well, cook very well and taste excellent. *Late season cultivar.*

'Purple Peruvian' — This is a very productive South American fingerling with a very rich, intense purple skin and equally dark, fine grained flesh which retains its color when cooked, and has delicious flavor. It has excellent storage qualities, and is vigorous and disease resistant. *Late season cultivar.*

'Ratte' syn. 'Asparagus Potato', 'Quenelle de Lyon', 'Corne de Mouton', and 'Princes' — This popular French cultivar from 1872 has waxy textured, golden flesh much prized for its use in salads. *Late season cultivar.*

'Red Gold' — This is an excellent all rounder, as delicious boiled or steamed as it is fried. The medium sized tubers are light red with yellow flesh. This is a very productive cultivar with disease resistance. *Mid-season cultivar.*

'Red Sangre' — This is a delicious cultivar for mashed potatoes, with red skin and white flesh, producing quantities of small tubers. It is also a favorite with chefs when dug as small new season potatoes. *Early season cultivar.*

'Skerry Blue' — An old variety from c. 1846, this is a favorite of home gardeners in the United Kingdom on account of its blight resistance and superb flavor. The long-oval tubers are violet colored with rich purple flesh mottled with cream-white. *Mid-to late season.*

'Spunta' — This excellent Dutch all-rounder has become very popular in many parts of the world. The tubers are medium to large, long, sometimes kidney shaped, with pale yellow skin and pale gold flesh. *Mid-season variety.*

'Russet Burbank' syn. 'Netted Gem', 'Idaho Potato' — This 1873 American cultivar is one of the world's most important potatoes. It forms large, russet-skinned, white fleshed potatoes with a richly nutty flavor, ideal for baking and for chips. It needs a cooler climate, reliable soil moisture, and a sandy loam to perform at its best. *Late season cultivar.*

'Russet Nugget' — A superb russet-skinned cultivar that is equally good as a new season variety or as a keeper. *Late season cultivar.*

'Russian Banana' — This is an ideal heirloom cultivar for the Pacific North West, United States, thought to have been introduced by early settlers from the Baltic states. It is a very disease resistant, long keeping, highly productive cultivar with yellow skinned, yellow fleshed fingerling tubers excellent for salads. *Late season cultivar.*

'Yukon Gold' — This long-keeping, productive, and much applauded Canadian cultivar has large rounded tubers, yellowish skin with shallow pink eyes, and rich, finely textured, delicious yellow flesh. *Early season cultivar.*

Sweet Potato

Ipomoea batatas   Zones 9–12

The sweet potato, or kumara, is tropical to sub-tropical in origin. It flourishes in warm, humid climates where the true potato fails to grow, and serves similar culinary purposes. It is a member of the *Convolvulus* family and was grown in various forms in Meso and South America. The tubers were carried around the world, to the islands of the South Pacific, India, Sri Lanka, Egypt, New Guinea, New Zealand, China (where it reputedly reached at the end of the16th century), and Japan. It is probable that it was grown in Polynesia by the mid-13th century and had reached New Zealand by the 14th century. Sir Joseph Banks recorded the sweet potato as an item in the Maori diet when Captain Cook made landfall on the North Island in 1769. It reached southern Europe by the early 16th century, before the introduction of the true potato. The sweet potato is thought to have been domesticated from *I. trifida* which is native from Mexico south to Venezuela.

Sweet Potatoes, Ipomoea batatas, flourish in warm, humid climates where the true potato fails to grow. There are a huge number of varieties developed for different cooking purposes.

Like the potato, there are a huge number of varieties developed for different cooking purposes around the world. Some are very high in starches, ideal for crisp chips of all kinds, and for roasting and candying, having a characteristic sweet nutty flavor; others are ideal for mashing, for soups, and for stews. The two groups are sometimes refered to as 'dry fleshed' and 'moist fleshed', refering to starch levels. They also come in a remarkable variety of shapes and colors. Local markets in many parts of the tropics and sub-tropics are stocked with varieties never seen in supermarkets.

The word *batata* was the name given to the sweet potato by the Taino Indians of the Greater Antilles and the Bahamas. The same name was given by the Spanish to the Andean tuber, and by corruption of batata they both became known as 'potato', the sweeter tropical tuber later becoming distinguished as 'sweet potato'. To add to early confusions, the yam (which belongs to the genus *Dioscorea*) also became known as sweet potato in some places, for instance in Louisiana.

Sweet potato grows as a trailing vine and may produce lilac or white morning glory-like flowers in hot, long summer areas. Some semi-trailing or almost bush types have been developed which are particularly useful for those with limited garden space. Trailing varieties root down into the soil in a similar manner to squash vines, often forming additional tubers wherever they root. The young tips of the vines are chopped and steamed or cooked in similar ways to spinach. The whole plant is very handsome with leaves that are shiny and three or five lobed, green, or suffused purple, or in a few instances are a handsome black-purple. Plants can be grown in large pots in warmer areas as a patio or decorative plant for the summer months before harvesting. A few pots are well worth growing in a greenhouse in cooler climate areas.

Growing and Harvesting

Under true tropical conditions there is no stopping the sweet potato. Once tubers begin to shoot, they can be planted sprout side up in the soil and a new plant rapidly develops. Sometimes the sprouted tuber is split lengthwise, placed cut side down in the soil, and covered. Plants grow all year round in frost free conditions and tip cuttings from vines can be

The running vines of sweet potato should be gently lifted and moved around during the growing season to prevent them putting down roots.

struck directly where they are intended to grow, burying the cuttings about halfway and watering well and regularly. Particularly in rich volcanic soils and with adequate watering, nothing more is required for an abundant crop in due course.

But gardeners outside the tropics can use a few additional steps to achieve a good harvest. In these areas, sweet potatoes are grown from rooted shoot cuttings which in some places are available from suppliers. But it is easy to grow your own plants and this allows you to raise many varieties that might never be offered by mail order suppliers and nurseries. Prop the sweet potato eye side upward in a warm, sunny place like a window sill. They will sprout, and when the shoots (sometimes called slips or draws) are about 6 in (15 cm) long they are gently twisted off and planted in a seed raising mixture in a protected, warm, and very regularly watered area or, in cooler climates, in a heated frame. Some gardeners sprout sweet potatoes in a container half filled with water, and also root the resulting cuttings in a container partially filled with water. This technique is usually successful, although occasionally rotting may occur with some varieties.

Other gardeners partially bury the tubers in moist sand to sprout in a warm, well lit place. Once the cuttings or slips have developed a cluster of small roots and are about 6–8 in (15–20 cm) with fully developed leaves, they are ready to be planted. Discard any rotted, or small, or very spindly rooted slips.

Rooted cuttings should not be planted until the soil has fully warmed after winter. The sweet potato prefers a loose, well drained, slightly acidic soil. Dig the soil over, incorporate a moderate amount of compost (they are more productive in soil which is not too rich) or plant into a soil that was well composted for a previous crop. Make a raised ridge or bed about 6–8 in (15–20 cm) high to provide good drainage and a warmer soil. Alternatively, create a number of separate hills for planting. Hills should be about 39 in (1 m) away from each other. If planting into raised beds, the rooted cuttings should be spaced 18–20 in (45–50 cm) apart. Rows should be 3–4 ft (900–1,200 cm) apart.

Alternatively, if planting in hills, use one rooted slip to each hill. Water well after planting and maintain a regular watering program. Reduce

Sweet Potato, Ipomoea
batatas, *can be dug as
soon as they have
reached a useful size.*

watering toward the end of the growing season at the end of summer to prevent cracking of the tubers. The running vines should be gently lifted and moved around during the growing season to prevent them putting roots down as otherwise the plants can grow too vigorously. In cool climates, the soil can be warmed to increase the growth rate of the plants by covering the raised ridges with black polythene, anchoring the sides with soil. Slits are cut into the polythene and the rooted slips planted through the slits. Few varieties of sweet potato compete at all well with weeds, and this method also has the bonus of controlling weeds.

Harvesting of mature tubers begins when the vines have turned yellow and before any frosts. In cooler areas, the plants are left in the ground to maximize the growing season until the first frost which will blacken the vines. The tubers are immediately lifted that day with a garden fork, using considerable care because the skin is still very tender, and bruised areas are prone to rot. Small or damaged tubers can be used immediately, but large tubers intended for winter use need to be cured. Tubers are left to dry in the sun if possible. Without treatment, the tubers have a useful life of about 10–20 days, and

to prolong their lives the tubers are stored in boxes of moist sand.

Like true potatoes, sweet potatoes can be dug at any time once they have reached a useful size. By mid-summer, tubers should be sufficiently large for use and are known as first sweets, the equivalent of first early potatoes. Sweet potatoes are as well regarded by wild animals as they are by humans, and temporary fencing around the sweet potato site is often advisable.

Recommended Cultivars

There are hundreds of sweet potato cultivars throughout the warm climate areas of the world. Few are available through nurseries (a small number can be obtained through mail order specialists), but a good collection can soon be accumulated by exchanges with local gardeners and farmers, and visits to markets and even supermarkets.

'**All Gold**' — An exceptionally good, early maturing and reliable vining cultivar that is grown in the South and Midwest of the United States, New Zealand, and Australia. It has golden-orange skin and excellent moist, sweet, fine-textured, orange-gold flesh with rich flavor. It is heavy yielding, a good keeper, disease resistant, and has high levels of vitamins A and C..

'Beauregard' — This is an American cultivar with sweet, moist, orange flesh and thin skin.

'Boniato' syn. Cuban Sweet Potato — This cultivar produces short, plump tubers with a dull reddish skin, and white flesh that is dry with a nutty flavor. It bakes and makes chips to perfection.

'Centennial' — This is one of the standard, moist fleshed, early cultivars for home gardeners and also market gardeners in the American South. It is reliable even on heavy soils, producing quantities of small tubers ideal for baking.

'Copperskin' syn. Porto Rico Copperskin, 'Copperskin Running Porto Rico' — This is a highly productive, very vigorous cultivar with many runners and smooth, copper colored tubers containing moist orange flesh. This is a long term favorite of the American South and Australia. There is a bush form producing similar tubers, known as **'Bush Porto Rico'** syn. Vineless Porto Rico and Red Yam, ideal for baking, and an old favorite, forming short runners and maturing about three weeks earlier.

'Georgia Jet' — This is an exceptionally early cultivar that performs well in the northern states of the United States. It has high productivity but is not a good keeper. The tubers are rose colored with moist orange flesh. Heavy mulching to maintain even soil moisture and prevent cracking is necessary. The foliage is handsome, dark red, and ornamental.

'Japanese' — This cultivar is widely distributed. The vines are extensive with heart–shaped leaves, and the tubers are large with white skin and white flesh. It is a high starch variety, excellent for frying and roasting, as well as for boiling.

'Nancy Hall' syn. Yellow Yam A favorite old cultivar, this is a long season runner type, moderately productive

of cream colored tubers with dry, light yellow flesh.

'Old Kentucky' — This very good keeping, late maturing cultivar has large white tubers and fine textured, sweet, cream flesh.

'Red-skinned Kumara' — This superb culinary variety is ancient in origin and was grown in New Zealand long before European occupation. The tubers are plump and long with deep red skin and fine textured white flesh. High in starch, it makes superb chips. The flavor is nutty.

'Tokatoka Gold' — This is a popular cultivar in New Zealand, favored for making excellent potato crisps. It is very plump, almost spherical with pale golden skin and pale golden flesh. It is also known there as the Golden kumara and was bred in Northland in the 1950s.

'White Maltese' — This is a reliable standard for Australian market growers in the south, producing good yields of dry white fleshed, white skinned tubers.

'White Yam' syn. Southern Queen, White Triumph, Poplar Root, and White Bunch — This is a sweet potato and not a true yam. It is one of the oldest

A favorite Chinese Sweet Potato cultivar.

cultivars in the United States and forms a semi-bush with short runners. The tubers are white skinned and white fleshed.

'Yellow Jersey' — A popular old cultivar for the Middle Atlantic states and the North East of the United States. An heirloom variety first recorded prior to 1780, it is very productive with dark green, ivy-like foliage, and yellow skinned, yellow fleshed tubers which are potato-like in flavor when cooked.

Taro

Colocasia esculenta   Zones 10–12

The plant of taro, or dasheen, or eddoe, somewhat resembles that of the arum lily (it was once classified botanically as *Arum colocasia*) with large, up to 3 ft (90 cm) long, inverted heart-shaped, dark green to purple-green, peltate leaves. It forms a large central tuberous root underground (strictly speaking a corm) with numerous smaller lateral tubers described as cormels

It is believed to have originated in wet areas of the Indian sub-continent. Several parts of the plant are eaten. The tuber is very high in starch and is prepared in any way that the true potato is prepared. The tubers have a rough, brown skin and are white, pale green, purple, or grey fleshed. They are boiled, sliced and fried to make nutty tasting taro chips, steamed, and also included in stews and soups. Savory puddings are prepared from taro tubers, and a much loved food called *poi* in Hawaii and *poe* in Tahiti, is created from mixing the cooked, peeled, pounded flesh with a little water. This is one of the world's most healthy starches and *poi* has a faintly tangy taste. In Cuba, delicious taro fritters flavored with garlic and called malanga are very popular. Classic Carribean dishes incorporating taro include 'Run Down', a dish of what are locally called 'ground provisions' (root vegetables), simmered with mind blowing Scotch bonnet chilies, garlic, and onions in seasoned coconut milk to which is added salt meat or salt fish which has been soaked to remove excess salt. 'Pepperpot Soup' which is a native Jamaican and West African fusion dish is created from ground provisions, coconut milk, chilies, callaloo, scallions and fish.

The young unfolding leaves are also eaten, tasting rather like a slightly bitter spinach; they are known in the Carribean as 'Callaloo'. Callaloo soup is a spicy and very popular dish throughout the Caribbean with every island having its own variation; callaloo with crab is a favorite in Trinidad, Guadeloupe and Martinique. The leaves are also used as an edible wrapper for food such as fish which is to be steamed. A dish universal to the Pacific and South East Asia under various guises is *luau* or, under its Tahitian name *fafa*, a creamy concoction of taro leaves and fish or chicken steamed in coconut milk. A related dish, *laulau*, is prepared with pork and chopped young taro leaves wrapped in more taro leaves and steamed. Callaloo fritters are a popular street and festival food. The leaves used must always be young.

A taro crop on Moorea Island, Tahiti.

All parts of the taro plant, including the leaves, contain poisonous calcium oxalate crystals. This can be a severe irritant. The oxalate crystals are considerably reduced by cooking and no part of taro should ever be eaten uncooked. Stems and leaves should be boiled before use in recipes. The stems are popular in Vietnam in sour soups. The cooked leaves are a valuable source of vitamin A. Selected cultivars are available and many have been selected for lower levels of calcium oxalate but must still be boiled to be safe.

Taro goes by a number of names around the world including dasheen, malanga, eddo, edo, tannia, cocoyam (a name also applied to *Xanthosoma* species which are closely related), and also elephant's ear. The closely related giant taro *Alocasia macrorrhiza* originated in Sri Lanka and is altogether larger with upright growth and a taro-like, edible, starchy root. Another relative originating from Indonesia, the giant swamp taro *Cyrtosperma chamissonis*, is destined to become particularly valuable in many coastal and island communities as global warming causes coastal inundation and salination of coastal groundwater supplies. It is tolerant of brackish water, and forms very large tubers. It is already an invaluable plant for the Gilbert Islanders.

For Polynesians, taro is far more than a vegetable. It is a powerful source of mana, a beautiful plant that offers a home to the nature spirits, a plant that honours the gods, and a magical gateway from the present to the ancient past. To plant taro is to honour the spirit of the land. For Hawaiians, taro is at the mysterious heart of their island home.

Growing and Harvesting

Taro is planted year round in the tropics, and in the spring in the semi-tropics, small tubers being planted approximately 14–36 in (35–90 cm)

apart in rows 36 in (90 cm) apart, and 3–4 in 7. 5–10 cm) deep. Taro needs constantly moist conditions to flourish and a number of varieties are grown in swampy conditions. The soil should be rich as taro is a heavy feeder, and rotted manures or generous quantities of compost are dug into the soil before planting.

The tubers chosen should have clearly visible growth points which look like small green knobs on the skin. The crop is watered generously and frequently, and some waterlogging should be of no concern. A second application of rotted manure or compost is made halfway through the growing season when the crop is about 2 ft (60 cm) high, the compost being applied to the surface as a mulch. Taro needs a minimum of 200 days with temperatures in the range of 77–95°F (25–35°C) to mature. Plants grown only for their stems or leaves, can be grown in somewhat cooler areas.

Taro is only tolerant of very light frosts which may cause the plants to die back. Heavier frosts will kill the plants. Once mature plants begin to yellow, the tubers can be progressively dug as needed. Upland taro is usually ready to harvest at between 8–10 months. Leaves can be harvested at any time during the growth of the crop. The new crop is begun

Taro, Colocasia esculenta, has large, inverted heart-shaped, dark green to purple-green, peltate leaves. It forms a large central tuberous root underground.

Taro flower.

by rowing out the cormels which should not be allowed to dry out before planting. Taro has no significant pests or diseases. Leaf hoppers and aphids can be a problem but rarely do serious damage.

Recommended Cultivars

Taro has been cultivated for more than 2,000 years in Asia, Africa, and Polynesia and some 200 cultivars have been selected around the world. The list below is a small number of those available, but among the finest for eating. For production purposes, taro varieties are divided into dryland types which are cultivated under normal irrigation, and those which are grown in temporarily flooded fields

Taro is a very hardy and resilient vegetable which can turn into an annoying weed.

and are known as wetland varieties. A third division is sometimes made, of upland varieties, those which grow well at higher altitudes, for example around 1,500 ft (450 m) in the tropics under dryland conditions.

'Akado' — This is a Japanese cultivar with purple skinned, white fleshed tubers and around 20 cormels which are excellent steamed and baked. Produces a sturdy medium sized plant.

'Apuwhai' — A Hawaiian cultivar much valued for its young leaves. The cream colored, white fleshed tubers are excellent steamed or baked, and also make excellent *poi*. It is a short growing variety and usually grows under wetland conditions.

'Bun Long' syn. Betel-nut — This Chinese cultivar is also popular in Hawaii. It is grown both as a wetland and dryland variety. The corms are cream with white flesh containing purple fibers. The young leaves are prized for their lower level of calcium oxalate. The corms have an excellent crisp texture which make them a popular commercial variety for taro chips. It also is an excellent choice for boiling and baking.

'Kakakura-Ula' — Excellent for baking, steaming and boiling, this is one of the most ornamental taros with creamy white tubers, creamy white flesh, and stems that are striped with light and dark green and overlaid with bright, rich purple-red. It is a dryland culture variety, maturing in 9–12 months, originating from Polynesia.

'Mana Eleele' — This cultivar is prized for baking, steaming, and boiling. The tuber is dark purple, the flesh white. The plant is erect growing, of medium height, and grows under dryland conditions, having good drought resistance.

A number of taro cultivars are prized for the high quality of the poi they yield. Among these are the royal Hawaiian strains, so called because they were once for the exclusive use of the royal family. They include '**Lehua Palaii**' (red poi), the royal black taro '**Eleele Naioea**' (red *poi*, upland culture), and '**Piialii**' (red *poi*). Other prized poi varieties are '**Lehua Maoli**' (red Lehua *poi*, wetland and upland culture), '**Kai Kea**' (amber *poi*, wetland culture), and '**Ohe**' (grey *poi* of excellent quality, upland variety).

Ulluco

Ullucus tuberosus   Zones 8–12

Ulluco (pronounced ooh-**yoo**-ko) is one of the three most important tuber crops in the Andes, and is the most important of all in a number of areas. The markets in Andean towns often display large baskets full to overflowing with a profusion of ulluco. Shaped like potatoes, smallish, rounded or curved fingerling in shape, they have waxy, polished skins and come in a rainbow array of bright red, rich pink, orange, purple, yellow, and candy-striped. The skin is paper thin and tender, requiring no peeling, and the silky-textured flesh is white to lemon, retaining its crispness after cooking, and having a sweet nutty flavor. The tubers are boiled, mashed, grated, added to stews, used to make a smooth textured soup, pickled, or sliced, boiled and cooled to make a dish equivalent to potato salad. Ulluco is a useful source of protein as well as carbohydrate, and is unusually high in vitamin C. Ulluco has been a domesticated crop for a very long period of time, and has been found in archeological excavations of Peruvian coastal ruins dating to 4,450 B.C.

Ulluco is at the beginning of a surge of popularity and, of all the Andean crops, so many of which have already changed the diets and even the history of the modern world, it offers some of the greatest promise for the 21st century. Drought resistant, frost resistant to 23°F (–5°C), capable of producing good yields even in marginal soils (and equivalent yields to potatoes in good conditions), it is also a crop that is markedly pest and disease resistant. As a crop it has ever gaining popularity in South America where it is sold extensively in supermarkets. It has been field grown in

The rainbow colors of ulluco. One of the most widely grown and economically important tuber crops in the Andean region.

England, and under greenhouse conditions in Canada and in other high latitude areas such as Japan and Finland. It is a crop with great promise for China and the high altitude tropics everywhere.

Growing and Harvesting

Ulluco is propagated in the same manner as potatoes and sweet potatoes. Whole tubers can be planted, or segments of a tuber each with an eye (node) can be planted and will grow readily, or cuttings of shoots can be taken in the manner of sweet potatoes. The tubers sprout and grow readily once the temperature reaches 64°F (18°C). Tubers are planted at a depth of 3 in (7–8 cm) and 12 in (30 cm) apart. They are tolerant of quite poor soil conditions, but respond to thorough preparation of the soil and the incorporation of generous quantities of compost, and require a sunny position and good drainage.

The plants are short and semi-vining to bushy, with somewhat fleshy, cordate leaves and small racemes of tiny reddish-yellow to yellow-green flowers formed directly from the leaf axils. The plants are earthed up with soil once or twice during the latter part of the growing period to encourage additional layers

of tubers to form, in the same manner as potatoes. In fall, once the daylength has dropped below 9 hours, the plants send out a number of stolons each of which forms a tuber at the end. The stolons emerge predominantly from below ground but can emerge from any level on the stem, which is earthed up in the manner of potatoes when field grown, greatly improving both the quantity and quality of yield. Growing time varies with the selection planted and may be 5–8 months.

The tubers have similar thin skins to those of new season potatoes and need to be lifted with some care. Yields are high and the tubers can be stored year round under dry, cool, dark conditions. If exposed to light in storage, they will gradually lose their rainbow of colors and turn green in a manner similar to potatoes.

Some 70 selections appear to be grown in the Andes, but only a few are available as yet in countries outside South America. Finland has been actively involved in developing new cultivars.

Water Chestnut
Eleocharis dulcis syn. *E. tuberosa*   Zones 9–12

Once considered too exotic for the home gardener to even contemplate growing, water chestnuts, or Chinese water chestnuts, or matai, are now quite commonly propagated by gardeners in areas with warmer climates, and are popular with permaculture gardeners for their ability to adapt to a multiple cropping system. A native of tropical Asia, it is a common crop in China, South East Asia, tropical Africa, and is now being cropped commercially in areas such as Queensland, the Northern Territory and northern New South Wales in Australia, as well as being successfully grown in the Deep South, the South East of the United States, and California.

The plants grow in rich, light soil covered in shallow water, making a

The leaves of the ulluco plant.

tuft of cylindrical reed-like leaves, and forming a number of runners each terminating in plump, dark brown, round, tuber-like corms which are approximately 1.5 in (4 cm) in diameter. The corms can be eaten raw and have a sweet, nutty crunchiness that adds much to salads. They are also sliced and used in stir fry dishes, and used to add textural contrasts to pork or prawn balls, Thai fish cakes and Chinese omelettes. The corms are also dried and converted into a starch which gives a crisp texture to fried foods and is also used to thicken sauces.

Growing and Harvesting

Chinese Chestnut requires a growing season of approximately 180–220 days depending on the region, but can be pre-sprouted in water on a sunny window sill to gain an extension of time in areas with shorter seasons. To gain about 4–6 weeks advantage, corms can be grown in individual pots in a greenhouse or in a sunny position in the house where the temperature is maintained at a minimum temperature of 60°F (15.5°C), until the weather is suitable for planting. A daytime temperature range of 85–95°F (30–35 °C) is optimal during the main growing season.

When field grown, the corms are planted in spring in well tilled soil enriched with rotted compost or manure during the previous fall/winter. The field is built up around the perimeter with soil to a height of 12 in (30 cm), and flooded to a depth of approximately 3–6 in (7.5–15 cm). At the end of the growing season, the water is drained away and the corms dug. They are stored in a cool, dry area through the winter months.

Chinese water chestnuts can easily be adapted to grow in a much smaller container than a flooded field. If you have a small pond in the garden, water chestnuts can be grown around the margin, in wide, shallow, sunken pots. They will even grow in an aquarium to which about 7 in (18 cm) of enriched sand or sandy loam (see below) has first been added, followed by 3–4 in (7.5–10 cm) water. Even gardeners with no more than a patio or balcony garden can enjoy an occasional harvest of water chestnuts by using an aquarium, and will have the additional pleasure of being able to watch the corms grow.

Easiest of all, gardeners have been experimenting very successfully in the United States, the UK, and Australia with growing crops in small, cheap, soft plastic, children's wading pools. Most come with a plug to allow drainage. These pools vary but have dimensions of approximately 5 ft (1.5 m) diameter and 10 in (25 cm) depth. Of course you can use more aesthetic containers if you wish. Even gardeners in warm, but not hot, summer areas have had great success using this technique. Growers using this system are often rewarded with large crops of around 25 lbs (11–12 kg) of plump corms from just one pool. So rewarding is the water chestnut, it can earn a side income as a specialty crop for the organic gardener.

An ideal soil for the bottom of the pool is a 1:1 mix of very sandy loam, or even river sand, with a mixture of well rotted manure and compost, with some added dolomite or lime,

The water chestnut can be grown in an aquarium or even a children's wading pool.

and a little ground rock phosphate. The recipe need not be precise, but it is desirable to ensure that the mixture it is light and sandy and approximately 7 in (17.5 cm) deep in the plastic pool. The corms can be pre-sprouted, as discussed above. They are planted equidistant, no more than 3–4 to the pool, and 2 in (5 cm) deep, shoot upwards as soon as the last frost date has passed. This may seem to be a sparse arrangement of the corms, but if they are placed any closer the plants will eventually be overcrowded and fewer, smaller corms will result. The pool is flooded after planting to thoroughly wet the soil, then drained via the plug.

The corms are then left to grow away until they reach a height of about 10 in (25 cm), when the crop is flooded and remains so until harvest time. A nutrient boost is often given once additional plants begin to arise from the runners and have made good growth. This boost may be in the form of manure or compost soup or diluted seaweed emulsion. Another

application is made in late summer when the reed-like plants flower. Rapid corm growth takes place in early to mid-fall, and in late fall the soil is drained and the plants allowed to continue to grow and gradually dry for 4–6 weeks.

During these last few weeks, stored starches are converted to sugars so that the corms are sweet and crisp. The soil, now filled with water chestnuts, is gently sieved with a wide mesh screen to separate out all the corms. They are quite easily bruised at this stage and harvesting should be done with care. The corms are then cleaned, washed, and carefully dried out of sunlight, before storing in a cool, dry area. There are specialty suppliers of water chestnuts to gardeners, but if you have difficulty in locating them, corms appear in many markets and can be used as a start. Many growers' groups, permaculture groups, and gardeners' societies in warmer areas are also useful sources.

Yacon
Polymia sonchifolia   Zones 6–11

Related to the sunflower and not unlike it, the plants of yacon reach 4–6 ft (1.2–1.8 m) in height with large, softly furred, hastate leaves and winged petioles, with a cluster of yellow or orange flowers resembling small sunflowers at the top of the plant and the tops of the lower lateral branches. Below the ground, it produces large tubers resembling those of a dahlia, up to almost 4$^1/_2$ lbs (2 kg) in weight, that are crisp, juicy and succulent and a combination of apple and watermelon in taste and texture. The most commonly available selection is white fleshed, but in the Andes selections seen in the marketplaces can have orange, yellow, purple, or yellow flesh flecked with maroon. Some of the selections are as sweet as candy.

Yacon, Polymia sonchifolia, produces large tubers below the ground which resemble those of a dahlia and are crisp, juicy and succulent.

Like the Jerusalem artichoke, the yacon accumulates large amounts of sugar in the form of inulin which makes the yacon an ideal food for diabetics. Yacon is usually eaten raw, but can also be boiled and baked. It is native to Peru, Colombia and Ecuador and is one of the Incan crops. Almost unknown outside the Andes until recently, the yacon has become an exciting new crop for Australia, New Zealand and the United States. Yacon was trialed in Northern Italy prior to World War II, introduced from the Dominican Republic by an Italian agronomist, Mario Calvino, who saw it as a future forage crop or source of sugar for industrial fuel production. It grew quite superbly despite the lowland conditions in which it was trialed, and crops were subsequently planted in other parts of southern Europe. The war years interrupted this valuable crop trial and sidetracked it into history. Apart from its great culinary potential today, the yacon may prove to be an excellent source of alternative sweeteners.

Growing and Harvesting

Yacon requires a relatively long growing season of 5–6 months, although the growing season can be extended by the use of frames or by growing the tubers in large pots and transfering them to a glass house or polytunnel as cool weather sets in. The plants are frost sensitive but the tubers survive underground unless frozen. Tubers are planted in spring in a sunny, well-drained position into soil which has been well dug over and to which generous amounts of compost have been added. The tubers are placed at a depth of about 4 in (10 cm) and 18 in (45 cm) apart in rows. Harvesting can take place progressively through fall in the home garden, lifting carefully under the plant with a garden fork to reveal the ring of large tubers at the base of the stem. Yacon can be grown at sea level in temperate to cool temperate areas as is done in the United States, New Zealand and Australia or at elevations up to approximately 11,500 ft (3,500 m) in tropical areas. It is drought resistant and is virtually disease and insect proof. Yacon also appears to be virus free. Only one selection appears to be readily available in non-South American countries, a vigorous and productive, sweet, white fleshed type.

Yams
Dioscorea spp.   Zones 10–12

Yams are tropical and sub-tropical tuber crops. There are a number of types belonging to different species of the genus *Dioscorea*. All contribute reliable, high carbohydrate, generous crops which are cooked in the same ways as potatoes and sweet potatoes.

Yacon, Polymia sonchifolia, *produces large tubers below the ground which resemble those of a dahlia and are crisp, juicy and succulent.*

Growing and Harvesting

Yams are cultivated in the islands of the South Pacific, in India, China, Japan, Australia, Africa, South America, the West Indies, and southern Florida and are very easy to grow anywhere with an all year round very warm to hot climate. In cooler areas, a few might be grown in a greenhouse, both for pleasure and for an interesting, exotic meal or two. Yams grow best in sandy soils, are perennial, and can vary in terms of where the useful tubers are formed. Some are formed above ground in the leaf axils and are often known as air potatoes. Others are formed underground. A number of species have both edible aerial and subterranean tubers.

Yams are rowed out, planted into ridged up soil or into individual hills, at any time of the year in tropical regions and in spring in sub-tropical and dry tropics areas. Depending on the species, aerial bulblets or small tubers are used for planting. Some varieties are prone to nematodes, and a crop of marigolds *Tagetes* planted prior to planting a crop of yams is effective in cleaning the soil of this pest. A barrier planting of marigolds around a crop will also reduce attacks. Just one species will grow in fairly cool areas, the cinnamon vine *Dioscorea batatas* syn. D. opposita which is worthy of culture for the delicious

cinnamon fragrance of its beautiful flowers. This species, also known as the Chinese yam, needs to be dormant in the winter and unlike other yam species will not grow in the tropics.

Recommended Cultivars

Dioscorea is a widespread, largely tropical genus which forms a very valuable food resource. Some of the more commonly cultivated yams are:
Dioscorea alata **Air Potato, Great Asiatic Yam, White Yam, Water Yam, Greater Yam** This is the most commonly cultivated variety. It is perennial, forming a large white tuber just below the ground and numerous small white tubers in the leaf axils. The small air tubers and the underground tuber are both eaten, and can be roasted, baked, boiled and mashed, fried as chips, or used to make a flour. This yam is also an ingredient in sweet puddings made with coconut milk, and in Japan is grated into soups and used in tempura. A number of newer cultivars exist.

'Florido' This is a very productive Peurto Rican cultivar which produces one or two high quality tubers of excellent flavor. It can be susceptible to nematodes.

'Gemelos' — Originally another Puerto Rican cultivar, it is productive, with a number of smooth, even, cylindrical tubers of excellent culinary quality.

D. bulbifera **Air Yam, Air Potato, Potato Yam** — It is the aerial bulbils that are commonly consumed in this species, in preference to the underground tuber.

D. batatas syn. *D. opposita* Cinnamon Vine or Chinese Yam — For those in cooler areas, this species offers the opportunity to grow edible underground yams of good quality with the additional benefit that the fast growing vine will happily cover a pergola, verandah or gazebo in a single growing season and its white flowers scent the air around with

Yams, Dioscorea spp., *are cooked in the same way as potatoes and sweet potatoes.*

cinnamon. Hundreds of edible bulbils are also formed in the leaf axils and have a chestnut flavor, while the taste of the underground tuber is compounded of potato and butternut squash (butternut pumpkin). New plants can be started with the bulbils. The plant is perennial, and portions of the tuber mass can be harvested each year. It was introduced to the United States by Chinese settlers during the California gold rush and into Europe via France in 1848 by the French consul in Shanghai. Immensely popular as an ornamental in 19th century gardens in the United States and Europe, plans to use it as a substitute for the potato during the onset of potato blight in the 1840s never succeeded, probably because it required great effort to dig the underground tubers which can be 39 in (1 m) long.

'**Tororo-Imo**' — This is an excellent selection of Cinnamon Vine, productive, hardy, and of very good flavor.

D. cayennensis **Yellow Guinea Yam, Yellow Yam, Attoto Yam** — This is a cultivated, tropical species with underground tubers that have a dry, mealy texture, and pale yellow flesh. They are baked, fried, boiled, mashed and roasted as well as being used in soups and stews. A tea is prepared from the leaf tips.

D. esculenta **Lesser Asiatic Yam, Goa Yam, Fancy Yam** — Notable for its delicious flavor reminiscent of chestnuts mixed with sweet potatoes, this tropical species is cultivated for its underground tubers which can be roasted, fried, boiled, mashed, baked, and used in soups and stews. Various selections have been made including '**Doli**' and '**Muni**' both of which have good yields of white fleshed tubers.

D. japonica **Glutinous Yam, Jinenjo** — This East Asian species is high in starch content and eaten boiled, baked and added to soups, and used as a binding agent. The aerial bulbils are also eaten, and the vine tips eaten as a cooked leafy vegetable.

D. trifida **Cush Cush Yam** — Widely cultivated in the Carribean and other regions, this is a gourmet yam with a smoothly textured, richly flavored, moist flesh which varies from white to purple. It is usually baked or boiled.

Yams are easy to grow in any area that has a warm to hot climate all year round.

Salad Greens

Celtuce *Lactuca sativa* var. *augustana* syn. *L.s.* var. *asparagina*; **Chicory** and **Endive** *Chicorium intybus* and *C. endivia*; **Corn salad** *Valerianella locusta, V. eriocarpa*; **Dandelion** *Taraxacum officinale*; **Gotu Kola** *Centella asiatica*; **Lettuce** *Lactuca sativa*; **Mallows** *Malva* spp. **Miner's Lettuce** *Claytonia perfoliata* syn. *Montia perfoliata*; **Mitsuba** *Cryptotaenia japonica*; **Nasturtium** *Tropaeolum majus*; **Perilla** *Perilla frutescens*; **Primroses** and **Violets** *Primula* spp. and *Viola* spp.; **Purslane** *Portulaca oleracea*; **Rice Paddy Herb** *Limnophila aromatica*; **Rocket** *Eruca sativa*; **Scurvy Grass** *Cochlearifolia officinalis*; **Shungiku** *Chrysanthemum coronarium* var. *spatiosum*; **Watercress** *Nasturtium officinalis*; **Wild Rocket** *Diplotaxis muralis*

One of the greatest pleasures of owning an organic food garden is the incredible diversity of fresh, crisp, and nutritious salad greens available almost year long. Lettuces alone offer huge variety, and a mixture of leaves from even a few different types can look very enticing. By combining a diversity of greens with different toppings and dressings, no meal need ever be the same.

When it comes to dressings, you can opt for a classic French or Italian recipe, or concoct your own from an almost infinite variety of ingredients including fresh lime, lemon, or orange juice, chili peppers, raw sugar, extra virgin olive oil, natural yoghurt, garlic, sea salt, freshly ground pepper, grated fresh green ginger, and herbs such as sweet marjoram, oregano, dill, lemon thyme, mints of all kinds, lemon and lime balms, chervil, chives, basils, and parsley. Ideal, flavor-packed, healthy toppings include shavings of parmesan cheese, toasted seed and nut sprinkles, sliced shallots and sweet red onions, black olives, peeled orange segments, edible flowers, and garlic croutons (preferably made with organic multigrain bread and fresh garlic). To create a robust, earthy salad, try adding deep fried, peeled garlic cloves. These are addictively good when fried to a light to mid-brown, but keep an eye on them as they burn easily.

Many seed suppliers now offer products that allow you to harvest the mixed salad seedlings that have long been a favorite of French and Italian cooks. For example, Provencal Mesclun usually combines choice lettuce and fine curled endive with rocket and chervil. It originated in Provence, France, but is now appreciated worldwide. Mesclun,

One of the most popular commercially available seed mixes, Provencal Mesclun comprises lettuce, curled endive, rocket and chervil.

The garden nasturtium, Tropaeolum majus, is a bushy annual. It rises to about 12 in (30 cm) and its trailing stems spread out up to 3 ft (1 m).

which is sold throughout northern France, contains a wider variety of greens and may include cress, corn salad, and spinach in addition to various lettuce and endive cultivars. As its name indicates, Mesclun Nicoise comes from Nice in France; it includes favored salad leaves of the Mediterranean such as dandelion, together with upland cress, rocket, chicory, lettuce and curly endive. These seed mixes allow even gardeners using container pots to obtain an attractive variety of leaves.

Aside from the following, other commonly used salad greens include kang kong, tree spinach, tampala spinach or leaf amaranth, the various sorrels including wild sorrel, sorrel, French sorrel, herb patience and sheep sorrel, houttuynia and orach. For information on all of these, *see Vegetables: Spinach of Every Kind.*

Celtuce

Lactuca sativa var. *augustana* syn. *L.s.* var. *asparagina*   Zones 7–12

Celtuce was developed in China and introduced to Europe in the second half of the 19th century. Also known as asparagus lettuce, Chinese stem lettuce and Chinese lettuce, it resembles a plain-leaved, loose-leaved lettuce

when young, but soon sends up a thick, central stalk that is harvested when about 12–16 in (30–40 cm) high and 1 in (2.5 cm) across. The 'heart' at the top is eaten as a kind of cos lettuce, and the peeled stem is sliced thinly and eaten fresh (it tastes like cucumber) or used in stir-fry dishes. The peelings exude a bitter latex, also present in wild lettuce and to a much lesser degree in modern lettuce after it bolts.

Growing and Harvesting
Celtuce is grown in the same manner as lettuce and under the same conditions (see below). It is a winter crop in warm areas and a spring and autumn crop in cooler climates. It has some frost tolerance.

Chicory *and* Endive
Chicorium intybus and *C. endivia*   Zones 4–10

Chicory and endive are closely related plants that are grown in much the same way. Endive is also called escarole.

The various kinds of chicories can be used to add a slightly bitter flavor to winter salads. They can be divided into a number of subgroups.

Heading chicory forms a large conical head like a small, pointed 'Sugarloaf' cabbage. The folded and wrapped inner leaves are self-blanching

'Rossa di Treviso' chicory is prized for its richly colored leaves. Like other chicories, it will grow in almost any soil and can be cultivated easily in the kitchen garden.

Verona' are sold as beautifully deep-red-colored winter field chicories, or are grown to form pale pink chicons. Non-forcing forms of radicchio produces full, dense heads in the field and are also used for salads.

Witloof chicory, also known as French endive or chicons, is grown specifically for forcing. The tops are cut off at the end of the growing season and the emerging, tightly formed shoots are blanched to produce crisp, ivory to white chicons, which are crisp, tender and sweet with a trace of bitterness.

The final subgroup consists of cultivars that are grown primarily for their plump roots. They are usually boiled until tender, sliced, and deep fried or served in any other way that parsnip might be used. Some forms are roasted to provide coffee chicory.

Endives are all green-leaved, but they too have been developed in various ways and can be grouped according to their appearance. Curly-leaved endive, also called *chicorée frisée*, forms double flat rosettes of narrow leaves, which are fringed or deeply indented or finely curled. Broad-leaved endive, also referred to as or escarole or Batavian endive, is characterized by larger, taller heads with broader, plainer leaves.

and sweeter than the outer leaves.

Loose-leaf chicory is principally an Italian group, and much favored for winter and early spring salads. The Catalogna types are also known as asparagus chicory or radichetta.

Radicchios are the red-leaved chicories. They are widely grown around the world, and prized for their beautiful colors, crisp textures, and edgy, slightly bitter flavors. Some cultivars such as **'Early Treviso'**, **'Rossa di Treviso'**, and **'Rossa di**

The heads of witloof chicory should be plump, firm and pure white with yellow leaf tips. If the tips are green, the endive is not fresh and likely to taste bitter.

Growing and Harvesting

Curly-leaved endive should be sown in spring, with repeat plantings in mid- and late summer in warmer areas. The fine seed should be sown thinly into shallow drills in a flat of soil and covered with a mixture of sand and finely sieved compost. Keep the flat moist until the seedlings have emerged and grown to approximately $1^1/_2$ in (4 cm) high. Then transplant them into a raised bed to which generous amounts of compost have been added—and well-rotted poultry manure, too, if it is available. The seedlings should be watered regularly and a weak liquid foliar feed of seaweed fertilizer or 'compost soup' added every two to three weeks.

To produce the preferred ivory color and sweet flavor, the plants must be blanched. Pull the leaves up and tie them at the top with raffia or a rubber band two weeks before picking. Only a few plants should be blanched at a time as they run to seed rapidly afterward.

Broad-leaved chicory is grown in the same way, but should be planted in autumn for harvest in winter (it is

cold-resistant) and the following spring. It is not usually blanched. However, it can become bitter when the weather warms and should either be blanched or eschewed entirely at that point, allowing it to go to seed for the next crop.

Chicory should be planted in spring. The beautiful, deep red colors of radicchio cultivars develop as colder weather approaches, so they should be planted for field harvesting in mid- to late summer.

To produce plump, ivory, sweet, crisp witloof chicory chicons, harvest the plants in autumn, choose only plump roots, and trim the roots and

Curly-leaved endive is characterized by double flat rosettes of deeply indented leaves. These provide the attractive pale leaves in mescluns.

Broad-leaved endive is distinguished by its wide leaves and dark color. It is not normally blanched.

'Sugarloaf' chicory is an upright, light green variety with a large, slender, tight head.

leaves in the manner of carrots. Then place the roots vertically in a pot of moist potting mix, with the crown exposed above the soil, and cover with a second inverted pot. The chicons will form in around four weeks. Many growers blanch Catalogna cultivars in the field by simply inverting a large pot over them.

Recommended Cultivars

'Florida Deep Heart' — An excellent, very large, broad-leaved endive with a creamy white heart.

'Rossa di Verona' — This classic Italian chicory produces tight, deep red, rounded heads with white veins; these are excellent in late-autumn and winter salads. It should be planted in late summer.

'Sugarloaf' syn. 'Pan di Zucchero', 'Pain de Sucre' — This chicory looks like a large, somewhat twisted cos lettuce, measures up to 20 in (70 cm) high, and is self-blanching. It has sweet, crisp, tender inner leaves that are delicious with cheeses or in a salad.

'Très Fine Maraichère — This is a fine endive with creamy, well-blanched hearts and delicate, mild, crisp flesh. The leaves are deeply lacinated.

'Variegata di Chioggia' — This chicory is green in summer but becomes variegated red and white in the cool weather of autumn. It forms solid, tight heads.

Corn Salad

Valerianella locusta, V. eriocarpa   Zones 4–9

Also known as lamb's lettuce and mache, these two species are winter crops. *V. locusta* is the northern species; *V. eriocarpa* (Italian corn salad) is native to the Mediterranean. *V. locusta* var. *oleracea* is a cultivated variety of corn salad. All have been grown in the USA for at least a century and a half, and are also cultivated in parts of the UK, Europe and Australasia. The leaves are often steamed as a spinach substitute.

'Variegata di Chioggia' is an Italian heirloom chicory that originated in Venice. The round heads are pale green with red streaks or speckles.

Growing and Harvesting

Corn salad should be propagated by seed sown in late summer to mid-autumn, depending on the district. Although cold hardy, in areas with severe winters they should be covered with hay in mid-winter, the covering being removed in early spring. Seed can be saved from a few plants left to run to flower in summer. Corn salad has no significant enemies.

Dandelion

Taraxacum officinale   Zones 3–10

Dandelion greens have long been used in spring salads. In the Mediterranean, they are particularly prized for the bitterness of the young green leaves, though the plants are sometimes blanched to reduce that bitterness.

All parts of the plant are used. The flowers make a delightful dandelion wine. The leaves can be steamed, braised, and fried—try serving the steamed leaves cold with lemon juice, extra virgin olive oil, and a little freshly ground sea salt. The roots can be peeled, sliced, cooked in two lots of water to remove any bitterness, and then served with a little melted butter. The flower buds are incorporated in sweet dishes such as sugared fritters and pancakes, and the roots have long been roasted and ground to make an interesting coffee substitute.

Dandelions produce a number of flowering stems directly from the dense basal rosette of leaves, and one flower per stem. They are often confused with other, similar yellow flowers, usually annual thistles. A number of named seed cultivars are available, including **'Broad Leaved'**, **'Ameliore à Coeur Plein'**, and **'Vert de Montmagny'**. The last is treated as an annual.

Growing and Harvesting

It's important to have a sunny, well-drained, well-composted site. The seeds should be sown in spring.

Dandelion, Taraxacum officinale, *is a highly versatile food crop, with almost every part of this widely naturalized plant having a culinary use.*

Gotu Kola

Centella asiatica   Zones 9–12

This is a creeping stoloniferous herb which roots into the ground as it spreads, sending up a rosette of fleshy, fan-shaped leaves. The flavor is a little like a combination of parsley and celery. It is known variously as gotu kola, Indian pennywort, Asian pennywort and Indian ginseng.

In many Asian countries and Hawaii, it is thought to promote longevity. Indeed, legend has it that a Chinese professor, Li Chung Yon, reached the age of 265, outliving 26 wives, as a result of regular consumption of tea made with gotu kola. Not surprisingly, the tea is known in China as 'long-life tea'. In Thailand, a juice is prepared from leaves ground with palm sugar. In Hawaii, it is said that if you eat two leaves a day, you will add 50 years to your life; three leaves a day will add 100 years. Gotu kola has been shown in laboratory studies to act as an adaptogenic in the manner of ginseng, though as with other adaptogenics it takes some time for the beneficial effects to manifest themselves. Gotu kola is also reputed to increase energy, improve the performance of the brain and memory, improve circulation to hands and feet, and discourage negativity. It is, however, important that pregnant women, people with high blood pressure, and people on blood-thinning drugs avoid gotu kola.

The best way to consume gotu kola is to add the raw leaves to salads, soups and stews, or steam them and serve them with rice.

Growing and Harvesting

Although gotu kola can be grown from seed, it is easier to start with clonal material, either a potted plant or a handful of rooted rhizomes from an Asian market or a friend's garden. Plant the material in a cool, partially shaded, moist position after adding generous quantities of compost to the soil (the plant can also be grown in a wide pot.) Water frequently. Harvest a few leaves at a time, as needed. In cool areas, gotu kola will die back a little in winter and renew itself in spring.

Reputed to have anti-aging properties, gotu kola, Centella asiatica, *is a creeping plant found in swampy areas of Asia, Africa and Australia.*

Lettuce

Lactuca sativa   Zones 7–12

All modern cultivated lettuces are descended from the wild lettuce *Lactuca serriola*, which is widely distributed in North Africa, Asia Minor, Iran, Turkestan, and northern Europe. The wild lettuce germinates in autumn, in cooler weather, forming rosettes of leaves. During the following spring, it begins to bolt, forming panicles of tiny, pale yellow flowers followed by gray seeds that are shed on the wind to begin the cycle again. A closely related species, *L. virosa*, was the source of the huge variety of lettuces around today.

Early varieties cultivated by the Greeks were more bitter and had open, rosette-like hearts made up of narrow, pointed leaves. Some of our oldest cultivars, such as **'Bunyards Matchless'** and **'Rabbit Ear'**, have a similar form.

A number of classes of lettuce are now available to suit every taste, season and use. Popular throughout Europe, Batavian lettuces form heavy, dense heads at maturity and remain very sweet; they have the crispness of iceberg and romaine lettuces.

In contrast, butterhead (or bibb) lettuces have a soft, tender, buttery texture and form loosely packed, rounded heads, reminiscent of perfect, semi-opened, cabbage rose flowers. The centers self blanch to a delicate cream color. Probably the most popular lettuce type in Europe, butterheads are exceptionally easy to grow; however, because they require careful, rapid transport to market, relatively few are sold widely. Both green- and colored-leaved forms are available.

Loose-leaf lettuces are easiest of all to grow, and include many wonderful cut-and-come-again varieties, which allow you to harvest a few leaves at a time from each plant. The group also contains many delicious heirloom cultivars and many of the newer frilled and colored cultivars.

Romaine lettuces are also called cos lettuces; the former name derives from the plant's popularity in ancient Rome, the latter from the Greek island of Kos, where the plant is said to have originated. Romaine lettuces form narrow, upright heads packed with leaves. The inner leaves are self-blanching and stand up to summer heat and dryness better than other types, being slow to bolt. When well grown, they are crisp and sweet, with a distinctive taste. This is the type of lettuce normally used in Caesar salad.

Lettuces that grow quickly are more likely to remain soft and sweet. Supply regular doses of nitrogen-rich fertilizers and abundant water.

The soft textures and delicate flavors of butterhead lettuces make them a favorite with gourmet gardeners.

Crisphead lettuces are the most popular type in the USA and Australasia. They are characterized by cabbage-like heads of densely packed leaves with a crisp, sweet, juicy flavor. Though they resist heat, they are perhaps the most challenging group to grow well. On the other hand, they withstand transport and short term cool storage well, making them a favorite with retailers.

That lettuce is a mild soporific has long been known: Hippocrates noted it in medical treatises he wrote on his home island of Kos. Lettuce is also rich in vitamins A and C, and romaine lettuce is a source of folic acid.

Growing and Harvesting

Lettuce will not germinate in temperatures above approximately 58°F (20°C). In hot areas, store seed in the refrigerator in a sealed container such as a zip-lock bag for a week before planting. Romaine lettuces are a good choice for summer as they are heat-resistant. Other lettuce types can be planted in early spring, mid-autumn and winter. In hot areas, lettuce can be grown under a layer of light shade cloth.

In cool areas, early spring seedlings should be raised in flats indoors for four to six weeks before the last frost and then planted out in rows. Late-spring to early-autumn plantings can be sown into the ground sequentially, every three weeks. Winter crops can be raised in the protection of a greenhouse or cold frame in all but the coldest areas, providing the most cold-hardy cultivars are chosen.

Lettuce requires a rich soil with plenty of compost, both to feed the plants and to retain moisture. Plants that are allowed to dry out are liable to run to seed prematurely. The application of nitrogen-rich seaweed or fish emulsion made up to the recommended strength and watered over the crop when half grown will help maintain the lettuce at the vegetative stage and boost the growth and health of the crop.

Lettuces prefer a neutral pH (7). Acidic soils should be adjusted with an application of lime or dolomite. Mulch should be applied once the plants are well established and the rows should be maintained weed-free. Lettuces are self pollinating and need a separation distance of only 6–10 ft (2–3 m). Wild lettuce can cross with cultivated lettuce growing nearby.

Like any highly selected vegetable, modern lettuce varieties are prone to pests and diseases that did not trouble their wild ancestors. Slugs and snails should be removed, either by capturing them at night as they feed or by using slug and snail beer traps. A barrier of any sharp-edged material, such as coarse sand, broken-up eggshells or diatomite, will also act as a deterrent. Cutworms can be kept out by placing a cardboard collar around each seedling (you can make collars by cutting a hole in the base of a paper cup).

Lettuce may suffer from root aphids. 'Bottom rot', a disorder causing the plants to rot from the bottom up, can also be a problem, but only on wet, poorly drained soils; it does not occur in raised beds. Because it is caused by a soil-borne fungus that remains in the ground for several years, its effects can also be minimized by crop rotation. The same good drainage and crop rotation will inhibit another soil-borne fungal disease, 'fusarium yellows.' It causes the leaves to yellow and fall off; the woody inside of the stem then turns brown.

Mosaic is a viral disease that causes leaves to turn mottled green and yellow. The virus is carried by aphids and is incurable, so the only treatment is to pull out any affected plants and burn them. Downy mildew may be a problem in prolonged wet weather, and grey mould can attack young seedlings. Adequate spacing between plants reduces the problem, and some cultivars have resistance. Watering in the early morning—on the soil rather than the plant top—is also helpful.

Lettuce is best harvested in the morning when it is crispest. Heading lettuce should be cut when the head is firm. Put the bottoms of the plants in the compost bin: if left in the soil, they are likely to cause problems in the future.

Recommended Cultivars

'Bibb' syn. 'Limestone' — The classic mainstay of home and market gardeners as well as glasshouse production, this is a small butterhead type with tender, brown-tinged, deep green heads.

'Bunyards Matchless' — This ancient cultivar has dense rosettes of small, pointed, smooth-edged leaves.

'Black-seeded Simpson' — For over a century, this has been a home gardeners' and marketers' favorite. It forms a high-quality, large, upright, loose-leaf lettuce with crumpled, light green, frilled leaves. It is very heat-resistant.

'Buttercrunch' — Produced by Cornell University, this reliable, tender, long-standing bibb-type lettuce was the 1963 All America Selections winner.

'Craquante d'Avignon' syn. 'Craquerelle du Midi' — A semi-romaine, open-hearted lettuce with crisp, deep green leaves. Resistant to bolting, it is ideal for warm regions such as Florida, where it is grown for an early-summer harvest.

'Darwin' — A beautiful lettuce from the Northern Territory of Australia, this is a large, buttery, tender, light green, oak-leaved type.

'Deer Tongue' syn. 'Matchless' — Still popular, this loose-leaf heirloom cultivar is perfect for home gardens. Of excellent quality and flavor, it is slow to bolt.

'Freckles' — A beautiful heirloom cultivar available in the USA and Australasia, this is a tender-leaved

A favorite with the ancient Romans and Greeks, cos lettuces have been cultivated as vegetables for almost 5,000 years.

As well as being heat-resistant, 'Black-seeded Simpson' matures quickly, usually within about 40 days.

cos type. It is light green with maroon speckles and splashes. For spring and autumn planting.

'French Laotian' — This is a superb, delicately flavored, savoyed lettuce with light green, tender leaves and butterhead conformation.

'Gold Rush' — This is a superlative heirloom cultivar from Australia. A loose-leaf type with intensely wavy, tender, flavorful leaves, it is also heat-resistant. The 1952 All America Selections winner 'Salad Bowl' is similar.

The 'Gwenda White' lettuce with large, upright leaves has been a gardeners' favorite for many years.

'Great Lakes' — The standard iceberg-type lettuce, it is cold hardy, widely adapted and excellent for home gardens. It is also resistant to bolting and tipburn.

'Green Mignonette' — A favorite in hot climates such as Hawaii, Florida and Queensland, Australia, this is a butterhead type that will reliably form small, firm, rounded heads with self-blanching inner leaves. It is crisp, tender and sweet. There is also a **'Brown Mignonette'**.

'Grosse Blonde Parerreuse' syn. 'White Stone', 'Non Pareil' — Appropriately, the last name translates as 'incomparable.' Still widely available, this pre-1885 French cultivar remains a paragon. It forms large, tall heads of buttery green leaves with superb flavor.

'Gwenda White' — This remarkable traditional Chinese cos cultivar is the tallest of all lettuces. The heads are elegant, slender, and tender.

'Italian' — This traditional Italian cultivar is a loose-leaf form. It develops a dense rosette of lightly frilled, tender, dark green leaves.

'Mescher' syn. 'Schweitzer's Mescher Bibb' — Introduced to the United States from Austria in the 19th century, this 18th-century heirloom

is still popular. A butterhead, it forms small, crisp, heads with wonderful flavor. It has marked cold resistance, reportedly to 28°F (−2°C).

'Merveille des Quatre Saisons' syn. 'Marvel of the Four Seasons', 'Meraviglia delle Quattro Stagioni' — As the name indicates, this is a favorite cultivar in France, Italy, and the UK; it is also grown in Australasia. Dating from before 1885, it can be planted in all seasons in milder climates, although it is at its best in spring and autumn. It is a butterhead type, forming rounded heads of spoon-shaped leaves tinged throughout with brownish red.

'Oakleaf' — This is a loose-leaf lettuce forming a compact rosette of narrow, tender, thin, oak-shaped leaves that never become bitter with age. It is an excellent cut-and-come-again lettuce. **'Everlasting'** is a light green form that can withstand occasional plucking of leaves. **'Purple Oakleaf'**, **'Red Oakleaf'**, **'Baby Oak'** and the deep green **'Royal Oakleaf'**, are all excellent in salads.

'Rouge d'Hiver' — This is a famous romaine-type French lettuce that was introduced before 1885 and is still grown around the world. Very productive, it is also hardy and

heads perfectly. It is deeply tinged with reddish brown.

'Tennis Ball' — One of the oldest lettuces still available, it is highly cold-resistant and forms small, solid heads if grown in cool weather. The outer leaves are savoyed and the heart self-blanches to a tender, creamy-white.

'Tom Thumb' — This is another much-loved and still widely available baby butterhead from the latter half of the 19th century. It is perfect for the small home garden and containers, forming tight heads, no larger than an orange, of sweet, tender, flavorful leaves that are perfect for single servings.

'Victoria' — This high-quality Batavian type is heat-resistant, crisp and deliciously sweet.

'Webbs Wonderful' — Famous and reliable, this old variety forms large, deep green leaves that are sweet and crisp. It is slow to bolt.

Seed Saving Notes

Lettuce seeds ripen progressively, and a mix of ripe and unripe seeds can make harvesting difficult. When seeds are clearly present in half the flowers, cut the plants down and dry them upside down over paper; the seeds will then fall onto the paper. The seeds will last for five years if kept in an airtight container in a cool, dry place.

Allow lettuce to 'bolt' in order to collect seed. When seeds are clearly present in half the flowers, cut the plants down and dry upside down in a bunch over sheets of paper to catch the seeds when they fall.

A well-known butterhead, 'Brown Mignonette' has crisp, curly, red-purple to green leaves that have a slightly tart taste.

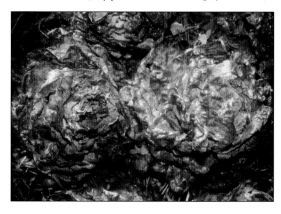

Whorled mallow, Malva verticillata, *is adaptable to most soil types. Its flowers are white or pale purple.*

Mallows
Malva spp.   Zones 4–10

Whorled mallow, *Malva verticillata*, and curly mallow, *M. crispa*, are European annual plants, closely related to true marshmallow, *Althaea officinalis*. They are cultivated in France for their leaves, which are used as a spinach substitute and garnish. When well grown, these mallows can reach 6 ft (1.8 m), and have leaves about 5 in (12.5 cm) in diameter. The margins of the curly mallow are lobed and beautifully frilled.

Rich in vitamins and other nutrients, mallow plants are widely used in herbal remedies.

The tender shoots of common mallow, *M. neglecta* (sometimes known as dwarf mallow), are eaten as a salad; the leaves are steamed as a spinach sustitute and added to soups. In some regions, the immature fruits are known as 'cheeses' and eaten raw in salads, or pickled, or fried. The leaves of cheese weed, *M. parriflora*, another member of the mallow species, are eaten raw in salads or steamed for use as a spinach substitute. The immature fruits are used like peas and can replace peas in almost any pea recipe, including pea soup. Hibiscuses are near relatives of mallows, and the flowers of the Chinese hibiscus, *Hibiscus rosa-sinensis*, can be used as an exotic garnish or ingredient for a summer salad.

Growing and Harvesting
Mallow seeds can be sown in spring. The plants require a modicum of compost and regular watering, and produce large, tender leaves. Mallows are naturalized in many parts of the world, so if some appear in your garden, don't rip them out; instead, use them as a ready source of greens.

Miner's lettuce

Claytonia perfoliata syn. Montia perfoliata
Zones 6–10

This exquisite small plant from the same family as purslane carpets damp, shady places on the west coast of North America, from southern California to British Colombia, in spring. The plant forms a posy-like, upright rosette, each stem having a cupped set of perfoliate leaves supporting tiny white flowers that appear as a cluster in late spring. The plant's common name derives from its use as a salad green by miners during the California gold rushes.

Growing and Harvesting

Miner's lettuce seeds are readily obtainable from specialist seed suppliers. They should be sown in moist, shady, cleared areas in autumn. The plant does not cope well with weed competition or dryness.

Mitsuba

Cryptotaenia japonica   Zones 10–12

Mitsuba is a perennial herb that also goes under the names of Japanese parsley and Japanese wild chervil. Its trifoliate leaves have a delightful, subtle flavor that lies somewhere between sweet angelica (particularly the hollow stems) and parsley. The leaflets are about 2 in (5 cm) long and 1 in (2.5 cm) wide. They add delicious flavor to green tossed salads. As well, they can be used in omelettes and other egg dishes, in tempura, sukiyaki, and sushi, in pickles, and as a substitute for parsley.

Growing and Harvesting

Mitsuba is frost-sensitive and in cool areas two crops are usually planted, in spring and in early autumn. In warm to tropical areas, crops are planted sequentially all year round. The plants flourish in a lightly shaded position and require a rich, moist soil—in

In its natural habitat in western North America, miner's lettuce, Claytonia perfoliata, usually blooms following spring rains.

warm climates, they should be planted into shallow trenches to increase moisture retention. The leaves can be harvested progressively once the plant reaches about 6 in (15 cm). Flowering stems should be cut off to encourage leaf production. Regular watering is required.

Nasturtium

Tropaeolum majus   Zones 8–11

The leaves of the nasturtium, also called Indian cress, have a delicious peppery, watercress-like taste. They can be torn up and tossed through green salads, used like watercress in sandwiches, and used to wrap nibble food. The flowers are piquant with a touch of nectar and are a delightful garnish for salads and other dishes. The tender, crunchy young fruits are borne in clusters of three; they can be pickled and used in salads like capers.

The leaves and flowers of nasturtiums such as 'Golden King' will add color and piquancy to a fresh spring salad.

Growing and Harvesting

Nasturtiums are hearteningly easy to grow plants, requiring little more than a reasonably sunny position; they even thrive in dry conditions and poor soils. However, the lush, tender foliage will benefit from moderate amounts of compost and regular watering, especially in hot conditions.

Sow the seeds directly into the ground once the last frost date has passed, or raise the plants in small pots indoors then plant them out when the weather warms. A second sowing can be made in summer.

Recommended Cutivars

'Alaska' — This cultivar is splashed and variegated with creamy-white and comes in a variety of colors.

'Whirlbird' — Separate color strains of this dwarf cultivar are available.

'Creamsicle' — This beautiful cultivar has creamy white flowers delicately tinged with peach.

Other attractive dwarf cultivars include the intense crimson-scarlet **'Empress of India'**; the intensely dark crimson to chocolate **'King Theodore'**; **'Golden King'**; and the salmon pink, dark-spotted, deep blue-green dwarf **'Vesuvius'**.

Companion-planting the magnificent 'Empress of India' nasturtium with cabbage, cucumbers and herbs will deter whitefly and cabbage caterpillars.

Perilla

Perilla frutescens   Zones 8–11

The young leaves of this plant, also called beefsteak plant, are used in Vietnam in fresh green salads, and served with sashimi in Japan. They are also incorporated in tempura, pickles, and miso. Red-leaved forms are used to color and spice salad vinegars, and the leaves are also used to wrap meat and seafood prior to cooking. The seed sprouts are also used widely as a garnish.

Perilla is a fast-growing annual. It forms a small, leafy, subshrub reaching 32 in (80 cm). The leaves are large with serrated edges, and may be green, red, or purple-red. There are a number of named forms each with its own distinctive flavors, fragrances, and colors; the different forms should be planted as far apart as possible to prevent cross-breeding. **'Green Cumin'** has a cumin-like scent and is excellent for all culinary uses. **'Lemon'** has curled green leaves with a lemon-spice fragrance. **'Curled'** has small, ruffled, dark purple leaves with a mild peppermint fragrance.

Growing and Harvesting

Perilla seeds should be planted in spring when the soil has warmed. The soil should be supplemented with compost and, if available, well-rotted manure. A sunny, well-drained position is required. Sow the seeds thinly, approximately $1/2$ in (1 cm) deep, leaving 8 in (20 cm) between plants. Water regularly. In very hot climates, provide crops with some shade. In tropical areas, plantings should be made in autumn, not spring.

'Green Cumin' perilla has a remarkable spicy flavor that can add an extra dimension to mesclun salad mixes and pestos.

Many forms of perilla are highly ornamental. Ideal for landscaping, they do not look out of place in a flower garden.

The flowers of the true, or English, primrose, Primula vulgaris, are used in various sweet dishes, teas and syrups.

Sweet violet, Viola odorata, is prized for its attractive flowers, sweet scent and tender green leaves which make a fine addition to spring salads.

Primroses and Violets

Primula spp., Viola spp.   Zones 6–9

Primrose, cowslip, and sweet violet leaves and flowers have long been a part of spring salads. As well as the inner, tender young leaves, the flowers are edible and are often used to add color and flavor to spring salad greens. The leaves and flowers are also incorporated in teas and syrups.

The flowers of the cowslip, *Primula veris*, are used to make cowslip wine,

pickles, tea, and a fragrant vinegar used in the manner of a refreshing cordial. The flowers of the true primrose, *P. vulgaris*, are sometimes incorporated in sweet dishes such as custards and can be crystallized; the leaves are also cooked as a vegetable.

The leaves of sweet violets, *V. odorata*, birdsfoot violet, *V. pedata*, Canada violet, *V. canadensis*, and the marsh blue violet, *V. cucullata*, are rich in vitamins A and C. The young leaves can be added to green salads. The leaves are also used as steamed or cooked greens. The leaves of birdsfoot violet are also dried to make a type of tea. Although the flavor is stronger, the tender young leaves of pansies, Viola, are also used as a spring salad green.

None of these plants should be gathered from the wild as their natural habitats have been greatly reduced.

Growing and Harvesting

When cultivating these plants, take care not to rob them of too many leaves or they will lose their vigor. For more information, *see The Flower Garden and The Herb Garden.*

Native to woods and meadows in Europe, the cowslip can be identified by its sweet scent and by the clusters of flowers that crown its tall stalks.

Purslane

Portulaca oleracea   Zones 9–11

Purslane is a popular salad green in France and the Mediterranean region, and is grown to a lesser extent elsewhere. The green-leaved form is naturalized throughout much of the world, growing as a 'weed' with a succulent rosette. Its memorable alternative name was noted in Dr Herklot's ground-breaking 1972 pulbication *Vegetables of Southeast Asia*: 'Buttocks-of-the-wife-of-a-chief'. A cultivar '**Golden**' is grown in the Mediterranean area. A cultivated form, var. *sativa*, has more upright growth and larger leaves than the wild species.

Growing and Harvesting
Seeds of the cultivar '**Golden**' can be obtained relatively easily. They should be sown in spring and planted in rows $1/4$ in (0.5 cm) deep on sunny, well-drained, raised beds. The plants have no notable enemies and grow rapidly. Their young shoots, measuring up to 2 in (5 cm), should be harvested regularly.

Rice Paddy Herb

Limnophila aromatica   Zones 8–11

This is one of those terrific Southeast Asian plants that have only become more widely available in the last decade. Known as *rau om* in Vietnam and *phak khayaeng* in Thailand, it is a wonderfully fragrant, semi-aquatic, herbaceous plant. The tender green shoots are eaten raw with salads, conferring a delicious curry, mace and lemon scent to dishes, and are added to fragrant Vietnamese clear soups, cooked as a side dish with rice, and used in several Vietnamese sweet and sour dishes including a famous soup containing melon and tamarind.

Growing and Harvesting
Rice paddy herb can be easily grown in the same way as watercress (see below) or in a shallow trench that is flood-irrigated every few days.

Rice paddy herb, Limnophilla aromatica, is distinguished by the attractive whorls of small leaves that curl around its slender stems.

Rocket, Eruca sativa, forms rosettes of long, lobed leaves in the manner of an open-leaved lettuce.

Rocket

Eruca sativa   Zones 7–10

Until a decade or so ago, rocket—also known as arugula, roquette and rucola—was relatively unknown outside of Mediterranean countries; since then, it has become a hugely popular salad green. The taste of the tender leaves is meaty and smoky and lightly spicy, and adds great depth of flavor and indispensible interest to salads. It is also the flavor of spring in Turkey, when it is served with many memorable dishes, and is an important ingredient in salad mixes such as mesclun.

Growing and Harvesting

High-quality rocket is easy and quick to grow provided a sunny position and well-composted soil are available. The seed should be thinly

If harvested while still young, the small leaves and yellow and white flowers of shungiku, Chrysanthemum coronarium, add spice and variety to salads.

sown in rows in spring and can be treated as a cut-and-come-again crop. Additional plantings can be made until the end of summer in cooler areas, and until mid-autumn in warmer areas. Rocket has no serious pests and diseases, but can suffer from snails and slugs.

Scurvy Grass

Cochlearifolia officinalis   Zones 4–9

The smooth, delicate, succulent, slightly salty green leaves of scurvy grass, a member of the cabbage family, are high in vitamin C. It was this attribute that led the plant, also known as spoonwort, to be used to cure subclinical scurvy, caused by long winters without fresh food, and full-blown scurvy in sailors who had been at sea for long periods. The leaves and flower heads can be used in salads, sandwiches and soups.

Growing and Harvesting

Scurvy grass seeds should be planted in spring, into well-composted soil in a lightly shaded position. Regular watering is required.

Shungiku

Chrysanthemum coronarium var. spatiosum
                                   Zones 7–11

Originating on the shores of the Mediterranean—this is the beautiful cream and yellow wildflower that covers the landscape of Greece in April—this species is also naturalized in cool, higher altitude areas of Southeast Asia, and in China and Japan. As well as shungiku, it is known as edible chrysanthemum, chop suey greens and garland chrysanthemum.

Shungiku is harvested as a food crop when the plants are still young. The tender young leaves are high in vitamin A and are eaten fresh in salads, as are the flower petals. The shoots are braised, stir-fried, used to season soups, and made into fritters. In Japan, a pickle is made from the petals.

Growing and harvesting

This is an annual plant grown from seed in spring. To grow as a vegetable crop, it should ideally have a sunny, well-drained site and soil that has been enriched with compost, but it will grow under far less ideal circumstances. Regular watering is needed to produce leaves and shoots with the desired tenderness; the leaves become bitter if they are water stressed and also when they age.

Plants should be thinned to 6–8 in (15–20 cm) apart to allow for proper development. Although the plants should be harvested when young for their leaves and foliage, a few should be allowed to flower as the flowers can also be used and the seed collected.

A number of cultivars have been selected: **'Ohba'** has thick, soft leaves and is suitable for all uses; **'Flavon'** is ideal for salads; and **'Hua Ye'** is widely adapted and delicately fragrant.

Watercress

Nasturtium officinalis   Zones 6–10

Watercress is native to Europe, including the UK. It grows naturally at the margins of clean streams, particularly in limestone-rich regions. It adds tang and zing to salads and is also used in sandwiches, watercress soup, and Japanese tempura.

The fresh, succulent leaves are high in vitamins A, B1, B2, C, and E and in calcium, iron, magnesium and copper. Like dandelion and scurvy grass, this plant was once prized for its positive health effects at the end of long winters.

Watercress should never be collected in the wild in sheep country as a life-cycle stage of the liver fluke may be associated with the foliage.

Growing and Harvesting

Watercress can be planted by seed, but it is a simple thing to propagate it by cuttings. Obtain a bunch from a grocer's or Asian store and place it in a jar of fresh water (which should be

changed twice daily) until roots have formed. Watercress does not need to grow in water, and you can plant it into a large pot of 8 in (20 cm) diameter or more, filled with a mixture of clean loam and compost in a ratio of 2:1 along with a small handful of lime or dolomite; it's also advisable to place 1 in (2.5 cm) of charcoal at the base.

The pot should be kept in a cool, semi-shady area, and can be placed on a large saucer of fresh water to help maintain moisture. It should be watered regularly. Once the plant is well established, the foliage can be collected at any time.

Wild Rocket

Diplotaxis muralis   Zones 7–10

Although it belongs to a different genus and its leaves are far smaller, wild rocket—also referred to as wall rocket—has the same flavor as rocket. Its leaves are used in the same way.

Growing and Harvesting

Wild rocket is grown in the same manner as rocket. It is, however, especially important to provide a sunny, well-drained growing site.

Watercress is a hardy, perennial, European herb which grows naturally in wet soil.

Spinach

The cartoon character Popeye ate spinach to make him strong and it's true that spinach contains iron in soluble form. It also has very high levels of beta carotene and chlorphyll, believed to prevent some forms of cancer. As well, in Japanese studies spinach has been found to lower blood cholesterol. Spinach is also a significant source of folic acid, vitamins B2, B6, and C, calcium, and magnesium. While most research has been concentrated on true spinach, dark green, spinach-like substitutes are also believed to be good for the health.

Good King Henry Chenopodium bonus-henricus; **Hastate Orach** Atriplex hastata; **Houttuynia** Houttuynia cordata; **Lamb's Quarters** Chenopodium album; **Madeira Vine** Boussingaultia cordifolia syn. Anredera cordifolia; **Malabar Spinach** Basella alba syn. B. rubra; **Mountain Spinach** Atriplex hortensis; **New Zealand Spinach** Tetragonia tetragonoides syn. T. expansa; **Sorrel** Rumex acetosa syn. Acetosa sagittata; **Spinach** Spinacia oleracea; **Strawberry Spinach** Chenopodium capitatum; **Tampala Spinach** Amaranthus gangeticus; **Tree Spinach** Chenopodium giganteum

Gathered together here are vegetables that are not only commonly called spinach, but share much in terms of culinary use and cultivation. Most are derived from the one botanical family, Chenopodiaceae. The classic spinach of European culture, *Spinacia oleracea*, has many mimics throughout the world, both in taste and usage, and many of these thrive where the true spinach cannot. They can be used interchangeably in any of the classic spinach dishes.

Good King Henry
Chenopodium bonus-henricus   Zones 4–9

From the same family as spinach, this perennial is an ancient vegetable which is thought to have been spread through northern Europe by the Roman legions. It is also known as mercury or allgood. The leaves are tender with excellent flavor, but it is that very tenderness which has seen it displaced commercially by spinach because it tends to wilt after harvest. They can be steamed like asparagus

Studies have shown that high carotene dietary intake, particularly in the form of spinach and carrots, is associated with lower rates of common forms of cancer.

Both the leaves and the young, tender flowering shoots of Good King Henry, Chenopodium bonus-henricus, *can be eaten.*

and served with a Hollandaise sauce or melted butter.

Growing and Harvesting

Plant in spring when the ground has warmed up, spaced 6–8 in (15–20 cm) apart. Prepare the soil by digging through compost. Leaves can be gathered from plants at any time after full size is reached. Good King Henry is cold-tolerant and has no significant pests or diseases. It can be grown in warm areas if treated as a winter vegetable, planting the seed in early fall.

Hastate Orach
Atriplex hastata   Zones 6–10

This temperate climate species is a close relative of true spinach and a popular spinach substitute. The leaves have a naturally salty flavor and are often served mixed with other greens to be steamed and finished with a squeeze of fresh lemon juice. The seeds can be ground to make a nutty flavored flour. It is grown in the same manner as mountain spinach.

Houttuynia
Houttuynia cordata   Zones 5–11

Also known as fish plant, this once rare species is now grown from the Himalayas to China, Japan, and Java in Indonesia. It has a delicious complex lemon fragrance and can be added to soups, fish stews, and eaten raw in salads. The roots and fruits are also edible. The plants are creeping perennials found naturally in moist woodland, forming a mat of heart-shaped leaves. The most commonly found cultivar is '**Chameleon**' syn. 'Variegata' which has very pretty green, deep rose-pink, and white variegated leaves. It is easily grown in moist soil to which plenty of compost has been added. It has no major pests or diseases.

Lamb's Quarters
Chenopodium album   Zones 4–9

The leaves and tips of this plant make an excellent spinach substitute and in many areas of the world are grown for this purpose. Plants are also selected for their seed which can be ground to

The houttuynia, Houttuynia cordata, makes an excellent—and edible—ground cover for cool, shady areas.

Madeira Vine

Boussingaultia cordifolia syn. *Anredera cordifolia*
Zones 8–12

This looks superficially like Malabar spinach and is a vigorous climber, growing to as high as 20 ft (6 m). The flowers are sweetly scented, and the plant forms tubers below the ground as well as aerial tubers. It is propagated from the tubers. Despite its common name, Madeira vine is South American in origin though it has been naturalized in the western Mediterranean area.

Malabar Spinach

Basella alba syn. *B. rubra*   Zones 9–12

Grown in warmer climates, this plant is native to South East Asia and the Indian subcontinent and is grown as a perennial scrambling climber. It is known by many other names—country spinach, Ceylon spinach, vine spinach, and basella. The heart-shaped leaves are small, smooth, and very thick. To eat, they are succulent with a delicious flavor that is milder than true spinach. In Asia the leaves are added to soups, or steamed. The leaves are rich in iron, beta carotenes, and vitamin C.

Growing and Harvesting

In temperate regions Malabar spinach can be cropped as an annual as it does not require a long growing season. Plant it in late spring for cropping through the summer and early fall months. It is totally intolerant of frost. Seed can be planted under glass in cooler areas and seedlings planted out when the ground temperature is sufficiently warm to grow melons, tomatoes, and eggplants. Where the plants are perennial, cuttings can be taken; they will root in water in a few days.

Malabar spinach is best suited to sandy loam soils with a pH of 6.0–6.5, but is quite tolerant of a range of soils if they are well supplemented with the

make a nutty flour for pancakes, muffins, breads, and biscuits. The young inflorescences are eaten like broccoli or dipped in a very light batter and fried, while the seeds are used in salads and cooking after sprouting. It is native to Eurasia and naturalized in Australasia and North America.

A distinctive cultivar supplied to Californian restaurants and grown in home gardens is called '**Magenta**'. As the name suggests, the foliage is a brilliant purple. A Eurasian subspecies, *amaranticolor* (sometimes called Anserine amarante), is also used as a spinach substitute. It has brilliant purple-red young foliage and panicles of red flowers. All forms are grown from seed planted in spring and respond to well-composted soil and regular watering. Seeds of the cultivated forms are available from a number of seed houses. None suffer from any significant pests or diseases.

Malabar spinach, Basella alba, *can be trained along a fence or wall to form an attractive cover.*

addition of compost. Crops should be given supports as they climb to about 4 ft (1.2 m), and they require regular watering. Occasional applications of fish emulsion or seaweed fertilizers which are rich in nitrogen will promote lush growth and abundant harvests. Occasionally, Malabar spinach may suffer from a fungal leaf disease that also attacks beets. The two crops should be well separated in the garden and any infected leaves removed and burned.

Harvesting should be resisted until the plants have begun to branch. By the time plants are three months old they can be regularly harvested for shoot tips up to 5 in (12.5 cm) long. In hot climates where the vines are grown as a perennial, regular picking should be maintained in the flowering season to ensure the production of green shoots. Seeds are quite widely available from specialist growers in the United States, Australasia, and Europe, usually marketed as Malabar spinach. Two types are available, one green, the other with a reddish tinge.

Mountain Spinach
Atriplex hortensis   Zones 6–10

Also known as butter leaves or orach, the mild-flavored leaves of this hardy annual plant are valued as a warm weather spinach substitute. In France, where it is known as *arroche*, it is often cooked in combination with sorrel to reduce the lemony acidity of the latter. The green-leafed form is cultivated, but it is the cultivar **'Red Mountain Orach'** which is currently sought after for its beautiful ruby-colored foliage. The seeds are traditionally used to add protein and flavor to soups and baked goods such as muffins.

Growing and Harvesting
Mountain spinach is exceptionally easy to grow. Plant the seed 6 in (15 cm) apart, in rows 12 in (30 cm) apart and cover with $1/_2$ in (1 cm) of soil. Although mountain spinach will survive well in less than perfect conditions, enrichment of the soil with compost and regular watering produces larger leaves and retards bolting.

'Red Mountain Orach' mountain spinach, Atriplex hortensis, has ruby-red foliage which turns green when steamed.

New Zealand spinach, Tetragonia tetragonoides, has high levels of vitamin C and was used by Captain James Cook in the 18th century to combat scurvy in his crew.

With the exception of an occasional leaf-eating insect, mountain spinach has no notable pests or diseases. It will grow to 4–6 ft (1.2–1.8 m) high. The leaves, which can be harvested on a cut-and-come-again basis, may grow up to 3 in (7.5 cm) in diameter.

New Zealand Spinach

Tetragonia tetragonoides syn. *T. expansa*
Zones 8–10

Few vegetables are easier to grow than New Zealand spinach, also known as Warrigal greens. It is capable of thriving in hot and dry

conditions and occurs naturally along the sea coasts of Australia, New Zealand, and other Pacific Rim countries and islands. Sir Joseph Banks, botanist to James Cook's expedition to the South Pacific in the late 18th century, discovered it and brought the seed back to England. It is a succulent, matting, grey-green plant that is an excellent substitute for true spinach, having a similar flavor and habit of 'melting down' in the pot when cooked.

It requires full sun and good drainage. Despite its ability to survive demanding conditions, it responds well when supplemented with compost and regularly watered. It is grown commercially in Australia and became known as part of the fashionable 'bush food' culinary movement. In Australasia it has always been a minor crop. It is treated as an annual in cooler areas, but is a short lived perennial in hot places. It has no pests or diseases of any significance.

Sorrel

Rumex acetosa syn. *Acetosa sagittata*   Zones 3–9

Several closely related species are eaten under the catchall name of sorrel. They all share a refreshing, tart, lemony flavor and make an excellent addition to early spring salads, as well as being used in soups. Sorrels are rich in vitamin C, and were valued as spring greens in the days when many people suffered marginal scurvy after a long winter of being deprived of fresh vegetables.

The most prized species for culinary purposes is French sorrel, or buckler-leaved sorrel, *Rumex scutatus*, which has a particularly fine lemony flavor. It is native to sub-alpine areas from France to Iran, and thrives in well-drained and fairly dry soils. It has also long become naturalized in places as far apart as Australasia and North America, and is prized by

gourmet foragers for wild food. It can be grown on well-drained soil in spring and responds with very tender, somewhat larger foliage. Herb patience, *R. patientia*, also known as spinach dock, is the earliest of the sorrels to produce a crop of leaves, and is milder flavored than the more commonly cultivated garden sorrel. It responds well to culture. The leaves are harvested when young. Other very acceptable spinach substitute species of *Rumex* include curled dock, *R. crispus*, rich in vitamin C and beta carotenes, and used raw in salads and cooked, and sheep sorrel, *R. acetosella*, with sour little tender leaves that are added to salads. Only the young leaves are used from these two species.

Garden sorrel or broadleaf sorrel, *R. acetosa*, is the most commonly cultivated species, and it is used in the manner of spinach, in soups, pureéd, in omelettes, ragouts, fricaseés, sauces, stuffings for fresh water fish, and in the classic *soupe aux herbes* and cream of sorrel soup.

Growing and Harvesting

All sorrels are perennial, and a small bed should be set aside to grow your chosen variety. Plant the seeds into well-drained, well-composted soils in spring or fall. They should be sown $^1/_2$ in (1 cm) deep and 6 in (15 cm) apart in rows 18 in (45 cm) apart. Sorrels prefer an acid soil, and require abundant nitrogen and regular watering. They require little care, growing quickly and vigorously.

Rarely bothered with any pests or diseases, a monthly feed with seaweed or fish emulsion in summer will produce very abundant supplies of tender leaves. Plants should be mulched once they are half grown. If they are left in the ground as a perennial, a spring dressing of well rotted manure or compost should be applied along the rows to supply a fresh source of nitrogen for the following season's growth. Sorrel wilts quickly after cutting so be sure to have your planting close at hand. It rarely appears in stores for this reason.

Recommended Cultivars

'Belleville' — This is a small-growing, productive French cultivar widely adapted in terms of soils and climate with large, lightly puckered, pale green leaves.

'Blonde de Lyon' syn. mammoth Lyon — This is probably the most widely grown cultivar, with rounded, large, thick, pale green leaves which are tender and mild in flavor. It is resistant to bolting and a good choice for warmer areas.

French sorrel, R. scutatus, is a low-growing perennial with pale green leaves and tiny flowers.

Sorrel, Rumex acetosa, belongs to the same family as rhubarb and rau ram (Vietnamese coriander).

Spinach

Spinacia oleracea   Zones 5–10

Spinach is thought to have originated in the western Himalayas, and was first cultivated by the ancient Persians. From there it spread eastward to China and westward to England, reaching there by the 16th century. There are two different strains of spinach: an older, more primitive group that is prickle-seeded and handles heat and cold well, and the more modern smooth-seeded group that contains the majority of the currently available cultivars. More than one species of *Spinacia* may well have been involved in breeding our modern crops. Spinach cultivars are also divided according to whether they are smooth-leafed or savoy-leafed, the latter having broader, thicker, puckered leaves that yield more bulk.

Spinacia oleracea, the classic spinach, is partial to cool climates though some varieties can be grown in warmer areas.

Growing and Harvesting

Spinach is a member of the goosefoot family Chenopodiaceae. It prefers cool temperatures— most of its cultivars have a tendency to bolt in warm weather. In warm but not tropical areas, spinach can be planted in early fall for late fall and winter harvests. A late winter planting is also feasible, but it should be harvested when young or it will run to seed. In cool climates, seeds of tender varieties are sown in very early spring and in progressive plantings throughout summer, while the winter hardy sorts are planted in late summer or early fall for winter harvests. Spinach is tolerant of light shade, and midsummer plantings should receive some shading to prevent sun scald. With the assistance of cloches or frames, winter crops can be carried through to the end of the following spring.

Seeds should be sown approximately $1/2$ in (1 cm) deep in rows and thinned to the strongest plants, allowing a final spacing of 6 in (15 cm) between plants and 12 in (30 cm) between rows.

Spinach is a fast-growing vegetable requiring a good, rich, moist soil and very regular watering to prevent it being held back in growth. It is tolerant of a fairly wide range of soils, but it is essential that generous amounts of compost be incorporated. One or two applications of a soluble seaweed fertilizer during the growth period is recommended in order to supply readily available nutrients, particularly nitrogen, to maintain rapid growth. Weeding is also necessary and once the summer and fall plants are established, they should be mulched to maintain cool moist soil and a weed-free growing environment.

Spinach, when well grown, has few enemies. Downy mildew can prove to be a problem and affected leaves should be removed and burned. The crop should then be given a boost with a seaweed foliar spray to promote healthy new growth. Caterpillar attacks are rare and can be controlled by hand picking.

Spinach can be treated as a cut-and-come-again vegetable, removing just a few of the outside leaves from each plant at a time; alternatively, whole plants can be harvested. At the first signs of bolting, the crop should be quickly cut and used as it takes little time from flower initiation to seed formation.

Recommended Cultivars

'King of Denmark' — Popular in the United Kingdom, this cultivar has thick, slightly puckered, deep green, arrow-shaped leaves, excellent for salads and as a cooked dish. It is heavy yielding, resistant to bolting, very hardy, and matures very early.

'Monnopa' — This is a very low oxalate level cultivar with a markedly mild flavor, suitable for babies and young children. It is winter hardy and quite bolt-resistant.

'Sigmaleaf' — Planted both in early spring and fall, this is a moderately savoy-leafed, upward-growing, early-maturing cultivar resistant to bolting and with a good flavor.

'Virginia Savoy' — This is a sturdy, erect-growing cultivar with dark, heavily puckered leaves, resistant to blight, and very cold-hardy.

'Winter Bloomsdale' — As its name indicates, this is a very cold-resistant strain which overwinters well, and has dark-green, thick, savoyed leaves. It is blue mold and virus-resistant.

Seed Saving Notes

Save seed from strong, healthy, productive plants that have been the last to run to seed so that you select a strain that will do best in your district and yield for as long as possible. Plants can cross with other spinach cultivars up to 533 yds (500 m) away, and it is better to grow just one

In warmer areas, spinach plants should be harvested young, before they run to seed.

cultivar to the seed production stage. Other cultivars can be grown but should not be allowed to run to flower. Seed will keep 3–5 years in zip-locked, plastic, labelled bags stored at the bottom of the refrigerator, or in airtight bottles in a cool dark place.

Strawberry Spinach

Chenopodium capitatum   Zones 4–9

Popular in the Victorian garden, but almost forgotten until recent times, this quaint spinach relative has mild-flavored leaves and extraordinary, red, berry-like clusters of fruits, borne up the stems. Both the leaves and tender young shoots can be eaten in salads and cooked; the succulent fruits are also edible and can be boiled or tossed into salads. A number of specialist seed companies now stock the seed.

Growing and Harvesting

This is an exceptionally easy plant to grow. In spring, sow the seed into well-composted soil and regularly water it. The crop should be thinned to 6 in (15 cm) apart when about 3 in (7.5 cm) tall. It has no major pests or diseases, although you may find that birds offer stiff competition for the berries. There are no selected varieties currently available.

Tampala Spinach

Amaranthus gangeticus   Zones 8–11

Also known as Chinese spinach, leaf amaranth, *yin tsoi*, and *bayan*, this is a very popular substitute for spinach in sub-tropical and tropical climates, where true spinach will not survive. It is extensively grown for sale in Asian vegetable markets throughout warmer areas of the world. It has also become popular among home gardeners. The flavor of most cultivars is like spinach with a touch of horseradish, and the leaves are exceptionally rich in iron, calcium, and leaf proteins.

Growing and Harvesting

Tampala spinach is an annual plant growing to 40 in (1 m). It is sown from spring onward in a succession of plantings each of which is totally harvested. Alternatively, the original planting can be encouraged to remain productive for the entire growing season. Seed is usually broadcast over a bed which has been prepared with generous additions of compost, and the seed then raked into the soil and watered well. The seedling thinnings can be used as a pot herb when they reach about 3 in (7.5 cm) high, leaving a spacing of about 8 in (20 cm) in all directions between the plants that are left to grow on to maturity. In cooler climates, it is still possible to grow this type of spinach by planting in early summer and thinning to a spacing of 4 in (10 cm),

the crop being harvested while still young, 6–8 weeks after planting.

To maintain growth, this nitrogen-hungry plant should be given a generous soaking to the roots with compost or manure tea (prepared by soaking a tied full bag of either in a large container of water for a week) during the growing period. In hot climates where plants may grow on to be repeatedly harvested over many months, the application of a foliar spray of seaweed-based fertilizer at the recommended rate, once or twice duing the growing season, is beneficial. Tampala spinach has no significant pests or diseases, although the leaves should be monitored for chewing insects on a regular basis.

Harvests may be made of successive plantings while they are still young and tender. In hot areas, provided that plants are prevented from flowering by regular harvesting of the young shoot tips, and provided with supplementary feeds of nitrogen, regular harvests may be taken from the same plants until colder weather arrives in fall. The side stalks can also be harvested. Peeled and cooked, they have a similar flavor to artichoke.

Recommended Cultivars

'Hartman's Giant' — A beautiful, tall, purple plant to 6 ft (1.8 m) used in salads, and cooked like spinach. The seeds can also be popped and used as a cereal.

'Hijau' — Characterised by brilliant lime green, rounded leaves with exceptional flavor which can be used fresh in salads or steamed and used as spinach, this cultivar forms a strong, upright plant.

'Merah' — Pretty enough to grow as an ornamental and perfect for edible landscaping, this bicolor cultivar has heart-shaped, slightly puckered, dark green leaves with rich red veins and a delightful walnut flavor perfect for salads. The large leaves, up to 6 in (15 cm), can be used as wraps for steaming or braising food in the manner of tender grape leaves.

Tree Spinach

Chenopodium giganteum   Zones 4–9

The leaves of this plant have long been used in Asian cooking and as a pot herb in Europe, but it is the cultivar **'Magentaspreen'** which has become so popular. Related to true spinach, the leaves are a beautiful mixture of magenta-red, rose-pink, lilac, and purple. The plants grow to 6 ft (1.8 m) and are perennial in mild climates. The seeds are planted in rows as soon as the soil has warmed and thinned to 10 in (25 cm) when 6 in (15 cm) high. The plants prefer a soil which has been well enriched with compost, but they will perform satisfactorily on quite sandy soils provided they are very regularly watered. The plants have no major pests or diseases. The leaves should be harvested when young, and it is advisable to cut all flowering stems back (saving one good plant for seed harvesting), or it may spread to other garden beds by seed. **'Magentaspreen'** is available from specialist seed suppliers.

Water Spinach

Ipomoea aquatica   Zones 9–12

This warm temperate to tropical crop which originated from India and South East Asia is also known as *kang kong* or *ong choi*. It is produced under greenhouse conditions (particularly by hydroponics) in places like Holland. In cooking, the succulent, tender green tips are used; they are rich in protein and iron and hence an old remedy for anaemia. They can be steamed and stir-fried, and are used in soups, curries, and stews, and are a favorite in Asian cooking. The youngest leaves can also be used in salads.

Growing and Harvesting

Seedlings are raised in spring and grown in moist beds on land. It is, an important commercial crop in many parts of the world but is regarded as a weed in others. It is not a problem when land grown, or confined to small pools for harvesting in the manner of water chestnuts. It has no notable pests and diseases.

A single water spinach plant can grow at a rate of 4 in (10 cm) a day and grow stems to a length of 70ft (21 m). It is therefore regarded as an invasive weed in many aquatic areas.

Squash, Marrows, Pumpkins and Zucchini

Summer Squash *Cucurbita pepo*;
Winter Squash *C. maxima, C. moschata, C. pepo*

Names like marrow, squash, and pumpkin are really quite confused around the world and are used more or less interchangeably. For instance, while the term 'pumpkin' in Australia implies a fine textured, golden or orange colored, well flavored, 'dry' fruit that is prized, elsewhere it is a term of derision for cultivars only suitable for cattle fodder. One country's winter squash is also another country's pumpkin, so common names are of limited value. The situation is further complicated by the prefixes 'summer' and 'winter', and descriptions of shape or usage to define groups of cultivars.

Gathered here are closely related, popular food cultivars derived from the plant genus *Cucurbita*. *C. pepo, C. moschata* and *C. ficifolia* all originate from Central America, and *C. maxima* originates from South America.

Some forms of *C. pepo* are regularly harvested when the fruits are immature, including zucchini or courgettes, and custard or scallop squash. *C. pepo* also includes winter squash such as the many acorn squash and the equally highly rated, turban shaped, buttercup-type squash with their curious protruding 'button' and the beautiful **'Turks Turban'**, vegetable spaghetti, the sweet potato squash **'Delicata'**, vegetable marrows, and crookneck squash. The seed of cultivars such as **'Lady Godiva'** are eaten raw, roasted, ground, or used

Above right: 'Turks Turban' is a winter squash that is very popular for ornamental use. The fruit is vertically striped with orange, green and white.

Below: Pumpkins are summer squashes that vary from the elongated to the broad and flattened with scalloped rims. Many have ornamental skins.

A harvest of pumpkins in Maine, USA.

as a source of cooking oil. The roasted seed are known as pepitas. The flowers and flower buds are stuffed or made into fritters. The seeds are also sprouted for salads. A number of cultivars are bush types. Popular Halloween pumpkins such as 'Jack O'Lantern', 'Jack-be-Little', and 'Connecticut Field' also come from this group.

C. *moschata* has been cultivated for more than 5,500 years and is characterized by sweet flavored flesh which is eaten raw, or in pumpkin pies, puddings, soups and cakes, as well as roasted, fried, baked, and boiled. The seed are roasted and salted. Included in this group are the excellent butternut squash and trom-bone pumpkin type cultivars, and the very sweet 'Pawpaw' pumpkin, its relative the 'Queensland Gramma', and 'Tahitian Melon Squash'. Some pumpkin cultivars including 'cheese' types like 'Kentucky Field' also belong to this group. Most cultivars are long trailing plants with large, soft, shallow lobed leaves, but some bush forms have been developed.

C. *maxima* is an enthusiastic trailer-climber with almost round leaves and includes the monster cow pumpkins such as: 'Atlantic Giant' which has reached over 612 pounds (280 kg) and wins giant pumpkin competitions around the world (otherwise being designated as a fodder crop); some of the finest 'pumpkins' such as 'Queensland Blue', 'Crown Prince', 'Triamble', 'Rouge Vif d'Etampes' and 'Hundredweight'; and the hubbard squash and banana types. Some of the best-loved pumpkins for Halloween carving are also derived from this group.

Growing and Harvesting

Bush forms of squash such as zucchini can be grown and fruited in cooler areas with short summers, but the long vining cultivars of squash and pumpkins require a growing season of 4–5 months of warm to hot weather. All have exactly the same growing requirements which are a sunny position, warm, fertile soil enriched with plenty of compost and well rotted manure too if it is available, and regular, generously applied water.

All are grown from seed which is planted directly into the soil in warm to hot climates, but should be raised in individual pots indoors in early spring in cooler areas to provide a head start on the growing season, and then planted out after the last frost date. Early plantings in cool districts are protected with cloches which increase the soil temperature and provide protection against aberrant frosts.

Small 'hills' are created of soil highly enriched with rotted down compost and manures, and the seed or seedlings are planted into them. The hills should be about 24 in (60 cm) across and 10 in (25 cm) high. The spacing of plants, and the number of seed planted, depends on the cultivar (size indicated below) and the amount of space available. In small gardens, extra space can be found for vigorous climbing forms by training them up and along fences, or as a temporary green and gold cloak over summer houses, garden sheds, and pergolas. Once established, there is little more to be done but regular watering. When the canopy of the crop has closed over, do not water the crop in the evening as it will encourage mildew to which many cultivars are prone, particularly as fall approaches. Instead, water in the morning so that the sun will quickly dry the leaves.

Cucurbits are very brittle so be careful when handling them at both the seedling and adult stages. Many of the cultivars that form runners will root down into the soil at nodes on the stem. It is a good idea if you have

limited space to guide the vines in the direction you wish them to grow every 2–3 days as their growth rate in hot weather can be as much as 39 in (1 m) in the same period. Weeding is difficult once vining types begin to develop and good weed contol and a mat of mulch for the plants to grow on is advisable in the garden. Once growth is well established and some fruits are formed, it is a good idea to pinch out the leader which will force side branching to take place.

The sexes of squash plants are separated into male and female flowers and the male flowers begin flowering first, so abortion of the first few flowers should be ignored. Female flowers have a swollen ovary beneath the petals and are easily distinguished. Bees are normally responsible for cross pollination but are not always obliging, particularly in districts where spraying programs have been carried out. It is a simple manner to hand pollinate the female flowers as they open by snapping off a fresh male flower and transfering some pollen onto the sticky green top of the protruding central, female stigma.

There is no need to wait for late fall to enjoy the fruits of squash and pumpkin. Many are truly delicious when harvested young before the skin hardens. This is one of the rewards of growing your own; these immature fruits are rarely seen in greengrocers as they bruise easily. If the vines are harvested lightly and regularly, they will also produce more fruit. However, leave some early fruit of winter squash and pumpkin to fully mature for winter storage.

Winter storage pumpkins and winter squash should be 'cured' before storage by leaving them out in the sun for 3–4 weeks on racks, raised wire netting, or clean hay. They should be checked underneath regularly for any damage from slaters or slugs. Once curing is complete, they are stacked on shelves or racks in a dry place. Other than the occasional predations of slugs and slaters, and the development of mildew as mentioned above, squash and pumpkins have relatively few problems. A number of the field grown, commercial cultivars are dryland farmed in warm areas, relying on seasonal rainfall alone, and remain highly productive despite any fuss.

Zucchini will continue to grow until they become marrows unless they are harvested when small.

Button or scalloped squash have become very popular. They should be harvested when small and tender.

Summer Squash

Cucurbita pepo   Zones 8–11

This group includes varieties known as patty pan, or custard, or scallop squash.

The scallop edged fruits of this type of summer squash have become so popular as to rival zucchini. The fruits should be picked constantly once the plants come into bearing, and are harvested as small as possible for cooking.

Recommended Cultivars

'Benning's Green Tint' — Popular in home gardens and for markets, this older cultivar has pale green, tender, prolific fruit. Bush.

'Sunburst' — This 1985 hybrid cultivar has rich golden yellow fruits and remains a firm favorite for its tender, buttery flesh. Bush.

'Yellow Bush' syn. Golden Bush — is another deep yellow skinned cultivar readily available and dating to prior to 1860, having finely textured, excellently flavored, yellowish flesh. Saved seeds of 'Sunburst' will not breed true. Bush.

'White Bush' syn. Early White Bush, White Patty Pan — This old garden cultivar of ancient origin remains one of the most popular and most readily available. The skin is palest green when the fruit are young, and later pure white. Eaten as a summer marrow, the tender flesh is milky white with a unique, delicious flavor. Harvested at all stages, it can be boiled whole when mature and the flesh scooped out to serve with a smooth, creamy white sauce. Bush.

Zucchini or Courgette

All zucchini cultivars should be constantly harvested when very young, no more than 4–6 in (10–15 cm) long. Most cultivars enlarge at an astonishing rate, rapidly losing their culinary attraction, and once a few have been allowed to grow productivity rapidly drops away.

Recommended Cultivars

'Butterblossom' — This is a hybrid which is very useful for those who enjoy eating squash blossoms. The male flowers form prolifically and are sold in bunches for stuffing, while the female flowers are sold with tiny fruits attached. Bush.

'Cocozelle' syn. Italian Vegetable Marrow, 'Cocozella di Napoli' — The long, slender, cylindrical fruit are pale green and ribbed, striped with deep green, and have firm delicious flesh. Bush.

'Costata Romanesca' syn. Roman Ribbed — This gourmet cultivar looks beautiful sliced on a plate. It is a distinctive strain with fluted fruit that are long and striped green. Unlike most zucchini, it remains delicious and tender even if the fruit become fully grown. It is usually picked while the fruit is about 6 in (15 cm) long and cooked with the blossom attached. Large vining plant.

'French White' — Becoming readily available from specialist seed firms, this older French cultivar has white fruits that are delicious when harvested while still tiny, around 3–4 in (7.5–10 cm) long. Semi-bush.

'Golden' syn. 'Burpee's Golden Zucchini' — A heavy bearing cultivar with

'Ronde de Nice' is a delicious cultivar that has almost perfectly round fruits that are pale green with firm white flesh.

cylindrical, glossy, pure golden fruit of excellent and distinctive flavor used both raw grated into salads and cooked. Bush.

'**Ronde de Nice**' syn. Tonda di Nizza — This is a highly productive, tender, delicious cultivar which forms almost perfectly round fruits that are pale green with firm white flesh. It is exceedingly easy to grow. Bush.

'**White Lebanese**' syn. Lubano — This is an excellent old cultivar widely grown in Europe, the Middle East, the United States, Mexico, and Australasia. The fruits are palest green, slightly fatter at the blossom end, and tender and sweet. Bush.

Other Summer Squash

'**Green Bush**' — This very popular, heavily productive old cultivar forms uniform long, pale green marrows with deeper green stripes. It can be steamed and served with a creamy white sauce, and also stuffed with savory fillings. Compact bush. 60 days. '**Long Green Trailing**' syn. Long Green Striped Vegetable Marrow — is similar but the fruit are borne on moderate vines.

'**Spaghetti Squash**' syn. Vegetable Spaghetti — So called because, when cooked, the flesh breaks up into spaghetti-like strands. The fruit are small and oval and harvested up to 10 in (25 cm) long. It was introduced from Japan in 1934 and is boiled or baked whole. Bush and climbing forms exist.

'**Tromonchino**' syn. Zuccheta Rampicante d'Albenga — This sweet and truly delicious summer marrow forms very long, slender, pale green fruits which are bulbed at the blossom end. It is harvested when 8–18 in (20–45 cm) long. It is a strong vine to approximately 38 ft (12 m), and is a *C. moschata* cultivar.

'**Yellow Crookneck**' syn. Early Golden Summer Crookneck — This very popular old cultivar from before 1828 forms golden yellow, warted, curved fruits bulbed at the blossom end and hooked over at the stem end with pale yellow-white flesh. It is excellent eating when picked young. Bush.

'**Goldarch Crookneck**' — is a closely related cultivar with greater uniformity of shape. Almost smooth skinned, it has a longer bulb to the fruit. Bush.

Top left: 'White Lebanese' and 'Golden' zucchini are becoming increasingly popular with organic gardeners.

Below left: The 'Yellow Crookneck' squash forms golden yellow, warted, fruits that are excellent to eat when young.

Cucurbita maxima includes a large group of pumpkins with very hard blue-gray or orange skins.

'Green hubbard' squash, Cucurbita maxima, are large, rounded in the center and tapered at both ends, with deep green, slightly warted, very hard skin that turns bronzed green.

Winter Squash

Cucurbita maxima, C.moschata, C.pepo Zones 8–11

Recommended Cultivars

'Buttercup' — The fruits are turban shaped with a distinctive 'button', dark green striped grey, weighing over 4 lbs (2 kg) when mature, with very finely textured, deep orange, sweet flesh of excellent quality and flavor. The vine grows to 10–13 ft (3–4 m).

'Chestnut' — Treasured for its rich orange, thick, very sweet and dry flesh, the long keeping fruits of this cultivar are small to medium, about 4 lbs (2kg), flattened, and green overlaid with slate.

'Crown Prince' — This is an excellent cultivar, widely popular, with large, somewhat flattened, grey-blue skinned fruits with excellent quality, dry, delicious flesh. The superb quality, long keeping **'Queensland Blue'**, now grown around the world, is of the same type, as is another fine quality, long keeping Australian cultivar **'Jarrahdale'**. **'Ironbark'** is an old cultivar of this type, found mainly in Queensland and northern New South Wales. It has unbelievably hard skin, traditionally opened by splitting with an axe. Very long-keeping indeed, it has extremely good flavor and a fine, dry texture.

'Delicata' syn. Sweet Potato Squash — Introduced at the end of the 19th century, this cultivar produces small, cylindrical, plump, ribbed fruit, pale cream striped green, with dry, sweet, rich flesh of good quality. A highly prolific small vine.

'Ebony Acorn' — Shaped like an acorn, this is a small fruit to almost 4 lbs (2 kg), with a dark green skin turning golden yellow at full maturity. The flesh is pale gold, quite thick, sweet, tender, dry and beautifully flavored. Short vine. **'Jersey Golden Acorn'** is similar and has high beta carotene levels, and a delicious nutty flavor. **'Bush Table Queen'**, **'Ebony Acorn'**, and **'Bush Table Queen'** are other acorn types of excellent quality.

'Green Hubbard' syn. True Hubbard — The long keeping fruits are large, rounded in the center and tapered at both ends, with deep green, slightly warted, very hard skin that turns somewhat bronzed green when mature. The flesh is thick, fine grained, dry, and semi-sweet. A vigorous, very productive climber. There are a number of closely related cultivars, **'Blue Hubbard'**, **'Golden Hubbard'**, **'Chicago Warted'**, the miniature **'Golden 'Little Gem'**, **'Blue Kuri'**, and **'Baby Blue'**. The last named is a semi-bush type.

'Gros Jaune de Paris' syn. Yellow Large Paris — The fruit of this pepo cultivar are large, flattened, and ribbed with a salmon-yellow skin and fine, sweet, yellow flesh. It is popular in France for soup and for pumpkin pie.

'Neck Pumpkin' syn. Trombone Pumpkin — Very popular in Australia and also grown the United States, this is a large, curved fruit up to 4 ft (1.2 m) long more bulbous at the blossom end, with smooth pale brown hard skin and thick, solid, orange, sweet and dry flesh. Climbing vine.

'Pawpaw' syn. Papaya Pumpkin — Very popular in sub-tropical to tropical Queensland, and grown also in the United States and Taiwan. Shaped like an oval pawpaw, it is thin skinned, dull green mottled with khaki-yellow, and with flesh that is thick, orange, tender, superbly flavored and very sweet. Excellent for roasting and pumpkin pies. Vigorous and disease resistant climber.

'Pink Banana Jumbo' — The fruit are very long, up to 4 ft (1.2 m), cylindrical, slightly bent at the stem end, pink when mature, and can weigh up to about 50 lbs (23 kg). The flesh is fine textured, sweet, and of excellent quality for baking and roasting. Popular in California and Australia.

'Queensland Gramma' — This very large fruit is pear shaped and ribbed, about 2 ft (60 cm) wide and 14 in (35 cm) high. It is usually pale brown but may be mottled khaki, with thick, meaty, deep orange flesh of superb flavor and sweetness. It is ideal for roasting and for pumpkin pies. Vigorous climber.

'Rouge Vif d'Etampes' — Beautiful to look at, this large, flattened, ribbed, glossy, bright, glowing orange-red fruit is unsurpassed for appearance. The moist richly colored flesh is tender but best reserved for soup— and Halloween.

'Tahitian Melon Squash' — An exceptionally sweet fleshed, excellent keeping, large cultivar weighing up to 40 lbs (18 kg) that continues to sweeten on storage. This cultivar needs a 5 month growing season and produces large slightly curved fruits with deep orange, rich, very sweet flesh which is used both raw and cooked. A vigorous vine.

'Tennessee Sweet Potato' — This is a medium to large, pear shaped, lemon fruit with greenish stripes. The pale yellow flesh is thick, sweet, and of excellent flavor. Climber.

Top left: Pink banana squash are very popular and have cylindrical fruit and are pink when mature.

Below left: The spectacular 'Rouge Vif d'Etampes' pumpkin.

'Triamble' — A splendid, vigorously vining cultivar with 3-lobed, dark skinned, long-keeping fruits with thick, sweet, excellently flavored and textured flesh.

'Turk's Turban' syn. Turk's Cap — This very distinctive cultivar is very popular for ornamental use. The fruit is up to 12 in (30 cm) in diameter, and is vertically striped with orange, green and white. The flesh is fine grained, juicy, and pale orange but lacking the flavor of other cultivars listed.

'Waltham' — The butternut pumpkins are an excellent group for all culinary purposes with dense, fine grained, sweet flesh of excellent flavor. Waltham is one of the best forms with uniform, blocky fruit up to almost 4 lbs (2 kg) with a very small seed cavity and excellent storage ability. Moderate climber.

Tahitian melon squash are exceptionally sweet fleshed.

Tomatoes

Cherry Tomato *Lycopersicon esculentum var. cerasiforme syn. L. lycopersicum var. cerasiforme;* **Currant Tomato** *L. pimpinellifolium;* **Tomatillo** *Physalis ixocarpa;* **Tomato** *Lycopersicon esculentum syn. L. lycopersicum*

Life is too short to waste on tasteless, mass-produced tomatoes. Far better to enjoy the intense flavors and fragrances of natural tomatoes grown as they should be: in an environment free of chemicals, and in rich, composted earth and warm sunshine.

Imagine spilled before you, like an upturned casket of precious jewels, a heap of tomatoes, ranging in size from the pearl-like to fruits as large as the great hearts of oxen; tomatoes shaped like bananas, pears, globes, plums, or valentine hearts; tomatoes that are smooth or exquisitely ruffled; tomatoes that are translucent apricot, jade green, ivory white, purple, black, chocolate, cherry, or with stripes and slashes of gold on richest red, or emerald on amber. Imagine overwhelming flavors: rich, tangy, sweet, sometimes laced with spice, smokiness, salt or with counterpoints of lemon, raspberry, strawberry or plum. All these sensations are yours for the savoring when you devote just a little time to growing your own tomatoes.

Tomatoes generally belong to the genus *Lycopersicon* and what we think of as a 'normal' tomato is derived from a wild ancestor, native to South America, *Lycopersicon esculentum.* Members of the same genus include the cherry tomato, *L. esculentum* var. *cerasiforme* and the currant tomato, *L.pimpinellifolium.* More distantly related is the distinctive Mexican tomatillo, *Physalis ixocarpa.*

The world's great storehouse of heirloom tomatoes was once almost lost. But the actions of individual seed savers around the world managed to rescue it and the old varieties are now among the produce most sought-after

There is a tomato for every occasion and growing them organically will enhance both flavor and color.

by the world's great restaurants. Specialist seed firms increase their offerings of heirloom and old tomato varieties annually. Among them you will find no tough-skinned, bounceable tomatoes with thick white cores. Nor will you find genetically modified plants. The old tomatoes are not 'all-purpose' fruits. In the past, there were different tomatoes for every occasion: tomatoes for sauces and pastes; flavor-filled cherry and currant tomatoes for salads; richly flavored beefsteak and oxheart tomatoes for slicing and frying; and fluted and hollowed tomatoes for stuffing and baking.

Today, there are literally a thousand or more superb nonhybrid and nonbioengineered heirloom varieties to choose from, and those listed below are but a small selection. Having been bred before the advent of artificial fertilizers, heirloom tomatoes are 'low-response' plants and were intended to be grown in composted soils, so they are the ideal choice for organic gardeners. And, as tomatoes normally breed true to type, you can save some seed and pass your favorite varieties on to friends, thereby helping to perpetuate these wonderful plants.

Although it is possible to turn tomato culture into an art form and the following description of how to grow these tomatoes may seem highly detailed, the procedure is really quite simple and the results among the most rewarding in all kinds of gardening.

Even if you only have a few pots on a balcony, you can grow a number of these best-loved of all salad vegetables, harvest them for months, and eat in a gourmet's paradise.

Growing and Harvesting
Increasing numbers of specialist nurseries sell seedlings of heirloom tomatoes in mid- to late spring, and you may well be able to buy healthy young plants. In most cases, however, you will have to begin with seed.

The cherry tomato, *Lycopersicon esculentum var. cerasiforme, can be highly productive. Single vines of certain varieties yield up to 1,000 fruits.*

Tomato plants are classified as either determinate or indeterminate. Determinate tomatoes stop growing once they reach their genetically predetermined maximum height. Indeterminate tomatoes, on the other hand, continue to grow until frost kills the plant. Like the original wild tomato, the majority of heirloom varieties are indeterminate.

The two types have their advantages and disadvantages. Indeterminate plants require careful staking to support growth but are usually more resistant to disease. They crop a little later and continue to produce over a long period. Determinate plants require less staking but are generally less disease-resistant; they come into bearing early, fruit heavily, then die. They suit cool-climate gardens, but can also be useful as an early crop in warmer climates, where they can be followed by a principal crop of indeterminate varieties that will grow through to the first frost.

In districts prone to frost, find out your last frost date (local nurseries and garden groups will be able to tell you). For determinate varieties, sow your seeds six weeks before the last frost date; for indeterminate varieties, start eight weeks before the last frost date. In subtropical and tropical areas, it is possible to plant year-round, though only a limited number of varieties will thrive. In areas with long, hot summers, tomato seeds can be planted until the end of spring. In very cool areas, tomatoes will still succeed if grown under tall frames in a sheltered sunny position or in glasshouses, provided suitable varieties are used.

Tomato seeds need warm soil to germinate—75–85°F (24–30°C) is ideal. Seedlings should appear above the soil 10 to 14 days after planting. Many relatively cheap commercial seed propagators are available which will provide the necessary protective warmth. Seeds can be sown in flats or in pots, or you may prefer to use cell pots, which should be planted with one tomato seed per pot.

If you wish to prepare your own seed-raising mixture, use coarse, washed river sand mixed with finely sieved compost in a ratio of 2:1. To sterilize your mix, place enough to fill a flat in a heavy, clear plastic bag, seal it by turning the end in and clipping it, then leave it in a low oven—122°F (50°C)—for 30 minutes. In areas with plenty of sunshine, you can simply leave the bag outside in the sun for approximately 45 minutes. Water gently and allow to drain.

When seedlings have their first two or three true leaves (do not count the first pair of smooth-edged seed leaves), it is time to transfer the plants to individual 2–3-in (5–7.5-cm) pots. Tomato seedlings are easily bruised or broken so handle them gently, and only by the leaves. If they were raised in a flat, use something like a pencil to lift them out gently so that the root system is not destroyed.

Fill the pots with potting mix (one-third coarse sand, one-third fine loam and one-third fine-sieved compost is an excellent combination). Gently firm the soil in the pot, make a hole in the center (the pencil will be useful again) and insert the roots into the hole. Gently press soil around the seedling so that it is slightly deeper than it was in the seed flat. Make up a dilute seaweed emulsion solution (one tablespoon to a large watering can of tepid water is about right) and gently water all your transplanted seedlings.

Keep the seedlings away from frosts in a warm place that receives plenty of sunlight during the day, such as a greenhouse or cold-frame. Plants should look thick, green and sturdy. Water them regularly and add the diluted seaweed every 10 days. Gradually expose the plants to air to harden them.

Wait until you are certain the cold weather is over before you plant the seedlings out into the garden. The minimum night temperature should be 53°F (12°C). Tomatoes enjoy rich root conditions and appeciate the addition of plenty of well-decayed compost. You could also fork into the soil well-washed and composted seaweed, rotted straw, aged horse or cow manure, or even rotted leaf mould, if they are available. If your soil is fairly acid, incorporate some dolomite—a handful to 1 sq yd (1 sq m) is adequate for most soils. Tomatoes like slightly acid to neutral soils.

Allow a week or more for the soil to settle before planting, and check that it is moist below the surface. If it

The 'Zapotec Ribbed' tomato is ideal for stuffing.

The delicious 'Green Zebra' derives its name from its striped skin. Inside, it is emerald green.

is dry, water well the day before planting, and water the seedling pots thoroughly at the same time. Make sure you have chosen a sunny and reasonably protected position.

Tap individual pots out and insert the plants with the soil ball attached, so that the new soil level is higher than it was in the pot. Tomatoes readily produce adventitious roots on their stems. Placing the young plants a little deeper in the soil causes them to quickly form a second set of roots which improve plant establishment and water and nutrient uptake.

Determinate plants should be spaced about 24 in (60 cm) apart; indeterminate tomatoes in warm areas need at least 40 in (1 m) spacing. This is further than often recommended, but allows good air movement.

Firm the tomato plants in gently and limit any possibility of transplant shock by thoroughly soaking each plant with a dilute seaweed solution. Young plants are vulnerable to cutworms, so place a collar of stiff paper around each seedling—paper cups with the bottoms cut out are excellent for this purpose; for even greater protection, surround the collars with a ring of wood ash. Place mulch around each plant to help prevent water stress, but only when the soil has warmed. Rotted lucerne hay is ideal but spoiled straw is also useful. Keep the mulch away from the stem. If the weather turns cold, seedlings should be protected overnight.

Tomato plants need stakes, not only to prevent anyone walking on the new shoots, but to provide support for the rapid growth that will now occur. If stakes are not used in the early stages, considerable root damage can occur. Ideally, stakes should be placed in a triangle around the plant to upport it on all sides.

Staking is essential for tomatoes, especially for indeterminate varieties, which may grow to 4–5 ft (1.2–1.5 m) and carry abundant fruit.

Continue to feed the plants at 10-day intervals with the dilute seaweed solution or manure tea and regularly retie the plants to their stakes (old pantihose cut into lengths makes good ties), making sure the stems are not bound tightly. Water regularly around the base of the plant.

Pruning should only take place in cool areas with short summers. Pruning out side shoots in young plants concentrates growth and minimizes the time to flowering and fruiting; the judicious removal of lateral shoots later in the growing cycle prevents unnecessary shading of fruit. To avoid having to prune, Russian growers often bred heirloom tomatoes to have almost carrot-like, finely divided leaves.

If you have a tiny garden, try growing small varieties such as 'Tiny Tim' and 'Silver Fir' in window boxes or pots. You can make a second planting a few weeks after the first one to extend the tomato season. Companion-planting sweet, lemon and Thai basils will deter insect pests and allow you to harvest a perfect salad combination. Conveniently, tomatoes and basils share the same growing requirements. Some of the big indeterminate tomatoes can be grown in large pots (half wine barrels

Check tomato plants regularly for blight, caterpillars, beetles, whitefly and, in warm, humid areas, fruit fly.

are ideal). They will continue growing and bearing for many months in warm areas but must be securely staked. One or two plants grown in tubs can yield enough fruit to feed a whole family.

Where space is a problem, you might also like to try the now-famous technique of growing tomatoes in bales of straw. This has the additional advantage of keeping tomato plants away from any soil-borne diseases. One bale of straw will grow two tomato plants. Soak the bale with water for several days in succession. Use a stake and pierce several holes in the bale to allow water to soak in well. Place the bale on a sheet of polythene and water thoroughly with seaweed solution—this will cause the bale to start composting and heat up considerably. When it has cooled down, make two widely spaced holes in the top of the bale, about 1 ft (30 cm) deep by 6 in (15 cm) wide. Fill the holes with good, rich compost. Water well and place a tomato plant into each hole, firming down gently. Water every day as the bale will tend to dry out quickly, and provide stakes to support the plants. The bale will gradually sink earthward as it continues to gently compost, but the tomato plants will grow very well, particularly if given a watering can full of diluted seaweed or other organic feed solution every 10 days.

Troubleshooting

A few sensible precautions will help you avoid most problems associated with tomatoes. The first is that no-one tending tomatoes should smoke. Just like humans, tomatoes suffer from 'passive smoking'. The mosaic virus of tobacco (also a member of the family Solanaceae) can cross-infect tomatoes. If you smoke, do so well away from the plants and always wash your hands before touching them.

Tomato seedlings are prone to a fungal disease known as damping off. Treat with a liquid copper fungicide.

Nematodes, or eel worms, are almost-microscopic, transparent wormlike organisms that can bore into the vascular system of tomato plants, clogging them and causing wilting. Fortunately, nemtaodes can be effectively cleaned from your soil by planting it first with a crop of colorful French marigolds—the root exudates of the marigolds deter nematodes. When the marigolds stop flowering, turn and chop them into the soil with a spade; this will cause the plants to break down and release their active nematocide agent. If you do not have time to wait, plant French marigolds amid your tomato crop.

A second cause of wilting in well-watered tomato plants is a soil-borne fungus, fusarium. Members of the family Solanaceae, such as tomatoes, peppers, eggplants, tamarillos, tomatillos, okra and potatoes, should never be grown consecutively in the same soil, nor should any of these crops be grown in the same soil for two years running. If they are, fusarium is likely to occur. It's therefore important to rotate your crops and a good idea to keep an annual map of your plantings. Try following Solanaceae crops with onions, leeks and shallots, or with members of the cabbage group, or carrots and parsnips. Professional tomato growers use at least a six-year cycle of soil rotation to avoid problems.

Anthracnose and blight can be threats, too, in some places. Blight appears as yellow-ringed brown spots on the leaves, which then wither and die. Some tomato varieties are far more prone to this problem than others. It can be inhibited by using a heavy mulch. The mulch and crop debris should be removed from the vegetable garden in autumn. Also inspect the plants regularly and remove any affected plants from the garden.

French marigolds not only add color to a garden, but also repel nematodes, a significant threat to tomatoes.

Ranging in color from pale yellow through green to dark red, tomatoes also grow in a wide variety of shapes.

Some varieties are prone to rot at the bottom, a condition known as blossom-end rot. This can be caused by calcium deficiency or by uneven soil-moisture levels. For protection, crumble eggshells around the plants, or add dolomite. A mulch should prevent severe changes in soil-moisture levels.

The most usual pests of tomatoes around the world are caterpillars of various kinds, such as Heliothus and tomato hormworm, which are best controlled by the use of the biolog-ical control Dipel; whitefly, partic-ularly in glasshouse-grown crops; and, in tropical areas, fruit fly, which is best avoided by growing exceedingly vigorous old strains of cherry tomato. In some regions, flea beetles are a problem; these should be controlled with rotenone. Colorado potato beetles are also controlled using rotenone and pyrethrum, and by squashing the orange egg clusters under leaves during inspections.

If the leaves of tomatoes show a distinct purple or general yellowing coloration, this is a nutritional deficiency. Fertilize with fish emulsion at the recommended rate.

Large tomato plants can blow over after heavy storms or severe winds. To prevent this, hill soil up around the base of the stems when the tomatoes reach about 2 ft (60 cm) in height. This will not only provide extra support but also encourage the plant to develop another set of roots.

The cherry tomato, Lycopersicon esculentum *var.* cerasiforme, *grows wild in parts of the tropics and subtropics.*

Cherry Tomato

Lycopersicon esculentum var. *cerasiforme* syn.
L. lycopersicum var. *cerasiforme*   Zones 8–12

Small and round like cherries, though they can vary from grape-sized to as large as a golf ball, these tomatoes may be green, yellow, orange or red. They contain high levels of natural sugars, providing a delicious, sweet taste.

Growing and Harvesting

Cherry tomatoes grow as indeter-minate vines which need to be staked, and can be highly productive if grown well. In most areas, they can also be cultivated in pots or hanging jars.

The trusses of tiny fruits produced by the currant tomato, Lycopersicon pimpinellifolium, *can be used as garnishes or as a decorative element in floral arrangements.*

Recommended Cultivars

'Cuatomate' — For warmer areas, this heirloom Mexican cherry tomato is one of the most vigorous, healthy and abundantly productive of all tomatoes. Indeterminate, it builds into a very large bush before bearing exceedingly heavy crops continuously until the first frost. In the subtropics and tropics, it is a short-lived perennial.

'Gardener's Delight', syn. Sugar Lump — A popular European cherry tomato, this prolific producer has small, very sweet, well-flavored red fruits borne in trusses of six to twelve. Indeterminate, it's a prolific bearer up until frost arrives.

'Green Grape' — Exquisitely beautiful and one of the most superbly flavored of all tomatoes, this variety bears clusters of up to 12 translucent, golden-green fruits that resemble large green grapes. It is a heavy producer and semideterminate.

'Red Cherry' — This vigorous tomato, introduced prior to 1840, soldiers on when all else in the tropics fails. Even the dreaded fruit fly is seldom a problem. A single vine of this indeterminate variety can cover several square yards (sq m) and produce over 1,000 cherry-sized red tomatoes of intense flavor. Plant one in a compost pile and let it sprawl.

'Yellow Pear' — Commercially released in the late 19th century, but almost certainly dating to the 1600s, this indeterminate variety will yield for six months or more in warm areas. It also performs well in cool areas, bearing abundant pear-shaped, bite-sized, golden fruits that are sweet and juicy.

Currant Tomato

Lycopersicon pimpinellifolium   Zones 8–12

The currant tomato belongs to a different species from the common tomato, but the delicious flavor and form is close to that of the original wild tomato. The bushes are tall, requiring solid staking, and are unbelievably prolific, bearing grapelike trusses of tiny fruits that are intensely flavored and sweet. Children find grazing on them irresistible, which is handy as the fruits need to be picked almost every day to keep up with the crop!

Growing and Harvesting

Currant tomatoes usually begin bearing about 65 days from planting out and are very successful in short-summer gardens; in warm to hot summer areas, they yield continuously for many months, on tall, healthy bushes.

Recommended Cultivars

Two forms are available: **'Red Currant'** and **'Yellow Currant'**. Both look wonderful used whole in salads.

Tomatillo

Physalis ixocarpa   Zones 8–10

A relative of the tomato and from the same family, Solanaceae, the tomatillo is distinguished by its papery, lantern-shaped husk (the calyx), which enlarges to completely enclose the developing fruit, only splitting when fully ripe. The cape gooseberry and Cossack pineapple are close relatives.

Mexican food is unimaginable without tomatillos. They are usually simmered for about 10 minutes before being used in salsa verde, in chile rellenos, in guacamole, or in other regional dips and sauces. They are also delightful in salads or eaten fresh.

Growing and Harvesting

Tomatillo plants typically grow to 2¹/₂ ft (75 cm), forming a lax, spreading vine (staking is beneficial) with softly furred leaves and pale golden, parachute-shaped flowers. Tomatillos are more sensitive than tomatoes to day length and temperature and some varieties set fruit late in the

Ideal for cool areas, the 'Golden Sunrise' tomato is named for its rich yellow-orange color.

season or not at all in cold areas. When mature, the fruits are about the size of a small tomato, up to 2 in (5 cm) in diameter, and pale green. They are fully ripe when they fall to the ground, still in their protective case.

Recommended Cultivars

Only two varieties of tomatillo are readily available:

'Purple de Milpa' — This vigorous variety is a prolific bearer of small, purple-tinged fruit. The flavor of the fruit is more acidic and stronger than most varieties.

'Tomate Verde' — This vigorous variety bears large, smooth, pale green fruits of superb quality, and is excellent fresh as well as cooked.

Tomato

Lycopersicon esculentum syn. *L. lycopersicum*
Zones 8–12

The wild tomato, *Lycopersicon esculentum*, was introduced to Europe in the 16th century. Initially, however, it was grown only as an ornamental plant; this was because it was a member of the nightshade family and therefore thought to be poisonous. It wasn't until the early 19th century that it began to be widely cultivated for food in Europe and America.

There are now hundreds of varieties of the garden tomato, differing widely in color, size and shape. They are generally highly productive and relatively adaptable to different climatic conditions. For information on growing and harvesting, see the introduction to this chapter.

Recommended Cultivars for Cool Areas

'Anna Russian' — This is an heirloom variety discovered in Oregon but originally from Russia. Indeterminate, it is vigorous, with large, pinkish red, heart-shaped, meaty fruits, consistently about 1 lb (450 g) in weight, with a superb sweet, intense flavor and feathery foliage.

'Black Russian' — An amazing heirloom with superb flavor, this is a semi-indeterminate variety. The abundant fruits have a dark chocolate skin with dark maroon flesh, are very juicy, and have an intense, rich flavor.

'Good Old Fashioned Red' — This indeterminate American heirloom produces big, rich, red beefsteak tomatoes borne prolifically on a large multistemmed bush. It grows superbly in cool- to warm-summer areas with abundant sunshine.

'Mr Stripey', syn. Tigerella— A highly productive English heirloom tomato, this determinate plant yields flavorful, medium-red, orange-striped fruits. ('Schimmeig Creg' from the Isle of Man is close in form and flavor.)

'Silver Fir' — So pretty it could be an ornamental plant, this Russian variety has finely dissected silvery-green foliage and abundant medium-sized, round red fruit with excellent flavor. It is determinate.

'Stupice' — This Czech variety is now widely available. Indeterminate, it produces smallish, red, juicy fruit with rich flavor and a perfect balance of sweetness and acid. It is early-maturing, productive, disease-tolerant—and wonderful in salads!

Other recommended varieties for cool areas include 'Abraham Lincoln' (excellent in areas where foliage disease is a problem), 'Earliest of All', 'Golden Sunrise', 'Marglobe VF', 'Outdoor Girl' (good for frame and cloche growing, and popular in the UK), 'Riesentraube', 'Rutgers' (developed by the Campbell Soup Company in 1928), 'Seville', 'Sigmabush', 'The Amateur', and 'Tiny Tim'.

Recommended Cultivars for Warm to Hot Areas

'Banana Legs' — An excellent yellow paste tomato for both salads and sauces, this determinate variety is meaty and sweet. The fruits are up to 4 in (10 cm) long and 2 in (5 cm) wide, and colored green to orange with yellow stripes. The foliage is finely divided and lacy.

'Black Krim' — Originating in the Crimean Peninsula and ideal for areas with long, warm summers,

An English heirloom plant, 'Mr Stripey', or 'Tigerella', has good flavor and is low in acid.

'Verna Orange' originated in Indiana, USA, but is now popular worldwide, most notably in Australia.

'Jeff Davis' produces large, flavor-packed fruit. It is disease-resistant in hot, humid areas.

this indeterminate variety grows into medium-sized bushes with a mixture of potato leaves and regular leaves. It bears prolifically, and its medium-sized, deep reddish-brown fruits have a distinctive, smoky, salty flavor.

'**Brandywine**' — An Amish heirloom dating from prior to 1885, this indeterminate plant yields abundant large, reddish-pink fruits on potato-leaved vines. Considered by many to be the most superbly flavored tomato of all, it is the standard by which other tomatoes are judged. (A '**Red Brandywine**' and '**Yellow Brandywine**' are available and have the same superb flavor.)

'**Brimmer**' syn. Brimmer Pink — An indeterminate variety, this tomato dates from around 1905 and has won numerous prizes. Its fruits can weigh over 2.2 lb (1 kg) and are pink- or purple-skinned, meaty, perfect for slicing, and extra sweet. Late-maturing, it yields prolifically.

'**China Flat**' — A superb performer in humid subtropical to tropical coastal areas, this indeterminate heirloom tomato from Queensland, Australia, produces large quantities of small red tomatoes that are juicy, flavorful and keep well. The plant bears year-round in the tropics.

'**Costoluto Genovese**' — This indeterminate heirloom tomato from the Italian Riviera has found favor in Australia and the USA for its rich, sun-drenched flavor. The vigorous, drought-tolerant plant yields well into autumn, producing large, deeply ribbed, red fruits.

'**Evergreen**' — One of a number of varieties that is actually green when ripe, this indeterminate plant is highly productive. Its beefsteak tomatoes have outstanding flavor, and are perfect for stuffing, or for adding color contrast to salads.

'**Garden Peach**' — Named for its resemblance to a peach, this indeterminate variety was first cultivated more than a century ago. It yields smallish fruits of deep blushed pink, with faintly fuzzy skin. It has outstanding keeping quality (the fruits will store for months if properly cared for), and is prolific, juicy and full of flavor.

'**German Johnson**' — An outstanding heirloom tomato from Virginia and North Carolina, this indeterminate variety is highly productive. Its large to very large, meaty, pink-red fruits, are full of flavor and resist disease.

'**Grosse Lisse**' — This French indeterminate variety grows as a tall, reliable, vigorous plant. The red fruits are richly flavored and medium to large. It continues bearing throughout summer and is especially popular in Australia.

'**Homestead 24**' — Homestead, south of Miami, is famous for its

tropical fruit plantations and this almost-indeterminate tomato was developed to cope with hot, humid, coastal conditions. It's an excellent producer of medium-sized, round, red fruits of good flavor.

'**Jeff Davis**' — An indeterminate variety from the southern USA, this prolific bush yields flavorful red fruit.

'**Marmande**' — The standard of excellence on the French Riviera, this is a productive indeterminate plant. The fruits are large, ribbed and red, and have a rich, sweet and lively flavor that typifies much Provençal cuisine.

'**Mission Dyke**' — A favorite in the Caribbean, Alabama, Louisiana and Florida and excellent in other hot, humid areas, this indeterminate variety produces large, pink, perfectly shaped tomatoes in trusses of between three and six fruits.

'**Mortgage Lifter**' — Developed by 'Radiator Charlie', M.C. Byles, in the early 1930s, this indeterminate variety yields huge, meaty, pink-red fruits with few seeds, weighing up to 4 lb (1.8 kg). It is disease-resistant and highly productive.

'**Oxheart**' — An old favorite dating from 1925, this indeterminate variety is well adapted to hot, humid summers. It produces trusses of two to seven meaty, firm, heart-shaped, mild-flavored, pink-red fruits. It is excellent for slicing, frying or sauces. (The variety '**Giant Oxheart**' bears fruits that are often twice as large.)

'**Peron Sprayless**' — This Greek variety was introduced over 50 years ago. Indeterminate, it is renowned for its disease- and crack-resistance and its large, round, deep red, vitamin-rich fruits. It is ideal for hot, dry summers.

'**Ruffled Yellow**' — Resembling '**Zapotec Ribbed**', this indeterminate variety is huge and has excellent flavor. The fruits are good for stuffing and a single slice is as large as a normal slice of bread.

'**Tropic**' — Developed originally by the University of Florida and resistant to virtually every disease known to tomatoes, this variety has sweet and highly flavored fruits. Indeterminate, it is ideal for hot, humid, disease-prone areas.

'**Verna Orange**' — This indeterminate heirloom variety produces huge, apricot-orange-colored fruits with a sweet flavor and meaty texture.

'**Zapotec Ribbed**' syn. 'Zapotec Pleated' — A beautiful ancient tomato from Oaxaca in Mexico, this indeterminate variety supplies large, evenly ribbed ('ruffled'), pink fruits with a sweet flavor. Its size makes it ideal for stuffing.

'**Zebra**' — This is a striking, intensely flavored, indeterminate tomato dating from the 1980s, when it was bred from two heritage varieties. The fruits are amber, striped with green when ripe, and medium sized. The bushes are prolific bearers.

Other recommended varieties for warm to hot areas include '**Amish Paste**' (excellent for sauces), '**Big Rainbow**', '**Burbank**', '**Cherokee Purple**', '**College Challenger**', '**Ponderosa**', '**Pruden's Purple**', '**Striped German**', '**West Virginia Hillbilly**' and '**White Beauty**'. None of these, however, is suitable for tropical conditions.

Ideal for warm to hot areas, 'White Beauty' yields large pale fruits with prominent ribbing.

Uncommon Gourmet Vegetables

Asparagus *Asparagus officinalis*; **Asparagus Pea** *Tetragonolobus purpureus*; **Bitter Melon** *Momordica charantia*; **Capers** *Capparis spinosa*; **Chayote** *Sechium edule*; **Chickpea** *Cicer arietinum*; **Globe Artichoke** and **Cardoon** *Cynara scolymus, C. cardunculus*; **Korila** *Cyclanthera pedata*; **Luffa** *Luffa acutangula, L. cylindrica*; **Mushrooms and other fungi** *Agaricus* spp., *Pleurotus* spp., *Flammulina* spp., *Lentinus* spp.; **Okra** *Abelmoschus esculentus* syn. *Hibiscus esculentus*; **Rhubarb** *Rheum x cultorum* syns. *Rheum x hybridum, R. rharbarbarum*; **Seakale** *Crambe maritima*

Asparagus

Asparagus officinalis   Zones 4–9

Asparagus is associated with luxury, and so it would seem only natural that it should be almost impossibly difficult to grow, and a real challenge for the gardener. The truth is that growing good asparagus is really easy—provided you have lots of

Asparagus spears are a favorite of gourmet cooks.

patience and can sacrifice a piece of your garden in perpetuity. However, once your asparagus bed is established, it should yield more and more of this delicious symbol of spring with every passing year.

Asparagus occurs wild all over Europe as well as North Africa, and is associated with sandy soils near the sea. Wild-gathered, slender, deep green spring asparagus is considered a very special seasonal dish in the restaurants of Italy and France. This gourmet vegetable was already domesticated by the first century A.D. in Italy, when Ravenna was noted for the superb quality of its luscious, huge, blanched stalks. By the 16th century, Venice had a leading reputation for superlative asparagus, and the growing season was extended by many weeks thanks to cultivation techniques.

The asparagus plant is closely related to the lily family. It is a perennial, with a central crown and fleshy roots radiating out from the center. The plant is not deep rooted but it does form plenty of feeder

roots. Uncut shoots grow rapidly, unfolding into feathery, fernlike foliage about 39 in (1 m) high.

Growing and Harvesting

The procedure for making a good asparagus bed may seem a little demanding, but remember that once the work is done it should be at least another 20 years before it needs to be repeated. If you decide to move to another house and garden, think what a selling point your well-established asparagus bed will be. The effort will never be wasted.

Asparagus needs very good drainage and an open, sunny position. Heavier soils on a slope will grow good asparagus provided they are loose and friable, and well supplemented with compost, but the ideal soil is a sandy to very sandy loam, well dug over and enriched with plenty of humus. Soil that drains poorly will cause the asparagus crowns to rot, but there is a solution. Free-draining beds can be made, raised well above the normal soil level. Begin by marking out the asparagus beds and digging them over thoroughly, incorporating coarse grit or gravel and wood ash. Build the

beds up by piling onto them a mixture of gritty sand, compost, leaf mould and well-rotted manure, together with wood ashes. As these beds are intended to remain for many years, a retaining edge of boards or bricks or tiles is advisable to retain the soil.

Asparagus plants can be raised from seed pre-soaked for 24–48 hours and planted in spring in a very well-drained seedbed outdoors. They will germinate and grow into small, ferny plants during the first season. The seedling crowns will fruit if they are female. Female asparagus bears less well, and the females should be rogued out.

A small family requires about 25 asparagus crowns, but more should be planted if asparagus is popular in the family. Only a small crop can be harvested in the second year, and harvesting begins in earnest in the third year. While it is more expensive, you might prefer to buy two or three year-old crowns from a nursery, requesting male crowns, and save the first two frustrating years of waiting.

To plant the crowns, which resemble starfish, open up a trench about 8 in (20 cm) deep and a spade wide in the prepared bed. The 'arms'

To grow edible asparagus, it is critical to select the correct garden bed. It should be in full sun, well dug over and manured, and have good drainage.

Asparagus officinalis 'Mary Washington' is an excellent, uniform, high-yielding strain of asparagus.

Female asparagus plants will produce many red-berried fruit, which should be removed before self-seeding occurs.

Each fall, cut the yellowing tops down. Many growers feed their crop with additional well-rotted manure or compost each year. Well-washed and composted seaweed washed up on beaches is rich in the nutrients required by asparagus and is an excellent annual enrichment for the soil. Any of these soil additives can be applied at the end of winter.

Recommended Cultivars

'**Argenteuil**' — Highly esteemed in Europe for its early, succulent, large white stalks and superb flavor.

'**Connover's Colossal**' — This is a very old asparagus but considered by many to remain unsurpassed as an early, high quality, vigorous, very productive, long-stalked cultivar. Female plants can be identified before setting berries as they are noticeably more spindly in this cultivar.

'**Mary Washington**' — An excellent, uniform, high-yielding strain, popular for marketing, with long, straight, thick shoots. A sport of this cultivar, 'Paradise', is also ideal for home gardens, producing long, tender, mildly flavored stalks.

of the crown should be spread out and rested on a ridge of earth created along the bottom of the trench, and the soil back-filled to cover the roots with a 2 in (5 cm) layer of soil. Crowns should be planted in spring, with a spacing of 18 in (45 cm) between crowns. When the shoots begin to grow away, continue to back-fill the trench until it is filled.

In spring, the rows are hilled over, the depth depending on whether you wish to harvest green asparagus or blanched white asparagus. The former should be hilled over with 8 in (20 cm) of soil mix, while for blanched stalks twice that depth is required. Once stalks protrude about 3–4 in (7.5–10 cm) above the ground, they should be harvested, cutting them as far beneath the surface as possible. Leave at least a third of the shoots to grow away each year to ensure healthy growth of the crowns.

Once the asparagus stalks have protruded about 3–4 in (7.5–10 cm) above the ground, they should be harvested.

Asparagus Pea

Tetragonolobus purpureus   Zones 3–10

The asparagus pea, also known as winged pea or bin dow, is native to the Mediterranean area and is a small creeping plant about 22 in (55 cm) in diameter. It is related to the garden pea, but the handsome small flowers are scarlet touched with black and the pods that follow have curious longitudinal wings.

The young pods are eaten raw in salads, and are also stir fried, added to soups, or gently braised. Pods should be harvested when less than 1 in (2.5 cm) long as they quickly develop fiber. The mature seed are also used, eaten like peas, and dried seed are roasted and used as a coffee substitute.

Growing and Harvesting

Asparagus pea requires a sunny, well-drained, open position and a humus-rich soil. It prefers neutral to slightly alkaline soils. Seeds are planted in spring, sown directly into the soil about 8 in (20 cm) apart in rows 12 in (30 cm) apart.

Despite their origin, the plants should be watered regularly. They have few enemies, although slugs and snails can be a problem in wet weather. A mulch should be applied once the plants are well established, and plants should be regularly weeded. The crop should be very regularly picked to prolong its productive life. Allow 4–6 plants per consumer, as the pods are very small when harvested.

Bitter Melon

Momordica charantia   Zones 9–12

Bitter Melons, also known as bitter gourds, balsam pears, bitter cucumbers or alligator pears, have a fruit somewhat resembling cucumbers but with rows of much modified and blunted spines over the green surface. Both the young, and already quite bitter, fruits and the tender shoots are eaten. The flowers are delightfully scented of vanilla.

Bitter Melon, Momordica charantia, is a fruit that resembles a cucumber but with rows of blunted spines over the green surface.

Capers

Capparis spinosa   Zones 8–12

The flower buds, and sometimes
the young shoots, of this species are
pickled in vinegar or granular salt and
used as a piquant addition to smoked
salmon, egg salads, pizza, meat and
other dishes. The exquisite white
flowers are used as a garnish in
salads, and the sprouts are used like
asparagus. Capers contain considerable amounts of an antioxidant
bioflavenoid called rutin. It has been
reported to be useful as a diuretic,
as a stimulant of kidney function and
in improving liver function.

This is a Mediterranean species
which thrives in dry, very hot
summers and easily copes with
temperatures of 104°F (40°C). It is a
small shrub to 39 in (1 m) and can
grow in very stony soils. It is
cultivated in Spain, Italy (particularly
in Sicily), and in Provence, Greece,
Algeria, Asia Minor, Egypt, Morocco,
Tunisia, Cyprus, the coastal Black Sea
area, Iran and California.

Growing and Harvesting

Propagation is usually by tip cuttings
as the very small seed become dormant
and are difficult to germinate. To
break dormancy, the seed are cold
stratified. Seed are treated with hot
water at 104°F (40°C), then wrapped
in damp paper toweling and sealed in
a glass jar in the refrigerator for 8–12
weeks. The seed are again placed in
hot water at the same temperature as
before, then planted $^2/_5$ in (1 cm) deep
in a loose medium.

Alternatively, cuttings are collected
in early spring, and they should be
basal stem portions about $^2/_5$ in
(1 cm) in diameter with 5–6 buds. The
cuttings are rooted in a freely draining
mixture, preferably with bottom heat.

The young plants are planted in
the following winter, and in the spring
are mulched with stones. The plants
are spaced about 6 ft (2 m) apart and
reach full production in 3–4 years,
continuing for up to 30 years in all.
The unopened flower buds need to
be hand-harvested every 7–8 days
in season.

Capers are often pickled in wine vinegar and are used as garnish and in sauces and butters.

At least 10 good selections exist around the Mediterranean, the most prized forms producing the tiniest buds. Germplasm collections are held at the universities of Palermo and Naples, and the National Council of Research at Bari in Italy, and in the agricultural research institute in Cordoba in Spain. A number of specialist seed firms offer seed, and a number of herb nurseries supply potted plants in suitable areas.

Chayote
Sechium edule

Few plants are more rewarding or easy to grow in sub-tropical to tropical climates than the chayote, also known as choko or chocho or mirleton or vegetable pear or christophene. Once established, they bear constantly, almost remorselessly, heavy crops of fruits that have a tender texture when cooked and the delicate flavor of a good, sweet squash. The single flat white seed has the flavor and taste of a chestnut. Plants can easily grow to 40–50 ft (10–15 m) in a season. The fruit are produced most prolifically in fall and winter.

While the common cultivars seen in Australia and the Deep South of the United States are either a smooth-skinnned or a slightly prickled green form of moderate size, far greater variations are seen in the markets in places like Oaxaca in Mexico, where cultivars can be 10 in (25 cm) long, and may be ivory white, tan or green, often with intimidating armatures of spines.

Growing and Harvesting
Plants are grown from the mature whole fruits, which are propped stem

Chayote or choko, Sechium edule, is very easy to grow. This is a Mexican variety with brown skin that is very prickled.

A commonly found cultivar in Australia and the Deep South of the USA is the green, smooth-skinned and slightly prickled form of choko.

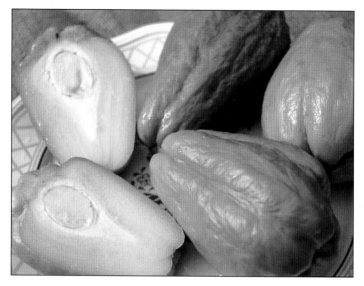

Raw and roasted chick peas, Cicer arietinum, *and hummus dip.*

side up in a sunny position. In time, the large white cotyledons of the single seed will appear at the top of the fruit, and the young plant emerges. It is then planted with the top of the fruit level with the soil. A good, strong trellis should be provided for the plant to grow on as it carries great weights of fruit. This species is very frost sensitive. The soil is prepared with moderate amounts of compost as excessive nitrogen favors leaf growth over fruit production. A few spadefuls of well-rotted manure or compost can be put around the plant when fruit production begins, keeping it clear of the stem as it may cause rotting.

Chickpea

Cicer arietinum   Zones 7–12

The chickpea, also known as garbanzo or Indian gram or Bengal gram or chana dal, is very old in cultivation and has been found associated with 9,000-year-old levels of excavation at the site of Jericho, and from sites 7,500 years old in Turkey. In India, their cultivation dates back at least 4,000 years. The cuisines of all these areas are rich in recipes for chickpeas, and they are field grown in hotter, drier areas of North Africa and southern Europe, east to India. Large quantities are also grown nowadays in

Mexico. In suitable climates, chickpeas are easily grown on well draining, sandy soils, planted at the end of winter when soil moisture is still high and the plants can develop well before the early heat begins. Once developed, the plants have good drought resistance. The pods are allowed to fill and dry before being harvested.

The fresh or dried seed are used in soups and stews, dips and sweetmeats. In India, the split peas are known as 'chana dal'. The flour ground from the chickpea is known as 'besan' and is used to make crisp batters, fritters, pancakes and sauces. Crisp, deep-fried chickpea noodles are a popular snack food in India. The seeds are also sprouted for use in salads. Members of the Seed Savers Exchange in the United States are currently listing a remarkable 20 cultivars and many more are held in collection.

Globe Artichoke and Cardoon

Cynara scolymus, C. cardunculus   Zones 6–10

Globe artichokes belong to the sunflower family and originate from the Mediterranean region. The addictively delicious part eaten is the receptacle or base of the unopened buds together with the green bracts. In the heart is the mass of the unopened thistle flower, which is extremely irritating if eaten and is scooped out during preparation. It is aptly called the *choke*. After the top or king flower has been harvested, a number of smaller buds will develop on the lateral shoots, and these are often marinated whole after being cooked. If the flowers are allowed to open, they develop into huge, double purple thistles that contrast perfectly with the handsome, architectural, silvered-green foliage. The flowers are excellent for cutting or can be hung upside down in a well-aired shaded place to produce dried flowers for winter vases.

Globe artichokes do not exist in the wild, but they are very closely allied to cardoons and are thought to have been developed from them. Cardoons closely resemble artichokes but are much larger, to 6 ft (1.8 m) or more, and form smaller heads. The flowers are similar to those of globe artichokes. Rather than the immature buds, it is the fleshy leaf bases that are the desirable edible part. The plant forms a giant rosette of basal leaves, and these are tied together and blanched to reduce their bitterness. They are then eaten raw or steamed.

Growing and Harvesting

Globe artichokes and cardoons require open, sunny, quite rich, well-drained soils and warm areas such as the coastal farm lands north of Monterey in California. (Castroville is the artichoke capital of the world, and can boast that the first Artichoke Queen crowned in the town was Marilyn Monroe.) The Brindisi coastal plain in Italy and the Brittany coast in France are famed for the superb quality of their globe artichokes. Both plants have some frost resistance but will not take hard frosts without protection.

While both crops may easily be raised from seed, the crops are quite variable and may include plants with

Globe Artichoke, Cynara scolymus, *has handsome, silvered-green foliage.*

The decicious part of the artichoke that is eaten is the receptacle or base of the unopened buds together with the green bracts.

an undesirable throwback to the earlier, more prickly types. It is perfectly possible, but time consuming, to select the best plants from a seed planting and eliminate undesirable types. On the other hand, as the plants are perennial it could be worth the effort. Most growers plant suckers from exceptionally good types, available through nurseries and specialist firms.

The young cuttings from side shoots are rowed out in spring, usually in double rows, and grow

rapidly with regular watering. The soil should be enriched with compost and manure too if available in the season before planting, and the soil well loosened. Artichokes are left in the ground for at least 5 to 6 years and need adequate feeding. Top dressings of an organic fertilizer each spring are helpful in producing high quality heads, and a layer of well-rotted manure (poultry manure is traditionally favored) is placed around the plants in spring also. Protection from hard frosts should be given when necessary in winter with a thick layer of straw.

Recommended Cultivars
Globe Artichokes
'**Grand Beurre**' — This is a very tall cultivar cropping well in its first year, with consistently large, spineless, tender, fleshy, delicious heads.

'**Green Globe Improved**' — This is a commonly available type with large globe-shaped heads of good quality.

'**Purple Globe**' — This is a purple budded type similar to the above.

Cardoons, Cynara cardunculus, *being blanched, in order to reduce their bitterness. They are eaten raw or steamed.*

'**Purple Sicilian**' — This is the cultivar harvested in France and Italy while still very young and tender, and is eaten raw, or sometimes steamed and marinated. It is also popular pickled. While it has excellent heat resistance, it should be protected from cold.

'**Purple Roscoff**' — This cultivar is grown in Brittany and the United Kingdom, and is harvested when the buds are small to be used for pickling.

'**Violetto di Chioggia**' — This is available as a seed line. Plants can be selected in their first year for their very desirable, elongated, purple heads.

Korila
Cyclanthera pedata   Zones 9–11

Korila, or achoccha, is native to South America, but is cultivated to some degree in Australia and also in Taiwan. It is a strong, attractive climber with slender stems and deeply lobed and incised, maple-like leaves. The small yellow female flowers are followed by ovoid, pale green fruit that are partly hollow and are eaten raw or cooked for their cucumber-like flavor. The vine can easily reach 16 ft (5 m). See *Bitter Melon* in this section for tips on growing and harvesting.

Luffa
Luffa acutangula, L. cylindrica   Zones 9–11

The angled luffa, *Luffa acutangula*, also known as Chinese okra, is indigenous to India. It is cultivated for its longitudinally ridged fruits, which are harvested when they are young and non-fibrous, and then sliced and boiled. The smooth luffa, *L. cylindrica*, also known as vine okra or loofah, which is probably also indigenous to India, is harvested for similar use when very young. The mature fruits are the source of the bathroom loofah or loofah sponge, the fruits being immersed in water until the flesh has rotted away from the fibers, which are then cleaned before being bleached in hydrogen peroxide and dried. See *Bitter Melon* in this section for tips on growing and harvesting.

Luffa, Luffa acutangula, *is cultivated for its fruits, which are sliced and boiled.*

*Button Mushroom,
Agaricus campestris,
can be grown indoors or
outdoors, as long as the
conditions are fairly
warm and humid, with a
constant temperature.*

Mushrooms *and other* fungi

Agaricus spp., *Pleurotus* spp., *Flammulina* spp.,
Lentinus spp.   Zones 5–11

The first mushrooms that were
cultivated in the Western world were
species of *Agaricus*, the common field
mushroom, and its near relatives.
Since that time, many other species
have been cultivated for commercial
purposes. Even the king of the
mushroom world, the truffle, has
finally yielded its secrets to a group of
fungi researchers in Tasmania.

Growing mushrooms from the raw
product stage is relatively easy in the
case of *Agaricus*, but other species
need technical knowhow and
controlled conditions that are difficult
to achieve at home. Instead, many
specialist firms have released
mushroom raising kits for a number
of popular mushrooms, including
various strains of field mushrooms
Agaricus, the Shiitake mushroom

*Enoki, oyster
and shimeji cultured
mushrooms.*

Lentinus edodes, various oyster
mushrooms *Pleurotus*, and Enoki or
Pearl mushroom *Flammulina
velutipes*. These kits are available
from specialist suppliers, and kits for
the more common species are sold
through nurseries.

Most varieties of okra will start yielding about 60 days after planting. Each flower will bloom for just one day.

Okra

Abelmoschus esculentus syn. *Hibiscus esculentus*
Zones 9–11

Okra, or gumbo, is an annual vegetable of tropical origin and suitable for areas with hot summers, forming upright bushes with small, hibiscus-like flowers followed by usually 5-sided pods. It is the pods that are eaten, and they have a delicate flavor and mucilaginous quality that is used to thicken soups and stews. It is very popular in the cuisine of Louisiana, as well as that of India, Sri Lanka and many African countries.

Growing and Harvesting

Okra requires an open, sunny position and a fertile, well-composted soil to which plenty of wood ash or another source of potash has been added. Seeds are sown once the temperature has reached 75°F (24°C). The seed is pre-soaked for 24 hours and planted $4/5$ in (2 cm) below the soil and 2 ft (60 cm) between plants as a final spacing. Allow 36 in (90 cm) between rows. In more marginal areas, plants can be started in pots and planted out when the weather is warm. The pods are harvested when very young, and sliced for cooking.

Recommended Cultivars

'Burgundy' — This cultivar yields beautiful, tender, burgundy pods up to 8 in (20 cm) long, and the plant is also suffused with burgundy.

'Clemson's Spineless' — This is a South Carolina cultivar and an abundant producer of slightly ribbed, spineless pods.

'Louisiana Green Velvet' — This is a large, vigorous, prolific producer of slender, green, smooth pods.

'Star of David' — This is a highly productive cultivar from Israel with a distinctive flavor and unusual shape.

'Louisiana Green Velvet' Okra, Hibiscus esculentus, *is a large, vigorous, prolific producer of slender, green, smooth pods.*

Rhubarb, Rheum
x cultorum, *is a tough,
vigorous perennial, with
stems ready to eat when
reddened. Eat the stems
only as the leaves
are poisonous.*

Rhubarb

Rheum x cultorum syns. *Rheum x hybridum,
R. rharbarbarum*   Zones 3–9

Rhubarb was once more highly valued
as a laxative than as a sweet dish, and
only in the 18th century did it become
popular as a food. Blanching techniques finally set it on the road to quite
universal acceptance. Only the leaf
stalks are used as the rest of the plant,
including the leaves, is poisonous,
with high levels of calcium oxalate.

Growing and Harvesting
Rhubarb is a very long-lived perennial
in cooler climates, although its life
expectation drops somewhat in
warm to hot climates. It is also
renowned for its hardiness and

virtual indestructibility, and makes
one of those indispensable fall-back
plants for hard times. However,
this does not mean that plants
should not be cosseted to obtain
high quality harvests.

Rhubarb can be raised from seed
planted in spring, but the plants will
be somewhat variable. It is possible to
select the best of the seedlings at the
end of the first season for future
crops. But a number of excellent
named cultivars are available that can
be expected to have low stringiness,
succulence, size, and the highly
desirable cherry red colored stems
when blanched. Nurseries often
supply barerooted plants in the winter
and potted specimens at other times
of the year.

The soil should be prepared with
plenty of compost and rotted manure
dug through as the plants are gross
feeders and will occupy the same
place for many years. The soil should
be moist but never waterlogged. Each
spring after harvesting the blanched
stalks, rotted compost and manure is
placed around the plants to encourage
strong growth.

Borrow a trick from the old growers
who piled compost or manure around
the sides of the forcing pots to create
additional warmth and produce extra-
early crops. The summer flower stalks
can be retained and enjoyed for their
beauty but should not be allowed to
run to seed.

Pick a few single stems at a time
from mature plants, and at the end of
spring allow plants to grow away and
gain reserves once more. In warmer
areas, mulch is advisable in summer.

Recommended Cultivars
'Canada Red' — Prized for its long,
thick, very tender stalks which are
deep cherry red on the outside and
strawberry red inside throughout
their entire length, and require no
peeling. This is a sweeter cultivar
requiring less sugar in cooking.

'Early Victoria' — This is an early maturing form of the excellent 1852 cultivar **'Victoria'**. The leaf stalks are very broad and up to 3 ft (90 cm) long. Green inside, the stalks are suffused with red, and are a little less sweet than some other cultivars but remarkably productive.

'Glaskin's Perpetual' — This cultivar has probably the lowest oxalate levels of any rhubarb so that the stems never become bitter. The greenish stalks have excellent flavor.

'Strawberry' — This cultivar has all the virtues for a home garden, with tender, mild-flavored, string-free, large stems that are rich strawberry red both inside and outside.

Seakale

Crambe maritima   Zones 5–9

As both its English and French names indicate, this long-lived perennial species is a member of the cabbage family that grows naturally by the sea, usually in shingle but even in crevices in beach rock just out of reach of the sea. Seakale, or chou marin, was exclusively developed as a vegetable by the English, although it has become far more widely grown in the past 150 years.

Growing and Harvesting

Seakale is easily grown from seed rowed out in spring. It prefers a very well-drained, deep, sandy soil and an open, sunny position.

The blanched emerging spring shoots are eaten raw or prepared in any way suitable for asparagus. In winter the plants die away, but in summer they form low-growing rosettes of handsome silvered foliage. The young leaf stalks and emerging flower heads are blanched in the field under forcing pots in early spring in the manner of rhubarb, or in well-composted and mulched beds placed under frames covered in black

plastic to exclude the light. Up to 3 harvests can be made from mature individual plants as they emerge, then the plant is allowed to grow away for the summer.

The ideal harvest size is about 8 in (20 cm). Most growers allow plants to build up reserves in their first season, harvest fairly lightly in the second, and heavily thereafter. Seakale has no significant pests or diseases under the correct growing conditions. A few selected forms are available, including **'Lily White'**.

The young leaf stalks and emerging flower heads of Seakale, Crambe maritima, are blanched in the field under forcing pots in early spring.

The blanched emerging spring shoots of Seakale or Chou Marin are eaten raw or prepared in any way suitable for asparagus.

Winter Root Crops

Arracacha *Arracacia xanthorrhiza*; **Burdock**
Arctium lappa; **Carrots** *Daucus carota*;
Evening Primrose *Oenothera ssp.*; **Hamburg
Parsley** *Petroselinum crispum tuberosum*;
Parsnip *Pastinaca sativa*; **Radishes** *Raphanus
sativus*; **Rampion** *Campanula rapunculus*;
Salsify *Tragopogon porrifolius*; **Scorzonera**
Scorzonera hispanica; **Skirret** *Sium sisarum*;
Swedes *Brassica napus napobrassica*; **Turnips**
B. rapa rapifera

Carrots, parsnips, turnips, and swedes
are the most popular of the winter root
vegetables. While most are harvested in
summer from successive plantings, it is
in winter that they really come into
their own, storing well and becoming
the basis of warming winter stews,
casseroles, and soups. Less well
known, but popular particularly in

Europe, are skirret, salsify, scorzonera,
Hamburg parsley, rampion, and
burdock. They share similar cultural
requirements and all perform best in
cooler weather. All of the above are
hardy and can be planted in spring for
harvesting in fall.

Growing and Harvesting

Soils need to be deeply dug to ensure
that the roots can develop easily
below the ground. Add generous
quantities of compost, and use a
mulch once the plants are
established. Fresh manure should
never be used with these crops as it
causes forking of the roots. All root
crops are directly planted into the
ground. Transplanting, particularly
of carrots and parsnips, often results
in poor root formation and forking.
All root crops tend to develop slowly
in the first few weeks and cannot
cope at that stage with weed
competition. Mulching will reduce
this work considerably. Superficial
watering is of little value as it
discourages roots from penetrating
deeply into the soil. One deep
watering per week will be of far
greater value. Ideally, regular
waterings are best.

All carrot cultivars readily cross with
each other and with wild carrot when
they flower in the following spring. To
prevent this, either cage a few plants of
each cultivar for which seed are to be
saved, or select only one cultivar to
flower and set seed each year. Seed
viability remains high for three years if
the seed is kept in an airtight container
in a cool, dry place. Whole
inflorescences can be harvested when
about half the seed is ripe and hung
upside down inside large paper packets
to complete ripening. The seed will fall
into the bag. Parsnip, salsify, scorzonera,
skirret, and Hamburg parsley seed can
be saved in the same way.

Radish plants cannot self-
pollinate, and a group of plants
should be allowed to flower together

*Winter root crops that
have gone to seed can
be useful for cut flower
arrangements.*

Some experts believe that the cultivated carrot originated in Afghanistan and that the purple Afghan carrot, left, is an ancestor of the traditional orange carrot.

to set seed. Cultivars will readily cross-pollinate with each other and with wild radish. Caging is the best technique for isolation. Similarly, turnip plants, which are from the same family, cannot self-pollinate and a group of plants should be allowed to flower together, isolated in a cage. Turnips will cross-pollinate with swedes, rutabagas, wild turnip, and rape (canola).

Arracacha
Arracacia xanthorrhiza   Zones 9–12

Related to both carrots and celery, arracacha looks a little like a cross between the two, forming a cluster of smooth white roots below ground that resemble a bunch of carrots. The roots have a crisp texture with white, yellow, or sometimes purple flesh and a flavor that is similar to freshly roasted chestnuts combined with mild celery. They can be eaten in any way that potatoes are prepared. Above ground, the shoots somewhat resemble green celery (sometimes being streaked purple) and are eaten raw or cooked like celery. It was once limited in cultivation to its native South America, and to the Caribbean, but deserves to take its place beside its more famous European relatives. For some reason, it was overlooked by the Spanish despite the fact that it is easier to produce than potatoes. It is very productive, with a longer growing season than potatoes, and is now being trialled in a small way by a number of Australian, New Zealand, and North American gardeners. In Brazil, it is rowed out as a field crop.

Arracacha was originally associated with the Andean region at fairly high elevations, but crops in Brazil have demonstrated that it also does well at low elevations equivalent to warm temperate areas of the world.

Growing and Harvesting
Arracacha is propagated by offshoots produced by the crown of the plant. The base of the offshoot should be lightly sliced several times to promote shoot formation and a uniform root system. Leave it in a protected area for a couple of days for the base to dry, then plant it out 3 ft (90 cm) apart in rows a similar distance apart, in raised beds. It can be interplanted with a spring potato crop. The roots can be harvested before full development, from about 120 days onward, but the crop is usually harvested a year after planting, the entire plant being lifted. Plants should not be allowed to flower. Each plant yields up to $6^{1}/_{2}$ lb (3 kg) of roots. Arracacha appears to have no significant enemies.

Burdock

Arctium lappa   Zones 7–12

Burdock is native to both Europe and Asia, and in some countries is used more for medicinal than culinary purposes. Also known as gobo, lappa, and Japanese burdock, it was most probably introduced into Japan from China, where it was developed into an important commercial vegetable crop. It is now grown commercially in small quantities in the United States for sale in natural food stores. It is also stocked in Asian markets, and a number of greengrocers in Australia, notably in New South Wales, Victoria, Tasmania, and Western Australia. It also appears commercially in small quantities in Europe.

Burdock grows into a clump with large, wavy, gray-green leaves. The fleshy, parsnip-like roots may grow to 40 in (1 m) long and have a flavor which has been described as somewhere between Jerusalem artichokes, parsnips, and scorzonera. The young roots are used raw and peeled like radish, often with a little sea salt; older roots can be stir-fried, braised, roasted, added to stews and soups, pickled, made into a tea or incorporated into a soft drink. The mature roots are peeled and soaked in cold water for about an hour before use. The young leaves can also be used as a green, as can any thinnings from the rows.

Burdock is believed to help in the treatment of gout and ulcers, arthritis, rheumatism, and skin conditions such as acne and psoriasis.

Growing and Harvesting

Burdock has wide temperature adaptability, growing in warm and humid as well as temperate climates. In cold climates the plants will lose foliage in winter but will survive underground to approximately –4°F (–20°C), reshooting in the spring. Typically in subtropical and tropical areas burdock is planted as a winter crop.

Burdock prefers well-drained, deep sandy to sandy loam soils as the root often penetrates very deeply. It also needs an open, sunny position. The crop is susceptible to nematode damage and a previous crop of French marigolds or, less decoratively *Tagetes minuta*, should be grown and turned into the soil to rot down fully before planting, as a preventative measure. Parasitic fungi are also available as a biological control. This crop does not thrive on acidic soils—its preferred soil pH is 6.5–7.5, around neutral. Avoid using fresh manures and composts, which cause forking of the roots. If possible, burdock should be grown in a site that has been composted for a previous crop. High phosphorus levels promote root growth and can be supplied in the form of ground rock phosphate applied at the rate of 11 lb (5 kg) per 30 sq yd (30 sq m), or bone meal.

Seed needs to be gently scarified with sandpaper or pre-soaked for half a day to assist in breaking dormancy, then rowed out directly into the soil and planted at a depth of $^3/_5$–$^4/_5$ in (1.5–2.0 cm) when the soil has warmed up in spring. Plants should be spaced 8–10 in (20–25 cm) apart in rows 10 in (25 cm) apart. Expect the seed to emerge within 14 days. High

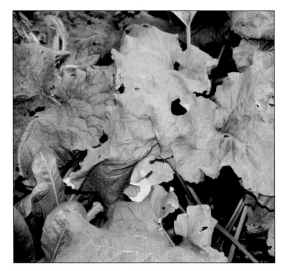

temperatures will inhibit germination. Water regularly to maintain ground moisture in the early stages of the crop. A weekly deep soaking rather than a light daily soaking should be carried out once the plants are established to encourage the roots to grow downward. Careful weeding should be carried out in the early stages. Thereafter, the crop should be mulched, to conserve soil moisture and suppress any weed growth. The plants have no enemies of significance.

Burdock can be harvested at any stage, but mature roots are harvested from late summer to fall, depending on the climate. The soil should be loosened by digging deeply with a garden fork around the plant and pulling gently on the tops to ease the roots which may be as long as 2–3 ft (60–90 cm). Plants should not be left in the ground after reaching maturity as the roots will become woody and fibrous. Most of the cultivars available are of Japanese origin and are becoming quite readily available from specialty seed companies.

Recommended Cultivars
Excellent cultivars include '**Watanabe Early**', '**Sakegake**', and '**Takinogawa Long**', the last being the most favored cultivar in Japan.

Carrot
Daucus carota   Zones 3–12

While it's true that carrots are readily available commercially, taste tests come out strongly in favor of organically grown samples. As well, baby carrots are not always easy to obtain and tend to transport poorly to stores. There is also the pleasure of growing a range of different colors and shapes, as well as the carrot's glorious lacy flower heads that are so tempting to flower arrangers. You could plant a small patch of carrots

Carrots contain high levels of beta carotenes, which are believed to reduce the risk of some cancers. Eaten raw, carrots also help to lower blood cholesterol levels.

'Pakistan', with its large colorful heads, is the ideal carrot cultivar for cut flower arrangements.

just for use as cut flowers. They are biennial and will bloom in their second growing season. **'Pakistan'** is the perfect choice for this use as the heads are huge and come in white, pinks, and purples to match the roots.

Carrots are believed to have many health benefits when eaten. They contain high levels of beta carotenses which convert to vitamin A and are also good sources of vitamins C, D, E, and K (potassium). As well, the fiber in carrots has been shown to be valuable in promoting regularity.

The root is the part that is eaten, either raw or cooked. Try grated carrot dressed with fresh orange juice or carrot sticks marinated in lemon juice with a touch of sea salt. Carrots steamed and mashed with a little butter and freshly ground pepper will often appeal to those who dislike boiled carrots; or try mashing half and half with orange sweet potato or orange squash for a new flavor. julienned carrots simmered in a little water until tender, then finished off with a touch of honey, fresh orange juice, and a little butter simmered down to a syrup is a dish which has converted many sceptics.

Growing and Harvesting

Carrots need some care and effort to grow and many gardens, particularly those with naturally shallow soils, or

sites that have heavy soils or where clay lies close to the surface, will be unsuitable. The large maincrop cultivars require a deep, well dug, fine soil. Raised beds will help to increase soil depth. However, there is now such a variety of carrot cultivars available that it is possible to get mini carrots and tiny beet-shaped cultivars requiring no more than 4 in (10 cm) of top soil.

Ideally, carrots prefer a sandy loam soil with a pH of 6.0–6.5. Soils which have been prepared with copious quantities of compost six months previously will produce abundant crops. However, the use of fresh manures and compost may induce malformation of the roots.

If the urge to grow monster carrots overcomes you, but your soil depth or type is unsuitable, carrots respond very well to container growing. Some growers have experimented with drainpipes. To do this, bury 18 in (45 cm) lengths of drainpipe vertically into the garden bed, fill them with a good soil and compost mix, and sow seed into the top. The roots can grow the entire depth of the pipe and then explore into the garden soil.

Seed is sown directly into rows in late winter in warm climates and mid-spring in cool climates. As the seeds are small and it is difficult to control the density of the planting, mixing the seed with dry river sand before planting is helpful. The plants should be thinned when they reach a slender but usable size. The tops will be around 4–5 in (10–12.5 cm) tall. Leave a space of 2 in (5 cm) between plants. A second thinning is done two to three weeks later to leave a final spacing of 3 in (7.5 cm).

Constant moisture is essential during germination and some growers like to create a 'sandwich' at the bottom of the drill of two thin, waterholding layers of finely sieved compost, seed raising mix, or other

moisture-retentive material with the carrot seed lying between. Press down firmly so that the seeds make good contact. In areas with hot dry climates, even germination will be attained with this technique provided the rows are gently watered each day. An alternative method is to cover the seed drills with hessian bags or old carpet, checking them each day and removing all cover once seedlings appear. Mulch can be placed around the rows to retain soil moisture. In areas with a long summer, a second major planting can be made in early fall for late fall harvests and winter storage. Smaller successive plantings can be made in cooler areas up to midsummer.

Carrots in the home garden are not much troubled by many diseases or pests though slugs and snails can be an occasional problem. Carrot white fly can be eliminated by covering the crop with fine mesh tucked into the soil all around. Interplanting the crop with onions will deter carrot fly, and the carrot root maggot can be discouraged by sprinkling coffee grounds or diatomaceous earth around the roots. Nematodes are rarely a problem if crop rotation is followed. The infestation cycle is broken by planting crops not affected by nematodes such as nitrogen-fixing legumes. A planting of French marigolds (*Tagenes*) dug back into the soil when flowering is at peak will clean the soil of nematodes. Parasitic fungi are also now commercially available to trap nematodes.

Carrots are quite cold-hardy and in cold winter areas may be left in the ground in winter, covered with a deep mulch of dried leaves. The old practice of inverting weighted down bushell baskets over the leaf-piled row adds further protection and marks the row. In mild climates with few frosts, the existing mulch around the crop is all that is required. As an alternative in cold climates, the carrots can be lifted after loosening the soil with a garden fork, the tops twisted off, and the carrots stored in sand under cool, dry conditions.

Recommended Cultivars
While most modern cultivated carrots are orange, it is possible to find them in white, yellow, red, purple, and

As seeds are small and difficult to sow evenly, carrot seedlings will need to be thinned out.

Constant attention to weeding is essential as carrots cannot contend easily with competitors. Mulching will help keep the weeds away, as well as retaining moisture.

A fine soil with plenty of well rotted compost should produce good harvests of carrots.

The evening primrose family is a cosmopolitan plant group that is well represented in North America, especially in the western regions.

crimson. A maroon carrot called 'BetaSweet' was created in 1989, a throwback in color to early cultivars.

'Amsterdam Forcing' — Grown as a miniature, or baby carrot, this variety has blunt-ended, cylindrical, reddish-orange roots that are very smooth, with sweet, crisp, tender flesh.

'Belgium White' — An old, pure white, mild cultivar. It will not over-winter.

'Early Horn' — Finely textured and delicately but richly flavored, this baby carrot dates back to 1865. It is ideal for shallow soils, and has resistance to whitefly.

'Golden Ball' — Golden-orange in color with excellent sweet flavor.

'Guerande' syn. 'Oxheart' — The short orange roots are fast growing on shallow and clay soils.

'Jaune Obtuse' — Still a favorite in France, with tapering golden-yellow roots. It is resistant to carrot root fly.

'Juwarot' — This is the most favored juicing carrot, having up to twice the carotene level of other cultivars.

'Lady Finger' — A highly productive gourmet carrot with small, cylindrical, orange, nearly coreless roots of excellent sweet flavor.

'Parisian Rondo' syn. 'Parisian Ball', 'Rondo', 'Round Paris Market' — This 19th century French cultivar is still very popular. It has small, uniform, almost spherical, deep orange roots that are sweet and delicious.

Evening Primrose

Oenothera ssp.   Zones 4–10

The fleshy roots of evening primroses were eaten in France in the 19th century, as they long have been in their native North America. Since then they have become almost a forgotten vegetable, but are returning to fashion. The roots are similar to salsify and parsnip and can be cooked in the same manner. The plants are biennial or perennial, a rosette of leaves forming in the first year and flowering commencing the following

year. A number of species are suitable for growing in home gardens including *Oenothera erythrosepala*, the common evening primrose *O. biennis* which has also become known as the German rampion, and Hooker's evening primrose, *O. subelata* ssp. *hookeri*. The young shoots can also be blanched and used in salads or boiled as a pot herb, and the young pods can be steamed. The flowers of *O. biennis* are sometimes used as a fragrant edible salad garnish.

Growing and Harvesting

All these evening primrose species are easy to cultivate in well-drained soils in a sunny position. As with any root crop, the more deeply the soil is dug and the more finely textured the soil, the straighter and finer the root formation will be. Even on poor soils, they grow well as they are indigenous to sand dunes and semi-arid areas. However, they do respond to a richer diet and the inclusion of compost in the soil. Sow the seed in early spring. The final spacing between plants should be about 12 in (30 cm). The roots can be harvested at the end of fall.

Hamburg Parsley

Petroselinum crispum tuberosum　　　　Zones 5–11

Also known as turnip-rooted parsley, parsnip-rooted parsley, and German parsley, this form of true parsley differs from the herb in developing a particularly thick, fleshy, parsnip-like root. The foliage is the same as the culinary herb and it can be used to flavor cooked dishes, although its use should be limited or root growth will be affected. The roots have a delicate and delicious flavor somewhere between celery and parsley, and are slightly nutty as well. They can be grated and eaten raw in salads, made into french fries, mashed, roasted, or used to flavor soups and stews.

Growing and Harvesting

To obtain good roots, the soil should not be too rich and it also needs to be loose. Compacted soils should be well dug over to ensure easy, unforked development of the roots. Dressing the soil with ground rock phospate will encourage strong root development. Seeds should be sown thinly $^3/_4$ in (2 cm) deep in drills about 14 in (35 cm) apart. Thin the seedlings to 6 in (15

The fleshy roots of evening primroses can used in salads or boiled as a pot herb.

Hamburg parsley is grown for its enlarged edible root which has a slightly nutty taste.

cm) apart when they are approximately 3 in (7.5 cm) high. The plants can then be cultivated in the same way as carrots. It has no major pests or diseases.

Roots can be harvested progressively from early fall and should be dug before winter, the foliage cut off, and stored in dry sand in a cool place for winter use. In milder climates, a few roots can be left in the ground for the plants to flower and run to seed in spring, thus providing fresh seed for the next season's planting.

Recommended Cultivars

Among the best are **'Early Sugar'**, for use on heavier soils, the high quality **'Berliner Halblanger'**, and the long storing **'Hungarian Felhosszu'**.

Parsnips were used as a source of sugar before the development of sugar beet.

Parsnip
Pastinaca sativa   Zones 7–10

Parsnips have had their admirers for over 2,000 years. The Emperor Tiberius accepted part of Germany's annual tribute in the form of a shipment of parsnips. So sweet is the parsnip that at one time it was used as a source of sugar. Parsnip wine has long been made in England, its high sugar levels contributing to a beverage somewhat like a sherry and not to be underrated for potency. Apart from wine, parsnips are also used to make beer, a honey-like syrup, and marmalade. The roots can be baked, boiled, steamed, and puréed, and used in casseroles, stews, and salads. Parsnip french fries are delicious.

Growing and Harvesting
Fairly deep soil is essential for parsnip production. A few cultivars such as **'Offenham' and 'Avonresister'** are shorter and also easier to dig on heavy soils. However, parsnip afficionados can use the techniques for drainpipe culture described above for carrots, the latter often producing exceptionally fine, large, show-worthy specimens. Seeds should be sown in drills as soon as the soil has warmed, thinning to 3–5 in (7.5–12.5 cm) apart. A second sowing can be made in early summer.

Parsnip seed is unusually short-lived, viable for only one year, so check that the seed you use is fresh. The seed must not be allowed to dry out during germination. If planting in a dry, fairly warm climate, create a $^1/_2$ in (1 cm) base layer of vermiculite or peat substitute down the length of the drill, row out the seed, then top with another $^1/_4$ in (0.5 cm) layer of vermiculite or peat substitute. Water in well. Regular deep watering of the crop is essential for good results but it is better to do this once a week as rots can develop with overwatering.

Parsnips can be affected by carrot fly and this should be prevented as described for carrots. Parsnips also suffer from canker which appears as cracks and blackened areas on the shoulders of the roots, later developing into a rot. Later sowings appear to be somewhat less affected, but choosing canker-resistant varieties is recommended. Parsnips are best harvested after a few frosts as the flavor becomes sweeter and more intense. Use a garden fork to loosen them in the ground before pulling.

Recommended Cultivars
'Avonresister' — Perhaps the smallest of the parsnips and best suited to shallow soils, this cultivar has very good resistance to canker.

'Cobham Improved' — Outstanding for its flavor, high sugar content, its smooth, white appearance, and canker resistance.

'Hollow Crown' syn. Long Jersey, Hollow-crowned Guernsey — An excellent older cultivar with long, smooth, tapered cream-colored roots up to 18 in (45 cm) long and 4 in (10 cm) across the shoulder.

'Offenham' — Of similar shape and size to 'Avonresister', with sweet tender flesh.

Parsnips, like carrots, are biennials, and share the same soil requirements as carrots.

The mild, white flesh of 'Hollow Crown' is fine-grained and has a sweet, nutty flavor.

'Tender and True' — This is a giant, suitable for the show bench with even, uniform, tapered roots at least 3 in (7.5 cm) in diameter at the shoulder. It can be grown in drainpipes if garden soil is not sufficiently deep. It is of excellent quality, tender and sweet, and resistant to canker.

'The Student' — This 1860 heirloom is a firm favorite on both sides of the Atlantic with mellow, superlatively flavored, medium sized roots.

Daikon tends to be sweet and juicy, but some varieties will be slightly hotter than the traditional radish.

Radishes

Raphanus sativus   Zones 6–10

While the crisp radishes of summer salads are well known, the large, hot winter radishes are not so familiar. Chinese and Japanese cultivars are now regularly seen in stores and markets, and it's worth becoming acquainted with them for their sweetness, juiciness, and crispness which they retain even when of huge dimensions.

Radishes are an old vegetable and there are records of them being issued as rations to workers on the Great Pyramid. It is doubtful that they dined as well as the French who eat them with a little unsalted butter, a touch of sea salt, and a fresh loaf of crusty bread. The cultivar 'French Breakfast' is perfect for this purpose.

Winter radish or black radish belong to an ancient group, the first type to be cultivated. They are much larger, with hot-tasting roots which may be either cylindrical or globose and can be left standing in winter. Modern cultivars of winter radish come from Spain and Italy. The rat-tail radish, *Raphanus caudatus*, which also goes by the names of monkey-tail radish, serpentine bean, mougri, and singri, is prized for its exceptionally long, slender pods that can be stir-fried, used fresh in salads, boiled, cooked in curries, and made into pickles. They are harvested when 5–8 in (12.5–20 cm) long. Two cultivars are easily accessible—'**Long Purple**', with long delicious purple pods, and the German cultivar '**Munchen Bier**', designed as a crisp, mildly hot, crunchable radish to serve with beer in the manner of nuts.

Radishes are believed to have found their way to Asia quite early, being cultivated in China by 500 BC, and reaching Japan two centuries later. There they were selected to produce vegetables that seem superficially to be a different species to the European radish. Although they are certainly mild, sweet, tender, and crisp enough to use sliced in salads or as a finger food, in Asia they are more likely to be eaten sliced and cooked, most usually in soups. They are very cold-resistant and many are designed to stand in the ground through winter. Many of the Chinese cultivars are round and white or green-skinned with pink, red, or purple flesh and are quite beautiful to look at. Specimens can reach an almost inconceivable 100 lb (45 kg). Long-rooted cultivars are particularly favored in Japan where they are known as daikon, and are usually white-skinned and white-fleshed, reaching up to about 50 in (125 cm) in deep, sandy soils.

Growing and Harvesting

With the exception of sprouts, this is the first vegetable you will harvest from a new garden. They can be ready for an early feast in just three to four weeks, providing crisp, sweet, fresh, healthy food for the absolute minimum of effort. They are also an ideal crop for children to grow as they are so quick and rewarding. They require a moist, rich soil, kept cool with the use of mulches to ensure

rapid growth, maximum sweetness, and succulent tenderness.

Dig the soil over well and incorporate compost, then create a raised garden to a height of 10 in (25 cm). Long-rooted European cultivars will require the full depth provided by the raised bed, while small globe and turnip-rooted cultivars require only 4 in (10 cm) of soil depth. Seeds should be sown in shallow drills, $^2/_5$ in (1 cm) deep, in rows 6 in (15 cm) apart. Water regularly and thin to 2 in (5 cm) apart.

Weed carefully so as not to disturb the young roots and apply mulch on either side of the rows once the crop is thinned. Pull roots once they have swollen and while still at their tender peak. It is better to make small regular sowings for home use. Radishes are also very useful as a catch crop planted

'French Breakfast' is the almost perfect salad radish. Its oblong roots are crisp, tender, and only mildly hot.

Popular cultivars with round, scarlet roots include 'Rex', 'Round Red' and 'Tarzan'.

between rows of slower growing vegetables to optimize space and help suppress weed growth. Daikons and large round Chinese cultivars need up to 40 in (1 m) of soil depth, and are suited to lighter, deeper soils. They need regular watering. Daikons are also ideal for painlessly breaking up and aerating soils without the highly undesirable soil inversion that occurs when the work is mechanized.

Recommended Cultivars

'China Rose'. A good keeper and an important winter source of vitamin C.

'China Rose' syn. 'Chinese Red Winter' — This winter radish is long and turnip-shaped, growing up to 5 in

(12.5 cm), with bright rose-colored skin and firm, pungent, white flesh.

'French Breakfast' — 'Flamboyant', 'Lanquiette', 'Flamivil', 'D'Avignon', and **'Pontville'** are all more modern forms of this pre-1885 cultivar. The last named stays crisp and sweet long after maturing.

'German Giant' syn. 'Parat' — This a favorite German garden cultivar with very large, bright red, round roots with crisp, white, mild-flavored flesh. Equally large and also from Germany, the white skinned, white fleshed variety **'Beer Garden'** is traditionally sliced and dipped into sugar or salt and nibbled with beer.

'Long Red Italian' — This succulent, tender, red-skinned, white-fleshed cultivar can grow to 12 in (30 cm) long.

'Minowase' — A summer harvested Japanese cultivar with crisp white roots up to 24 in (60 cm) long and a mild flavor.

'Sparkler' — A round-rooted form with the same coloration pattern as 'French Breakfast' but more contrasted, retaining its crispness long after maturing.

Rampion

Campanula rapunculus   Zones 4–10

Rampion is an old vegetable from southern Europe and England. It is an attractive biennial, flowering in its second spring and can be planted as an ornamental. As food, it has a pleasant nutty flavor and the young roots can be sliced and eaten like radish, while the older roots can be boiled, fried, or roasted. Use the young leaves in green tossed salads or steamed as a pot herb. The young shoots can also be blanched and served steamed like asparagus.

Growing and Harvesting

The soil for this crop should be rich and loose, and the plants should be grown in the cool part of the garden. If necessary, fork the soil over well and incorporate plenty of compost. The surface should be raked over finely and the seed sown in mid-spring in very shallow drills, lightly covered with finely sieved compost, and pressed down gently before watering. Alternatively, the seed can be raised in flats indoors for late spring planting. The final spacing between plants should be 4 in (10 cm). An even soil moisture should be maintained throughout the growing period with the use of mulch and regular watering, otherwise the roots become fibrous. Roots are dug progressively from mid-autumn and the remainder of the harvest can be lifted and stored in sand for winter use.

Salsify

Tragopogon porifolius   Zones 5–10

Salsify is a member of the daisy family Asteraceae (previously the Compositae family) and has long, slender, white roots, long grass-like leaves, and large, pretty, rich purple flowers rather like 'Cupid's dart'. It is native to the Mediterranean but is naturalized in North America and in cooler areas of

Creeping Bellflower, Campanula rapunculoides, *is closely related to rampion, and has sweet fleshy roots that can be picked young and eaten in salads.*

Australia. It is thought to have first been cultivated in Italy in the 16th century and was described in cultivation in England in the 17th century. The root is the part most eaten and it has an oyster-like flavor, hence its other names, vegetable oyster and oyster plant. The young leaves and buds are also used in Italy. The Spanish oyster plant, *Scolymus hispanicus*, also called golden thistle, is cultivated in the

Salsify is commonly referred to as the 'oyster plant' because, when boiled, its flesh has a similar texture and flavor to oysters.

same way as salsify and has a milder flavor. It has pinnate (feathered) leaves.

Growing and Harvesting
Salsify is a hardy biennial. Seed remains viable for four years. It is cultivated in the same way as carrots, and can only be grown deep: either fine-textured sandy soils or sandy loams are perfect. Soil that has had compost or rotted manure added for a previous crop is ideal. Fresh compost or manure, or stones in the soil, will all cause forking of the roots. Seeds should be sown in early spring and thinned to 4 in (10 cm) apart. Roots can be harvested from mid-autumn onwards. Salsify can be left in the ground for winter harvesting. Any roots not harvested can be left to form flowering shoots and buds for harvest in spring together with the leaves. In very cold areas, a protective mulch should be applied over the crop. It has no notable pests or diseases.

Recommended Cultivars
The most easily obtained cultivars are **'Improved Mammoth Sandwich Island'**, **'Mammoth Long Island'**, and **'White French'**, which are fairly similar. The latter has the finest flavor but all share salsify's delicate oyster-like taste and have tender white flesh.

Scorzonera
Scorzonera hispanica   Zones 5–9

Scorzonera, also known as black salsify, mock oyster, and coconut root, is a hardy perennial with long, blackish roots. These can be boiled or steamed, and also fried in batter, baked, or added to stews and soups. The roasted roots are used to make a coffee substitute. The tender young shoots, known as chards, are used in salads. The flowers can be cooked or eaten raw in salads, the petals being distinctively flavored and used in French cuisine.

Recommended Cultivars
Unselected seed was the only option until recently. Some improved forms are now available including the excellent **'Maxima'**, **'Gigantia'**, which is delicious served raw, the nutty (almost coconut) flavored **'Flandria'**, and the delicious, long-rooted **'Duplex'**.

Scorzonera is grown for its edible taproots, which are long, thin, and black.

Skirret

Sium sisarum var. sisarum   Zones 5–10

This northern European species, also called crummock, was once commonly grown as a root vegetable but has drifted a little out of favor. The seeds are short-lived and remain viable for no more than two years. It is related to celery and lovage which it somewhat resembles, but differs in producing a bunch of long fleshy roots about the thickness of a finger joined at the crown of the plant. The roots are brown, and the flesh within white, and very sugary. Skirret is prepared by cleaning the roots and slowly braising them in butter. Alternatively, the roots can be cleaned and floured before frying, or baked, boiled, creamed, or used in soups and stews. They are delicious mashed with potatoes, or dressed with a sharp French dressing. Roasted skirret roots are used as a coffee substitute. This is truly a fine vegetable—and just rare enough to annoy any competitive gardening neighbors!

Growing and Harvesting

Skirret is grown in a manner similar to celery, preferring light but humus-rich soils. Some older books recommend propagation by division to produce slips but this results in inferior-quality roots.

Sow the seeds in mid spring, about 1 in (2.5 cm) deep, in rows 12 in (25 cm) apart. Harvest before winter, cutting the foliage back to near the crown, and store in sand in a cool dry area. A few plants should be left in the ground to flower the following spring and produce seed for the next season's planting. It has no serious pests or diseases. A closely related species, water parsnip, *Sium cicutaefolium*, occurs in the eastern United States and has roots with a nutty flavor that have been part of the diet of Indian tribes in Canada and North America.

Swedes

Brassica napus napobrassica   Zones 5–9

Swedes, rutabagas, and Swedish turnips are essentially the same vegetable. They have turnip-like roots that are prepared in the same way by boiling, steaming, mashing, roasting, baking, and frying. Rutabagas differ in being somewhat cold-hardier (although all swedes have good cold resistance),

Skirret is believed to help with chest complaints and is regarded by many as being superior in flavor to the carrot.

The 'American Purple Top' produces globes with a light-yellow skin and purple on top. Flesh is light yellow, firm, fine-grained, and sweet.

elements will establish if your soils suffer from this deficiency.) This should be dealt with as described for turnips below.

Sow the seeds directly into the soil in mid to late spring through to early summer. The holes should be $1/2$ in (1 cm) deep. Seedlings are thinned to 6 in (15 cm) apart. The tops of the thinnings can be used for greens. Swedes are quite easy to grow under the right conditions but it is important to keep the rows weed-free so a mulch should be applied once the plants start to grow.

Flea beetles can attack spring plantings. A dusting with rotenone can be used or, better, wood ashes. As advised elsewhere, care should be taken with rotenone. Clubroot can be a problem and it is important to include swedes in any plant rotation scheme as a member of the brassicas to prevent the build-up of soil-borne pests. Mildew can also be a problem.

Swedes and rutabagas can be harvested from fall onward. While they are very cold-resistant, the quality of the roots will drop for most cultivars left in the ground during winter, and it is better to dig the roots, twist off the tops, and store the roots in dry sand in a cool storage area, or in a clamp in cold areas.

are often larger, and require 21 to 28 days longer to mature. The whole group is characterized by yellow to deep gold flesh which has a rich buttery flavor. The tops can also be used as greens, in a similar manner to kale. Swedes and rutabagas are believed to have the same valuable anti-cancer qualities as turnips, and are a good source of vitamin C and potassium.

Growing and Harvesting
Swedes prefer a light, fertile soil. A site where the soil was prepared with compost in the previous season is ideal, as swedes do not like high levels of nitrogen. They are also sensitive to boron deficiency. (A test for trace

Recommended Cultivars
'American Purple Top' — This cultivar produces large, bright yellow, globose roots with purple shoulders. The flesh is fine-grained, sweet, tender, and mild. It is an important cultivar in Australia and North America.

'Champion Purple Top' — Very popular in Australia and North America, this cultivar with rose colored skin and yellow flesh has a rich flavor and color. It is very reliable and long-keeping.

'Gilfeather' — This famed Vermont heirloom has a large, creamy white root with a delicate, sweet, mild flavor. It can be harvested when young through to the very large root stage without losing any quality. Used like kale, the greens are excellent.

'Laurentian' — This is a very good quality storing type developed in Canada before 1860. It has almost globe-shaped, pale yellow roots with purple shoulders. The texture is fine and the flavor mild and sweet. This is North America's favorite cultivar.

'Marion' — Developed in Wales, this is a vigorous newer cultivar producing uniform crops of globose, purple-topped roots with fine-textured flesh and excellent flavor. It is highly resistant to club root, mildew, and root crack.

Turnips

Brassica rapa rapifera   Zones 7–11

Brassica rapa is one of those extraordinary species that have given rise to many vegetables including turnips, broccoli raab, field mustards, Japanese mustards, Chinese cabbages of many kinds and, through an ancient natural hybridization with kale, swedes. In turnips, the root has been developed by selection to become enlarged. Earlier cultivars were longer and more tapering compared with modern cultivars which have globose or flattened globose forms. The flesh is white or creamy yellow, and skin color, concentrated around the shoulders of the root, varies from green to cream, yellow, rose-pink, red, and purple. The tops are also edible when steamed or braised. Some varieties have crisp sweet roots that can be used fresh in salads. Others are suitable for soups and stews, or cooked like potatoes (with which they can be mixed half and half for a dish with milder flavor), or pickled.

Turnip greens are rich in calcium, phosphorus, and potassium. The roots and tops contain vitamin C and are a good source of folic acid.

Growing and Harvesting

Turnips are markedly affected by boron deficiency. A soil test is well worth performing for this trace element as its absence also affects many other vegetables. A once-off application of mixed trace elements should suffice to restore this nutrient to your soil. Compost made from recycling garden waste will not solve this problem as the compost will be

Turnip greens are rich in glucosinolates, believed to block the development of cancer. The 'Shogun' variety has tender leaves and smooth, globe-shaped roots.

The 'Waldaboro' long-neck turnip is an heirloom cultivar with a huge underground root.

The 'Green Stone Top Turnip' can be left underground for extended periods.

equally deficient, coming from the same soil. However, once you give the soil the necessary minute amount of trace elements, composting all garden wastes should ensure that no further applications are necessary for many years.

Turnips need an open, sunny position and preferably a site which has been well composted for a previous crop as they are relatively light feeders. Sow the seed in rows in early spring, protected by cloches in cool to cold areas. Thin the seedlings to a spacing of 3 in (7.5 cm) one to two weeks after emergence. Successive plantings can be made until late summer. Bolt-resistant cultivars should be used for spring plantings. Water the plants regularly as they tend to bolt if allowed to dry out. A good, thick mulch should be applied to help retain soil moisture, moderate the soil temperature, and suppress weed growth. Radishes can be intercropped with turnips to maximize use of the land. They are harvested five to six weeks after planting before the turnips require the space. Turnips should be included in the garden rotation of brassicas to prevent a build up of diseases in the soil.

Turnips tend to become woody with age so should be harvested while relatively young—for most cultivars when they are about the size of a tennis ball. Harvest only one to two leaves per plant once or twice during the season as they are required to feed the growing roots. Turnips planted for late fall or winter use can be stored in a shed or in clamps as they have good winter hardiness.

Recommended Cultivars

'Golden Ball' — This old cultivar from 1855 is widely grown for its globose, sweet, pale golden flesh. It has some bolt resistance. It is a selection of the even older **'Orange Jelly'**.

'Green Stone Top' — A white-fleshed, green-topped, uniform, globe-rooted cultivar which is very cold-hardy and keeps well if left in the ground. It can be planted in fall and left in the soil for spring harvests in milder areas. It keeps well and has firm, tender flesh and a mild sweet flavor.

'Purple Top White Globe' — A pre-1880 cultivar which is still the standard home and market cultivar, with globose white roots that are bright purple on the upper half and have a sweet mild flavor.

'Seven Top' syn. 'Southern Prize' — This is a fast-growing crop used for cool weather greens. The roots are suitable only for fodder, but the deliciously tender, dark green tops are a favorite in the southern United States.

'Tokyo Cross' — This semi globose, pure white-skinned and fleshed cultivar has superb, sweet, crisp, fine flesh and can be grown to its full size of 6 in (15 cm) diameter with no loss of quality. Harvested at 2 in (5 cm) diameter it is good in salads, used in similar ways to radish. The leaves are excellent used as greens. It has good disease resistance and is used for spring and fall sowings in warm areas, spring and summer in cooler climates.

'White Egg' — Introduced before 1888, this forms egg-shaped, pure white, medium-sized roots that are fine-textured, dense, sweet, tender and with a mild flavor. It is a fast-growing cultivar for spring and fall.

The 'Purple Top White Globe' is a popular cultivar but like most turnips will become tough if conditions are too dry.

Section 2

HERBS

Herbs

Agastache *Agastache* spp.; **Aloe** *Aloe vera*; **Angelica** *Angelica archangelica*; **Basil** *Ocimum* spp.; **Bay** *Laurus nobilis*; **Bergamots** *Monarda* spp.; **Borage** *Borago officinalis*; **Catnip** *Nepeta cataria*; **Chamomile** *Chamaemelum nobile*; **Chervil** *Anthriscus cerefolium*; **Cilantro** *Coriandrum sativum*; **Comfrey** *Symphytum officinale*; **Dill** *Anethum graveolens*; **Elecampane** *Inula helenium*; **Fennel** *Foeniculum vulgare*; **French Tarragon** *Artemisia dracunculus*; **Horseradish** *Cochlearia armoracia*; **Hyssop** *Hyssopus officinalis*; **Lady's Mantle** *Alchemilla molliss*; **Lavender** *Lavandula* spp.; **Lemon Balm** *Melissa officinalis*; **Lemongrass** *Cymbopogon citratus*; **Lemon Verbena** *Aloysia triphylla*; **Licorice** *Glycyrrhiza glabra*; **Marigolds** *Tagetes* spp.; **Marshmallow** *Althaea officinalis*; **Meadowsweet** *Filipendula ulmaria*; **Milfoil Yarrow** *Achillea millefolium*; **Mint** *Mentha* spp.; **Parsley** *Petroselinum crispum*; **Rosemary** *Rosmarinus officinalis*; **Rue** *Ruta graveolens*; **Sage** *Salvia* spp.; **Salad Burnet** *Sanguisorba minor*; **Savory** *Satureja* spp.; **Scented Geraniums** *Pelargonium* spp.; **Soapwort**, *Saponaria officinalis*; **Society Garlic** *Tulbaghia violacea*; **Southernwood** *Artemisia abrotanum*; **Sweet Woodruff** *Asperula odorata*; **Tansy** *Tanacetum vulgare*; **Thyme** *Thymus* spp.; **Valerian** *Valeriana officinalis*

Herb gardens are very personal. The power of a herb's fragrance can capture and hold memories as fresh as if imprisoned in crystal; the taste of a herb can bring the comfort of familiar flavors that link us to our pasts. In short, herbs are touchstones for our lives. To walk among herbs is to unlock doors in the mind. So the herb garden can never be an open space. There must always be a special sense of place, a feeling of welcome, of intimacy—both in the plants grown and in the garden design.

Formal, geometric, Tudor herb gardens are a delight. There is something about all that patterning that is very pleasing and soothing. The gentle

A formal herb garden at Ballymaloe near Cork, Ireland.

colors of herbs seem so at home there. It is no coincidence that these lovely, patterned gardens continue to be built around the world. They are usually enclosed gardens, denying the outside world and its troubles, and at the same time protecting the plants within, creating a microclimate in which the winds blow less cold and the warmth of the sun is trapped.

If you want to create your own herb garden, but have little room to spare, it is possible to do it using only planters and pots, with a garden seat for two so that it can be enjoyed with a friend. Gardening in pots actually has many advantages. The pots can be moved in accord with the season, lifted onto bricks to catch the pale rays of a winter sun, and all the imperfections of real garden soils overcome as you create the perfectly tailored soil mix for plants.

If you have a little more space, consider planting herbs everywhere.

They don't need to be confined to only one place. An advantage of this approach is that many herbs have a strong fragrance that interferes with the ability of some insects to target plants for food, so they are useful companion plants. And while they discourage the insects you don't want, they're attractive to those you do—bees love herbs.

Some herbs can remedy minor medical problems. A pot of aloe vera can help sooth sunburn. Harvest a leaf, break it open, and squeeze the gel onto the sunburnt area. It can also be used to soothe insect bites, or minor burns when cooking. A sore throat can often be improved by sipping hot sage or thyme tea sweetened with honey. For nausea, upset tummies, indigestion and fever, peppermint or spearmint tea will bring relief. Feeling anxious? Nothing could be better than lavender flower or lemon balm tea. Just smelling those fragrances is restful.

Herbs spill over the pathways in profusion in this informal garden at Heritage Farm, Iowa, USA.

The flowers of anise hyssop, Agastache foeniculum, *are attractive to bees.*

Agastache
Agastache spp.   Zones 8–10

Agastache species are native to the Americas and many have a delightful scent locked in their leaves. Anise hyssop, *Agastache foeniculum,* was the first to be widely distributed and has sweet anise-scented leaves and dense spikes of rich deep lavender-blue flowers. The leaves make an excellent herbal tea, and can be used to flavor cold drinks and fruit salads, and added to pot pourri. It requires full sunshine to light shade, and an enriched soil. **'Licorice White'** and **'Licorice Blue'** are perennial cultivars. A hybrid of *A. cana,* **'Heather Queen'**, has showy heather-lilac flowers and sweetly aromatic leaves. A hybrid of *A. mexicana,* **'Champagne'**, has pink champagne flowers and sweetly scented leaves.

Aloe
Aloe vera syn. *A. barbadensis*   Zones 8–11

This is the aloe renowned for its medicinal qualities. The fresh juice has long been used to heal wounds and help regenerate skin tissue. The gel that contains the active substance oozes from the broken leaf. Aloe requires full sun, and reproduces by budding off new plants from the base.

Angelica
Angelica archangelica   Zones 4–9

This handsome herb eventually reaches 5 ft (1.5 m) or more in its second year of growth as a biennial. It requires a moist, protected position. All parts of the plant have a sweet, clean fragrance. The stems are candied

The thick, fleshy leaves of Aloe vera *help to conserve moisture during hot dry summers. Its medicinal qualities qualify it for inclusion in a herb garden.*

for delicious green sweets, and a delightfully refreshing tea is made from the fresh or dried leaves.

Angelica is a substantial plant and a gross feeder, requiring a well-composted soil. This will also assist in the necessary soil moisture retention. The seed is of short viability and should be replanted reasonably quickly.

Basil
Ocimum spp.   Zones 10–12

There are about 35 species of basil found through tropical Asia including tropical Australia, as well as tropical Africa. They all have aromatic foliage, the majority sharing the clove scent of sweet basil. In the last decade as interest has grown in basils, more and more species have come into general cultivation. The official hybridists for the seed companies and the unofficial hybridists, the bees, have produced many new species and new cultivars are being released continually. Until recently, virtually all the cultivars of sweet basil *Ocimum basilicum* were developed in Italy. There are now two lemon-scented species, *O. gratissimum* and *O. americanum*. The richly lemon-scented cultivar '**Mrs Burn's Lemon**', now marketed world wide,

and '**Lime**' with true lime fragrance, are both cultivars of *O. americanum*. Perennial cultivars possess much of the flavor and fragrance of sweet basil.

Both the annual and perennial cultivars of basil need a well-composted, moist soil, and a mulch supplied once the plants are established will improve productivity. Basils are outstanding bee attractors, and are excellent companion plants for tomatoes, their perfect complement.

Bay
Laurus nobilis   Zones 7–10

The bay, bay laurel, or sweet bay is native to the Mediterranean area. It forms a broad tree over a period of about 40–50 years, reaching a height of around 40 ft (12 m). As it is so slow growing, it is an ideal subject for tub culture, as well as for topiary work, with the additional advantage that the clippings are a harvest that can be dried and used in the kitchen to flavor casseroles, stews, and soups.

Bergamot
Monarda spp.   Zones 4–10

Bergamots are native to North America and are characterized by whorled arrangements of their twin tubular, nectar-filled flowers, and by warmly aromatic foliage which was

Angelica archangelica has a sweet fragrance and a refreshing tea is made from its leaves.

There are dozens of basils now available. Sweet basil, Ocimum basilicum, *is still the most widely used.*

Bergamot, Monarda spp., has edible flowers and leaves that can be used to make tea.

The foliage of lemon bergamot, M. citriodora, makes an excellent herbal tea.

traditionally used for tea. The plant is also known as bee balm as the flowers are attractive to bees. They are edible and can be used on salads and as a garnish for sweet dishes. The famous Oswego tea that sustained Bostonians through withdrawal symptoms after the Boston Tea Party was made from bergamot.

Bergamots have been subject to selection and hybridization and a number of cultivars are available, many of great beauty but less aromatic than the wild species. They include **'Croftway Pink'**, **'Crimson'**, **'Thundercloud'**, **'Cambridge Scarlet'**, **'Enfield Gem'**, and **'Kardinal'**.

Lemon bergamot, *Monarda citriodora*, also known as lemon mint and purple horse mint, is an annual species. Commercial varities have lilac colored flowers with lemon-scented foliage that makes an excellent herbal tea. It prefers a well-drained site with no additional compost or mulch. Watering is important, however.

Spotted bergamot, *M. punctata*, also known as horse mint, is a plant of subtle beauty with large, dense whorls of showy flowers of pale cream delightfully spotted and speckled with purple, and a ruff of lavender bracts.

Wild bergamot, *M. fistulosa*, is a species of great loveliness which carpets the hills of a number of US states from July onward. It is so common that it is the visual equivalent of the heather of Scotland. The leaves are very aromatic. Oregano de la Sierra *M. fistulsa* var. *menthaefolia* is a beautiful, deep green foliaged, lavender flowered perennial. The foliage is scented of oregano and is used to flavor meats, wild game, and cheeses.

The young leaves of borage, Borago officinalis, *are delicious dipped in a light batter and fried.*

Borage

Borago officinalis   Zones 5–10

With starry flowers in the richest, truest blue, borage was also known as the herb of gladness. The old saying 'Borage for courage' may come from the medieval tradition when ladies of crusading knights would embroider this blue flowered symbol on a scarf for their departing lover. The flowers are cucumber-flavored and can be floated in long summer drinks after removing the hairy calyx.

Catnip

Nepeta cataria   Zones 3–10

Catnip is related to the mints, and forms a bushy herbaceous perennial of soft grey-green leaves with dense spikes of pinkish-white small flowers in summer. A lemon-scented form is available. The dried foliage can be used

to stuff catnip mice, balls, and other feline toys. Catnip requires a sunny, well-drained situation.

Chamomile

Chamaemelum nobile and *Matricaria recutita*

This chamomile has come to be known as 'the plant doctor'. For reasons that no-one is yet able to fully explain, if this species of chamomile is planted beside an ailing plant, it appears to improve its chances of recovery. This is particularly true for roses. Presumably some root exudate is responsible.

This type of chamomile, also known as Roman chamomile, forms a matting, dense, perennial clump with a fresh apple scent when touched. It blooms in summer with prolific single

The tea from Roman chamomile, Chamaemelum nobile, *is called manzanilla and is used to soothe the stomach.*

While catnip, Nepata cataria, *has a stimulating effect on cats, a tea made of the leaves is believed to have tranquilizing properties for humans.*

Chervil

Anthriscus cerefolium   Zones 6–10

This is an exceptionally pretty plant, its leaves resembling a dainty Italian parsley. The leaves have a delicate flavor like sweet anise and can be used as a garnish to many dishes. Chervil is one of the *fines herbes* of French cooking.

A chamomile plant threatened by caterpillars will produce a natural repellent for protection.

Right: Essential to the cuisines of South East Asia and the Middle East, cilantro, Coriandrum sativum, adds flavor to curries and seafood. The leaves, roots, and stems of the plant can all be used.

white daisy flowers. *Chamaemelum nobile* **'Flora Plena'** is a double-flowered form, and **'Treneague,'** which is flowerless, is ideal for a bee-free chamomile lawn that is safe to walk on barefoot.

German chamomile is another plant, *Matricaria recutita*. It is an annual, growing to 2 ft (60 cm) with aromatic, finely divided foliage. It flowers with small white daisies which can be regularly harvested, dried, and used for a tea. The same tea cooled makes a good final rinse for blond hair, lightening it just a fraction and adding lights. This is a self-seeding plant so sacrifice the last few flowers to provide the seed bank for next year's plants.

Right: Chervil is used as a garnish and also in French cooking.

Cilantro

Coriandrum sativum   Zones 7–12

Known also as coriander, cilantro has been used for more than 5,000 years by the Chinese, and is also called Chinese parsley. It is an annual plant, forming a rosette of leaves which are very aromatic. Even greater flavor is to be found in the roots, which are also used in Asian cooking. The plants flower at a height of about 24 in (60 cm) and bear tiny round fruits. It requires well-composted, moist soil in full sun and regular watering or it tends to run to seed early.

Two other plants bear the name 'coriander'. Mexican coriander, *Eryngium foetidum*, is also known as *ngo gai*. The leaves have an intense flavor and should be eaten when tender and young. It requires a sunny position and grows well if rowed out in the vegetable garden. Vietnamese coriander, *Polygonum odoratum*, also called Vietnamese mint and *rau ram*, is a quintessential element of Vietnamese cooking. Requiring a moist, well-composted soil, and a protected position, it is a spreading groundcover.

Comfrey
Symphytum officinale   Zones 5–10

Boneset, healing herb, knitwort, and bruisewort are other names for comfrey and testify to its qualities as a healing herb. Used for centuries to speed the healing of broken bones, sprains, and minor burns and bruises, it contains a substance called allantoin, which is now used in commercial ointments to treat some of these conditions. Comfrey forms rosettes of large, rather coarsely textured, leaves about 1 ft (30 cm) long, from which emerge tall racemes of nodding bell-shaped flowers. It is propagated by root cuttings taken in fall. Be careful where you grow it as it is difficult to remove all those potential root cuttings later. It will grow happily on less than perfect soil, provided it receives water.

Dill
Anethum graveolens   Zones 5–10

Dill is an annual herb of Mediterranean origin. Related to fennel, it has long been in cultivation. It forms upright plants that have very fine, filamentous leaves with a unique fragrance and flavor that marry perfectly with fish. The seeds are prized for their role in creating pickles such as dill pickles. It is said to be a good trap plant to lure green tomato worms from their prey. Certainly they are attractive to many desirable insects which predate on pests. Compost should be added to the soil before planting. Sow the seed where it is to grow, in spring.

Nibbling on dill seed was considered to help stop hiccups. A tea of the seed was a traditional cure for indigestion.

Elecampane
Inula helenium   Zones 5–10

Elecampane is a tall, handsome perennial with large leaves that flowers at a height of 5–6 ft (1.5–1.8 m). The blooms are yellow-rayed and resemble a branched sunflower, to which it is related. The roots were candied as a sweetmeat in the past, and found use in some wines and liqueurs in Europe. In days gone by it was also used to treat various respiratory disorders.

Fennel
Foeniculum vulgare   Zones 5–10

Fennel is an anise-scented perennial herb growing to 5–6 ft (1.5–1.8 m) that goes perfectly with seafood. When cooking fish, stuff the fern-like leaves in the body cavity or add the stalks, dried or fresh, to barbecue coals when grilling. The lacy heads of the tiny yellow flowers form flat seeds that can be used to make a tea.

The leaves are all compressed in the base of the plant and have become

Above right: Comfrey, Symphytum officinale, growing as a green manure.

very fleshy, forming a bulb-like structure. The taste of the bulb is sweet and combines celery with mild sweet anise. The texture is tender and crisp, like the finest blanched celery. It is used in slices raw (perfect for healthy dips) or in a wide variety of cooked dishes. The bulbs take between 80 and 110 days from seed.

All fennel plants appreciate a well composted soil, ample water, good drainage, and full sunshine.

A highly ornamental bronze

foliaged form is also available. Through centuries of selection a vegetable called Florence fennel, or sweet fennel, or finnochio has been developed from the herb.

French Tarragon
Artemisia dracunculus   Zones 6–9

Tarragon, called estragon by the French, is a staple of French cuisine. The plant has multiple stems and small slender green leaves that have a delicate and inimitable taste of sweet anise. Tarragon combines well with chicken, egg dishes, fish, shellfish, and green salads.

To eat with chicken, mash some chopped tarragon into a knob of butter and work it down between the breast skin and the flesh of a plump, corn-fed organically raised fowl. Add another knob of the butter to the cavity with a little salt, a quartered lemon, and the cloves of half a bulb of garlic that have been been broken with the side of the blade of a heavy knife. (There is no need to peel the garlic.) Drizzle a little extra virgin olive oil over the chicken and roast gently until the juices run clear when a toothpick or similar is pushed into the deepest flesh.

Horseradish

Cochlearia armoracia   Zones 5–10

The grated root, harvested in the
second year of growth, is used to
make horseradish cream, traditionally
served with roast beef. Excess grated
root can be stored in vinegar in the
refrigerator. Horseradish is a
vigorous, large-leafed perennial. It is
propagated from seg-ments of root in
fall. It is best planted somewhere out
of the way. Although it is not
invasive, once established it will
probably be permanent.

Hyssop

Hyssopus officinalis   Zones 3–11

This is a very pretty and ancient plant
related to the mints. Its bitter mint-
flavored leaves can be finely chopped
and added to game meats, soups, and
stews. It is a neat shrub growing to
20–24 in (50–60 cm) with many
spikes of small lipped, deep blue
flowers. Occasional white and pink
forms occur in the wild. It requires a
well-drained, sunny position.

Lady's Mantle

Alchemilla molliss   Zones 4–9

Originally grown to treat muscular
ailments and rheumatism, lady's
mantle, named for the Virgin Mary,
is now grown for its simple beauty.
The fan-shaped leaves are pleated
and form drops of water evenly
around the leaves (a process called
guttation) each morning, resembling
tear drops. The flowers are tiny,
yellow-green, and borne in cloudy
panicles in late summer. A second
flush follows in fall. It makes a
delightful groundcover for semi-
shaded areas.

*French tarragon,
Artemisia dracunculus,
is one of the classic
fines herbes used in
French cooking.*

*The grated root of
Cochlearia armoracia is
the part used to make
horseradish cream.*

Lavender

Lavandula spp.   Zones 6–10

Lavender belongs to the mint family Lamiaceae, and there are approximately 30 species of the plant, originating from the Canary Islands in the west, across southern Europe and North Africa, though Asia Minor to Western India. Many of these are only in specialist culture. The species usually encountered as herb garden plants are true lavender (sometimes called English lavender), *L. angustifolia* which, despite its name is endemic to France

Recently developed cultivars of Lavandula stoechas *have been bred for different colors, multiple flower heads, and new bract formations.*

English lavender, Lavandula angustifolia, *should be planted in well-drained soil to prevent rot. Good air circulation will help to prevent foliage diseases.*

at altitudes above 1,625 ft (500 m), spike lavender, *L. latifolia,* which occurs at lower latitudes, and in between a hybrid group called Lavandins or Intermedias *L.* x *intermedia.* The finest quality lavender oil comes from the true lavender.

L. stoechas has been subject to much effort by Australian plant breeders and this species has become an important landscape lavender for warmer areas. The United States and New Zealand have also been very active in breeding lavender for garden plants. Other species to plant in milder climate gardens include green lavender *L. viridis,* woolly lavender *L. lanata,* fringed lavender *L. dentata,* fernleaf lavender *L. multifida,* and Canary Island lavender *L. canariensis* together with their many cultivars.

All lavender plants require full sunshine and excellent drainage. They should be mulched annually which will provide the light nutritional boost that they require.

Lavender has many uses. Interleave the dried flowers between stored bed linen. Its scent will ensure that you will

sleep well, even on the the hottest nights. Fold away winter woolens and blankets with a mixture of equal quantities of dried lavender leaves and flowers, and dried southernwood. Drink lavender flower tea to relieve stress headaches. Use a bath bag filled with lavender for the most relaxing of baths and to ease tired muscles.

Lemon Balm
Melissa officinalis   Zones 4–10

Also called bee balm, lime balm, and liqueur balm, lemon balm is a close relative of the mints. It forms a soft shrub that dies back each winter. The leaves have a delicious fresh lemon fragrance and the tiny white flowers in spikes are attractive to bees. The leaves are used to flavor a number of European liqueurs, and the tea is used to combat nausea. Lemon balm also has a wide variety of culinary uses. Two named cultivars, **'Lime'** and **'Liqueur'**, are available and there is a variegated form, and a pure gold leaf form. It requires a moist, well-composted soil in sun to half shade.

Lemongrass
Cymbopogon citratus   Zones 10–12

This deliciously scented grass, also called West Indian lemongrass, smells strongly of fresh lemons. It is used in the cuisines of South East Asia,

particularly those of Thailand and Malaysia. It will grow in areas from the tropics to warm temperate areas, provided it is supplied with a well-composted soil in a sunny position, and is adequately watered. Small clumps can be harvested from around the edge of the plant as needed. It is also propagated by side shoots. It forms a large clump of leaves to around 2 ft (60 cm) in height.

Lemon Verbena
Aloysia triphylla   Zones 8–11

This deciduous shrub grows to as high as 10 ft (3 m) with light green pointed leaves covering the branches, and large, cloudy terminal panicles of tiny white to lavender flowers in summer. The leaves have a delicious lemon fragrance which is captured in perfumes, toiletries, pot pourri, sleep pillows, and in one of the most delicious of the herbal teas. In frosty areas, the bush can be grown in a pot and brought indoors for the winter months. It will take a few moderate frosts but not a severe one. It appreciates regular watering and the provision of a mulch.

Lemon verbena, Aloysia triphylla, *can be grown in pots if space is limited. It thrives in full sun in cool climates or light shade in warmer areas.*

The fleshy white, bulbous base of lemongrass, Cymbopogon citratus, *is the part that is used in cooking. When dried, the leaves make a refreshing herbal tea.*

Glycyrrhiza glabra *is the source of commericial licorice. Its flowers are pale blue, yellow, violet, or purple.*

Licorice
Glycyrrhiza glabra   Zones 8–10

This plant is the source of commercial licorice. It is a southern European plant, cultivated in Italy, and forms a slender shrub to 4 ft (1.2 m) high, with lilac pea flowers. It grows in full sun and a wide range of soils. A perennial legume, it is harvested in its third or fourth year for its roots. The seeds need to be scratched between two sheets of sandpaper before planting.

Marigolds
Tagetes spp.   Zones 9–11

The marigolds contain several remark-ably talented plant mimics. *Tagetes lemmonii* is native to Arizona and south into Mexico, and forms a sub-stantial shrub to 5 ft (1.5 m) high and somewhat wider, in a neat, rounded shape provided it is planted in full sunshine. It flowers spectacularly and over a long period of time, covering in bright golden single flowers. The scent of the foliage is quite remarkable, released at the slightest touch, and unmistakably that of ripe passionfruit.

T. lucida is an equally successful mimic, having almost the exact same sweet anise scent and taste as French tarragon. It forms a small, upright growing bush with dark green foliage and in summer is bright with terminal clusters of tiny golden flowers.

Both plants are tough and will survive on quite poor soils, but they respond very well to moderate additions of compost.

The marigold, Tagetes spp, *is a composite herb, also known as winter tarragon or sweet mace.*

Marshmallow

Althaea officinalis   Zones 6–10

Althaea is a hardy perennial that
resembles a small hollyhock, to which
it is closely related. It is still widely
used today in herbal medicine for its
soothing properties for the throat and
digestive system. The Romans also
regarded it as a delicious vegetable,
the roots (which were the source of
true marshmallow) being boiled until
tender then finished in butter. The
tender young shoots were eaten in
salads. It is easily grown in full sun,
and requires moderately composted
and loosened soil.

Meadowsweet

Filipendula ulmaria   Zones 2–9

Also known as queen of the meadow,
meadowsweet forms rosettes of
deeply incised, fern-like leaves. In
summer it sends up flowering heads
to 24 in (60 cm) with creamy masses
of tiny flowers which have an
almond scent. It is an ancient
strewing herb from the days when
floors were covered with sweet
smelling herbs. It is also a source of
salicylic acid, the basis of aspirin.
It was used in the past to reduce

*Left: Meadowsweet,
Filipendula ulmaria,
grows best in a
protected position with
cool, moist soil and
protection from direct
sunshine.*

fevers, and relieve the symptoms of
migraine, rheumatism, and arthritis,
in the way we would use pharmaceutical aspirin today. It requires a
protected position with cool, moist
soil and protection from direct
sunshine. A thick mulch and well-
composted soil are best for this species.

Milfoil Yarrow

Achillea millefolium   Zones 3–10

Milfoil yarrow was traditionally used
to staunch the flow of blood from
wounds, particularly those caused by
knives or swords. The last battle it
was reputedly used in by an army
medical corps was the American Civil

*Milfoil yarrow, Achillea
millefolium, forms a fine,
ferny groundcover and is
tolerant of partial shade
to full sun.*

Above: There is a large range of mint species and cultivars to choose from. Mentha x piperita 'Chocolate mint' is among those recommended for a beginner's collection.

Right: Curly-leafed parsley, Petroselinum crispum, is a must in any herb garden. It is also attractive enough to grow as a decorative border.

War. Among its many names are herbes militaris, staunchweed, and carpenter's weed. It flourishes on quite poor ground, provided there is adequate soil moisture.

Mint
Mentha spp.   Zones 4–10

While most gardeners are familiar with spearmint and perhaps applemint, the sheer range of mint species and cultivars could keep a collector active for many years. They are all rhizomatous creeping herbs and live in moist soil to which plenty of compost has been added. Among those recommended for a beginner's collection are **'Lime'** *M. x piperita cv.,* **'Chocolate mint'** *M. piperita* var., **'Lemon'** *M. aquatica* var. *citrata,* **'Moroccan'** *M. spicata* cv, and **'Grapefruit'** *M. x piperita.*

Australia has some interesting native mints rarely seen outside the country including native peppermint, *M. australis,* which has a delicious peppermint fragrance and is used like true peppermint to relieve the symptoms of an upset stomach. Like pennyroyal, this should not be taken by pregnant women. In addition to the quite remarkable range of true mints and their hybrids on offer (currently in the region of 70), there are a number of related species which bear the name of mint.

Parsley
Petroselinum crispum   Zones 5–11

Parsley is a biennial, forming a lush rosette of green, stalked, compound leaves, then sending up flowering stalks. Parsley takes an inordinately long time to germinate. Of the two varieties (continental plain-leafed and common curly-leafed) the plain-leafed parsley is the easier of the two forms to grow. They should both be given a well-composted soil, and regularly watered. Always harvest from the outer leaves or you will hasten the plant running to seed. Parsley seed is short lived and should be stored in an airtight bottle or small zip-locked bag in the crisper of the refrigerator until ready for use. Leave some of the flowering plants to seed, as the best plants always seem to be the self-sown ones.

Rosemary
Rosmarinus officinalis   Zones 6–11

Rosemary is one of the finest of all bee-attracting plants and is an excellent planting in orchards and gardens to attract large numbers of bees for the pollination of crops. Rosemary is said to improve the memory. If so, this may be due to its antioxidant levels. Bride's bouquets at one time regularly contained a sprig of rosemary, and the sprig was planted to grow into a bush which was the symbol of fidelity. The scent, though,

Rosemary, Rosmarinus officinalis, *is a good companion plant. Its strong scent is believed to deter the flies that attack some root crops.*

has long been considered a masculine one and it has been used in male toiletries for centuries. Rosemary (along with holly and ivy) was a plant which, since it remained fresh and evergreen in the depths of the longest and bitterest days of winter, was looked on symbolically as a promise that summer would reign once again.

Although attempts have been made to establish the existence of more than one species in the genus, the attempted revisions have not been accepted and rosemary remains a solitary species genus.

The resinous fragrance of rosemary has long been of value to chefs. It is an excellent flavoring for pork, lamb, and chicken dishes.

Rosemary forms a neat, upright, woody shrub that may live for 30 years or more in suitable areas. Clippings can be used fresh, or alternatively dried for convenience. Rosemary needs a well-drained, sunny position, and in colder areas, the backing of a brick wall provides re-radiated heat at night to give some cold protection.

While there is only one species, there are many cultivars available, including the beautiful, semi-prostrate, mid-blue Californian cultivar **'Santa Barbara'**, **'Majorca Pink'**, the rich blue flowered bush **'Collingwood Ingram'**, the giant **'Tuscan Blue'**, the semi-prostrate, cascading **'Lockwood de Forest'**, and the gold splashed **'Genges Gold'**.

Rue

Ruta graveolens   Zones 5–10

This was Shakespeare's 'herb of grace', and it is an ancient biblical herb symbolic of repentance. It is a moderately frost hardy species, upright growing to 3 ft (1 m). Rue was used medicinally in the past, and was one of the herbs in the 'Four Thieves' Vinegar', a concoction used

Rue, Ruta graveolens, *is a pretty addition to the herb garden with its lacy, foliage and yellow flowers.*

Salvia officinalis
'Purpurascens' is an
attractive purple-leafed
form of sage.

Sage

Salvia spp.   Zones 5–10

Sage is one of the most important culinary herbs. It forms a soft grey-green leafed, aromatic shrub which is very attractive when it flowers with handsome spikes of lavender, and rarely pink or white flowers. It requires full sun and good drainage. It is also a good choice for pot culture. In addition to the common grey-leafed sage, *Salvia officinalis*, there are a number of variations such as **'Holt's Mammoth'** and **'Berggarten'** both of which have extremely large leaves. Color variations have been particularly valued and include **'Painted'** or **'Tricolor'** sage which has leaves mottled in cream, mulberry, and gray-green. **'Icterina'** is a golden variegated form. There is also a purple-leafed form, **'Purpurascens'**.

Sage finds use in stuffing poultry and pork (a good practice as it increases the digestibility of fatty food) and is used in a classic sauce for pasta. It is also used in soups and stews, with grilled cheese dishes, and to make the delicious sage-marbled English Derby cheese. A tea made from the leaves is attributed with conferring longevity provided the tea is drunk more or less daily. Salvia is also believed to have antioxidant properties.

by a notorious gang who robbed the dead and dying during the Great Plague. Apparently the preventative qualities of the herbs in the vinegar allowed them to carry out their nefarious activities with impunity. For some time in England judges carried posies containing rue to ward off the jail fever which killed many before they even received a trial.

Two interesting cultivars of rue are **'Jackman's Rue'** with lacy, very pretty foliage in a markedly blue shade, and **'Harlequin'** with cream variegated foliage.

Rue should be handled with some caution as many people are allergic to the leaves, developing a reaction on the skin from simply brushing against it.

The foliage of pineapple
sage, S. elegans, *smells
intensely of the ripe
fruit. It has brilliant
crimson flowers.*

A number of species of salvias are found in the herb garden, and are used to add their scent and flavor to various dishes. Some are also used in the making of pot pourri. Some species are also grown for their high protein, energy supplying seed. Two species find medicinal use, *S. officinalis* and *S. miltiorrhiza*, known as red sage or *tan shen*, and is used to reduce cholesterol levels and blood pressure.

Cleveland's sage, *S. clevalandii*, originates from the chapparal of California and forms a many-stemmed shrub growing to 4 ft (1.2 m) with aromatic gray-green foliage. Numerous long, upright flowering stems are massed with whorls of lavender-blue flowers. It is used in pot pourri, craft work, and floristry.

S. dorisiana is a Honduran species and one of the most spectacular of the sages growing to 5 ft (1.5 m) in sunny conditions. It is more shade tolerant than most sages and will reach a greater height in such conditions. It is a many stemmed species with large, heart-shaped, soft hairy leaves that release an astonishing scent of tropical fruit salad when brushed or even watered, giving rise to one of its common names, fruit salad sage. The flowering spikes are particularly eye-catching, long and dense with large soft magenta-pink flowers.

The pineapple sage, *S. elegans*, is an open shrub growing to 4 ft (1.2 m), and the foliage is intensely scented of ripe pineapple. The brilliant crimson flowers are borne in elegant racemes and are filled with nectar. They are edible and can be use as a garnish. Pineapple sage needs better conditions than garden sage, so enrich the soil with compost. There is a cultivar derived from it called '**Honey Melon Sage**' which is similar to the parent but of smaller dimensions; it has the distinct scent of ripe honeydew melon.

Grapefruit sage, *S. gesneriifolia*, from Colombia and Mexico is quite close in type but with heart-shaped leaves that are strongly scented of grapefruit. Both of these salvias have the same growing requirements as pineapple sage.

White sage, *S. apiana*, is strikingly lovely, with pointed white colored leaves that give a silvered effect. The foliage is intensely aromatic, and in summer the plant puts forth long spikes of delicate flowers. This sage requires full sun, good drainage, and no weed competition.

Salad Burnet

Sanguisorba minor   Zones 5–9

The salad burnet comes from moist, mountainous areas in Europe and responds to compost or well-rotted manure dug through the soil to form a moisture retentive medium. The leaves are compound and the plant forms an attractive, dense, grey-green, ferny rosette.

Fruit scented sage, S. dorisiana, is also known as fruit salad sage for the amazingly fruity scent it releases when brushed or watered.

The leaves of salad burnet, Sanguisorba minor, smell of fresh cucumbers and can be used in salads and sandwiches and as an attractive garnish.

Pelargonium crispum 'Variegatum' is a lemon scented geranium cultivar that has a wonderful fragrance and cream-edged leaves.

Savory

Satureja spp.   Zones 6–11

The savories are a group of culinary herbs that, like the thymes, have a range of scents to offer. Lemon savory, *Satureja biflora*, is a low-growing dense South African plant that smells of fresh lemon with thyme and oregano notes in the background. In summer, its tiny mauve flowers are very attractive to bees. Greek savory, *S. thymbra*, sometimes sold under the name of pink savory as a reference to its attractive flowers, is a stiff little gray-green shrub, slightly spreading, with fairly sparse leaves and a warm, mouthwatering scent of oregano with thyme. Matting winter savory, *S. repens*, forms a dense mat across the soil. It grows to about 2–3 in (5–7.5 cm) high and has a warm spicy scent. It is more than worthy of the ornamental garden, with densely arranged tiny bell-like flowers which resemble white heather. Winter savory, *S. montana*, forms a neat, tufted, dark-green shrub which is excellent in stuffings and in combination with bean dishes. All four of these are quite long-lived perennials. A fifth, summer savory, *S. hortensis*, is the most significant in culinary terms, a classic herb often included with the *fines herbes*. It is a slender upright annual with a spicey scent.

The leaves of savory, Satureja montana, go well in stuffings and in combination with bean dishes.

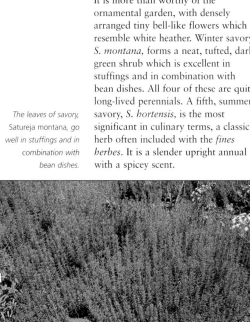

Scented Geraniums

Pelargonium spp.   Zones 9–11

The origins of the group known as scented geraniums go back to the 19th century. Some species of *Pelargonium* collected in Africa and taken back to England had scents that were strongly reminiscent of well known fragrances such as rose, lemon, spice and lime. In the greenhouses of England, it was soon found that crosses between these species resulted in an entire pot pourri of new fragrances in combination with exciting new leaf forms. The flowers were more dainty than dashing, but with such wonderful fragrance released at a touch that everyone wanted to grow the scented geraniums. At one time there were hundreds of named cultivars. There are perhaps around 70 of these amazing cultivars left. They include intensely lemon sherbert scented 'Mabel Grey', 'Nutmeg', 'Attar of Roses', 'Peppermint', 'Lime', mint-and-rose scented 'Dr Livingstone', 'Ginger', 'Spice', 'Tutti Frutti' and 'Lemon Balm'. Many of the scented geraniums are admirably suited to pot culture. However some, such as 'Lemon' and 'Lemon Balm' are large shrubs in warm climates. In cooler areas, cuttings should be taken every fall to guarantee the following season's planting. They are sensitive to frost and should be brought under cover for winter. Potted plants ahould be repotted every 1–2 years and a supplementary feed with seaweed meal

or equivalent should be given each spring once active growth has begun.

Soapwort
Saponaria officinalis   Zones 5–10

Few herbs have such old-fashioned charm as soapwort, also called bouncing bet. It earned both its botanical name and one of its common names from the saponins in the plant. Saponins create soaping

effects in water. Soapwort was long considered the only safe cleansing agent for old and delicate fabrics including tapestries, and is still considered the only acceptable cleaner by many museums.

Soapwort is also an exceptionally pretty plant when in flower, with beautiful single or double pink flowers that are evening scented. It spreads by rhizomes and is easily propagated from a few roots. It is particularly undemanding and will occupy an area that many plants would consider beyond the pale.

Society Garlic
Tulbaghia violacea   Zones 7–10

This plant looks like garlic chives, and the leaves taste the same, but in place of the starry white flowers that are borne by garlic chives there is an inflorescence of nodding mauve bells. There is a very pretty, variegated form with cream edges. Many gardeners in Texas are using society garlic to great effect in beautiful spring mixes with such plants as mealy sage, Mexican hat, and prairie coneflower.

The roots of the soapwort, Saponaria officinalis, *were once used, mixed with water, to clean delicate fabrics. Some museums still use the technique on ancient tapestries.*

Society garlic, Tulbaghia violacea, *looks and tastes somewhat like garlic chives except for its distinctive mauve-colored flowers.*

Southernwood

Artemisia abrotanum   Zones 4–10

This small, upright-growing shrub is also known by the romantic names of lad's love, maiden's ruin, and old man. It has very finely divided gray-green foliage that is almost filamentous, with a lemon and camphor scent, very refreshing to the senses. It is a moth repellent, and can be dried for pot pourri, and also for moth-repellent mixes for stored clothing. It is an excellent companion plant for the orchard and vegetable garden. It will grow on a wide range of soils, but the soil should be well drained, with added organic matter, and the bed or pots should be in full sun for much of the day. This can become a rather straggly bush, and the secret of beautiful plants is to cut them back by two-thirds in spring.

Sweet Woodruff

Asperula odorata   Zones 5–9

Sweet woodruff likes a fairly moist, shady place to grow, and threads the ground with ruffs of leaves and tiny white star flowers. Its scent is of new mown hay. The fragrance increases on drying with an added hint of vanilla. The plant is valued for its dainty elegance as a groundcover. It is used dried in pot pourri, to give fragrance to stored linen, and is added fresh in the famous German *maibowle* punch made to celebrate May Day.

Tansy

Tanacetum vulgare   Zones 4–10

Tansy is a perennial which grows to approximately 3 ft (90 cm) when in flower, and has ferny, dark-green foliage with a strong, clean-smelling aroma. The foliage is renowned for its insect repellent properties, particularly of ants. It bears dense heads of rich golden, button flowers that are bitter tasting and were once used to make tansy pudding at Lent. A very attractive curly-leafed form also exists known as 'Crested Tansy'. Tansy is easily grown, being unfussy as to soil. It enlarges the clump slowly by means of rhizomes.

Thyme

Thymus spp.   Zones 7–10

The thymes are a huge group of plants with over 300 species known, and with the possibility of more to be discovered. They are native to southern Europe through to Asia, and are mainly herbaceous perennials, or small to spreading shrubs. Of those in cultivation, one group is prized for culinary purposes, while the others find use as fragrant ornamentals, for creating carpets of flowers and spillovers, and also for fragrance based crafts. It is a group which is eminently collectable, and in addition to the very large number of species, accidental and and deliberate crosses have resulted in a very large number of fragrant cul-tivars. You would never be bored if you collected thymes. Among the culinary thymes are the cultivars **'Oregano'**, **'Bush BBQ'**, **'Spanish'**, **'West-moreland'**, and **'Sauce'**.

Lemon-scented thyme, Thymus x citriodorus, has tiny oval lemon-scented leaves that can be used fresh or dried in meat, fish and vegetable dishes.

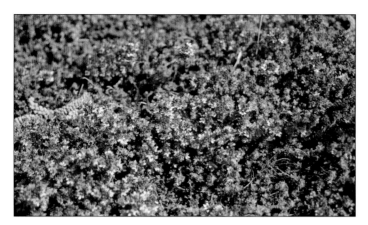

The citrus-scented thymes include 'Orange' or 'Fragrantissimus', 'Lemon Curd', 'Lime', and 'Lemon Thyme'.

The best known of the thymes is *T. vulgaris* which is used widely as an ingredient in savory dishes. It contains thymol, which was used in traditional treatments for sore throats; a tea brewed from the leaves is administered sweetened with honey, or it can be taken in honey into which generous amounts of the herb have been infused.

All thymes require full sunshine. While most come from naturally rocky or poorer soil areas, they respond to the incorporation of modest quantities of compost in the soil.

Valerian
Valeriana officinalis   Zones 3–9

This is an attractive perennial plant forming a mounded rosette of leaves which are deeply cut. The flower stalks are 4 ft (1.2 m) and bear tiny white flowers resembling Queen Anne's lace. The plant has long been used as an analgesic, but is equally at home in the ornamental garden for its attractiveness.

An attractive addition to the herb garden, valerian, Valeriana officinalis, has tiny white flowers.

Section 3

FRUIT AND NUTS

Berries

Alpine Strawberry *Fragaris vesca*
'Semperflorens'; **Blackberry** *Rubus* spp.;
Blueberry *Vaccinum* spp.; **Cape Gooseberry**
and **Cossack Pineapple** *Physalis peruviana*,
Physalis spp.; **Currant** *Ribes* spp.; **Gooseberry**
and **American Gooseberry** *Ribes grossularia*,
R. hirtellum; **Raspberry** *Rubus* spp.;
Strawberry *Fragaria x ananassa*

Alpine strawberries, Fragaria vesca 'Semperflorens' have small fruit with an intense flavor. A straw mulch will keep the soil cool and moist and prevent weeds from invading the planting site.

Alpine Strawberry

Fragaria vesca 'Semperflorens'　　　Zones 4–10

The larger and longer fruiting wood strawberry that entered into European gardens in the 18th century was a distinctive form with elegant, long, pointed fruits. These were selected and bred to become a class of straw-berries in their own right now known as Alpine strawberries. They are char-acterized by having prolific small fruit with an intense flavor and aroma far surpassing that of most modern large fruited strawberries. They are prized by the chefs of Europe who use the intensely flavored fruits in preference to the common strawberry. The plants are grown from seed *(see Strawberries for technique)* or by division in the

Alpine strawberries are as suited to the ornamental garden as they are the vegetable patch

manner of peren-nials. They do not form runners and this makes them gourmet food of the highest order and also very easy to manage compared to the common strawberry. They are also immune to many of the problems that beset strawberries.

Because they are runner free (not technically correct because the clump enlarges with tiny runners), and because they are long-lived, these very attractive plants are suited to the ornamental garden as well as the vegetable garden. They make ideal garden edgings and most attractive plantings for pots and even hanging baskets. As the species originated from woodland areas, it should not be planted in full sun. An area receiving only morning sunlight is ideal.

Recommended Cultivars

'Alexandria' — This cultivar has long, conical fruit which are rich red, very aromatic, and sweet.

'Alpine Yellow' — The tiny fruits are pale gold and highly aromatic, and have the most intense flavor. Birds tend to miss the yellow fruits.

'Ruegen' syn. Benary — This is a long bearing strain, particularly prolific in fall, with medium sized fruits that are deep red, aromatic and intensely flavored.

'Tutti Frutti' — This strain is highly ornamental and forms a dwarf creeping plant ideal as a groundcover with round, richest red fruits with a delicious flavor.

'White' — The small white fruits do not attract birds, but chefs flock to it for its sweet fragrant fruit which are very elegant for desserts.

Blackberry

Rubus spp.   Zones 5–10

Blackberries have an excellent flavor, even when gathered unimproved from the wild. There are a number of species of *Rubus* around the world that are called 'blackberries', many of them cultivated. The first to be designated botanically was *R. fruticosus* which is the most commonly cultivated species. Native to Europe and the British Isles, it has naturalized in South Africa and Australia where it has become a serious pest in some areas. Relishing the milder climate and completely taking over areas of farming land, using its habit of bending long cane tips to the earth, taking root and

Some varieties of blackberry have almost no thorns.

sending up new bushes. This looping progression across the land is difficult to control manually as the plants are armed with vicious arrays of thorns. They can also regenerate with some ease from sections of plant left behind in the soil. Other species from Europe which have excellent eating qual ities are *R. schlechtendahlii* and the parsley-leaved blackberry *R. laciniatus*. Among the finest of the many North American blackberries are the alleghany blackberry *R.alleghaniensis* and the highbush blackberry *R.argutus*.

The blackberry, Rubus spp., is an aggregate, consisting of over 2000 microspecies, all differing in small details. The cultivated blackberry's prickly, arching stems grow to 10 ft (3 m).

Blackberries attract birds and should be netted to ensure heavy cropping.

the strength of the supporting trellis. Bush blackberries can be trained reasonably easily within a double row of trellis which makes harvesting a pleasure. Trailing cultivars are the more difficult group and need to be pruned and then trained onto supports. In areas with milder climates this can be done in early fall after harvesting is complete, but in areas with very cold winters the pruning is done in spring . Blackberries are self-fertile. Until fully ripened the berries remain fairly astringent and they should 'pick themselves', as country people once said, falling into the hand when gently touched.

A large number of commercially important and exceptionally fine hybrids created between raspberries and blackberries are discussed in the section *Raspberries*. Some of these may make a better choice where space allocation is limited.

Growing and Harvesting

Blackberries are adaptable plants but prefer moist, very rich soils. They are markedly cold hardy as a group, although selections vary in their cold tolerance. If severe winters affect your garden, check that the cultivars you have chosen are tolerant to low temperatures. In small gardens these berries cannot be recommended as most of the cultivars are invasive to some degree and the less invasive and smaller raspberry would make a better choice.

Blackberries and their hybrids require the same soil preparation and maintenance as raspberries. They are pruned in the same manner as summer raspberries, allowing no more than 10 canes to develop on each bush. Particular attention needs to be paid to

Recommended cultivars

'**Brazos**' — This is an erect growing cultivar producing very large, slightly tart fruit which are fairly firm and good for marketing as well as home use.

'**Lawton**' — Wonderfully rich flavored and sweet when fully ripened, this 1854 cultivar is still widely grown around the world. The fruit are large, elongated, and shining jet black. The bush is tall, upright, and very productive.

'**Merton Thornless**' — This is a far less vigorous form than most and will fit well into the average garden.

'**Waldo Thornless**' — This is a high yielding cultivar originating from the Oregon Agricultural Experiment Station in Corvallis, Oregon. The flavor is intense and the bush remains thornless even from suckers, unlike some thornless cultivars.

'**White**' — Perversely creamy-white berried, the flesh tender and delicately blackberry flavored, this is a berry of the highest quality and worth seeking out. The bush is tall, vigorous, and very productive. It would make an excellent niche crop to supply directly to good restaurants.

Blueberries

Vaccinum spp.   Zones 2–9

Blueberries are a modern introduction to the garden. In North America they were treated as wild harvested fruit, and came from several species that were closely related. The rabbiteye was picked in swamps in Florida to Georgia, other species were harvested in the Appalachians north to New England, others still in Oregon, Alaska, Michigan and elsewhere. It was not until Dr Coville of the United States Department of Agriculture began collecting blueberry species and carrying out interspecific hybridization and cultural research on the group in 1909 that progress was made in the domestication of the genus.

Most of today's cultivars are descended from the rabbiteye blueberry *V. ashei*, the highbush blueberry *V. corymbosum*, and the lowbush blueberry *V. lamarckii*. Lowbush cultivars are ground huggers with a height between 6–18 in (15–45 cm). Highbush cultivars usually vary between 4–6 ft (1.2–1.8 m) but may grow smaller or taller. Highbush cultivars have high chilling hour—hours spent below 45° F (7°C)—requirements, often in excess of 1,000 hours. Rabbiteye cultivars require around 500 hours of chilling, and a few require less. They are smaller berried, but more productive, and also more heat and drought tolerant,

Rasberries, blueberries and blackberries. Most berries freeze nicely, keeping for up to ten months in the freezer.

The blue ray blueberry has delicious sweet, juicy fruit. It has a preference for boggy soils and has fine scarlet fall foliage.

Earliblue is a tall and vigorous blueberry with very large berries.

of the compost. If leaves turn yellow, the plants may be suffering from iron chlorosis caused by the soil pH being too high. If your soil is not acidic enough, blueberries can be grown in an acidic soil and compost mix in large pots. Never use concrete pots which will leach lime into the soil, and check that the water you use for the garden is not alkaline.

Recommended cultivars

For those with high chill hours, some excellent highbush cultivars include 'Blueray', 'Coville', 'Earliblue', and 'Jersey'. 'North Country' is useful in smaller gardens with a height of 18–24 in (45–60 cm). Some good rabbiteye cultivars include 'Premier', 'Tifblue' (very tall), 'Brightwell', and 'Climax'.

although no blueberry will tolerate excessive heat or soil dryness.

Growing and Harvesting

Blueberries grow naturally in acid conditions and thrive in soils rich in organic matter, with heavy mulches to create a cool root run. They prefer a light loam, but heavier soils well supplemented with compost to aerate them will still succeed with blueberries. Very acidic soils with a pH of 4.0–5.0 are ideal. If your garden grows excellent rhododendrons, the soil should have a pH suitable for blueberries. Except in areas with fairly hot, dry summers, they should be planted in full sun.

The bushes are planted out in late fall in milder areas, and in early spring as soon as the soil can be worked in cold winter areas. The bushes are planted approximately 4–6 ft (1.2–1.8 m) apart depending on the cultivar, and should be trimmed back gently to allow for the reduction in the root system. Highbush cultivars should be thinned each year at the end of winter to remove older wood and any entangled branches. Bushes should be given a generous mulch of compost each spring, but no lime or dolamite should have been used in the making

Cape Gooseberry *and* Cossack Pineapple

Physalis peruviana, P. pruinosa   Zones 8–11

Closely related to the tomato, these fruits differ in being enclosed in a persistent calyx shaped like a Chinese lantern, which surrounds and protects the fruits until they are fully ripe. The calyx then becomes papery and partly splits open. It is an excellent bird-foiling device. Both of these fruits are short lived perennials in the warm climates where they prefer to grow. The Cape gooseberry, or ground cherry, forms a soft, herbaceous shrub to 3 ft (90 cm), while the cossack pineapple is lower growing. Both can be propagated either by tip cuttings or by seed. The fruits of both are aromatic and richly flavored, the cossack pineapple having a distinct fragrance of ripe pineapple. They are eaten fresh as a dessert fruit or can be used to make excellent preserves. Both appreciate a well drained, sunny position. When harvesting, look on the ground as well as on the bush as when ripe, the fruits fall from the bush and lie there fully protected by their calyx cover.

The Cape gooseberry, grows to around 3 ft (1 m) tall and produces berries that are bright yellow to purple.

Currant

Ribes spp.   Zones 5–10

Currants never went wholly out of favor, but their highly ornamental tart little fruits are enjoying a gastronomic resurgence.

Growing and Harvesting

Currants are notably cold tolerant. They prefer cool, moist summers and perform poorly in warm summer areas. Black currants prefer acidic, cool soils to which plenty of organic matter has been added. (Black currants are a potential host of white pine blister rust and in states in North America where the white pine is a significant resource, they are a prohibited planting.) All currants are self fertilizing. Red and White currants are less demanding and will grow in average soils.

The ground is prepared by digging through generous amounts of compost and granite or basalt rock dust together with ground rock phosphate. The bushes are planted in fall in all but very cold climates as currants commence growing very early in spring. Depending on the cultivars chosen, the bushes are rowed out

5–6 ft (1.5–1.8 m) apart. Trim any broken roots before planting and position the bushes so that they are slightly below the soil level they previously occupied. Trim the tops back by 6–12 in (15–30 cm). Currants bear most heavily on canes that are

The pale amber berries of the white currant *Ribes silvestre*. Racemes of small flowers open in spring, followed by clusters of small, very juicy fruit.

Gooseberries come in a wide variety of sizes and shapes, bearing green, russet green or yellow green fruit.

2–3 years old. They should then be removed for younger canes to take over fruiting. Apply nutrients to the bushes each year at the end of winter.

Recommended cultivars

'**Baldwin**' — This is the leading commercial black currant in England. The medium to large juicy fruits have a fairly tough skin. It is particularly high in vitamin C and is well suited to small gardens, forming a medium bush. It is a late 19th century cultivar.

'**Boskoop Giant**' — This is a tender, large to very large berried black currant with juicy, richly flavored, fairly sweet fruit. It was raised in the Netherlands prior to 1895.

'**Consort**' — Originating from Ottawa, Canada, this is a self pollinating black currant cultivar

This vigorous, open-bushed redcurrant 'Jonkheer van Tets', Ribes silvestre syn. R. robrum, flowers and fruits very early.

with medium to large, tender, intensely flavored fruit.

'**Jonkheer van Tets**' syn. Von Tets — Originating from the Netherlands, this is a widely grown red currant in Europe and the United States with deep red, medium to large fruit of excellent quality and flavor.

'**Noir de Bourgogne**' — The fruit of this black currant are medium sized with an excellent flavor and the bush is very productive.

'**Red Lake**' — This is an excellent, late ripening red currant originating from Minnesota in 1933. The bright red fruits are juicy and of good quality, its clusters particularly well filled.

'**White Imperial**' — This is a white currant of the highest quality with medium to large, round, cream-white, juicy firm fruits with a rich sweet flavor. The bush is very productive.

'**Wilder**' — This is a very vigorous and productive red currant from Indiana in 1877, still very widely grown for its tender, deep red, juice, and excellently flavored berries.

'**Willoughby**' — A black currant from Saskatchewan with very good quality, juicy fruits. Highly resistant to pine blister, rust and mildew, it is also very cold hardy, and is self pollinating.

Gooseberry *and* American Gooseberry

Ribes uva-crispa syn. *R. grossularia, R. hirtellium*
Zones 5–9

European gooseberries have been in cultivation for many centuries, used mainly as a dessert fruit in England and for conserves and preserves. It evokes particular fondness in the form of Gooseberry Fool, the puréed fruit being mixed with whipped cream to produce an aromatic creamy dessert. A number of English preserves and syrups combine the muscatel fragrance of elderflowers with gooseberries, an irresistible and ancient summer combination. Smaller cultivars have largely been developed for cooking, and the larger cultivars for fresh eating. They range in color from translucent green to gold and red. American gooseberries are smaller and less flavorful, but the darker fruited forms are considered to have the sweetest flavor.

Growing and Harvesting

Gooseberries are particularly cold hardy and tolerate a wide range of soil types. The ground is prepared as for currants. The bushes are self pollinating and reach a modest 4 ft (1.2 m), making them an ideal choice for smaller gardens. The plants send out long feeder roots and the plants should be mulched annually to beyond the driplines when the soil warms. The bushes are pruned in winter, an essential job as they become an impenetrable mass of stems and spines by their third year if left untouched. For this reason, they are best trained to a single stem, the remainder being removed. Each stem will bear for 4–5 years and can then be replaced by a new stem.

Recommended Cultivars

A number of cultivars are available including **'Roaring Lion'** which is popular in Australia, with large, pale green, dessert-type fruits, the

American gooseberries **'Pixwell'** and **'Poorman'**, both with pinkish-red fruits, the latter having very high quality. aromatic sweet fruits, and the European types **'Bedford Yellow'**, **'Catherina'**, **'Early Sulphur'**, **'Crown Bob'**, and **'Red Champagne'**.

The gooseberry, Ribes uvacrispa syn. R. grossularia, *develops pinkish flowers followed by greenish fruit covered with soft bristles.*

Raspberry

Rubus spp.   Zones 4–8

The extremely large genus *Rubus* occurs in both the northern and southern hemispheres and contains a remarkable number of edible berries, many of them little known outside the area to which they are endemic, but many having claim to being outstanding fruits. The Ceylon or hill raspberry *R. niveus* has juicy, purple-black fruits that are of high quality and have an intense sweet raspberry flavor. A selected form is **'Mysore'**. The Andes black raspberry *R. glaucus* is large, deep purple, and of excellent quality. The yellow Himalayan raspberry *R. ellipticus* has an excellent flavor and good quality. The list of raspberries would be very long if completed. The European red rasp-berry common to many cooler gardens is *R. idaeus*. The Black raspberry of common cultivation is *R. occidentalis*, while the purple raspberry is *R.x neglectus*, arising from a cross between the European red and the black raspberries. The purple raspberry group tend to be reserved for juice and jam.

The raspberry, Rubus spp., is a perennial shrub which grows to 5 ft (1.5 m) tall and wide. The succulent, aromatic berries, borne from mid-summer to mid-fall are usually red but can occasionally be white or yellowish in color.

The European red raspberries are divided horticulturally into two broad types: everbearing, also called fall bearing raspberries, which bear their fruit on the current season's growth and have the considerable benefit of not requiring training or trellising, and come into bearing within a year of planting; and the summer bearing raspberries which bear fruit on canes that have been made the previous summer and overwintered.

Some interesting intergeneric crosses have been made between raspberries and blackberries. They include a number of significant commercial types including the tayberry with large, deep purple fruit

The loganberry, Rubus loganobaccus, is a hybrid between a blackberry and a garden raspberry; its crimson, tart fruit is excellent for cooking.

with a sweet intense flavor, the loganberry with large maroon fruit and slightly tart, juicy, large berries, the marionberry with superb eating quality medium to large fruit, and the youngberry with large, rounded, black-crimson fruit with intense flavor. Thornless forms exist of all but the tayberry. They are grown on the same system as raspberry.

Growing and Harvesting

Raspberries prefer an acid soil from pH 6.5–5.0 enriched with compost, and a well drained sunny position. Grown on alkaline soils they develop iron deficiency symptoms and are shorter lived and less productive. Raspberries will continue to bear plentiful fruit for at least 12 years once the bed is made, and any effort in establishing the bushes and in soil preparation is amply rewarded. To feed an average family with generous quantities of raspberries for dessert, the equivalent of about 100 ft (30 m) of raspberries should be planted. In the small garden, this could consist of three short 33 ft (10 m) rows. A garden which has been in use for some time is ideal as all perennial weeds should have been eliminated. Very generous quantities of compost or well rotted manure should be mixed into the topsoil along with a heavy application of basalt or granite rock dust and rockphosphate dust. A supporting trellis system should be built, remembering that it will be in place for at least 12 years. A row of posts should be put in and a simple wire trellis made about 3 ft (1 m) above the ground. A second wire at 5 ft (1.5 m) is helpful. More elaborate systems use a trellis on either side of the row with canes trained evenly out to the two sides.

Certified disease free plants should be purchased through a reputable source. Never let the roots dry out when planting. Mail ordered plants may arrive a little on the dry side.

Soak them in a very weak seaweed solution for 3 hours before setting them out. If they arrive when you are unable to plant them, temporarily heel them in to moist soil. The plants are most easily managed if planted in rows. Everbearing cultivars are much simpler to manage. They are cut down to the ground each year at the end of fall, and as a result they also develop few diseases. The new canes that emerge in spring are tied in to supporting wires.

Summer bearing raspberries are a little more complicated to manage. During the season the plant has a mixture of overwintered canes that are bearing fruit and newly formed canes that will bear the following year. At the end of the season the canes that bore fruit should be cut down to the ground while the new canes should be trained onto supporting wires. Also cut down any new season canes that are weak. At the end of winter tip prune the canes back to 5 ft (1.5 m) before they begin to flower in spring.

Raspberries appreciate plenty of organic matter in the soil and a thick mulch should be maintained. Include generous amounts of fall leaves in the mulch as they are a very good source of nutrients. Fishmeal or cottonseed meal can be added annually. Any

canes that appear away from the rows should be removed.

Birds can be a problem and the crop should be protected by netting. Atypical plants with curling, mottled leaves are likely to have a virus and should be removed and burned. Plant something other than a berry fruit in the space it occupied as the soil will probably be contaminated. Aphids and raspberry beetle can be a problem in some areas. Raspberries grown the organic way, well mulched and well fed, just do not seem prey to the vast list of ills that can be suffered by commercially grown crops. They also appear to live well beyond the use-by date of commercial crops grown the conventional way.

Raspberries will bear fruit for 12 years so it is esssential that any supporting trellis should be robust.

Raspberries have small, 5 petaled flowers and serrated leaflets 6 in (15 cm) long.

Raspberries are easy to harvest as the berries slide off the plant without pressure.

prolific bearing and sturdy, growing to almost 8 ft (2.5 m), and is freestanding requiring no support. It is an everbearing type, suitable for cooler gardens.

'Malling Jewel' — This is an early to mid-season, summer bearing cultivar of good eating quality and virus resistance.

'Meeker' — This is an excellent home garden cultivar and is also ideal for local fresh markets. The bush is very tall and productive, the fruit being extra large, bright red, firm fleshed, with good flavor, and suitable for freezing and jam. It requires a mild winter.

'September' — This is a raspberry of excellent dessert quality with medium to large, bright red, sweet and juicy berries. It is a reliable and heavy bearer, summer fruiting, and an everbearing type.

'Williamette' — This is a summer-bearing cultivar with very large, round, berries that are dark red, firm, with fair flavor. The bush is exceptionally productive and vigorous.

Recommended Cultivars

'Fallgold' — This is an everbearing form producing large, round, yellow, juicy fruits which are very sweet. The bush is exceptionally high yielding and very cold hardy.

'Heritage' — This is an excellent home garden cultivar popular both in the United States and Australia with bright red, conical fruit of excellent quality if firm. It is

'Fallgold' is a beautiful golden raspberry from a cold hardy plant.

Strawberry

Fragaria x ananassa   Zones 4–10

Strawberries are—or should be—one of the great pleasures of the summer garden. They were once luscious, rich red, juicy, and melted in the mouth. Then came the commodity marketers, and newer cultivars were released, looking perfect, but with none of that fragrance and intense flavor that begged for fresh cream. In place of melting juiciness, strawberries became crisp like apples. They developed a tough core. They transported well, the commodity sellers were delighted with the low wastage that was involved, but our love affair with strawberries declined—or we grew our own. And instead of the modern cultivars we went back a few decades to try older types that were reliable and produced quantities of excellent quality fruit that tasted as strawberries should, and were tender and juicy. Plants of these older cultivars are still relatively easy to find from specialist suppliers and nurseries.

Our modern strawberries are a happy blending of the Old World and the New World. Wild strawberries *Fragaria vesca* were first brought into the garden in the Medieval period. In the 14th century, wild strawberries were also planted *en masse* in the royal gardens of the Louvre in Paris at the behest of King Charles V. The larger fruited and longer season strawberry *F. vesca* 'Semperflorens' made its way into European gardens in the 18th century, joining two other desirable species already there, the Haut bois *F. moschata* with a sweet musky scent and *F. viridis*.

The New World had its strawberry species too. The scarlet strawberry *F. virginica* was introduced into France in 1624, and into England in 1629. It is still grown, under the name '**Little Scarlet**' and is used to make excellent conserves. A form of the scarlet strawberry known as the **Pine** strawberry was named for its pineapple scent. A much larger fruited species *F. chiloensis* was discovered in Chile by a French naval officer who returned with a few surviving plants to France

Strawberries should be planted in weed-free soil and the plants replaced every three years to guarantee a good crop.

Strawberries need acidic soils and full sun or light shade. They should be protected from snails, strawberry aphids and birds.

many famous hybrids quickly followed, most sadly now ghosts of gardens long gone having become prey to various diseases and viruses. The most famous of them all, Thomas Laxton's **'Royal Sovereign'** bred in 1892, is still with us although less vigorous. For those who knew it at its peak, 'Royal Sovereign' is rated the greatest strawberry of all time.

Growing and Harvesting

A few cultivars of strawberries are available as seed. These can be planted in flats or pots filled with a good, fine textured seed raising mix, just covering the seed with soil. They need to be watered from the bottom, and should be raised under protection. When the plants have 6–8 small leaves, they can be gently loosened in the pot with a pencil, and individually potted into small pots. When they have filled the pots, they can be planted into a larger pot, or if they have reached a good size, directly into the garden. They have the advantage of being guaranteed to be virus free as they have been raised from seed. A number of viruses are transmited with relative ease in the strawberry world, and if you plan to start your strawberry garden with purchased plants it is important to ensure that they are certified virus free.

Strawberries can be grown conventionally, rowed out in raised beds, but they also lend themselves to use in planter pots, for edging gardens, or for making edible groundcovers in sunny areas. Nothing is prettier than mounded pots spilling over with strawberries with their pure white flowers, trifoliate green leaves, and plump red berries in the summer sunshine. Traditional terracotta strawberry pots are an effective way to plant strawberries in a limited space and look wonderful. Fill the pot gradually with soil enriched with plenty of well rotted compost, planting each pocket progressively,

in 1714 after a 6 month sea voyage. This species is by no means restricted to Chile. It grows on the Pacific Coast of North and South America and is easily found by those travelling Highway 1 in California, particularly north of San Francisco where it grows beside the sea in large patches. The fruits are pale pink as a rule, and have a definite hint of pineapple in their scent.

In a French garden, by good luck, *F. chiloensis* encountered *F. virginica*, a North American strawberry it had never before met because they had been separated by the length of a continent. It was a marriage made in strawberry heaven for gardeners and gourmets alike. The two species were compatible and able to cross pollinate.

The **'Pineapple'** strawberry was the most noted of the early hybrids, but

Strawberries have palmate leaves with 3 toothed leaflets and cymes of white or pink, 5-petaled flowers..

and then adding another layer of composted soil and firming down. Water thoroughly, and then very regularly as the soil inside pots can dry quite fast. The strawberry pot should be where it receives morning sunshine rather than blazing afternoon heat. An old wine barrel makes an excellent strawberry planter too, if holes are cut out at appropriate intervals. The tops of either container can also be planted once filled with the soil mix.

The secret of strawberry production is good soil preparation. They thrive in a slightly acidic soil, well enriched with compost. They also need a thorough watering once a week during the season, more if the weather is intensely hot. The plants are shallow rooted and need the protection of thick mulch to maintain an even soil moisture and temperature. (It would seem a reasonable guess that their name came from the straw mulch traditionally applied around the plants as the berries started to form. How-ever, it apparently comes from an old Anglo-Saxon word *streawberige* meaning that it is inclined to stray, a reference to its runners.) Weeding shallow rooted plants disturbs them unnecessarily, and a thick straw mulch also suppresses all weed growth.

The fruits are also kept clean, raised off the soil on mulch, and in cooler climates the light color of the straw reflects sunlight under the ripening berries.

Strawberry plants should be well spaced when planted out. As the season progresses, the plants will send out runners. Most of these should be pinched off so as not to rob the fruiting plants of energy. Transplant a few to another garden bed to make plants for the next season. Some gardeners bury small pots of soil halfway into the garden and plant the young runners into the pot while still attached to the parent. They root easily and once they have done so

Strawberries thrive under an organic gardenng system

they can be cut free of the parent plant and raised elsewhere. Add extra straw mulch as the season progresses to ensure a constant, even coverage of mulch. In areas with shorter growing seasons, the season can be extended with the use of cloches.

Most gardeners run their strawberry beds on a 3 year rotation. A new row is planted every year, and each row is removed when it completes its third year of production.

Birds are one of the greatest aficionados of strawberries. Scarecrows may work for some crops, but the scarecrow hasn't been made that will stand between birds and strawberries. Use floating row covers to protect beds of strawberries. Slugs can also be a problem and should be attracted away with beer traps. A night patrol with a torch is not an unpleasant task on a summer night and often pays handsomely with a harvest of strawberry filled slugs. Strawberries should be picked regularly as they can mould if left. In humid or wet weather rot can spread quickly among fruit.

Recommended cultivars

'**Cambridge Late Pine**' — Currently considered the finest flavored strawberry in England, this is a mid-season cultivar with rich red berries and good productivity.

'**Kent**' — This is an exceptionally large fruited type with dark skin, firm red flesh, and good flavor for both dessert use and freezing. It is a very cold hardy cultivar and produces healthy, vigorous plants.

'**Red Gauntlet**' — This is one of the great standards for Australian conditions. The fruits are large, mid-red, tender and flavorful while the plants are very productive.

'**Redchief**' — Although strawberries should largely be a seasonal pleasure, there is a place for frozen fruit. This is a multi-purpose cultivar producing deep red, firm, large cone-shaped fruits that have good dessert quality and also freeze well.

'**Royal Sovereign**' — Dating to 1892, the mention of this early cropping cultivar brings sighs of memory from older English gardeners. The fruit are large and bluntly conical, the skin lacquer red, the intense sweet flavor truly memorable. The plants are vigorous and compact but, sadly, susceptible to disease.

'**Senator Dunlap**' — This is an old favorite for both domestic gardens and local markets with plump, conical, medium to large fruit. The skin is a shiny deep red when fully ripe, red to the centre, and the flesh is juicy, sweet and true strawberry.

'**Sequoia**' — This is an older cultivar with the melting tenderness to be expected of a home grown strawberry. The fruit are large and conical, deep red, very attractive, with wonderful flavor.

'**Sweetheart**' — This is an everbearer style of strawberry and one of the first seed cultivars to be commercially released. The fruits are small but of excellent flavor. Seed is available in the United States, Australasia, and Europe.

'**Torrey**' — This is a favored home grown strawberry in Australia. It has a quite tender texture and excellent flavor.

Strawberries can be grown conventionally but lend themselves to use in planter pots, for edging gardens, or as edible groundcovers.

The elderberry plant, Sambucus nigra, *bears large, flat clusters of white flowers before the fruit appears.*

The Unofficial Berries

A number of ornamental trees and shrubs bear berries that are quite choice and can be harvested. It is possible to plant your garden with many double duty plants that look beautiful and also put food in the larder. Many make excellent conserves, jellies, and syrups. Among these are the rowanberry or mountain ash *Sorbus aucuparia* with its clusters of bright red berries. The berries are high in pectin and are used to make a clear red, rather acid jelly that is a favorite in England and Scotland to serve with richly flavored meats like roast venison. Rowanberry trees grow well in areas with cold winters, and are high in vitamin C.

Elderberries have a delightful, rich flavor and fragrance of muscatel grapes. They are used to make an excellent, richly flavored wine, pies and jams, and a syrup known as ederberry rob. Both the European elderberry *Sambucus nigra* and the western elderberry *S. caerulea* from Western North America can be used. Elderberries are undemanding small trees, and are pretty in spring with their huge lacy heads of creamy white, fragrant flowers that make delicious delicate fritters for a special spring dessert, and a delicately flavored sparkling wine. Elders prefer a moist soil with plenty of compost in the soil, which mimics its natural ecological niche in moist, self mulched hedgerows.

Rowanberries, Sorbus aucuparia, *are high in vitamin C.*

Citrus

Australian Finger Lime *Microcitrus australasica*; **Bergamot Orange** *Citrus aurantium* ssp. *bergamia*; **Calamondin** *C. madurensis* syn. *C. mitus*; **Citron** *C. medica*; **Cumquat** *Fortunella* spp.; **Grapefruit** *Citrus x paradisi*; **Kaffir Lime** *C. hystrix*; **Lemon** *C. limon*; **Mandarin, Tangerine** and **Satsuma** *C. reticulata*; **Orange** *C. sinensis*; **Pummelo** *C. maxima*; **'Rangpur' Lime** *C. limonia* var. *rangpur* syn. *C. x limon*; **Seville Orange** *C. aurantium* ssp. *aurantium*; **Tahitian Lime** *C. latifolia*; **West Indian Lime** *C. aurantifolia*

Above right: 'Tangelo'. This evergreen is a cross between the tangerine and the grapefruit, and is renowned for its juice and as a superb dessert fruit.

Below: 'Ruby' and 'Marsh Seedless' grapefruit, limes, mandarins and lemons.

Citrus fruits are native to Southeast Asia and they have been cultivated there for over 4,000 years. As a group they have been developed and domesticated to such a degree that their botanical nomenclature is severely entangled and is subject to almost constant debate and revision. But if they are a botanical nightmare, they are also among the world's most significant and delicious fruits, and a major source of vitamin C. They are of largely subtropical to tropical origin and although some show a degree of cold tolerance, they are not suited to cold climate gardens. A number can be overwintered in pots in a glasshouse, as the old orangeries of grand houses proved.

Where they are climatically suited, few fruit trees are easier or more rewarding to grow. Except for cool climate areas there are citrus to suit most gardens. Even lack of space is no great problem as many smaller citrus adapt well to being grown in large tubs. The least hardy of the citrus are the West Indian and Tahitian

The navel orange, so-called because the shape of its blossom resembles the human navel.

limes. The citron also lacks cold hardiness. Some lemons such as 'Meyer' and 'Lisbon' will recover from even repeated mild frosts. The sweet oranges and mandarins can also take repeated mild frosts to around 23°F (-5°C), particularly if budded onto cold-resistant rootstocks.

Citrus worked onto Trifoliata *Poncirus trifoliata* rootstock can resist cold conditions considerably better. Even though the fruit may freeze and sometimes the leaves even blacken, the trees quite often recover in spring. An additional benefit of the Trifoliata rootstock is that it produces a degree of dwarfing in many citrus, which is desirable in the home orchard.

The hardiest of the common citrus are cumquats. In marginal citrus areas, gardeners sometimes hill soil up around the base of the tree before winter sets in, making sure the soil is above the graft union. Even if the tree is killed back by an unusually cold winter, there should be enough buds in the trunk beneath the soil to initiate growth once more.

Apart from frost considerations, citrus will grow on a wide range of soils provided they are well drained. A sunny and reasonably protected situation is required for all citrus.

Australian Finger Lime
Microcitrus australasica   Zones 9–11

The genus *Microcitrus* contains 7 species, of which 5 are found in the coastal rainforest of New South Wales and Queensland north to Cape York Peninsula. The other 2 species are endemic to New Guinea. One species, *Microcitrus australasica*, the finger lime, is found both in the Northern Territory and also on the eastern coast of Australia. This species has excited considerable interest in recent times, with a number of excellent new selections being released, with pink, ruby, gold, purple or green flesh. The individual, juice-filled cells are particularly large and have little adherence to each other. When the fruit is cut, the cells spill forth like individual jewels, making a most attractive and versatile addition to everything from elegant drinks to toppings for seafood, chicken, lamb and salad dishes. It can be used in much the same way as pomegranate seeds. It eventually forms a tall, slender tree to about 32 ft (10 m) if left to its own devices. *M. australis* is also of interest to the bushfood industry, with golf ball-shaped, dryish, but highly aromatic fruits.

A healthy calamondin orange branch.

Bergamot Orange
Citrus aurantium ssp. *bergamia*   Zones 9–11

The bergamot orange, or bergamot or bergamot lemon, is a dwarf form of the Seville orange. It is cultivated mainly in southern Italy for the production of bergamot essential oil, while the essential oil distilled from the clustered masses of fragrant, waxy white flowers is oil of neroli, both of which are used in the creation of perfumes. 'Orange Flower Absolute', obtained by fat or solvent extraction, is an important ingredient at the upper end of the perfumery trade. Petitgrain oil is obtained from the distillation of the foliage and immature fruits, and is used in good formulations for eau-de-cologne. Oil of neroli also finds use in candies, liqueurs, ice-cream and baked goods. The bergamot orange is also the secret source of the flavoring of the famous 'Earl Grey' tea.

The fruits are small, ovoid to pear-shaped, and sour. The bergamot orange is grown in the same manner as the sweet orange and has the same requirements. It is very susceptible to drought, and to extremely wet or dry soils.

Calamondin
Citrus madurensis syn. *C. mitus*   Zones 9–11

Calamondins, or Calamondin oranges, are greatly prized in the Phillipines where they are called '*Kalamansi*'. The tree resembles that of a small sweet orange, and the fruits resemble globose, thin-skinned, orange-gold, miniature oranges about 1 in (2.5 cm) in diameter. They peel easily and also break easily into segments. The flavor and taste is distinctive and deliciously sweet-tart, and the fruits are high in vitamin C. The juice is used to make

Calamondins, C. madurensis, are used in many Chinese and Southeast Asian dishes.

drinks similar to home-made lemon-
ade, and it adds wonderful taste and
fragrance to fish and chicken dishes
when used as a marinade. It is also
used in sauces, Asian soups, cakes,
desserts and sweet pies. A distinctively
fla-vored and fragrant marmalade is
made from the fruits, and they are
also crystalized whole. The thin skins
can be dried and added to containers
of dried black or green teas. It is left
for at least a month for the fragrance
to infuse the leaves. The tea made
from this mix is particularly refreshing, fragrant and reviving. Alternatively,
add some fresh juice to a cup of tea
instead of a slice of lemon.

A small, neat tree, the calamondin
is very ornamental. It is more cold
hardy than most citrus trees, tolerating
a few degrees of frost, although it still
requires a warm temperate to tropical
climate range to grow. It flourishes in
most of coastal mainland Australia, the
North Island of New Zealand, the
Phillipines, much of Africa, the coastal
Mediterranean, the southern USA and
subtropical Asia. It is rarely without
flowers and fruit all year round, is self-
fertile and does not need another tree
nearby to set fruit. Calamondins will
fruit in their first year of planting.
There are several named cultivars
developed for their ornamental or fruit
value, including a beautiful cream variegated form, and they are becoming
increasingly valued in Europe as a
conservatory and indoor ornamental.
While the fruits are not usually available in greengrocers, they are regularly
carried in Asian stores and used in many
Chinese and Southeast Asian dishes.

Growing and Harvesting

Calamondins are grown in the same
way as oranges. They also respond
well to tub culture, and are becoming
a popular house plant in Europe. (*See
Cumquat section below for information on tub planting.*) The plants,
particularly when pot grown, are
susceptible to chlorosis (yellowing

of the leaves) arising from a lime
induced locking up of iron, or a
magnesium deficiency. Neither should
be a problem with organically grown,
unstressed plants given regular foliar
seaweed feeding.

*The variegated
calamondin flowers
profusely and fragrantly.*

Citron

Citrus medica   Zones 9–11

This species is grown primarily for its
fragrant thick rind, which is candied
and used in puddings, fruit cakes,
confectionery and baking. The rind
is also used in the making of liqueurs
such as *kitrinos* and *cédratine*. The
fresh-sliced rind is added to salads.

There are several cultivars of citron
available including '**Corsican**',
'**Diamante**', '**Earle**' and '**Palestine**'.
The intensely fragrant and famous
'**Buddha's Hand**', also known as
'**Buddha's Fingers**' or '**Fingered**', is
another a form of *C. medica*, with the
fruit deeply divided into 5 fingerlike
projections. The fruits are lacking in
pulp but are sliced for candying. In
China and Japan they are also used as
temple altar offerings and as a room
perfumer. Another famous citrus used
for religious purposes, '**Ethrog**', is the
official citrus fruit used in the Jewish
Feast of the Tabernacles. Previously
classified as a form of citron, it has
been reclassified from *C. medica* to
C. limonimedica.

Citrus medica, 'Buddha's Hand'.

in spring, intensifying its flavor as the daily temperatures climb. It is sweet, juicy and richly flavored, used for late spring and summer eating. It is tolerant of quite heavy frosts. The tangelo is a cross between the grapefruit and common mandarin.

'Wekiwa' syn. 'Lavender Gem' — Considered to be the finest flavored of all citrus by some, this early ripening cross between a grapefruit and a tangelo has pear-shaped fruit with pale golden to amber-pink tender flesh that is juicy, sweet and delicious.

Cumquat

Fortunella spp.   Zones 9–11

Cumquats, or kumquats, have the appearance of a small orange, an intense sweet-acid flavor and delightful fragrance. They are principally made into jam, crystallized and pickled. The very thin skins are quite sweet and mildly spicy, and the fruit is eaten whole without peeling. The small fruit keep very well for months on the highly ornamental dwarf bush with its shiny, small foliage. The abundant blossoms are very fragrant.

Native to China, the cumquat with its golden-orange color is a symbol of good fortune and prosperity, and potted cumquats are commonly used as a household gift during the Chinese New Year. Hotels in Hong Kong take no chances, and walking through a main lobby during the Chinese New Year can be an obstacle course of potted cumquats.

Three different cumquats are quite commonly grown, each being a species of *Fortunella*, a genus closely allied to *Citrus* and in the same family *Rutaceae*. The most widely grown in the United States, China and Japan is **'Nagami'** or **'Oval'** or **'Pearl Lemon'**, which is *Fortunella margarita*. It has ovoid orange-yellow fruit. The other two cumquat types are **'Meiwa'** or **'Sweet'** or **'Large Round'** *F. crassifolia*, and

Recommended Interspecific Hybrid Citrus

'Eustis Limequat' — This is a delightful new fruit created by crossing the cumquat with a Key lime. It has the small oval shape of the cumquat and the flavor of lime. The small, neat-leafed tree is very attractive, everbearing and very productive. It is less cold sensitive than the Key lime. It should be clipped back evenly and lightly each year to keep its dense form.

'Minneola' syn. 'Honeybell' — This tangelo cultivar has bright, rich, deep reddish-orange skin and ripens

The 'Nagami' cumquat, with its oval-shaped fruit, has a sweeter taste than other cumquats and looks very decorative on the tree.

'**Marumi**' *F. japonica*. '**Marumi**' has small, round fruit that are considerably sweeter than '**Nagami**', but with similar very thin skin which does not need to be removed. The fruits are quite delicious when crystalized. Other less well known cumquats include '**Malayan**' *F. polyandra* and '**Jiangsu**'.

Growing and Harvesting

Cumquats are grown in the same manner as oranges. They also respond well to tub culture (half wine cask size is needed) provided they are regularly and deeply watered, and are grown in a freely draining mixture enriched with compost. They require a sunny but not baking hot site if grown in a tub. Supplementary foliar feeds with seaweed fertilizer applied at the recommended rate will alleviate any additional stress from pot life, and will keep the foliage wonderfully healthy and glossy.

Citrofortunella microcarpa. *A hybrid between a mandarin and a cumquat, this is the least edible of all citrus fruits. However, it makes an attractive ornamental shrub.*

Developing 'Marsh Seedless' grapefruit.

Grapefruit

Citrus x paradisi   Zones 10–12

Grapefruit are characterized by flesh that is sharper flavored than oranges. Apart from the older, tart, yellow-fleshed, seeded cultivars, there are also pink-fleshed, virtually seedless and quite sweet cultivars available.

Growing and Harvesting

Grapefruit, like oranges, are self-fertilizing and need no additional nearby grapefruit for fruit set to occur. In general, they have a somewhat higher nutritional demand than oranges, but otherwise are grown in the same manner.

Recommended Cultivars

'Marsh Seedless' — This is an exceptionally fine cultivar with very large, smooth, yellow-skinned fruits. The fruits are juicy with a nice balance of acidity and sweetness. This is a handsome and reliable older cultivar for the home orchard as well as for commercial use.

'Rio Red' — This Texan cultivar is a large, well-formed fruit with yellow flesh suffused with ruby-pink. It is an excellent choice for warm areas, including near the coast.

'Oro Blanco' — This is a large-fruited cultivar with clear yellow skin and exceptionally sweet flesh, which is lemon-yellow. The blossoms are remarkably large and very fragrant.

'Star Ruby' — This is a heavily cropping cultivar for spring harvesting. The fruit hold well on the tree, and are clear yellow-skinned with flesh that is blushed ruby.

Two of the most popular varieties of grapefruit: 'Marsh Seedless' (upper) and 'Star Ruby' (lower).

Kaffir lime foliage is dark green and very glossy.

Kaffir Lime

Citrus hystrix   Zones 10–12

The Kaffir lime, or Leech lime or Caffre lime or Mauritius papeda, is a small, rather spiny bush-tree grown principally for its delightfully fragrant leaves, which are pinched in to the mid-rib halfway along the leaf to give a 'waisted' effect. Dark green and very glossy, the leaves are essential to Thai cooking and give incomparable flavor to soups such as *Tom Yum Kung*, curries and salads. They are used for the same purpose in other Southeast Asian countries such as Malaysia, Singapore and Indonesia. The fruits are thick-skinned and curiously knobbled, and the skins are also used in cooking after the white pith has been scraped away. The whole fruits are also used medicinally, boiled until very soft,

and the pulp rubbed into the hair as a dandruff treatment.

Growing and Harvesting

The Kaffir lime is grown in the same manner as the sweet orange. It lends itself to pot culture as it is an attractive bush, but its thorns should be considered in terms of locating it. *(See Cumquat section above for planting information.)* It requires a warm temperate to tropical climate.

Lemon

Citrus limon   Zones 9–11

Lemons are highly productive trees and tend to crop for much of the year. In areas that are marginal for lemons, the excellent hybrid 'Meyer' lemon can be grown in a pot and overwintered in a conservatory or glasshouse as a very attractive and fragrant ornamental. It is more disease free than many other cultivars and will survive in temperatures down to 14°F (–10°C).

Growing and Harvesting

Lemons are intermediate between oranges and limes in terms of hardiness. Young plants of most cultivars will show leaf damage at less than 28–30°F (-2 to -1°C). The trees are almost everbearing. They are

Crushed kaffir lime leaves are used extensively in Asian cooking.

The 'Lisbon' lemon
originated in Portugal
land is one of the most
productive cultivars.

modestly pruned annually to keep the trees reasonably compact, and any wayward branches are removed as they occur. They require greater distance between trees as they are larger plants. Otherwise lemons are grown in the same manner and have the same requirements as oranges.

Very old lemons that have reduced productivity can be 'skeletonized', a practise in which the tree is cut back evenly all over, removing the foliage and leaving the main branches bare. Any larger cuts are closed with wound healant. The branches are then white-washed in order to reflect heat from the exposed branches. Under the bark are a surprising number of bud initials, and skeletonizing encourages them to break dormancy, shoot from the bare branches, and form a clean new full canopy within a year. It is a drastic process but can rejuvenate old trees remarkably. The price, however, is that the tree yields no fruit for at least a year.

Recommended Cultivars

'Eureka' — Popular as an attractive container tree as well as for lemon production, this cultivar forms large, plump, smooth, golden yellow fruit of excellent clean flavor. It has few thorns.

'Lisbon' — This cultivar originated in Portugal and is an excellent, very productive, heat-resistant type carrying fruit heavily in late winter and spring. The fruit are large, smooth, clear lemon in color, juicy and fragrant, with a clean tangy flavor. It will recover from frosts down to 23°F (−5°C), and when well established will survive the occasional somewhat more severe frost.

The 'Eureka' lemon tree.

'**Meyer**' — The Meyer is a smooth, very large, thin-skinned, juicy lemon but lacks the clean bite of some cultivars. It fruits very abundantly in winter, but carries some fruit for most months of the year. The small tree has a mounding habit, is almost thornless and lends itself to pot culture. It has quite good cold resistance, growing well in coastal areas.

Mandarin, Tangerine *and* Satsuma

Citrus reticulata   Zones 9–11

Mandarins originated in southeastern China and have been cultivated there since at least the 12th century B.C. The most common species is the **Common mandarin** C. *reticulata*, but three other closely related species are grown: the **Satsuma** or **Japanese mandarin** C. *reticulata* var. *unshiu*, the **King mandarin** C. *nobilis* and the **Mediterranean mandarin** or **tangerine** or **Italian tangerine** C. *reticulata* var. *deliciosa*. Satsumas are the hardiest of the mandarins, and are seedless and easy to peel. The tree is a slow grower.

The '**Clementine**' is a mandarin that was selected in North Africa, ripening in spring and having few seeds. It is an excellent coastal cultivar in Mediterranean climates and belongs to the cultigroup Tangerine.

Citrus limon 'Meyer'.

Mandarins originated in southeastern China in the 12th century B.C.

The 'Dancy Tangerine' or 'Red Tangerine' belongs to the same cultigroup.

Growing and Harvesting

Mandarin trees are grown in the same way as oranges and have the same requirements. (See **Orange**.)

Recommended Cultivars

'Dancy Tangerine' — This is a winter-ripening mandarin with good, sweet flavor and loose peel.

'Ellendale' — This cultivar can be grown in inland tropical to warm temperate areas. It is richly flavored, very juicy, medium to large sized and thin skinned.

'Fremont' — This is an excellent mandarin cultivar with intense reddish-orange skin and superbly flavored, juicy flesh with occasional seeds. The fruit holds well on the tree until spring.

'Honey Murcott' — This cultivar grows well in warm temperate to tropical areas with occasional light frosts. The skin is fine, thin and clear orange, the fruits medium sized, and the flesh very sweet.

The 'Jaffa' orange is a sweet, juicy, medium-sized orange with few seeds. It is easy to peel, ripens in spring and stores well on the tree.

Orange *or* Sweet Orange
Citrus sinensis   Zones 9–11

Two species of oranges are grown: the sweet orange and the bitter or Seville orange. The sweet orange requires a mild to very warm climate, ideally one with distinct seasonal variation but not an extreme one.

Growing and Harvesting

A number of orchards in the USA, especially in California, and also in Australia and New Zealand, are now producing top grade organic fruit on land that was once biologically dead, and on its way to being salinized, by using organic techniques such as the annual addition of manure or compost, and of pulverized rock minerals such as greensand, rock phosphate and granite dust. If the soil is excessively acidic, dolomite can also be added to bring the pH up to around 6.0. The orchards are inter-rowed with nitrogen-fixing cover crops such as alfalfa (lucerne), which is slashed approximately 3 times in the growing season to make mulch for the trees. If manures are to be used as an annual fertilizer, as a guide each orange tree needs a yearly application of 10 oz (300 g) of nitrogen from a nitrogen-containing organic top dressing for every year of the tree's life up to 10 years of age. Thereafter, they require the same annual fertilizing as for the 10-year-old tree for the rest of their hopefully very long life. This works out at the equivalent of approximately 3 lb (1.4 kg) of poultry manure or alfalfa (lucerne) hay or twice that weight of dried cow manure multiplied by the age of the tree in years. A 10-year-old tree, for instance, would require 30 lb (14 kg) of poultry manure if that was the top dressing of choice.

The same organic techniques can be used in the home orchard as in the larger organic orchard and are even more effective. Some organic gardeners

Sooty mould on mandarin leaves.

belong to the 'do no harm' school and simply withdraw all chemicals from the crop and its soil. Provided watering is adequate, the fruit that comes from their trees often looks a little the worse for wear, with probably mite or scale damage and perhaps sooty mould, but inside they will usually be fine. Real organic gardening, however, means positively building the health of the soil and of the plant. The outside of the fruit should look appetizing too as a result of good organic practises. Eulogizing the presence of sooty mould on fruit as evidence of a lack of spraying is close to praising a lack of thinking and caring for the wellbeing of plants. Equally importantly, any nutritional deficiencies present in the fruit are passed on to those consuming it.

The best choice of plant material to buy is a strongly growing, 1-year-old budded tree that will quickly settle into its site. Genuine 1-year-old trees should still have leaves growing on the main trunk below the first branches. (Trees that have been through an extremely hot period may have dropped these leaves.) Discuss your choices with a good local nursery that is familiar with the best orange cultivars and rootstocks for your district. Four trees would keep a family in fruit all year round; choose two for fresh eating and two for juicing.

Blood oranges are a specialty orange with dark red to burgundy flesh. The skin is usually tinged with red, giving an indication of the color beneath. Most blood oranges have a thin skin.

Prepare the soil well with plenty of compost before planting. Rotted manures can also be used if available, and washed seaweed that has been composted is particularly helpful. Powdered rock fertilizers such as greensand can also be added at this stage. Citrus are heavy feeders and require regular nutritional boosts. The tree should be planted in a hole about $2^1/_2$ ft (75 cm) wide. Loosen the soil at the bottom of the hole, then add enough of the loam and compost mix so that the tree can be planted at the same depth in the soil as it occupied in the pot. The bud union should be well above the ground. Fill in with the compost and soil mix around the tree, firming down well. Water deeply until you are satisfied that the soil is saturated and no more air bubbles rise to the surface. Several buckets of water are generally required. Prune the tree very gently with sharp secateurs to reduce the leaf area, just tipping back by 2–3 in (5–7.5 cm).

This will also reduce transpirational stress on the young tree and allow it to grow away strongly. Heavy pruning is totally unnecessary. In mild to hot climates, trees can be planted at any time other than mid-summer when the plants would be heat stressed.

Trees are planted in pots in the same way, using a mixture of loam and compost with washed river sand added to facilitate good drainage, and added rotted manure, composted seaweed and pulverized natural rock minerals. The final ratio depends on the type of soil you have, but aim for a fairly heavy but freely draining mixture. Lighter mixes dry out too easily.

Heavy mulches should be regularly applied to the ground around trees to mitigate moisture loss, but the mulch should not touch the trunk as that will cause collar rot. A stone mulch taken out to the drip line is very helpful in drier climates. A regular organic mulch can be applied beneath

Healthy-budded citrus plants at 2 months. These will be planted out after 12 months

Chlorosis of citrus leaves. Citrus crops frequently develop lime-induced chlorosis, which shows up on the leaves as a dark green vein pattern against a pale green leaf.

the stone mulch. Regular deep watering is essential in the summer months in particular. Light watering is often of little value and a hot summer wind can irreversibly dehydrate the tree, particularly in its establishment years. In the first growing season, trees should be watered to saturation every 7–10 days. In the second year, watering to field capacity is done every 2–3 weeks. Depending on how hot and windy the weather is, watering can be cut back to every 3 weeks of the growing season from the third year onward.

Regular applications every 2–3 weeks of a seaweed foliar fertilizer applied at the recommended rate, or of compost or manure 'soup' diluted 1 in 10, will supply the necessary nutritional boost during the growing season. A side-dressing of blood and bone could replace the seaweed application occasionally. Once growth has ceased for the winter months, applications can stop completely. To make the 'soup', fill a hessian sack with rough compost, or weeds and comfrey leaves and herb clippings, or washed seaweed from the beach, or manure. Tie at the top, and suspend in a bin filled with water for about 2 weeks. The nutrients leach out into the water. It is a trifle ripe smelling but does wonders for the plants. Stir before using. Oddly, some birds fancy it too.

Any growth that appears at the base of the plant below the graft union should be removed by pushing down and snapping the shoot out of the trunk. Cutting back, no matter how closely, often leaves a couple of buried buds to reshoot. Never let whipper-snippers near the tree trunk area.

The experience of organic citrus growers seems to verify the strongly held belief by organic growers that healthy plants do not attract pests and diseases. Most of the pests and diseases of citrus affect the appearance of oranges rather than their flavor or productivity, but if citrus are grown in the appropriate climate with good air movement and soil drainage, and good cultivar choice, the fruit should be clean and minimally affected by any problems.

Aphids of several types can be a problem. These tiny sap suckers can be present in very large numbers on tip growth and cause distortion of the young foliage. Their sugary exudate, honeydew, provides the ideal medium

Distortion of young tips of citrus foliage caused by bronze orange bug.

Gall on citrus caused by gall wasp.

such as ladybugs, lacewings and parasitic wasps are not in the firing line. Natural predators normally control aphid populations. Plants grown with high-release inorganic fertilizers are most at risk in spring because the new foliage is so tender.

The citrus leaf miner is a very small moth whose larvae feed and develop inside young leaves. The silvery larval tunnels cause twisting and curling of the leaves, and a characteristic general silvering or bronzing of affected leaves, setting back the development of young trees. An integrated approach is taken by pruning young trees, reducing any sources of plant stress with heavy mulches for weed and moisture control, and using only slow-release feeding via organic composts or manures. Because the larvae are within the leaf, they are not easily reached by sprays (even chemical alternatives) and any spray might affect the good work of natural predators, which are the best control. Prune off any affected branch tips and dispose of them.

for disfiguring sooty mould to grow on. Aphids may also act as vectors for various viral diseases. They can be controlled with sprays of insecticidal soap, or home-made garlic and chile spray, or lemon spray. Pyrethrin/rotenone sprays, often combined with oil, are also used. Before using any spray, check that natural predators

Red scale on the fruit are tiny round (female) or oval (male) protective covers of insects that are sessile in almost all stages of their lives. Their protective covering is white when young, turning brown or red when older. Their natural enemies include predatory mites and ladybugs. Petroleum oil sprays are used together with parasitic wasp release in commercial organic orchards. In the home garden, the best solution is to hand-brush or wash the fruit. In California, both red scale and yellow scale are a problem.

The Crusader bug, with its characteristic cross on the back in mature specimens, is widely distributed; it is a voracious sucking insect causing the juicy new tip growth to wither. All citrus cultivars can be attacked. Sprays of pyrethrum, insecticidal potassium soap, or pest oil are used if the problem becomes

severe, after checking that natural predators are not present. Hand-removal is effective in small groves. Its natural enemies include praying mantises, birds, assassin bugs and parasitic wasps.

The spined citrus bug is a problem in lemon crops, but populations are sustained on any citrus. They feed on the fruit of lemons at all stages, sucking and browning one or more internal fruit segments dry. Their enemies include lacewings and assassin bugs, and they are controlled in the same manner as Crusader bugs if their population is becoming large.

Recommended Cultivars

'**Jaffa**' syn. Shamouti, Palestine Orange — Popular in Israel, this is a sweet, juicy, medium-sized orange with few seeds. It is easy to peel, ripens in spring and stores well on the tree.

'**Maltese Blood**' — A classic, very productive, richly flavored blood orange favored in many parts of the world.

'**Moro**' — This is a highly productive blood orange grown in coastal areas, with an orange skin but very deep red flesh, as if soaked in a dark red wine. It has a rich berry-like flavor and exotic aroma.

'**Sanguinelli**' — This is a blood orange with a spicy, tart flavor and few if any seeds. The rind is blushed to a deep sunset orange-red and the flesh is deeply suffused and flecked with red.

'**Valencia**' — This is a medium-sized, golden orange, excellent for juice that is rich and very sweet at the end of the season.

Citrus sinensis cultivar.

'Valencia' oranges have very few seeds and a sweet flavor. Their thin skin makes them difficult to peel.

'Washington Navel' — This 18th century cultivar continues to be the standard with seedless, sweet, juicy fruit that separates easily into segments. The tree is winter ripening, and will grow in relatively cool climates. It is thought to have been created as an improved selection of the **Bahia Orange** or **Brazilian Navel** *C. sinensis* var. *brasiliensis*. Various named selections of the **'Washington Navel'** have also been released.

Pummelo
Citrus maxima   Zones 10–12

The largest of the citrus fruits, the pummelo is native to Southeast Asia. Also known as the Shaddock, West Indian or Thai Pomelo, the fruit was seemingly named after Captain Shaddock, an English sea captain who introduced the seed to the West Indies in the 17th century. Its seeds produce a fruit that grows in bunches or clusters.

The pummelo is an ancient ancestor of the common grapefruit, with a shape that can be fairly round or slightly pointed at one end. They have very thick, soft rind, a skin that is green to yellow and slightly bumpy, and a flesh color that ranges from pink to rose.

Like grapefruits, they can range from almost seedless to very seedy, from juicy to dry, from sweet to sour. Sweeter than a grapefruit, the pummelo can be eaten fresh, although membranes around the segments should be peeled. The pummelo usually has 16 segments, compared with most grapefruit that have about 12. Pummelos are grown in the same way as grapefruit with similar requirements.

The sweet, juicy fruit of the 'Washington Navel'

'Rangpur' Lime

Citrus limonia var. *rangpur* syn. *C. x limon*
Zones 10–12

The 'Rangpur' lime is an orange-colored fruit with something of a rough, small mandarin appearance and a taste of lime mingled with a mild orange flavor. The flower buds are quite purple in color, opening white. It requires a warm temperate to tropical climate to grow, and is grown in the same manner as Tahitian lime. The cultivar **'Kusaie'** is a yellow-fruited form of 'Rangpur'. It has a true wild lime flavor. The fruits of both are only about half the size of Tahitian lime. The trees are quite small, growing to only 6½ ft (2 m) over a number of years, and make excellent tub specimens in half oak wine barrel containers or pots of equivalent size. They should be given a loamy soil well enriched with compost. Both of these limes are more cold-resistant than either Jamaican or West Indian limes, and are grown in the same manner as sweet oranges.

Seville Orange

Citrus aurantium ssp. *aurantium*   Zones 9–11

The Seville orange, or Bitter or Sour orange or Bigerade, is golden-orange fruited, but sour and unpalatable when raw. It is in demand for making premium breakfast marmalades that are deliciously tangy and help wake the weary, and the fruits are largely exported to Scotland and England for this purpose. The dried peel, particularly of the cultivar **'Jacmel'** in Jamaica and the very aromatic **'Curaçao Orange'** is the source of the essential oil that is used to flavor the liqueur curaçao. They are also a popular street planting in southern Italy and Spain, having all the beauty and fragrance of the sweet orange but offering no temptation to the passers-by. As a result, the oranges hang on the trees for months.

The trees range in size from a modest 10 ft (3 m) to 30 ft (9 m). The aromatic leaves have markedly winged petioles. The species is thought to

The Seville orange 'Bouquet' is popular throughout California for its large clusters of fragrant blossoms.

have reached Polynesia very early, and Arabia by the 9th century AD. It was cultivated around Seville in Spain by the end of the 12th century. Sir Walter Raleigh introduced Seville oranges to England, and 3 trees planted in Surrey were bearing in 1595 but were killed by the great winter of 1739. The Spanish introduced the Seville or bitter orange into St Augustine, Florida. It was the first orange introduced into the New World, becoming naturalized in Mexico by the mid-16th century. It became an important rootstock for budding sweet oranges for early pioneer settlers in the southern states of the USA. Today, two rootstocks 'Vermilion Globe' and 'Leather-head' are also popular rootstocks for sweet orange cultivars in China.

A number of good cultivars exist including 'Standard', 'Oklawaha' (which originated in the USA), 'Rubidoux' and 'Brazilian'. The dwarf, almost thornless 'Taitai' is popular in China and Japan for its abundant, fragrant blower buds, which are dried and mixed with tea for their scent. 'Bouquet' is a popular ornamental cultivar in California for its large clusters of fragrant blossoms borne on a small, neat tree. In France,

'Riche Défeuille' is grown for oil of neroli. The Myrtle-leafed bitter orange is a mutation of the bitter orange found in Florida and also grown on the French and Italian Riviera, its fruits being candied.

All bitter oranges are grown in the same manner as the sweet orange and have the same requirements. They have remarkable survival powers (old plants can be found growing on hummocks in the Florida Everglades, remnants of Indian dwellings), and some trees in Spain are reputedly 600 years old. The Versailles Palace in France has a pot-grown specimen said to have been planted in 1421. The Seville orange can withstand several degrees of frost for short periods, and unlike the sweet orange is moderately tolerant of high watertables.

Tahitian Lime
Citrus latifolia   Zones 10–12

Also known as the Persian or Pond's or Bearss lime, this is the most commonly grown lime. It has large, smooth-skinned, lime-green, virtually seedless fruit which are very juicy. The lime-green, high quality flesh has a fragrant, refreshing, clean lime taste ideal for drinks and cooking.

The 'Tahitian Lime', also known as 'Persian Lime' and 'Pond's Lime'. These limes are botanically the same and are the variety usually found in shops.

Growing and Harvesting

Lime trees should be positioned in a protected site away from wind. They are cold sensitive, and many growers make use of the rootstock citrus *Poncirus trifoliata* or its hybrid 'Flying Dragon' to allow Tahitian lime to grow in cooler areas than is normally possible. The rootstock stops growing under cold conditions, and so does the plant canopy. As a result the lime develops tough, winter-hardened leaves rather than the soft leaves it continues to produce if grafted onto Rough Lemon rootstock. Limes are otherwise grown in the same manner as the sweet orange. A light trim each year at the end of spring is beneficial, but 'skeletonizing' is unnecessary.

West Indian Lime

Citrus aurantifolia   Zones 10–12

The West Indian lime, or Key or Mexican or Sour lime, is strictly for very warm to tropical gardens if it is to be grown outside. The fruits are seedy and smaller than the Tahitian lime, and less juicy, but have an excellent flavor and fragrance. The species is very thorny and makes an excellent edible and highly repellent hedge to exclude anything from cows to unwanted intruders, but a number of thornless clones have been developed. The Key lime is quintessential to the cuisine of the Florida Keys, and gives its name to the justifiably acclaimed Key Lime Pie. It is grown in the same manner as the sweet orange.

The lime grows best in tropical and subtropical climates. It is stronger in acidity and flavor than the lemon.

The thorns on 'West Indian Lime' make it the ideal plant for hedging.

Melons

Cantaloupe Melon *Cucumis melo* var. *cantalupensis;* **Muskmelons** *C. melo* var. *reticulatus;* **Watermelon** *Citrullus lanatus;* **Winter Melons** *Cucumis melo* var. *inodorus*

Muskmelons (the common name for cantaloupes and honeydew melons) originated in valley lowlands of south-western Asia, whereas other melons were first cultivated in the Nile Delta. They did not find their way into Europe until at least the 15th century.

Growing and Harvesting

Given their origins, it's not surprising that melons prefer to grow in areas with warm, preferably dry and hot, summers. However, plant breeding has created cultivars that will grow in quite short summers and somewhat cooler conditions. The use of cold frames and glasshouses allows melons to be grown successfully in areas that otherwise would be too cool.

Melons require full sun, a well-drained position, and good air circulation to minimize fungal diseases. Most cultivars are trailing plants, but some dwarf cultivars have been developed in which the vine length has been reduced to around 40 in (1 m), making them suitable for small gardens. In warm climates, a few of these plants could even be grown on a sunny balcony.

Melon plants require soil enriched with modest quantities of broken-down compost. This not only provides nutritional benefits, but also improves the soil structure. If the soil is too sandy, water stress is likely to occur; wilted vines then cease to photo-synthesize and growth can be set back badly. The compost acts like a sponge, retaining extra water for the plants which will see them through dry spells. The addition of compost to heavy soils will greatly improve aeration.

The optimum pH for melon production is 6.5–7.0; acid soils should be adjusted with lime or dolomite before planting. A sprinkling of bonemeal can also be incorporated.

In warm to hot districts, seeds can be planted into individual hills, with two or three seeds in each hill. You can then select the strongest seedling to continue to grow on, or plant them all out on a raised bed.

Raised soil warms quickly. This is significant as melon seeds will not

Cantaloupe melons, Cucumis melo *var.* cantalupensis, *usually have a round or oval shape, netted rinds and deep orange flesh.*

germinate until the temperature rises to 64°F (18°C), and they require a minimum temperature of 70°F (21°C) to grow successfully.

Most cultivars require two and half to three months to produce ripe fruit. In cooler areas, seedlings can be raised in individual pots in a heated greenhouse until they have reached a good size and all danger of frost has passed. Only the strongest seedlings should be planted on into larger 5-in (12.5-cm) pots. This stage of potting can be eliminated where a reasonable growing season of three months or more is expected. Otherwise, it is essential to raise the plants to a good size in order to make the most of the field growing time available.

The first blossoms that open will be male flowers, so do not worry when they abort. However, if the female flowers, which have a distinct swelling below the petal tube, also continue to abort, it means that bees (the main pollinators of melons) are probably absent. Temperatures may be too low, or local populations may have been reduced by neighborhood spraying. In the bees' absence, you may need to pick male flowers and carry pollen to the tip of the female stigma.

It's worth making a concerted effort to attract and protect bees. Cultivate bee-attracting plants throughout the vegetable garden and orchard. Try annual flowers like sweet alyssum, *Lobularia maritimum*, and old-fashioned forms of snapdragons, *Antirrhinum majus*; poppies, *Papaver species*; and Californian poppies, *Eschscholtzia californica*. Many of the flowering herbs, including lemon balm, rosemary, basils, thymes, oregano, mints and hyssop will also draw the insects. Hedging your garden with bee attractors such as elderberry, *Sambucus*, and Rugosa roses will not only attract bees, but also form a windbreak that in turn creates the calm, warm conditions that bees enjoy. The same hedges will also provide the birds and you with food and pleasure. The best insurance policy, however, when it comes to pollinating melons is to add a beehive to your garden.

The commonest threats to melons are powdery mildew, downy mildew, spider mites, and, in some areas, cucumber beetles. The use of a seaweed spray twice during the growing stages appears to maintain plant growth, reduce stress, and make the melons less vulnerable to these problems. Pest-resistant melon cultivars have also been developed.

Because fruiting takes place on side shoots, growers in marginal areas, especially, tend to pinch the vine back two or three times to encourage side

The myriad colors of melon flesh range from the reds and pinks of watermelon to the rich orange shades of canteloupes and the yellow hues of honeydew.

growth and rapid production. Mulch is essential for reducing water stress in hot-summer areas. It should be applied after the soil has fully warmed. Regular watering should be carried out under hot conditions.

Cantaloupe Melons

Cucumis melo var. cantalupensis   Zones 8–11

This group derives its name from the castle of Cantalupo near Rome in Italy, where these melons were reputedly first cultivated. They are characterized by a hard rind which is never netted but may be roughened or scaled. The group provides some of the finest eating of all melons.

Growing and Harvesting

Even when ripe, cantaloupes do not partially separate from the stem in the manner of muskmelons; they must therefore be cut with a knife.

In some regions, the cantaloupe 'Charantais' is served for dessert, filled with port or madeira wine.

Recommended Cultivars

'Charantais' — This is the legendary cantaloupe melon of Provence. It is smallish, plump and rounded, with a smooth grey-green skin. The thick, fine-textured, deep orange flesh is very aromatic. It is often served as a first course in summer with sliced ham or other cold meats, or with a fruity iced white wine.

Muskmelons

Cucumis melo var. reticulatus	Zones 8–11

Muskmelons are characterized by a delightful fragrance that is perceptible from some distance away when they are ripe. They are sometimes referred to as 'netted melons' because many cultivars have a raised, net-like pattern on their skin. Often, they are referred to incorrectly as cantaloupes, and in Australia they are called rockmelons.

Growing and Harvesting

When ripe, muskmelons partially dehisce, or separate, from the stem. This is called 'the slip stage' and it allows for easy harvesting.

Recommended Cultivars

'Ananas' syn. Sharlyn — This is an oval fruit with a thin, pale grey-green rind that turns yellow-orange. The flesh is white, tending to gold just around the seed cavity, and is juicy, sweet and perfumed. The vine is vigorous and mildew-resistant.

'Banana' — The long fruits of this cultivar are pale green or creamy yellow, with sparse netting and prominent ribs. The flesh is deep salmon to orange, very sweet and juicy, and mildly aromatic.

'Blenheim Orange' — This traditional greenhouse cultivar was first raised in England, in 1881, in the gardens of Blenheim Palace. Sadly, it does not perform well when grown outdoors, even in hot-summer, melon-growing areas. Raised under glass, it forms a medium-sized, plumply oval, thin-skinned, creamy yellow and finely netted melon with juicy, thick, almost red flesh that is sweet and highly aromatic.

'Green Nutmeg' — This is a valuable cultivar for those who live in cooler climates as it will grow and ripen in about two months. The fruits are heavily netted and lightly ribbed; the flesh is pale green near the skin, orange near the seed cavity, and very sweet and aromatic.

'Hale's Best' — This is a popular shipping cultivar but fully deserves consideration for the home garden where the season suits. In that setting, it is a different fruit—small, round, heavily netted, with sweet, aromatic, salmon-colored, high-quality flesh. It is susceptible to powdery mildew. 'Hale's Best Jumbo' is larger and coarser.

Top: The pale green skin of the 'Ananas' cultivar will eventually turn a yellow-orange color.

Above: The 'Banana' melon derives its name from its pale yellow skin and elongated shape.

The 'Haogen' melon originated in Israel. The fruit normally weighs 3–5 lb (1.5–2.5 kg).

it is exceptionally sweet, tender, and mild-flavored.

'Minnesota Midget' — This is an ideal choice for smaller gardens. The fruits are small and rounded, deeply lobed, and only sparsely netted. The flesh is golden and very thick, leaving only a small cavity, and sweet all the way through to the skin. It makes a dwarf vine that grows to 40 in (1 m).

'Haogen' syn. Ogen, Israel — Considered one of the greatest of all melons, this cultivar forms smallish, rounded fruits with smooth green skin striped with lighter green. The flesh is a pale greenish white suffused with salmon around the small seed cavity. It is exceptionally sweet and full-flavored. The vines are vigorous and prolific.

'Jenny Lind' — This cultivar was introduced in 1846 and is still popular. The fruit is small, orange-brown in color, and mottled with green. Flattened at both ends, with a small knob at the blossom end,

Watermelon

Citrullus lanatus   Zones 8–11

Although we think of watermelon as having pink or red flesh, some of the most delicious cultivars in this group have creamy-white, orange, or yellow flesh. And though we associate watermelon with the peak of summer heat, there are cultivars that can be saved for winter eating.

If you find the idea of spitting out watermelon seed offputting, you can even buy seedless varieties. These melons were developed by Dr Warren Barham, who completed his PhD in plant breeding in 1949. He began with a small 19th-century heirloom cultivar that had tiny seed, then used

The 'Cream of Saskatchewan' watermelon cultivar was introduced to Canada by Russian immigrants.

highly inbred lines to create 'seedless' fruits. Seedless hybrids include 'Jack of Hearts', 'Queen of Hearts', 'King of Hearts', 'Fummy', 'Honey Yellow', and 'Honeyheart'. Of course, the problem with seedless watermelons is that, by definition, they cannot be propagated; they need to be recreated with another round of hybridization. It's not only nature that's been thwarted but also the seed-saving gardener!

Growing and Harvesting

To an even greater extent than other melon types, watermelons depend on hot summer weather to flourish. For the fruit to succeed in cooler areas, special attention must be paid to cultivar selection. Even then, no cultivar will survive outdoors in the ground without a minimum of 75 frost-free, sunny days. Watermelon development is hindered by water stress, and gular watering (preferably not overhead) and mulching are important. You can check whether the melon is mature by rapping on it: a hollow sound means it is ready to be harvested. The stem should be cut with a knife. Store the melons in a cool place, where they will keep for at least two to three weeks.

Recommended Cultivars

'Charleston Grey' syn. Candy Red — This remains an excellent early-producing cultivar that has long, light green fruits striped with dark green and bright red, crisp, sweet flesh. The vines display resistance to most ills of the watermelon world including anthracnose, fusarium wilt, and sunburn.

'Cream of Saskatchewan' — This famous cultivar will grow well in cooler areas. The fruits are of medium size, about $8^1/_2$ lbs (4 kg), with pale green skins striped with dark green, a thin rind, and cream-white, very sweet, delightfully flavored, crisp and juicy flesh. The vines are prolific.

'Golden Honey' — Popular with home gardeners, this is an oval fruit, with thin, green, striped rind and clear, bright yellow, crisp, flavorsome flesh.

'Kleckley Sweet' syn. Monte Cristo — This old favorite forms long fruits weighing up to 40 lbs (18 kg). The rind is thin, deep blue-green, and glossy. The flesh is extremely sweet, bright red, fine-grained, and crisp.

'Moon and Stars' — This cultivar was believed to be extinct until it was rediscovered in Missouri by Kent Whealy, the founder of the Seed Savers Exchange. The skin of the oval fruit is dark green splashed with small and large gold spots; it has been likened to a constellation of stars with one or more moons.

'Navajo Winter Red Seeded' — This cultivar was developed by the Navajo people as a winter-keeping cultivar and was traditionally stored in sand. The melon is plump oval in shape, the skin is pale green striped with a deeper green, the rind unusually thick, and the crisp, deep pink flesh particularly sweet. A more recent cultivar suited to long-term storage is **'King and Queen'** syn. Winterkeeper, Christmas Melon. It is often eaten at Christmas in the northern hemisphere.

'Northern Sweet' — This is an early cultivar suitable for shorter summer

In traditional Navajo culture, the 'Navajo Winter Red Seeded' was regarded as a prestigious gift at ceremonies and other celebrations.

areas. Its round fruits have a dark and light green striped rind and sweet, orange-red flesh.

'Sugarbaby' syn. Icebox Midget — Popular with home gardeners and commercial producers since its release in 1955, this is an early-maturing, small, dark green, round melon, with a thin, tough skin and very sweet, crisp, deep red flesh.

'Texas Giant' — This large, rounded melon has a blue-green skin and very sweet, crisp, red flesh.

'Warpaint' syn. Crimson Sweet — This is a round to oblong melon weighing 22–26 lb (10–12 kg). Its skin is light green with darker green stripes, and it has a thick, hard rind, and bright red, sweet flesh with a fine texture.

Winter Melons

Cucumis melo var. inodorus   Zones 8–11

This group contains the casaba melons and the honeydew melons, as well as a third group including the various Crenshaw and Canary types.

Casaba melons have a rough wrinkled skin, the wrinkles forming longitudinal ribs, and a hard rind. They are thought to have originated in Turkey. Honeydew melons are usually smooth-skinned with a hard

rind and green flesh. The third group is more diverse, but typified by a hard rind and good keeping properties.

Growing and Harvesting

Winter melons ripen late. To harvest these fruits, cut them carefully from the vine; pulling them off can cause rot to develop during storage. Winter melons can be stored for a longer period than other melons.

Recommended Cultivars

'Earli-Dew' syn. Early Honeydew — This is an excellent cultivar for the small garden and will ripen in slightly cooler areas. It produces medium-sized, round fruits, with a smooth greenish-gold skin and outstanding, thick, emerald green, tender, sweet flesh. The vines are vigorous, exceptionally productive, and resistant to fusarium.

The exquisite, aromatic fruit of 'Indian Cream' is delicious when served with ice-cream or drizzled with honey.

'Indian Cream' syn. Cobra Melon —
This is an extraordinary traditional cultivar long grown on the north coast of New South Wales and in south-eastern Queensland in Australia, and also in the southern USA. It forms long-oval, pale cream fruits which split lengthwise when fully ripe. The flesh is dryish, tender and superbly aromatic.

'Green Fleshed' syn. honeydew — This heavy melon can weigh as much as 6 lb (3 kg). It has a hard, ivory white rind, and thick, very juicy, fragrant, green flesh.

'Sungold' — This Casaba-type melon is plump, almost round, with a golden skin. The flesh is greenish-white, very juicy and sweet, and of high quality. The dwarf vine measures 40 in (1 m).

'Yellow Canary' syn. Jaune des Canaries — This melon has long been popular in the Mediterranean area. It has elongated, slightly wrinkled, canary yellow fruits which can weigh over 6 lb (3 kg). The flesh is white, tinged with orange around the seed cavity, very thick, aromatic, crisp and sweet.

The 'Sungold', a wintermelon, has a thick, yellow rind with highly distinctive ribbing.

Nuts

Almonds *Prunus dulcis*; **Butternut** *Juglans cinerea*; **Chestnuts** *Castanea* spp.; **Hazelnuts, Cobnuts, Filberts** *Corylus* spp.; **Macadamia** *Macadamia integrifolia*; **Pistachio Nut** *Pistacia vera*, **Peanuts** *Arachis hypogaea*; **Pecan** *Carya illinoensis*

While fruits of some kind are usually included in gardens, nuts are often forgotten, although many are easy to grow. Some are only suited to large gardens, but hazelnuts, almonds, pistachios, and even pecans can be considered for the small to medium garden. Rather than planting a conventional shade tree for the house, consider planting one of the smaller walnut cultivars, or one of the *Pinus* species which produce good sized pine nuts, or a smaller cultivar of chestnut (although everyone will need to take care of fallen, spiny cases in fall). They can look as handsome as any ornamental, and in due season will yield abundant fresh food. Make sure that larger trees have sufficient room to grow. In small gardens it is better to choose bush and small tree nuts to prevent shading the house or the vegetable garden.

Stalkless pink almond blossoms are borne in clusters on the leafless branches in late winter or early spring.

Almonds
Prunus dulcis   Zones 6–9

There are two major groups in the almonds which are believed to have originated in the eastern Mediterranean. Those with bitter nuts which find use mainly as rootstocks, and those with sweet kernels which are used for food. The bitter character crosses the barriers between the two groups and some commercial cultivars have slight bitterness, a characterisic which appeals to some consumers. Experimental cultivars often throw a percentage of fully bitter nuts, a characteristic which will eliminate them from commercial consideration.

The trees, which closely resemble peaches, bear leathery, flattened, furry fruit which resembles a dried peach. The fruit eventually splits to release a stone which may be hard walled, or paper shelled, a characteristic which makes the wall of the stone thin enough to break in the hand. All degrees of hardness exist between the two extremes in commercial cultivars. The almond is the pit or kernel that lies inside the stone.

Almonds are an excellent sustenance food. They are rich in protein, fat, and vitamin B complex, and store well in the shell in a dry cool area for a few months.

Growing and Harvesting
Almonds will grow anywhere that peaches flourish, and most have much the same chill requirements as the older peach cultivars. However they bloom between 2–4 weeks earlier than peaches, and the blossoms are vulnerable to frosts. The unopened flower buds are equally vulnerable to a period of sustained cold occuring at any time after the flower buds begin to swell. As a result there are limited areas where almonds are grown successfully on a commercial scale. Areas of Provence in France, South Australia, warmer areas of the Pacific

Almonds are an excellent sustenance food, being rich in protein, fat and vitamin B complex.

North-West of the United States, parts of the Middle East and the Aegean region have the necessary Mediterranean climate and sufficiently warm temperatures at bud swell and flowering time to provide consistent growing conditions for commercial production. Despite this, some success is often achieved in home gardens where high-chill peaches will flourish.

Most cultivars of almonds require a cross pollinator to set fruit, and compatible pairings have been included in the list provided below. However some very good cultivars which are later flowering have been developed for the home gardener in recent times; these are exceptionally pretty in spring, and self pollinating. Dwarfing genes are also being included in breeding programs, and the almond is now far more adaptable for inclusion in gardens. Almonds also prefer a deep sandy loam enriched with plenty of humus. Heavy soils and clay will not support almonds. It is always possible to containerize a dwarf almond, providing a freely draining mix well enriched with compost, and they are very ornamental additions to the garden.

Almonds are grown in the same manner as peaches *(see section 'Stone Fruits')*, in terms of soil preparation, planting procedure, training, and maintenance. In designing your nuttery,

allow for a mature spread of 20–30 ft (6–9 m). Dwarfed plants usually have a spread of only half that estimation. If the soil in which almonds are to be grown is at all heavy, it is advisable to purchase almonds budded on to peach seedling stock which will thrive considerably better than plants on almond rootstock.

Recommended cultivars

'All-In-One' — This is a very attractive cultivar with an outstanding show of beautiful white blossom in spring. It is self fertilizing and heavy yielding, with soft shelled nuts of excellent quality and very good, sweet flavor.

Almond trees bear leathery, flattened, furry fruit, which eventually splits to release a stone with the almond lying inside the stone.

'Butte' — This cultivar can pollinate 'Non Pareil'. The shell is medium hard and thick, the kernels plump, medium sized, and sweet.

'Garden Prince' — This is a useful genetic dwarf growing to only 8–10 ft (2.5–3.0 m). As an added bonus, it is self pollinating. It makes a good container plant. It is productive and the nuts are soft shelled with sweet, medium sized kernels.

'Mission' syn. Texas — This is a late blooming cultivar which will pollinate 'Non Pareil'. The nuts are hard shelled and rounded, of good quality with a slightly bitter flavor.

'Ne Plus Ultra' — This is a fairly low chill cultivar used as a pollinator for 'Non Pareil'. The nuts are soft shelled and the kernels are flat and only of average quality.

'Non Pareil' — This is an extremely important commercial cultivar of high quality with paper thin shells and smooth, even sized, sweet nuts.

'Thompson' — This is a Californian cultivar with soft to paper shells with plump kernels of good quality. It is a pollinator for 'Mission'.

Butternut
Juglans cinerea   Zones 4–9

This is an exceptonal walnut (also known as the white walnut) too little known outside its North American homeland. It has no trace of the bitterness associated with the European walnut, and has a rich, buttery, smooth flavor that is irresistible.

Butternuts are much hardier than the black walnut. They are native to northern parts of North America including Quebec and Ontario. Trees grow to approximately 26 ft (8 m). Three other species well worth growing if room can be found are the very fine **Black walnut** *J. nigra*, the **Persian** or **Common** or **English Walnut** *J. regia* of which perhaps the best cultivar is **'Wilson's Seedling'**, and the **Heartnut** *J. ailantifolia* var. cordiformis.

Recommended cultivars
'Bountiful' syn. Stark Bountiful — This is a very well flavored nut, and is easily shelled. The tree is hardy, self pollinating, and very producive. It was bred in Missouri and released in 1982.

'Craxeezy' — Despite the truly terrible name, this is a superior cultivar with a medium sized nut that easily cracks down the suture line to yield twin halves. The flavor is excellent, and the tree is a heavy bearer, cold hardy, and vigorous. It was bred in Michigan and released in 1934.

'Kenworthy' — This is an exceptionally large nut with excellent texture. The tree is a semi-dwarf, vigorous and cold hardy.

The common walnut, Juglans regia, has a sturdy trunk and a broad leafy canopy. The edible nut is enclosed in a green husk that withers and is cast off.

The sweet chestnut or Spanish chestnut, Castanea sativa, finds its way into many famous dishes.

Chestnuts

Castanea spp.   Zones 4–9

Few trees give so much for so little as the chestnuts. At least 12 species provide excellent nuts, and unlike almost all the other nuts, they are high in stored carbohydrate rather than oils. The Chinese chestnut *C. mollissima* produces nuts that are eaten raw, or roasted, boiled or puréed. The American chestnut *C. dentata* is credited with having the sweetest nuts of all. They are small, but they are used to great effect in all the ways the Chinese chestnut is used. Blight has destroyed many of the native trees but the excellently flavored cultivar '**Kelly**' has good resistance to blight. The Japanese chestnut *C. crenata* is boiled like potatoes, cooked with rice, roasted, and sugared. The Spanish or Italian chestnut *C. sativa* finds its way into many famous dishes, from marrons *glacés* to desserts, stuffings, purées, and in the form of the flour *farine de chataigne* is used in puddings, bread, and sweet, delicate fritters. The Chinquapin *C. pumila* has small but very sweet nuts that can be eaten raw or roasted. This is a dwarf tree and amazingly prolific. Selections are available together with a hybrid called '**Jane**'.

Chestnuts prefer a deep sandy loam with high humus levels. The incorporation of good quantities of organic matter into the soil and the addition of ground rock phosphate and granite or basalt rock dust before planting will help ensure that the young tree grows away healthily. The addition of a heavy straw mulch is also necessary to prevent drying out of the topsoil.

Chestnuts are high in stored carbohydrate rather than oil.

Spiky chestnut cases split to reveal glossy brown chestnuts.

but would be a clever way of putting a number of hard to place plants together. (The same idea will work with any garden, mixing together useful plants that are fairly compatible for soil and climate. It might be a hedgerow of rainforest native plants to be used for fruits, seeds, nuts and teas, or an array of useful semi-arid zone plants.) The only management required apart from the occasional light pruning is to renew a thick layer of mulch around the roots as required. On the other hand, if ease of picking and optimizing yield is important, prune the bush to a single stemmed tree and let it bush out at the top to make a standard.

Watering should be done during the first year until the roots reach the moister, deeper soil layers. Training consists of progressively removing any lateral branches that emerge from the base of the plant so that it has a clean lower trunk to a height of 39 in (1 m) above the ground, and growth is concentrated at the top of the plant.

Hazelnuts, Cobnuts and Filberts
Corylus spp.   Zones 4–9

These nuts form deciduous bushes to small trees, and are among the easiest of the nuts to grow. They are tolerant of relatively poor soils and can be used as part of an unofficial hedgerow. Rather than a neat, conventional hedge in the garden, create a hedgerow from all those wild and semi-wild plants that yield harvests for little effort, for both the household and the birds and wildlife. In cooler areas, a mixture of several hazelnuts, elderberries, wild roses, honeysuckle, hawthorns, sloes, Guelder rose *Viburnum opulus*, the Yellow Guelder-rose *V. opulus* 'Xanthocarpum', and perhaps High-bush Cranbury *V. trilobum* and Stagbush *V. prunifolium* would not only be beautiful from spring to fall,

Hazelnuts are among the easiest of nuts to grow The nut is ripe when it readily turns in the husk.

Hazelnuts should receive full sunshine and they prefer a slightly acid pH of 6.0–7.0. The hazelnut is very cold hardy, but it flowers early and may be caught by a late frost. The bushes should be planted in a sheltered, frost free place. Hazelnuts are not self-fertilizing and pollinators must also be planted. The list of recommended cultivars given below suggests cross pollinators that are appropriate. Your local nursery will also be able to advise you.

Prepare the soil by incorporating some compost, basalt or granite rock dust, and some bone meal into the soil. Dig holes for each bush, making the hole larger than the root ball, and use a garden fork to plunge into the soil at the bottom of the hole. Gently rock it backward and forward to just crack the lower stratum. Do not disturb it in any other way. Plant the bushes after trimming back any broken roots. Make sure that the plant remains at the same depth in the new hole as that at which it previously was planted. Fill the hole in and firm down gently. Water until no further air bubbles rise to the top. The bushes are planted at the end of the season after the leaves have fallen. Hazelnuts are a desirable food for rabbits so if you have rabbit problems, place treeguards around each bush.

The nuts need to be eaten within a relatively short period of time as they do not store well. If there is room, store the nuts sealed in ziplock bags in the bottom of the refrigerator. They will last at least 3 months.

Recommended cultivars

'Barcelona' — This is an exceptionally good eating nut, medium to large, rounded, with a good, sweet flavor. It remains the leading cultivar.

'Butler' — This is an excellent medium to large oval nut. It acts as a pollinator for 'Barcelona' and for 'Ennis'.

'Ennis' — This is an excellent cultivar with large, long nuts.

'Kentish Cob' syn. Du Chilly — Bred in England in 1830, this cultivar has long nuts and a fairly hard shell. The quality is excellent, and the flavor superb. It performs best in cold climates. Cross pollinators used for this cultivar include 'Butler', 'Royal', and 'Daviana'.

'Royal' — This was bred from Barcelona and has large oval nuts that are thin walled. The kernels have good flavor.

In winter, the bare twigs of the hazelnut are draped with the developing male catkins, which start to show their yellow pollen at winter's end.

Macadamia

Macadamia integrifolia   Zones 9–11

This is a handsome, long lived, evergreen tree with rather holly-like, dark green leaves which can reach 50 ft (15 m) in time and when grown on rich, deep soils such as in their native rainforest habitat. Macadamias, or Queensland nuts, require a sub-tropical to tropical climate. They flower in spring, bearing catkins of many tiny flowers only a few of which develop into nuts. The nut develops within a husk which turns from green to brown when matured, splitting longitudinally to release the excepionally hard shelled nut. Commercial plantations are in New South Wales and Queensland. The largest plantations in the world are in Hawaii.

The Macadamia nut is an easy tree to grow given the correct climate and a good, deep, rich soil. It is in plantation plantings that pests and diseases become a problem. The site chosen should not be too exposed and should be on deep, well drained soils. The soil should be prepared with the addition of generous amounts of compost and rock dusts worked into the topsoil. Basalt rock dust and ground rock phosphate are ideal. Regular deep watering should be provided weekly until the tree is well established. Good selections of Macadamia integrifolia are available in both Australia and Hawaii. The closely related bopple nut or rough shell macadamia nut is also grown for its nuts which have a similar taste. It forms a smaller tree to about 40 ft (12 m).

Peanuts
Arachis hypogaea   Zones 9–12

The seeds of peanuts, or groundnuts, form an important part of the diet of many warm to sub-tropical areas and are eaten raw, boiled in slightly salted water (best loved by many who come from peanut producing areas), roasted, made into peanut butter, used in satay sauces, cooked in the everpopular groundnut soup of Africa, fermented in Asia, or used for the extraction of peanut oil. The plants are rather remarkable in that the pollinated lower blossoms, which alone are responsible for forming the pods, arch down and bury themselves into the ground to a depth of about 6 in (15 cm) to mature the seed. The whole plant is dug up when harvesting to reveal masses of brown pods containing the peanuts.

Growing and Harvesting
The plant succeeds best in a warm, light, deep loam that has been brought to a fine tilth. The seeds are planted out about 9 in (22 cm) apart in rows, and at a depth of 2 in (5 cm). Weeding must be well maintained early in the season as it cannot be carried out after flowering without damaging the crop. Once flowering commences the vines are earthed up from time to time in the manner of potatoes which greatly increases the yield. The vines are killed by the first frost.

Recommended Cultivars
'Spanish' — This is a reliable older cultivar popular for commercial culture in many parts of the world. It is very productive, grows rapidly, and is tolerant of cooler climates than most. 'Early Spanish' is similar but harvests 10 days earlier.
'Virginia' syn. Virginia Bunch — This productive cultivar is popular in Virginia and the Carolinas in the United Staes and produces large, high quality kernels. It is popular for roasted and salted nuts, as well as raw eating. It is also grown in Australia. A selected form 'Virginia Jumbo' produces even larger kernels with excellent rich flavor. It forms runners and the plants have a spread of about 39 in (1 m).

There is some evidence that planting corn alongside peanuts reduces the risk of disease and ensures a bountiful harvest.

Pecan

Carya illinoensis   Zones 6–11

The pecan is one of the most important nuts in commercial cultivation. The trees need a long, hot summer to succeed in maturing the nut crop. A minimum of 220–270 frost free days have been estimated to be necessary for successful ripening of the nuts. The trees are relatively cold hardy and flower late enough to avoid the damaging effects of a late frost.

Different races of pecans have been developed from different parts of the United States. Pecans from the south are more frost tender but include some of the finest large, thin shelled cultivars, such as 'Schley', 'Moneymaker', and 'Success'. Northern cultivars are in general smaller with thicker shells. They include 'Indiana', 'Devore', 'Major', 'Peruque', and 'Green River'.

Pecans occur naturally on deep alluvial soils that may occasionally flood but will drain quickly. The trees have a deep tap root in combination with long lateral roots. Pecans produce male and female flowers but the blooming time is offset so that cross pollinating trees need to be nearby. This is one of the most handsome of nut trees with the added attractions of good fall color and one of the finest of nuts, but the combination of needing at least two trees and the considerable spread of their lateral roots mean that only large gardens can accomodate them. They are an admirable farm tree where the

The pecan is not suitable for all gardens as it has large lateral roots.

Young pecans, Carya illinoensis, *developing on a tree. The nuts are borne in small clusters and form within a green leathery coat.*

soil is suitable and a planting can be quite profitable if well managed. The wood is quite brittle and pecans do better grown in a stand on a site that is not too exposed.

Nursery trees are dug with a long tap root or propagated in deep containers. The hole to accomodate the tree needs to be able to take the taproot with no bending. Approximately half the top growth should be removed as the root system has been severely disrupted. Regular watering should be supplied during the first year of establishment. A thick mulch needs to be applied around the plant to help retain soil moisture, keeping the mulch away from the trunk. The tree usually has its lowest branch removed each year until there is a 6$^1/_2$ ft (2 m) clearance to the first branch. Trees should be fertilized annually with generous amounts of rock dusts and a thick mulch of straw. Stable straw with manure through it is optimal. The nuts are borne in small clusters and form within a green leathery coat. When fully matured, the outer covering shrinks and splits, spilling the nuts to the ground.

Pistachio

Pistacia vera   Zones 8–10

Pistachio trees can be an ideal choice for gardeners in more arid areas, particularly those with a Mediterranean climate. The species is native to western Asia and Asia Minor as far east as the Caucasus and Afghanistan. Archeological excavations in Turkey have shown that pistachios have been eaten for at least 7,000 years in that area.

The trees slowly attain a height of around 20–23 ft (6–7 m) and have handsome compound leaves. They are usually trained to develop around five scaffold branches. The species is dioecious with male and female flowers on separate trees. For home garden purposes, nurseries often supply female trees which have been grafted with a branch of a male tree so that only one tree need be planted. In commercial plantings one male tree is planted for every 12 females. Trees should be allowed a spacing of 20–26 ft (6–8 m). Pistachio cultivars are grafted onto the more vigorous **Chinese Pistachio** *P.chinensis,* or preferably the Verticillium resistant rootstock *P. integerrima*. Trees are slow to come into bearing, producing lightly in the fifth year but not reaching full productivity until the fifteenth year. The fruits are deep red and wrinkled, somewhat like a ripe olive, and are arranged in grapelike clusters. When the nuts are ripe, the husk around the shell loosens and the nuts will shake out. A groundsheet should be placed under the tree to catch them.

Trees are planted in spring, taking some care when handling the plants as the grafts are unusually easy to knock at this stage. They have very specific requirements for optimum production and require a district where the winters are sufficiently cold to break bud dormancy, yet the summers are long and hot. Their chill requirement is between 600–1,500 hours. The trees have comparable cold resistance to almonds, but with an advantage in that they flower approximately two weeks later than almonds and are less likely to be damaged by frosts. They are extremely drought resistant. Much of the southern half of the Australian continent is suited to their cultivation, and parts of California are also growing pistachios. The world's major producers however are all in the pistachio's area of origin, Iran being the largest single producer.

Pistachios require full sun and a deep, well drained soil that retains moisture. Watering should be deep and occasional, once the trees are established. High alkaline soils are tolerated. The trees should be fed with rock dusts and light organic fertilizing. They do not need high nitrogen inputs. There is a tendency to biennial production which also occurs in areas in which the pistachio is native, and indicates that it is a natural phenomenon, not caused by crop management problems.

Pistachio nuts are eaten raw, or roasted and salted, and are also used

in a wide range of confectionery, baking, and to flavor ice-cream. A superb pistachio marmalade is an Iranian specialty food. Pistachio oil, butter and paste are also produced.

Pistachio nut trees are slow to come into bearing. The fruits are deep red and wrinkled and are arranged in grape like clusters.

Recommended Cultivars

'Kerman' — This female cultivar originated in California as a chance seedling arising from an importation from Iran. The nuts are large, and of high quality. The shells split easily to allow easy opening.

'Peters' — This is used as a male pollinator. It originated in California.

Pistachio nuts are eaten raw or roasted and salted, and are also used in a wide variety of confectionery.

The Pome Fruits

Apple *Malus x domestica;* **Asian Pear** *Pyrus pyrifolia* var. *culta;* **Crabapple** *Malus* spp.; **Medlar** *Mespilus germanica;* **Pear** *Pyrus communis;* **Quince** *Cydonia oblonga*

Of all the fruit trees, there are few more rewarding than the pome fruits. Without exception they are very long-lived, the lifetime of some being measured in centuries. Nothing could be simpler to manage with a little organic know-how. At a time when we are trying to replant the earth to reduce carbon dioxide levels, planting an orchard of such long lived and rewarding plants is an ideal choice for the home garden. And in an age of uncertainty, the seasonal bounty of fruit bowing branches with their weight has the same comfort and reassurance as a well stocked larder.

If the pome fruits are long lived, they also take a while to come into production. The first good harvests from apples are often not until their third or fourth year (although you should get a small harvest in the second year), and of pears in their seventh. Some say that it is too long to wait, and put the idea of an orchard aside. But if you don't plant this year, in four years' time you still won't be eating fabulous fruit under your own trees. An hour or so of work each year is all it takes for endless baskets of spray-free fruit.

Above: Apple blossom time.

Below: The magic of a small orchard is within the reach of any organic gardener, whatever size garden they own.

Apple

Malus x domestica   Zones 3–9

Apples as a group are very tolerant of a wide range of soils and climates. There are even apples that have been

bred to succeed in warm temperate to sub-tropical conditions, and despite their very low chill requirement they are crisp, large, and have good flavor. However, most apples have been bred for cooler climate areas. They are the most popular fruit in the United States, Europe and Australasia. 'Cox's Orange Pippin', for instance, is deservedly England's most loved apple. Choosing the right cultivars for your climate and soil is vital. An apple of highest repute in one area can perform indifferently in another. There are literally thousands of cultivars available, but your local nursery, and also local farmers and gardeners, will be able to quickly narrow the choice for you, based on their local experience. But whatever your choice, apple trees that are planted now may still be supplying harvests for many generations into the future.

In recent times there has been a great resurgence of interest in the heirloom apple cultivars. Offerings in shops are so limited and standardized, often based more on appearance than flavor. The range of apples known to 19th century and early 20th century apple lovers was vastly larger than today. The subtle flavors of apples and their cooking and eating qualities were at least as well appreciated as their appearance. In fact some rather unprepossessing kinds were near the top of the list for many cooks and connoiseurs. Subtle and amazing flavors—of pineapple, bananas, apricots, strawberries, roses, cloves, spices, wine, nuts, and berries—were treasured. The flesh was white, sometimes like snow as in the 'Snow Apple' syn. 'Fameuse' (France, 1739), or pale golden, or suffused rose pink. To read the beautifully illustrated *The Apples of New York*, one of the best and most extensive records we have of apples of the past, is to mourn for what might have been. As apples are so long lived, considerable success has been had in finding and gathering

these older apples into collections around the world. Nevertheless, probably 60% of the apples grown in apple districts in the past are now lost. Many homes had their own orchard, and it was common to have 15 or more cultivars, all with their special flavors and uses. In the last 50 years, 300 of the 500 cultivars once grown have disappeared.

Apples can be divided into three groups on the basis of usage: sweet or fresh eating apples, cider apples which are usually too tart for eating out of hand, and cooking apples. Good cooks further distinguish between apples that hold their shape when sliced and cooked, and those which disintegrate. Many cultivars find use in more than one group, for instance fresh eating and sweet cider making. If the huge diversity in shapes and colors in the old apples, and their sometimes tender flesh that travelled poorly made them undesirable for standard fruit growers, it made them ideal for home gardeners.

Apples are also popular for their reputation as health protectors and are quite variable in nutritional content according to the cultivar, and where and how it was grown. But it is the high pectin content which appears responsible for its therapeutic effects. The juice of fresh apples is a long recommended cure for constipation. Apple vinegar—fermented apple

It can be three years before an apple tree bears significant fruit.

Apples which are not good enough for eating can easily be made into delicious pies.

juice—has long been a popular folk cure for reducing arthritic pain and is believed to act on the crystallized deposits formed in the joints of the body. A number of laboratory trials have looked at the effect of pectin on levels of cholesterol and tryglycerides in the blood.

Growing and Harvesting

Apples are propagated by grafting them on to a suitable stock. They will not come true from seed. The seed can be removed from the fruit, placed in a ziplock plastic bag with some damp sand, and placed in the refrigerator for 10–12 weeks. At the end of that time, the pips can be planted in a seed raising mixture in individual small pots, and will germinate in a couple of weeks. They should be repotted when they outgrow their pot, always moving to a slightly larger pot. Some seedlings will be weak and can be eliminated. When the seedlings are 1 year old and well hardened off, they can be planted outside. Use them as a hedge,

The fruit of the 'Blue Pearmain' can be beautiful in colour but the tree is not a reliable cropper.

or as a living screen. If nothing else they will be pretty in spring, but there is a chance that a really exciting new apple may be among them.

If this is all too much effort, consider tossing apple cores around the edge of your land! In places with fairly cool winters, the seed will be naturally stratified during winter and at least a few plants should come up. Some of the world's most successful apples were discovered in gardens as seedlings. For instance, **'Granny Smith'** occurred in a Sydney back yard in 1850 although the coast of New South Wales is noted for its balmy climate.

Despite these possibly profitable diversions with seed raising, if land is limited you will want to ensure that the orchard space is devoted entirely to highly desirable types of apples. In large gardens, apples would be grafted one cultivar to one stock. But multiple grafted trees will ensure good pollination, and allow a large variety of apples to be grown in a small place. Some specialist apple nurseries will multigraft to your requirements, from 3–7 cultivars per stock. Some can offer choices of cultivars in the hundreds, many of them rare heirlooms.

It is true to say that the choice of stock is almost as important as the choice of apple cultivar. The correct choice of stock can make a real difference to the success of your orchard. There are 3 main categories of stocks: standard, semi-dwarf, and dwarf. The first allows the cultivar to express its full potential height which may be very large indeed; the semi-dwarf stock reduces its height to about 60–75% of its potential; and the dwarf creates a small, easily managed tree about 50% of the potential size. Dwarf stocks are particularly favored for small gardens. They come into the fruit-bearing stage of their life sooner, and they are easier to prune and harvest, and to maintain good pest and disease inspection and control. A higher density planting can also be achieved, allowing more variety of planting in a small space.

Different stocks suit different soils and climates. Discuss the type of stock and its suitability for your garden with your supplier. Many rootstocks are available, and it is part of the science of plant propagation to design trees that will perform as required by manipulating the rootstock. To give examples, the rootstock designated M 27 is extremely dwarfing, resulting in trees that are no more than 6 ft (1.8 m) high. M9 and M26 are dwarfing and trees reach a height of 10–12 ft (3–4 m), while MM106 is semi-

dwarfing, producing trees that reach 13–18 ft (4–5.5 m). Rootstocks also control other factors, including adaptability to different soils and onset of cropping. For instance the much used MM106 allows trees to be grown on quite poor soils as it rapidly creates a strong root system. The tree also comes into bearing early, often in two years.

In choosing cultivars for your garden, consider the spread of your harvest, as well as the purposes your apples must serve. Apples fall into 3 categories; early season harvesting, mid-season, and late season, the last

Although apples can be grown from seed they are more usually propagated by grafting.

The all-purpose 'Granny Smith' apple with green skin, firm, crisp flesh, and a tart flavor. Named after Maria Ann Smith an Australian gardener who developed it.

generally being very good keeping types that may keep through the winter until early spring, and which are often of excellent quality and rich flavor. In general, it is desirable to have a good spread of maturity dates, so that you can enjoy eating your own apples for much of the year. If you have special requirements for multigrafted or heirloom cul-tivars, make sure you place an order well ahead of time with a firm that custom buds trees. Some apples are multi-purpose, like 'Golden Delicious', but most have a specific use.

Make sure you have chosen a range of cultivars so that some will make sauce, some will bake well, and some will be good for fresh eating. If you are thinking of trying your hand at cider-making, include 2–3 cultivars suited for that purpose.

Plan the orchard before you begin to dig holes. The trees should be there for a long time to come, so it is well worth while calculating the eventual size of each tree and the cross pollinator(s) required, and then working out a design on paper to optimize the space available. Apples are self sterile and require a cross pollinator. (A few require two cross pollinator cultivars.) Your supplier will work out the pollinator requirements for the apples of your choice. For home use, a cross pollinator is often budded onto the stock together with the desired cultivar.

Warm brick walls can provide an ideal place to train ornamental espaliered plants. At night, the walls re-radiate the warmth they have absorbed from the sun during the day. Trees on such walls can ripen fruit considerably earlier, and marginal fruit cultivars for a district may flourish against a warm wall

where freestanding specimens would not. Espaliered fruit allow even ripening of the fruit as they are well exposed to warmth and light, and even a very small garden can accomodate them. When you have drawn your orchard plan to scale, the holes for the young trees can be prepared. The holes should be at least 6 in (15 cm) wider and deeper than the rootball of the tree.

Plants may be supplied bare-rooted or container planted. Cut back any broken roots before planting, making a clean cut. If trees have been supplied bare rooted, the roots will have been damaged and shortened in the process of being dug. The diminished root system will be unable to sustain the top of the tree in the first few months of growth, and the top should be cut back proportionally with a sharp pair of secateurs, making the cut about $^2/_5$ in (1 cm) above an outfacing bud. Apart from breaking up the soil dug from the holes, and adding about half a spadeful of granite, greensand, or basalt dust, resist the temptation to enrich the soil. The tree needs to make an active effort to send out roots in search of moisture and food in order to establish in the ground. Place the rootball in the hole so that it is at the same depth in its new soil as it was in the soil it was produced. Fill the hole in with the soil and gently firm the soil down. Standing on the filled hole and jumping is an interesting and often observed technique but can break the root framework. Water thoroughly. Keep adding water until bubbles no longer emerge from the filled hole.

'Root rock' is an important cause of slow establishment of trees. As wind blows, the plant moves in the ground and tender new roots moving out into the soil are broken. It can be like a continuous form of root pruning for the tree, and impedes its ability to establish well and explore adequately for water and nutrients.

A double staking is preferred. Hammer a 6 ft (1.8 m) stake on either side of the young tree about 10 in (25 cm) from it. Loop a tie to the tree from each stake, so that the tree is evenly and firmly strained between the two ties. The material that the ties are made from needs to be flexible. Professional webbing is available, but sections of old pantyhose will do very well. Never use rope or twine. It will rub through and partially ringbark the

'Starkspur Compac Mac' has been bred as a singled stemmed columnar form, enabling it to be grown close to walls and fences.

A staked 'McIntosh Rogers'. Staking your fruit tree will reduce root rock and give the tree a better chance of survival.

A Step-over or Horizontal Cordon. This pruning technique produces a very attractive garden border which is covered in blossom in spring and fruit in autumn.

each year just two horizontal branches are allowed to grow, with all others being removed. The tree is stopped once it has reached a maximum of 6 lateral branches. All side shoots are pruned away each year to maintain the shape. The beautiful candelabra shape is created by allowing each lateral branch to grow one upward pointing branch. All upward branches are then stopped at the same level.

Once established and maintained, they become a very attractive structural feature of the garden. Free standing espaliers make charming garden screens. A variation on the espalier is the very simple Step-over or Horizontal Cordon, in which the top is removed and just one lateral is allowed to grow, trained at a height of about 1–2 ft (30–60 cm) above the ground along a wire. When it meets the trunk of the next apple planted in the row, the tip is grafted to the trunk. An alternative idea is a Double Horizontal Cordon in which only two lateral branches emerging from the same position on the trunk and again about 1–2 ft (30–60 cm) above the ground are trained along the wire in opposite directions. When the tips meet with the growing tips of the next apple plants, they are grafted together. These cordons are used as a permanent, very attractive and productive garden border; covered in blossom in spring and fruit in fall, they are ideal space savers for the small garden. Single whip latticework is also very ornamental. A row of yearling trees is pruned to a low bud which will grow away as a single lateral at the desired angle of about 45° from the vertical, and all in the same plane. Alternatively, the one year tree is again cut down, but a pair of opposite buds are allowed to grow away to form a letter 'Y'. By repeating a planting of these in a row, spaced 1 ft (30 cm) apart, the branches form a latticework pattern.

Very pretty and rapidly formed freestanding screens and windbreaks

tree. Once the tree is firmly established in its site, the support can be removed.

Weed regularly in the spring, and as soon as the soil has warmed, mulch the tree out to the dripline, keeping the mulch away from the trunk. Water on a regular basis. Failure to supply adequate watering means that the trees come into bearing at least a year later, even if the plant survives. After 4 years, the tree should need supplementary watering only under stressful conditions. Once the tree is established, it can be fed around the dripline with compost, and mulch should be regularly checked and supplemented as it will not only gradually compost down, but the dripline of the tree will be expanding. A couple of spadefuls of rock dust placed around the dripline annually will supplement the mineral supply.

Pruning

The first few years are critical to the shaping of the tree. Trees planted against walls are trained so as to make a two dimensional framework that will stand flat to the wall. The principle is to train the tree into an open framework pruned regularly into a flat plane. Espaliers can be very ornamental and the art of espaliering is ancient. Various patterns such as fans and candelabras and interknotted branches, symbolic of love in the home, have been used. In general, can be constructed using this same technique using 6 ft (1.8 m) lengths of white willow from which all but the top buds have been removed. They root very easily if pushed into damp soil. They are evenly planted in a row, about 12 in (30 cm) apart and trained to cross and form a diamond pattern. This idea was popular in the medieval period and was a major feature at the 1992 Floriade in Holland where living tunnels and even houses of willows had been woven from much to the delight of children. Since then it has once again become a fashionable—and useful—garden art. Temporary wire supports are usually provided for shaping the various patterns of espaliers. Fans are created by training a number of basal branches into a fan shape, tying them to wires for support. All other branches are regularly removed.

In the regular orchard area, the same objective of opening the tree to sunlight and good air movement is most usually achieved by cutting the central leader, the main stem, back

and allowing usually 5 side shoots to grow out evenly from the main trunk. Once the vase shape has been established, an annual pruning is carried out in late winter to remove secondary branches and tip back the original frame branches. Nothing else needs to be done.

'Starkspur Supreme Red Delicious' form an impressive windbreak.

White willow can be used to form freestanding windbreaks between trees.

Pests and Diseases

Orchards well supplied with appropriate rock dusts, well mulched, and watered as required, are considerably less likely to be subject to pest and disease attack. Only a couple of generations ago, almost everyone grew their home garden apples organically, and expected good harvests. The problems found in large orchards are also less likely to occur in small domestic plantings due to isolation factors. However apples have acquired a number of pests during their thousands of years of domestication.

The use of many sprays in the commercial orchards constantly upset the natural balance, suppressing one insect problem only to allow another to reach serious levels of infestation. A balanced ecosystem with plenty of natural diversity such as in an organically managed home garden does much to reduce such problems. Choosing disease resistant cultivars is also a practical measure to take.

A number of natural predators—including various wasps, spiders, and birds—are helpful. Biological controls are currently being sought for most pests. Apple scab is one of the major problems and the currently approved organic measure is to spray with a lime, sulphur and copper mix. Codling moths are controlled with pheromones. These are available commercially and, diffused through the orchard, give off a scent which mimics that of the female moth. The bewildered male moths can no longer detect where the females are and fail to complete the breeding cycle. Companion planting has had some successes too in improving apple tree health. Suitable plants are chives, nasturtiums, garlic, and wallflowers. With a mulch system in place, it is simple to plant a few of these near the tree.

When Do Apples Ripen?

The flavor of unripe apples is sharp and sour, but also surprisingly starchy. As an apple ripens, the starch in its tissue is converted into sweet sugars and those aromatic characters we seek in a good apple develop. Apples may be fully grown and fully red, in other words fully matured, yet not also fully ripe. There are a few tests that can be applied, but no single test is infallible. It is the answer you get from a combination of tests that is most accurate as a predictor of ripeness. The apple stalk should separate with reasonable ease from the branch, the seed in the centre of a sample apple should have turned brown (although that isn't always true for early harvested apple cultivars), and the fruit should 'give' slightly when squeezed, unlike unripe fruit which is hard.

Apples are harvested when fully ripe on the tree, unlike European pears. The apple should be held in the palm of the hand and then twisted off the branch. Holding the apple with your fingers will cause bruising. The worst offence is to rip the spur that the apple is attached to off the tree. Fruit are borne on the same spur branch year after year, provided that it remains undamaged. Treat early season cultivars as apples to be used for immediate fresh eating. Mid-season cultivars can be stored or eaten fresh. Apples for winter storage should be picked when fully ripe, taking care not to bruise the fruit, and either stored in single layers, or individually wrapped in tissue paper and then packed in layers, ideally at about the temperature of the domestic refrigerator, 39°F (4 °C). Slatted boxes were traditionally used for this purpose, and wooden crates make a good substitute.

Recommended Cultivars

The list provided below is short, but each apple listed is exceptional of its kind. If it is a suitable choice for your soil and area, then it will not disappoint.
'Ashmead's Kernel' — This apple has a very intense, nutlike flavor with a balance of sweet and tart, and is usually rated among the very finest—if not as the finest— flavored heirloom apple in the U.K. according to the taste tests at the Royal Horticultural Society in the U.K. It dates to c. 1780, and improves with storage.
'Baldwin' — The 'Baldwin' has been grown in Massachusetts since 1740. It is a bright red late cultivar stored for winter eating. The tree is long lived and vigorous, tolerant of a variety of soils and widely adapted.

Named after Loammi Baldwin, the 'Baldwin' apple is sharp tasting and juicy. It was highly regarded for its keeping qualities in the days before refrigeration.

'Beauty of Bath' — This is an excellent early dessert type with golden skin flushed with red, and sweet, juicy flesh. It keeps poorly.
'Bramley's Seedling' — This is one of the greatest cooking apples, very large, yellowish-green with broken brown and red stripes, and perfect for pies, tarts, and sauce. It was released in 1809 in England and remains that country's favorite cooking apple. It needs two pollinators.
'Caville Blanc d'Hiver' — This is one of the great dessert apples of France, tasting of spice and banana, with tender, sweet flesh. It dates to 1590.

'Caville Blanc d'Hiver'. This winter apple is medium to large, and has pale green skin speckled with light red on the sunny side. It has flattish sides, a banana-like fragrance, and more Vitamin C than an orange.

'Cornish Gilliflower' — Still grown by collectors around the world, this apple was named for the delightful fragrance of clove pinks (or gilliflowers as they were called in the Elizabethan era) that the tender flesh emits. It was mentioned by Shakespeare. If you prefer the scent of roses to carnations, **'Chenango Strawberry'** (c. 1850), tender skinned and ideal for dessert eating or apple sauce would be your choice.

'Cortland' — Bred in 1898 in New York, with a large, dark red fruit, this is an excellent fresh eating apple, perfect in salads, and also good for cooking. It is of very high quality in all respects.

'Cox's Orange Pippin' — This is an excellent late apple with superb flavor and excellent keeeping properties. It can be used in every way, and is considered the finest flavored eating apple in England.

'Esopus Spitzenberg' — This was Thomas Jefferson's favorite apple. It has crisp, sweet, tender pale golden flesh renowned for its rich, complex, fruit and spicy flavor. It keeps well too. Originating in 1790 in Esopus, New York, it is not the easiest apple to grow, but where it suits, it is a treasure.

'Fameuse' syn. Snow, Snow Apple — Reputedly bred in Canada in the late 17th century and introduced into the United States in 1730, and later into Australasia and Europe, this is a small to medium apple with glowing deep red skin and purest white flesh tinged pink near the skin. It is popular with florists for arrangements, and is sweet and juicy.

'Golden Delicious' — From West Virginia in 1890, thought to be a seedling of **'Grimes Golden'**, introduced in 1900, with large, pure golden fruit with a unique flavor and wonderful aroma. The flesh is firm and crisp. It can develop scab.

'Golden Russet' — This apple was known to George Washington, and originated in 1804 in England. It is the complete all-rounder, excellent for eating, cooking and making cider, and also keeps well.

The 'Cortland' has fine-grained juicy flesh which stays white longer than most other apples. Ideal for snacking, salads, and baking.

The flesh is firm and yellow, the skin russeted and golden, and the flavor rich and aromatic.

'Gravenstein' — This was a favorite in Northern California and also became a favorite in the orchards of Tasmania and on the Granite Belt of South East Queensland. It is a wonderful, crisp, fine flavored apple but needs 'to be eaten close to the tree'. It remains a favorite for local markets.

'Grimes Golden' — Originating in West Virginia prior to 1804, this was one of the parents of **'Golden Delicious'** — The fruits are of excellent quality, medium to large, with clear yellow skin and yellow, crisp, richly aromatic, juicy, sprightly flavored flesh. The tree is productive and vigorous.

'Jonathan' — Introduced in 1826 by a grower in New York, and a market leader, this apple is a benchmark for rich, true apple flavor. It is scab free.

'Laxton's Fortune' — Bred in 1904 by Laxton Bros., this is considered the finest of apples for Scotland, and hence ideal for cold districts. It is a richly flavored dessert apple and is scab resistant.

'Lord Lambourne' — From England, and raised in 1907 by the famed fruit breeder Thomas Laxton of Bedford, this is a fine, large dessert cultivar of perfect rounded shape.

'McIntosh' — This apple was first grown in Ontario in 1796. It is an excellent, juicy, aromatic dessert apple.

'Margil' — Renowned for its sugary, richly aromatic yellow, firm flesh, and cultivated since c. 1750, this English cultivar is also a good keeping apple, with orange-red skin with dark red stripes.

'Michelin' — This is an exceptional cider apple with highly colored, perfumed, richly flavored juice.

'Northern Spy' — Released in 1800 in New York, this is a good baking type but suitable for all uses other than drying, and with excellent cold resistance.

'Stayman Winesap' — An excellent cooking apple, with a delicious spicy taste, introduced in 1866.

The 'Michelin' apple is prone to mildew but its sweet, mildly astringent flavor makes it ideal for cider production.

The 'Tower of Glamis' apple originates from Scotland and is used for culinary purposes.

The 'D'Arcy Spice' apple was named after the English village in which it was first found and is a late russet variety which is ideal for baking.

Other recommended cultivars

'**Belle de Boskoop**' (Holland, 1856); '**Blue Pearmain**' (New England, 1833); '**Canada Reinette**' (Canada, 1817); '**Chenango Strawberry**' (New York, 1800s); '**Court Pendu Plat**' (France, 1613); '**D'Arcy Spice**' (England, 1785); '**Kandil Sinap**' (excellent dessert type, Turkey, 1887); '**King David**' (cider apple, Georgia, 1893); '**King of Tompkin's County**' (excellent dessert and cooking and sauce apple, New York, c. 1730); '**Kingston Black**' (cider apple, England, 1820); '**Tower of Glamis**' (Scotland); '**Twenty Ounce**' (huge premier cooking apple, New York, 1822); '**Tom Putt**' (excellent cider apple, England, 1700s); '**Wagener**' (New York, 1791); '**Wolf River**' (very large baking and pie apple, Wisconsin, 1875); '**Liberty**' (good general disease resistance, including to scab).

Note

For those who would like to explore the world of heirloom apples and taste the wonderful flavors that were once readily available, there are a number of options including: Petty's Orchard in the Yarra Valley in Victoria, Australia; the Royal Horticultural Society's National Collection of apples in Brogdale, U.K. which contains apples the Romans would have known (the Apple Festival with more than 300 heirloom cultivars for taste-testing is held in mid-October each year); the fruit orchards of Monticello in Virginia, once the home of Thomas Jefferson; White Oak Cidery (organically managed, including a large collection of Perry pears in Newberg Orlando); Tower Hill Garden in Boylston, Massachusetts with 120 19th century cultivars on display; the amazing preservation farm of heirloom apples at the Seed Saver's Exchange in Iowa which houses 700 different 19th century apples; Weston's Apple Orchard Herefordshire, U.K. with its rare collection which now functions as a foundation, and websites 'Applesource', and 'Tree-mendous', both of which contain a large number of relevant links. A website 'Orchard Trail', part of the 'Apple Journal' site, at <www.applejournal.com/trail.htm> is an amazing compilation of thousands of small family owned fruit orchards around the world. Wherever you visit, you can find places to see and taste our amazing heritage of fruits.

Asian Pear

Pyrus pyrifolia var. *culta*   Zones 4–9

Asian pears are derived from the somewhat unpromising sand pear or Japanese pear *Pyrus pyrifolia* which produces small, round fruits with a gritty texture. The Manchurian pear has been involved in the breeding of some of the Asian pear cultivars, and some complex hybrids have been created. The Asian pear has been cultivated in China for 3,000 years.

P. pyrifolia is native to central and southern China and has moderate cold hardiness. The Manchurian pear is native to northern China and Siberia and has excellent cold hardiness. Most of the domesticated cultivars are intermediate in cold hardiness. They have also inherited excellent fall coloring of the foliage, making them true three-season trees for the garden.

The Asian pear has been grown in Australia and elsewhere outside of Asia for a century or more, but it attracted real interest for commercial production in the Western world in the 1980s.

Growing and Harvesting

Asian pears are grown in the same manner as European pears in terms of ground preparation, installation, and maintenance. In their harvesting requirements Asian pears are similar to apples. They should be allowed to reach maturity, are harvested when ripe and then stored. Ripening indicators are subtle. When the skin begins to lighten and the fruit lenticels turn brown, the fruit is ready to be picked.

Recommended cultivars

'Chojuro' — This is a very productive cultivar with medium sized fruit that is russeted, and white mildly sweet flesh. The scent and flavor is unique.

'Hosui' — The fruit are medium sized, globular, with a russeted green skin and crisp, sweet. juicy, fine textured flesh. It requires cross pollination.

The term "Asian pear" describes a large group of pear varieties having crisp, juicy fruit. There are three types of Asian pear: round or flat fruit with green to yellow skin; round or flat fruit with bronze-colored skin and a light bronze-russet; and pear-shaped fruit with green or russet skin.

Crabapples can lose their ornamental charm if pests and diseases are not kept under sufficient control.

'Kosui' — The fruit are small to medium sized, russeted and golden. The flesh is quite exceptionally sweet and juicy with a rich flavor. This is Japan's premier cultivar.

'Seigyoku' — This is a highly productive tree with large fruit that are greenish yellow, with sweet, crisp, tender white flesh.

Crabapple

Malus spp.   Zones 4–9

Crabapples are species closely related to apples. They are a group of beautiful ornamental trees which offer spectacular spring flowering with white, pink or wine colored petals in single and double flowers, followed by quantities of ornamental fruits. The fruits are tiny in some species, unsuited for culinary use, but provide food for wildlife. In others the fruits may be as large as 2 in (5 cm) in diameter, and are used for making spiced crabapples and for crabapple jelly.

Crabapples are unsuited for culinary use, but provide food for wildlife and spectacular displays of spring flowers.

Growing and Harvesting

Crabapples are tolerant of a wide range of soil types and are particularly adaptable, but prefer a pH of 5.0–6.5. They should be planted in full sun. Unlike apples, crabapples are left to develop their natural form and pruning is restricted to removing any unwanted branches and any suckers that may occur from the stock.

Recommended species and cultivars

'Baskatong' — This is a spectacular and disease resistant cultivar with dark wine-purple buds opening slightly lighter with large, dark purple fruits.

'Gibb's Golden Gage' — This is a very disease resistant cultivar with pink buds opening to single white flowers followed by clear yellow fruits 1 in (2.5 cm) in diameter.

'Indian Summer' — This is a tree to 20 ft (6 m) with rose colored single flowers in spring followed by globe-shaped bright red fruit that are $^3/_4$ in (2 cm) in diameter.

M. *floribunda* — A widely adapted species forming a beautiful ornamental tree to 20 ft (6 m), flowering spectacularly with rose pink buds opening white followed by quantities of gold to amber small fruits relished by birds as the winter approaches.

M. *hupehensis* — This species forms a tree to 20 ft (6 m) high, and a little wider, smothered in pink buds that open white, followed by small $^2/_5$ in (1 cm) gold and red fruits.

M. *sargentii* — This is a large shrub to 8 ft (2.5 m) with rose pink buds opening to fragrant white flowers with masses of tiny, bright red fruit which are much appreciated by birds as winter approaches.

Medlar

Mespilas germanica   Zones 4–9

Like the apple tree which it resembles, the medlar is a member of the family *Rosaceae*. In spring it bears exquisite, large, white single blossoms with deep rose stamens which are as showy as wild roses. Unlike apples, they are self fertile, and the flowers are followed by russeted, plump, round fruits that are classified as pomes, but differ from pears and apples in that the calyx is persistent, resembling a

Medlars have been cultivated since ancient times for their edible fruit.

crown. The small tree is deciduous, and it is only as the leaves fall that the fruit begins to ripen. The first frosts soften the fruit on the tree, a process called 'bletting'. If the fruit is harvested and kept for some time, it has the same effect. The fruits are picked when the leaves are falling, and are stored on a bed of hay in a well ventilated area for up to two months, by which time they are fully softened. The flesh becomes soft, buttery, brown, fragrant, and absolutely delicious even though it looks dubious. They are best eaten fresh, served after a meal with a dessert wine, accompanied only by a small spoon to remove the pulpy contents of the fruit.

Growing and Harvesting

They are grown in the same manner as apples and are remarkably easy to cultivate with no major pests or diseases. Medlars are tolerant of a wide range of soils

Recommended cultivars

'Dutch' — This is a large fruited form on a spreading tree.

'Nottingham' — This is an erect small tree with smaller, but very well flavored, fruits.

'Doyenne du Comice'. A large, juicy, richly flavored pear, with yellowish-green skin covered with speckles and frequently displaying a reddish blush.

Pear

Pyrus communis   Zones 2–9

Pears are one of the most rewarding of all fruit trees, with spectacular displays of snowy blossom in spring, followed by fruiting, and finally a superb fall foliage dispay. Most cultivars tend to be medium to larger trees. Although many are reasonably self fertile, to obtain a good crop a second pear is often planted as a pollinator. Like apples, a tree can be budded with two pear cultivars. Triploid cultivars, on the other hand, have no viable pollen and are reliant on the pollen of two other pollinating cultivars to ensure cropping.

As with apples, pears can be divided into three groups, depending on the purpose they serve. There are dessert pears, cooking pears which can be stored through winter, and perry pears. The last named are used to make perry, a popular drink in Europe similar to apple cider. Giant old trees of cooking pears are the pride of many farms, especially in warm climate areas. The fruit are hard and require long stewing or baking, but the flavor of many is rich and sweet, and they turn a delicate blush pink after the cooking process.

Because pear trees are a substantial size, dwarf stock is often used for smaller gardens.

Growing and Harvesting

Pears are grown in much the same way as apples. They are better adapted to warmer and more humid climates than apples. Pear trees are substantial in size and require deep and fairly good soils to grow well. A reasonably sheltered, sunny place should be selected to plant trees as the early blossom is damaged by late frosts and by wind. An east facing slope is ideal. Dwarfing stocks are available for pears grown in smaller gardens, and trees will then reach a more modest 13–16 ft (4–5 m). In warmer areas, pears can be planted out in fall and winter, but in cool districts planting is best done in very early spring while the trees are still fully dormant.

When setting a bare rooted plant out, follow the guidelines in *apples*. One year old plants should be cut back to about 3 ft (1 m) when planting to allow the formation of a good shape. Five to a maximum of 8 strong lateral branches are allowed to develop. These become known as 'scaffolds'. Once the scaffolds are established, light shaping is all that is required for the tree thereafter. The only pruning required as the tree ages is the removal of any suckers and any storm or wind damaged wood.

Pears should not be fed a lush diet of manures. A continuous straw mulch can be used, kept away from the trunk, and extended to the dripline, with the addition of rock dust every few years to the dripline area, and wood ashes scattered around annually. Where fireblight is a problem, as it is in Europe and the United States, it poses a major fungal problem causing the trees to look scorched. There is no known organic treatment, and the only thing to do is regularly inspect trees from spring onward and remove infected wood along with some sound wood and burn it. Cut back into at least 6 in (15 cm) of good wood. The knife or saw used should be thoroughly sterilized in alcohol or 10% bleach after each cut is made.

Whereas apples are picked when fully ripened on the tree, pears are best picked when fully matured in size, but still hard. They are stored in a single layer, in the light.

Recommended cultivars

'Anjou' — This is a mid-season cultivar bearing medium to large fruit with blushed pale green skin.

The flesh is very fine flavored and sweet. It is a good storing cultivar.

'Beurré Bosc' — This is an elegant, elongated cultivar with a russeted skin and a superb, juicy, melting texture, with richly aromatic, sweet juices. It is a late cultivar, and makes a large tree to almost 25 ft (8 m). It is quite cold tender.

'Concorde' — was raised at East Malling and is a cross between **'Doyenne du Comice'** and **'Conference'**. It is similar in appearance to conference but slightly less elongated. The flesh is very juicy, and firm.

'Conference' — This was released by the great fruit breeder Thomas Rivers of Sawbridgeworth in Hertsfordshire, England in 1885. The fruits are large, very elongated, and golden green with brown russeting. They are juicy and of excellent flavor. It was exhibited with great success in the National Pear Conference in 1885, hence the name.

A display of 'Beurré Bosc', 'Red Williams' and 'Bartlett' pears. Pears are best picked when fully matured in size, but still hard.

A small, russet-colored fruit with a sweet, spicy flavor, the Seckel's firm flesh makes it excellent for both cooking and canning.

Doyenne du Comice — Raised in Anger in the Loire Valley in France in 1858, this is the Rolls Royce of pears, juicy, meltingly tender, and richly flavored. The fruits are large, rounded, greenish-gold to gold, and delicately blushed. It is self fertile, but an irregular bearer. It is a mid-season cultivar for fresh eating.

'Seckel' — This is a very fine cultivar, mid–to late season, with small, rounded fruits of delightful flavor. It is particularly good for cooking. The tree is very vigorous and productive, very cold hardy, and is sometimes self-sterile, needing a pollinator.

'Williams' Bon Chretien syn. Bartlett — Known around the world as 'Williams', this excellent commercial pear acquired the name 'Bartlett' in the United States where it is produced in large quantities. The fruit are large, green turning golden when fully ripe and very juicy. A good keeper, it is a widely adaptable cultivar, forming a large, upright tree. It is only very modestly cold hardy. It requires cross pollinators, and 'Anjou' and 'Beurre Bosc' are among those commonly used. The original name translates as 'Williams' Good Christian'.

'Winter Nellis' — As its name suggests, this is a winter keeping, very late pear with small, rounded fruit that are slightly russeted. They are exceptionally juicy and richly flavored when fully ripened.

Quince
Cydonia oblonga   Zones 6–9

Quinces are one of the most ancient fruits. They are native to the area from Iran to the Caspian Sea, and were very popular in ancient Greece and Rome. In fact, supping from cooked quinces was a part of marriage ceremonies long ago, and the fruit was dedicated to the goddess Aphrodite. Quinces grow only in mild

The flesh of the quince is hard, and is never eaten raw. Instead, the fruits are stewed, taking on the texture of firm pears,

climates, and have fairly similar climatic requirements to peaches. Depending on the cultivar, the plants vary from a large shrub to a small tree. The solitary flowers are large, single, and delicately beautiful in spring. The fruits are large to very large, resembling lumpy pears, and are golden yellow when fully ripened. The flesh is hard, and is never eaten raw. Instead, the fruits are stewed, taking on the texture of firm pears, and having a delicate rose and pear fragrance. They are sometimes combined with apples in pies, to which they lend their delicate fragrance. Quince jelly, made from the fruit, is another gourmet treat.

Growing and Harvesting
Quinces are commonly propagated by aerial layering or by suckers. The trees are slow to come into bearing, with light crops at about 4 years of age and heavy cropping beginning at about 8 years af age. Quinces are self fertile. Little other maintenance is

required and the trees, which have a naturally open pattern, need only gentle shaping.

Quinces particularly like high clay, heavy soil conditions with a well drained slight slope. Like pears, they should not be fed a rich organic diet. But they do appreciate both potassium and phosphorus and wood ashes and appropriate rock dusts can be applied from time to time to supply these elements.

Recommended cultivars
'Champion' — This is a large, pear shaped, golden fruit with a mild flavor. Turns pale pink when cooked.

'Orange Quince' — This is a large, irregularly shaped, fruit of excellent flavor and fragrance.

'Pineapple' — This is a medium sized, pear-shaped cultivar with good flavor.

'Rea's Mammoth' — This is an irregularly shaped, large fruit with golden skin and flesh which has a rich fragrance and flavor.

The quince 'Burbank' was bred by Luther Burbank and has large, smooth skinned fruit best used for drying and cooking

Stone Fruits

American Plum *Prunus nigra, P. americana,*
P. hortulana, P. munsoniana; **Apricot**
P. armeniaca; **Cherry** *P. avium, P. cerasus;*
Damson and **Bullace** *P. insititia;* **European**
Plum *P. x domestica;* **Japanese Plum**
P. salicina; **Mexican Bird Cherry** *P. salicifolia;*
Peach and **Nectarine** *P. persica;* **Plumcot**
P. domestica x armeniaca; **Sloe** *P. spinosa*

Stone fruits can be a demanding crop
to grow, even for the most dedicated
organic gardener. The fragile fruits of
the plum, cherry and apricot are easily
bruised, and early or late frosts can
damage buds, roots and stems. They
are also require the right soil balance
and growing temperatures to flourish.
However, the pleasures that these
fruits can bring are enormous. Because
they are delicate and perishable, the
home-grown, fresh-picked fruits
always taste far better than their
commercial equivalent, which may
have been picked many days earlier.

The stone fruits are so-called
because they have large pits or stony
seeds. They are particularly susceptible to brown rot, which first
appears on the twig of the plant
but later appears as a small brown
spot on the fruit. These spots can
eventually cover the entire fruit,
turning the flesh hard and brown,
and causing the fruit to drop from
the tree.

American Plum

Prunus nigra, P. americana, P. hortulana,
P. munsoniana   Zones 2–9

A number of cold-hardy American
species have undergone selection or a
degree of hybridization (usually with
the Japanese plum *P. salicina*). Some
of these can be used in extremely cold
areas and will take temperatures as
low as an incredible –50°F (–45°C).
Particularly valuable in Canada, they
are grown in the same way as
European plums.

Recommended Cultivars
'Dandy' — This is a prolifically
   bearing Canada Black plum *P. nigra*
   selection from Saskatchewan, with
   early ripening, medium-sized,
   golden fruit blushed red, and very
   good fresh eating qualities.
'Dropmore' syn. 'Dropmore Blue' — This
   is a vigorous and cold-hardy
   cultivar from Manitoba, with
   medium to large, purple-red fruit, a
   dark grape bloom and thick, sweet,

*Flowering peaches
generally produce small,
hard fruit that are of
little use for eating.*

yellow flesh used mainly for fresh eating, but also for preserves.

'Grenville' — This very cold-hardy hybrid of *P. nigra* from Ottawa has large fruits with golden-yellow skin suffused with red, and high quality golden flesh for fresh eating.

Other recommended American plum cultivars include **'Monitor'** (a hybrid of *P. americana*), **'Aitken'** (*P. nigra*), **'Assiniboine'** (*P. nigra*), **'Patterson's Pride'** (a hybrid of *P. nigra*), the hardy, very productive, good quality freestone **'Wolf'** (*P. americana*), and the superb, apricot-flavored, hardy cultivar **'La Crescent'** syn. 'Golden Minnesota' (a hybrid of *P. americana*, and sometimes classified as a Japanese plum).

Apricot
Prunus armeniaca   Zones 5–10

Apricots are a richly flavored fruit that have been widely adapted. Cultivars exist for warm through to moderately cold areas. Orchards were largely grown from seedlings until the 19th century. Even today, seedling orchards are common in many of the main apricot growing areas. By growing seedlings, the orchard has greater resistance to disease and the crop has greater vigor, an ideal situation when economic sustainabil-ity and genetic diversity are priorities. On the other hand, the crop will yield over a pro-longed time and the fruit is not uniform, factors that Western farmers dislike. The center of origin of apricots is the area of north-eastern China near the Russian border. Some remark-able variants, which have been known since ancient times, still exist in that area including a very large tree with peach-like leaves and white, apricot-appearing and apricot-tasting fruits. Apricots have been cultivated in China for at least 3,000 years. The major apricot growing countries are all warm climate areas such as Turkey, Iran, Iraq, Syria, Afghanistan, south-ern France, Pakistan, Spain, Italy, Morocco, Australia and California.

Apricots can be divided into those with sweet seeds, which can be substituted for almonds and in some countries are crushed for apricot oil, and bitter-seeded kinds. The seeds of most Mediterranean and Central Asian types are sweet-seeded. The blanched kernels are sometimes known as Chinese almonds. Bitter-seeded stone fruits all contain a group of compounds called cyanogenic glycosides in the seeds, and to some extent in the bark and roots. Apricots are particularly high in these compounds, and have been involved in tumor therapy since the early 6th century, and were used in attempts to regress tumors and ulcers in England in the 17th century. In the 20th century there was a revived interest in bitter apricot seeds, and the drug Laetrile was derived from the seeds. It became a controversial treatment for cancer, although unfortunately clinical trials in the United States showed no benefit.

A number of hybrids have been created by crossing apricots with peaches. The resulting fruits, called Peachcots, are trees similar to apricots in most instances, with the sweet flavor of the peach enriched with apricot. The best form of Peachcot

Mid-summer apricots are richly flavored fruit that can be eaten raw, cooked or dried.

currently is probably **'Bill's'**. A cross was made with the Western Sand Cherry *P.* besseyi to produce the Cherrycot, the best known cultivar of which is named **'Yuksa'**. It was released in 1908 and is very free flowering, with the fruit of an apricot, but with enhanced cold-hardiness. Various crosses have been made with plums resulting in what have been called Plumcots and Pluots. Among the best of these are **'Flavor Delight'**, **'Parfait'** and **'Flavor Queen'**. A natural hybrid with *P. cerasifera* resulted in the Black Apricot or Purple Apricot, with soft, juicy fruits that are purple-black and eaten fresh or used to make conserves.

There are a number of species closely related to apricots. These include the **Japanese Apricot** or **Ume** *Prunus mume*. This species flowers in early winter in mild climates and forms large trees which may have single or double, very fragrant, white or pink flowers. The fruits are eaten raw, candied, preserved in syrup, pickled in salt, flavored and colored with Perilla, and dried to a kind of salty prune called *umiboshi* or salt

Japanese Apricot, Prunus mume 'Geisha', is closely related to apricots and may have single or double, very fragrant, white or pink flowers.

plums that are irresistible, or used to make a sourish conserve and also a liqueur. The Manchurian Apricot is native to northeast Asia and forms a large self-pollinating tree with small fruit that are sweet and juicy.

Growing and Harvesting

Apricots are all self-pollinating. They vary in the number of hours of chilling required, and local advice should be sought as to the best types for your soil and the number of chilling hours in your garden. Some of the list of cultivars below would suit any apricot growing district. Various rootstocks are used to propagate apricots, and semi-dwarfing St Julien A will restrict trees to a height of about 13 ft. (4.5 m). Seedling peach rootstocks are used on lighter soils and can result in larger fruit. Trees grafted to myrobalan plum do best on clay soils. Seedling apricot stocks are best used on heavy soils.

The ground should be prepared as for peaches, and the pH adjusted as close as possible to neutral (7). In cold climates, apricots can be grown in fan shapes trained against a warm wall.

Apricots are intensely flavored and scented, and are all self-pollinating.

In milder climates, they are grown as orchard trees, usually trained into the vase shape as described for peaches. Apricots are particularly vulnerable to dry soils in spring, and attention should be given to regular watering to ensure good crops.

In heavy fruiting seasons, the closely arranged fruit provide an admirable opportunity for brown rot to develop in the humid interstices between the fruits. Hand-thinning the developing fruits when they are about the size of a thumbnail or a little larger will control this problem, and the fruits will be well formed and large. Leave just one developing fruit for every 2–3 in (5.0–7.5 cm) of branch.

Recommended Cultivars

'**Early Golden**' — This is an early ripening freestone with small to medium, plump fruit, very juicy with good flavor. The tree is vigorous and hardy.

'**Goldrich**' — This is an excellent, large-fruited cultivar with firm, deep orange, high quality fruit ideal for cooking and freezing.

'**Harcott**' — This is an early apricot of medium size and rich color that cooks and freezes well.

'**Moorpark**' — This is a fruit of exceptional quality and has long been the benchmark for apricots.

The fruits are large, rounded, deep clear apricot in color, with firm, juicy, sweet, richly flavored fruit. It originated in England in 1760.

'**Royal**' syn. Blenheim — This is a highly productive tree with low chilling requirements. The fruits are large, oval, with golden-apricot flesh that is firm, juicy and aromatic.

'**Sungold**' — This is a high quality, semi-freestone, dessert apricot with rounded fruits that have tender, juicy, aromatic, sweet flesh.

'**Tilton**' — This is an excellent cultivar for colder districts and has a high chill requirement. The fruits are very large, freestone, of moderate flavor, and widely used for drying.

Apricots, Prunus armeniaca 'Story', have been cultivated in China for at least 3,000 years and are now grown in many other parts of the world.

Sweet Cherry, Prunus
avium, *is the major
parent of the cultivated
sweet cherries and can
reach 60 ft (18 m) tall.*

Cherry

Prunus avium, P. cerasus   Zones 3–9

Two closely related wild species have
been involved in the development of
our modern cherries. The first is the
Sweet cherry *Prunus avium*, native to
Europe and the Caucasus, which
includes bird cherries, mazzards and
wild cherries. The second is the Sour
cherry *P. cerasus*, which is native to
Europe and Asia. The two species are

able to cross easily, and sweet
cultivars can be budded onto sour
cherry rootstocks and vice versa.

Three strains of cherries were
developed from the sweet cherries: the
Biggareaus, which are sweet and
relatively firm-fleshed, such as **'Royal
Ann'** syn. 'Napoleon', which is widely
used for maraschino cherries and
canning; the Hearts or Geans, which
are tender-fleshed, very juicy, sweet
and intensely flavored, such as **'Bing'**,
'Cavalier', **'Hedelfingen'**, **'Lambert'**,
'Blackheart' and **'Black Tartarian'**;
and the important group of rootstocks
known as mazzards.

Two strains of cherries were
developed from the species *P. cerasus*:
the amarelles and the morellos.
Amarelles produce pale red fruits
on small trees and include the cultivars **'Carnation'**, **'Richmond'** and
'Montmorency'. Amarelles are also
known as Kentish cherries and in
France as *griottes*. They have colorless juice and light-colored, less acidic
flesh. In France, they find extensive

Japanese Cherry,
Prunus serrulata, *is a
cherry from China that
is a spreading tree,
which bears pink-
flushed white flowers.*

use in confectionery and in the production of the cherry version of *eau-de-vie*. The morellos are dark-skinned and dark-fleshed, and include cultivars such as '**North Star**' and '**English Morello**', which is prized not only in England but also in Tasmania, where it has been grown for almost two centuries.

In addition, a number of inter-specific hybrids have been bred between these two species. These are called Duke or Royal cherries and include cultivars such as the richly flavored '**May Duke**', '**Royal Duke**', '**Belle Magnifique**' and '**Brassington**'.

Cherries are excellent snacking food, with very useful levels of vitamins A, B-complex and C, as well as iron, potassium and sodium. They have long been considered by herbalists to be a good stimulant of the kidneys and colon, and therefore useful in the removal of wastes from the body. The juice has also been recommended to relieve the symptoms of gout and arthritis. The herbalists are right. Research at Michigan State University has established that the juice of tart cherries contains natural anti-inflammatory compounds that are ten times more active than aspirin.

Growing and Harvesting

Most cherries have a fairly high chill factor. For gardeners living in coastal and warmer areas who have long dreamed in vain of growing this fruit, recent breeding research has produced a number of promising new cultivars that are currently being trialed. It may soon be possible to grow good quality cherries in Florida, coastal Queensland and even the Caribbean, places where only a raving optimist would plant currently available cool temperate cultivars. For those in very cold areas, the morello is a good choice, although its uses are largely confined to baking, cooking and wine.

Cultivar selection is critical for success with cherries, and your local

Cherry leaves that have shothole.

supplier of fruit trees will be able to advise on choices for your district, and also on the right pollinators to use if they are required. Most of the *P. cerasus* cultivars are self-fertilizing, while the majority of those belonging to the group *P. avium* require another cultivar for cross-pollination. A warm, friable loam with a pH of 6–8 is ideal, and in general cherries need a well-drained soil that is high in organic matter and minerals, and is moisture retentive.

Cherries are planted in the same manner as for plums *(see below)*, and with the same soil preparation and fertilizing regime. In dry springs, water-ing must be attended to if the crop is to be heavy. An even soil moisture in the last few weeks before harvesting is also important. Sour cherries are perhaps the least affected by pests and diseases of any stone fruit crops. Sweet

Sweet Cherry, Prunus avium, has profuse white flowers that appear in late spring before the leaves and are followed by black-red fruit.

White-fleshed cherries ripen in mid-summer.

cherries are more prone to problems, but by far the biggest problem will come from birds, which love cherries with a passion. Trees need to be netted if your labors are to be rewarded. A diversion for feathered friends can be provided by planting a mulberry nearby. It is the fruit that birds will forsake all others to eat.

Recommended Cultivars

'Bing' — This is a very productive, vigorous, spreading tree that originated in Milwaukee, Oregon, where it was raised by Seth Lewelling in 1875. It has become one of the world's most important cultivars. The fruit are very large, heart-shaped, dark red to almost black, very meaty, rather coarse textured, and sweet. 'Sam' is widely used as a pollinator for 'Bing', as well as for 'Lambert'.

Morello Cherry, Prunus cerasus var. austera, has pendulous branches and bears blackish fruit with purple juice.

'Carnation' — Thomas Jefferson grew this cherry along the Long Walk of the vegetable garden terrace of 'Monticello', so much did he love it. Popular since it was bred in the 17th century, this is an amarelle cherry with medium-sized, rounded fruits, deep red-skinned with some golden-yellow, pale golden-white fleshed. It is a meltingly tender, very juicy freestone, with a wonderfully fresh, clean cherry flavor. The tree is medium sized, ripens in mid to late season, and is moderately productive.

'Early Rivers' — Bred in England in 1872 by Thomas Rivers, this is a very popular cultivar in England, with large to very large, luscious, melting, juicy, deep red cherries of very good quality. It makes a large tree of semi-weeping habit and is only suited to a medium to larger garden.

'Giant' — Luther Burbank, the world-famed plant breeder of Santa Rosa, California, considered this to be one of his finest releases. The tree is large, quick growing and productive. The fruits are large, luscious, very sweet and juicy, and richly flavored. All that a cherry should be, it was released in 1900.

'Hardy Giant' syn. 'Starking Hardy Giant' — This is a dark, large cherry, of high quality, with firm sweet flesh. It ripens early to mid-season. The tree is large, vigorous, a reliable bearer and a good pollinator.

'Merton Biggareau' — This is an outstanding home garden cultivar with large, rounded fruits that are deep red, with an intense rich flavor and tender flesh. The tree is vigorous and spreading. It is not self-fertile. 'Black Tartarian', 'Van', and 'Black Republican' are commonly used as pollinators for this cultivar.

'Stella' — This is the first self-pollinating, high quality, black cherry released, and its qualities make it popular with home gardeners everywhere. The fruits are large, heart-shaped, black-skinned, medium firm, with good flavor. It is a good pollinator of other cherries.

Note

Any of the cherries mentioned in the introduction to this section are very fine cultivars and are recommended for planting. Dwarfing rootstocks such as Gisela 5 are available to tame the exuberance of some larger species, and there are also semi-dwarfing rootstocks available. In small gardens, it is better to choose a couple of dwarf cultivars for the orchard.

Damson *and* Bullace

Prunus insititia   Zones 5–9

These two styles of plums both belong to the species *P. insititia*. Bullaces are the older form and have been found at excavated prehistoric sites in mainland Europe, England and Wales. The small fruit are round to ovoid, and are palatable eaten out of hand. The fruits are normally blue-black in color, but white-fruited forms are in cultivation. Cultivars include **'Black'**, a cooking plum and one of the oldest plums still in cultivation, and **'White'** syn. 'Gold',

with amber fruits heavily covered in a white bloom and having firm, juicy, amber flesh that is slightly sour, but excellent in pies and stewed. More modern cultivars include the early 20th century **'Langley'**; with medium purple fruit, its green flesh is acid but this is balanced with sweetness. They have good cold-hardiness.

Damsons are a class of plums believed to have been derived from the bullaces, but they differ from bullaces in their famously rich, sweet flavor. The fruits are usually oval and purple-black, and they differ from the bullace in having only a light bloom on the fruit. They also differ in that they ripen approximately 6 weeks before bullaces. They are widely used in cool climate areas, where they thrive, for making the prized damson jam, damson jelly and damson wine. About a dozen cultivars are fairly easily obtainable including **'Damson'** syn. 'Blue Damson', a cultivar brought to Italy from Damascus prior to the 1st century B.C. that remains very popular. The tree is upright growing, vigorous and productive.

'Merryweather', from Nottinghamshire in England and released in 1909, has excellent quality clingstone fruit with good damson flavor and is excellent for jams. The tree is spreading and vigorous. They are grown in the same manner as European plums.

European Plum

Prunus x domestica   Zones 5–9

European plums are smaller than those in the widely marketed Japanese plum class, having denser, slightly drier flesh that lends itself to cooking and to drying. The prune cultivars belong to this group, as do all of the great plums used for conserves. The many cultivars are cold-hardy and require a high number of chilling hours to give of their best. They can be divided into

Damson Plums have a famously rich, sweet flavor. The fruits are oval and purple-black.

European Plum, Prunus x domestica 'Stanley', bears large, purple-black, sweet and juicy, yellow-fleshed fruit in mid-season.

might carry on year after year producing remarkable harvests despite receiving no more kindness than simply digging a hole and watering it. As always, the less perfectly a plant fits its ecological niche, and the more highly bred it is, the more effort must be made to care for it, and the more likely the plant is to be vulnerable to diseases. The damsons are the hardiest group of all, and will adapt well to sandy soils.

European plums are more deeply rooted than Japanese plums, which spread their roots more widely, and they appreciate deep, fertile soils. Good drainage is necessary for both groups of plums, and regardless of the soil type they respond to, they thrive on the addition of a large amount of humus supplied in the form of well-rotted manures and compost. The optimum pH range for plums is 6–8. Some plums require pollinators, but by no means all. European plums are more likely to be partially or wholly self-sterile; when ordering your trees, check with your supplier to receive a list of pollinators. Planting a mixed group of plums in the home orchard, if space is available, would almost certainly ensure adequate cross-pollination takes place, provided their blooming times overlap.

As with all stone fruits, 1-year-old trees are the best to buy. The under-stocks most commonly used are peach, almond or myrobalan plum seedlings, St Julien A for semi-dwarfing of cultivars, and Pixy for full dwarfing. The myrobalan has long been favored for nematode resistance and for producing a long-lived tree that is slightly dwarfed and copes well with clay soils. Peach stock is an advantage on poorer or shallower soils.

In milder areas, bare-rooted plums are planted in autumn, and in warm areas in winter. This allows the plants to begin establishment while water stress is low. In cold winter areas, planting is done as soon as the soil

several subgroups, including the delectable gages, the many mirabelles of France that make intensely, almost apricot-flavored preserves and desserts, the prune cultivars, and the richly flavored and far from fairly described 'common plum', which contains most of the greatest classic cultivars of the plum world such as 'Coe's Golden Drop', 'Reine Claude de Bavay', 'Green Gage', 'Prune d'Agen', 'President' and 'Victoria'. The very cold-hardy damsons are usually reserved for the making of exceptional jams and jellies.

Growing and Harvesting

Plum trees are exceptionally easy to grow. They are tolerant of a wide range of soils including heavy soils and clay soils, will tolerate temperatures of 113°F (45°C) and beyond, and some of the old European cultivars can tolerate very cold winters. There are plums for almost every garden, and many individual cultivars have exceptionally wide tolerances. In kinder climates, although it is any-thing but optimal, a poor plum tree

Fruiting plum 'Santa Rosa' in blossom. Planting a mixed group of plums would ensure adequate cross-pollination, provided their blooming times overlap.

can be worked and before bud break. The soil is prepared by clearing the turf (which can be added to the compost heap), in an area about 5 ft (1.5 m) wide, and incorporating into the topsoil generous quantities of rock dusts such as basalt, rock phosphate and granite dust, as well as wood ashes if available. These will release nutrients including phosphorus and potassium to the developing tree over a number of years.

Before planting, make sure you have designed the orchard site and made allowances for the eventual size of your trees. Those one-year whips will one day occupy a space of around 18–23 ft (6–7 m) diameter. A zigzag planting design offers the best packing and pollination pattern for trees in a small space where no tractor access is required. Dig the holes at least 6 in (15 cm) deeper and wider than the opened-out root ball. Use a fork to just loosen the soil at the bottom of the hole without disturbing it. Cut back any damaged or overlong roots with sharp, sterilized secateurs and plant the tree, making sure that it is at the same level in the ground as it was previously grown. Firm the soil gently but well, then water slowly. Continue to water until no air bubbles emerge.

In more exposed situations, provide initial support with a stake on either side and soft looped ties. These can be removed once the plum's root system is re-established. The cleared soil should then be mulched with clean hay.

Plums should be pruned back to about $2^1/_2$ ft (75 cm) when planting, making the cut slightly above a lateral branch. This allows the much-reduced root system to supply adequate water and nutrients to the upper portion of the plant. It balances out supply and demand for the tree. They are then trained in the manner of peaches. Although any orchardist would shudder, where a tree is wanted as much for its beauty and landscaping purposes as for its fruit, the tree can be allowed to assume its natural shape, with some minor intervention to remove any branches rubbing over each other, and to open the inside of the tree to sun and air movement by removing most internal laterals. The fruit is smaller and less easy to harvest, but the technique feels more in accord with nature.

Whether using minimal pruning or orchard style pruning, in good plum seasons the trees will be heavy with developing fruit. The branches should be thinned while still very small and

Right: Always cut branches at an angle so that water flows away easily from the exposed cut.

Far right: Cuts should be clean and close to the stem. Leaving stubs can encourage rot and diseases.

green, and wooden props placed under the branches of ripening fruit to support them if needed. When thinning, ideally no two plums should be touching. This minimizes brown rot, which develops in the spaces between bunched fruits. Unless trees are netted in areas of high bird populations, more will be lost to them than to any license taken in pruning patterns. If you are working with nature, figure on losing one-third of the crop to the birds, much of it just pecked. In a bigger garden, plant a couple of extra trees and consider it the birds' share. Another possibility is to plant a distracting mulberry, as birds prefer them to plums and other stone fruit. Even so, after about 3 years, you will have more fruit than a family can eat coming from your orchard—and preserves, chutneys and jams piled up in the pantry.

Fruit trees feed through active feeder roots concentrated around the dripline of the tree. In milder climates, slow-release organic nutrients can be supplied around the dripline at any time in the growing season, and particularly in spring. Plums can suffer from various pests and diseases, although they are more resistant with the incorporation of rock dusts in the soil and the slower nitrogen release of organic practises which make for trees of strong constitution. San Jose scale can be a problem in Australia and the United States, and a dormant oil spray

can be used. Plums are susceptible to heart rot if poorly pruned. Always cut a branch back as closely as possible. If a long stub is left, it is difficult for the tree to heal and fungus may enter.

Recommended Cultivars

'Belle of Louvain' — This is an excellent plum for stewing, and for pies. It has a rich flavor. The fruits are very large, oval, purplish-red skinned, with yellow flesh.

'Coe's Golden Drop' — This is the ultimate plum, the greatest of its kind, a very late ripening freestone that distils the entire summer into its rich plum and apricot flavor, and drips with sweetness. The fruit are rounded, clear pale yellow, and heavily bloomed. The tree is a regular bearer. It was raised in Suffolk in 1809.

'Greengage' syn. Reine Claude — Irrevocably linked with the book and movie *Greengage Summer*, this cultivar has been considered the benchmark for plums since it was first released in 1699. The tree is small, self-pollinating, vigorous and productive, bearing richly aromatic, intensely juicy, semi-freestone, transparently golden-fleshed fruits that are a distillation of all that the rich flavor of the gages can capture.

'Pearl' — Bred by Luther Burbank in Santa Rosa, California, in 1898, this is a lower yielding tree but the fruits are of superb quality, rounded, golden-yellow flecked with crimson, clingstone, with deep golden, juicy, sweet, tender flesh. **'Alabaster'**, originating from Michigan, is a close form. It is a pale golden cultivar of excellent quality that comes into fruit two weeks earlier.

'President' — One of the world's most famous plums, this freestone has large oval fruit, black-purple skin and yellow, dryish, richly and sweetly flavored flesh. It is used widely for cooking of all kinds including conserves, and can be dried as a prune. Another highly recommended cultivar for bottling whole is **'Warwickshire Dropper'**, with large golden-yellow fruits on a productive, self-compatible, very cold-hardy, large tree.

'Prune d'Agen' — The prunes are a group of plums with high density flesh that dries rather than molds. They have small pits and a very rich flavor which intensifies with drying. This is the best-known French cultivar, grown worldwide for its superb quality. It is semi-freestone, late ripening, with long, oval, rich violet fruits and sweet, aromatic, tender, yellow-green flesh, excellent used fresh and for drying. The tree is medium sized and spreading, and cold-hardy. It was brought into France by the Benedictine monks when they returned from Persia during the Crusades.

'Reine Claude de Bavay' — This superb c. 1843 compact, small tree is admirable for small gardens. Named after one of Napoleon's cavalry officers, it has medium to large, oblong fruit, of translucent pale yellow-green skin with tiny white dots. The deep amber-yellow flesh is richly aromatic and juicy.

'Victoria' — Considered the best of all the canned plums, giving a tender, juicy product that is ruby colored with a slight almond flavor. It is also excellent for jam. The fruits are large, oval, light to deep red, freestone, firm, juicy and quite sweet.

A European Plum, Prunus domestica 'Mount Royal', espaliered against a wall to take advantage of the warmth stored in the bricks.

Japanese Plum

Prunus salicina   Zones 6–10

This group is characterized by large, juicy fruit used mostly for fresh eating. The fruit have a good balance of acid and sweet, although the flavor is often less rich. As a group they bloom earlier, which makes them susceptible to late frosts, but they are an ideal choice for gardeners in milder climates such as much of Australia, California and the southern states of the United Staes. They are good cross-pollinators with other Japanese plums, and with many American plums. They are cultivated in the same way as European plums.

Prunus x domestica 'President' bears very sweet and juicy, purple, oblong fruit with a heavy bloom.

Recommended Cultivars

'**Elephant Heart**' — Bred by Luther Burbank at Sebastopol in California and introduced by Stark Brothers in 1929, this is a blood plum of the highest quality, with medium to large, freestone, late ripening, heart-shaped fruit with black-purple skin and exceedingly juicy, deep red flesh with a rich, sweet flavor. They do not come any better than this. The tree is vigorous and healthy, but requires a pollinator.

'**Mariposa**' syn. 'Improved Satsuma' — This upright-growing cultivar, originating in Pasadena, California, ripens in mid-season and has large, round, dark purple, freestone fruit with deep red, thick, tender, juicy, sweet flesh.

'**Santa Rosa**' — This is considered one of the world's greatest plums and is grown extensively in Australasia and the United States. The tree is widely adapted, highly productive, large, upright growing and vigorous. The fruits are large, very early ripening, rounded, dark crimson-purple, with red skin, juicy, and wonderfully balanced for acid and sweetness. '**Weeping Santa Rosa**' is an ornamental, very productive cultivar with a low chilling requirement of only 150 hours.

'**Shiro**' — Bred by Luther Burbank in 1897, this is an exceptionally popular cultivar for the larger garden, with very fine, clingstone, medium-sized, rounded fruit that are juicy, melting, translucent yellow and early ripening.

'**Burbank**' — Raised by Luther Burbank from a seed sent to him from Japan, this has become an important cultivar with medium to large, dark red, early ripening, clingstone fruit that have rich yellow, aromatic, sweet, tender but firm flesh. The tree is highly productive, vigorous and unusually cold-hardy for this group.

Mexican Bird Cherry
Prunus salicifolia   Zones 6–10

The Mexican Bird cherry, or Capulin cherry, is native to Mexico through to Peru. The large, juicy fruits with deep maroon to purple skins have green flesh that is juicy and refreshing, and slightly tart. They are eaten fresh or stewed, or made into preserves and jams. Capulin cherries have a very low chill requirement and can be grown in areas with warm winters.

A number of cultivars have been selected including the heavy-bearing '**Ecuadorian**', with very large cherry fruits up to nearly $1^{1}/_{2}$ in (4 cm) wide; the delicious '**Fausto**', with large, green-fleshed fruits and a rich, sweet flavor, borne on a reliably producing tree; and the heavy pro-ducer '**Huachi Grande**', with large, rounded, sweet fruit.

The Blood Plum has fruit used mostly for fresh eating. It has purple skin and is exceedingly juicy.

Prunus persica 'Rekord aus Alfter' is a juicy peach cultivar.

Peach *and* Nectarine

Prunus persica   Zones 5–10

Although the fruit of peaches and nectarines look dissimilar, the trees that bear them are indistinguishable and betray the fact that they are derived from the one species, separated by a single minor genetic difference. The skin of the peach fruit is covered by a faint furring of hair, while that of the nectarine is smooth. Breeding patterns have created a size difference, nectarines being smaller on average than peaches. Nectarines are also notable for a distinctive and delicious fragrance, quite different from that of the peach. Peaches and nectarines will happily interbreed. Peach seeds will produce nectarines, and nectarine seeds will produce peaches, a conundrum commented upon by Charles Darwin.

Peaches originated in China and have been in cultivation there for at least 3,000 years. They have come to represent longevity and immortality, and bushes in bud are given as Chinese New Year gifts. If they flower, it is an omen of good luck for the coming year.

Spring blossoming of the famous fragrant white peaches.

The Chinese Honey
Peach is grown for its
flavorsome fruit.

Peaches were carried to Persia along the ancient silk route, so that early botanists thought of peaches as being of Persian origin, hence their botanical name. From there, the peach was carried by the Greeks and Romans through Europe.

The Spanish had introduced the peach into northern Florida by 1865, and by the mid-19th century Georgia was noted for its lush groves of peaches. Expert horticulturists that they were, the Georgians could not have chosen a better place to grow peaches, and Georgia is now known as the Peach State. Virtually two-thirds of the mainland states of the United States now grow peaches, and they are also found growing wild to the point that visiting botanists in the 19th century assumed them to be endemic. So prolific were peaches in the early 1800s before pests and diseases caught up with them, that the fruit became hog fodder or were converted into 'mobby', a fairly lethal peach brandy in terms of potency, and common in states such as Virginia. Thomas Jefferson grew 160 peach trees in the South Orchard of his

beloved 'Monticello', and in 1811 listed an astonishing 38 cultivars including early American and imported Italian ones. So readily did they grow, that he used peach seedlings as ornamental and fruitful hedges to his fields.

White-fleshed and yellow-fleshed forms are found in both peaches and nectarines. The old blood peaches, such as **'Indian Blood'** syn. Blood Cling, **'Indian Cling'** and the almost black-skinned, much sought after and highly priced French cultivar **'Peche de Vigne Rouge'**, which is grown to mark the end of vineyard rows, have flesh suffused with rose-pink to wine-red, usually concentrated just under the dark purple-red skin or around the stone. Modern breeding is working to create evenly distributed red coloring throughout the flesh. In China, peaches with pink flesh are known as **'Chicken's Blood'**, while those that are deep red inside are called **'Pig's Blood'**. Some of the old peaches, such as the Mississippi **'Blood Leaf'** syn. General Tilghman Peach, have very ornamental purple-red foliage. Dwarfing genes have also been introduced into peaches, and cultivars such as 'Honey Babe' and the UK Terrace series 'Terrace Amber' and 'Terrace Diamond' are popular for growing in pots.

An ancient Chinese peach, the 'Peento' syn. 'Pen-tao', is very compressed in shape, so much so that it is reminiscent of a flying saucer. It has been grown in Queensland and in the United States (presumably its entry coinciding with goldrushes), since the second half of the 19th century, and is valued not only for its aromatic, sweet, melting flesh but also for its earliness, which allows it to be harvested before fruit fly becomes a problem. It has a very low chill requirement, and is also grown in the Gulf states of the United States. Modern cultivars derived from it include 'Australian Saucer' and 'Stark Saturn'. Two other groups from China are the honey peaches, with the taste of nectar, and the ancient winter peaches. 'White Heath' syn. Heath Cling originated in America before the War of Independence. It is considered to be the oldest named American peach still in cultivation, and also the closest representative of the ancient winter-keeping Chinese peaches. Trees are still commercially available.

Both peaches and nectarines are characterized by groups of 'melting' and 'non-melting' genes. Western tastes favor luscious, melting flesh, and this characterizes all the old cultivars. Japanese tastes often prefer a firmer, even crunchy, fruit. The food commodity business agrees happily with the latter style of fruit, and many cultivars in recent times can be carried three times around the world without bruising, but go from hard to rotting without ever passing through the 'soft ripe' stage. If you prefer fruit so luscious that the flesh melts in your mouth and the juice runs down your arms, this is an admirable reason for planting peaches and nectarines in your home orchard. Peaches also carry genes that control the adhesion of the flesh to the stone, effectively dividing them into two types: freestone and clingstone.

Growing and Harvesting

Peaches and nectarines are grown in the same way. Selection of appropriate cultivars is essential to success with both groups. Many of the peach cultivars currently used around the world have been selected for their ability to grow in cooler conditions than are natural to the species. Some fruit breeders in research centers, such as the University of Florida at Gainesville and the Horticulture

Prunus perica 'Red Haven' bears medium-sized, yellow-fleshed peaches over a long season.

Espaliered fruit trees, Chicago Botanical Gardens.

Section of the University of Western Sydney (Hawkesbury) in New South Wales, have concentrated their breeding programs on the development of low-chill cultivars capable of growing well in very warm to subtropical climates, and these programs have released a number of cultivars popular with growers in such areas. The Gainesville releases are prefixed by 'Florida'. Horticulturists talk in terms of total chilling hours for cultivars, which is a calculation of how many hours a cultivar must spend below 45°F (7°C) in order to set fruit. Lack of chilling hours will prevent a tree from setting fruit. The minimum chilling hour requirement is provided in the descriptions of recommended cultivars, with the exception of dwarf forms, which are not usually grown in the ground.

Flowers are initiated early in spring, and spring frosts can damage the buds severely. The buds of young trees are more easily damaged by cold than those of mature trees, but even the hardiest cultivars will not take temperatures of below –18°F (–28°C), and many are severely damaged at –12°F (–24.5°C). To prevent this, peaches are often espaliered against brick walls in marginal peach growing areas to take advantage of the warmth that is stored in the bricks in daylight hours and reradiated at night. The few degrees of warmth afforded by the wall is often the difference between success and failure when growing peaches in a cool garden. *(For descriptions of espalier designs and how to create espaliers, see the section 'Apples' in Pome Fruits.)* In areas marginal for peach culture, the soil type becomes an important factor. Trees grown in sandy soils are more likely to thrive than those in stiff, cold clay.

Most peaches are self-fertilizing and need no pollinator. A notable exception is '**J.H. Hale**', a successful commercial cultivar requiring a cross-pollinator. In choosing peaches for your garden, take into consideration the average number of chilling hours, the intensity of frosts experienced and the micro-climate effects of the site. Local gardeners will be able to make recommendations, as will your local fruit tree supplier. Trees begin to bear at 2–3 years of age and come into full bearing at about 5 years in good peach growing areas. The trees remain fruitful up to 12–15 years of age, although some trees may continue bearing well for another 5 years with good care.

Peaches need a well-drained position with the incorporation of plenty of organic material. This material should not be high in nitrogen, and rotted hay is ideal to be mixed through the topsoil. Rock dusts can be incorporated at this stage, and if the soil is markedly acidic (below pH 5.5), dolomite can also be added. Peaches do best around a neutral pH of 7.

In milder areas, bare-rooted trees are planted in late autumn to late winter, but in cooler areas they are planted in spring, as soon as the ground can be prepared. The hole provided should be at least 6 in (15 cm) wider and deeper than the root ball. Trim off any broken roots using clean cuts, and then cut the top down to a height of 2½ ft (75 cm).

Technically, this is referred to as 'heading out the leader'. It may seem disastrously wasteful when you see most of the tree lying on the ground, but bare-rooted peaches do not transplant particularly well, and the reduced root system that results from lifting the tree will not support the full top growth. Old fruit growers used to call it 'cutting them down to their socks', and it is a fair description. Make the cut just above a side branch. Now cut each side branch back to about 1–2 in (2.5–5.0 cm) long. By now, you will be wondering why you paid so much for this bit of stick! Spread the roots out in the hole and check that the tree is at the same height in the hole as it was when propagated. Fill the hole in and press down gently to firm the plant into the ground. Resist the temptation to bounce up and down around the tree. Even gardeners of sylph-like proportions will break some of the underground roots. Water the site thoroughly. When no further air bubbles rise to the surface, the soil is

Vase-trained peach trees with beautiful pinkish blossoms.

The peaches of Prunus persica *cultivar have a velvety down, are delicious and contain a stone that is deeply pitted and grooved.*

make three side or secondary branches. They are headed back (cut back) again every year.

In the early years, peaches are exceptionally attractive to rabbits and other wildlife, and a temporary cage made from rectangles of wire netting formed into cylinders can be placed as wire guards around the trunk, held in place by a pair of wooden stakes. Rabbits can and will ringbark a tree in a single night on occasions.

Once the tree is well established and growing away, it can be regularly fed with compost. However, in marginal peach growing areas with short summers, trees need to be encouraged to make their annual growth spurt between early spring and early summer, tailing growth off after mid-summer to allow trees to harden off adequately to withstand the rigors of the next winter. For this reason, while compost is used freely and regularly on trees in mild to hot climates, a concentrated high-nitrogen boost needs to be given to peaches in marginal areas in early spring. Fishmeal, granulated seaweed preparations, seaweed extracts, cottonmeal or similar is fed around the dripline to boost nitrogen levels and growth.

Some peach cultivars are obligingly self-thinning, but they are few and far between, and most trees should be thinned by hand after they have dropped the first round of excess

fully saturated. Once the trees begin to grow actively, they should be watered regularly. The trees should be mulched, but the mulch should be kept free of the trunk.

Different peaches have different natural shapes. As the tree throws out new laterals, it will form either a fairly upright structure or a naturally open structure, and it is better to allow the tree to dictate the correct form into which it is to be shaped. Pruning is done in winter, and in the case of low-chill cultivars in early winter. If an unusually severe winter affects your trees, it is better to wait until flowering begins in spring to indicate the extent of the cold damage. If damage has been severe, avoid any pruning in that season other than to remove the dead wood. Open-growing cultivars are pruned to a vase shape by allowing 3 lateral branches to grow outward from the young tree after the leader has been removed. These three laterals will become the frame of the tree. Each branch is then allowed to

Prunus persica 'Robert Blum'.

fruit. The general rule is to remove all excess fruit, leaving behind one fruit for each 4 in (10 cm) of branch. For prize-winning fruit this is expanded to 6 in (15 cm). Trees that are not thinned often break major branches under the load of fruit, particularly in winds or a storm.

Peach leaf curl is a problem wherever peaches grow. It is caused by a fungus, *Taphrina*, and can damage a tree severely. The only organic protection is to use three cover sprays, one applied after leaf fall, one in early to mid-winter, and one just before the new flower buds open. A lime sulfur or Bordeaux mixture should be used.

Peaches are quite delicate when ripe, and the fruit should be harvested with care. Cup the fruit with your hand, push up and twist it off. Pulling the fruit causes bruising and results in a very short shelf life for the fruit.

Recommended Cultivars

Peach cultivars in particular are emerging in very large numbers from breeding programs in California, Florida and the University of Western Sydney's Hawkesbury campus. Some of these have now been widely grown and evaluated, and a representative is included here for warm climates. Older established cultivars are the main listing.

Peach Cultivars

'Belle of Georgia' — This old cultivar from Georgia, the Peach State, is still very popular and forms a large, vigorous tree bearing large oval fruits with milky-white skin delicately blushed red. The fruit is juicy and sweet, and has a semi-freestone habit. *850 hours chilling*

'Dixired' — This is a very popular clingstone cultivar with round,

Prunus persica 'Dixired' bears small, red-flushed, yellow-fleshed fruit.

medium-sized fruits with a bright red skin when ripe and golden, and firm yellow flesh. *950 hours chilling*

'Flordaking' — Bred by the University of Florida, this has very low chilling requirements and has proved excellent in the Deep South of the United States and in Australia. A clingstone, it has yellow skin with a red blush, and juicy, sweet, firm, golden-yellow flesh. *150 hours chilling*

'Garden Lady' — This is a genetic dwarf ideal for small gardens and tub culture.

'Halehaven' — This is an excellent freestone cultivar for home use, with medium to large, well-formed, round fruit with a deeply colored skin and exceptionally sweet, juicy, melting yellow flesh. The tree is highly productive and vigorous. *850 hours chilling*

'Honey Babe' — This is a genetic dwarf and a very attractive ornamental. It is also a serious eating peach with large golden fruit blushed deep red, and highly aromatic, sweet, juicy, firm yellow flesh flecked red.

'Loring' — This is an early blooming cultivar bearing large, sweet, yellow, freestone fruit of very good quality. The tree is upright growing, vigorous and dependable. *850 hours chilling*

'Nectar' — This is an exceptionally fine white-fleshed freestone cultivar with large to very large fruit blushed pink to carmine, with sweet, melting, juicy, aromatic white flesh suffused with pink. The tree is healthy and vigorous. (Along the same lines is the more difficult to obtain 'Stark Early White Giant'.) *1050 hours chilling*

'Peregrine' — This is an excellent, heavy-cropping, white-fleshed cultivar.

'Redhaven' — Excellent for canning and freezing, as well as fresh eating, this is a reliable peach with medium-sized, yellow, freestone fruit. It is a good home garden type. Early thinning of the fruit on the branches ensures good fruit size. It has resistance to bacterial leaf spot. *850 hours chilling*

'Stark Saturn' — Shaped like a flying saucer with highly blushed creamy

The nectarine, Prunus persica var. nectarina cultivar, is almost identical to the peach in habit and flowers.

skin, this cultivar has melting white flesh that is very sweet. The tree is tall and highly vigorous.

Nectarine Cultivars

'Garden Beauty' — This is a genetic dwarf cultivar with large fruit, suited to growing in a well-sized pot or tub, particularly if thinned. A clingstone, it has yellow skin blushed red, and yellow flesh that is full of flavor. It is highly ornamen-tal in flower. Another genetic dwarf nectarine of compa-rable appear-ance is **'Southern Belle'**, which has a low chilling requirement.

'Nectarose' — Ideal for colder regions such as the New England area, this vigorous, upright-growing, very productive cultivar is early blooming.

'Nectar Babe' — This is an excellent genetic dwarf suited to pot culture, with large, very attractive fruit with bright red skin and richly flavored, sweet, golden flesh, ripening in mid-summer.

Plumcot

Prunus domestica x armeniaca   Zones 5–10

Created as a result of a cross between a plum and an apricot, this richly flavored fruit has never had the fame it deserves. This may be under-standable in fruit fly areas as the fruits ripen mid-season to late, and are prone to stings. In other areas, however, they are well worthy of planting. The trees are vigorous and large, the fruits resembling very large plums but with an apricot fuzz on the skin. They are grown in the same way as apricots, and cultivars exist for all but very cold districts. Recommended cultivars include the original Burbank hybrid, **'Rutland'**, which is favored for the US Pacific coast and New South Wales; **'Stanford'** and **'Sharp'**, which are excellent for the same areas; and **'Apex'**, **'Silver'** and **'Triumph'** for cool areas.

Sloe

Prunus spinosa   Zones 4–10

The Sloe, or Blackthorn, is native to Europe and Asia, and is a wild plum considered to have been involved in the breeding of the European domestic plum, *P. domestica*, the other major contributor being the Cherry plum or myrobalan. The fruits make a potent alcoholic drink when fermented, which may explain the remarkably large numbers of sloe stones excavated at archeological sites such as Silbury and Glastonbury in southern England and also in Caerwnt in Wales. Sloes are also added to gin with sugar to make a highly regarded fine liqueur. The trees are found in surviving hedgerows in many parts of Europe, and form a substantial bush to around 8 ft (2.5 m), with typical plum foliage and bark, bearing small, rounded-oval, blue-black fruits that are heavily covered in a bloom. In France, the flowers are crystalized, the leaves and fruits used to make herbal teas tisanes, and the immature fruits pickled. Sloes are grown for such uses outside their area of origin, and an ornamental, purple-leafed form, **'Purpurea'**, is also cultivated. The tree is cultivated in the same way as the European plum.

Sloe, Prunus spinosa, is a wild plum with small, rounded-oval, blue-black fruit that are heavily covered in a bloom.

Uncommon Fruits

Avocado *Persea americana* syn. *P. gratissima;* **Banana** *Musa* ssp.; **Common Fig** *Ficus carica;* **Japanese Persimmon** *Diospyros kaki;* **Kiwi Fruit** *Actinidia deliciosa* syn. *A. chinensis;* **Papaya** *Carica papaya;* **Passionfruit** *Passiflora edulis, P. edulis* var. *flavicarpa, P. mollissima;* **Pineapple** *Ananas comosus;* **Pomegranate** *Punica granatum;* **Prickly Pear** *Opuntia ficus-indica*

The past 10 to 20 years have seen an enormous increase in the availability of exotic fruits, many of which originated in the tropics and parts of Asia. Gone are the days when such delicacies were restricted to specialist sellers. Nowadays, general fruit stores and markets stock a great many varieties, and the never-ending supply sometimes gives the impression that certain exotic fruits are more common in our area than they are in reality. Bananas are a good example. We can easily find a bunch of bananas at our local grocery store, and might well think that they are grown nearby. Bananas, however, usually grow en masse only in very warm areas, and it is purely due to their propensity to ripen off the plant that they can easily be transported and consumed in cooler areas. When we buy a can of pineapple, do we ever think about the great distance that the pineapple has traveled? Who knows where their nearest kiwi fruit plantation is? By and large, the sweet and juicy kiwi fruit you cut up for fruit salad has made a long trip in a fast airplane to get to you.

As improvements and innovations are made in global transport, and countries continue to improve trade relations, we will find more and more fruits and vegetables that we have never seen before, or even heard of, on display at our local grocery store. It's great to try out new and exciting tastes and textures, so be sure to query your grocer next time you see an unusual fruit or vegetable. You never know, you may like it and may decide to plant one in your garden! Remember to research the growing requirements carefully, to make certain you have, or can create, the right conditions for your choice. For instance, if you live in a colder region, tender crops such as tropical fruit can be grown in a greenhouse. While this protects against birds and frost to a great extent, the downside is it tends to create more pest and disease problems.

The fruits in this chapter are just a few from around the globe that you may want to try growing in your garden. Each one is distinctive in taste and texture, can easily be incorporated into fruit salads and cooking, and can be appreciated as fresh alternatives to the usual diet.

Cultivated by Central American Indians for centuries, the pineapple's wild origin is believed to be in Brazil.

Avocados have widespread culinary use in spreads and dips and as a salad ingredient.

Avocado

Persea americana syn. *P. gratissima*   Zones 10–11

Avocados are the perfect substitute for imperfect protein foods such as meat, eggs, cheese and poultry. The fruit contain high quality essential fatty acids and proteins that are easily digested, and they are also rich in vitamins. For babies and growing children, they are an excellent source of energy. Avocados have widespread culinary use, from salad dressings or as a spread, to dips and as a major salad ingredient.

Growing and Harvesting

The species, native to Mesoamerica, is an evergreen tree that can reach a height of 60 ft (18 m). It bears dark green, leathery leaves and small, greenish flowers held in the axils. Pear-shaped fruit are borne 2 to 3 years after planting and ripen at most times of the year, depending on the variety and region. Being a tropical to sub-tropical tree, the avocado is sensitive to both frost and drought but if cared for can adapt to mild climates well outside the tropics. There are many named cultivars, each with different growth patterns and requirements, which fall into three major groups. 'West Indian' varieties have poor cold tolerance, with large fruit ripening in the summer of the same year of planting, and bear a thin, usually smooth skin. 'Guatemalan' varieties have moderate cold tolerance and tend to ripen in the spring/summer period of the year following planting. The fruit is medium-sized with a thick, often rough skin. 'Mexican' varieties are hardy, with fruits ripening in the summer/fall the year after planting, and produce a thin, usually smooth skin.

The avocado tree is an evergreen that can reach a height of 60 ft (18 m). The pear-shaped fruit are borne 2 to 3 years after planting.

*The banana is a
herbaceous perennial.
When a flowering shoot
of the banana has risen
and borne fruit, it dies.*

Banana

Musa spp.   Zones 10–12

Grown across the globe throughout the tropical zones, bananas constitute the world's fourth largest fruit crop. They have been a domestic crop since before recorded history, so it is difficult to accurately say where they originated. Many banana species, however, are native to the Indo-Pacific region.

Although the banana looks a lot like a tree, and grows to 20 ft (6 m), it is actually a herbaceous perennial whose 'trunk' is made up of leaf bases. When a flowering shoot of the banana has risen and borne fruit, it dies.

Bananas are said to contain all of the 8 amino acids our body cannot produce itself, and are considered extremely healthy fruit, full of potassium, vitamin C and fiber. A banana is sometimes likened to a full meal.

Growing and Harvesting

Banana crops require fertile, moist soil and full sun, and protection from winds, which will cause new growth to shred. Some of the smaller species can be cultivated as house plants or in greenhouses in temperate climates. Banana plants are bisexual, with female flowers borne at the base of the flower spikes, and male ones further up. Propagate from ripe seed or by division of clumps.

*Bananas are considered
an extremely healthy
fruit and are sometimes
likened to a full meal.*

There are many different cultivars of banana across the world. Here is a small selection that would do well in a home garden. '**Orinoco**' is a popular landscape plant in California, very cold-hardy, and bears plentiful fruit. '**Lady Finger**', growing to 15 ft (4.5 m), is well suited to domestic gardens; it also tolerates more temperate gardens. '**Dwarf Cavendish**' grows only 6–10 ft (1.8–3 m) high, with short broad leaves. The fruit of the '**Apple**' (or '**Silk**' or '**Manzana**') is about 4–6 in (10–15 cm) long and has a slight apple flavor when ripe. This cultivar grows to about 10–12 ft (3–3.6 m).

Common Fig

Ficus carica   Zones 8–11

The fig, although not a true tropical fruit, is a favorite among all fruit growers. It is a fruit of antiquity, with remnants having been found in excavation sites traced to at least 5,000 B.C.. Figs can be eaten fresh or used for preserves and other types of desserts, and also dry particularly well.

Growing and Harvesting

The fig, with its distinctive 3-lobed leaves, is indigenous to Turkey and western Asia, and has been cultivated for millennia. A small deciduous tree, it reaches 30 ft (9 m) and needs a sunny site in a warm climate with dry summers, as rain can split the ripening fruit, usually harvested in summer and autumn. Nematodes can be a problem, and so figs will benefit through heavy mulching and light. If limited space is an issue, they can be grown as a container plant or on a porch or patio.

There are many named cultivars. **'Black Mission'** is the well-known black fig grown in California; the fruit is of excellent quality and in warm regions it bears two crops per year. **'Brown Turkey'** is a productive, vigorous tree with large, purplish-brown fruit with pink flesh and a rich flavor. **'Genoa'** bears a greenish-yellow fruit with a rich flavor and amber flesh. **'San Pedro'** is prized for its large and early first crop of fruit, which may be followed by a second, smaller crop.

Japanese Persimmon

Diospyros kaki   Zones 8–10

This highly prized East Asian native has been cultivated in China and Japan for hundreds of years and in the Mediterranean basin for more than a century. Europeans refer to the persimmon by the Japanese name 'kaki'. While they may not be the most visually tempting fruit,

persimmons are certainly a delightful taste sensation and are enjoyed in all corners of the globe. Unripe persimmons are inedible and must be kept until almost rotting before eating. The fruit is generally eaten fresh but can be frozen, canned or dried, and is sometimes used in oriental cooking.

Growing and Harvesting

The deciduous tree grows to about 20 ft (6 m) tall with spreading branches, and prefers warm temperate to sub-tropical areas, although it can tolerate hot and humid coastal areas. Persimmons are grown on a wide range of soils but produce best on deep, fertile, medium-textured soil with good drainage. Being brittle, they need good shelter from strong wind. Its dark green, oval leaves turn yellow to deep orange in autumn, and it produces small cream flowers, which are followed by orange or yellow fruit about 3 in (7.5 cm) across. The fruit is sweet, but most cultivars have an astringent taste until fully ripe. Propagate from seed and, for good crops, grow plants of both sexes.

The 'Black Mission' cultivar is a well-known black fig that is popular among gardeners.

Japanese persimmons or kaki are enjoyed in all corners of the globe. The fruit must be very ripe before eating.

Kiwi fruit are ripe when just soft, and the green flesh tastes like a combination of citrus, melon and strawberry.

Kiwi Fruit

Actinidia deliciosa syn. *A. chinensis*   Zones 8–10

The kiwi fruit, or Chinese gooseberry, is native to China's Yangtze Valley, and it was first cultivated there in 1900. It was a New Zealander, however, who developed the plant and marketed it. The name 'kiwi fruit' arose as the fuzzy brown skin of the fruit is reminiscent of the feathers of the kiwi, a native bird of New Zealand.

Kiwi fruit is said to have double the vitamin C content of an orange. The fruit is ripe when just soft and the green flesh, which is sweet and tart, tastes like a combination of citrus, melon and strawberry.

Kiwi fruit vines need a strong trellis, a strong support or even a dead tree on which to climb.

Kiwi fruit thrive in moderate conditions where they can be given a chilling period in winter, but don't like frost. In suitable conditions, kiwi fruit can astonish by their vigor and speed of growth, the long writhing canes reaching the thickness of a thumb in one season and forming a dense tangle that can break a trellis not built strongly enough.

Growing and Harvesting

In order to produce fruit from the vine at least one male plant is required, planted in the company of several female plants. The different cultivars are divided into either male or female plants. The '**Hayward**' is the standard female kiwi fruit. The fruits produced are large and keep well. For cooler climates, the '**Saanicheon**' is a good alternative to the 'Hayward'. For a male plant, consider '**The Matua**' (meaning 'father' in the Maori language). It is the foremost male plant in orchards, and its flowering cycle works in well with the 'Hayward'. The '**Chico**' is a male plant commonly found in California and is also recommended.

Kiwi fruit vines need a strong trellis, a strong support or even a dead tree on which to climb. They grow best in a sheltered but sunny position, and need fertile, well-drained soil and plentiful water throughout the growing season. Propagation is normally from cuttings. Prune during winter for optimum fruit production.

Papaya

Carica papaya   Zones 10–12

Of the 22 species existing of *Carica*, five bear edible fruit; but only one, the *Carica papaya*, is the true papaya or pawpaw. Originating from Central and South America, the papaya grows to 21 ft (6 m), and is usually a single, branchless stem with an umbrella of leaves emerging from the top. The papaya leaves are large and deeply

The papaya or pawpaw grows to 21 ft (6 m) and is usually a single, branchless stem with an umbrella of leaves emerging from the top.

lobed, and provide some shade for the large sweet fruit that grows from the stem in large numbers. The unripe fruit can be cooked like squash. The fruit turn golden when ripe, and are perfect to eat fresh, as well as in salads and as a side-dish to curries.

Growing and Harvesting

Papayas can only be grown outdoors in frost-free or near frost-free climates. Plant in rich, moist, well-drained soil in sun or part shade. Most papaya plants are either male or female, but hermaphrodite plants have been developed in cultivation. It is advisable to plant papayas in a clump to ensure pollination. Young plants bear ripe fruit about 11 months after germination. While papayas live up to 25 years, it is best to plant a new crop every 3–4 years as productivity declines with age. Propagate from seed or cuttings, or by grafting.

There are two types of papaya: Hawaiian or Mexican. The Hawaiian type has yellow skin when ripe and generally weighs about 1 lb (450 g). The Mexican fruit are a lot larger and

heavier at 10 lb (4.5 kg), grow much taller than Hawaiian plants (so are harder to harvest) and can have yellow, orange or pink flesh. 'Waimanalo' is a Hawaiian type, high in flavor and quality, and keeps well. The 'Mexican Red' is obviously of the Mexican type, contains pink flesh, but is generally not as sweet as the 'Waimanalo'.

Large sweet fruit grow from the stems of the papaya in large numbers. When ripe, the fruit turn golden and are perfect to eat fresh.

The 'Panama Red' passionfruit has reddish-purple fruit, whose skin stays smooth when ripe.

Passionfruit

Passiflora edulis, P. edulis var. *flavicarpa,*
P. mollissima   Zones 10–12

When Spanish Catholic missionaries came across the Passiflora in the Amazon in the 16th century, they likened the spectacular flowers to the 'Passion' (or suffering) of Christ. Believing that the flowers' stamens represented the five wounds of the crucifixion of Christ, the missionaries named the plant *flor passionis*, or Passion Flower.

The flower of the banana passionfruit, which has long, golden-yellow fruit.

Of over 400 species of Passiflora existing, most are native to the Amazon region, and many are inedible. Of the few edible species, *P. edulis* is known as the passionfruit, and is considered the most delicious. It produces oval-shaped fruit about 2–3 in (5–7.5 cm) in diameter, with a tough rind and white pith that encases a tasty pulp along with pas-sionfruit seeds. The pulp has a sweet and tart taste, and can be eaten along with the seeds, or used to make drinks, ice-cream or preserves.

Growing and Harvesting

The passionfruit is an evergreen or semi-evergreen climbing vine growing to 15 ft (4.5 m). Most varieties of the passionfruit are frost-tender, and are best suited to warm areas. Plant in rich, well-drained soil in full sun and provide support. If planted in the right spot, the vine will grow quickly. Water regularly in summer. Prune congested or over-grown plants in spring. Propagate from seed in spring, or from cut-tings or by layering in summer. The Passiflora flower requires insect pollination in order to fruit. The vine is susceptible to nematodes.

There is a purple and a yellow variety of *P. edulis*. A popular cultivar of the purple variety is the **'Australian Purple'** (or **'Nelly Kelly'**). Pick this fruit when the skin is still smooth, and wait until the skin wrinkles before eating. **'Panama Red'** has reddish-purple fruit whose skin stays smooth when ripe. **'Noel's Special'** is a vigorously growing yellow passionfruit (*P. edulis* var. *flavicarpa*) that was developed from a vine discovered in the 1950s in Hilo, Hawaii, by Noel Fujimoto. The yellow passionfruit is ripe when the skin is still smooth. *P. mollissima* is the Banana passionfruit, featuring long, golden-yellow fruit, although not as sweet as the fruits of *P. edulis*.

Pineapples have sweet, tender and juicy fruit.

Pineapple

Ananas comosus   Zones 11–12

Pineapples are thought to originate from Brazil, and have been cultivated by Central American Indians for many centuries. Christopher Columbus first saw the pineapple on his travels in the 15th century, and these sweet, tender, juicy fruit were soon lauded by early Europeans as the finest of all.

The plant is part of the Bromeliad family, and has large rosettes of narrow, tapering, tough leaves with sharply toothed edges. Cultivars with smooth-edged leaves have been developed. The flowers, which develop into the familiar pineapple shape, are usually reddish-purple, each backed by a bract and borne in a crowded head at the top of a short, stout stem that emerges from the center of the leaf rosette.

Growing and Harvesting

All pineapple species are very frost tender and can be grown outdoors only in the tropics and sub-tropics; in cooler climates they can be grown as indoor or conservatory plants, but must have strong light. Plant in full sun in fertile, well-drained soil. They

are usually propagated from the basal suckers that develop on mature rosettes. Alternatively, you can remove the leafy top from the fruit and treat it as a cutting, either rooting it in soil (leave it to dry out first) or water.

Pineapples can be grown outdoors only in the tropics and sub-tropics because they are very frost tender.

*Pomegranates grow
to 15 ft (4.5 m) tall
and 10 ft (3 m) wide,
with blunt-tipped,
glossy leaves.*

The '**Smooth Cayenne**' (3–5 lb or
1.5–2.5 kg) is a cultivar whose leaves
are spineless; it is used in the canning
process due to its cylindrical shape. It
has a high sugar and acid content. The
'**Kona Sugarloaf**' (5–6 lb or 2.5–3 kg)
has white flesh that is well-known as
delicious, sweet, and acid-free. '**Natal
Queen**' (2–3 lb or 1–1.5 kg) is perfect
for eating fresh, and once ripe will
keep well. It has a mild flavor.

Pomegranate
Punica granatum   Zones 9–11

Native to the Middle East and one
of the oldest known edible fruits,
the pomegranate has been cultivated
extensively throughout the
Mediterranean, southern Asia and to
some extent the United States. Records
are found in the *Book of Moses*,
together with figs and grapes, and it is
also understood that the pomegranate
was buried in Egyptian tombs. These
unusual fruits were considered holy or
mystical by many civilizations, quite
possibly because of their appearance.
Pomegranates have a distinctive sweet-
sour taste and the seeds are good in
salads, cold soups and desserts.

Growing and Harvesting
Pomegranates grow naturally as a
bushy shrub or small tree, and despite
developing in a wide range of climates,
from tropical to warm temperate, the
fruit will ripen only where summers
are hot and dry. Plant in deep, well-
drained soil, preferably in a sheltered,
sunny position. They can be pruned as
a hedge and are also good in tubs.
Propagate from seed in spring, from
cuttings in summer or by suckers.

*Pomegranates have a
distinctive sweet-sour
taste. The seeds are
good in salads, cold
soups and desserts.*

This deciduous tree grows to 15 ft (4.5 m) tall and 10 ft (3 m) wide, with blunt-tipped, glossy leaves 3 in (8 cm) long. Its large, 8-petaled, red-orange flowers are borne at the branch tips in spring and summer. These are followed by the apple-like fruit, which have a thick rind and a mass of seeds, each enclosed in a reddish, acid-sweet envelope. Many cultivars are available, the fruit varying from very sweet to acidic and the flowers from red to pink or white. *P. granatum* 'Nana', a dwarf cultivar to 3 ft (1 m) high, has single orange-red flowers and small fruit. The commercially grown **'Wonderful'** has double, orange-red flowers and large fruit.

Prickly Pear
Opuntia ficus-indica   Zones 9–11

The prickly pear, or Indian fig cactus, is native to Central America and has been cultivated in Mediterranean countries and India for centuries for its delicious fruits. In addition to the consumption of the fresh fruit, jams, alcoholic and juice drinks, syrups, candied fruit and flour can be produced from the plant, and oil extracted from the seeds. The flowers were traditionally used and taken internally as medicine for male discomforts.

Growing and Harvesting
The cactus grows to 10–18 ft (3–5.5 m) tall and wide, each branch made up of several flat, oval segments that may be almost the size of a tennis racquet head, and bears rather attractive yellow flowers in early summer. These develop into the oval, red or orange fruit 2–3 in (5–7.5 cm) in diameter, their skin studded with bristles which must be stripped, taking the utmost of care and wearing gloves. The flesh inside may be red or yellow with a pleasant, bland taste that is heightened by the texture of the fruit's small, crunchy seeds. Spineless cultivars exist, but connoisseurs insist they are not as sweet as the prickly ones.

Prickly pear is a delicious fruit. It is eaten fresh and is also used for jams, alcoholic and juice drinks, syrups and candied fruit.

Section 4

FLOWERS

Annuals

Annual Clary *Salvia horminium*; Annual Phlox *Phlox drummondii*; Baby's Breath *Gypsophila paniculata*; Bachelor's Buttons *Centaurea cyanus*; Bells of Ireland *Moluccella laevis*; Blanket Flower *Gaillardia* spp.; Blue Lace Flower *Trachymene caerulea*; Bluewings *Torenia fournieri*; Calendula *Calendula officinalis*; Californian Poppy *Eschscholzia californica, E. caespitosa*; Canterbury Bells, and Cups and Saucers *Campanula Medium*; Chinese Aster *Calistephus chinensis*; Chinese Pinks *Dianthus chinensis*; Clarkia and Godetia or Farewell-to-Spring *Clarkia unguiculata* syn. *C. elegans, C. amoena*; Cleome or *Cleome hassleriana* syn. *C. spinosa* (of gardens); Cosmos *Cosmos bipinnatus, C. sulphureus*; Dame's Violet *Hesperis matronalis*; English Wallflower *Erysimum cheiri* syn. *Cheiranthus cheiri*; Flowering Tobacco and Woodland Tobacco *Nicotiana alata* syn. *N. affinis, N. langsdorfii, N. sylvestris*; Garden Forget-me-not *Myosotis sylvatica*; Garden Snapdragon *Antirrhinum majus*; Garden Verbena and Sweet Verbena *Verbena x hybrida*; ; Larkspur *Consolida ajacis* syn. *C. ambigua*; Linaria *Linaria maroccana*; Lobelia *Lobelia erinus*; Love-in-a-Mist *Nigella damascena*; Lupin *Lupinus* spp.; Marguerite Carnations *Dianthus caryophyllus*; Marigold, *Tagetes* spp.; Meadow Foam *Limnanthes douglasii*;

Nasturtium or Garden Nasturtium or Indian Cress *Tropaeolum majus*; Petunia *Petunia x hybrida*; Pink Strawflower and Swan River Everlasting Daisy *Rhodanthe chlorocephala* subsp. *rosea, R. mangliesii*; Poor Man's Orchid *Schizanthus x wisetonensis*; Poppy *Papaver* spp.; Primula *Primula malacoides, P. obconica*; Prince of Wales Feathers and Cockscombs *Celosia argentea* syn. *C. pyramidalis, C. cristata*; Rose Moss *Portulaca grandiflora*; Stock and Night-Scented Stock *Matthiola incana, M. longipetala* ssp. *bicornis* syn. *M. bicornis, M. tristis*; Sunflower *Helianthus annuus*; Sweet Alyssum *Lobularia maritima* syn. *Alyssum maritimum*; Sweet Mignonette *Reseda odorata*; Sweet Pea *Lathyrus odoratus*; Sweet Scabious and Sternkugel *Scabiosa atropurpurea, S. stellata*; Sweet Sultan *Centaurea moschata*; Sweet William *Dianthus barbatus*; Tidy Tips *Layia platyglossa*; Tree Marigold *Tithonia diversifolia*; Viola or Pansy and Wild Pansy *Viola x wittrockiana, V. tricolor*; Violetta *Viola cornuta*; Zinnia *Zinnia haageana* syn. *Z. angustifolia, Z. elegans, Z. peruviana*; Edible flowers

Annual flowers have been the poor cousins of the garden world for some time now. 'Cheap and cheerful' was the kindest remark to be heard in their favor. They were victims of the ever swinging fashion pendulum, displaced by the perennials which had in their turn been in the plant fashion wilderness for the previous couple of decades.

Deep down inside, however, we seem to love all those simple flowers from our childhoods, flowers with the sweet, green rush of summer in them. We love great patches of nasturtiums, sunflowers like benevolent suns, and the intoxicating scent of old style petunias in the midday heat. We love the honeyed scent that dense cushions of tiny flowered alyssum pour on the air, and the ethereal fragrance of sweet peas.

And just in time, the pendulum has swung once more and annuals are back in fashion. There are perfectly good reasons why we put the annuals

Godetia and poppies add color and life to the organic garden

behind us. When a garden consists almost entirely of annual vegetables and annual flowers, it is a case of flood or drought. By the time they are all in place, the inner world of the garden sparks with color and overflows with bounty. But when they have come to the end of their lives, the garden seems to die with them.

It is easy to rationalize annuals out of our gardens as time wasters, and advocate perennials which do not need annual planting and ground preparation. It isn't completely true, of course. A garden is an act of creation, a living artwork. If we want to do no work and harvest no fruits,

herbs, or vegetables, then we must hand the land back to nature. After all, perennials come with their own cultivation demands, and they retire to the subterranean depths when winter approaches, leaving space almost as bare as that vacated by annuals.

Annuals were a firm-favorite in the Victorian and Edwardian eras when armies of under gardeners maintained them to perfection. The 1950s brought a surge of love for annuals. This was a decade of hope, and the reconstitution of family life after the bitter years of World War II. Annuals with their bright colors and freshness symbolized the renewal of life and hope. Then they became seriously unfashionable. Those glorious herbaceous perennial borders of England became the benchmark of the elegant garden in the New World as well as the Old, and annuals became the province of unsophisticated council gardens. But these days annuals also once again symbolizing the sort of world we are wanting; they represent a need to turn the clock

The vigorous, climbing sweet pea has sweetly scented flowers. It is ideal for covering walls or fences.

Bright and attractive annuals used to great advantage at the Butchart Gardens, British Columbia, Canada.

Feverfew is an aromatic plant which was once used to dispel fevers and agues.

back to a feeling of security and peacefulness and innocence.

This is fortunate, because never have our gardens needed annual flowers more. Climate warming is making seasons increasingly unpredictable, and sprays and land clearing have done their damage to the insects that we rely on for pollination of our food crops and as natural predators of pests. The butterflies that were once so prevalent are fewer. Annuals with their brilliant flowers and soft, sweet, fragrances are both attractors and sustainers of these insects. So too are some weedy species that the average gardener frowns on. A small wild place out of sight in larger gardens and filled with food plants for bees and butterflies would make a good garden project to try to redress the balance.

Rather than the older idea of carpet bedding the entire front garden—which had its charms but also its drawbacks—annuals are used as fillers and brighteners now. They are far less susceptible to pests and diseases simply because they do not live very long. They are in for the season, then out, the soil renewed with well rotted

Annuals give any gardener the chance to 'paint' their garden as this herbaceous border featuring Lychnis coronaria *and* Salvia x sylvestris *illustrates.*

compost and other organic additives, and replanted. Their growth rate is very fast. In a month, seedlings may be breaking into early flower.

Use them wherever you would like a splash of color—in pots, on balconies and patios, lining paths and framing gates and doorways, in hanging baskets and wall mounted pots, in window boxes and on green strips, and as fillers wherever there is bare ground. They should be a part of the vegetable patch and orchard too, bringing with them pollinators for the crops, and predators of unwanted insect pests. They turn your production patch into a magical place, humming with life and energy. Let the vegetable annuals reciprocate and spill into the front garden. Corn, eggplants, peppers, tomatoes, potatoes, lettuce and endive are beautiful in their own right and add interest and height to annual plantings. So too do annual herbs like basils and dill, coriander, and the white daisy flowered feverfew and chamomile.

Beautiful color schemes can be created with annuals. Unlike perennial flower color schemes which can fall apart easily if the timing of flowering is miscalculated, annuals flower in such a tight window ot time that your scheme will always work. Whether you live in a hot climate and dream of cool color schemes such as mixes of lavender, blue, green, and white flowers, or romantic mixes of chiffon and silken pinks, or brilliant golden gardens or fiery clashes of bold reds

Pot marigold, Calendula officinalis, *is a brightly colored flower that provides food for bees and butterflies.*

and oranges and purples, they are all yours with annuals. Or create a bold and beautiful effect with a cascade or a massed planting of a single cultivar.

This time around, there is a larger choice than ever. Try to vary the height of your plantings, too, so that there is greater diversity of form. Plant breeders see public gardens as their principal clients as plants are bought in bulk quantities, and the demand has been for dwarf to ultra dwarf forms, the opposite to that which private gardeners need. Older, tall cultivars of stocks, snapdragons, poppies, calendulas and other mainstays of the annual flower garden are still available, to meet the requirements of the cut flower growers. Some annuals, like lavatera, cleome or spider flower, and sunflowers, are naturally tall and will add height and interest.

Annuals almost all belong to a plant group called 'ephemerals', plants that must take advantage of temporarily good growth conditions to germinate, grow, flower, and set viable seed before the environment shuts down on their growth cycle. Many of our ephemerals come from the tundras and alpine regions where the window of opportunity for active growth is a summer of around 6 weeks or a little more. A second group of ephemerals come from the desert where rare thunderstorms bring with them sufficient soil moisture to allow annual flowering plants to complete their entire life cycle, and create a seed bank for the next growing cycle, before dying back into the earth.

Butterfly Gardens

Butterflies set a garden in motion, and give it another dimension. Planting butterfly attracting plants in the garden is the perfect way to ensure their presence. Butterflies, like many wild creatures, are threatened by human activity. Age old plants with which they have co-evolved are being lost to weedicides and modern agricultural practises. Ancient migratory pathways are being inter-rupted. Gardeners around the world can help reverse this considerably by offering congenial habitats and providing appropriate food resources to keep these lifecycles turning.

Butterflies are creatures of color and light. Even brightly colored pots,

Aster novi-belgii, a
Michaelmas daisy,
attracts many butterflies.

painted pebbles, or bright splashes of color on a summer shirt will attract their attention. They are particularly attracted by rich pinks, crimsons, blues, mauves, and bright yellows. Butterfly flowers are often heavily scented as butterflies are strongly attracted by sweet scents. Not surprisingly, they are drawn to such plants as honeysuckles *Lonicera* spp., the Chilean jasmine *Mandevillea laxa*, wallflowers *Erysimum* spp., lilac *Syringa* spp., jonquils *Narcissus* spp., and jasmines *Jasminum* spp.

There are two guaranteed butterfly attractors in the garden—the butterfly

Lonicera x americana *is ideal for attracting butterflies and it is also simple to grow.*

bush *Buddleja davidii*, and the butterfly weed *Asclepias tuberosa*. Although *Buddlleja davidii* is known as the butterfly bush, all species of *Buddleja* are very attractive to butterflies. The very sweetly fragrant, lavender blue *B. fallowiana*, the honey fragrant orange ball tree *B. globosa*, and the fountain butterfly bush *B. alternifolia*. are also excellent butterfly attractors.

Asclepias has clusters of curiously turreted golden-orange flowers. The leaves contain a milky exudate which is distasteful to birds but it is an ideal larval diet for the Wanderer butterfly. All species of *Sedum* are very attractive to butterflies, as are the Michaelmas daisies *Aster novi-belgii* and *A. novae-angliae*.

Old-fashioned plants which are particularly attractive to butterflies include:

cherry pie *Heliotropium arborescens*
dandelion *Taraxacum*
hyssop *Hyssopus officinalis,*
lantana *Lantana camara, L. montevidensis,*
leadwort *Plumbago auriculata*
mock orange *Murraya paniculata*
sea holly *Eryngium maritimum,*
tree marigold *Tithonia diversifolia*
valerian *Centranthus ruber,*
yarrow *Achillea millefolium*

It isn't always remembered that these glorious creatures of summer days were once unadmired caterpillars nibbling on leaves, and silent enameled pupae undergoing transmutation. In a butterfly garden, then there can be no poisonous sprays, no moans at the occasional tattered leaves. It is also a good idea to have a little wild patch somewhere out of view where butterflies can still find the wild plants they need.

Bee Gardens

The humming of bees among nectar rich flowers is part of the pleasures of the summer garden. It was a pleasure that was once taken for granted but increasingly in many parts of the world bees are found to be in lower populations than in the past. And the ramifications for orchardists and vegetable farmers are serious. The use of non-discriminating insecticides for several decades has had its impact, and though progress is being made in reversing these practises, farmers in many countries are faced with

reduced yields as bees become fewer and the pollination service that we all took for granted and depended on is no longer there.

In the past gardeners were not so likely to take bees and their services so lightly. Gardens were with tall hedges to provide protection from the wind, and supply a warm sunny place.

Colors that attract bees include blues, purples, and yellows. Nectar guides are streaks of color that lead into the heart of the flower. We can see them simply as colors but for the bee it is as if a 'flare path' has been lit in welcome. The colors we see are nothing to the blaze perceived by bees. Only when we place a plant under ultraviolet light do we glimpse its powerful hues.

Plants that are not too changed from the original are the most attractive to the bees. Bees and flowers co-evolved, finding a way to proceed though many possible design options to one that met the needs of both the pollinator and the plant. The radical changes in design which we impose are often less attractive to

First flick out the sting as quickly as possible. Then crush the leaves of either balm, houseleek, hollyhock, ivy, or mallow and hold it over the area.

Growing Annuals

Annuals are easy to grow and, given the right conditions, are also quite easily raised from seed.

The nursery industry has geared itself to our changing lifestyles and seedlings of hundreds of different cultivars are available to us now, strong and healthy and ready for us to use. If the time to plant seedlings has passed us by, there are now potted instant color offerings available from nurseries, flowering annuals that we can transfer to a garden bed to create an instant, delightful effect. This is what gardeners did in Victorian times, conjuring up instant gardens with masses of flowering annuals that had been raised in pots inside greenhouses. The fortunate owners of grand houses would wake to a springtime miracle of color.

Whatever you do, don't miss out on the pleasures of annuals, even if it is just a few planters and a window box that you can afford, or have time to fill. There is only so much all of us can fit into our busy schedules, and if that means cutting corners we shouldn't feel guilty. It is desirable, to buy organically raised seedlings but if the only seedlings we can buy have been raised with artificial fertilizers, it will make relatively little difference as long as the garden beds they are planted into are rich and organically managed.

Most modern seed raising firms use individual plastic cells to grow seedlings. The cells are gently squeezed between the fingers, and the seedling with its rootball and attached soil can be lifted out and planted with minimal root disturbance. Older style punnets in which the roots of plants became tangled lead to inevitable severe root damage as plants were teased apart.

bees, and annual flowers which have received less attention from plant breeders or are less malleable are the most powerful attractors. These are some of the most irresistible of our garden flowers for bees:

Annual Phlox *Phlox drummondii*
Blanket Flower *Gaillardia spp.*
Blue flowered cornflower *Centaurea cyanus*
Blue Woodruff *Asperula orientalis*
Californian Bluebell *Phacelia tanacetifolia*
Love-in-a-Mist *Nigella damascena*
Meadowfoam *Limnanthes douglasii*
Sweet Mignonette *Reseda odorata*
Sweet Sultan *Centaurea moschata*

Many of the sweet scented herbs attract bees to the garden and then to your orchard and vegetable garden. Thymes, sages, aniseed, catmint, sweet marjoram, hyssop, basils of all kinds, pennyroyal and all mints, the various savories, nectar rich borage, lavender, cedronella, and above all lemon balm are markedly attractive to bees. Bee masters rubbed their hives with lemon balm to keep the hive from swarming. In the vegetable garden, chives are the favored plant, giving yet another reason to place them around pome and stone fruits. For bee stings in the garden, many of the bee attracting plants will also soothe the inflammation.

If you would like to grow your own seedlings, again there are compromises possible. Store bought seedling mix can be supplemented with sieved compost to make a more acceptable mixture. In some areas, organic seed mixes can be bought. Always dampen the mixes down before handling. Watering the seedlings each week with a fish or seaweed emulsion diluted to the recommended strength will give your young plants an excellent start in life. When you garden on a balcony, this is by far the best solution.

If your garden allows the space, your own seed raising mix can be created using a fairly fine garden sieve. You will need sharp sand, a reasonably good garden loam, and a well seasoned compost pile. You should also have dolomite available. The compost should be sieved and the finings gathered together. The remainder can be returned to the compost pile. Next sieve the loam. Make a heap with equal quantities of sieved compost, sieved loam, and sharp sand. Add a small handful of dolomite or lime to the pile and mix it through thoroughly.

Various micro-organisms can cause disease in trays of young seedlings and wilt a pot full of previously healthy young plants overnight. The soil mix needs to be sterilized to kill such organisms. The easiest way to do this in cool climate areas is to put the soil into trays spread out to a depth of about 4 in (10 cm), cover with foil, and place in the oven at a temperature of approximately 175°F (80°C). Leave the tray in the oven for 30 minutes, and then remove. It would be better if you are also the cook in your household, because an interesting, distinctly earthy odor lingers for some time afterward. For everyone's sake, if you choose to microwave the soil instead of using a conventional oven, check that there are no stones in the mix. They may explode if there is moisture trapped in a crack. A weight of 2.2 lbs (1 kg) of soil in a covered bowl requires 2$^1/_2$ minutes on maximum setting. Immediately spread the mix out to bring the temperature down quickly. In warm to hot areas, the method of soil sterilization is easier as the sun can do the the the cooking. Use black rubbish bin liners; fill each a quarter full with the seed raising mix, and put out in the sun for 4 hours. Leave the mix in the tied bags and only open as needed so that the mix sterile.

Annuals can provide a riot of color in the most confined spaces.

The hollyhock is a traditional cottage garden plant that will self seed.

Salvia horminium, 'Pink Sundae' is a sow-and-forget annual, tough and easy to grow.

Annual Clary
Salvia horminium   Zones 8–10

This species should not be confused with true clary sage *S. sclarea* grown in Provence and other areas for an oil used by the perfumery trade and for aromatherapy. This species is grown for its most attractive, petal-like bracts in several beautiful colors. The plants grow to 20 in (50 cm) and are available in separate colors, notably **'Pink Sundae'**, **'Oxford Blue'**, and **'White Swan'**. These are literally sow-and-forget annuals, tough and easy. All they require is full sun, good drainage, and fairly regular watering.

Annual Phlox
Phlox drummondii   Zones 6–10

Few annuals are as rewarding, or as sweetly fragrant as phlox. It is planted as seedlings in fall in warm gardens, and in spring in cool gardens. They grow away quickly to become low, densely mounded plants that competely cover in flower and the unique scent from a bed floats far and wide. There are two basic flower types, those with round, five-petalled flowers and those with star-shaped flowers.

There are many excellent strains of phlox including **'Twinkles'**, a striped and splashed strain of the star-shaped type. A new star shaped form is **'Petticoat'** which has flowers of the star type but with each petal drawn

If you can find (or recycle) plastic cell trays, fill the cells with soil, press down, insert a seed into each cell, cover to twice the depth of the seed's diameter with mix, and water from the bottom. Place in a cold frame, glasshouse, or protected area and ensure that the tray does not dry out. Most annuals are above ground in 5–10 days at the most. The old ephemeral genes persist, and they are anxious to grow. The same procedure is used with flats and pots of seedlings. Tiny seed are difficult to handle, and seed can be mixed with fine sand to make it easier to handle and spread evenly.

Suggestions for Annual Plantings
Included here also are species that are biennials. In mild to warm gardens, these are planted in fall, grow through the winter, and flower in the spring. In cooler gardens they are planted in spring and spend the first year building reserves and forming a rosette on the leaves. In the second spring the plant elongates and forms inflorescences.

Sweetly fragrant and very attractive, Phlox drummondii 'Sternenzauber' is a very rewarding annual to grow.

out into a long, elegant ray. The **'Mount Hampden'** mixture, recently released, forms densely mounding plants that are very floriferous; it comes in a range of clustered semi-double and double flowers. **'Chanal'** is stunning with fully double flowers in a deep pink. It flowers through the first frosts before giving up. **'Promise'** is similar, but in shades of soft peach.

Phlox are raised from seed and the seedlings transplanted into the garden in spring in cooler climates, or planted in fall in warmer areas. They respond to soil enrichment with compost and prefer a soil with a near neutral pH. Phlox should be given full sunshine, preferably in the morning.

Baby's Breath
Gypsophila paniculata   Zones 4–10

This is an excellent annual for providing a soft, cool, misting effect in the garden. It is both a lime and compost lover and both of these substances should be incorporated into the soil before planting. Its small flowers are arranged into delicate open panicles and they may be white or pink. It requires full sun and good drainage. Seed may be planted directly into the garden, covered with $1/2$ in (1 cm) of soil and watered daily to promote germination, or seedlings can be raised elsewhere and transplanted into the garden. **'Covent Garden'** is a large, single white flowered strain, **'Deeprose'** has clouds of deep rose flowers while **'Kermesiama'** is an unusual crimson-red cultivar.

Bachelor's Buttons
Centaurea cyanus   Zones 5–10

This beautiful flower was known in the United States as bachelor's button because it was once a popular *boutonniére* of Victorian gentlemen. In Australia and the United Kingdom, it was known as cornflower because in the days before weedicide, these

beautiful flowers were seen in the wheatfield along with the red corn poppy. They can still be seen in the ancient 'Mother of Wheat' fields in the Alpes de Haute Provence. The cornflower is used principally as a bedding plant. Older cultivars grew to 3 ft (90 cm) but many semi dwarf and dwarf cultivars have been developed. Plants are usually raised as seedlings and transplanted into the garden. They need full sunshine and good drainage.

The original cultivated plants were a rich blue. However today amythyst, pink and white are all sold in formula mixes like **'Double Mix'**, **'Polka Dot'** which is a dwarf, double flower color mix, and **'Frosty Mixed'** with blue, pink, maroon, and crimson flowers with the flower tips appearing frosted.

*Baby's breath,
Gypsophila paniculata
has small flowers, white
or pink, providing a
misting effect in the
garden.*

*Centaurea cyanus,
bachelor's buttons.*

Bells of Ireland

Moluccella laevis   Zones 7–10

Native to Syria, Turkey and the Caucasas, this species is prized by florists for its pale green 'flowers' borne evenly up the 3 ft (90 cm) stems. The true flowers are small, white, and borne in the center of the saucer-like apple green calyces. It is one of those plants that always attracts attention and adds an elegant, cool note in the garden. Seedlings can be raised and transplanted but Molucella germinates particularly well in the garden and is usually directly planted. Seed can de sown directly $1/4$ in (0.6 cm) below the soil surface. It is one of those plants which are particularly tough and undemanding and requires no additions to the soil other than dolomite if the soil is markedly acid. Water should be supplied regularly. Also known as Molucca balm or shell flower

Blanket Flower

Gaillardia spp.   Zones 8–11

Gaillardia is a genus of some 30 species all but two of which are North American in origin. Their common name comes from the resemblance of the flower's coloring to the desert colored dyes and patterns used in First Nation weaving. There are both annual and perennial species, including firewheel *G. pulchella* and the Texan *G. amblyodon*. The annual species come into flower before the perennial species of gaillardia. *G. amblyodon* grows to a height of approximately 3 ft (1m) and bears maroon flowers. *G. pulchella* is smaller growing to a maximum of 60 cm (24 inches), very showy, with downy, deeply incised leaves, and large flowers 3 in (7.5 cm) across or more, in a range of colors from deep purplish-red to yellow with the central disc a matching color and the petals often tipped yellow or white. An unusual variation in this species is *G. pulchella* var. *lorenziana* with quilled petals gibing the effect of a round head. These are two very hardy plants and they require little more than watering.

Blue Lace Flower

Trachymene caerulea   Zones 9–12

Reminiscent of the pincushion flower, this annual is now admired around the world. Originating from Western Australia, it grows to 15–20 in (38–50 cm) high with pincushion heads of lavender blue flowers. They need a good garden soil with additional

Gaillardia x grandiflora is appropriately named the blanket flower.

Blue lace flower is an annual that is admired around the world and has pincushion heads of lavender blue flowers.

compost, and a reasonably protected position away from the wind, with exposure to morning sun only. They are planted where they are required to flower. The plants should be mulched and composted stable hay is perfect for this plant, but clean, new or spoiled hay would also be excellent.

Bluewings
Torenia fournieri   Zones 9–12

This is a frost tender annual widely grown in the tropics and sub-tropics. It forms a soft, small plant to 10 in (25 cm) and bears racemes of bell-shaped flowers that are an exquisite

lavender-blue with a yellow nectar guide framed with an almost black-purple, velvety petal edge giving a startling contrast. Only the pansy can offer such a color mix, apart from torenia. They should be given light shade and a well enriched soil.

Calendula
Calendula officinalis   Zones 6–11

Calendulas, pot marigolds or English marigolds, are ancient in cultivation and were used both for celebratory purposes and to make a useful balm and ointment. The name 'marigold' came from 'Mary's Gold', a reference

Bluewings, Torenia fournieri, *has bell-shaped flowers that are an exquisite lavender-blue.*

Calendula, Calendula officinalis, *track the sun with their flowers and so have become known as 'the sun's bride"*.

The Californian poppy, Eschscholzia caespitosa, *is very beautiful and is an undemanding plant to grow.*

to the Virgin Mary. It was only one of its Medieval names. It was also known as 'marybuds', or 'gold ruddes', or just 'goldes'. Because they track the sun with their flowers every day, they also became known as 'the sun's bride'. The original herbal flowers cultivated in monastery and nunnery gardens had only one row of ray petals. We have lost many old horticultural plants, and one that would have been expected to have been lost was the old Victorian cultivar **'Hen and Chickens'**. Sometimes listed as *C. officinalis* var. *prolifera*, it is a quaint, charming plant with many miniature marigold flowers surrounding the base of the

double, golden parent flower, like satellites of a sun. Fortunately it is still available from some suppliers.

Calendulas are one of the mainstays of the modern annual garden. They are particularly obliging plants, quick to grow and quick to flower. However, compost should be added to the topsoil along with a sprinkling of dolomite if the soil is below pH 6.5. The quite large seed can be planted directly where they are to grow. Older cultivars grow to about 18 in (45 cm) but many cultivars now offered are semi or fully dwarf. Calendulas can suffer badly from rust disease and sulphur may be used to combat it. Badly infected plants should be burned. Good cultivars include **'Kablouna Intense Yellow'**, **'Tangerine Dream'**, the old but reliable **'Radio'**, and the slightly younger **'Pacific Beauty'**. The English marigold should not be confused with the genus tagetes from Mexico.

Californian Poppy
Eschscholzia californica, E. caespitosa   Zones 6–11

Californian poppies were born for the sun and heat. They are very undemanding provided they are in full sunshine, weed competition is under control, and they receive watering. These beautiful poppies are anything but weedy, but they have a way of returning year after year and a little pool of cream or gold or satin pink appears somewhere the following summer. A mulch of straw looks raw for a little while, but if it is chopped it will settle down well at the end of a week. It is the ideal clean, quickly drying mulch for this plant that originates from the hot, dry climate of the state of the United States it is named for. The plants form a rosette on the ground of finely ferny, grey-green leaves from which emerge a never ending display of single or double cream, lemon, gold, or pink poppy flowers with a glowing silken sheen.

Named cultivars are available including **'Mission Bells'** with a mixture of mainly double flowers in shades of white, rose, orange, pink, copper, gold and lemon, **'Purple Gleam'** in a beautiful new shade of rich lilac-purple, **'Ivory Castle'** with pure white flowers, **'Apricot Chiffon'**, and a brilliant. scarlet-red **'Red Chief'**. **'Thai Silk'** forms compact plants with large single or semi-double flowers with frilled, striped petals in a glowing combination of pink, orange, and bronzed red.

California poppies can be transplanted as seedlings while small, taking care not to damage the tap root; however, they are much better raised where they are to grow. Firm the soil down, scatter the seed thinly, cover with a thin layer of soil, firm down and water with as fine a nozzle as possible so as not to disturb the seed. After the seedlings emerge, control any weeds by scuffling the soil while they are still very small. The California poppy will look quite different. Mulch can be applied once the poppies have developed a sturdy rosette of leaves, keeping it away from the plant or they may rot.

The tinier species, the sundew *E. caespitosa*, has great charm and is largely overlooked by gardeners although the seed is commercially available. It is grown in the same way, and forms dwarf compact plants of finely divided, threadlike leaves, and in the cultivar **'Sundew'** prolific tiny lemon yellow flowers.

Canterbury Bells and Cups and Saucers
Campanula medium   Zones 6–10

This is a biennial if planted in spring, but an annual if planted in milder areas in fall. It is a mainstay of the English garden and suitable for cool to mild garden areas everywhere, forming a rosette of leaves from which emerge stems that are clad along their length with large bell-like flowers which may be single or double. In **'Cups and Saucers'** the outer layer of petals is flanged back to create a form reminiscent of daffodils. They are very easy to grow in the correct climate areas, and are planted in spring in a well composted garden to which lime has been added if the soil pH is below 6.5. Despite the seed industry's preoccupation with the dwarfing of plants, the old fashioned, tall Canterbury bells are still available either as mixed colors or as single blue, white, or rose pink colors. The dwarf, deep pink **'Chelsea Pink'** can flower in 3 months from sowing and is a true annual. **'Cups and Saucers'**, sometimes listed as *C. medium* var. *calycanthemum* is available in the old, taller forms which were so charming, and also in the mixed color, dwarf strain **'Ringing Bells'**.

A roadside planting in North Carolina of Californian Poppy, Eschscholzia californica.

Canterbury bells, Campanula medium, have large bell-like flowers and are the mainstay of the English garden.

Chinese Aster,
Calisstephus chinensis.

Chinese Aster

Calisstephus chinensis   Zones 7–10

This is the very beautiful and floriferous annual aster, not to be confused with the various species of *Aster* which includes the Michaelmas daisy and the Easter daisy. They are summer annuals and flower from the height of summer onward, peaking in early fall. They are widely adapted and will grow and flower well from cool climate gardens to the sub-tropics. Older cultivars include the

Dianthus chinensis,
Chinese pinks originate
from China and are
dense, low, spreading
plants with green
spear-shaped leaves,
ideal for lining paths or
edging gardens.

beautiful **'Ostrich Plume'** which is one of the the the tallest cultivars, growing to 2ft 6 in (75 cm), with huge, fully double, informal flowers in lavender, pink, purple and rose. Of similar height is the **'Giant Princess Aster'** with very large, long stemmed flowers, and the dependable old cultivar **'Crego Giant'** with fully double, large flower heads in many shades of pink and purple. Close in height is the newer **'Giant Ray Aster'** with needle-shaped petals, and up to 6 in (15 cm) across. A good blend of colors for this newer aster is found in the **'Quadrille'** mix. Compost should be added to the soil before planting, but avoid the use of rotted manures. A mulch should be used to conserve soil moisture. A number of dwarf cultivars have been brought out in the last two decades, and good bedding forms include the **'Dwarf Thousand Wonders'** mix, and **'Starlet'**.

Chinese Pinks

Dianthus chinensis   Zones 7–10

The annual pinks will often flower for a second year but they are treated as annuals in most gardens. Originating from China, they are dense, low, spreading plants with green spear-shaped leaves, ideal for lining paths, edging gardens, or for use in garden pots and tubs. They are the perfect choice to tuck into spaces between stones, and for use in rock gardens. The soil should be prepared with lime or dolomite. Excessive nitrogen causes the plants to elongate and it is better to plant them in an area to which compost was added the previous year. The round, single or slightly double, lightly scented flowers form a cushion of gently blended colors in shades of pink, rose, lilac, crimson and white. They require full sun. **'Magic Charms'** is a good cultivar, readily available, and containing the full color range. Plant seedlings 12 in (30 cm) apart. Also known as Indian pinks.

Clarkia *and* Mountain Garland, *and* Godetia

Clarkia unguiculata syn. C. elegans, C. amoena
Zones 7–11

Previously in two genera, and rather confusing for gardeners, the old-fashioned annual clarkias have been reclassified and joined with the annuals commonly known as godetias. They are now *C. unguiculata* and *C. amoena* respectively.

Clarkia, as many gardeners still call it, or mountain garland, has tall, slender stems to 3 ft (90 cm) or more. The flowers are about 1 in (2.5 cm) across, usually very frilled and double, arranged up the length of the stem. The most popular strains include three 1931 selections, **'Appleblossom'** with palest pink, double flowers tinged with salmon, **'Chieftain'** in a double mauve, and **'Salmon Queen'** in warm salmon pink.

Godetia or Farewell-to-Spring is one of the loveliest of all annual flowers, with large, shallow cupped, flowers with a satin sheen in colors of lilac, crimson, rose, and pink with deeper regular rouging of color in the center of the petals. It is a fast growing annual to 2 ft (60 cm) and, despite its common name, on the cooler coastline around Elk and Mendocino in northern California where it grows to full perfection, the farewell to spring is in fall. Dwarf cultivars are also available.

Cleome hassleriana *are valued for their unusual spidery flowers.*

Cleome *or* Spider Flower

Cleome hassleriana syn. C. spinosa
(of gardens) Zones 9–11

Native to Central and South America, and introduced into the United States c. 1810 and Europe later, the original cultivar **'Rose Queen'** released in 1846 is still available, and has been joined by **'Cherry Queen'**, **'Pink Queen'**, **'Violet Queen'**, and the pure white **'Helen Campbell'**.

Cleomes are without doubt one of the finest of all the annual flowers, growing to a height of 4–5 ft (1.2–1.5 m) in full sunshine and on good soil. The flowers have long stamens about 3 in (7.5 cm) in length and it is an excellent attractor of butterflies. Cleomes are used at the back of flower borders to give height. They require a well drained soil and full sun and are sown directly into the garden in mid- to late spring. Cleomes will usually reseed themselves annually.

Cosmos

Cosmos bipinnatus, C. sulphureus Zones 8–11

Cosmos are the solution when you need a beautiful effect on thin, poor soils in summer. They will flower their hearts out with little more assistance than planting and watering. Plant the seed directly into the soil where they are to flower. A mulch in summer is a luxury for them, but they will repay this indulgence with even geater beauty. Cosmos will flower

Farewell-to-Spring, Clarkia amoena, *is inappropriately named as it flowers until the end of summer.*

abundantly, always looking springtime fresh, until the cold of late fall finally finishes them. They make tall, sturdy plants that range in height from 3–4 ft. (90 cm–1.2 m). Recommended cultivars of *C. bipinnatus* include the pure white, **'Purity'** and the charming **'Seashells'** with each petal rolled from side to side to form individual trumpet shapes in shades of white, pink, and crimson. **'Psycho'** is not quite as alarming as it sounds. The mixture consists almost entirely of semi-double and double flowers in white, pink, and maroon. **'Picotee'** contains bicolor flowers, white painted with deep pink around the edge. **'Gloria'** has flowers the size of a tea saucer in rose pink with a deeply rouged pink base to the petals. There are several cultivars of *S. sulphureus* including **'Crest Lemon'** with double lemon flowers, **'Sunset'** with bronzed orange flowers, and the dwarf **'Cosmic Yellow'** and **'Cosmic Orange'** with strong, stocky, branched plants to only 12 in (30 cm).

Dame's Violet
Hesperis matronalis   Zones 3–9

All the common names of *Hesperis* (dame's violet, sweet rocket, damask flower) refer in some way to its beautiful scent which emanates on the night air. It is related to stocks and the

flowering plant is reminiscent of graceful, single stemmed, purple, lavender or tall white stocks with which it shares its sweet, spicy scent. It is a biennial and in suitable districts can act as a short lived perennial. But it is often used as an annual in mild to warm districts, planted in autumn and flowering the next summer. In North Carolina there are superb highway plantings of this brilliant flower. Such a massed planting is the way this annual used to be grown. But even a few plants will give pleasure. The seed can be sown in place, or raised as seedlings and transplanted. Prefering dryish conditions and sunshine, dames violet is often offered in the two separate colors, purple and white.

English Wallflower
Erysimum cheiri syn. *Cheiranthus cheiri*   Zones 3–9

The perfume of wallflowers is not to be missed in spring. It floats far and is unique to this species. Although classified as an annual, it is a short lived perennial under good conditions. The old-fashioned tall, single wallflowers are still the most fragrant kind, beautiful though some of the old perennial forms of this species are. There are also squat forms developed for the bedding industry but they lack the grace of the tall cultivars which at 18–20 in (45–50 cm) occupy a useful intermediate height in the garden. **'Fair Lady'** is the strain most likely to be found with an excellent mix of subtle color and good scent. The tall, branched, **'Double Flowered'** strain is also still available. Some older single color strains include dwarf, deep velvety crimson **'Vulcan'**, **'Cloth of Gold'**, and deep red **'Fire King'**. Among the best of the dwarf forms are **'Dwarf Primrose'**. But the old, tawny, russet shaded, tall, incredibly richly scented kind have disappeared from the shelves. **'Fair Lady'** is the closest. A beautiful, perennial, double form with excellent scent and frilly, small, golden

'Monarch Fair Lady' Erysimum cheiri, has an excellent mix of subtle color and good scent which makes it ideal for many gardens.

flowers was bred from English wallflower crossed with the Canary Island wallflower *E. bicolor*; it is called **'Harpur Crewe'** *Erysimum x kewensis*.

Wallflowers are undemanding, other than for the need for full sun and regular watering. They were called walflowers because they voluntarily seeded into the stone walls and crumbling structures of abandoned cottages and old castles, so they are well able to cling to life. However they are responsive to the inclusion of modest amounts of com-post in the soil, and the pH should be adjusted upward to neutral with dolomite or lime if you garden on acid soil.

Flowering Tobacco, Nicotiana langsdorfii, is currently popular becaause of its green flowers and foliage.

Flowering Tobacco *and* Woodland Tobacco

Nicotiana alata syn. N. affinis, N. langsdorfii,
N. sylvestris   Zones 7–11

Flowering tobacco or night-scented tabacco, *N. alata* is a native of Brazil. Earlier forms closed their flowers during the day but many newer cultivars remain open. At night the flowers have a powerful sweet scent, making tobacco an ideal plant around a porch or patio.

N. langsdorfii is a Brazilian species also being sold as **'Lime Tree Nicotiana'** that is now exceptionally popular due to the ever increasing interest in green flowers. It is a quickly growing annual to 3 ft (90 cm) or a little more. The flowers are bell-like, pinched near the mouth, and small, no more than 1 in (2.5 cm) long, in a clear green. Although small, the flowers are beautifully displayed and the impression is charming. A recent new seed strain has been released with cream splashed variegation on the leaves under the name **'Cream Splash'**.

Woodland tobacco *N. sylvestris* is a perennial from Brazil, but in most gardens it behaves like an annual as it is intolerant of cold. The season can be extended by planting in a warm position against a brick or stone wall.

It will grow comfortably to a statuesque 5 ft (1.5 m) and can grow beyond that under optimum conditions. The leaves are scented of petunias when touched. Terminal clusters of very long, slender, white flowers remain open during the day and are elegant. As night draws on, the sweet daytime scent becomes intense and floats far beyond the plant, a mixture of jasmine and freesia.

All three species enjoy a cool root run, rich soil, and preferably morning sunshine. Plants are raised from seed. Firm the sterilized soil in the seedling tray, scatter the seed over the surface, and cover with a thin layer of sand. Water from the base by placing in a tray partially filled with water, using capillary action to moisten the soil. Transplant the seedlings at the 4–6 leaf stage into individual small pots, and plant out when they are healthy small plants. Once each species is established in the garden, there should be small batches coming up every year with no further effort by the gardener.

Forget-me-not
Myosotis sylvatica   Zones 5–10

Once introduced to your garden, you should never be without this indispensable garden annual. It prefers a cool area with morning sun and a well enriched, moisture retentive soil.

Garden forget-me-not, Myosotis sylvatica 'Blue Ball', is grown as an annual for its bright lavender-blue, yellow-eyed flowers

The seeds are raised in trays or pots, and are sown with a thin covering of soil, either in fall or in spring. The seedlings are spaced 10 in (25 cm) apart. Seed is unusually slow to germinate, taking 3–4 weeks, and the seedling pots must not dry out during that time. A small sheet of glass put over them will maintain moisture.

Forget-me-nots or English forget-me-nots, are used extensively as an interplanting for spring bulbs but perhaps look their best planted more naturally, forming small pools of blue in protected areas.

Garden Snapdragon
Antirrhinum majus   Zones 6–10

Although snapdragons are true, if short lived, perennials and are treated as such in many village gardens around the Mediterranean, for most gardeners these are grown as annuals and so are included here. Rust on snapdragons in some areas is another reason for gardeners to clear all their snapdragons at the end of the season and rotate their crops for the next year.

Originating from Spain, snapdragons make upright, bushy growth. In the tough, old village strains that are close to the original domesticated forms, they reach 4 ft (1.2 m) with ease, growing among stones, and with no sign of rust even at the end of the season. The original flowers have a closed trumpet to ensure self pollination—and every child who ever has the opportunity squeezes the 'dragon faces' open and shut, hence the name 'snapdragon'. Breeding has concentrated on dwarfing, creating subtle color ranges that would seriously puzzle a 19th century gardener, opening the trumpet to create azalea-flowered forms, doubling the flowers, and then increasing disease resistance to cope with the decreased vigour. Among the best is the old strain **'Monarch'** which is medium sized, vigorous, and rust

'Tall Snapdragon',
Antirrhinum majus.
Originally from Spain
these upright and bushy
plants have a spectacular
closed trumpet.

resistant, and the F1 hybrid **'Madame Butterfly'**. Pure white **'White Wonder'** is an old strain with vigour. **'Appleblossom'** is also vigorous with pale pink coloring. **'Sawyer's Old-fashioned Snapdragon'** was found growing in old stone walls and is as tough in constitution as it sounds, but also very attractive.

Snapdragons now come in a range of heights and a very wide range of colors. Plants showing any sign of rust should be dusted with sulphur. They should be given full sun and a soil that is not too rich. The very finest of blooms can be grown on quite lean ground, so long as there is adequate moisture.

Garden Verbena *or* Sweet Verbena

Verbena x hybrida   Zones 9–10

Strictly speaking, this group of hybrids are short lived perennials, but in practise their blooming falls away after the first year and most gardeners remove them at the end of the season. Unlike most verbenas, the garden verbena or sweet verbena, have a distinct sweet fragrance detectable at some distance. They make excellent spillovers for garden edges, rock embankments, and for use in window boxes and large tubs. The plants are low growing, dense and spreading, and are virtually covered in flowers for several months after coming into bloom. The inflorescences are dense and shallowly rounded, and the individual flowers are tubular, usually with a white eye in the center. Strains selected for a single color, as well as mixed strains, are available. **'Peaches & Cream'** is one of the newest and perhaps the prettiest of all. It flowers constantly and rings the changes on cream with every shade of peach in the same inflorescence. **'Derby'** is one of the finest mixed color strains, coming into flower early and flowering continuously with rich, clear colors of red, rich rose, purple and white. The most pronounced sweet fragrance is in the old pure

Easy to care for, garden
verbena, Verbena x
hybrida 'Sissinghurst' is
an ideal plant to use for
ground cover.

white cultivar '**White Queen**'. Other worthwhile cultivars include '**Sissinghurst**' with flamingo pink flowers and '**Homestead Purple**' with an excellent display of rich lilac-purple flowers.

Verbena does best on a soil that has been enriched with compost for a previous crop. However it is a very willing plant and will do well provided it is regularly watered and receives full sun for most of the day. If the ground is markedly acidic, the pH should be adjusted upward with lime or dolomite to close to pH 7. If the plants are mulched once they are fully established, they will soon cover the mulch and no weeding will be required for the season.

Larkspur
Consolida ajacis syn. C. ambigua   Zones 7–11

This species is native to the Mediterranean region and has been grown in English gardens since the late 16th century. Larkspurs are tall growing with slender, upright stems to 4 ft (1.2 m). The flowers which may be single or double are arranged evenly up the flower stems. They are excellent for the back of borders, giving height and a feeling of airiness with their soft pastel colors of pink,

white, lavender and purple. The stems keep very well as cut flowers as long as the lower leaves are stripped. The individual flowers dry perfectly for pot pourri, and they also press beautifully, perhaps the easiest flower of all for this purpose.

Larkspurs require full sun, good drainage, and the addition of organic matter in the form of compost.

Linaria
Linaria maroccana   Zones 6–10

This charming species, also known as baby snapdragon or toad flax, is native to Morocco and despite its delicate appearance is heat and dry resistant, flowering profusely in spring. It comes in usually bicolor flowers in cream, apricot, purple, mauve, gold and pink, no two plants the same. Planted en masse they look like an exotic oriental carpet. Seed is sown where the plants are to flower, usually in fall in milder climates and in spring in cool areas. The old strain '**Fairy Bouquet**' is still the one planted, and any attempt to enlarge the flowers would defeat the purpose. The plants grow to 12 in (30 cm), and require an open, sunny position and no weed competition. They take 10 weeks from seed to flowering.

Right: Larkspur, Consolida ajacis, is excellent for the back of borders giving height. They have soft pastel colors of pink, white, lavender and purple.

Far Right: The fairy bouquet, Linaria maroccana, is a hardy annual but is susceptible to root and stem rot. No two plants have the same coloring.

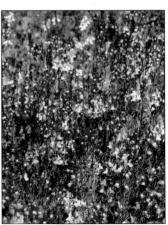

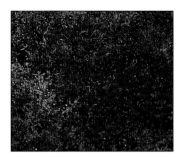

Far left: Lobelia erinus 'Crystal Palace' is a blue cultivar, excellent for edging and for use in window boxes and mixed pot plantings.

Left: Nigella damascena, 'Love-in-a-Mist', has fine and lacy foliage.

Lobelia *or* Edging Lobelia
Lobelia erinus   Zones 7–11

This is one of the most useful plants in the spring and summer garden, not least because of its intense blue color. New colors have been available for some time in pinks, lilac (**'Lilac Fountain'**, **'Riverina Lilac'**), white (**'White Lady'**), and and red (**'Rose Fountain'**, **'Rosamond'**) but these are colors easily found elsewhere. Excellent blue cultivars include **'Riviera Sky Blue'**, **'Cambridge Blue'**, **'Blue Fountain'**, and **'Crystal Palace'**. Lobelia was traditionally used as a path and gardening edging, but it also finds use as spill-overs, interplantings, and for window boxes and mixed pot plantings.

Love-in-a-Mist
Nigella damascena   Zones 6–10

This species entered into culture in the latter half of the 16th century, and was included together with an illustration in Gerard's *Herbal*. It had many country names including Lady-in-the-Green and Jack-in-the-Bush. The foliage is fine and lacy, and the flowers nestle within to give a misted effect. The seed cases that follow are horned and interesting, often used by flower arrangers. The semi-double **'Miss Jekyll'** is an older strain, still unsurpassed with rich, double blue flowers. Newer strains are **'Mulberry Rose'** which opens creamy white turning to deep rose. A good standard mixed color range is **'Persian Jewels'**.

Love-in-a-Mist is planted where it is to grow and will usually self seed satisfactorily in future years if flower arrangers do not reach the seedheads first.

Lupin
Lupinus spp.   Zones 7–11

A number of North American lupin species are grown as annuals for the summer garden including the delightful rich blue **'Texas Blue Bonnet'** *L. texensis*, the low growing *L. nanus* of California, particularly in the strain **'Pixie Delight'**, and the Mexican *L. hartwegii*. Lupins run to leaf rather than flower in rich soil, and soil that has not been composted

Lupinus texensis 'Texas Blue Bonnet' is a bushy annual that has a delightful rich blue flower.

African marigolds set against green grass at the Butchart Garden, British Columbia, Canada.

for a while is best. All lupins are nitrogen fixing plants and will enrich the soil if dug back into the soil at the end of flowering. They all appreciate the addition of lime or dolomite to the soil. Sow where they are to bloom, approximately $1/2$ in (1 cm) deep.

Marguerite Carnations
Dianthus caryophyllus   Zones 8–10

This is a true annual form of carnation, flowering reliably in summer if seedlings are planted in spring. The seedlings should be started under cover in late winter in cool climates, and in mild, almost frost-free climates can be planted in fall. The flowers are mainly double, intensely and spicily fragrant, and come in a wide range of colors including lemon. Many of the old carnation color patterns can be seen in this group, including 'flakes' with their irregular fine dots, stripes, and splashes. They require full sun, the modest addition of compost (or can be planted in a site composted for a previous crop), and the addition of dolomite or lime to the ground as they prefer an alkaline soil.

The single flowers of signet marigold, Tagetes tenuifolia, have a wonderful citrus scented foliage.

Marigold
Tagetes spp.   Zones 9–11

The African Marigold is an excellent plant in the right place, which is to say that it is so, brilliantly golden or orange that it can be difficult to blend other than in the bright light near the seaside. Two memorable gardens—one in England built at the height of the 1920s, the other the 'Butchart Garden' near Victoria in British Columbia— discovered the same secret. They isolated the planting completely and set the color against green grass. The English garden was planted as a checkerboard of gold and green, the perfect feature for a stylish, jazz age garden. The 'Butchart Garden' placed two long solid rectangles of gold to mark the edge of a shallow, formal, walled terrace. Use these sunshine flowers in a solid block of a single color. Plants are easily raised either in seedling trays or directly planted where they are to flower. They will grow without much assistance, but a finer and much more lasting display will result from the incorporation of a generous amount of compost to the soil. The old strain '**Crackerjack**' is still an excellent choice, as is the newer

'Sunset Giants'. 'Inca' is an early flowering hybrid with huge, brilliant colors available separately.

French marigolds *T. patula* resemble a dwarf African marigold. Like the African marigold, the French marigold is native to Mexico. It entered England via France, hence the common name. They are used as nematicidal plants, notably in the field cropping of garlic in Gilroy, California. They also find extensive use in the ornamental garden and in planted tubs and window gardens. Good strains include the crested flowered **'Honeycomb'**, **'Bonita'** mixed, and **'Legion of Honour'** with pretty, single gold flowers marked with brown.

The Signet marigold *T. tenuifolia* is much more refined than the other two annual marigolds. It is low and dense and spreading, covering in small, single flowers. The foliage is distinctly citrus scented in some strains such as **'Lemon Gem'**, **'Golden Gem'**, and 'Tangerine Gem'. The fragrance is fresh and lingers. In small amounts it has been used as a culinary herb to flavor custards, sorbets and other dishes, and also in *pot pourri*.

Meadow Foam

Limnanthes douglasii   Zones 8–10

Indigenous to the west coast of North America, meadow foam carpets the soil in spring with low growing, delicately fernlike, light green, foliage and masses of single, cupped, small, round flowers about 1 in (2.5 cm) across which are cream with a golden yellow center. The plants grow to only 6 in (15 cm), and do indeed resemble a delicate foam. A pure golden variation also occurs in wild populations. It is easily grown from seed sown where the plants are to flower in early spring, covering the seed very lightly with soil and watering with a fine nozzle to prevent soil disturbance.

Meadow foam carpets the soil in spring with low growing, fernlike, foliage.

Nasturtium, Garden

Nasturtium *and* Indian Cress

Tropaeolum majus

(See 'Salad Greens'.)

Petunia

Petunia x hybrida   Zones 9–11

The common garden petunia arose from hybridization of two South American species which were both in North America by the 19th century. The perfume for which the petunia is famed was passed down through one parent *P. integrifolia* syn. *P. violacea*. The other parent was the white flowered *P. axillaris*. The petunia is closely allied to *Nicotiana*. The scent of the leaves of some species of *Nicotiana* like *N. sylvestris* clearly reveals the relationship. The slightest touch releases the same delicious scent as that of petunia flowers. Modern petunias remain fragrant but the old, semi-vining, pink, lavender and white types that filled gardens until the 1960s shed fragrance far and wide, and during the last 50 years have traded some of their fragrance for size, brilliant colors and patternings, and doubling of the petal. Fortunately the Seed Savers Exchange in Iowa, which has a section of its biodiversity conservation gardens devoted to the old flowers and herbs, has taken the almost lost early petunias under its protective wing.

Petunias grow well on sandy through to heavy loam soils and require full sunshine. They can be raised from seed, but as it is very fine it should be mixed with washed river sand so that they can be spread fairly evenly over the surface of the seedling mix. Water the tray from beneath by immersing the base in a shallow tray of water and let capillary action draw the water upward. Cover the seed with sand and place a sheet of glass over the tray until germination commences.

Modern petunias can be divided into two major groups: the grandifloras which have very large and somewhat vining plants as they age and which includes types such as 'Color Parade' and 'Picotee', and the more compact, very floriferous multifloras such as 'Celestial Rose', 'Fire Chief', and 'Snowball'. Some petunias have been bred for hanging baskets and spilling from pots—both these forms of gardening are enjoying a revival—rather than for bedding. These belong to the pendula group, of which the very fashionable 'Lady Purple' and the recently released 'Lady Blue' are good examples, flowering well into fall. The search for ultra-compact dwarf petunia cultivars is largely driven by gardeners managing public parks and gardens. The group developed for such bedding purposes are called nana compacta.

The most popular of the new releases is the wave series, which have the habit of rolling over the ground in wave after wave of richly colored, dense flowers. 'Lavender Wave', 'Tidal Wave Silver' and the 'Ramblin' also popular. series are also riding high on the garden charts. The latter are low growing to only 8 in (20 cm) but spread to four times that width, and are covered in bright flowers. The equally new supertunias are grown on a richly composted diet to keep up with their extraordinary growth rate.

Petunias are well known for their fragrance, size, color and vivid patterns.

about 3 ft (1 m). They require a very well drained but moisture retentive soil and full sunshine. In warmer areas the plants should be rowed out in autumn as they flower quickly once the temperatures begin to rise.

The Swan River everlasting daisy *R. mangliesii* is widely cultivated in spring to summer gardens and is a desert ephemeral, forming great carpets across the desert after rains. The plants have several shades of pink flowers simultaneously creating a charming effect.

Pink strawflower, Rhodanthe chlorocephala subsp. Rosea is one of the mainstays of the dried flower trade.

Pink Strawflower *and* Swan River Everlasting Daisy

Rhodanthe chlorocephala ssp. *rosea, R. manglesii*
Zones 7–11

This South Western Australian annual is popular in warm gardens around the world, particularly in Mediterranean climates. It produces exquisite, shiny flowers in shades of soft, clear pink to white. The petals are thin and feel as if made from paper. The flowers dry with great ease, and together with statice this is one of the mainstays of the dried flower trade. It is also used extensively in craft work. This species flowers profusely in spring on slender plants to

Poor Man's Orchid

Schizanthus x wisetonensis   Zones 7–11

With their pretty butterfly-like flowers and rich tapestry colors, poor man's orchid, or butterfly flower, from Chile is a delightful annual that gives an outstanding display. In cool climates it is greenhouse grown, but in warmer areas it is easily raised, reaching about 3 ft (1 m). The plants are susceptible to frost and should be planted out after all risk has passed. Seed is sown in winter or spring. '**Hit Parade**' and '**Star Parade**' are recommended strains. They dislike excessive heat but are usually tolerant of sub-tropical areas mitigated by the sea, or by altitude.

An annual that produces an outstanding display in any garden is Poor Man's orchid, Schizanthus x wisetonensis, which has pretty butterfly-like flowers.

The 'Iceland Poppy', Papaver nudicaule is a beautiful poppy that has been cultivated in many parts of the world.

Fairy Primrose, Primula malacoides, will thrive in damp conditions.

Poppy

Papaver spp.   Zones 5–9

A number of poppies that are part of our spring gardens are annuals or biennials. The wild red corn or field poppy, has enjoyed a return to gardens, appreciated for its extraordinary glowing silken red petals. The Shirley poppies were developed from the corn poppy by the Reverend Shirley for whom they are named. They come in singles and doubles, and are long-stemmed, medium to large flowered, with subtle, silken changes of color blending white with pinks and crimsons, and lacking the dark cross that marks the base inside the flower of the corn poppy.

The old peony poppy is a tall, silvered-green annual with huge powderpuff heads of very double flowers in a stunning range of colors from scarlet to pinks, white, mulberry, and subtle mixes of pearl grey with pink or purple. Iceland poppies *P. nudicaule* have been the focus of intensive breeding from time to time in the last century and recent work using traditional breeding methods has taken this beautiful poppy to new dimensions of color, health, strength, and beauty.

Primula

Primula malacoides, P. obconica   Zones 8–11

Both the Fairy primrose *P. malacoides* and *P. obconica* are grown as bedding annuals for spring, and also for pot culture. Seedlings should be spaced approximately 9 in (23 cm) apart. Both species come in the same color range of rose, pink, mauve and white and superficially differ mainly by the larger flowers in *P. obconica*. Both are candelabra style primula.

For this reason, they are very compatible species and often used together. **'Postford White'** is an old cultivar but still very widely used and nothing compares with it for ethereal beauty when planted in a small drift in a glade.

Prince of Wales Feathers *and* Cockscombs

Celosia argentea syn. *C. pyramidalis, C. cristata*
Zones 10–12

Coming from tropical Asia, Prince of Wales feathers forms upward pointing, feathery plumes of flowers usually in brilliant gold or lush regal crimson. The foliage of the golden yellow form is green, but the entire plant of the deep red celosia is suffused with crimson. The plants grow to about 3 ft (1 m). More recent releases have included apricot, cream, and purple in the colors available. A tall growing mixed color range of quality is **'Century Mixed'**. The cultivar **'Flamingo Feather'** has bicolor plumes that are rose pink on the upper half, and pale pink or white at the base.

Cockscombs are curiosities with fasciated flower spikes forming waved, crested inflorescences that strongly resemble the comb of a cock or some fanciful coral. The original colors supplied in this form are a velvety crimson red and gold, and these are still the colors seen in the tropics, but the same range of colors now available in Prince of Wales feathers is also available in cockscombs. A good strain containing all the modern colors can be found in *Celosia* **'Coral Fountains'**.

Both types need full sun and regular watering. While seedlings are available, many gardeners sow seed directly into the garden bed, ensuring that regular watering occurs. The beds should be prepared with generous amounts of compost and smoothed over before planting. Cultivars range in height to around 2–3 ft (60–90 cm), but dwarf forms are also available.

Rose moss

Portulaca grandiflora   Zones 10–11

Rose moss, Portulaca grandiflora, is also known as the sun plant.

This is one of those annuals regaining popularity. With our interest in conserving water these days, this is an ideal ground hugging, succulent plant spreading to about 8 in (20 cm) with brilliantly enameled single or semi-double flowers in saturated colors of Thai pink, pure gold, clear red, and others. The hottest summer day cannot faze it, and it will be one of the last annuals to succumb to drought. It is one of the least fussy of plants, and should be raised from seed, either

Celosia argentea, Prince of Wales feathers (Plumosa group) produces feathery plumes of flowers.

planted in punnets or directly sown in the garden. It is ideal as a trailing plant, in pots, or planted among rocks. Rose moss or sun plant, is highly adaptable in terms of soil provided it is well drained, and although they are arid zone succulents, they appreciate watering, particularly during the establishment phase.

Stock *and* Night-Scented Stock

Matthiola incana, M. longipetala ssp. *bicornis* syn. *M. bicornis, M. tristis*   Zones 6–10

The beautiful stock is powerfully scented with a warm, rich, spicy fragrance. They were introduced into cultivation in England early and were common in Elizabethan gardens where they were known as 'stock gillofers', later to be gillyflowers. All flowers that shared the rich spicy clove scent were known at that time as gillyflowers, so that wallflowers were wall gillyflowers, clove pinks were clove gillyflowers, and stocks were stock gillyflowers. Fragrance was perhaps even more important in that century than color. By the end of the 16th century, double stocks were in gardens and all the common colors of stocks available. Four major types

were developed: the Brompton stocks introduced in the 18th century, planted in mid-summer to bloom the following summer, and of which the formula mix **'Brompton Lady'** is an example; the ten week stocks or summer flowering stocks, of which the giant Excelsior column stocks are an example; the autumn flowering or **'East Lothian'** stocks, for which the **'Kelvedon'** strain and the **'East Brompton finest mixed'** are seed strains; and the winter flowering or beauty of Nice type. All four groups are still grown to provide almost year round stocks. A beautiful perennial, single white flowered *M. incana* is also available which must be close to the original.

The night–scented stock pours forth a powerful, rich, spicy scent at night that is exotic, warm and oriental, entirely at variance with its rather drab daytime look. It is native to southern Europe and is treated as an annual. The seed is scattered where it is to grow and covered with a thin layer of soil, then watered in. It is somewhat insignificant, slender and grows to about 20 in (50 cm), with very small white to brown flowers, yet they perfume the air from a distance as the temperature falls and evening draws on.

Matthiola incana is powerfully scented with a warm rich spicy fragrance and has long spikes of mauve flowers.

The common sunflower, Helianthus annuus, is one of the most popular plants in any organic garden.

Sunflower

Helianthus annuus   Zones 4–11

Apart from the giant sunflowers and others grown primarily for seed but very acceptable in the flower garden, there are annual sunflowers that are grown purely for pleasure. Indeed, few plants are as rewarding and simple to grow—or create more impact.

A great deal of research is currently underway to develop new forms of sunflowers. The first of these, 'Discovery Mix', is now available,

Other cultivars well worth finding are 'Italian White', the gorgeous 'Lion's Mane' which was painted by Van Gogh, and 'Gloriosa Polyheaded', often seen depicted in old garden paintings.

Sweet Alyssum

Lobularia maritima syn. *Alyssum maritimum*
                                        Zones 7–10

Found growing wild in places like the high cliffs of Provence and elsewhere beside the sea, this is not only one of the indispensable annuals for garden edgings, spillovers, pots and window boxes in all climates except the true tropics, but also one of the best choices for seaside gardens. It has an

exceptionally sweet, honey fragrance that is very attractive to bees, and forms a dense, low, cushioning, spreading plant that may grow to 12 in (30 cm) wide. The inflorescence is composed of densely arranged tiny, four-petalled flowers. The pure white form is the best known, and to many noses the most fragrant, but there are many charming variations available in shades of pink, lilac, and purple.

'Snowcloth' remains one of the finest cultivars and is a compact, densely flowered white form. 'Rosie O'Day' has very pretty, fragrant pink flowers and is densely carpeting.

Sweet alyssum Lobularia maritima, *is an indispensable annual for garden edgings, spillovers, pots and window boxes.*

'**Oriental Nights**' forms dense mats of rich purple.

Sweet alyssum or sweet alice, is extremely tough once it is established, and will also produce a pleasant number of seedlings in the following year in places you may not have thought of. Leave them in their chosen places. They do wonderfully well when self sown. Provide a sunny, well drained position for sweet alyssum. While they cope with a wide range of soil, they prefer a neutral to slightly alkaline soil and acid soils should be adjusted with dolomite or lime.

Sweet Mignonette
Reseda odorata   Zones 6–10

Originating from North Africa, this is an annual of modest garden charms visually, but it is grown for its delicious scent. It requires a sunny, well drained position, and can be used for bedding in areas where its fragrance will be appreciated, such as around garden seats, below open windows, and near patios. It is also excellent in pots. The flowers are yellow to reddish and small, appearing from spring to late autumn, and the plant will grow to around 2 ft (60 cm). Three cultivars are fairly readily available,

Sweet Mignonette, Reseda odorata, is grown for its delicious scent. The flowers are yellow to reddish and small.

'**Ameliorata**' which is excellent for pot culture and has very fragrant, deep rose flowers, the very old '**Grandiflora**' with large, very fragrant heads, and '**Machet**', a dwarf French cultivar from the 1890s well suited to pot culture.

Sweet Pea
Lathyrus odoratus   Zones 4–10

The first sweet pea was discovered by a Franciscan monk, Father Cupani, in Sicily in 1696. He was led to the place where it scrambled among the rocks by a scent of extraordinary sweetness, and discovered a climbing plant with stems of large pea-like flowers in rich maroon and purple. He subsequently forwarded seeds to an English schoolmaster Dr Robert Uvedale and the first commercial release in 1724 was '**Cupani**'. Sweet peas breed true and it remained one of the few cultivars until the 1870s when plant breeders began to deliberately cross the different strains that had emerged as chance mutations. One of those chance mutations was the beautiful pink and white flowered '**Painted Lady**' from 1737. Both are still available.

Henry Eckford created the grandiflora class in 1877, among the finest of these being the deliciously scented pink '**Prima Donna**'. This sweet pea subsequently sported three times in the same year and the famed class of Spencer sweet peas were founded by a then gardener at Althorpe, the estate of the Earl and Lady Spencer. Named '**Lady Spencer**', it too is still available. The second sport '**Gladys Unwin**' founded the fortunes of the great English seed house of Unwin which remain leading specialists in sweet pea breeding, and the third sport was found by Eckford himself.

By 1910, the Spencers reigned supreme, and in the United States Mr. Atlee Burpee of the famous seed firm popularized the sweet pea. Natural dwarf sports also arose such as

Apart from the dwarf cultivars, all sweet peas require trellising. Teepees constructed of a circle of thin bamboo canes pushed into the ground and tied at the top are a spectacular way of growing this annual. Sweet peas should be supported with branched twigs in their first stage of growth to encourage climbing. They need a sunny, open, well drained site to which generous amounts of compost has been added. If the soil is acid, dolomite or lime should be added. Once the plants have begun to climb, they should be mulched, keeping the mulch away from the base of the stems.

Sweet peas, Lathyrus odoratus. Apart from the dwarf cultivars, all sweet peas require trellising.

Sweet Scabious *and* Sternkugel
Scabiosa atropurpurea, S. stellata   Zones 7–11

'Cupid' found at Santa Barbara in California. Around 25 of these amazingly fragrant early cultivars have been rediscovered around the world and are now commercially available once again. The modern sweet peas derived from these heirlooms are somewhat larger and often much frilled, but the striped and flaked types were already available in the early 20th century. Among the finest of the more modern, named sweet peas are the very fragrant, multiple award winning '**Leamington**' with very frilly, clear, deep lilac flowers, vanilla scented '**Mabel Gower**' with lavender blue flowers, deep lilac '**Patience**' with a truly delicious scent, '**Rose Fondant**' bred by Unwins, and having intense fragrance, and the lovely '**Rosy Frills**', a very large flowered white broadly edged with deep rose-pink and superbly fragrant. Sweet peas are largely sold today as mixes and among the best are '**Unwin's Striped**', '**Old Spice**', '**Royal Family**', the older but very reliable (particularly in hot summer areas) '**Seventh Heaven**' and the dwarf '**Knee High**' which lends itself to pot culture.

The pincushion flowers are characterized by lightly but very sweetly scented, dense flat heads of small flowers with protruding filaments that give the impression of an old-fashioned pin cushion packed with pins. Their alternative name of mourning bride (or mourning widow) refered to the often somber colors of the flowers. This species occurs on

Sweet scabious looks like an old-fashioned pin cushion packed with pins.

chalky soils in full sun, and to grow it successfully in the garden acid soils need to be adjusted in pH. An irresistible cultivar is '**Chat Noir**'; it is very dark and also very sweetly scented. The strain '**Mixed Giant Hybrids**' are large, sweetly scented, and in an excellent color range including deep maroon.

Sternkugel *S. stellata* bears spherical heads up to 4 in (10 cm) in diameter and composed of about 20 pale blue flowers. When the flowers drop and the head dries it has a parchment texture and delicate moulding much admired by flower arrangers. It grows to about 12 in (30 cm).

The flowering stems of sweet william, Dianthus barbatus, *are topped with a densely clustered head of small, carnation-type flowers.*

Sweet Sultan
Centaurea moschata   Zones 6–10

This charming old-fashioned annual flower was introduced 350 years ago and remains a favorite. The plants are bushy and bear large, sweetly scented, fluffy cornflower style flowers.The strain '**Imperialis**' is the most popular and contains a mixture of pink, purple, white, and yellow flowers. They are raised and used in the same way as Bachelor's buttons.

Sweet William
Dianthus barbatus   Zones 4–10

Although Sweet William is classified as a biennial, it is often quite long lived in mild climate gardens. It was not mentioned in the literature until Dodeons, Flemish physician to Emperor Charles V, wrote of it in 1554 in the *Historie of Plants*. He described it as growing on the hillsides in Germany. It was not in English gardens until the 16th century, when it showed up as a recorded purchase for the additions made by Henry VIII to Hampton Court. Gerard described it in his *Herball* in 1597. It has been sug-gested that its common name was given in hon-our of St. William of Aquitaine. It also went by the name of 'London tufties'.The name is apt as the plant first forms a low, dense tuft of coarse, grasslike leaves. In its second year if spring planted, it puts forth flow-ering stems about 18 in (45 cm) tall in most cultivars topped with a densely clustered head of small, carnation-type flowers, single or double. The auricula-eyed forms have been available since the 17th century and have a clear white eyepot, while other types are in one solid color or subtly laced with other colors. Sweet william is indeed sweetly scented. The species also gave rise to a group called mule pinks, for their sterility, not their obduracy in the garden,

The flowers of tidy tips are clear golden with a splash of white at the tip.

and were derived from a cross with carnations. '**Napoléon III**' is the best known of this old group.

Most of the named cultivars have disappeared but '**Nigricans**' is still available, and well worth growing with purple foliage and stems, and the darkest red flowers imaginable. The strain '**Auricula Eyed**' is still available, as is the tall '**Double Flowered**', and '**Harlequin**' has a mix of shades in every head.

Sweet william responds to cultivation in moderately composted soil, and prefers an alkaline pH. Acidic soils should be adjusted with lime or dolomite. They need a well-drained, sunny position.

Tidy Tips
Layia platyglossa   Zones 8–11

The genus *Layia* consists of 15 species endemic to California, and one of the most beautiful sites of the American spring are huge, open, valleys in the north carpeted to the horizon with this beautiful plant. The flowers of tidy tips are charming when inspected. Clear golden, medium sized, each flower tip is precisely painted white, hence the name. They require full sun and moist but well drained soil. They are ideal for bedding out, excellent for

cutting and long lived in vases, and flower through from early spring to the end of summer summer.

Tree Marigold
Tithonia diversifolia   Zones 9–11

This glowing Mexican species is a butterfly attractor in a class of its own, comparable only to the butterfly bush *Buddleja*. It is a strong and rapid grower, forming a tall, open branched, herbaceous bush with large, furred, hastate leaves, and producing a constant supply of brilliant burnt orange flowers that resemble large zinnias. It normally reaches about 10 ft (3 m) in the garden, and is best suited to the back of a border.

The tree marigold is particularly effective in attracting a butterflies to your garden.

Viola *or* Pansy *and* Wild Pansy

V. x wittrockiana, V. tricolor,   Zones 4–10

The tiny faces of wild pansies, or Johnny-jump-ups or heartsease as they are commonly known, rarely fail to charm with their whiskered faces and perky looks. They are also exceptionally easy to grow, often naturalize in the garden, returning to greet the early spring each year. They love the cool weather and the first real heat of summer quickly dispatches them. Early colonists carried the seed around the world with them. It was introduced into America in the 17th century and there took its name from its habit of scattering its seed around the garden and 'jumping up' the next season in the most unexpected but always becoming places. It was introduced into Australia very early in the colony's settlement but retained its old English name of 'heartsease'.

In warmer areas the plants are set out in autumn. In cool gardens they are planted in spring, and while they make a later start they will often survive the summer to go on and flower in the autumn. Cut the plants back in such areas to encourage a new flush of flowering. They are not fussy about soil although it should be well drained. They grow best in a sunny position. No two plants of heartsease are entirely alike. They all have a yellow lower petal, cream middle petals and two deep purple upper petals, hence their specific name 'tricolor', but ring endless subtle changes on the theme.

Pansies, bred in part from *V. tricolor*, are a little more demanding as they are more highly bred and refined to produce those exquisite patterns and colors. They prefer to grow on a rich, well drained soil. Compost should be incorporated before planting, together with lime or dolomite if the soil is very acid. They can take three weeks to germinate if you are raising your own seedlings.

Pansies are among the annuals that have attracted a great deal of attention from plant breeders for over 150 years. New strains appear regularly. Reliable cultivars that have proved themselves for some time include **'Aalsmere Giant'** with huge flowers in a wide range of

Viola x wittrockiana is a hybrid group that offers flowers of a great many hues. They grow slowly reaching about 8 in (20 cm) in height and spread.

colors, 'Majestic Giants' with flowers up to 4 in (10 cm) wide, and 'Swiss Giants'. If you are less interested in size than in beautiful markings or unusual forms, 'Rococo' would appeal. Also known as 'Germania', it comes in a range of darker, velvety flowers which are frilled and refrilled. The 'Black' pansy is as close to black as any flower reaches and has a velvety sheen. The recently released 'Padparadya' is an extraordinary deep glowing orange, and nothing could be perkier than 'Jolly Joker'. It is a multiple award winner and has intense but soft orange lower petals that contrast quite startlingly with the dark purple upper petals. The 'Crystal Bowl' strain has medium sized flowers that are in pure clean colors with no markings. 'Accord Red Blotch' is an intense burgundy red. Perhaps the most charming in recent times is a pansy close to the original 19th century strain, 'Penny Azure Wing' which is not much larger than Heartsease, and has a white eye shaded heavenly blue. For a rich blue pansy, the old 'Ullswater' is still readily available and a mass planting creates the effect of a deep blue pool on a

summer day. Many of these recent releases have blurred the line between the classes of viola.

Recent breeding efforts have been directed at extending the lives of garden pansies by reducing their sensitivity to heat. The result has been the development of the heat tolerant 'Universal' series which allows flowering to persist well into summer in places that never grew pansies at that time of the year, even persisting into the cooler autumn.

Viola tricolor 'Bowles' Black' is as close to black as any flower reaches and has a very velvety sheen.

Johnny-jump-up Viola cornuta (Violaceae) is a compact annual or short-lived perennial, native to Spain and the Pyrenees Mountains.

Violetta

Viola cornuta   Zones 6–9

The horned violet *V. cornuta* has given
rise to a class of small, perennial,
pansy-like flowers called violettas.
Many of these are reliably perennial
and are propagated by cuttings or
division. Others are treated as annuals,
sold as seed and grown in the same
way as pansies to which they are
closely related. *V. cornuta* was involved
as a major contributor to the pansy
class. The seed propagated violettas
include: '**Helen Mount**' which resembles Johnny-jump-ups but comes in
a soft blend of lavender blue, lemon
and white; '**Admiration**' with medium
sized, deep velvety blue flowers; the
old '**Blue of Paris**' with beautiful,
medium sized, heavenly blue flowers;
velvety purple, small, very floriferous
'**Prince Henry**' and his royal, pure
golden brother '**Prince John**'; pure
apricot, medium sized '**Chantryland**';
and sky blue '**Baby Lucia**'. They are
all grown in the same way as pansies.
(See above.)

*Viola 'Baby Lucia' has a
sky blue flower and is a
seed propagated violetta.*

Zinnia

Zinnia haageana syn. *Z. angustifolia, Z. elegans,
Z. peruviana*   Zones 6–9

The hotter it gets, the more zinnias like
it. With their sitff petalled flowers, they
always look fresh while all else wilts
around them. In hot or dry climates
they are indispensable and if the
brilliant colors of the tall '**Dahlia
Flowered**' and '**Giant Cactus-Flowered**'
strains are not for you, perhaps the
tall, chartreuse green flowered, dahlia
type '**Envy**' would fit the garden
scheme, or the hybrid-flowered
'**Dreamland Ivy**' with faintly green
suffused cream flowers. For those who
need cheering up or want to get in
touch with their 'inner child', plant the
innocent and joyous '**Candy Cane**'
mix. The flowers are the happiest of
striped flowers, no two alike, and grow
to 24 in (60 cm). The rainbow colored
tall, large flowered zinnia to 3 ft
(90 cm) or more is *Z. elegans*. The
Peruvian zinnia *Z. peruviana* has
rich red or yellow flowers on approximately 3 ft (1 m) stems. Despite the

The flowers of Zinnia elegans always look fresh whatever the temperature.

name, it is endemic from Arizona south to Argentina. Narrow-leaved zinnia *Z. haageana* syn. *Z. angustifolia* is virtually foolproof in drought and heat, and grows to 2 ft (30 cm). It has a profusion of small yellow, orange or bronze flowers and the most readily available cultivar is **'Old Mexico'**.

Sow zinnia where they are to flower, firming the soil down gently before you begin planting. They require only sunshine, good drainage, and watering. However they will grow larger and flower better if compost is incorporated into the soil before planting. If the soil is acidic amend it with lime or dolomite so that it approaches a neutral pH of 7.

Edible Flowers

Edible flowers are one of the rediscovered delights of the flower garden. It sounds strange at first, but many flowers are grown or gathered around the world not only for their beauty but because they provide an essential ingredient in traditional dishes. Almost all the edible flowers belong to the annual flowers, although a few of our flower flavorings like rose petals and flower teas such as linden come from shrubs and trees.

Not every flower is safe to eat. We are tapping into thousands of years of accumulated wisdom and traditional knowledge in eating the flowers that are listed here. Experimenting with others could be dangerous. As a further caution, it is very important to make sure that the flowers you gather have not been sprayed or are not in the fallout zone of a busy highway. Flower petals are among the purest culinary delights from the garden and it is sad to have them contaminated. Edible flowers include:

Artichoke, Globe — *Cynara scolymus*
The vegetable is a giant thistle bud.

Bergamot *Monarda didyma* — The leaves and flowers are used to make the famed Oswego tea (consumed at the Boston Tea Party).

Borage *Borago officinalis* — Borage has the most beautiful starry blue flowers which are cucumber flavored. Remove the hairy calyx at the back of each flower and float the flowers on long summer drinks, or use them to garnish salads.

Calendula *Calendula officinalis* — The petals have long been used as a turmeric substitute. Food cooked with calendula petals turns a rich golden color and picks up the spiciness of the petals.

Day lilies, Hemerocallis *spp., are edible flowers that have been eaten by the Japanese in particular for many hundreds of years.*

Chrysanthemum *Chrysanthemum* spp. — Use chrysanthemum petals in the same way that they are used in Japan where they are added to give a warmly aromatic, spicy flavor to broths. The petals are also blanched and scattered over salads. The old-fashioned tawny and gold cultivars are best.

Clove Pinks and Carnations *Dianthus caryophyllus* — The petals give a clove fragrance to food and drinks.

The flowers of the hollyhock are edible and are frequently used as a garnish in salads.

They add a delicious fragrance to an apple pie. Try adding a handful to mulled wine before it is simmered and strained.

Cowslips *Primula veris* — The fragrant tiny flowers are scattered over salads. In the past the buds were pickled.

Day Lily *Hemerocallis* spp. — Buds of day lilies are prepared in the same way as the flowers of courgettes, and have been eaten in this manner by the Japanese people for many hundreds of years.

Elderflower *Sambucus nigra* — The lacy white flower heads make delicious fritters. Whole heads are dipped into a very light batter and deep fried. They are served sprinkled with vanilla sugar.

English Daisy *Bellis perennis* — The whole tiny heads are scattered over salads.

Hollyhock *Althaea rosea* — Both the whole flowers and the cooked flower buds have been traditionally used in salads.

Lavender *Lavandula angustifolia* — The flowers of lavender are tranquilizing and are used to make a relaxing tea. Use lavender in any recipe that calls for rosemary and prepare for a surprise. But halve the quantity that is quoted for rosemary.

Nasturtiums *Tropaeolum majus* —
Nasturtium flowers have the same
peppery flavor as their leaves. Fill
them with a little cream cheese for
an entrée. Scatter the flowers over
a tossed salad, and also use them
as an edible garnish

Pansies and Violets *Viola x
wittrockiana* — All pansy flowers
are edible but the little faces of
heartsease are perfect to scatter over
salads, as are the tender young
leaves of violets and their flowers.
They can also be crystallized by
using a little paint brush to paint
their faces with slightly beaten egg-
white, then sieving over with castor
sugar. Dry in a very cool, half open
oven or in the sun. Use them to
decorate cakes and special sweets.
Violet flowers make a delightfully
fragrant, naturally sweet tea.

Primrose *Primula vulgaris* — The
flowers of the species primrose
were candied in the past, and both
the young spring leaves and flowers
are added to green salads. Gerard
wrote in his 1633 *Herbal* that
primrose root tea 'drunk in the
month of May is famous for curing
phrensie'. Given the anxieties of the
modern world we should all probably be robbing the flower patch.

Roses *Rosa* spp. — Rose petals are the
perfect touch floated over a cool
dessert of almost any kind. Added
before serving, they also give an
oriental touch to lamb dishes. Use
them as a final addition to salads.
Rose petals make a delicious jam,
reminiscent of rosella jam, which is
perfect to sandwich small individual
sponge cakes with (along with some
fresh whipped cream), or place in
the heart of miniature meringues.
A couple of handfuls of deep red
rose petals added to apples when
making apple or quince jelly creates
an exquisite flavor. When making
a cherry tart, line the bottom of the
pastry case with rose petals for a
fragrant twist on an old recipe.

Modern roses are for the most part
tough petaled and the white heel is
bitter and needs to be removed. The
older roses from previous centuries
have a delicacy and fragrance which
is perfect for these culinary ideas.

Zucchini or Courgette *Cucurbita pepo*
— The flowers of young zucchinis
can be dipped into a very light
batter (gently fold through two egg
whites beaten until they hold peaks
of add even more lightness) and
deep fried. The tiny finger-like
attached baby courgette will be
tender enough to cook in the given
time. Drain well and serve. The
blossoms are also delicious filled
with cooked savory rice stuffings
and finished in the oven with a
little white wine and butter. It is
too delicate a flavor to swamp in
strongly flavored sauces.

*Both the young leaves
and flowers of* Primula
vulgaris *'Gigha White',*
Primrose, *are added to
green salads. They can
also made into a tea.*

*The flowers of the
courgette or zucchini,*
Cucurbita pepo, *can be
battered and deep fried.*

Bulbs, Corms, and Rhizomes

Agapanthus *Agapanthus campanulatus, A. praecox* var. *orientalis, A. africanus, A. inapertus;* Amaryllis *Hippeastrum* spp.; Belladonna Lily, *Amaryllis belladonna;* Canna *Canna flaccida, C. indica, C. x generalis;* Clivea *Clivea miniata;* Crinum *Crinum x powellii;* Crocus *Colchicum autumnale, C. byzantium,C. bivonae;* Cyclamen *Cyclamen* spp.; Daffodil *Narcissus* spp.; Day Lily *Hemerocallis* spp.; Fairy's Fishing Wand, *Dierama* spp.; Fritillary *Fritillaria* spp.; Ginger Lily *Hedychium* spp.; Grape Hyacinth *Muscari* spp.; Hyacinth, *Hyacinthus* spp.; Iris, *Iris* spp.; Lily *Lilium* spp.; Lily of the Valley *Convallaria majalis;* Montbretia *Crocosmia* spp.; Red Hot Poker *Kniphofia;* Snowflake *Leucojum aestivum, L. vernum;* Trout Lily, Dog-Tooth Violet and Tuolumne Fawn Lily *Erythronium* spp.; Tulip *Tulipa* spp.; Wild Iris *Dietes*

This section includes some of the loveliest and most fragrant of all plants chosen for their total relia-bility when grown in appropriate areas. Many beautiful plants have not been included simply because they require more care than plants in organic gardens should. Almost all multiply via side shoots, and it is these that are generously passed among garden friends and family. They are a group receiving much more attention in recent times, both from landscapers and plant breeders, as their sturdiness has become appre-ciated by gardeners looking for easy care, spray free gardens that can look stunning and provide that most desirable feature, fragrance.

Agapanthus
Agapanthus campanulatus, A. praecox var. *orientalis, A. africanus, A. inapertus*   Zones 8-10

Agapanthus is a genus of 10 species, native to southern Africa. They are remarkably drought tolerant and many century old plantings on country properties in eastern Australia attest to their survival capacity. The flowers, sometimes known as the African blue lily, are borne in umbels which in some species are spherical, and in others drooping, for instance *A. inapertus.* Flower color ranges from white to all shades of blue including the richest violet blue, and a few rare pale pinks. Dwarf and semi-dwarf forms with proportionately smaller heads of flowers are available. A winter mulch can improve their cold survival.

Amaryllis
Hippeastrum spp.   Zones 10-11

This group of bulbs is largely available today as modern Dutch hybrids, which are very striking but lack the staying power of the original species and their early hybrids. These have a grace and considerable charm of their own and require no attention whatsoever when grown in a suitable climate. Particularly worthy of

African Blue Lily, Agapanthus praecox subsp. orientalis, has large dense umbels of blue flowers.

planting is the **'St. Joseph's Lily'** *H. johnsonii* that is seen in spectacular clumps of deep scarlet-red flowers with white stripes in old gardens in the Deep South of the United States and north-eastern Australia, which has an almost identical climate. The **'Mexican Lily'** *H. reginae* with its smooth, red trumpets which have a white blaze inside is equally worthy of culture. The bulbs remain in place for many years after planting, slowly multiplying from side shoots.

Belladonna Lily
Amaryllis belladonna   Zones 8-11

This is a bulb of the Cape Province region of South Africa. It flowers before the leaves emerge, hence one of its common names, naked lady. The umbels of long, trumpet shaped flowers are fragrant and borne on 2 ft (60 cm) stems. They require full sunshine and a well drained position. It is a common bulb on old properties on the Australian east coast, and in the Deep South of the United States. A number of color variations are present in the pink form and **'Hathor'** is a white cultivar. This is one of the most reliable of bulbs, flowering in situ for decades with little or any assistance.

Canna
Canna flaccida, C. indica, C. x generalis
Zones 10-11

Native to the North and South American tropics and sub-tropics, these are fast growing, reliable, colorful garden performers with lush broad foliage which is usually green or a deep bronzed red, or purple, but in cultivars such as **'Striata'** may be handsomely striped. The leaves are sheathed and wrapped around each other up the stem in the manner of a banana plant. The flowers are tubular with usually wide, soft petals.
C. flaccida is a small, yellow flowered native of Louisiana. *C. indica*, known as **'Indian Shot'**, is a tall, red flowered, green leafed species that has naturalized in both the American south and Sydney northwards in

The spectacular trumpet-shaped tropical lily Hippeastrum 'Cocktail'.

Belladonna lily, Amaryllis belladonna 'Hathor' is a white cultivar with long, trumpet shaped flowers.

Indian Shot, Canna indica, *is a tall, red flowered, green leafed species.*

coastal eastern Australia. The dark, hard seed was reputedly used as shot by natives of the West Indies, hence the common name. A large number of flamboyant and beautiful hybrids have been bred from several species with large flowers in shades of yellow, apricot, red, pink, white, and orange, often spectacularly spotted. Dwarf cultivars have also been developed, such as **'Tropical Rose'** with lovely, open rose pink flowers. Beautiful varieties for colorful foliage include **'Wyoming'** with bronzed purple leaves and orange flowers, **'Red King**

Humbert' with reddish bronze leaves and scarlet flowers, and the spectacular **'Bengal Tiger'** with green and yellow striped leaves edged with dark crimson. Cannas are planted in spring after the last frost date and require a moist, friable soil to which compost has been added.

Clivea

| *Clivea miniata* | Zones 10-11 |

Clivea, or Kaffir Lily, originates from South Africa and forms a dense clump of deep green, strap-shaped leaves from which emerges the flowering stem bearing a cluster of usually soft, pure orange, trumpet shaped flowers. A number of beautiful hybrids have been released in recent years, largely originating from France and Belgium, including an outstanding series in primrose to golden yellow. These lilies are particularly valuable in the garden as they will in time form attractive groundcovers for half to full shade. Most cultivars commence blooming in very early spring. Kaffir lilies should be left to multiply undisturbed for many years once established and are modest in their requirements, other than the provision of regular watering. They adapt well to pot culture.

Clivea, Clivea miniata, *forms a dense clump of deep green leaves from which emerges the flowering stem bearing a cluster of pure orange, trumpet shaped flowers.*

Crinum

Crinum x powellii   Zones 6-10

Crinum x powellii is a popular larger bulb with lush, broad, strap-like foliage with tall umbels of flowers to 4 ft (1. 2 m). The common form has pendulous, long bell-like flowers in a soft pink with a delightful rich, sweet fragrance. They can be subject to both caterpillar and slug damage. A rarer white flowered form **'Album'** is also available. They require a well drained site in sun although they will tolerate to half shade. Crinums are a feature of old gardens in the southern United States and much of eastern Australia, and New Caledonia. A number of other crinums are to be found in old gardens including those that are called **'Milk and Wine'**, of which there are at least a few forms, with large, pendulous, white trumpet flowers with red stripes and beautiful fragrance, the very deep rose **'Ellen Bosanquet'**, the **'Longneck Crinum'** *C. moorei* with pinkish red bells, and the lovely lavender **'Peach Blow'** which is widely distributed in the old gardens of the Deep South of the United States. **'St. John's Lily'** or the **'Grand Crinum'** *C. asiaticum* is widely distributed from Sydney north along coastal eastern Australia and in the Deep South of the United States. It is a popular planting in many Pacific nations and Singapore. The flowers are borne in heads of up to 50, and the large, spidery individual white flowers are up to 8 in (20 cm) and very fragrant. It forms a massive plant in time. All crinums prefer to be left undisturbed for many years after planting. The ground should be well enriched with compost before planting, which is usually done in spring or fall. The bulbs should be buried to a depth of 6 in (15 cm) beneath the enriched soil, and watered regularly. The bulbs die down in winter. All parts are poisonous.

Crocus

Colchicum autumnale, C. byzantium, C. bivonae
                                   Zones 5-9

Colchicums are one of those pleasant surprises each year when they erupt unbidden from the ground. The largest of the group is the Byzantine crocus which is a feature of Monet's garden at Giverny, which has been restored and opened to the public. Colchicums reach a height of 5 in (13 cm) and have open, rather shaggy lilac-pink flowers. *C. autumnale* grows to a height of 6 in (15 cm), has regular goblet flowers in lilac-pink; it is hardy to zone 5. *C. bivonae* originates from Italy and Turkey and is perfumed; its flowers are pink-purple with cream centers. All parts are poisonous. It is hardy to zone 6.

Cyclamen

Cyclamen spp.   Zones 7-10

There are approximately 20 species of cyclamen, or sowbread, originating largely from the Mediterranean area and Iran. They are members of the primula family, and have distinctive, easily recognized flowers with five fully reflexed petals, reminiscent of an umbrella blown inside out. Some species such as *C. repandum* are renowned for their sweet perfume. The foliage is often outstanding with delicate patterning or rich marbling. Cyclamen species originate from warm low to high altitude areas, and their cold hardiness should be checked when purchasing plants. The florists' cyclamen *C. persicum* is the most tender of the group, and all other species have daintier flowers and con-siderably greater cold hardiness. All have a preference for very high levels of compost and fiber added to the soil, which preferably should be sandy. Many of the lower altitude species form delightful groundcovers in sum-mer if planted below shade trees.

Cyclamen persicum has heart-shaped leaves and large waxy flowers in shades of white, pink, red or purple.

Daffodil

Narcissus spp.   Zones 4-9

Narcissus is a genus containing some 50 species, many of which have been subjected to considerable selection and hybridization. They are divided horticulturally into 11 groups: the trumpet daffodils, the large-cupped daffodils, the small-cupped daffodils, the double daffodils, the triandrous hybrids, the cyclamineus hybrids, the jonquilla hybrids, the tazetta, the poeticus group, the species, their direct hybrids, and wild forms, and finally a miscellaneous group. In cooler climates daffodils are long lived and multiply reliably. They require good drainage and a humus rich soil that is moist during the flowering season. They are ideal bulbs for naturalizing and can be left in place for a number of years. Many are persistent around old homes long after they have ceased to be habitable. Among those found on old properties are the 'Hoop Petticoat' *N. bulbocodium*, the 'Campernelle Jonquil' *N. odorus*, the 'Jonquil' *N. jonquilla* with its fine, rushlike

foliage, the **'Pheasant's Eye'** *N. recurvus* syn. *N. poeticus recurvus*, and *N. pseudonarcissus* **'Telemonius Plenus'**, which is almost identical to **'Van Sion'**. In warm climate areas, by far the most persistent forms are tazetta hybrids, the bunch-flowered daffodils with intense fragrance. The ancient **'Paperwhite'** is by far the longest lived in the sub-tropics, often remaining and multiplying for many decades.

Day Lily
Hemerocallis spp.   Zones 4-11

Day lilies have proved to be one of the most genetically malleable of all species in the hands of the hybridists. They are a genus of about 15 species, native to temperate areas of east Asia of which the most significant in terms of plant breeding were *H. fulva* and *H. lilio-asphodelus* syn. *H. flava* which were at least as significant as food items as they were as flowers. *(See Potatoes and Other Tuberous Crops.)* Although some species of hemerocallis were in cultivation from the 16th century in Europe and various new species entered England in the 18th and 19th centuries, the first breeding work was not done until the 1890s, **'Apricot'** being the first release. The United States is currently the leading producer of new daylilies. Today there are an estimated 30,000 cultivars or more. They are, as the name indicates, flowers of a day, but a long succession of blooms occurs in early to mid-summer with some cultivars repeat flowering in fall. There are flowers now in every shade but true

Daffodil, Narcissus *papyraceus 'Paperwhite', has white, fragrant flowers with pointed petals, the corona is frilled and the stamens are orange-yellow.*

Hemerocallis Hybrid 'Rose Tapestry' is a modern hybrid that has a very elegant flower.

blue; they include fully double forms, dwarf cultivars, and fancy forms such as the spider-flowered class. Recently more attention has been devoted to fragrance and a number of very fragrant cultivars have emerged. There is also a breeding line developing nocturnal day lilies for the evening garden.

Day lilies are propagated by division of the clump, preferably when the deciduous forms have died down in fall or in spring, but they can be divided at any time of the year in milder climates. They require a well drained site and a sunny position are more drought hardy than most species but appreciate good moisture retention in the soil. This can be achieved by the addition of moderate amounts of compost before planting.

Fairy's Fishing Wand
Dierama spp.   Zones 8-10

Originating in southern Africa this is a group of cormous perennials, most with wiry, arching flower stems arising from a clump of long grassy leaves. The flowering stems may reach 5 ft (1.5 m). Their ungainly look has led to a number of descriptive names including angel's fishing rod, wand flowers, fairybells, wedding bells and wandflower They require a position in full sun, with a well drained site enriched with compost.

Fritillary
Fritillaria spp.   Zones 4-9

There are some 100 species of fritillaries of which by far the best known is the '**Crown Imperial**', whose beauty is limited only by its distinctly foxy smell. They originate from Europe, Asia, and western North America, and as a result no generalizations can be made about their culture. The 'Crown Imperial' grows under Mediterranean conditions with a dry summer, and requires a sunny growing situation. The site should be well drained, and the soil neutral to alkaline. The 'Crown Imperial' has been in gardens since c. 1570 and was introduced from south-eastern Turkey where it had been in cultivation for some time. It is a bulbous species reaching 4 ft (1.2 m) in modern cultivars, flowering in spring with a tall umbel of nodding, large, open bell flowers in either tawny orange or yellow. The umbel is crowned with a tuft of leafy bracts that match the lance-shaped, glossy stem foliage. It is propagated by bulb offsets which are planted 8–10 in (20–25 cm) deep.

Ginger Lily
Hedychium spp.   Zones 9-11

The ginger lilies thrive in humid, subtropical conditions, although some are tolerant of somewhat cooler conditions. They have the typical lush foliage of the ginger group, and mass quickly to give a tropical feeling to the garden. Many are intensely fragrant. Included in this group is the **'White Ginger Lily'** *H. coronarium* with perhaps the most ethereal and beautiful fragrance in the world and crystalline white flowers of utter purity borne in terminal clusters. **'Kahili Ginger'** *H. gardnerianum* is cultivated widely and is more tolerant of cooler conditions than most species. It bears dense cylindrical heads up to 18 in (45 cm) long of golden, intensely fragrant flowers with crimson stamens. The **'Golden Butterfly Ginger'** *H. flavum* has richly fragrant, large golden flowers borne in terminal clusters. The **'Red Ginger Lily'** *H. coccineum* lacks fragrance but forms dense, spectacular, rich red spikes. **H. greenei** is more slender but bears spikes of rich, intense, soft orange flowers. Moderate frosts not infrequently kill many of these species back to the ground, but they often recover by shooting from the rhizome.

Grape Hyacinth
Muscari spp.   Zones 3-10

The common grape hyacinth *M. botryoides* is among the most widely adapted and persistent of the spring flowering bulbs, capable of surviving for several years in a sheltered position in frost free, hot summer gardens and yet able to survive snow cover. Under less stressful conditions they survive indefinitely and multiply by seed. The foliage is grass-like and low growing, the dense spikes of rich, heavenly blue, tiny, rounded bell flowers reminiscent of a bunch of grapes. There are several other species in cultivation including the fringe or tassle hyacinth *M. comosum*, *M. armeniacum* with bright blue flowers, the showy and larger *M. latifolium*, and the fragrant *M. azureum*.

'Red Ginger Lily', Hedychium coccineum, lacks fragrance but forms dense, spectacular, rich red spikes.

Ginger lily, Hedychium gardnerianum 'Kahili Ginger' bears large dense cylindrical heads of golden, intensely fragrant flowers with crimson stamens.

'**Lady Derby**', all of which are beautifully scented.

Hyacinth bulbs are planted in the fall in cooler climates, and early winter in warm gardens. Except in such areas, the bulbs should be planted in a sunny position. Soil should be prepared with the addition of moderate quantities of compost, and the bulbs are planted 4 in (10 cm) below the soil. Hyacinths are particularly amenable to pot culture, allowing the fragrance to be fully appreciated in spring.

A rich blue stream of grape hyacinth.

Above right: Hyacinthus orientalis *'King of the Blues' is popular with gardeners all over the world.*

Hyacinth

Hyacinthus spp.   Zones 5-9

Hyacinths are native from Asia Minor to Central Asia, and there are 3 species in the genus. The common hyacinth *H. orientalis* is the one best known to gardeners and is grown extensively in spring gardens for its fragrance. It entered into cultivation in western Europe in the 16th century. A wide range of cultivars now exist including double forms and previously unknown colors such as primrose yellow. Recommended cultivars for general garden culture include the older '**King of the Blues**', the pure white '**L'Innocense**', and light pink

Iris

Iris spp.   Zones 4-10

Iris constitute a very large genus of between 200 and 300 species and are found in many parts of the northern hemisphere. Closely allied genera are found in the southern hemisphere. They are all variously bulbous or rhizomatous. The iris is also known as flag or fleur de lys. The Royal Horticultural Society classifies them into five major horticultural groups: the bearded iris which are rhizomatous and require good drainage; the Aril group which become summer dormant and include oncocyclus, regelia, regeliocyclus, and the arilbred

types; the beardless iris which include the Pacific coast iris, spuria, siberian, laevigatae, Loiuisiana, and unguiculares, all of which are rhizomatous and in general require moist soil; the crested iris which are rhizomatous and prefer moist soil; and the bulbous iris which are summer dormant, beardless, and prefer well drained soils.

The bearded iris *Iris. germanica*, *I. pallida*, *I. albicans (Hybrid cultivars)* is one of several important horticultural species and groups.

There are many thousands of these hybrids, of complex breeding involving *I. germanica* and *I. pallida*. *I. albicans* is a sterile natural hybrid bearded iris of ancient usage from the Yemen. It was introduced via Europe in colonial times into warm to sub-tropical gardens in eastern Australia, and into the southern states of the United States. It multiplies rapidly and is the most persistent of the bearded iris in hot, humid areas. The delicate white flowers borne on stems about 18 in (45 cm) long have a sweet, almost vanilla fragrance. This iris is frequently confused with the Florentine iris *I. germanica* var. *florentina* which it superficially resembles.

Bearded iris require typical Mediterranean conditions with a cool winter and a hot, dry summer to flower at their best. They are divided on the basis of height both for exhibition and sales purposes into tall

bearded, medium bearded, and dwarf bearded types. The beautiful oncocyclus and regelia iris of eastern Mediterranean and central Asian origins are included in some hybridizations with these species. Hybrids that have been created between these two types of iris are known as regeliocyclus irises, and hybrids between either group and the bearded iris cultivars are known as arilbred iris.

The bearded iris require good drainage and if this is provided they are tolerant of a wide range of soil types. Rhizome rot is a frequent problem in poorly drained gardens. They also require a warm sunny position, and it is essential that the rhizomes be planted just below the surface. These hybrids are cold hardy to zone 6, but in severe winter areas, clumps should be mulched to prevent winter heavage.

Pacific Coast hybrids are a complex hybridized group bred from various West Coast species in the United States. Similarly, the Louisiana iris hybrids have been created from interbreeding between a group of five species from the lower Mississippi River and Gulf Coast. The former

Iris bracteata has flowering stems that are short and bract-like. Its flowers are usually cream or yellow.

Iris germanica has a sparsely branched stem that produces up to 6 yellow-bearded, blue-purple to blue-violet flowers.

Crested iris, Iris japonica *bears sprays of ruffled, pale blue or white flowers.*

warm climate gardens. Use seaweed liquid fertilizer in spring rather than blood and bone with these iris. The rhizomes grow rapidly where they are suited and become crowded, reducing the yield of flowers. To prevent this, plants are subdivided every 3–4 years. Louisianas are also easily adapted to growing in bog gardens and growing in pots submerged shallowly in an ornamental pool or planted along a stream margin where available.

The crested iris *Iris japonica* is an excellent cultivar for dry shade, the most difficult of all areas to plant. It does however appreciate both the addition of compost to the soil and regular watering if available. Rapidly forming a dense groundcover, in spring it gives an outstanding display of single, pale lavender flowers formed in profusion over the much branched, wiry stems.

The Japanese iris or beardless iris, *Iris ensata,* prefers soil that is moist to wet, acidic, and rich in humus, and is used as marginal plantings for pools and beside garden streams. The rhizomes are planted in fall or spring, approximately 2 in (5 cm) below the soil surface. A border that has been

group require moist, well enriched soil, and perform best in Mediterranean climate conditions. The Louisiana iris hybrids require sun to half sun and will flower spectacularly in a rich, moist, well composted, acid to very acid soil. Gardens that grow azaleas well are ideally suited to the culture of Louisiana iris, and they are the optimum choice for humid, mild to

Japanese iris, Iris ensata, *has purple flowers with yellow blotches.*

Lily
Lilium spp.   Zones 5-10

There are almost 100 species in this genus which includes some of the most important horticultural and floricultural plants. They are mainly native to Eurasia, the Phillipines, and North America. The closely related *Cardiocrinum* was once classified with the genus Lilium.

Among the most commonly planted of the lilies are the Asiatic hybrids *Lilium*. This group contains a large number of hybrids between Central and Western Asian species. They have proved to be useful potted color material for European gardens, and are also extensively used for cut flowers. In many gardens, these are the easiest lilies to grow and are early flowering. The form is variable, but the plants are very sturdy, with open flowers which can be upward facing. They can be propagated by the stem bulbils which form in fall. They also form bulb offsets and can be propagated by bulb scales. They are available in a rainbow of bright colors and are often spotted within. Well known examples include 'Enchantment', 'Golden Pixie' and 'Sancerre'.

The beautiful Formosa lily *Lilium formosanum* from Taiwan can reach 6 ft (1.8 m) and bears numerous long, trumpet-shaped white lilies stained with pink to purple on the outside

Siberian iris, Iris sibirica *'Ruby', is one of the most popular beardless irises and has purplish blue flowers.*

Lilium, Asiatic Hybrid, *'Golden Pixie' has deep golden-yellow flowers.*

well composted, is moisture retentive, and receives regular watering will also grow this group of iris satisfactorily. They are also ideally suited to a bog garden. The lovely irises 'Freckled Geisha' and 'Silken Parasol', are in this class.

Cultivars of the Siberian iris *Iris sibirica* are not for cold climate gardens only, they are easily grown in moist soils in areas with a cool to mild winter, forming a dense, deciduous clump of narrow, upright, almost grass-like leaves and many tall, slender flower stems each bearing 2–5 flowers with upright standard petals and drooping falls. Most cultivars available involve a degree of hybridization. The flowers are white, or in a rich range of colors from violet to mulberry and in lighter shades of rose. In the border, the Siberian iris should be planted into well composted soils and watered regularly.

Cultivars of the Spuria iris *Iris spuria* have flowers reminiscent of the Dutch iris in form and are medium to tall growing, up to 6 ft (1.8 m), requiring a rich, well composted soil with a pH 7–8 in a sunny position. The rhizomes should be planted very shallowly, approximately 1 in (2. 5 cm) below the surface. They usually require 2 and occasionally 3 years to settle into their regular flowering pattern after transplanting, and should not be disturbed for some time thereafter if possible.

Formosa Lily, Lilium formosanum, *has trumpet-shaped flowers with recurving, highly fragrant petals, pure white on the inside, pink or purple-brown on the outside.*

near the base of the flower. The color has been removed in cultivars. It can be raised fairly easily from seed. In eastern Australia it has naturalized along roadsides but is non-invasive in undisturbed forest. It prefers moist, acidic soils and full sun to half shade.

The Golden-rayed Lily of Japan *Lilium auratum* is arguably the most beautiful and fragrant of the world's lilies. It has huge flowers up to 10 in (25 cm) in diameter, each petal with a single golden stripe leading in to the heart of the flower. These lilies have a delicious, spicy fragrance. They may

grow to 10 ft (3 m). There are a number of named cultivars, including the pure white **'Casablanca'** and the deep rosy pink **'Stargazer'** with white petal margins.

Planted in gardens since the Medieval period, the Madonna lily *Lilium candidum* can grow to 6 ft (1.8 m) with white, sweetly fragrant, trumpet flowers in racemes of up to 20 flowers. It prefers an alkaline soil that is very well drained with good levels of organic matter. It should always be planted with the nose of the bud showing. Deep planting causes rotting of the bulbs.

The very fragrant regal lily *Lilium regale* from China grows to a height of 6 ft (1.8 m), with lance-shaped, glossy, deep green foliage arranged in spirals up the stem, and racemes of up to 20 open, white bells with a deep, golden yellow throat. It requires very well drained soils that are moisture retentive with moderate amounts of organic matter.

The tiger lily *Lilium lancifolium* is from the Far East. It is ideally suited to acid soil conditions in sun or half shade. The flowers are a rich orange marked with deep brown spots. It is propagated by bulbils.

Tiger Lily, Lilium lancifolium, *produces numerous bright orange pendulous flowers, spotted with purple on the lower parts of the petals.*

Lily of the valley,
Convallaria majalis, *is
renowned for its
delicious scent. It is best
grown in full sun or with
just light shade.*

Lily of the Valley

Convallaria majalis   Zones 3-9

Renowned for its delicious scent, this
species grows to 10 in (25 cm),
forming a lush ground cover of
smooth, deep green, broad foliage.
The flowering stems are one-sided
with nodding white bells. All parts of
the plant are poisonous. A number of
charming variations are available
including a pink flowered form, a
double white, and one with a green
and cream variegated leaf. It requires
moist, semi-shaded, fertile conditions
and generous quantities of compost
should be incorporated into the soil
before planting. The pips are set 4 in
(10 cm) apart and planted in fall.
Each year, cover the planting with a
layer of rich leaf mould in fall.

Montbretia

Crocosmia spp.   Zones 7-11

There are few easier or more reliable
plants in warmer climate areas than
the montbretias. They have been the
subject of complex interbreeding, not
all of it recorded, and a number of
cultivars are of unknown, or supposed
origin. They belong to the iris family,
and reproduce by means of corms and

require to be lifted from time to time
as the corms build into chains and
lose productivity. The leaves are long
and swordlike, and are pleated or
ribbed. The wiry flower spikes are
spiked or branched and set with
tubular flowers in a range of colors
from lemon, to gold, apricot, orange
or bronze. All montbretias are quite
hardy. Recommended cultivars include
Crocosmia '**Lucifer**' with intense but
soft red flowers and Crocosmia
'**Walburton Yellow**'.

Crocosmia should be planted in full
sunshine to partial shade. Good
drainage is essential and they flourish
on well composted, moisture retentive
soils. Their rapid growth allows them
to become self mulching rapidly.

Montbretia, Crocosmia
x crocosmiiflora *'Lucifer'
has bright red flowers.*

Red Hot Poker, Kniphofia x praecox cultivar reaches up to 5 ft (1.5 m) tall when in bloom. It has slender leaves and vivid red or yellow flowers.

Red Hot Poker
Kniphofia   Zones 7-10

There are some 70 species of kniphofia, all of them originating from soutern to central Africa. They are clump forming, bearing their flowers in dense racemes on top of stiff, upright, tall stems. They make a definite statement in the garden with usually brilliant, golden to red colors, although there are some cream and cream-shaded green cultivars. They

Snowflake, Leucojum aestivum. Unlike many other bulbs the snowflake can flourish in watterlogged soils.

are attractive to bees and butterflies. Most cultivars prefer a rich, fertile, well drained soil to which compost has been added. As a group, they are remarkably free of pests and diseases.

Snowflake
Leucojum aestivum, L. vernum   Zones 4-10

Appearing early in spring, these bulbous plants with lush, slender, daffodil-like leaves bear pendant white bells tipped with emerald green. They require a moist position to flourish, and will take full sun to half shade, but when suited can be persistent for decades. The spring snowflake *L. vernum* is relatively common in cool climate gardens such as England, and bears flowering stems to around 6–9 in (15–23 cm). It is hardy to zone 4. Much commoner in warm to semi-tropical summer areas with mild winters such as the southen states of the United States and north-eastern Australia is the summer snowflake *L. aestivum*. The name of this species relates to its flowering time in England, but in warm areas this plant is a herald of spring requiring little winter chilling. The flowering stems are up to 18 in (45 cm) tall with 3–5 flowers per stem. The cultivar **'Gravetye'** is more floriferous than the species and the flowers are larger.

Trout Lily, Dog-Tooth Violet, *and* Tuolumne Fawn Lily
Erythronium spp.   Zones 3-9

The trout lilies are native to North America and Eurasia. They flourish in well drained, acid soils that mimic their natural woodland habitats. They are variably hardy to zones 3–5, and all species need some winter freezing. The soil should be well enriched to grow these plants and they should be located under the canopy of existing trees. It is normal to have no flowers for the first 2–3 years as the corms

Left: Tulip, Tulipa, Gregii, 'Oriental Splendour'. Daffodils do not require 'dead-heading' but tuplips will go to seed if you do not clip off the faded blooms.

Far left: Tuolumne fawn lily, Erythronium tuolumnense, has abundant, yellow flowers with yellow anthers.

settle in to their new site. *E. americanum*, the trout lily, bears pale yellow flowers which are sometimes lightly suffused with purple. The dog-tooth violet *E. dens-canis* is a European species with blooms which are rose pink or purple, although other color selections have been made. *E. tuolumnense*, the tuolumne fawn lily, is a particularly good species from California, with abundant, gracefully displayed strongly recurved, yellow flowers with yellow anthers.

Tulip

Tulipa spp.   Zones 5-9

The genus Tulipa is Eurasian in distribution and contains almost 100 species. They are all hardy bulbous perennials, and are grown for their glowingly colored chalice– or bowl– or star-shaped flowers com-posed of 6 petals. In some species the petals are much elongated to create very elegant, exaggerated goblet shapes. Most benefit from being lifted immediately they have died down after flowering and then cold ripened under refrigeration every year, particu-larly the beautiful and very numerous hybrid classes created largely in Holland. Some tulips may be left in the ground each year to multiply. These belong to the Kaufmanniana and Greigii groups.

Wild Iris

Dietes   Zones 9-10

These are excellent, rhizomatous landscaping plants closely related to true iris, in flower for much of the year and tough beyond measure. The commonest species are *Dietes bicolor* with rounded, creamy yellow flowers with a chocolate blotch at the base of three of the tepals, growing to a height of 2 ft (60 cm), and a pale lavender species *D. grandiflora* which is of similar size.

Wild iris, Dietes grandiflora, has pale lavender, iris-like flowers marked with orange-yellow.

Perennials

Perennials are herbaceous (non-woody) plants that survive for a number of years, dying down to the ground each winter. They shoot forth again in spring. Long loved for their impressive reliability and spectacular flowering, few plants are so forgiving of our shortcomings as gardeners.

For gardeners in warmer climes, there is a limited repertoire of perennials that will perform reliably. Single shasta daisies, four o'clocks, various begonias, coreopsis, blue ginger *Dichorisandra thrysiflora* from Brazil, perennial blanket flowers, liriope, evening primroses, various salvias, herbaceous hibiscus and the shrimp plant are not an exhaustive list, but among the most commonly encountered. They combine with bulbous and rhizomatous plants such as alpinias, costas, hedychiums, crinums, cannas, arum lilies, red hot pokers, alstroemerias, agapanthus, day lilies, the Eucharis or Amazon lily, montbretias, gloriosa lilies, spider lilies *Hymenocallis*, and hippeastrums. It is a list that is quintessentially sub-tropical and totally interchangable between Louisiana and Queensland. But in cooler climates the list of

Aster *Aster* spp.; **Astilbe** *Astilbe x arendsii, A. chinensis*; **Bear's Breeches** *Acanthus mollis*; **Bellflower** *Campanula* spp.; **Cardinal Flower and Blue Cardinal Flower** *Lobelia cardinalis, L. syphilitica*; **Checker Mallow** *Sidalcea malviflora*; **Clove Pinks** *Dianthus plumarius*; **Columbine** *Aquilegia* spp.; **Common Sneezeweed** *Helenium autumnale*; **Evening Primrose** *Oenothera* spp.; **Foxgloves** *Digitalis* spp.; **French Hollyhock** *Malva sylvestris*; **Hellebore** *Helleborus* spp.; **Hollyhock** *Alcea rosea* syn. *Althaea rosea*; **Japanese Anemone** *Anemone x hybrida* syn. *A. japonica, A. hupehensis* var. *japonica*; **Jerusalem Sage** *Phlomis fruticosa*; **Mexican Hat** *Ratibida columnifera*; **Obedient Plant** *Physostegia virginiana*; **Pasqueflower** *Pulsatilla vulgaris*; **Penstemon** *Penstemon* spp.; **Perennial Phlox** *Phlox paniculata*; **Purple Coneflower** *Echinacea purpurea*; **Russian Sage** *Perovskia* spp.; **Sea Holly** *Eryngium* spp.; **Sea Pink** *Armeria maritima*; **Shooting Star** *Dodecathon* spp.; **Slipper Flower** *Calceolaria biflora, C. integrifolia*; **Tree Mallow** *Lavatera* spp.; **Violet** *Viola* spp.; **Yarrow** *Achillea* spp.

While there are many beautiful new perennials constantly appearing on the market, organic gardeners seek out reliable plants that have proved their resistance to harsh conditions and disease, and are largely immune to, or recover quickly from, insect attack. Many are true heirlooms, handed down through families, or passed over the fence between gardening friends. The same beloved old perennials often turn up, fresh and perky in pots, for fund raising events. Some true treasures can be found this way, and a perennial long considered to be the commonest of plants by a particular gardener may be a rare colonial period treasure, performing reliably in the garden for over a century with little help. Ousted from other gardens by the decrees of fashion, it may be all but extinct.

Like most perennials, Penstemon digitalis multiplies at the base of the stem and are fibrous rooted.

herbaceous perennials expands and it is there that the true glory of a well planned perennial flower border can be appreciated.

By their nature, perennial garden beds need thorough preparation as clumps are divided every three years on average. They should be well dug, incorporating generous quantities of well rotted manure and compost. Most perennial plants prefer a pH close to 7 and the acidity of the soil should be adjusted appropriately. Once the garden has been prepared add a heavy layer of mulch. There should be no need to repeat this effort. Each year the remaining mulch can be just turned in the top soil, and a layer of compost added along with some fresh mulch.

Most perennials multiply at the base of the stem and are fibrous rooted. They are lifted regularly every 2–3 years. The clump will often last almost indefinitely, but once it has enlarged to the point that flowering has become sparse or smaller, division is necessary to achieve the desired display. The clump is gently dug from the ground with a garden fork. Many species are easily teased apart into several good sized, well rooted segments, or a number of large, well rooted segments can be cut from the main clump with secateurs. Densely matted clumps are sometimes difficult to break apart. Place the clump on the ground and put two large garden forks back to back and plunged into the center of the clump. Push the two handles away from each other and force the clump to pull apart. This is the least damaging technique. All named cultivars of herbaceous perennials are multiplied by division. Perennials can be multiplied by seed, but usually will not be identical to the parent. A few perennials are propagated by root cutting.

Included in this list are the reliable perennials that will always perform well.

Aster

Aster spp.   Zones 3–9

The asters are among the most important garden perennials, and many are native to North America. Overwhelmingly a Northern Hemisphere genus, a few bush species also occur in South Africa. There are at least 150 species. Included here are ones with ray florets, clearly variations on the theme of daisy flowers. Their natural color range is limited to white, purple, blue and shades of pink. *A. utea* has lemon flowers. Among the most useful are the New England Aster *A. novaeangliae*, the New York Aster *A. novi-belgii*, the Alpine aster *A. alpinus*, the Italian Aster *A. mellus*, and the beautiful Frikart Aster *A. x frikartii*, particularly in its form 'Moench'. Michaelmas daisies are various selections from the New England daisy and the New York daisy, as well as hybrids between them. Good examples are 'Barr's Pink', 'Harrington Pink', and the rich deep red 'Crimson Glory'. Most of the asters are martyrs to slugs and powdery mildew. They make the 'pass along' list despite these faults because their role in the fall garden is impossible to replace; they are very

Aster alpinus is a popular rock garden perennial and is fully frost hardy. It bears large, violet-blue daisy flowers with yellow centers.

The flower spikes of Acanthus mollis can be over 6 ft (1.8 m) tall with the purple-pink bracts contrasting sharply with the crinkled white flowers.

attractive to butterflies, and they are hugely generous in their flowering. They are fairly strictly for the mild to cool garden, but a remarkably long lived and floriferous Michaelmas daisy survives with no effort in sub-tropical heat and has done so for at least a century. It is a very significant 'pass along' plant, but generally not seen in nurseries.

Astilbe

Astilbe x arendsii, A. chinensis   Zones 6-10

Astilbes score highly as perennials. They are long flowering with somewhat open, densely studded, panicles of tiny flowers that are eye-catching and, in cooler gardens, are the main plant of choice for the semi-shaded border. The foliage is similar to that of meadowsweet, ferny and handsome. *A. chinensis* is commonly grown, but various cultivars from the hybrid group *A. x arendsii* are the most likely choice. Good cultivars include the deep red **'Fanal'**, the soft salmon pink **'Peach Blossom'** and the lilac **'Hyacinth'**. All require a rich, moist soil and ample compost should be added to ensure good moisture levels are maintained.

Bear's Breeches

Acanthus mollis   Zones 7-10

These are among the most architec-tural of plants with large, polished, dark green leaves that are deeply incised, up to 2 ft (60 cm) long arising in a large clump. The flow-ering stalks may reach 3 ft (90 cm) with stiff, cylindrical heads of white flowers, each shaded with a lilac bract. Also known as Bear's breech, it grows rapidly and is tolerant of partial shade. Particularly suited to landscaping large modern and formal buildings, it requires a well drained soil and benefits from the addition of moderate quantities of compost.

Astilbe x arendsii 'Fanal' has long-lasting scarlet flowers and is an eye-catching choice for the semi-shaded border.

Bellflower

Campanula spp.   Zones 4-9

This is an exceptionally large group including many that are alpine or are sub-alpine. But there are a number of easy to grow perennials that have wide adaptability, and are perfect for a sustainable garden. These include the clustered bellflower *C. glomerata*, particularly in its beautiful white-flowered form *C. glomerata var. alba*, the great bellflower *C. latifolia*, **'Elizabeth'** (a selection from the excellent, large belled *C. takesimana*),

the Milky Bellflower *C. actiflora*, and the utterly reliable, tall to 3 ft (90 cm) Peach-leaved bellflower in several forms including the pure white '**Alba**', the white iced with pale blue '**Chettle Charm**', and in its large flowered, rich blue form '**Telham Beauty**'. These are all excellent perennials, quite undemanding, and spectacularly lovely. They require a well drained, moist soil, but will take full to half sun, and are hardy and long flowering.

Cardinal Flower *and* Blue Cardinal Flower

Lobelia cardinalis, L. syphilitica   Zones 3-10

Some very fine perennial species of lobelia grown in gardens for over a century are the lovely deep red flowered cardinal flower with dense, tall spikes of flowers to 4 ft (1. 2 m). It is a native of North America and a lover of moist rich soil. It attracts hummingbirds in the United States and honeyeaters in Australia. Equally beautiful is the richly blue flowered *L. syphilitica*, its dense flower spikes growing to 3 ft (90 cm). Some excellent hybrids have been bred between them including *L. x girardii*.

The checker mallow, Sidalcea malviflora, has lobed leaves and loose heads of pink or white flowers resembling hollyhocks.

Checker Mallow

Sidalcea malviflora   Zones 6–10

The checker mallow, or checkerbloom, is an airy flowered look-alike for a baby hollyhock and is native to the United States. It has been hybridized with other species, particularly *S. candida* and *S. malviflora*, and the result has been several perennials that are now widely grown around the world including rose pink '**Party Girl**', '**Croftway Red**', rich pink '**Elsie Heugh**', and clear light pink '**Loveliness**'. They are best grown in fairly dry climates in a sunny, well drained position.

Clove Pinks

Dianthus plumarins   Zones 3–10

Among the toughest, oldest, and most fragrant of plants are the pinks. Those most handed down are the cottage pinks, or clove pinks, which were derived from *D. plumarius*. They form a dense low mat of very neat, short, grass-like foliage. Their fragrance is legendary, and some dating to the Tudor period are still available, saying much for both the esteem in which these pinks are held and their remarkable staying power as named cultivars. Among the many splendid heirloom cultivars are: '**Dad's Favorite**', a 19th century cultivar with double white flowers that are edged

Blue Cardinal Flower, Lobelia siphilitica, has dense flower spikes growing to 3 ft (90 cm) and bears racemes of 2-lipped violet-blue flowers.

Clove Pinks Dianthus plumarius, *is a loosely tufted, evergreen perennial with strongly fringed petals. It has a legendary fragrance.*

Colarado's state flower the blue columbine, Aquilegia caerulea.

with ruby and have a maroon heart; **'Essex Witch'** which has semi-double, fragrant, rose pink flowers; the glorious mid-19th century cultivar **'Mrs Sinkins'** with very double, large, carnation-like flowers in pure white and the most intense fragrance, up to 50 stems being borne at the one time; and the classic 18th century **'Musgrave's White'** with large, intensely scented, single white flowers with a green eye. All the clove pinks require excellent drainage, full sun, and an alkaline pH. If your soil is acidic, place a couple of broken pieces of concrete near the roots. They will leach lime into the soil whenever the plant is watered, steadily maintaining an alkaline soil reaction.

Columbine
Aquilegia spp.   Zones 3–9

Aquilegias form a group of some 70 species found across North America, Europe, and Asia. They have long been a popular garden plant, easily raised from seed and quite unfussy with regard to soil provided that it is well drained. The foliage resembles that of maidenhair fern and would be a garden attraction even without the flowers which are richly colored, often two-toned, and with long, nectar filled, backward projecting spurs that add to the delicacy of their appearance. Species cross with avidity and should be separated as far apart as possible. The plants are not long-lived, perhaps 4 years, and self sown plants will replace them if allowed to do so. They have few potential enemies, and all parts are poisonous. Among many readily available and beautiful cultivars are the rich blue-flowered **'Alpine Columbine'** *A. alpina* and its taller stemmed hybrid the **'Hensoll Harebell'**, the **'Golden Columbine'** *A. chrysantha* with astonishingly long, delicate spurs, the miniature **'Fan Columbine'** *A. flabellata* from Japan, and the beautiful blue and white **'Colorado Columbine'** *A. caerulea.*

Common Sneezeweed
Helenium autumnale   Zones 3–9

The sneezeweed has been widely hybridized to form some of the finest perennials in the United States. The majority are tall growing to 5 ft (1.5 m) and are usually planted to the back of a garden border and sup-ported with a stake. The most famous among the hybrids is **'Moerheim Beauty'**, a smaller, neater, cultivar than most with very rich copper-red tints. All the hybrids in this group require average garden conditions. They have considerable drought tolerance.

Evening Primrose
Oenothera spp.   Zones 4–10

The evening primroses have long been cultivated in gardens for their delicious scent. Other species lack the legendary fragrance but are outstanding perennials for the garden. *O. biennis* and *O. odorata* are both wonderfully fragrant, the pure fine fragrance lying somewhere between that of tuberose and lemon. They both have large, light golden flowers. The former is biennial while the latter is perennial. *O. hookeri* is a majestic perennial species hardy to zone 4 for the flower border with a continuous succession of large, pure golden flowers on stems to 6 ft (1.8 m). Sundrops is the common name for the golden flowered, red stemmed perennial *O. fruticosa* syn. *O. tetragona*; it is hardy to zone 4. In dryland gardens such as those of inland Texas, the heat proof '**Mexican Evening Primrose**' *O. speciosa* comes into its own with an endless profusion of light pink, medium sized blooms of such fresh beauty that you would swear they would be crushed and wilted at the first morning heat. Instead they remain fresh throughout the day while all else wilts. There is a lovely white form available too. This species is hardy to zone 5. The evening primroses deserve to be featured far more in domestic gardens. Many very fragrant species exist apart from those listed here. They all thrive on sunshine and warmth.

Foxgloves
Digitalis spp.   Zones 4–10

Foxgloves are short lived perennials, but self seed unaggressively so that the plants are easily replaced. The best known species is *D. purpurea* the common foxglove, a much loved plant for the perennial border and old fashioned gardens. It readily naturalizes in the garden if provided with moist shade, and can reach 6 ft (1.8 m). All parts are poisonous. A number of other species have entered gardens in more recent times including the strawberry foxglove *D. x mertonensis* with large strawberry pink bells. It comes true from seed despite being a hybrid and is hardy to zone 5. The yellow foxglove *D. grandiflora* syn. D. ambigua is a foxglove of modest but quaint charm with large creamy yellow bells spotted inside with brown. It is hardy to zone 6. *D. laevigata*, also hardy to zone 6, is a longer lived perennial with dense, small, cream bells marked with brown-purple. The Grecian foxglove *D. anata* is a true perennial and a particularly charming plant with dense spikes to 3 ft (90 cm) of densely arranged cream flowers veined with brown. It is hardy to zone 7. All require moist, rich soil and a light shade.

Evening Primrose, Oenothera speciosa 'Rosea', has flowers edged and heavily veined in rose pink and yellow in the center.

Yellow Foxglove, Digitalis grandiflora has large creamy yellow bells spotted inside with brown.

French hollyhock, Malva sylvestris, is a perennial mallow with lavender pink flowers striped or veined purple.

French Hollyhock

Malva sylvestris   Zones 5–10

Often incorrectly described as *M. zebrina* this is a a lovely perennial mallow which smothers in light lavender pink flowers striped or veined purple so that the flowers do indeed look like zebras. It requires good drainage and full sunshine. This species appears in 19th century European mixed flower paintings, and is coming back to fashion.

Below right: Hollyhock, Alcea rosea, is popular for its tall spikes of flowers that come in a range of colors including pink, purple, cream and yellow.

Below: Helleborus argutifolius produces large clusters of cup-shaped, nodding green flowers on an upright spike above deep green, spiny foliage.

Hellebore

Helleborus spp.   Zones 6–9

The hellebores are excellent long-lived perennials and one of the classics of the shady garden. They bloom over an extended period and the flowers are often reminiscent of single roses. They thrive in rich woodland type conditions but prefer a pH around neutral. A number of beautiful species are available including the elegant Christmas rose *H. niger* with flowers 2 in (5 cm) wide and ice white or slightly suffused pale green. The lenten rose *H. orientalis* is equally beautiful with large saucer-shaped flowers in shades of white, or pale green, or pale or rose pink, or delicate washes of slate, or mulberry, or crimson. Some pale primrose forms are now being bred. The corsican hellebore *H. argutifolius* syn. *H. corsicus* has clusters of medium sized apple green flowers.

Hollyhock

Alcea rosea syn. *Althaea rosea*   Zones 4-10

The old single hollyhock of the past was reliably perennial for at least several years, but recent breeding efforts have produced several strains that are effectively grown as annuals including '**Summer Carnival**' which is double flowered and can grow to 6 ft (1.8 m), and the lower growing '**Marjorette**' strain, reaching 30 in (75 cm). A number of firms still list the perennial hollyhock but they are

getting fewer and this is a good time to locate and hold a sturdy old line of the original hollyhock. Sturbridge Village has offered an old strain interesting in that it has the figleaf shape of the figleaf hollyhock A. ficifolia rather than the rounded leaf of *A. rosea*. The colors are outstandingly rich and the plants resistant to rust. Small towns in the Alpes de Haute Provence have very long lived perennial strains to 6 ft (1.8 m) of exceptional vigor and health in a beautiful range of large single colors. They appear impervious to the rust that affects many gardens. Hollyhocks require full sun and respond to the addition of compost to the soil. If rust appears, remove all affected leaves to slow its progress.

Japanese Anemone

Anemone x hybrida syn. *A. japonica*,
A. hupehensis var. *japonica*   Zones 6–10

This is one of the finest of the late summer and fall perennials. Flowering over an extended period, it is a long lived, fibrous rooted perennial for a lightly shaded position. It is exceptionally tough yet it has an airy grace possessed by few plants. The plants, also known as Japanese wildflower, have lobed leaves and are relatively slow to establish, but then gradually expand the clump each year. The large flowers in white or shades of soft pink to wine, in singles or doubles, are born on branched, 4 ft (1.2 m) stems. A number of named cultivars are available including the single white '**Honorine Jaubert**', '**Prince Heinrich**' with double deep rosy red flowers on shorter stems, '**Queen Charlotte**' with tall stemmed, single pink flowers, '**Whirlwind**' with large, semi-double, white flowers, and the lovely '**September Charm**' with the softest silvery pink flowers. It can be propagated by division in fall once it has established. It should be mulched after flowering in severe winter areas.

Jerusalem Sage

Phlomis fruticosa   Zones 7–10

This is an excellent species for a sunny, well drained situation and bears a superficial resemblance to salvia to which it is related. It forms a handsome, compact shrub to 4 ft (1.2 m), with soft velvety silver-grey leaves and spikes of lipped, clear yellow flowers. It has very good drought and heat resistance. Other species well worth acquiring are *P. samia* with lilac flowers and *P. russelliana* with creamy-yellow flowers.

Mexican Hat

Ratibida columnifera   Zones 3–9

This is a delightful perennial too little known outside of the United States, with a quaint charm. It is native to prairie and the western states and is used to great effect in the many lovely dryland gardens of Texas. The individual flowers have a columnar brown disc surrounded by drooping, single, short, yellow and sometimes yellow tinged purple petals evoking for some drooping Mexican sombreros. It flowers to a height of 2 ft (60 cm) and requires a sunny, well drained position. The closely related prairie coneflower or yellow coneflower *R. pinnata* grows to twice the height at 4 ft (1.2 m), and the central brown disc is globular.

Jerusalem Sage, Phlomis *fruticosa, has soft velvety silver-grey leaves and spikes of lipped, clear yellow flowers.*

Obedient Plant

Physostegia virginiana   Zones 3–10

The obedience of this species lies in
the individual flowers, which somewhat resemble small snapdragons,
staying in whatever position they are
arranged. This is one of Australia's
favorite perennials (it is known as
Gallipoli heath) to pass on to other
gardeners. It is highly reliable
perennial even in the subtropics.
Native to the eastern United States, it
is available as **'Summer Snow'** (white),
'Vivid' (lilac pink), **'Bouquet Rose'**
(rose pink), and **'Variegata'** (white
margined leaves and lavender pink
flowers). It expands modestly by
rhizomes, dying down almost to the
ground each fall.

Pasqueflower

Pulsatilla vulgaris   Zones 5–9

This is a soft, herbaceous, clump
forming species, growing to 8 in (20
cm). The leaves are pinnate and each
leaflet is deeply dissected, light green,
and covered with silken hairs. The
flowers are borne singly, at the end of
the stems, and are cupped with a
prominent cluster of golden stamens.
The colors range from purple to lilac,
pink, lavender, and white. It requires a
sunny, sharply drained position. It is
propagated most commonly by seed,

but desirable color forms can also be
propagated by root cuttings taken in
winter.

Penstemon

Penstemon spp.   Zones 3–10

Penstemon or beard tongue, is
exclusively a North and Central
American genus of around 250
species, although relatively few have
passed into cultivation. Most
commonly found are a large range of
very fine, evergreen hybrids. They
have tubular to bell-shaped flowers
which are very attractive to
hummingbirds. They are propagated
by tip cuttings taken in fall. The
hybrids form tall clumps to 4 ft (1.2
m), with tall racemes of flowers.
Among the very fine cultivars are
'Sour Grapes', **'Port Wine'**, and
'Pennington Gem'. Other species
which are reliable in cultivation
include the charming *P. digitalis* and
its selected form **'Husker's Red'**, and
the Beardlip Penstemon *P. barbatus*.
All require excellent drainage and a
position in sun to part shade. They
grow easily in the flower border with
no particular attention.

Perennial Phlox

Phlox paniculata   Zones 4–10

The perennial phlox are treasured for
the sweet light fragrance that they
pour onto the summer air. They grow
to 3–5 ft (90 cm–1.2 m) with large,
compact, dome to cylindrical cymes of

typical 5-petalled phlox flowers.
They flourish in a moist, fertile soil
supplemented with compost and in
sun to half shade.

Peruvian Lily
Alstroemeria spp.   Zones 7–9

The alstroemerias number around 50
species all derived from South
America. Few of the species are now
available. The most commonly found
in old gardens is *A. psittacina* syn.
A. pulchella. It is certainly no rival in
the attention stakes with the widely
distributed, brilliantly colored Ligtu
hybrids which were derived
principally from *A. ligtu* and *A.
haemantha*. Quite a few of the named
hybrids are fairly tender being hardy
down to zone 7, but they perform
supremely well in the cool maritime
climate of coastal northern California.
Ligtu hybrids are propagated by seed,
while named cultivars are propagated
by division in fall. All alstroemerias
require fertile, moisture retentive, well
drained soil.

Purple Coneflower
Echinacea purpurea   Zones 3–10

The coneflowers have come to
prominence in recent times for their
use in assisting the human immune
system. But they are also widely
recognised for their charm as flowers.
They all have large, daisylike flowers
which in the case of the purple

coneflower are arranged on tall
branched stems to 5 ft (1.5 m). Named
cultivars exist, including the pure
white '**White Swan**' and the rosy pink
'**Magnus**'. The plants require a sunny,
well drained situation.

Russian Sage
Perovskia spp.   Zones 5–9

This is a woody based perennial genus
ideal for very well drained, sunny
areas. Two species *P. abrotanoides*
and *P. atriplicifolia*, together with
their hybrids are available. The plants
have a slight resemblance to lavender
with their grey green foliage and tall,
much branched, dense spikes of
lavender flowers.

Sea Holly
Eryngium spp.   Zones 5–9

The sea hollies belong to the celery
family, rather surprisingly for their
appearance is quite different
superficially. There are a large number
of species, all of them erect and stiffly
branched. The tiny flowers are
arranged into dense terminal umbels
subtended by very ornamental, finely
cut dramatic bracts. Most species are
in beautiful shadings of rich blue, but a
few are in ghostly shades of silver grey,
or in sea green. The more delicately
formed ones such as *E. x tripartitum*
are a mist of rich blue while large, lacy
ruffled species such *E. alpinum* are the
envy of all flower arrangers.

Sea Pink

Armeria maritima   Zones 4–9

With the possible exception of Gazanias and Rugosa roses, no plant performs better in gardens beside the sea than the sea pinks. The plants form small leafy tufts and send up several flower stalks each topped byspherical heads of tiny flowers in white, pink, or rose. The flowers are attractive to butterflies, and are excellent for edging paths and garden beds, and in rock gardens. They require excellent drainage. Two closely related species are *A. arenaria* syn. *A. plantaginea* and *A. girardii* syn. *A. juncea*. The plants require virtually no watering once established making them ideal for the xeroscaped garden.

Shooting Star

Dodecathon spp.   Zones 3–10

Shooting Stars are members of the primrose family, and like primroses the plants form a central rosette of leaves from which emerges a flowering stem topped with a cluster of flowers which have backward pointing petals and a prominent forward pointing cluster of stamens. It prefers a rich, shady, well drained position.

Slipper flower

Calceolaria biflora, C. integrifolia   Zones 8-10

Calceolarias are native to South America and include rhizomatous plants such as *C. biflora*, and small shrubs such as *C. integrifolia*. They prefer rich acidic soils in sun to full shade and are characterized by purse-like, two-lipped golden yellow flowers. *C. biflora* is short growing and is hardy to zone 9. They are among the most consistent and profuse flowerers.

Tree Mallow

Lavatera spp.   Zones 6–10

Tree mallows are the kind of plant that can rapidly add height and old-fashioned charm to the garden in summer and fall. They bear hollyhock-like flowers which in the case of the cultivar **'Loveliness'** selected from the annual mallow *L. trimestris* are a satiny, rich pink. The delightful perennial shrub *L. thuringiaca* is nearly ever-blooming

in a lilac pink, and the famous cultivar **'Barnsley'** is an eye-catching shell pink with a white heart.

Violet

Viola spp.   Zones 4–10

A number of true violets are excellent ground-covering perennials. Best loved among the violets is the fragrant species *V. odorata* which has been in gardens since the Medieval period and was also valued as a medicinal plant. Many old cultivars are still available including four old 19th century Parma violets and some of the true 19th century double violets. Violets are renowned for their heady fragrance and modest charms. Although they grow lushly in shady positions, sweet violets flower far better under very light, deciduous shade or morning sun.

Surviving from the 19th century is the beautiful silvery blue perennial viola **'Maggie Mott'**. It is one of the last of its class and period to be quite widely grown. It is propagated by cuttings.

Yarrow

Achillea spp.   Zones 3–10

The yarrows are a particularly useful group of plants, thriving in full sunshine. Drought resistant, cold hardy, very floriferous, and excellent bee and butterfly attractors, some species are also ideal for drying. All but one species are characterized by very finely divided, feathery foliage. The best known species is *A. millefolium* which has been developed in recent years into a rich and subtle color range. Particularly valuable for dried flower work and aarrangements are forms of the fernleaf yarrow *A. filipendula* **'Gold Plate'** and *A. f.* **'Parker's Variety'**, both of which bear large, flat, dense heads of golden flowers on long stems to 4 ft (1.2 m). A number of named hybrids are available of which **'Fanal'**

with a profusion of bright cherry flowers and **'Lemon Queen'** with heads of soft, cool lemon flowers are among the finest. Some very fine species include *A. ageratifolia* with heads of much larger, single white flowers, the finely carpeting woolly yarrow *A. tomentosa* and the diminutive *A. x lewisii* **'King Edward'**. Rather different is sneezewort *A. ptarmica* which is most readily available in a double white flowered form borne in airy, open panicles.

Violet, Viola odorata, is a popular fragrant species with white, violet or rose colored flowers.

Fernleaf Yarrow, Achillea filipendula 'Gold Plate', bears large, flat, dense heads of golden flowers on long stems.

Roses

It has taken the efforts of rose growers thousands of years to create roses that actually need us. There are about 130 species of roses, many of them not discovered and passed around the world of gardening until the 19th century or early 20th century. They occur throughout the Northern Hemisphere but none are native to the Southern Hemisphere. Many of the species roses have become very popular garden shrubs, having the vigor and health of the wild rose, and making perfect selections for a trouble-free organic garden. They come in an astonishing array of forms and an infinitely greater range of foliage, colors, flowers, and fragrances than could ever be imagined by those who have only grown modern hybrid tea roses. An entire garden might be planted with nothing else and give pleasure without effort every day of the year.

Relatively few of the wild roses have been developed in the past. In Europe, the Gallica or French rose *R. gallica* was very early in gardens together with its natural hybrids *R. x alba*, the alba rose or rose of Albion, and the damask rose *R. x damascena*. Archaeological evidence suggests that the Medes and Persians, the Myceneans, the Minoans, the Egyptians, Greeks, Carthaginians, and Romans all knew and grew the Gallica rose. It is an exceptionally tough, shrubby rose, short and suckering, with fragrant large pink or light crimson flowers. It conferred its toughness and fragrance on its progeny, the Gallica class of roses, and the rich purple-reds of the old European roses are derived from them. These roses are among the great survivors of old gardens, cemeteries, roadsides, and ghost towns of the world, tolerating drought, cold and heat, and total neglect. The albas are

Above: The 'Diamond Jubilee' hybrid tea rose has buff yellow, double cupped flowers with 28 petals.

Right: 'Pink Radiance' has semi-double scented flowers with 23 petals.

hardy plants of beautiful form, sweet fragrance and grace, while the damasks and autumn damasks have legendary fragrance to match their beauty. Like the gallicas, these two groups have the strength to survive climatic extremes and neglect.

Together, the Gallicas, albas, and damasks are known as the summer roses, flowering from late spring or early summer for about a month each year. But what a glory they create, bearing as many roses in that month as most modern roses bear in a year.

To this group may be added the slightly less vigorous cabbage or provence roses *R. x centifolia* and moss roses *R. x centifolia muscosa*.

These old classes of roses are the happiest of hunting fields for the organic gardener. Of thousands of varieties originally created we are left with a few hundred varieties at most. Their very powers of survival guarantee their extraordinary capacity to grow well with very little help once established. Spraying and pruning are unnecessary to their wellbeing. Very few are totally resistant to disease but they recover rapidly with no permanent damage.

Rugosa roses have remarkable resistance to fungal infection and are highly valued by organic gardeners world wide. The species *R. rugosa* is the ramanas rose or Japanese rose and it comes from China, Korea, and Japan. It is capable of surviving sub zero temperatures, sea salt, gale force winds, and growing in almost pure sand. It has profuse clusters of large, clove-fragrant flowers borne throughout the season, golden coloring in fall, and a neat shape and profuse thorns that make it a very handsome safety barrier or security hedging. The foliage is large and rugose and fungal diseases cannot take hold. In addition to these many virtues, single and slightly double forms bear a profusion of hips after each flowering that are huge and rich with vitamin C.

China and tea roses found their way to Europe early in the 19th century. These roses brought with them an immensely important genetic difference to the original summer roses. They flowered repeatedly until winter. The China and later developed hybrid China roses are exceptionally tough plants for the warmer garden and are among the most likely to be surviving in old gardens in the sub-tropics and tropics. They are often only lightly fragrant but are virtually

The Gallica rose 'La Belle Sultane' has flat, almost single blooms with heart-shaped petals that form around a crown of golden stamens.

'Blush Noisette' has loosely double, perfectly formed blush-pink blooms that open from dark pink buds.

disease free. Some varieties are tolerant of cool area gardens. Tea roses are a sad sight in cooler climate gardens requiring the greatest coddling to bring them through cold winters. But the same roses grow like small trees, sometimes up to 13 ft (4 m) high and almost as wide in gardens with reliable hot summers. It can even be drastically pruned with a chainsaw if it outgrows its allotted place, bouncing back to full size in less than two years. Even on tropical Pacific islands where most roses could not hope to survive, big, disease-free old bushes can be found. China roses, tea roses, and noisettes, a related class of climbing roses, are all exceedingly floriferous, almost never out of flower in the warm to hot garden, amazingly vigorous and very healthy, often living well past a century given the opportunity. The teas and noisettes are wonderfully fragrant with exquisite, mutable, silken colors within their large double flowers.

Organic gardeners are truly spoiled for choice. There are so many roses

'Le Vésuve' has very large, full flowers of carmine to pink and sometimes fiery red. The flowers will change color depending on whether they are planted in the sun or shade.

needing minimal maintenance, roses to suit almost any soil and almost any climate. With care and knowledge most roses in modern catalogs can be well grown in most gardens. But who really needs to be constantly spraying, or even pruning roses? It is better in the organic garden to consider a rose as a shrub to be planted, established with care, then largely left to is own devices. Be ruthless and remove bushes if they prove unsuitable. Choosing reliable roses matched to your climate is the secret to success, and this chapter is designed to help you make those choices.

There are many classes of roses available, and there are varieties of roses in every class which are long tested and thoroughly reliable in most situations. Some modern breeders have particularly concentrated on rose health, often using species roses to introduce new vigor into old, very highly bred classes such as the hybrid teas which began in the 1850s, and floribundas which were developed from the 19th century polyanthas. Once a rose garden is structured around highly reliable roses correctly matched to climate, it is always possible to introduce a few of the best roses from classes that are less tough, such as hybrid perpetuals, bourbons, and the hybrid teas.

Modern rose production is concentrated in the hands of a very few giants in the industry. They concentrate on the hybrid teas and floribundas, and only on the latest releases of these, because that is where money can be made. Smaller specialist growers and heritage rose societies exist everywhere now to supply and preserve all the rose classes overlooked by these giant rose producers. Take a walk around your district when you can, peering over garden fences to see what roses seem to be flourishing without any great care. When you see a thriving rose, ask for its name.

Why Species and Old-Fashioned Roses?

Species roses are survivors. Time has long ago weeded out the weaklings. These are the roses that many past generations loved, not only for their fragrance and beauty but because they survived everything to which Nature exposed them. These were the roses passed on by cuttings between neighbors, or dug up and moved from place to place by emigrants. They truly represent the very best we have inherited from the past. Old heritage roses are not the product of intense modern breeding programs and are closer to the wild forms, sharing more of their vigor.

Beautiful though many modern roses are, few of our newer roses with their intensive breeding could withstand the extreme situations that our heritage roses have survived, and time has not yet winnowed the very best from our current offerings.

Every region has its own heritage roses that have proved particularly resistant to the climatic extremes of the area and to the growing conditions. It can be one of the most exciting of all hobbies to collect these roses of the past, from long deserted graveyards and roadside plantings, and by begging cuttings from old farms and cottages. As well as col-

lecting, identifying, and preserving these genuine treasures, the heritage rose societies provide a wealth of experience for new gardeners to draw on.

Another important aspect of these heritage roses is that they were developed at a time when organic growing was the norm, when compost, manures, and wood ashes were the only fertilizers, so that these old roses grow optimally under modern organic techniques.

Growing Notes

Almost all commercial roses are propagated by a process called budding. A very strong species rose like *Rosa rugosa*, *R. canina*, or *R. multiflora*, or an exceptionally strong variety such as '**Dr Huey**', is chosen to form the root section of the rose, called the stock or understock. Selection is based on a consideration of soil and climate tolerance of the stock in combination with its physiological compatibility with the variety which will be budded on to form the rose bush, technically the scion. When you buy a rose bush, it is quite easy to see the bud union where the bush has grown away from the basal stub of the stock.

Experts are divided as to whether to plant a rose below or just above the bud union. Roses planted below the union may begin suckering from the buried lower branches but the deeper planting ensures less root rock of the young plant in windy weather. In small gardens, suckering may be discouraged, but it can lead to a large, healthy clump that will make a very fine display.

Roses are tolerant of a wide range of soils and pH. A good loam soil with a pH of 6.5 to 7.0 is ideal but most soils can easily be assisted to grow good roses. If your soil is very acid, pH 5.5 or less, incorporate dolomite to raise the pH. There is no need to be precise. A good large

Rosa ecae has single flowers that are bright buttercup-yellow in color.

handful of dolomite sprinkled over each square yard (square meter) and lightly turned through the upper soil is adequate. Some well-rotted compost forked through the soil is also a valuable addition, and should be added in good quantity to sandy soils which easily leach nutrients and retain water poorly.

Soft, sappy, lush growth is the opposite to what the organic gardener needs. Such growth is dependent on regular high watering levels and the addition of high levels of nutrient additives to the soil. The bushes are prone to fungal and insect attack because they are so soft.

The provision of an immensely rich soil for rose culture is only gradually being abandoned. A search through 19th century books reveals potions of the most dire, dark, and secret composition used by rival gardeners to grow show roses. The rose-loving dean of Rochester, Dean Hole, in 1869 advised the use of copious farmyard manures, explaining: '*By farmyard manure I mean all the manures of the straw-yard, solid and fluid, horse, cow, pig, poultry, in conjunction. Let a heap be made near the rosarium, not suppressing the fumes of natural fermentation.*'

Rosa canina is the common rose of the hedgerows in central and western Europe. It has small, scented flowers with color varying from white to pink.

Such excessively nitrogen-rich additions created such lush, sappy, weakened growth that the bushes were very disease-prone, cold and drought-sensitive, and easily wind damaged. Beautiful blooms were produced on weakling bushes. It is far better to rely on an annual addition of compost supplemented with bone meal, and in the growing season the use of regular foliar feeds of liquid seaweed fertilizer.

Instead of heavy regular watering, a heavy organic mulch such as lucerne or hay should be applied to conserve soil moisture and prevent soil temperatures becoming excessively hot or cold. Watering can then be restricted to one very deep soaking weekly which encourages the root system to search into deeper soil. In very hot, dry summer areas, create a shallow saucer-like depression in the ground before planting. This acts to hold every precious drop of water and ensure that it targets the roots. In areas with heavy rains, garden beds should be raised to allow for adequate drainage.

Soils which have previously grown roses should not be replanted with roses. The term 'rose sick soil' arose from the gardener's observation that replacement roses in a garden do not thrive, even when well managed. The cause of this problem lies in the accumulation of rose disease organisms and predators built up in the soil, possibly in association with auto toxins. This soil is not a problem for other plants which can be used to replace rose bushes when they are removed. But if you wish to grow more roses on the site, the only viable solution is to barrow the soil away and exchange it with soil from another part of the garden. Dig soil out to a depth of aproximately 2 ft 4 in (70 cm) and a diameter of 40 in (1 m) on the site of a previous mature rose bush.

Good soil preparation is wasted if roses are not properly planted. Roses can now be obtained all year round grown in containers, or in winter, when deciduous, they can safely be lifted from the ground, the top and roots pruned, and sold bare rooted. Mail order plants are sent out in the cool months of the year as bare-rooted roses.

The right time to plant roses depends on your climate. In very cold areas where temperatures drop well below freezing for some time, as they do in many areas of North America and northern Europe, planting should be delayed until spring. In areas with cold but not bitter winters such as southern England, Ireland, and parts of southern Australia and the southern United States, planting can be carried out in the winter months. Subtropical area gardeners should plant before what little there is of winter.

Most gardeners buy their roses bare-rooted. If for any reason you are unable to plant out immediately, the bushes can be temporarily heeled in by digging a short trough and laying the roses at 45° with the roots covered in soil. If roses are to be planted immediately after arrival in the post, shorten any long thick roots by about a quarter, cut any broken pieces off, and soak the bundle in a diluted seaweed emulsion (1 tablespoon to a bucket of water) for an hour or two before planting. This will rehydrate the roots and give them an excellent start in life.

With the exception of alba roses which have some shade tolerance, and a few species, roses should be planted in a sunny, well-drained, open but wind-protected area. Plantings under low eaves, or the heavy canopy of trees, will not flourish as they should and are prone to mildew.

To plant containerized roses is usually a simple matter of tapping the plant out with its soil ball attached. Place two fingers of your hand around the base of the stem with fingers spread out to support the soil, invert the pot, and give a

The color of a rose may vary with its position, the soil, the climate, and the age of the bloom.

Flower color and the 'character' of a rose are factors to consider when planting a rose garden.

couple of smart taps to the edge of the pot. The contents should slide out intact. Plant this soil ball into a prepared hole, at the same depth of the original planting, firming the soil down gently and watering the plant in very thoroughly before applying a mulch. Roses that have been in a container for a while or are very strong growers begin to exhaust the soil in a container and grow around the inside of the pot searching for nutrient. The roots become twisted and inward growing. If the rose is planted like this, the roots will continue to grow around the old root

When planting bare-rooting roses, follow these basic steps: 1: Check for damaged roots. 2: Dig a hole big enough for the roots. 3: Plant the rose, back-filling with crumbly soil. 4: Mulch well.

ball instead of exploring outward. To prevent this happening, use the back of a pair of secateurs to gently tease the largest roots outward before planting, ensuring that the hole dug is large enough to accommodate these teased-out roots, and finish planting as before.

Bare-rooted plants need a slightly different aproach. The main downward roots form a kind of rough cone shape. If these roses are simply placed in a hole and soil filled in, a large air gap is left beneath the bush. To avoid this, dig a hole a little wider and deeper than the root system and

create a conical pile of earth in the center. The roots fit snugly onto this cone of soil, and extra soil can then be placed around the plant to the correct depth. Press down firmly but gently with your hands. The old-fashioned idea of trampling around the plant to settle it only results in breaking the main root framework. Water the rose thoroughly, allow all the water to drain away, then water again. The roots should now be in good contact with the soil, all air pockets removed, and the roots able to grow away. A stake can be advisable in windy positions to minimize root rock which inhibits the establishment of a rose.

While roses are creating a new root system in the soil, they are easily water-stressed and attention to watering and mulch is essential. After the first year they should be strong enough to cope with some adverse weather provided mulch is regularly renewed each year. The tough roses which have been recommended here often survive well without watering, except during hot, dry spells, but a weekly soaking will yield far more blooms.

A gentle long soaking with a soaker hose or a spray system located at the base of the plant creates the minimum disturbance to the soil and mulch. Overhead watering is not harmful and (contrary to much advice) will deter mildew. The exception is the use of overhead watering late in the afternoon or evening when the leaves will remain moist and encourage the fungal disease blackspot. The active root zone of a rose is at least 2 ft (60 cm) deep. If you are concerned about soil moisture, use a hand trowel to gently dig down well away from the roots and check how deeply the soil has been moistened. Too much water can be as great a problem as too little. Excessive watering on heavy soils can cause waterlogging and make roses susceptible to disease.

'Mary Rose'. Beautiful in the garden but not a good rose for picking as the blooms shatter soon after they have reached full-blown stage.

Trouble-Shooting

If rose varieties have been well selected for the garden, very few problems should emerge. Roses that are debilitated by fungal attacks have no place in the organic garden. But even the best roses are not always trouble-free. An occasional minor problem may still occur. A first line of attack for all fungal diseases is a thorough spray with soft soap (not detergent) diluted in the ratio 1 part of soap to 100 parts of water. This should be followed up in the next few days with one or two foliar sprays of liquid seaweed fertilizer. Liquid soap performed outstandingly in trials on rose fungal diseases, equalling the effect of many toxic chemicals. The seaweed spray has a twofold effect, providing a nutrient boost to releaf the branches, and coating leaves with a dried gel which inhibits the penetration of germinating fungal spores.

Most common fungal diseases are easy to diagnose. Blackspot appears as irregular black blotches on the leaves which then turn yellow before falling. It is usually associated with periods of high humidity.

Powdery mildew looks exactly as if the young shoots and buds had been

Blackspot appears
as irregular blotches on
the leaves of roses,
which then turn yellow
before falling.

puffed with baby powder, and the mildew can extend quite rapidly over the upper half of the plant. The spores of powdery mildew germinate on dry leaves, so that climbers and bushes growing under eaves are particularly prone. Gallica roses often suffer some mildew on the necks of buds although it is rarely debilitating, and the much loved old rambler rose 'Dorothy Perkins' can be a martyr to this fungus. An interim solution is to apply wet-table sulfur followed a few days later by a seaweed emulsion foliar appli-cation. If the problem is shade, it should be addressed, by lifting the rose and replanting in winter or cutting back any overgrowth.

Downy mildew is usually associated with a cool wet spell during the growing season. It appears as dark, irregular, purple to brown patches on the leaves. It is controlled in the same way as powdery mildew with wettable sulfur and foliar seaweed application.

The fourth of the common fungal diseases of roses is rust. Rust appears as numerous bright orange pustules beginning beneath the leaves before spreading to the surface and causing the leaves to fall. Good aeration and light is again important, and the fungus can be controlled with wettable sulfur followed by foliar seaweed spray.

Roses are susceptible to a variety of viruses which are carried via the sap and can be carried by sucking insects like aphids, or in the processes of budding or pruning if equipment is not sterilized between working on each plant. Wiping down with alcohol or flaming the blade is ade-quate. Most viruses have little effect on the rose but any obvious, persis-tent, very eccentric growth is suspicious and severely affected bushes that are growing poorly should be burned. (The use of many herbicides can produce similar distortions so check that none has drifted over your garden before condemning a plant. It will usually recover from herbicide damage unless it is acute.) The commonest virus is mosaic disease, which looks like a checkerboard patterning of green and yellow on the leaves. It is more obvious in cool weather, and shows up much more easily with roses budded onto some rootstocks than others. ('Dr Huey', for instance, masks mosaic disease to a considerable degree.) Mosaic is usually more of an aesthetic issue than a problem for the rose.

Another problem, very largely associated with the modern classes of roses, is 'dieback'. Any one of several fungi may attack the stem, particularly of younger roses, reducing the flow of sap and causing the stem to die progressively from the top downward. There are several ways that dieback may be initiated, all of them preventable. First, even in the absence of fungus, water stress particularly of recently planted roses can cause shriveling of tender, unfurling leaves in spring. Once the buds have been shrivelled the stem automatically shuts down sap supply to the bud, and the stem dies back to the next lowest bud. If that too is irreparably shrivelled the stem dies back once again. Particularly in hot or windy spells, ensure that young plants are regularly watered, that the water is penetrating at least 2 ft (60 cm) into the soil, and that an adequate mulch is in place. Careless pruning and poor drainage can also abet dieback in susceptible varieties.

Attacks by fungi such as blackspot can cause defoliation of the bush, reducing its photosynthetic capacity. One attack is rarely a problem but two or three in quick succession over a season can cause dieback in susceptible varieties.

There is no magic bullet to cure dieback. The best preventative is to choose vigorous healthy varieties and manage the plants well so that they are not unduly stressed particularly when young. To deal with an existing case of dieback, cut the affected stem to well below the damaged area and $1/_5$ in (5 mm) above a healthy bud.

Frost Damage

There are any number of strange devices recommended for insulating the lower part of a rose bush to prevent freezing of the buds, usually a combinaton of hilling up with soil followed by an insulating layer of peat or cardboard, held in place with heavy fall branch trimmings. A few dearly beloved roses could be preserved this way but planting roses with the necessary level of frost tolerance is in general far easier for an organic gardener.

In spring, any frost-killed wood should be pruned down to strong live buds. The pith will appear brown inside when the stem is cut in frost killed wood. Do not prune until spring in cold districts.

The rugosa rose 'Scabrosa' is very cold-hardy.

Aphids can cluster very densely on sappy young growth of shoots and buds and cause serious distortion.

Insect Pests

Many insects are benign, or are actively predating upon pests and should be considered beneficial. It is important to be able to recognize problem insects, and to monitor their populations. A few insects of any species are certainly not worth worrying about. The commonest problems you will encounter are aphids, red spider, scale, thrips, and leaf-chewing insects.

Aphids, also known as greenfly, are tiny, plump, green insects which can cluster very densely on sappy young growth of shoots and buds, and cause serious distortion. They may also carry viruses between roses. Aphids can be gently squashed on leaves and stems. The smell of squashed aphid acts as a warning, and most aphids will immediately drop to the ground when disturbed. They can also be dislodged with a jet of water from the hose. Pyrethrum spray or a spray based on garlic is an effective control.

Red spider or spider mite is neither a spider nor necessarily red. They are tiny, almost microscopic, insects that live beneath rose leaves, building their population during hot, dry weather. While the insects are very tiny, the fine webbing under the leaves is easier to detect. They are leaf-sucking insects and mottled yellow and brown leaves are a probable indication of their presence, as is the curling over of leaves as they dry out. Regular, vigorous hosing under the foliage is very helpful in dislodging the mites. Biological controls are effective too, and lacewing larvae and predator mites are both used to control outbreaks of this pest. Garlic spray is also useful, as is a spray of whole milk diluted with an equal quantity of water, but be certain to aim the spray under the leaves.

Wax insects are disfiguring, and large populations, usually found on the lower stems, reduce sap flow by sucking and can severely weaken a rose bush. Wax insects look exactly like

Scale insects on rose can be disfiguring.

blobs of wax on the stem, in the form of oval, waxy, white to pale-brown mounds. When scraped off, under the thick protective carapace of wax will be found a small insect. Ladybirds are their natural predators, but in severe attacks an old toothbrush dipped in methylated spirits can be used to dislodge scale. Any heavily infected branches should be cut out and burned. Old-fashioned lime sulfur can be painted on the branches to prevent further infestation.

Thrips resemble tiny brown or black splinters crawling over rose blooms. They are far more attracted to pale colors than dark reds. Thrips are migatory, coming in on hot summer winds, and leaving with them. As they are migratory there is no point in trying to control them.

There are several minor leaf chewing insects which do cosmetic, but rarely extensive, damage to leaves. Leaf cutter bees are probably the most unusual, creating almost perfect round punch holes in leaves. Their population never becomes excessive and they represent a good case for the attitude of 'live and let live' in the garden. Leaf hoppers or jassids are short term visitors to the garden, rarely doing much damage in the few days they are visible. They somewhat resemble miniature jade-green cicadas, jumping sideways on bushes, and are another insect to be tolerated within

reason. Katydids look like slender green grasshoppers with exceptionally long green legs. They are rarely present in significant numbers and can be controlled by picking off manually.

Japanese beetles are small brown beetles which can be highly destructive in some places such as the United States, swarming and chewing on both flowers and leaves. Pyrethrum-based sprays can be tried, and hand picking will deal with smaller numbers.

On sandy soils, nematodes or eelworms may be a problem. They are tiny, colorless, soil-dwelling worms that can penetrate into the vascular tissue of the plant, blocking transportation of sap. The roots of an infected plant have gall-like protrusions. Nematodes are best controlled by interplanting roses with French marigolds, or pre-planting the soil with marigolds, chopping them back in as a green manure crop when they are slowing down their flowering, and allowing them to rot down before planting the soil with roses.

Companion Plants

Several plants are helpful in controlling problems with roses.

French marigolds *Tagetes* spp. — These are used to control soil-borne nematodes.

Garlic *Allium sativum* — Professional rose growers in many countries use garlic interplantings to deter undesirable insects. In Bulgaria, which is a major supplier of the precious essential oil attar of roses, many farmers inter-row plantings of the damasks, albas, and centifolias with garlic or onions, and swear that it not only improves the health of the roses but intensifies the fragance and increases the volume of attar produced. Some of the ornamental *Allium* species are exceptionally beautiful and retain the strong onion scent which acts as an insect

Thrips resemble tiny brown or black splinters crawling over rose blooms.

'Amélia' has bright pink flowers and golden stamens. Garlic, Allium sativum, is a good companion plant.

growing ornamental plant belongs to the cabbage family and is considered to have beneficial effects on roses. It is an annual grown from seed and can be used as a groundcover.

Parsley *Petroselinum* spp. — Both the moss-curled and plain-leaf varieties of parsley are considered to be beneficial to roses.

Pruning

Pruning, like all gardening, is based on a few sensible rules easily followed, and is not in the least complicated.

The first questions are why, and when, to prune roses. Species roses and most of the first generation hybrids of species roses require no pruning to sustain their health. Neither do the great majority of the Gallicas, damasks, albas and Portland roses. If they were never pruned, little harm would result. The major reasons for pruning these groups are to remove damaged branches, or to restrain branches from overgrowing paths or other bushes. The centifolia and moss roses are more highly bred than most members of the summer roses and can respond well to an occasional light pruning, but it is not necessary to their survival.

If pruning is to be carried out on these groups, it should be done soon after flowering has finished in summer. The reason for this is that they flower on mature wood, and

repellent. Chives, *Allium schoenoprasum*, which form neat lush clumps of hollow-leafed, onion scented foliage and dense heads of onion-flavored, lilac-pink flowers are an attractive perennial border for a rose garden, dying down each winter. Society garlic, *Tulbaghia violacea*, also known as mauve garlic chives, are strongly garlic-scented relatives of *Allium* with tall stems of nodding mauve bell flowers; they are equally acceptable as an ornamental pest-repellent edging.

Mignonette Reseda — This very sweetly scented, old-fashioned, low-

Right: Parsley, Petroselinum crispum, is considered to be beneficial to roses.

Far right: The conventional method of pruning is to cut about $1/2$ in (6 mm) above a bud, sloping away from it at a slight angle.

need to retain their autumn growth. Remove no more than a quarter to a third of growth, and prune any very twiggy, unproductive old wood, or broken or dead stems.

The repeat flowering roses including the classes Bourbons, hybrid perpetuals, floribundas, and hybrid teas are highly bred and annual pruning assists them in regenerating a new framework. Long, lush, often reddish shoots that emerge from **above** the bud union are watershoots which will form the new framework. They are spurred into growth by pruning. Never remove these branches. When hardened off they can be shortened back by up to one third. Pruning of this group depends on the climate, but it should be done before the new growing season starts. The tops of rose bushes help provide cover until frosts are over so the later the better in cold districts.

The old idea of pruning a rose 'down to its socks' as the saying went is no longer followed. It produces fewer roses the following season, although they are usually of good quality. Rather than cutting plants down to some prescribed height, let them keep as much as possible their natural form and height. Remove all dead (and frozen) wood. Good air movement through the bush reduces fungal damage and prevents damaging rub between branches, so look for inward growing crossing branches and remove them together with any old

twiggy unproductive growth. Head back the remaining stems by no more than a third, remove the prunings, and the work is complete.

Grown in warm to hot area gardens, tea, noisette, and China roses grow almost unchecked year round. They need no more than the removal of dead wood.

Only three other points need be made. First, always use very sharp secateurs and pruning knives or you will do far more harm than good. Second, always make cuts $^1/_5$ in (5 mm) above an outward-facing bud and slope the cut very gently away from the bud. Never allow a cut to be level with or dip **below** a bud. The bud will die and on susceptible varieties initiate dieback. Third, don't cut off suckers. They will leave behind deeply buried shoot initials which will in time form another sucker. Instead, use your thumb to press down firmly on the junction between stem and sucker, or gently pull the earth aside and press on the root sucker. When it breaks off, it usually carries the shoot initials with it. Sometimes long shoots come from below the bud union or from the roots. The former is sometimes the result of a bud on the stock not being removed, but suckers from the understock are usually caused by damage done when digging around roses. Never dig around roses. Once a rose is planted simply mulch or apply compost to the surface.

Left to right:
Long-handled secateurs for big pruning jobs can prevent fatigue in the pruner's arms.

Rose bushes can be rejuvenated by cutting out old growth.

Old twiggy growth should also be removed.

'Winterizing' with lucerne hay mulch provides insulation from freezing weather.

'Lafter' is a sub-zero rose that will grow in cold winter areas.

Roses for Cold Climates

With much effort and care, insulating roses from extremely cold conditions can be effective in maintaining them for many years. The Sangerhausen Rosarium in Germany, about 50 miles (80 km) from Leipzig and one of the oldest major rose gardens in the world, maintains a very significant collection of tea roses through bitter winters, although with great effort and some annual losses.

The most cold-tolerant groups of roses are Gallicas, albas, multiflora ramblers, rugosas, and many species roses. *R. wichuriana* and *R. pimpinellifolia* are both very cold-hardy as are the roses developed from them. Most species roses are hardy to 12°F (⁻11°C), yet can tolerate hot summers. *R. roxburghii* is an exception, being being unable to withstand temperatures in the region of 50°F (10°C). South China species of roses, which have contributed so much to the development of modern roses, are relatively tender so that classes bred with these species are often vulnerable.

For those who long for modern-style roses to grow in cold winter areas, there is plenty of choice. The *R. wichuriana* climber 'Dr W. van Fleet' has been used to introduce greater hardiness, producing a series of sub-zero roses such as 'Lafter' and 'Elegance'. The climbing rose 'New Dawn' has excellent cold resistance, insect-proof shiny foliage, and some of the loveliest flowers anywhere, very fragrant, double, and pale pink, borne throughout the season. The very hardy 'Max Graf' is an almost sterile hybrid and is a cross between *R. rugosa* and *R. wichuriana*. Climbers 'Dortmund', 'Leverkusen', 'Parkdirektor Riggers', 'Ritter von Barmstede', and 'Hamburger Phoenix', are all worthy of a place in cold-area gardens, and all virtually disease-free. 'Silver Jubilee' is an example of a hybrid tea involving *R. x kordesii*, and is an exceptional rose of outstanding vigor and cold resistance.

Roses for Hot and Humid Climates

Hot, humid tropical climates are a real test of most classes of roses. For those who garden in areas with such climates, it is an excellent idea to keep an eye out for old rose bushes in your area. You may be able to beg cuttings or find out the name of the rose. Some classes are much more success-ful in such subtropical to tropical areas. China, tea, and noisette roses are by far the best performers, togeth-er with some polyanthas and the banksia roses.

The *Old Texas Rose* newsletter recently nominated the following roses as most easy to grow in the very hot and humid South Gulf region of the United States: 'Mutabilis' (China), 'Old Blush' (China), 'Duchesse de Brabant' (tea), 'Chestnut Rose', 'Lady Banks Rose', 'Prosperity' (hybrid musk), 'Champney's Pink Cluster' (noisette), 'Cramoisi Supérieur' (China), 'Green Rose' syn. Viridiflora, (China), 'La Marne' (polyantha), 'Kronprinzessin Viktoria' (Bourbon), 'Mermaid' (climber), 'Paul Neyron' (hybrid perpetual) and 'Souvenir de la Malmaison' (Bourbon).

Many roses considered to be the most disease-resistant by the *Old Texas Rose* contributors are not surprisingly on the above list., but additional roses nominated were 'Monsieur Tillier', 'Mrs B.R. Cant', 'Mrs Dudley Cross', and 'Safrano' (all old tea roses), 'Russelliana' ('Russell's Cottage Rose'), and the 'Swamp Rose' *R. palustris*. Members also included among their best performing climbers 'Rêve d'Or' (noisette), 'Sombrieul' (climbing tea), 'Climbing Souvenir de la Malmaison' and 'Desprez à Fleur Jaune' (noisette). It should be noted, though, that 'Souvenir de la Malmaison' is undoubtedly a tough survivor, its very double pale-pink flowers ball easily in wet weather, the buds not opening and eventually rotting off.

In Tahiti and other islands of the Pacific, three roses consistently appear in the local markets and in the tropical gardens: 'Monsieur Tillier', 'Old Blush', and 'Cramoisi Supérieur'. The same roses are also found in old gardens and churchyard gardens of the Greek island of Corfu. In the Caribbean, 'Old Blush' and other early China roses such as 'Louis Phillipe' have persisted over long periods of time, often handed on to neighbors as cuttings. 'Bloomfield Abundance', an old polyantha, is found in some tropical gardens in New Caledonia.

In Australia, huge subtropical and tropical specimens of noisette roses such as 'Celine Forestier', 'Maréchal Niel', 'Rêve d'Or', 'William Allen Richardson', 'Cloth of Gold', and 'Claire Jacquier' grew in profusion around the graceful verandahs of spacious old colonial Queenslander homes. Tea roses were also excellent survivors and needed no care. They include 'Bon Silène', 'Mrs Dudley Cross', 'Lady Hillingdon', 'Maman Cochet', 'Red Maman Cochet' ('Niles Cochet'), 'Duchesse de Brabant', 'Perle des Jardins', 'Mrs Herbert Stevens', 'Catherine Mermet', 'Comtesse Riza du Parc', 'Anna Olivier', 'Baronne Henriette de Snoy', 'Etoile de Lyon', 'White Maman Cochet', 'Marie Van Houtte', 'Souvenir d'Un Ami', 'Isabella Sprunt', and the glorious climbing tea rose, 'Souvenir de Thérèse Levet'. Long surviving China roses include 'Old Blush', 'Cramoisi Supérieur', and 'Le Vésuve'. Old polyantha varieties that have survived unaided for many decades in these tropical gardens are 'Bloomfield Abundance', easily reaching $11^1/_2$–13 ft (3.5–4 m), 'Perle d'Or', reaching 8 ft (2.5 m) and 'Papa Hameray'.

Many gardeners in the tropics struggle with modern hybrid teas and floribundas in vain. The lack of a cool season forces hybrid teas into a relentless growth cycle resulting in poor spindly growth and a shortened life, as well as making them susceptible to every disease and in constant need of rejuvenation pruning. There are a few very well proven varieties that can be grown

The Old Texas Rose *newsletter nominated green rose of China,* Rosa chinensis *'Viridiflora', as one of the most easy roses to grow in a very hot and humid region.*

'Frau Karl Druschki' a huge white cabbage-flowered hybrid perpetual rose, the old Gallica rose **'Hippolyte'**, the double white climbing rose 'Fortuneana', **'Fisher Holmes'**, a crimson-red hybrid perpetual, **'Marchioness of Londonderry'**, an 1893 white hybrid perpetual faintly suffused with pink which is a survivor in the Mexican Gulf area of the United States, and **'Rose Edouard'**, the first Bourbon rose.

Uses Of Roses

No flower has found as many uses as the rose. Precious attar of roses, more valuable weight for weight than gold, has long been incorporated into many of the world's most valuable perfumes. Its fragrance has been captured in pot pourris and waxes to scent the home. Rose petals have astringent healing and skin moisturizing properties, and are still incorporated into many modern face lotions and creams. Glycerine and rosewater, rose cold cream, 'milk of roses', rose vinegar, 'cream of roses', and rose lipsalve were widely used in the past to nourish and moisturize the skin, and they are as effective, gentle, and natural today as they were then. The fragrance of roses was captured in many recipes for delicious foods in days gone by. With the return of interest in using edible flowers in modern cooking, roses once more are favored as one of the most delicious additions to innovative dishes from salads to roast lamb, exotic desserts and summer drinks. Rosehips are remarkably rich in vitamin C and can be used to make a vitamin-rich delicious syrup or incorporated into cooking. Try a baked apple pie into which the sliced, deseeded rosehips of rugosa or eglantine roses (with all the internal hairs carefully removed) have been added before baking. Not only is the pie better for you, but it has a tangier flavor and a tantalizing rose perfume.

successfully in tropical areas with little or no intervention. These are 'Crimson Glory', 'Etoile de Hollande', 'Red Radiance', 'Radiance', 'Chrysler Imperial', 'Laurent Carl', 'Mme Abel Chatenay', 'Mrs C.J. Bell', 'La France', 'Spek's Yellow', 'Sutter's Gold', and 'Talisman'. They are all old varieties but still so reliable, the strongest of their era, that they remain commercially available.

Other roses that have survived very well in tropical areas with little or no need for a gardener's intervention are

Species Roses

In general, the species roses are the toughest forms available and require little or no help from gardeners provided they are planted in fairly similar situations to that in which they flourish in Nature. Many are capable of withstanding far more extreme conditions than most varieties created by the plant breeders of the last few centuries and are usually highly vigorous and disease-resistant. Once established and mulched, many will survive on rainfall alone, with supplemented watering during hot dry spells.

For all the beauty of modern rose flowers, the bush on which they grow often lacks grace and has coarse and none too abundant foliage which is not infrequently disease-susceptible. Species roses offer many advantages to organic gardeners, and indeed to all gardeners. While modern roses have what at best could be called functional foliage, wild roses possess an amazing array of foliage textures, forms, and subtle color variations that will never fail to add to the beauty of your garden, even when the bushes are not in flower. Foliage may be bold and ferny, brilliantly burnished or silken in rugose, in a subtle range of silver and silver-greens, rich deep forest greens and olives, and fresh acid yellow greens. A number of species are noted for their translucent ruby or grape purple spring foliage and many have beautiful rich autumn coloring. Some even have fragrant foliage.

The abundant flowering of many of the species roses is fleeting, a matter of a few weeks, but the single flowers have a great delicacy and are followed by hips of every shape, size and color.

Rosehips are rich in vitamin C and the fruits of some species are used commercially to make rose syrup for children. Most organic gardeners are happy to share this autumnal bounty

'Nevada' is a striking species rose that bears white, yellow-centered flowers.

with birds which inevitably gather for the feast, but also bring life and music into the garden in fall and assist with insect control.

Species roses come in a wide range of sizes and shapes. Some make bold massed displays for larger suburban and country gardens, while others are small enough for tiny city gardens and balconies. And with their exquisite, sweetly scented flowers and array of foliages and fruits, they contribute to the garden for three seasons of the year.

The wild climbing roses have the same sweet simplicity as their shrub cousins and need no greater care. Like the wild shrub roses they are increasingly fashionable, being adopted everywhere as much for their beauty and bounty of blossoms and fruits as for their carefree ways. Most species are larger climbers ideal for pergolas or even for climbing

'Raubritter' flowers in summer and is quite spectacular bearing clusters of light pink, double, globular flowers.

'Village Charm', Rosa Brunonii group, is a hardy, wild climbing rose.

substantial trees to spill in cascades of fragrant flowers in late spring and early summer. They require no pruning or spraying, but their vigor and growth means that you will want to train them in early years to their eventual support which must be sturdy. Like the shrub species roses they have an array of foliage textures and subtle colors, extraordinarily varied fragrances, flower sizes from that of a tiny coin to a saucer, and wonderful hips in fall.

No roses are native to the Southern Hemisphere, but many wild roses are admirably suited to gardens in cool to warm areas in the Southern Hemisphere. As a general guide, the species roses of North America are successful in cool gardens, as are European species. Species from south China have some cold sensitivity. Species from Central Asia require warm

Rosa nitida has lush, highly polished neat green leaves and medium-sized lilac-pink flowers that are scented at night.

summers and cold winters. Gardens with Mediterranean climates grow them well, but not gardens with unreliable summers. Species such as *R. persica* from hot dry regions need both heat and a dry summer.

Recommended Cultivars

Most species roses can be grown with confidence, providing that the environment from which the rose originated is reasonably compatible with that of the garden in which it is to be grown. Listed here are a few highly reliable species but many, many more are very suitable. Also listed here are some of many first generation hybrids of wild roses that have proved themselves over a period of time in many parts of the world to be comparable in toughness to the species.

R. californica 'Plena', 'Californian Rose' — This is the double-flowered form of the Californian rose, eventually making a large shrub to 9 ft 9 in (3 m) with charming, semi-double, rich pink flowers around 1³/₅ in (4 cm) in diameter borne in corymbs. In the wild, *R. californica* occurs in Oregon and California, flowering over a long period from June to October. Zones 3–10.

R. cinnomomea 'Cinnamon Rose' — A rose from the 17th century and particularly treasured in American colonial gardens, it forms an upright-growing, branched shrub to 6 ft (1.8 m) with downy gray-green foliage and abundant single, soft pink flowers in spring followed by red hips. Zones 4–11.

R. ecae — This is a spectacular spring flowering shrub of Chinese origin with fern-like foliage and exceedingly abundant, single flowers that are pale gold and the size of primroses. It is tough and disease-resistant, and reaches 8 ft (2.5 m) as a freestanding shrub. Zones 4–11.

R. forrestiana — This Chinese species makes a splendid specimen shrub with attractive, disease-resistant

foliage which flowers abundantly in spring bearing very fragrant, cerise-pink single blooms with prominent golden stamens followed by a profusion of glowing hips. It was introduced in 1918. Zones 4–10.

R. hugonis 'Father Hugo's Rose' syn. Golden Rose of China — Introduced from central China in 1908 with good cold hardiness, this species forms a shrub to 6 ft 6 in (2 m) with many dainty but finely thorny arched branches covered in fern-like foliage and bearing along their length single, cupped, fragrant, golden-yellow flowers. Zones 4–10.

R. multiflora var. 'Bamboo Rose' — A very finely divided leaf form of the thornless Japanese rose, bearing large panicles of small sweetly scented white flowers. It is treasured for its willowlike or bamboo form and grows into a graceful, totally disease-resistant shrub to 5 ft (1.5 m) which is very hardy. Zones 4–11.

R. nitida — Commonly found on wet acid oils and around water edges in the New England area of the United States and north to Newfoundland and Quebec, this is a very resistant variety with lush remarkable, highly polished neat green leaves. The medium sized lilac-pink flowers are fragrant with a lily-of-the-valley scent at night. The hips are rich dark red and the fall foliage is a dramatic claret to purple. It forms a totally trouble-free, exceptionally

neat, low-growing shrub. It is an ideal choice for a gardener struggling with poor drainage, although it fares very well in normal garden situations. Zones 4–11.

R. primula syn. R. ecae subsp. primula, Incense Rose — From Central Asia with very good cold hardiness but also excellent in warm gardens, this is a very healthy bush to 8 ft (2.5 m) with fern-like, glossy very healthy leaves which are very aromatic, and abundant pale primrose yellow single flowers in spring. **'Golden Chersonese'** is an excellent hybrid with the same aromatic foliage and larger yellow flowers in spring. Zones 4–11.

R. roxburghii 'Plena', 'Chestnut Rose' — This is a handsome rose of great beauty from China with spectacular foliage composed of up to 15 or more leaflets beautifully arrayed on a medium-sized spreading shrub. it bears large, lightly scented, very

Rosa cinnamomea, the 'Cinnamon Rose', forms an upright branched shrub with downy gray-green foliage and abundant single, soft pink flowers.

Rosa roxburghii 'Plena', 'Chestnut Rose', is a beautiful rose from China that bears large, lightly scented rich pink flowers.

Rosa virginiana is a fine wild rose with charming pink, medium-sized single flowers.

double, flat, rich pink flowers opening from softly bristled green buds. The single form produces remarkable bristled hips resembling the case of chestnuts. It is a very healthy and vigorous species in cool to warm gardens, but will not survive below 12°F (⁻11°C). Zones 4–11.

R. rubrifolia syn. R. glauca — Introduced prior to 1830, this is a taller-growing famous species rose renowned for its superb foliage coloring. In spring it is rich and vinous, in mid-season glaucous and purple tinted, and in late fall there is a magnificent display of claret and rich purples. It is very disease-resistant and vigorous large bunches of ruby-red hips in fall are an added attraction. Small, rich pink flowers with light fragrance are borne in clusters in spring. It prefers drier situations. It is quite shade-tolerant. Zones 4–10.

R. rugosa *(See section on rugosa roses.)*

R. stellata mirifica 'Gooseberry Rose', 'Sacramento Rose' — This is an unusual and lovely rose forming a compact shrub to 4 ft (1.2 m) with gooseberry-like dense foliage and lilac-pink single flowers with prominent creamy-golden stamens. Zones 4–10.

Rosa rubrifolia is renowned for its superb foliage coloring. It has small, rich pink flowers with a light fragrance.

R. villosa 'Duplex', 'Wolly Dods' Rose' — A charming form of the apple rose which bears the synonym **R. pomifera** as its hips are large, up to nearly one in (2.5 cm) long, and pippin or pear-shaped. This form has large healthy foliage and medium-sized, semi-double, exquisite light-pink flowers followed by somewhat smaller hips than the species. It has excellent cold hardiness, the species being native to Scandinavia. Zones 4–11.

R. virginiana — One of the finest of the wild roses, unreservedly recommended on all counts, this makes a mounded bush to 6 ft (1.8 m) with graceful form and disease-free foliage clothing the bush to the ground. The charming lively pink, medium-sized, single flowers last over long periods and are followed by a spectacular display of red hips. The foliage shows excellent fall coloring from gold to rich red. This variety is superb as a hedge or as a specimen rose. It was almost certainly grown in England by 1640, and tolerates cold winters and hot summers. A hybrid 'Rose d'Amour', also known as 'St Marks Rose' and **R. virginiana plena,** is a double pink form with exquisitely scrolled buds and a fruity fragrance, growing to around 6¹/₂ ft (2 m) forming a densely mounded bush with beautiful fall coloring. Zones 3–11.

Recommended Shrub Hybrids

'Canary Bird' — This is a very fine, spring flowering shrub, a seedling of the Chinese species rose *R. xanthina*, most probably originating from the Botanic Garden in Edinburgh. It grows into a slightly arching tall bush up to 6 ft (1.8 m) with clear sunshine-yellow, small, single flowers with a pleasant fragrance, and the delicate fern-like foliage is a joy in summer. It is hardy although full exposure to chilly winds is not advisable. It performs well in warm gardens with cool winters, and is trouble free. Zones 4-9.

'Dupontii' — syn. *R. x dupontii*, *R. moschata nivea* — This cultivar from 1817 is not infrequently considered to be the finest shrub rose ever bred. It forms a large bush to over 6 1/2 ft (2 m) and bears abundant clusters of large milky white flowers up to 3 in (7.5 cm) across, deliciously fragrant, and opening from rose pink buds. The flowers are fol-lowed by an excellent display of orange hips. It is tolerant of cold to warm gardens, vigorous, and reputedly is a cross between *R. gallica* and the musk rose *R. moschata*. Zones 4-11.

'Frühlingsgold' — Released by Kordes in 1937, this is a vigorous healthy shrub to 6$^1/_2$ ft (2 m) created by a cross with the Scotch or burnet rose *R. spinosissima*. It is very drought and heat-resistant once established, has inherited good cold hardiness, and survives some neglect. It is long flowering with exquisite, large, semi-double pale gold flowers of sweet fragrance opening from elegant, furled, buff-gold buds. It is an excellent specimen shrub. Zones 4-9.

'Geranium' — This is the commonest selection of *R. moyesii* in cultivation, forming an upright strong shrub to 8 ft (2.5 m) with plentiful, very striking, rich red,

'Dupontii', Rosa x dupontii, is considered by some to be the finest shrub rose ever bred. It forms a large bush and bears abundant clusters of large milky white flowers.

medium-sized single flowers and leaves with 11 to 13 leaflets. The flowers are followed by magnificent, bright red, huge, flask-shaped hips in great profusion. It is exceptionally vigorous and is cold hardy. For gardens on limestone, it is one of the few roses that perform outstandingly well. Zones 4-9.

'Golden Wings' — This is a very valuable shrub which repeat flowers, tall growing to 5–6 ft (1.5–1.8 m), with very abundant, wide, creamy-yellow flowers with deeper stamens and sweet scent. It has good cold hardiness. Zones 4-9.

'Nevada' — For larger gardens only, but a splendid, vigorous, and spectacular shrub introduced in 1927. It grows to approximately 9 $^1/_2$ ft (3 m) with a glorious profu-sion of very large, single, creamy-white flowers almost totally hiding stems and leaves. It gives a minor repeat flower in fall. A variation of 'Nevada', 'Marguerite Hilling', is equally excellent but in a rich pink. Both are cold-hardy, but perform well in warm gardens. Zones 4-10.

'Raubritter' — This famous variety forms an arching rounded shrub to 5 ft (1.5 m) high and is the epitome of the old roses, cascading with sweetly scented, globular, rich rose pink flowers in early summer. It can be used to cascade over low walls

spinosissima and by presumption the damask rose, discovered in 1838 in Essex in the United Kingdom, this is an outstanding rose in every way forming an excellent and totally trouble-free shrub to 5–6 ft (1.5–1.8 m), repeat flowering with neat, fern-like, gray-green foliage, bearing charming double, medium, clear blush-pink blooms with the sweetest scent. It is adaptable to most climates, other than tropical. Zones 4-9.

Recommended Climbing Hybrids

'Francis E. Lester' — Recorded as a climbing mybrid musk, this is a tall stout strong climber for cool to warm gardens to 16 ft (5 m) bearing very large flower clusters with pink buds opening blush-pink to white. It has clean disease free foliage, a rich free-floating scent of oranges and bananas, and an excellent fall show of orange hips. It is one of the last varieties to flower. Zones 4-9.

R. banksiae 'Banksia Rose' — This is a completely thornless rose known in four forms, **'Single Yellow'** syn. Lutescens cowslip-scented, **'Double Yellow'** syn. Lutea, **'Single White'** syn. Normalis and violet-scented **'Double White'** syn. Lady Bank's Rose. All have vigorous growth to around 14 ft (4.5 m) and disease-free foliage, and are only mildly frost-hardy. **'Fortuneana'** is believed to be a Chinese hybrid of the 'Lady Bank's Rose' and the 'Cherokee Rose', having clusters of double white flowers about twice the size of the banksia roses and glossy, highly disease-resistant foliage. It will grow to about 18 ft (6 m). Zones 4-10.

R. bracteata 'Macartney Rose' — Introduced from south China in 1793, this is a modest branching climber to 8 ft (2.5 m) and its plentiful thorns are useful as a people (and stock) excluder. It has

'Golden Wings' has very abundant, wide and creamy-yellow flowers with deeper colored stamens and a sweet scent.

or as a feature shrub. Hardy and vigorous, it is a hybrid of *R. macrantha*. A susceptibility to mildew is its only fault. Zones 4-9.

'Sally Holmes' — This is an outstanding modern repeat flowering hybrid musk introduced in 1976, forming a magnificent shrub to 6¹/₂ ft (2 m) high and 5 ft (1.5 m) wide with healthy strong growth. The flowers, borne in trusses of about 12, are very large, single, pure white to faintly blushed apricot pink, exquisite as a piece of porcelain and sweetly scented. It is very temperature-tolerant, and drought-tolerant when established. Reverend Joseph Pemberton raised a series early in the 20th century known as the Pemberton hybrid musks. A number of these can also be recommended including **'Penelope'**, **'Felicia'**, and **'Prosperity'**. **'Moonlight'**, with massed sprays of creamy-white, lemon-scented flowers and fresh sweet musk scent, is excellent in difficult situations and tolerant of some shade. Zones 4-9.

'Stanwell Perpetual' — A chance hybrid of the Scotch rose *R.*

dark-green, highly polished, absolutely disease proof foliage and large, exquisite single white blooms. In cold climates it will only do well against a warm brick wall, but it is exceptionally to grow in warmer gardens. 'Mermaid', released in 1917, is a famous hybrid of the 'Macartney Rose', a vigorous, very healthy, cold-tolerant climber bearing huge single pale-gold flowers throughout the season. Zones 4–11.

R. brunonii 'Himalayan Musk Rose' — Another easy rose for the large garden in cool to warm garden areas. Left freestanding, it eventually forms a 'tree' to about 26 ft (8 m) with graceful gray-green, drooping leaves, covered in early summer with large panicles of single white fragrant flowers followed by sprays of small orange hips. There is no second fall flowering. Some strong hybrids include 'Village Charm', with huge clusters of sweet, musk fragrant, double, soft pink flowers, very vigorous and healthy to 16 ft (5 m)

as a freestanding bush. 'Tintagel' has larger white flowers than the parent and glossy foliage, and 'Orange-blossom' is almost in the 'Kiftsgate' class with healthy, very vigorous growth to 32 ft (10 m), and fragrant, philadelphus-like white flowers. Zones 3–10.

R. gentiliana — A strong, healthy, tall climber covering in large panicles of creamy-yellow buds opening to milky white flowers powerfully fragrant of oranges. There is no second fall flowering. *R. helanae*, native to south China, is another species in this vein growing to 20 ft (6 m)or more. Zones 4–11.

R. gigantea — Introduced into Europe in 1888 and native to south China and Burma, this is a spectacular and healthy climber to approximately 32 ft (10 m), bearing large, single, fragrant, creamy-white flowers followed by very large, fragrant, edible, pear-shaped orange hips (sold as fruits in Indian markets). It thrives in mild to very warm summer areas and is tolerant of coastal humidity and heat. Zones 4–11.

'Francis E. Lester' is a tall stout strong climber that bears very large flower clusters that are blush-pink to white.

Rosa banksiae 'Double Yellow' has vigorous growth and disease-free foliage.

R. laeavigata 'Cherokee Rose' — This is a rose of extraordinary beauty, and good health, native to south China and Taiwan, and excellent in warmer gardens. It will survive some frosting, but severe winters cut it to the ground. The very disease-resistant leaves are composed of only three leaflets, highly polished, and dark green. The flowers, pure as crystalline snow, are huge, up to 4 in (10 cm) or more across. They are among the earliest roses of the year, and are borne along the entire branches. Two excellent hybrids are

Rosa brunonii 'Himalayan Musk Rose' 'Orangeblossom' has very fragrant white flowers.

'**Anemone**' syn. Anemonoides, a soft pink and '**Ramona**', a rich pink, both with huge single flowers. This species performs superbly in the southern United States, Australia, and the Mediterranean region. The hybrids are more cold-tolerant and successful plantings can be made against sun-facing brick walls in southern areas such as England. Zones 4–10.

R. moschata — This is '**Shakespeare's Musk Rose**', long thought to be a delusion of the bard although the rose was certainly in England in his era, and he was equally certainly a knowledgeable gardener. It was rediscovered in E.A. Bowles' famous late Victorian garden at 'Myddleton House' by Graham Thomas. The true species bears on the one plant both huge panicles composed of only double milky white flowers and huge panicles of single white flowers, intensely scented of sweet musk, the scent being free on the air. It is virtually the last species rose to flower, persisting into fall. It builds to a substantial climber of 33 ft (10 m) or a large freestanding bush, and is disease-free. Zones 4–10.

R. multiflora '**Cathayensis**' — A rose of great beauty introduced from China in 1907. It is a climber to approximately 16 ft (5 m) bearing a great profusion of single, porcelain-pink flowers poised elegantly against the foliage. It is cold-hardy, vigorous, and healthy. Zones 4–11.

'**Silver Moon**' — This is a vigorous climber for cool to warm gardens. Growing to 32 ft (10 m) or more, it has magnificent, glossy, healthy dark-green foliage and large, slightly double white blooms shadowed with cream and filled with ripe apple fragrance. Zones 4–10.

Other Recommended Cultivars

R. filipes 'Kiftsgate', *R. indica major*, *R. macrantha*, 'Wedding Day'

Rose Classes

Alba Roses

Alba roses are more tolerant of light shade than other classes, although they too will fail if grown in heavier shade. The oldest forms are very sizable shrubs, enormously vigorous, healthy, and abundant blooming. All have considerable cold tolerance.

Recommended Cultivars
'**Amelia**' — A very beautiful, healthy, tough variety that is both hardy and drought-tolerant, growing to 5 ft (1.5 m). The abundant blooms are large, palest pink, semi-double with golden stamens and sweet fragrance. Zones 4–10.

'**Celeste**' syn. Celestial, Minden Rose — This is a hardy variety forming a large shrub to 6 ft (1.8 m) with gray-green, healthy foliage bearing masses of purest pale pink, large, ethereal blooms with delightful fragrance. Zones 5–9.

'**Mme Legras de St Germain**' — A superb almost thornless variety with prolific dainty buds opening to slightly cupped, perfect, ivory white petals with a faint lemon center that are very fragrant. It grows to 6¹/₂ ft (2 m) as a shrub and up to 16 ft (5 m) if trained as a climber. Zones 4–10.

'**Mme Plantier**' — An extremely hardy, healthy, very easy to grow rose that is exceedingly floriferous, bearing great swathes of sweetly fragrant, medium-sized, creamy-white flowers. Freestanding, it grows to 6 ft (1.8 m) with smooth stems. It can be trained over small trees to good effect. Zones 4–10.

'**White Rose of York**' — This is a large shrub growing to 6 ft (1.8 m) with very healthy gray-green foliage and abundant sweetly fragrant, semi-double, pure white flowers that are followed by elongated bright orange hips. Zones 5–10.

Other Recommended Cultivars
'**Chloris**', '**Felicité Parmentier**', '**Maiden's Blush**'

'White Rose of York'
is a very famous alba
rose that has abundant
sweetly fragrant pure
white flowers.

Bourbon Roses

Beautiful though this much loved, repeat flowering, very fragrant class is, many varieties are susceptible to black spot which can be debilitating. Grow these roses in full sun, never under eaves or overshadowed. Taller growing varieties can be trained on a pillar, or along a fence which forces the side shoots to break and create many more flower heads.

'Amelia' is an alba rose
that is hardy and
drought-tolerant and has
large, pale-pink flowers
with golden stamens.

'Mme Isaac Pereire' is a Bourbon rose with huge flowers.

open. It performs well in cool gardens but is adaptable, even coping with coastal subtropical conditions. A beautiful creamy-white variety with pale lemon depths, **'Kronprinzessin Viktoria'** is well worth planting. Zones 5–9.

'Variegata di Bologna' — A 1909 rose never equalled for its extraordinary beauty of form. It grows to 5 ft (1.5 m) with double cupped, large blooms in long sprays, white, beautifully striped and splashed with rich deep crimson-purple. It has ravishing fragrance. Sadly, there is little or no fall flowering. Zones 5–9.

Other Recommended Cultivars

'Bourbon Queen', **'Great Western'**, **'Honorine de Brabant'**, **'Mme Ernst Calvat'**, **'Mme Lauriol de Barny'**, **'Rose Edouard'**, and **'Souvenir de St Annes'**

Recommended varieties

'Boule de Neige' — The name, meaning 'snowball' in English, refers to the way the double pure white flowers reflex to almost form a ball. This cultivar is very floriferous, repeat flowering through-out the season, and very sweetly scented. It has some susceptibility to black spot, but good vigor. Zones 5–10.

'Mme Isaac Pereire' — Powerfully fragrant of rich raspberries blended with the old rose perfume, the flowers of this much loved rose are huge, very double, in a deep rich rose madder. Flowers are borne in several flushes over the season and the foliage is excellent. It is a tough hardy variety once established and will also perform well in warm gardens. Zones 5–10.

'Souvenir de la Malmaison' — A shorter-growing rose from 1843, growing to 4 ft 4 in (1.4 m), often best grown in the climbing form in high rainfall areas, with bountiful, large, very double, soft pale-pink blooms with a scent compounded of rose, cinnamon, and banana. The very double flowers tend to 'ball' in wet conditions, failing to

Centifolias

The centifolias, also known as the cabbage rose, the Provence rose, the rose des peintres, and the Holland rose, emerged as a class at the end of the 16th century and are quite hardy typically making large open shrubs although dwarf forms such as **'Petite de Hollande'** and **'Spong'** exist. Despite a susceptibility to mildew, the survivors of this class are vigorous and outgrow such problems. Good air movement around bushes reduces any problems.

The centifolia rose 'Unique Blanche' has sweetly scented double white flowers.

Recommended Cultivars

'Chapeau de Napoléon' syn. Crested Moss, Cristata — This is a very sturdy variety with an unusual mutation of the sepals which are fringed and crested, forming a shape like a cockaded three-cornered hat with clear pink, globular, very double, sweetly fragrant flowers. It forms a bush to 4 ft (1.2 m) or a little more. Despite the name, it is not a moss rose but a separate mutation. Zones 4–9.

'Fantin Latour' — A magnificent rose making a substantial, rounded bush. It grows to 5 ft (1.5 m) and has healthy foliage and abundant, large, saucer-shaped, very double blooms in delicate pink, filled with rich, sweet, old rose fragrance. Zones 4–9.

'Gros Choux de Hollande' — This is a tall rose growing to 5–6 ft (1.5–1.8 m). It is a vigorous, very tough plant of considerable beauty, very generous in flowering, with large, very full, pink blooms with out-standing old rose fragrance. Zones 4–9.

'Old Cabbage Rose' — An open shrub to 5 ft (1.5 m) bearing richly fragrant, globular, very double pink blooms singly and in clusters, and lush foliage. Zones 4–9.

'Unique Blanche' — This is a drought-resistant sort of old cabbage rose from 1885 with very sweetly scented double white flowers and more compact habit to 4 ft (1.2 m). Zones 5–10.

Other Recommended Cultivars

'Bullata', 'La Rubanée syn. Variegata, 'The Bishop', 'Tour de Malakoff'

China Roses

The Chinas and the later bred hybrid Chinas are ever-flowering, very floriferous roses. They are disease-resistant, some disease-free, and several are common survivors in 19th century plantings.

Recommended Cultivars

'Le Vésuve' syn. Lemesle — An exceptionally freely flowering drought and heat-resistant plant bearing large double silvery-pink blooms with richer pink depths.

'Old Blush' is a China rose that bears abundant clusters of clear pink informal flowers with a wild astringent fragrance.

It is almost never out of bloom and grows to 5 ft (1.5 m). Zones 6–10.

'Mutabilis' ('Tipo Ideale') — Introduced in the late 19th century but probably much older, this is an extraordinary rose, bearing masses of medium-sized single blooms that resemble a fluttering of many exquisite butterflies. Slender pointed buds begin a vivid flame color opening to soft buff yellow, then changing to a soft coppery pink and coppery crimson, all colors borne simultaneously on the bush. It is rarely out of flower, and it needs warmth and shelter to do well. It grows to 6 ft (1.8 m). Zones 5–10.

'Old Blush' syn. Old Pink Monthly, Parson's Pink — This is an ancient Chinese rose and was the original 'Last Rose of Summer'. It survives on roadsides and in old abandoned gardens despite heat and drought. It bears ceaselessly abundant clusters of medium-sized clear pink informal flowers with a sweet, wild astringent fragrance, mixed with that of sweet peas. It will not survive severe winters. Zones 6–9.

'Slaters Crimson China' syn. Semperflorens, Old Crimson China — Another very old Chinese rose growing into a low to medium bush to 3 ft (90 cm), this variety has continuous semi-double, deep-crimson cupped flowers. It has great heat and drought resistance. Zones 7–9.

Other Recommended Cultivars

'Archduke Charles', 'Cramoisi Superieur', 'Hermosa', 'Serratipetala', 'Single Pink China', and 'Sophie's Perpetual'

Damask Roses

These are roses of legendary fragrance and several varieties are commercially used to gather the fabulously expensive essential oil attar of roses. Typically, the plants form an open bush with light-green foliage.

Recommended Cultivars

'Gloire de Guilan' — Produced for attar, this beautiful variety grows to 5 ft (1.5 m) with masses of large, intensely fragrant, fully double clear pink blooms. It is

'Mme Zoetmans' is a damask rose that has big, ruffled, double creamy-white blooms flushed with pink and is very fragrant.

exception-ally vigorous and healthy. Zones 5–9.

'Mme Zoetmans' — A splendid lower growing variety to 4 ft (1.2 m) with big, ruffled, double creamy-white roses blushed with pink and very fragrant. Of the same height and type but with pure creamy-white, very double, very fragrant blooms faintly infused pink is 'Botzaris'. Zones 4–10.

'Quatre Saisons' syn. Autumn Damask, Alexandria Rose, Rose of Paestum, Pompeii Rose — This is an ancient rose, as its plethora of names indicates, and a great survivor in old plantings tolerating considerable heat and drought when fully established. It grows to 5 ft (1.5 m) with informal, double pink, very sweetly fragrant flowers borne in clusters in spring and again in fall. Zones 4–10.

'Rose de Rescht' — This rose was discovered in an old garden in the ancient town of Rescht in Iran and was introduced into England by Nancy Lindsay who described it as being 'a sturdy yard high bush of glazed lizard green, perpetually emblazoned with full camellia flowers of pigeon's blood ruby, irised with royal purple, haloed with dragon sepals'. It is all of that, and performs very well in gardens with warm to hot summers. 4 ft (1.2 m). Zones 5–9.

'Trigintipetala' ('Rose of Kazanlik') — This is the most important variety for attar production in Bulgaria, particularly around the town of Kazanluk in the Valley of Roses. It requires a warm summer climate where the upright bush grows to 6 ft (1.8 m), bearing informal, deep-pink, double blooms. Zones 5–11.

Other Recommended Cultivars

'Blanchfleur', 'Celsiana', 'Hebe's Lip', 'Holy Rose' *R. x richardii*, 'La Ville de Bruxelles', 'Leda' ('Painted Damask'), 'Marie Louise', 'Mme Hardy'

English Roses of David Austin

A happy compromise for some organic gardeners has proved to be the English roses bred by David

'Graham Thomas' is an English rose of David Austin that is tall-growing and bears large terminal clusters of fragrant, golden-yellow flowers.

Austin. This is an entirely new class of roses bred originally by hybridizing the old summer roses with modern roses ('**Constance Spry**', '**Chianti**', and '**Shropshire Lass**' are early non-repeat flowering varieties from the early stage of the program that are still widely planted), then continuing to breed from the progeny to produce roses that combine the form of the old rose classes such as Gallicas and Bourbons with the repeat-flowering qualities of the modern roses. A number of cultivars, certainly not all, have proved to be exceptionally vigorous and not infrequently perform far better in the hot sunny climates of places like California and south-eastern Australia than in their original home. Older cultivars have been sufficiently well trialled around the world to be recommended as being exceptionally vigorous.

'Leander' is an English rose that bears small to medium flowers of a soft, rich subtle apricot blend.

Recommended Cultivars

'**Chaucer**' — This was one of the earliest English roses, released in 1970. It is not immune to downy mildew but seems little the worse for an attack. It bears abundant, large, cupped, pale-pink cabbage roses, richly scented, until early winter. While it grows to 3 ft (90 cm) in England, it regularly reaches 5 ft (1.5 m) in warmer climate areas. Zones 4–9.

'**Graham Thomas**' — Released in 1973 and bred from 'Iceberg' crossed with an earlier, very strong yellow David Austin rose '**Charles Austin**', this is a tall-growing 6 ft (1.8 m) cultivar with clean stems bearing large terminal clusters of large, cupped, very fragrant, golden-yellow flowers. It is rarely without flowers until early winter. It only occasionally shows any disease (blackspot occurs in wet falls), and outgrows any problem rapidly. Zones 4–9.

'**Leander**' — This is a tall, very healthy, shrub from 1982 which can also be used as a short climber growing to 6¹/₂ ft (2 m). It has shiny, thick foliage, an arching habit, and bears large clusters of very double, cupped, small to medium flowers of a soft, rich, subtle apricot blend that have a strong fruity fragrance. Zones 4–9.

'**Mary Rose**' — Released in 1983, this bushy rose is particularly hardy and tolerant, bearing reliably and for many months flushes of large, soft, rich pink double flowers with sweet scent. It has given rise to the excellent white flowered variety '**Winchester Cathedral**' and the pale-pink '**Reduouté**' (1992). Zones 4–11.

'**Sharifa Asma**' — Released in 1989, this is perhaps the loveliest of all the English roses with large, saucer-shaped flowers full of delicate, translucent petals that despite appearances is quite hardy. The flowers vary from creamy-white

suffused with faint pink to a clear, pure pink. The bush has an excellent constitution, growing to 4–5 ft (1.2–1.5 m). Zones 4–10.

'Troilus' — This is a sturdy, medium-sized, healthy bush to 3 ft 3 in (1 m) with an abundant, large, very double, cupped creamy-honey flower with a honey fragrance. It is a very consistent flowerer. Zones 4–9.

Other Recommended Cultivars

'Charles Rennie MacKintosh' (1988), 'Eglantyne' (1997), 'L.D. Braithwaite' (1988) 'Sir Walter Raleigh' (1985), 'The Dark Lady' (1991), very good in warm climates, 'Fisherman's Friend' (1987), exceptionally hardy in cold areas, and 'John Clare' which is remarkably floriferous with cupped, semi-double, deep-crimson blooms.

Floribunda Roses

These roses were derived from the polyantha class and hybrid teas, bearing small clusters of medium to large usually hybrid tea style flowers.

Recommended Cultivars

'Apricot Nectar' — Perhaps the best performing widely grown floribunda, vigorous, healthy, very rarely out of flower, bearing small clusters of delightfully scented, medium-sized, clear buff to apricot blooms. It is not immune to fungal diseases but has sufficient vigor to outgrow them. It grows to 4 ft (1.2 m). Zones 4–9.

'Bonica' — A delicious fresh green apple scent emanates from very abundant, double, saucer-shaped, medium-sized blooms borne on a low dense bush, well clothed with glossy, small-leafed foliage that is very disease-resistant. It is an exceedingly good performer flowering repeatedly, equally resistant to cold and warm climates and was bred by Meilland. Zones 4–9.

'Gold Bunny' — This is a superb, free-flowering floribunda that is widely adapted. Flowers are a clear, pure, soft gold borne singly and in clusters on a compact small bush to 2 ft 8 in (80 cm) with healthy, light-green foliage. Zones 4–9.

'Iceberg' — It is a pity that this rose is now being dismissed by some because it is so universally planted. It has some susceptibility to black spot but this is less apparent when grown as a standard (stem) rose. It performs well in a wide variety of climates and is tough, abundant, and repeat flowering, bearing clusters of smallish white flowers. Zones 4–9.

Above left: 'Troilus' is an English rose of David Austin that has large creamy-honey flowers with a honey fragrance.

Below: 'Iceberg' is a Floribunda rose that bears clusters of smallish white flowers. It performs well in a variety of climates.

'Queen Elizabeth' — Sometimes classified as a grandiflora because of its height, it has enormous vigor that ensures a long life, easy growth, and outstanding performance. It grows very well indeed in an extraordinary range of climates, bearing abundant large, double rich fuchsia-pink blooms on exceptionally tall upright bushes to 8 ft (2.5 m). Pruning is best done by taking out the oldest stem at the base each year.

Other Recommended Cultivars
'Angel Face', **'Bella Rosa'**, **'Ferdy'**, **'Oranges and Lemons'**, **'Radox Bouquet'**

Gallica Roses

Among the excellent cultivated roses of the ancient world was the wild rose *Rosa gallica* and two of its naturally occuring hybrids, the alba rose *R. x alba* and the damask roses *R. x damascena*. These early roses brought beauty and fragrance to the gardens of Europe, north Africa, and the Middle East for thousands of years. As European countries colonized the New World, southern Africa, the Indian subcontinent, and South East Asia, treasured varieties of the Gallica rose and its relatives were carried into the new gardens of Spanish monasteries in the American southwest, French colonies in the southern United States, the Caribbean, and Africa, and into the English settlers' gardens of Australia, New Zealand, Cape Province, and the eastern United States. Such is their toughness that many bushes now a century or more old have survived totally uncared for, abandoned to drought, heat, even fire, in forgotten gardens, overgrown cemeteries, and ghost towns around the world. The foliage of Gallicas is tough, leathery, and disease-resistant, and the stems are typically covered in a mixture of straight thorns and prickles. The class has excellent drought resistance, is very hardy, and can survive quite high temperatures up to 122°F (50°C) and thrive in a cool climate.

Gallica roses are not disease-free. Particularly in late fall when the leaves are aging and preparing to drop you may see evidence of fungal disease, and in spring, Gallicas are prone to downy mildew. However, unlike some modern classes of roses, the Gallicas

'Duchesse de Montebello' is a Gallica rose with masses of sweetly fragrant medium-sized pale-pink blooms set off by fresh green foliage.

are not weakened by these attacks, bouncing back with ease and showing no tendency to dieback. They require no spraying despite the occasional fungus problem, simply dropping affected leaves and reclothing. The squat growth habit of many older varieties ensures that pruning is unnecessary. However, some Gallica hybrids, mainly those raised in France in the 18th and 19th centuries, can be taller growers which can be either pruned occasionally or constrained within a rose pyramid or other device. Some varieties give a light reflowering in fall but it is never the overwhelming abundant display of early summer which can last up to six weeks.

Recommended Cultivars

'Belle de Crécy' — This French rose forms a bush to 4 ft (1.2 m) with few thorns bearing abundant, very fragrant, soft parma violet shaded, very double, flat blooms that gradually age to to cerise and then lavender-gray. Zones 4–10.

'Belle Isis' — A tough, low-growing bush to less than 3 ft (90 cm), from 1845, this rose is ideal for the small garden, bearing an abundance of plump, winged, rosy buds opening to very full blooms in purest pink with creamy-pink edges filled with sweet fragance. Zones 4–10.

'Camaieux' — From 1830, this 4 ft (1.2 m) plant is tough and carefree, and one of the finest striped roses with large, crisp, sweetly scented double blooms of white striped and splashed with clear rose-pink which changes to gray and violet. It is heat and cold-resistant with some drought tolerance. Zones 4–9.

'Charles de Mills' — One of the best known and strongest Gallicas, this is a frequent colonial survivor in areas with high heat and drought coupled with cold winters. It bears profusely, the exceptionally fine fragrant flowers being very large, very double, colored in richest

crimson-red with subtle suffusions of smoky purple-gray as they fade, on an erect, medium bush to 5 ft (1.5 m). Zones 4–9.

'Complicata' — This is atypical of the class, and the flowers are the least complicated of any Gallica! It forms a large rounded bush to 8 ft (2.5 m) which blooms in early summer with single, gently cupped flowers of exquisite beauty in clear mid-pink. It is trouble-free, tough, and the flowering persists for some time. A glorious shrub with excellent cold hardiness, it is derived in part from its *R. canina* parent. Zones 5–9.

'Duchesse de Montebello' — A Gallica from 1829, this is an

'Belle Isis' is a Gallica rose cultivar that is ideal for the small garden. It has pink flowers with creamy-pink edges.

'Camaieux' is a Gallica rose that has sweetly scented blooms of white stripes, splashed with clear rose-pink that changes to gray and violet.

'Complicata' is a Gallica rose that forms a large rounded bush and has mid-pink exquisite flowers.

listed in most European pharmacopoeias for centuries. Zones 4–10.

'Rosa Mundi' syn. Versicolor, R. gallica variegata — In cooler climates, this beautiful color mutation of 'Officinalis', which arose prior to 1580, has gaily striped and splashed semi-double blooms of light crimson, white, and palest pink. It is low-growing to 3 ft (90 cm) and makes an excellent border plant. It is hardy. Zones 4–9.

'Tricolore de Flandre' — An 1846 rose with neat, upright, restrained growth that makes it perfect for small gardens and pots, bearing masses of large, full blooms of pale pink striped with rich, deep lavender-pink with a fresh sweet fragrance. It grows to a restrained, dense 40 in (1 m). Zones 4–9.

'Tuscany' — Almost certainly the velvet rose described in Gerard's *Herbal* of 1597, this variety grows to 4 ft (1.2 m) into a stiff upright tall shrub bearing semi-double velvety dark maroon-red flowers with old gold stamens. . A more double form, 'Tuscany Superb', exists. It performs particularly well in cool to warm climate gardens. Zones 4–9.

exceptional rose with masses of sweetly fragrant, very double, medium-sized pale-pink blooms set off by the fresh green foliage. Long sprays can be cut from the 5 ft (1.5 m) bush. Zones 4–10.

'La Belle Sultane' syn. Cumberland, R. gallica maheka Grown in the gardens of the Empress Josephine at Malmaison, this is a tall-growing, vigorous variety. The buds are enclosed with finely incised, lacy sepals and the flowers open semi-double, large, and velvety dark rich red with striking golden stamens and sweet fragance. It grows to 4–5 ft (1.2–1.5 m). Zones 4–10.

'Officinalis' syn. Red Rose of Lancaster, Apothecary's Rose, Rose of Provins — This is among the oldest of roses still grown, forming a sturdy, hardy shrub to 4 ft (1.2 m) of thicketing form, with semi-double, light-crimson blooms. Unlike most roses, the petals retain their fragrance long after they have dried. This rose has useful medicinal properties, being antiseptic, astringent, and containing good levels of vitamin C. This rose was

'Tuscany' is a Gallica rose cultivar that bears velvety dark maroon-red flowers with gold stamens.

Other Recommended Cultivars

'Gloire de France' syn. Fanny Bias,
'President de Séze' syn. Mme Hébert

Hybrid Perpetuals

Hybrid perpetuals can be glorious when fed a rich diet of compost and well-rotted manures. None are entirely disease-free, although the varieties listed are both disease-resistant and vigorous. Nor is the term perpetual quite correct, as these roses flower in a series of flushes. They should be regularly pruned, as much for their tall habit as for the creation of new basal growth. They send framework branches from the base of the plant, and pruning out the oldest branch each year is the advised method. All hybrid perpetuals are good performers when planted in enriched soil, but there are some very hardy 19th century varieties with cold hardiness and proven ability to survive drought, heat, and reasonable neglect, and to grow in a variety of soils and climates.

Recommended Cultivars

'Frau Karl Druschki' syn. Reine des Neiges, Snow Queen — Often used as a grave planting in Australia, and a great survivor in old gardens capable of withstanding severe heat, cold, and drought once established, this variety has plentiful, huge, ice-white double blooms on a bush to 5 ft (1.5 m). It is rarely out of flower but lacks scent. Zones 4–9.

'General Jacqueminot' — A colonial survivor in the United States, this variety bears large full, fragrant, vivid crimson-red blooms. It has excellent healthy foliage and grows to 5 ft (1.5 m). Zones 5–9.

'Mme Victor Verdier' — An opulent rose with huge buds opening to big, double, fragrant, cabbage roses of deep crimson on a bush to 5ft (1.5 m) with leathery leaves and great vigor. Zones 5–10.

'Paul Neyron' — An 1869 rose with huge bowl-shaped double flowers of a rich pink once known to the fashion world as 'Neyron Pink' with a sweet fragrance. It has good cold hardiness but is remarkably

Above left: 'Gloire de France' is a Gallica rose that bears pink blooms with cerise centers, the pink edges fading to light purple.

Above right: 'Frau Karl Druschki' is a hybrid perpetual that has plentiful, huge, ice-white double blooms.

'Paul Ricault' is a Hybrid Perpetual with saucer shaped, silken deep rose blooms.

'Crimson Glory' is a hybrid tea rose with magnificent dark-red, richly fragrant blooms.

tolerant of drought and heat, very vigorous and healthy. 5 ft (1.5 m). Zones 5–9.

'**Paul Ricault**' — An excellent colonial survivor in many southern Australian gardens and abandoned sites, this is a rose from 1845 with fully double, saucer-shaped, silken deep-rose blooms in clusters on an upright bush to 4–5 ft (1.2–1.5 m). It has China rose in its breeding, and is drought and cold-resistant. Zones 4–9.

Other Recommended Cultivars

'**Baron Prévost**', '**Ferdinand Pichard**', '**La Reine**' (exceptionally hardy), '**Mrs John Laing**', '**Mrs Wakefield Christie-Miller**', '**Reine des Violettes**'

Recommended Cultivars

'**Crimson Glory**' — A magnificent dark-red, large double rose that is richly fragrant and was released in 1935. Surviving in many old gardens, it is heat and drought-resistant, and can sometimes be found in thickets in graveyards. It is vigorous and healthy. Zones 4–9.

'**Golden Showers**' — This is an excellent tall bush or short climber, bearing very large pale to mid-yellow fragrant blooms. It survives in many gardens and old public plantings. It is at its finest in warm to hot climate gardens. '**Spek's Yellow**' is another very tough yellow-flowered survivor best grown in its climbing form. Zones 4–9.

'**Helen Traubel**' — A very healthy floriferous older rose with considerable stamina. The long, elegant, flame-colored buds open to exquisite, barely double roses of

'Mrs Wakefield Christie-Miller' is a hybrid perpetual cultivar that has fragrant double flowers that are a blush-shaded salmon color with vermilion-rose undersides.

Hybrid Tea Roses

This may seem to be a very small list, but these are the hybrid tea roses that have consistently survived and thrived in gardens from cool to hot climates around the world. There are others that have been included in the additional list that are less universally distributed but have been tested and found not wanting from regional rose selections. Beautiful though this group is, it is by no means the toughest or most disease-resistant, and with few exceptions the bushes require annual pruning. It is an old group which has its beginnings in the 1850s, but has been enduringly popular for the range of colors it offers and the beauty of the high pointed flowers.

'Golden Showers' is a hybrid tea rose that bears very large pale to mid-yellow fragrant blooms.

glorious rich apricot and peach tonings with a deep, fruity scent. It is rarely out of flower until the end of fall. Zones 4–9.

'Irish Elegance' — Still surviving in many old gardens, often fighting its way through overgrown shrubs, this rose bred by Dickson in 1905 in Ireland won the Gold Medal from the National Rose Show. It forms a tall bush bearing repeated flushes of large, single mandarin to flame-colored buds opening to soft apricot. Equally strong and beautiful is the single silken apricot rose 'Mrs Oakley Fisher' (1921). Zones 4–9.

'Radiance' syn. Pink Radiance — Released in 1908, this rose survives in many old gardens around the world, and is exceedingly free-flowering with cabbage-shaped (globular) silvery-pink roses with slightly deeper reverse, richly scented, and wonderfully vigorous and healthy. It is usually the first to bloom. What is more, it is heat and drought-resistant, and cold-hardy. Zones 4–9.

'Red Radiance' — This is a light-red form of 'Radiance', a variety released in 1916 with the same cabbage rose form, immense freedom of flowering, and rich sweet damask rose fragrance. 'Mrs Charles J. Bell' syn. Mrs C.J. Bell is a richly scented light-pink variety of 'Red Radiance' released in 1917 and shares all its virtues. Zones 4–9.

'Sutter's Gold' — This rose establishes more slowly, but is a great survivor in old gardens bearing fruity scented, rich gold, double flowers tinged pink. Zones 5–10.

Other Recommended Cultivars

'Captain Christy', 'Cherry Vanilla', 'Chicago Peace', 'Chrysler Imperial', 'Columbia', 'Dame Edith Helen', 'Diamond Jubilee', 'Etoile de Holland', 'Fragrant Cloud', 'Lady Huntingfield', 'Lady Mary Fitzwilliam', 'Mister Lincoln', 'Red Devil', 'Silver Jubilee', 'Shot Silk', 'Squatters Dream', 'Wendy Cussons'

'Irish Elegance' is a hybrid tea rose that bears soft apricot-colored flowers.

'Red Radiance' has light-red flowers and a rich sweet damask rose fragrance.

Miniature Roses

For all their diminutive apearance, most of the miniatures are quite hardy. They can suffer frost damage and should be pressed back into the ground as soon as detected. They are quite easily propagated by cutting and can be used as garden edgings, or rockery or pot specimens. In the larger garden they are often overgrown and shaded or overlooked, and so suffer a cruel demise. For that reason they are often better grown as a small standard.

Recommended Cultivars

'Antique Rose' —A taller, healthy variety with well formed rose-pink flowers, this is a reliable bloomer. Zones 4–11.

'Magic Carousel' —This is one of a number of bicolor forms, a very reliable variety with deep-rose buds opening to creamy-white double rosette blooms, each petal edged with deep pink. Zones 5–11.

'Mary Marshall' — A medium to tall form with soft, apricot-salmon, double flowers in clusters, this variety is a prolific flowerer. Zones 5–11.

'Rise 'n' Shine' — This is a prolifically blooming variety producing nicely shaped clear golden-yellow roses on a healthy, disease-resistant bush. Zones 5–11.

Other Recommended Cultivars

'Cream Gold', 'Easter Morning', 'Gidday', 'New Penny', 'Plum Duffy', 'Starina', 'Whipped Cream'

Moss Roses

The moss roses originated with a mutation of the glands of the calyx and upper stem, creating a soft, pine-scented, moss-like growth on the sepals. The growth is tall and rather lax and the class can be prone to mildew. Nevertheless, many are long-time survivors and some of the classes are excellent in growth and form.

Recommended Cultivars

'Baron de Wassenaer' — This is a vigorous upright rose to 6 ft (1.8 m), with large clusters of generous, globular, fully double, deep-rose blooms, well-mossed, with sweet fragrance. Zones 5–10.

'Eugenie Guinoiseau' — An excellent taller grower to 6 ft (1.8 m), this rose is very floriferous, with exceptionally lovely, large, double blooms in shades of violet, gray, and purple with deep green

mossing. It is highly reliable even in warmer gardens. Zones 4–9.

'**General Kléber**' — A vigorous, taller, upright shrub to 5 ft (1.5 m) with plentiful large, clear light-pink, double blooms with sweet scent, this is an exceptionally good variety for many areas. Zones 4–9.

'**Gloire des Mousseux**' syn. Mme Alboni — This is an excellent sturdy rose with enormous, full petalled blooms of clear pink borne very freely, strongly fragrant, and well mossed. It grows to 5 ft (1.5 m). Zones 4–9.

'**Louis Gimard**' — A smaller, neat, upright bush to a little over 40 in (1 m) with healthy dark foliage and large, sweetly fragrant, lilac-crimson blooms. It performs best in cool areas and is ideal for smaller gardens. Zones 5–10.

'**Mme Delaroche-Lambert**' — Reblooming in fall, this is an prolific sturdy rose with fragrant blooms of purple suffused with rose, and soft green mossing. It reaches 5 ft (1.5 m) in height. Zones 4–10.

'**Mme Louis Leveque**' — This is a very generous rose with 'a fragrance more Chanel than Chanel', bright green very healthy foliage, and large, full, cupped, warm-pink, well-mossed blooms on sturdy plants. It is one of the easiest and most adaptable of the moss roses growing to 4–5 ft (1.2–1.5 m). Zones 5–10.

'**Old Pink Moss**' — Often reflowering in fall, this old moss rose has rarely been surpassed with well mossed, globular, clear pink blooms that are exquisitely fragrant. It is a vigorous neat rose to 4 ft (1.2 m). Zones 5–9.

Other Recommended Cultivars

'**Alfred de Dalmas**' syn. Mousseline, '**Comtesse de Murinais**', '**Deuil de Paul Fontaine**', '**Felicité Bohain**', '**Henri Martin**', '**James Mitchell**', '**Mousseux du Japon**' syn. Japonica, '**Salet**', '**Soupert et Notting**', '**William Lobb**'

The moss rose 'Baron de Wassenaer' bears large clusters of deep rose blooms with a sweet fragrance.

'Felicité Bohain' is a moss rose that has pink blooms and bright, small green leaves.

The 'Blush Noisette' was the first noisette to be sold to the public and it is still highly regarded by rose gardeners.

Noisettes

These are by far the finest climbing roses for warm summer areas through to tropical gardens. The tea noisettes bloom in long flushes repeatedly throughout the entire growing season, even persisting through winter in frost-free gardens. The blooms, borne with overwhelming abundance, are usually large, and are double, very fragrant and have the same color-saturated, mutable, wild silk qualities as tea roses. The scent is outstanding in all noisette roses.

Recommended Cultivars

'Blush Noisette' — This is a modest, very healthy short climber that makes a good freestanding bush, repeat flowering with large sprays of intensely fragrant, pale-pink, very pretty, double small blossoms. It will tolerate light dappled shade. Zones 7–10.

'Celine Forestier' — One of the finest of the tea noisettes, this is a vigorous grower to medium height which is reliably repeat flowering once established with clusters of plump buds opening to medium, creamy pale-gold, very double blooms with a delicious spicy tea fragrance. Zones 7–10.

'Crépuscule' — A smaller growing climber or freestanding shrub remarkable for its abundance of silken, semi-double, medium-sized blooms of old gold to soft, almost translucent apricot, that are wonderfully fragrant. It will climb to 13 ft (4 m). Zones 6–11.

'Lamarque' — A vigorous climber from 1830 producing great swathes of large, double, white blooms shading to a tiny lemon heart, exquisitely fragrant, as many as a thousand or more borne at a time. This is simply one of the greatest roses ever bred, with excellent foliage, growing to 20 ft (6 m) in warmer areas. Zones 4–10.

'Maréchal Niel' — This rose was rightly a sensation when released in 1864 with endless nodding, elegant, chalice-like blooms of the purest, softest butter yellow unsurpassed for their rich scent of wild fresh

'Lamarque' is a noisette rose with large white blooms shading to a tiny lemon-colored heart.

strawberries. It survives in many hot summer gardens growing to 16 ft (5 m). Zones 6–11.

'Rêve d'Or' — A very vigorous, tough, drought-resistant, free-blooming variety growing to $10^{1}/_{2}$ ft (3.1 m) with fragrant, large, pale apricot-yellow blooms. Zones 7–9.

Other Recommended Cultivars
'Aimée Vibert', 'Autumnalis', 'Cloth of Gold' syn. Chromatella, 'Desprez à Fleur Jaune'

Polypoms and Polyanthas

These roses were the forerunners of the modern floribunda class, typified by clusters of small blooms, prolific blooming, and constant flowering. Many tough roses occur in this group, some of remarkable vigor with good cold hardiness, yet performing well in very warm areas.

Recommended Cultivars
'**Bloomfield Abundance**' syn. Shrub Cecile Brunner — Believed to be a variety of 'Cecile Brunner', the sweetheart rose, this tall shrub to 8 ft (2.5 m) forms a large graceful clump bearing abundant huge, airy panicles of 50 or more perfect, double, tiny pink flowers identical to 'Cecile Brunner' except that the sepals are long and foliose. It is sweetly scented and repeat flower-ing until late fall, the fall flowering being exceptionally fine. It is one of the commonest roses in older gardens in warm areas and large bushes thrive even in the tropical heat of New Caledonia in the Pacific. Zones 4–9.

'**Carabella**' — A very fine shrub rose from 1960 with large heads of milky white, single, sweetly scented flowers tinted pale-pink resembling apple blossom. It grows to 4–5 ft (1.2–1.5 m), repeat flowering constantly, as fresh looking in mid-summer heat as in spring. Equally

excellent is the related '**Honeyflow**' to 5 ft (1.5 m), which is never out of flower with excellent healthy, lush foliage. The flowers are single, milky white, and in large heads. Zones 4–9.

'**Mme Jules Thibaud**' — Thought to be a variety of 'Cecile Brunner', this tough little rose to 3 ft 3 in (1 m) carries sprays of thimble-sized buds opening to rich peach-pink flowers scented of old-fashioned sweet peas. It is rarely out of flower and excellent in cool to hot summer gardens once established. Zones 4–11.

'**Marie Parvie**' — From 1888, an excellent survivor making a low, tough, rounded bush to 3 ft (90 cm), almost thornless, completely covering with small, cupped, sweetly scented creamy blush blooms. Tolerant of cool to hot summer gardens, it flowers until late fall and is also excellent in a large pot. Zones 7–11.

'Bloomfield Abundance' is sweetly scented and bears tiny pink flowers.

The 'Gruss an Aachen' is a short rose variety, making it useful as a border edging, or for a small bed or group.

'The Fairy' has long panicles of thimble-sized double roses in clear mid pink.

'The Fairy' — A low-growing, spreading rose from 1941 with glossy, deep-green, very disease-resistant foliage bearing long panicles of thimble-sized double roses in clear mid pink. Zones 4–11.

Other Recommended Cultivars
'China Doll', **'Gruss an Aachen'**, **'Perle d'Or'**, **'White Cecile Brunner'**

Portland Roses

Characterized by forming smallish, neat shrubs growing to about 3 ft (90 cm) with large, double, deliciously fragrant blooms, the Portlands form an excellent disease-resistant, vigorous group that flower generously and for many months at a time. They are ideal for cool to warm summer areas and are tolerant of hot summers.

'Portland Rose' bears masses of light crimson-red, sweetly fragrant blooms.

Recommended Cultivars
'Compte de Chambord' — This 1860 rose bears very generous quantities of large, full, intensely fragrant blooms of mid-pink shaded with lilac. Zones 5–9.

'Jacques Cartier' — Perhaps the most famous of the group, this is an 1878 rose, very rarely out of bloom, bearing masses of pearl pink, very double blooms slightly deeper pink in the center, filled with exquisite fragance. Zones 4–9.

'Portland Rose' syn. Duchess of Portland — Originating from Italy c. 1790, this garden treasure was the first of the class, bearing masses of light crimson red, sweetly fragrant, semi-double blooms. It is rarely out of flower. Zones 4–10.

'Rose du Roi' syn. Rose Lelieur, Lee's Crimson Perpetual — From 1815, this rose bears highly fragrant flowers of intense, clear rich red. Zones 5–9.

Other Recommended Cultivars
'Arthur de Sansal', **'Delambre'**, **'Mme Knorr'**, **'Rose du Roi à Fleures Pourpres'**, **'Yolande d'Aragon'**

Ramblers and Climbers

For cooler areas, the superlative noisette climbers for warmer areas are supplanted by the multiflora and Wichuriana rambler roses that have considerable cold hardiness. Sempervirens rambler roses are less hardy but do well in districts that do not drop below 12°F (⁻11°C). All roses listed here are once flowering, in early summer.

Recommended Cultivars
'Albéric Barbier' — An outstanding variety, very vigorous and growing to 20 ft (6 m) with lemon buds opening to very double creamy-white blooms borne in spectacular profusion. The foliage is excellent, deep-green, healthy, glossy, and abundant. Zones 4–10.

'Albertine' — One of the world's greatest roses, exceedingly healthy and vigorous and a large climber, producing richly perfumed, large, double, soft pink blooms with a faint coppery shading, as if dipped in tea. It grows to 20 ft (6 m). There is a light fall reflowering in some districts, and the lush foliage is very disease-resistant. Zones 4–9.

'Francois Juranville' — This variety is a beautiful large-flowered rambler from 1906 growing to 20 ft (6 m) with flexible canes that are easily trained. It is very generous indeed in its flowering with delightfully scented large, double, glowing deep-pink flowers. Zones 4–9.

'Jersey Beauty' — This is an intensely fragrant, large-flowered rambler with glossy, dark-green, healthy foliage and vigorous growth to 16 ft (5 m). The flowers are double, rich cream with golden stamens, borne in clusters. Zones 4–10.

'New Dawn' — An exceptionally healthy, exceptionally cold-tolerant variety with shiny deep-green foliage, repeat blooming, with fragrant, exquisite, pale double pink flowers of lovely form borne freely. Zones 4–10.

'Nozomi' — This Japanese bred variety is a dainty, short climber, ground cover, or weeping standard rose, thornless and bearing single pale pearl pink flowers fading pearl white in overwhelming profusion. It is non recurrent. Zones 5–10.

'Paul Transon' — This is an apple scented, large flowered rambler to 16 ft (5 m), very vigorous, with rich pink double flowers, excellent cold resistance, and great generosity of bloom. Zones 4–9.

Other Recommended Cultivars

'Aglaia', 'Appleblossom', 'Auguste Gervais', 'Aviateur Bleriot', 'Goldfinch', 'Rambling Rector', 'Veilchenblau'

Rugosa Roses

Very tolerant of salt-laden sea winds, supremely tolerant of cold and heat, and of sandy soils, R. rugosa, the ramanas rose of Japan is the answer to many gardeners' prayers. Fall-colored foliage, and clove-fragrant large flowers borne from spring to late fall followed by exceedingly large, brilliant red hips rich in vitamin C are further virtues. But in addition to all this, the rugosas are supremely disease-resistant. Their handsome profuse foliage is tough and rugose. They are without doubt the ultimate rose for organic gardeners in many areas. The Grootendorst group, hybrids with R. multiflora, are excellent performers but less disease-resistant than the pure rugosa varieties.

Recommended Cultivars

'Alba' — A tall well-clothed shrub to 6¹/₂ ft (2 m), this rose bears many flushes of huge, clove-fragrant, single white flowers followed by prolific, very large red hips until early winter. Hips and flowers are often mixed on the bush. It is totally disease-resistant. Zones 3–9.

'Blanc Double de Coubert' — A magnificent tall shrub to 8 ft (2.5 m), producing an outstanding display of huge semi-double white flowers with a delicious scent,

'Albertine' is a vigorous and large climber, covered in large, soft pink blooms with faint coppery shading.

'Martin Frobisher' is a tall-growing rose with an abundance of soft pink, very fragrant flowers.

followed by some large red fruit. It is a superb hedge or specimen planting, has good fall coloring, and possesses outstanding disease resistance. Zones 3–9.

'Frau Dagmar Hastrup' — This cultivar bears clusters of huge saucer-shaped, fragrant single pink blooms in profusion followed by very large red hips. It has compact growth to $6^1/_2$ ft (2 m) and profuse clean foliage. The flowers and hips occur together on the bush. Zones 3–9.

'Martin Frobisher' — This is an excellent windbreak, high security hedging, or impressive specimen rose growing $6^1/_2$ ft (2 m) with very clean, abundant fresh foliage that is highly disease-resistant. It has abundant, soft pink, very fragrant flowers opening from plump, pretty buds. Zones 3–11.

'Scabrosa' This is a cultivar with richly colored, large, cerise-pink, fragrant flowers followed by prolific huge red hips and excellent

The blossoms of 'Anna Olvier' exude a delicate scent and make good cutflowers.

fall color. It is rarely out of flower and has outstandingly disease resistant handsome foliage. 6 ft (1.8 m). Zones 4–9.

Other Recommended Cultivars
'Belle Poitevine', 'Delicata', 'Honeysuckle', 'Roseraie de L'Hay', and 'Souvenir de Philemon Cochet'

Tea Roses

With few exceptions, these roses need much cosseting in a cool to cold climate gardens together with complicated efforts to create winter insulation. But they are the supreme class for gardeners in areas with very warm to tropical summers. Mature bushes can bear many hundreds of medium to large double roses at a time and they are in bloom almost 12 months of the year. They are tough and virtually disease-free, very fragrant, and their silken colorings are unsurpassed. Many have survived for over a century in gardens in Australia and New Zealand, the southern United States, South Africa, the Pacific, the Caribbean, and Mediterranean areas. A few more cold hardy varieties survive in warmer parts of the United Kingdom although occasional extreme winters are very damaging to their numbers.

Recommended Cultivars
'Anna Olivier' — A well-clothed bush to 5 ft (1.5 m), this variety bears abundant, large, elegant, high centered, double blooms of iced apricot with deeper reverse, filled with rich fragrance. Zones 5–10.

'Comtesse Riza du Parc' — This is a very floriferous variety with large, full, globular blooms of salmon-rose infused with copper. It forms a strong bush to 5 ft (1.5 m). Zones 7–11.

'Devoniensis' syn. Magnolia Rose Raised in Devon in England in 1838 and somewhat more cold-resistant, this has big, creamy-white flat blooms stuffed with thick petals and filled with rich warm fragrance. It is a lower-growing variety to 4 ft (1.2 m). An excellent climbing form also exists. Zones 6–11.

'Duchesse de Brabant' syn. Comtesse de Lambatha, Countess Bertha (in Australia), Shell Rose — From 1857, this is indisputably one of the most beautiful roses ever bred with a profusion of double, cupped, medium flowers with shell-like petals in a blend of tender pure pinks with a pearl-like sheen and a refreshing, delicious scent. The light profuse foliage is disease-resistant. It is a great survivor in colonial gardens, withstanding considerable heat and drought, and was much handed around in the southern Unnited States, Australia, and New Zealand as cuttings. It grows to 5 ft (1.5 m). Zones 5–11.

'Lady Hillingon' — Another great survivor, with rich claret-red juvenile growth and great quantities of elegant, long, copper-apricot buds unfurling to tulip-shaped, semi-double, soft apricot blooms that are scented of ripe apricots and tea rose. It has reasonable cold tolerance, and can grow to $11^1/_2$ ft (3.5 m) over a long period of time. Zones 5–10.

'Maman Cochet' — Very free flowering and rarely out of flower, this 1893 variety has high centered very double, large blooms to rival the finest hybrid tea, in a pale creamy-pink shaded with rose, and highly scented. It grows to 5 ft (1.5 m). A white flowering bush variety, **'White Maman Cochet'**, and a climbing white form also exist, both excellent. Zones 5–10.

'Mme Lombard' This is one of the many tea roses regularly chain sawed in hot summer districts by way of pruning only to rise again in perfection. From 1878, this rose bears enormous quantities of sweetly scented, large, very double rosy salmon flowers with deeper centers. It grows to $6^1/_2$ ft (2 m). Zones 6–11.

'Monsieur Tillier' – A common survivor in many very hot, humid areas and the tropics, this magnificent variety from 1891 is exceedingly vigorous, very floriferous, almost never without flowers, and the blooms are extraordinary, full of short petals cupped, the outer petals the color of a rich, subtle, deep rose washed with tea, with a coppery silken glow, and suffused with light. The fragrance is equally rich. The deep-green foliage is supremely healthy. It grows to 10 ft (3 m). Zones 7–9.

Other Recommended Cultivars

'Jean Ducher', **'Hugo Roller'** (more frost-resistant than most varieties), **'Marie van Houtte'**, **'Mrs B.R. Cant'**, **'Mrs Dudley Cross'**, **'Octavius Weld'**, **'Perle des Jardins'**, **'Rosette Delizy'**, **'Safrano'**, **'Sombrieul'** (a climbing tea), **'Souvenir de Thérèse Levet'**, **'Souvenir d'Un Ami'**

'Maman Cochet' is a tea rose that is rarely out of flower. It has large blooms in a pale creamy-pink shaded with rose.

Section 5

TREES, SHRUBS
AND CREEPERS

Trees, Shrubs and Creepers

Acacia *Acacia* spp.; **Beauty Bush** *Kerria*; **Bottlebrush** *Callistemon* spp.; **Butterfly Bush** *Buddleja davidii*; **Camellia** *Camellia* spp.; **Cassia** *Caesalpiniaceae* spp.; **Deutzia** *Deutzia* spp.; **Dogwood** *Cornus* spp.; **Eucalypt** *Eucalyptus* spp.; **Firethorn** *Pyracantha* spp.; **Forsythia** *Forsythia* spp.; **Frangipanni** *Plumeria* spp.; **Gordonia** *Theaceae* spp.; **Hawthorn** *Crataegus* spp.; **Hibiscus** *Hibiscus* spp.; **Honeysuckle** *Lonicera* spp.; **Jasmine** *Jasminum* spp.; **Lilac** *Syringa* spp.; **Linden Tree** *Tilia* spp.; **Maple** *Acer* spp.; **Mock Orange** *Philadelphus* spp.; **Mountain Ash** *Sorbus* spp.; **Peach** and **Nectarine** *Prunus persica*; **Silverbell** *Halesia* spp.; **Viburnum** *Viburnum* spp.

It is difficult to imagine any garden—even one in pots on a balcony—being complete without at least a tree or shrub and perhaps a climbing plant or two. Much has been expounded in recent times about the significance of these larger, more permanent plants to the environment as a whole. Trees and shrubs provide havens for fauna, particularly birds. They assist in the prevention—and rectifying—of soil erosion. Extensive plantings, even in inner cities, create wildlife corridors, significant not only for recreational purposes but also because they work towards filtering polluted air. A closely planted row can serve as a windbreak. Hedges provide privacy and create a sense of peace and seclusion from the stresses of the world beyond. And a quiet, shady spot is a must for summer—as well as for added protection against ultraviolet radiation. Creepers and climbers can enhance fences and walls, lattice screens, verandah posts and balcony railings; they can disguise sheds, carports and garages; they can cover a retaining embankment, smothering in it blooms.

Whether productive or ornamental, the placement of trees, shrubs and creepers, however, needs careful consideration. It is crucial to choose the right position—and the right plant, bearing in mind its height and growing habit when mature, as well as its impact on your neighbors.

Planted in a sufficiently sized hole, with plenty of compost dug in and a good layer of mulch spread about the base (avoid the trunk or stem), and in the right spot, however, a tree, shrub or creeper, once established, should need relatively little attention to provide years of pleasure. Here is just a small selection, all suited to organic cultivation.

Acacia
Acacia spp.   Zones 8–11

This large genus contains over 1,200 species of trees and shrubs from warm climates. Some are deciduous but most are evergreen. Ranging from low-growing shrubs to tall trees, many have been introduced to other countries. The tiny flowers range from deep golden yellow to cream or white, and crowd into globular heads or cylindrical spikes. Often fragrant, they produce abundant, bee-attracting pollen.

Knife-leaf wattle, Acacia cultriformis, *is a tall shrub has showy spring flowers in profuse short sprays of round, fluffy yellow balls.*

Beauty Bush

Kerria   Zones 5–10

This deciduous shrub from China
and Japan (and sometimes called the
Japanese rose) has many upright 6 ft
(1.8 m), deep green stems emerging
directly from the ground. The leaves
are 1 inch (25 millimeters) long,
bright green and roughly diamond-
shaped with finely serrated edges.
The true species has simple, bright
golden-yellow flowers up to 2 in
(5 cm) across.

A very tough, fully frost-hardy,
adaptable plant, it does well in moist,
well-drained soil in dappled shade.
Trim lightly after flowering to thin
out the older canes. Propagate from
basal suckers or cuttings in summer
or by division in fall. The golden
blossoms of *Kerria japonica*, which
appear in spring, make good cut flowers. The double form **'Pleniflora'** is
more common.

*Beauty bush, Kerria
japonica 'Pleniflora', has
bright colored flowers
that are delightful cut.*

help promote bushiness. Prune to
make a single trunk on tree-like
species. Propagation of species is
from seed (preferably wild collected),
cultivars and selected clones from
tip cuttings.

Scarlet bottlebrush, lemon
bottlebrush *Callistemon citrinus* syn.
Callistemon lanceolatus is widely

*Narrow-leafed
bottlebrush, Callistemon
linearis, has red flower
spikes with a tinge
of green.*

Bottlebrush

Callistemon spp.   Zones 9–11

Evergreen and native to Australia,
these shrubs and small trees bear
magnificent long-stamened, mostly red
flowers in dense cylindrical spikes
which are nectar rich and attract
birds. Many species have a somewhat
weeping habit; a few have striking
papery bark, similar to the related
genus *Melaleuca*. The 25 species
hybridize freely and seed from mixed
stands cannot be trusted to come true.

In recent decades many hybrid
cultivars have been named, with
flowers in a variety of hues in the
white, pink to red range. Shrubby
callistemons make a fine addition to
the shrub border. Larger species are
popular as compact street and park
trees for mild climates. They are only
marginally frost tolerant and prefer
full sun and moist soil; some,
however, will tolerate poor drainage.
A light pruning after flowering will

Butterfly Bush

Buddleja davidii   Zones 4–9

The butterfly bush is a deciduous shrub of about 12 ft (4 m). In late summer and early fall its arching canes bear at their tips long narrow canes of densley packed flowers which are mauve with an orange eye. They are particularly attractive to butterflies, which feed on the nectar. Prune hard in late winter to encourage stong canes with larger flower-spikes.

Camellia

Camellia spp.   Zones 7–11

Camellias are among the most popular of flowering shrubs and a profusion of beautiful varieties has been produced. Most of the many thousands of cultivars now listed are descended from *Camellia japonica*, introduced to Europe in the early 18th century from China. Two other species, *C. sasanqua* and *C. reticulata*, have also produced many cultivars. In the wild they are restricted to eastern Asia, from Japan through southern and central China into Indochina, with a few outliers in the eastern Himalayas and the Malay Archipelago. Discoveries by Chinese

Scarlet bottlebrush, Callistemon citrinus, was one of the first bottlebrushes to be taken into cultivation.

distributed through coastal south-eastern Australia. This stiff-leafed, bushy shrub was among the first bottlebrushes to be taken into cultivation. There is a barely detectable lemon scent in the crushed leaves. This tough, vigorous plant usually grows quite rapidly to 10 ft (3 m) but may remain at much the same size for decades after. The scarlet to crimson spikes are 4 in (10 cm) long and held erect, appearing in late spring and summer, often with an fall flush as well.

The long, narrow cones and densely packed flowers, of the rich, purple-pink butterfly bush, Buddleja davidii, 'Cardinal'.

'Ellie's Girl', Camellia reticulata, *is one of the most beautiful cultivars in this species.*

botanists in recent decades have tripled the number of known species, from under 100 in 1960 to almost 300. All species are evergreen. The flower color is always in the white-pink-red range, except for a small group that have pale yellow to bronze-yellow flowers.

Some species are very frost tender, but most cultivars are moderately frost hardy. They prefer well-drained, slightly acidic soil enriched with organic matter and generally grow best in part-shade, though some cultivars are quite sun tolerant. Good drainage is important to prevent phytophthora root rot, but they like to be kept moist. Many varieties make handsome tub specimens. Pruning is unnecessary, but trim them after flowering or cut back harder if rejuvenation is required. Propagate from cuttings in late summer or winter, or by grafting.

Cassia
Caesalpiniaceae spp.   Zones 10–12

This genus now consists of over 100 species of shrubs and trees from tropical and sub-tropical regions across the world. Some are evergreen, some deciduous. Most have ferny pinnate leaves and clusters of simple, bright golden yellow flowers with prominent stamens, often borne for a

long period and followed by bean-like seed pods. They grow under a wide range of conditions, but most prefer well-drained soil and a sunny position. Propagation is from seed.

Dwarf poinciana, Caesalpinia gilliesii, *has fern-like leaves and short spikes of pale yellow flowers with very long crimson stamens.*

Deutzia

Deutzia spp.   Zones 5–9

These summer-flowering, deciduous shrubs from east Asia and the Himalayas bear small, white or pink flowers in crowded sprays, with 5 pointed petals. Closely related to *Philadelphus*, the plants have long, straight, cane-like stems. The leaves occur in opposite pairs and are mostly finely toothed. There are many frost-hardy species and fine hybrids available.

Deutzias prefer a sheltered position, moist fertile soil and some sun during the day. Avoid pruning the previous year's short lateral shoots; thin out canes and shorten some of the thickest old stems after flowering. Propagate from seed or cuttings in late spring.

Deutzia scabra have thick canes to about 10 ft (3 m), and long, dull green, rough-textured leaves. Large panicles of white, bell-shaped flowers terminate upper branches from mid-spring to early summer. 'Flore Pleno' has double flowers, striped dull pink on the outside; 'Candidissima' is a pure white double. *Deutzia purpurascens* is a slender arching shrub to 5 ft (1.5 m) tall with flowers that are white inside and purple on the outside.

Dogwood

Cornus spp.   Zones 6–10

Widely distributed in temperate regions of the northern hemisphere, dogwood includes deciduous and evergreen species. Flowers are small, mostly greenish, yellowish or dull purplish; few are decorative. Another shrubby group has small panicles of flowers that are not at all showy, but the stems and twigs are often bright red or yellow. One such species is the common European dogwood, *Cornus sanguinea*. The fleshy fruits are also ornamental.

Dogwoods do best in sun or very light shade. Most appreciate a rich, fertile, well-drained soil. Many are quite frost hardy but *Cornus capitata* will tolerate only light frosts. The species with decorative red stems can be cut back annually almost to ground level to encourage new growths, which have the best color. Propagate from seed or rooted layers struck in a moist sand-peat mixture.

Popular for its beauty and reliability, Flowering dogwood *Cornus florida* reaches 20 ft (6 m) or more tall with a single, somewhat crooked trunk. In mid-spring it bears an abundance of flowerheads, each with 4 large white or rose-pink bracts; in late summer the scattered red fruit make a fine showing; and in fall the foliage is scarlet and deep purple with a whitish bloom on the leaf undersides. It prefers a warm summer and may not flower

well in cool-summer climates. **'Rubra'** has dark rose bracts that are paler at the base. **'Apple Blossom'** has pale pink flower bracts.

Table dogwood, giant dogwood *Cornus controversa*, native to China, Korea and Japan, is a handsome deciduous species which grows about 40 ft (12 m), with a straight trunk and horizontal tiers of foliage. The glossy, strongly veined leaves are arranged alternately on the reddish twigs. The fruit are shiny black, and fall foliage is red to purplish.

The tree species Cornelian cherry *Cornus mas* has tiny, golden yellow flowers, grouped in small clusters. Stiff and rather narrow at first, it becomes a spreading tree of 25 ft (8 m). Edible fruit ripen bright red in late summer. Native to central and south-eastern Europe, it provides winter color for streets, parks and gardens.

Eucalypt
Eucalyptus spp.   Zones 7–12

All but a few of over 700 species that make up this genus are native to Australia. Possibly the world's most widely planted trees, especially in drier sub-tropical and tropical regions,

they are renowned for their fast height growth and ability to thrive on poor or degraded land, providing shelter, timber and fuel. The leaves tend to hang vertically so the foliage provides only partial shade. Eucalyptus oil is an important product of certain species. The nectar-rich flowers are abundant, mostly white, but yellow, pink or red in a minority of species. Petals and sepals are fused into a cap-like structure (operculum). The bark of many eucalypts is smooth and shed annually. Some have persistent bark of varying texture, for instance, the stringybark and ironbark groups. The juvenile foliage characteristic of many species, with rounded, stalkless, waxy-bluish leaves, is popular with florists.

There are species to suit most climates except where winter temperatures fall below about 10 °F (–12°C), but the great majority will tolerate only the lightest frosts. Drought hardiness also varies greatly. Eucalypts are mostly grown from seed, which germinates freely. They should be planted out into the ground when no more than 18 in (45 cm) high, ensuring that roots have not coiled in the container at any stage. They seldom

Cornelian cherry, Cornus mas, *looks unlike any other dogwood tree when it flowers. The flowers are tiny and golden yellow.*

Narrow-leafed black peppermint, Eucalyptus nicholii, *has fine, sickle-shaped, blue-green leaves and bears white flowers.*

cider gum *Eucalyptus gunnii* syn. *Eucalyptus divaricata* is sometimes multi-trunked. It has light reddish brown bark that peels irregularly revealing white new bark. Young trees have the 'silver dollar' style foliage; mature trees have narrower stalked leaves. Small cream flowers in spring and summer are followed by tiny, goblet-shaped seed capsules. Quite frost-hardy, it is the most commonly grown eucalypt in the United Kingdom.

Firethorn

Pyracantha spp.   Zones 7–10

Tasmanian blue gum, Eucalyptus globulus, is a large tree that can grow to over 200 ft (60 m). A distinctive feature is the solitary, stalkless flowers in the leaf axils, with broad, wrinkled, bluish bud caps.

survive transplanting, and are not long-lived as container plants. They prefer full sun at all stages of growth.

The large tree Tasmanian blue gum *Eucalyptus globulus* can grow to over 200 ft (60 m), with a trunk to 6 feet (1.8 m) in diameter. The bluish bark is shed in long strips. Occurring naturally in coastal areas of Tasmania and far southern Victoria, it prefers moist conditions. **'Compacta'** reaches only 30 ft (10 m) and retains its silvery blue juvenile foliage for some years. From the highlands of Tasmania, the 80 ft (24 m) tall Alpine

Native to temperate Asia and the Mediterranean, these large shrubs are grown for their evergreen foliage and abundant, bright red, orange or yellow fall berries which are edible and much enjoyed by birds. Growing up to 20 ft (6 m), the branches are armed with spines; the foliage is usually glossy green. Clusters of small, white flowers are borne on short spurs along the branches in spring.

These temperate-climate plants adapt to a wide range of soils and need a sunny position for the brightest berry display, and adequate moisture in dry weather. Propagate from seed or

Scarlet firethorn, Pyracantha coccinea 'Lalandei' is a vigorous plant with erect branches that display abundant fruit that ripen to bright orange-red.

cuttings. Pruning is often necessary, but bear in mind that fruits are produced on second-year wood. They can be espaliered and make dense, informal hedges and screens. They tend to naturalize in favorable conditions. Check for fireblight and scab.

Forsythia
Forsythia spp.   Zones 7–9

Since their introduction to Western gardens from China and Japan in the 19th century, forsythia have been popular shrubs valued for their brilliant yellow or gold blossoms in mid-spring which make excellent cut flowers. Deciduous or semi-evergreen and of medium stature, they have soft-wooded stems branching from near the ground. The rather narrow, bluntly toothed leaves appear after the 4-petalled flowers.

Fully frost hardy, they are not fussy about soil type but well rotted compost encourages growth. They prefer a sunny position, but seldom flower in warm climates, requiring winter temperatures well below freezing point. Prune only to remove older branches. Propagation is normally from cuttings in early summer.

Border forsythia *Forsythia x intermedia* is an arching or spreading deciduous shrub with dark green, lance-shaped leaves. It grows 8–10 ft (2.4–3 m) tall and slightly wider. Some fine cultivars include **'Lynwood'** and **'Spectabilis'**.

Frangipani
Plumeria spp.   Zones 10–12

This genus contains 8 species of mainly deciduous shrubs and trees, originally from Central America. They can reach a height of 30 ft (10 m), though they are generally much smaller. The fleshy branches contain a poisonous, milky sap. In the tropics the fragrant, terminally held flowers (generally white, but also cream, yellow and shades of pink) appear before the leaves and continue for most of the year. In sub-tropical climates, flowers appear in spring after the leaves and continue growing until the next winter. Propagation is from cuttings in early spring. *Plumeria rubra* is a large shrub, distinguished by its pale pink to crimson flowers which are used extensively for decoration.

Border Forsythia, Forsythia x intermedia, is an arching shrub with dark green, lance-shaped leaves with large, brilliant gold flowers.

Frangipani, Plumeria obtusa, is one of the loveliest of all plumerias.

Gordonia
Theaceae spp.   Zones 7–11

The evergreen and deciduous trees and shrubs of this small genus are, except for one North American species, indigenous to East Asia. They have beautiful flowers with showy, golden stamens. They do best in sun or dappled shade on a good quality, friable, slightly acid soil.

Crataegus diffusa *has umbels of smallish white flowers in late spring or early summer.*

Hawthorn *or* May
Crataegus spp.   Zones 5–10

Native to cool-climate areas of the Northern Hemisphere, most of the 200 species have long, sharp thorns on the summer growths. The leaves are either toothed or lobed, and the white or rarely pink flowers are clustered in flat to rounded umbels in late spring or summer. They are followed in fall by fruits mostly in shades of red.

Hawthorns are robust, frost-hardy, deciduous trees, compact enough even for quite small gardens. Sun-lovers, they are not very fussy about soil type or drainage. Some are prone to fireblight, controlled only by prompt removal and burning of affected branches. Foliage may also be disfigured by the 'pear and cherry slug' (larva of a sawfly). Propagate from cold-stratified seed, or by grafting. In winter they are easily transplanted.

From the north-eastern United States, *Crataegus diffusa* grows up to 30 ft (10 m), the branches armed with long spines. Leaves are pale green and shallowly lobed. Umbels of smallish white flowers in late spring or early summer are followed by red fruit about $3/_8$ inches (9 mm) in diameter. Washington thorn *Crataegus phaenopyrum* syn. Crataegus cordata from south-eastern United States, is an elegant though very thorny tree reaching 20–30 ft (6–9 m). It forms a round-headed, densely branched tree with long, sharp thorns. The leaves are toothed and glossy green. Fragrant white flowers in mid-summer are followed in fall by profuse clusters of small, shiny orange-red berries.

Hibiscus
Hibisus spp.   Zones 9–12

This genus of around 220 species is quite diverse. It includes hot-climate evergreen shrubs and small trees, a few deciduous, temperate-zone shrubs, and some annuals and perennials. The leaves are mostly toothed or lobed and the flowers, borne singly or in terminal spikes, are of characteristic shape with a funnel of 5 overlapping petals and a central column of fused stamens.

Easy to grow, the shrubby species thrive in sun and slightly acid, well-drained soil. Water regularly and feed during the flowering period. Trim after flowering to maintain shape. Propagate from seed or cuttings or by division, depending on the species. Check for aphids, mealybugs and white fly.

A tall perennial species from the marshes of Georgia and Florida in the United States *Hibiscus coccineus* spp. has distinctively shaped petals, each petal narrowing at the base to a slender basal stalk. The elegant flower, up to 8 in (20 cm) wide, has the long column of stamens typical of many hibiscus.

Blue hibiscus, Rose of Sharon *Hibiscus syriacus* is an upright,

Blue hibiscus, Hibiscus syriacus, 'Blue Bird' is an upright deciduous shrub that flowers freely in summer.

deciduous shrub (evergreen in warmer climates). From temperate Asia it is the most frost hardy of the genus. Flowering freely in summer in varying shades of white, pink, soft red, mauve and violet blue, the single, semi-double and double flowers are bell-shaped and are borne in the axils of the leaves. It grows to 12 ft (3.5 m) tall with a spread of 3–6 ft (1–1.8 m). Popular cultivars include **'Blue Bird'** with single, violet blue flowers with red centers; and **'Woodbridge'** with 2-toned pink blooms at least 4 in (10 cm) across.

Honeysuckle

Lonicera spp.   Zones 4–10

There are around 180 species of shrubs and woody twining climbers, both evergreen and deciduous, in this genus. They have flowers that are 2-lipped with a short to long tube, usually sweetly scented and yielding nectar. Honeysuckle or woodbine, are valued garden plants, hardy, long lived and disease free though often becoming straggly unless pruned. They are easily grown in sun or light shade and not fussy about soil. Propagate from seed in fall or spring or from cuttings in summer or late fall. Watch for aphids.

The deciduous, woody everblooming honeysuckle, goldflame honeysuckle *Lonicera x heckrotti* is valued for its magnificent flower colors and exceptionally long bloom period. In bud, the flowers are brilliant carmine, revealing a lustrous yellow throat as the corolla opens. Once opened, the outside changes to a true pink.

Jasmine

Jasminum spp.   Zones 7–10

The name jasmine is synonymous with sweet fragrance, although many among this large genus, mostly from Asia and Africa, offer nothing to the

Everblooming honeysuckle, Lonicera x heckrotti, has brilliant carmine flowers, revealing a lustrous yellow throat.

Pink jasmine, Jasminum polyanthum, is a vigorous, evergreen climber that has fragrant white flowers with pink buds in spring and summer.

nose. The flowers are white, yellow or more rarely reddish pink. Most of the species cultivated for their fragrance are climbers.

Some species are frost hardy, although most thrive best in sub-tropical to tropical areas. Plant in full sun in fertile, moist but well-drained soil. Prune as required after flowering. In cold climates, they can be grown in pots and kept indoors in a well-lit position. Propagate from cuttings in summer.

Lilac
Syringa spp.   Zones 4–9

Lilacs are prized for their upright to arching panicles of small, highly fragrant flowers, which are massed in loose heads. They appear from mid-spring and range in color from white and pale yellow to all shades of pink, mauve and purple. Although new forms appear from time to time, not all are fragrant. Deciduous, most lilac reach about 8 ft (2.4 m) high and 6 ft (1.8 m) wide. They prefer moist, 'humus-rich, well-drained soil in sun or light shade and do best where winters are cold because they require at least a few frosts in order to flower well. Any pruning is best done immediately after flowering. Species may be raised from seed or cuttings. Named cultivars are usually grafted

Common lilac, Syringa vulgaris, 'Katherine Havemeyer' has fully double, large-flowered heads of lavender-purple buds opening to a soft mauve-pink.

but can sometimes be struck from hardwood or semi-ripe cuttings.

Common lilac *Syringa vulgaris* is the species from which most garden cultivars derive. It is native to south-eastern Europe and grows to about 20 ft (6 m) high. The flowers are strongly fragrant, white or pale mauve. '**Katherine Havemeyer**' has fully double, large-flowered heads of lavender-purple buds opening to a soft mauve-pink; '**Mme Lemoine**' is a double white with medium-sized tight flowerheads on a compact shrub; '**Primrose**' has single, soft lemon flowers.

Japanese tree lilac *Syringa reticulata* has small, creamy white flowers at the ends of the branches. Sweetly fragrant, they stand out against the dark green foliage and make excellent cut flowers. It can grow to 30 ft (9 m), forming a squat, wide-crowned tree, but is usually seen as a large shrub.

Syringa meyeri, from China, is a small, spreading shrub growing to about 6 ft (1.8 m) tall and wide. The deep purplish mauve flowers appear in spring in dense heads. '**Palibin**' is a slow-growing dwarf cultivar with violet to rose-pink flowers in small dense clusters. '**Superba**' has dark pink

which becomes fissured with age. Its young branches are green and form a compact, narrow crown. The heart-shaped, dull green leaves are up to 6 inches (15 centimeters) long and have toothed edges. Yellowish white, fragrant flowers in pendant clusters appear in summer, followed by small, hairy fruit. '**Redmond**', a selected form raised in Nebraska in about 1926, has a dense conical habit.

Small-leafed linden, little-leaf linden *Tilia cordata* syn. *Tilia parvifolia* grows to 100 ft (30 m) tall with a dome-shaped crown. Its leathery, round leaves are bright green on top with pale undersides. Its small flowers are pale yellow and sweetly scented; the fruit are gray. It makes a handsome specimen for parks and formal gardens where it has plenty of space. 'Greenspire' is fast-growing with an upright habit and oval-shaped crown. 'June Bride' is heavy-flowering with conical growth and glossy leaves.

Basswood, Tilia americana, *is an attractive tree that grows to 120 ft (36 m).*

flowers that fade as they mature; it is a long-flowering form with some flowers produced from mid-spring to mid-summer. All forms of *Syringa meyeri* may have a lesser flowering in fall.

Linden Tree

Tilia spp.   Zones 3–9

From temperate regions of Asia, Europe and North America, these tall, handsome, deciduous trees, are often planted in avenues and streets. Fast growing and able to withstand regular heavy pruning and atmospheric pollution, they are generally upright, with thick, buttressed trunks, and a tendency to sucker. The leaves briefly turn yellow in fall. The small, fragrant, cup-shaped cream flowers are borne in clusters in summer. Very frost hardy, they do best in cool climates and prefer full sun, neutral, well-drained soil and plenty of water in dry periods. Even quite large trees can be readily transplanted during their winter dormancy.

Basswood, American linden *Tilia americana* is an attractive, sturdy tree from eastern-central United States and Canada grows to 120 ft (36 m). It has an erect trunk with smooth gray bark

Maple

Acer spp.   Zones 4–9

Maples are unrivaled for their fall foliage coloring and variety of leaf shape and texture. They are also grown for shade and for timber.

Sugar maple, Acer saccharum, *in the arden makes a low-branching, broad-crowned tree. Its leaf adorns the Canadian flag.*

Many are compact enough for the average garden.

Most maples prefer a cool, moist climate with ample rainfall in spring and summer. Shelter from strong winds. For best fall color, plant maples in a neutral to acid soil. Propagation is generally from seed for the species, by grafting for cultivars. Cuttings are difficult to root, but layering of low branches can be successful. Seed germination can be aided by overwintering in damp litter, or by refrigeration.

Mock Orange
Philadelphus spp.   Zones 6–9

This genus of 60 species of deciduous shrubs comes from the temperate regions, mainly of east Asia and North America. The cultivated species, sometimes called syringa, grow to a height and spread of 10 ft (3 m) and have light green, roughly elliptical leaves about 3 in (8 cm) long. They flower in late spring and early summer, the scent strongly resembling that of orange blossom. *Philadelphus* '**Miniature Snowflake**' is a dwarf cultivar of the popular '**Snowflake**'. '**Natchez**' is another cultivar often grown.

Moderately to very frost hardy, they are easily grown, preferring moist, well-drained soil and a position in sun or light shade. They may be pruned after flowering and can be used for informal hedging.

Mountain Ash *or* Rowan
Sorbus spp.   Zones 5–9

From cool-climate regions of the northern hemisphere, ash are grown for their foliage, timber and decorative fruits. Most species have pinnate leaves and terminal clusters of small, creamy white flowers in spring. The flowers, which are often rather unpleasantly scented, are followed by showy berries. A few species have attractive fall foliage.

Ash are easily grown in sun or part-shade in any well-drained, fertile soil and are most at home in areas with distinct winters. The species may be raised from stratified seed; selected forms are usually grafted. They are susceptible to fireblight.

American mountain ash *Sorbus americana* is a vigorous tree to 30 ft (9 m) with ascending reddish branches and red sticky buds. The leaves turn bright golden yellow in fall. Large dense bunches of small red berries follow. Rowan, mountain ash, European mountain ash *Sorbus aucuparia* is the most common species. Growing to about 50 ft (15 m) high in gardens, it is much taller in its native European and Asian forests. The pinnate leaves turn rich gold in fall. The white spring flowers are followed by scarlet berries. '**Edulis**' is a large-berried form used for jams and preserves; '**Pendula**' has wide-spreading growth and a weeping habit; '**Sheerwater Seedling**' is narrowly upright.

Mock orange, Philadelphus 'Natchez', is a deciduous shrub that flowers in late spring and early summer, bearing 4-petalled white or cream flowers.

Silverbell
Halesia spp.   Zones 3–9

Found in eastern United States and in
China in rich, moist woodlands and
beside streams, silverbells, or snow-
drop tree, are grown mainly for their
attractive bell-shaped flowers, which
open in clusters as the leaves unfold.
Cool-climate plants, they prefer a
sheltered position in part- to full sun
and grow best in well-drained, moist,
neutral to acid soil. Propagation is
from seed in fall or from softwood
cuttings in summer. Halesias have little
trouble with pests and diseases and are
therefore ideally suited for organic
cultivation.

The ornamental, spreading
Carolina silverbell *Halesia carolina*
syn. Halesia tetraptera grows 25–40 ft
(8–12 m) high and somewhat wider.
It flowers profusely, even when young,
producing masses of drooping, bell-
shaped white or pink-flushed flowers
in mid- to late spring.

Viburnum
Viburnum spp.   Zones 3–9

These evergreen, semi-evergreen and
deciduous cool-climate shrubs or small
trees are primarily of Asian origin with
fewer species from North America,

Europe and Northern Africa. Many
are noted for their fragrant, showy
flowers and may also produce colorful
berries or bright foliage. In several
species, flowers are arranged with
small fertile flowers and large sterile
ones on the same plant; these have
given rise to cultivars with all-sterile
flowerheads known as 'snowball
viburnums'. The evergreen species are
often used for hedging.

Fully to moderately frost hardy,
most species are remarkably trouble-
free, growing in any well-drained soil
in sun or light shade. They can be
trimmed heavily after flowering, even
though this will prevent fruit forming.

*Carolina silverbell,
Halesia carolina, flowers
profusely, producing
masses of drooping, bell-
shaped white or pink-
flushed flowers.*

*Viburnum davidii
'Femina' spreads slowly
to form a densely
foliaged shrub. It has
pointed oval leaves and
spring-borne clusters of
white flowers.*

Organic Gardening

INDEX

ORGANISATIONS

North America

Abundant Life Foundation, P.O. Box
777, Port Townsend, WA 98368

The American Community Gardening
Association
100N 20th Street, 5th Floor,
Philadelphia, PA 19103-1495
www.communitygarden.org.

The Ark Institute
P.O. Box 142, Oxford, OH 45056

Biodynamic Farming and Gardening
Association Inc
Building 1002B, Thoreau Center, The
Presidio, P.O. Box 29135, San
Francisco, CA 94129-0135

California Rare Fruit Growers.
The Fullerton Arboretum - CSUF, P.O.
Box 6850, Fullerton, CA 92834-6850

Canadian Organic Growers
Box 6408 Station J, Ottawa, Ontario,
K2A 3Y6, Canada

International Herb Association
4456 Corporation Lane, #120,
Virginia Beach, VA 23462

The Luther Burbank Home and
Gardens
P.O. Box 1678, Santa Rosa, CA 95402

Thomas Jefferson Center for Historic
Plants
Monticello, P.O. Box 316,
Charlottesville, VA 22902

Maine Organic Farmers & Gardeners
Association
P.O. Box 170, Unity, ME 04988

Michigan Organic Food & Farm Alliance
P.O. Box 626, Gaylord, MI 49734
The Organic Consumers Association
6101 Cliff Estate Road, Little Marais,
MN 55614

Organic Farming Research Foundation
P.O. Box 440, Santa Cruz,
CA 95061

RAFI International Office
110 Osborne Street, Suite 202,
Winnipeg MB R3L 1Y5, Canada

Scattered Project
Box 1167, Farmington, Maine 04938

Seeds of Texas Seed Exchange
P.O. Box 9882, College Station, TX.
77842

The Seed Savers' Exchange
3076 North Winn Road, Decorah,
Iowa 52101

Seeds of Diversity Canada. P.O. Box
36, Station Q, Toronto ON M4T 2L7,
Canada
http://www.seeds.ca

Australia

Australian City Farms and Community
Gardens Network
David Stephen, Tasmania.
Phone:(03) 62278390

Australian Garden History Society
Royal Botanic Gardens, Birdwood
Avenue, South Yarra, Victoria 3141
http://home.vicnet.au/-aghs/

The Australian GeneEthics Network
c/- 340 Gore Street, Fitzroy, Victoria
3065

Australian Rare and Minority Breeds
Association
Lot 13, Read Road, Elphinstone,
Victoria 3448

Bio-Dynamic Agricultural Association
of Australia
Main Road, Powelltown, Victoria
3797

The Bio-Dynamic Farming and
Gardening Association Australia Inc.
P.O. Box 54, Bellingen, N.S.W. 2454

Bio-Dynamic Gardeners Association Inc.
P.O. Box 479, Leongatha, Victoria
3953

Heritage Roses of Australia
c/- Jean Reid, 1058 Port Road, Albert
Park, S.A. 5014

Heritage Seed Curators Australia
P.O. Box 113, Lobethal, S.A. 5241
www.ozemail.com.au/-hsca

National Association for Sustainable
Agriculture Australia Ltd. (NASAA)
P.O. Box 768, Stirling, S.A. 5152
www.nasaa.com.au

Organic Federation of Australia
c/- 452 Lygon Street, East Brunswick,
Victoria 3057
www.ofa.org.au

Organic Retailers and Growers
Association of Australia (ORGAA)
P.O. Box 12852,
A'Beckett Street Post Office,
Melbourne, Victoria 3000

Organic Herb Growers of
Australia Inc.
P.O. Box 6171, S.Lismore. N.S.W.
2480

Permaculture International Limited
P.O.Box 6039, South Lismore,
N.S.W. 2480

The Seed Saversí Network
P.O. Box 975, Byron Bay, N.S.W. 2481
www.seedsavers.net

U.K.
National Council for the
Conservation of Plants and Gardens
c/- Wisley Garden, Woking, Surrey
GU23 6QB

National Horticultural Society
Harlow Car Gardens, Crag Lane,
Harrogate, North Yorkshire,
HG3 1QB

The National Trust
36 Queen Anne's Gate,
London SW1
www.nationaltrust.org.uk/main/

The Royal Horticultural Society
Vincent Square, London SW1P 2PE

Soil Association
Bristol House, 40-56 Victoria Street.
Bristol, BS1 6BY

Tradescant
The Tradescant Trust, Museum of
Garden History, St. Mary at Lambeth,
Lambeth Palace Road, London, SE1
www.cix.co.uk/~museumgh/index.htm

RESOURCES

North America
Antique Rose Emporium
9300 Lueckemeyer Rd., Brenham,
TX 77833

Abundant Life Seed Foundation
P.O. Box 772, Port Townsend, WA
948368

Caprilands Herb Farm
534 Silver Street, Coventry,
CT 06238

Catnip Acres Farm
67 Christian Street, Oxford, CT
06483-1224

Chris Weeks Peppers
P.O. Box 3207, Kill Devil Hills,
NC 27948

Comstock, Ferre & Co.,
263 Main Street, Wethersfield
CT. 06109

Cooks Geranium Nursery
712 No. Grand Highway 14, No.,
Lyons, KY 647554

Deep Diversity Seed Catalog
P.O. Box 190, Gila,
NM. 88038

Dutch Mill Herb Farm
6640 NW Marsh Road,
Forest Grove,
ORE 97116

Far North Gardens
16785 Harrison St., Livonia,
MI 48154

Garden City Seeds
778 Hwy. 93 N, Hamilton, MT 59840

Gardens Alive
5100 Schenley Pl., Lawrenceburg,
IN 47025
Garden Research Exchange
61 South Bartlett Street, Kingston,
Ontario K7K 1X3, Canada

Goodwin Creek Gardens
P.O. Box 83 Williams, OR 97544

Greenmantle Nursery
3010 Ettersburg Rd., Garberville, CA
95542

Hardy Roses for the North
P.O. Box 2048, Grand Forks, BC,
Canada

Heirloom Old Garden Roses
24062 Riverside Dr., N.E. St Paul OR
97137

J.L. Hudson, Seedsman
Star Route 2, Box 337, La Honda, CA
94020

Johnny's Selected Seeds
Foss Hill Road, Albion, ME 04910
http://www.johnnyseeds.com

Jackson and Perkins Co
PO Box 1028, Dept. 883C., Medford
OR 97501

Le Jardin du Gourmet
P.O. Box 75, St. Johnsburg Center, VT
05863

Logee's Greenhouses
141 North St, Danielson, CT 06239

Lowe's Own Root Roses
6 Sheffield Rd., Nashua, NH 03062

Nichols Garden Nursery
1190 Old Salem Road, Albany, OR
97321
www.nicholsgardennursery.com.

Peaceful Valley Farm Supply
P.O. Box 2209 #OG, Grass Valley,
CA 95945

The Pepper Gal
P.O. Box 23006, Fort Lauderdale,
FLA 33307-3006

Richters Herbs Box
26, Goodwood, ON, LOC 1AO.
Canada

The Rosemary House
120 South Market Street,
Mechanicsburg, PA 17055

Roses of Yesterday and Today
802 Brown's Valley Road, Watsonville,
CA 95076-0398

The Flowery Branch Seed Company
P.O. Box 1330, Flowery Branch, GA
30542

The Sandy Mush Herb Nursery
Rt 2 Surret Cove Road, Leicester, NC
28748

Seed Savers Exchange
P.O. Box 70, Decorah, IA 5210

Seeds of Change
621 Old Santa Fe Trail, #10 Santa Fe,
NM 87501

Shepherd's Garden Seeds
30 Irene St, Torrington, CT06790

Shumway's
P.O. Box 1 Granitesville, SC 29829

Southern Exposure Seed Exchange
P.O. Box 158, North Garden, VA
22959

Spring Valley Roses
P.O. Box 7, Spring Valley, WI 54767

St Lawrence Nurseries
325 State Hwy., 345 Potsdam, NY
13676

Stokes Seeds, Inc.
P.O. Box 548, Buffalo,
NY 14240-0548

Territorial Seed Company
P.O. Box 157, Cottage Grove, OR
97424

The Cook's Garden
PO Box 535, Londonderry, VT 05148
www.cooksgarden.com

Thompson and Morgan, Inc. P.O.
1308, Jackson, NJ 08527-0308

The Seed Source
Route 68 (Box 301), Tuckasegra, NC.
28783

Vesey's Seeds, Ltd.
P.O. Box 9000, York, Charlottetown,
PE C1A 8K6,
Canada

Vintage Gardens
2833 Old Gravenstein Hwy.,
Sebastopol, CA 95472

Wayside Gardens
1 Garden Lane, Hodges, SC 29695-
0001

Well Sweep Herb Farm
205 Mt. Bethal Rd., Port Murray, NJ
07865

Weeks Berry Nursery
6494 Windsor Island Road N, Keizer,
ORE 97303

White Flower Farm
P.O. Box 50, Rte. 63, Litchfield, CT
06759-0050

William Dam Seeds Ltd
Box 8400, Dundas, ON L9H 6M1
Canada

Woodside Gardens
1191 Egg & I Rd., Chimacum,
WA 98325

Australia
Australian Bushfoods
38 Mountain View Road, Maleny,
Queensland. 4552

Cobber Seeds
Summerhill Farm, Nubeena,
Tasmania 7184
www.cobbers.com

Cornucopia Nursery
55 Station Street, Mullumbimby,
N.S.W. 2482
www://users.mullum.com.au/botanica

Cresswell Seeds
RMB 190, York Plains,
Tasmania. 7120

Diggers' Seed Club
P.O. Box 300, Dromana, Victoria
3936.

Dragonfly Aquatics
RMB AB 366 Via Colac. Victoria 3249

Eden Seeds
MS 316 Gympie, Queensland. 4570

Fairbanks Seeds
Melbourne Markets, Box 35, 542
Footscray Road, Footscray,
Victoria 3011

Fruit Spirit Botanical Garden
Lot 9 Dunoon Road, Dorroughby,
N.SW. 2480
www.fruitspirit.com.au

Goodman's Seeds
P.O. Box 91, Bairnsdale, Victoria 3875

Green Harvest Australian Organic
Gardening Resource Guide
52 Crystal Waters Permaculture
Village, MS 16 via Maleny,
Queensland 4552

Green Patch Seeds
P.O. Box 1285, Taree, N.S.W. 2430

Honeysuckle Cottage Nursery
Lot 35, Bowen Mountain Road,
Bowen Mountain, N.S.W. 2753.
Australia
www.honeysucklecottagenursery.com

New Gippsland Seeds And Bulbs
Catalogue
P.O. Box 1 Silvan, Victoria 3795

Petty's Orchard
Yarra Valley, Melbourne, Victoria

Phoenix Seeds
P.O. Box 207, Snug, Tasmania, 7044

Potager Seeds
P.O. Box 5089, Alphington,
Victoria 3078

UK
Allwood Brothers Mill Nursery,
Hassocks, West Sussex, BN6 9NB

Beth Chatto
White Barn House, Elmstead Market,
Colchester, Essex, CO7 7DB

Chase Organics
Ian Allan Group, River Dene Estate,
Molesey Road, Hersham, Surrey,
KT12 4RG

Chilterns Seeds
Bortree Stile, Ulverston, Cumbria.
LA12 7PB

David Austin Roses
Bowling Green Lane, Albrighton.
Wolverhampton, Staffordshire, WV7
3HB

Great Dixter Nurseries
Great Dixter, Northam, Rye, East
Sussex, TN31 6PH

C.W. Groves and Son
Grove Dorset Violets, The Nurseries,
West Bay Road, Bridport,
Dorset, DT6 4BA
Heritage Seeds
HDRA Sales Limited, Ryton-on-
Dunsmore, Coventry,
CV8 3LG

Hillier Nurseries (Winchester) Ltd
Ampfield House, Ampfield, Romsey,
Hampshire, SO51 9PA.

Hollington Nurseries Ltd
Woolton Hill, Newbury, Berkshire,
RG15 9XT

Iden Croft Herbs
Frihenden Road, Staplehurst, Kent,
TN12 0DH
www.herbs-uk.com

Jersey Lavender Ltd.
Rue de Pont Marquet, St. Brelade,
Jersey.
The Margery
Fish Plant Nursery East Lambrook,
South Petharton, Somerset, TA13 5HL

Norfolk Lavender
Caley Mill, Heacham, near Kings
Lynn, Norfolk, PE31 7JE
www.norfolk-lavender.co.uk

Peter Beales Roses
London Road, Attleborough, Norfolk,
NR17 1AY

Suttons Seeds
Hele Road, Torquay, Devon, TQ2
7QT

FURTHER READING

Andrews, Jean. 1984. *Peppers, the Domesticated Capsicums.* University of Texas Press, Austin. U.S.

Ball, J. 1983. *The Self-sufficient Suburban Garden.* Ballantine Books, U.S.

Bartholomew, M. 1981. *Square Foot Gardening.* Rodale Press, PA, U.S.

Bronlield, Louis. 1945. *Pleasant Valley.* Harper and Brothers, NY, U.S.

Bromfield, Louis. 1948. *Malabar Farm.* Harper and Brothers, NY, U.S.

Bronfield, Louis. 1950. *Out of the Earth.* Harper and Brothers, NY, U.S.

Cherikoff, Vic and Jennifer Isaacs. *The Bush Food Handbook.* Ti Tree Press, Sydney, Australia.

Cribb, A.B. and J.W. 1974. *Wild Foods in Australia.* Fontana, Sydney,

Australia.
Cundall, P. 1989. *Seasonal Tasks for the Practical Gardener.* McPhee Gribble/ Penguin Books, Sydney, Australia.

Falcciola, Stephen. 1990. *Cornucopia A Source Book of Edible Plants.* Kampong Publications, California. U.S.

Fedor, John. 2001. *Organic Gardening for the 21st Century.* Frances Lincoln, London, U.K.

French, J. 1989. *Organic Control of Common Weeds.* Aird Books, Sydney, Australia.

Foster, Catharine Osgood. 1972. *The Organic Gardener.* Vintage Books, NY, U.S.

Fukuoka, Masanoba. 1978. *The One Straw Revolution.* Rodale Press Emmaus, PA, U.S.

Gilbert, Allen. 2001. *Organic Gardening For The Home.* 2nd edition, Harper Collins Publishers, Sydney, Australia.

Hawkes, J.G. 1990. *The Potato: Evolution, Biodiversity and Genetic Resources.* Bellhaven Press.

Herklots, G.A.C. 1972. *The Vegetables of Southeast Asia.* George Allen and Unwin, London, U.K.

Larcom, Joy. 1990. *The Vegetable Garden Displayed.* Royal Horticultural Society, London, U.K.

Larcom, Joy. 1991. *Oriental Vegetables.* John Murray, London, U.K.

Leighton, Ann. *American Gardens in the 18th Century.* Houghton Mifflin, U.S.

Little, Brenda. 2000. *Companion Planting in Australia.* New Holland, Sydney, Australia.

Logsdon, Gene. 1981. *Organic Orcharding - A Grove of Trees to*

Live In. Rodale Press, Pennsylvania, U.S.
McKillip, Barbara. 1973. *Getting the Bugs Out of Organic Gardening.* Rodale Press, Pennsylvania, U.S.

McLeod, Judyth A. 1994. *Heritage Gardening.* Simon and Schuster, Sydney, Australia.

McLeod, Judyth A. 2000. *Lavender, Sweet Lavender.* 2nd edition, Kangaroo Press, Sydney, Australia.

Mességué, Maurice. 1975. *Maurice Mességué's Way to Natural Health and Beauty.* George Allen & Unwin Ltd., London, U.K.
Mollison, Bill and Holmgren, David. 1978. *Permaculture One: A Perennial Agriculture for Human Settlements* International Treecrops Institute.

Mollison, Bill. 1979. *Permaculture Two: Practical Design for Town and Country in Permanent Agriculture.* Tagari Publications, Tygalum, Australia.

Mollison, Bill. 1988. *Permaculture: A Designer's Manual.* Tagari Publications, Tyalgum, Australia.

Murray, David R. 1999. *Growing Peas and Beans.* Kangaroo Press, Sydney, Australia.

Murray, David. 2000. *Successful Organic Gardening.* Kangaroo Press, Sydney, Australia.

National Research Council. 1989. *Lost Crops of the Incas: Little-Known Plants of the Andes with Promise for Worldwide Cultivation.* National Academy Press, Washington D.C., U.S.

Phillips, Roger and Martyn Rix. 1993. *Vegetables.* Pan, London, U.K.

Riotte, Louise. 1987. *Sleeping With A Sunflower.* Garden Way Publishing, Vermont, U.S.

Roach, F.A. 1985. *Cultivated Fruits of*

Britain. Basil Blackwell, Oxford, U.K.

Roads, M. 1989. *The Natural Magic of Mulch, Organic Gardening Australian Style.* Greenhouse Publications, Syney, Australia

Simmonds, N.W. (Ed.). 1976. *Evolution of Crop Plants.* Longman, London, U.K.

Smit, Tim and Philip McMillan Browse. 2000. *The Heligan Vegetable Bible.* Victor Gollancz, London, U.K.

Stuart, David C. 1984. *The Kitchen Garden.* Robert Hale, London, U.K.

Stout, Ruth. 1979. *How I Have A Green Thumb Without An Aching Back.* Cornerstone Library, New York, U.S.

Stout, Ruth. 1971. *The Ruth Stout No-Work Garden Book.* Rodale Press, PA, U.S.

Sykes, Friend.1959. *Modern Humus Farming.* Rodale Press, Emmaus, PA, U.S.

Vilmorin-Andrieux, Mm. 1885. *The Vegetable Garden.* Trans. William Robinson.

Weaver, William Woys. 1999. *Heirloom Vegetable Gardening.* Owl Books, New York, U.S.

Yeomans, P.A. 1981. *Water For Every Farm.* Second Back Row Press, Australia.

A

B

C

All photographs Keith McLeod and Random House Picture Library except:
page 161, 162, 207, 211, 214, 217, 220, 223, 228, 237, 238, 243, 309 and 323
Nick Romanowski, Dragonfly Aquatics, Victoria, Australia.

Index: Monika Paratore